International Handbook
of Local and Regional
Government

International Handbook of Local and Regional Government

A Comparative Analysis of Advanced Democracies

Alan Norton

Institute of Local Government Studies
University of Birmingham

Edward Elgar

Published by
Edward Elgar Limited
Gower House
Croft Road
Aldershot
Hants GU11 3HR
England

Edward Elgar Publishing Company
Old Post Road
Brookfield
Vermont 05036
USA

British Library Cataloguing in Publication Data
Norton, Alan
    International Handbook of Local and
    Regional Government: Comparative Analysis
    of Advanced Democracies
    I. Title
    352

Library of Congress Cataloguing in Publication Data
Norton, Alan
        International handbook of local and regional government: a
    comparative analysis of advanced democracies/Alan Norton.
            p.   cm.
        Includes index.
        1. Local government.   2. Comparative government.   I. Title.
    JS67.N67 1993
    320.8—dc20   93–42472
                                                                          CIP

ISBN 1 85278 005 3

CONTENTS

Contents

Contents

Contents

Contents

LIST OF TABLES

List of Tables

xi

FOREWORD

This book originated from two comparative studies commissioned by British local authority associations in association with my employer, the Institute of Local Government Studies (INLOGOV) of the University of Birmingham. The object of both studies was to help to identify what might be learnt from systems abroad that could usefully contribute to British policy-thinking. The first, commissioned by the English metropolitan county councils in 1983, was a study of metropolitan governments abroad. The second, defined by the four main English and Welsh local authority associations in association with INLOGOV in 1985, had the wider objective of describing and comparing aspects of local and regional systems abroad and their relationships with state governments. It added the United States to the national systems covered on the understanding that in this case the description would be based on published literature and the advice of American experts on local government. Subsequently I agreed with the present publishers to develop the work into the form of this book and to add Japan to the countries covered, drawing on the help of several Japanese scholars who adopted INLOGOV as their base for study visits to Europe.

The book was originally planned to appear several years earlier than has been possible as a result of other major commitments to which I felt obliged to give priority. The delay has not been without its advantages. The advent of recent decades has brought unexpected changes. In Western Europe the end of the 1970s heralded a period in which major decentralisation of power was initiated in major countries, excepting the United Kingdom which, if anything, tended to move in the opposite direction. It was followed by the empowerment of democratic regional governments in important countries in Western Europe. The subject merits a book in itself, but I have described here briefly their nature and their place in the new European structures.

The early 1990s have brought more momentous changes — most conspicuously the establishment of new liberal democracies in Eastern Europe, leading to social and economic results that have carried deep consequences for countries throughout the world. Delaying the book has thus made it possible to take into account some immediate direct and indirect consequences, as well as the benefits of an expanding new literature on local and regional government issues.

This book is designed to meet several purposes. One central aim was to facilitate comparison. Learning is essentially by comparison at all levels, from that of individuals to that of nations and families of nations. If it is to be of positive value it must be well-informed learning.

While the book facilitates the systematic study of differences between nations, it is also a reference book to enable those seeking background information on major aspects of local and regional government in other countries to find key facts through the index or by turning to the relevant chapter and section.

A leading aim is to assist policy-making, especially in opening up vistas of what local and regional governments can achieve and how they might be better organised, thereby providing a stimulus to worthwhile innovations that may make significant contributions to efficiency and to the local and national quality of life. Although the direct copying of institutions and practices used abroad is not to be recommended without as thorough as possible a study of their possible impacts in a new environment, comparison often leads to a reconception of national and local problems and new ideas on how they might be overcome. History shows that it has been widely undertaken, sometimes, however, for the worse where it has not been preceded by sufficient care about the likely consequences in a particular situation.

Another main aim of the book is to contribute generally to international understanding about local and regional institutions and related matters. The need for mutual understanding on local government affairs became clear to me in attending a number of international conferences on local government issues in the 1970s, when attempts at intelligent discussion were frustrated by mutual ignorance between representatives of different countries about each others' institutions and problems. Since then international contacts have rapidly increased, and with them the size of the problem of meaningful communication, not only at governmental levels but also in the activities of trade and commerce, voluntary agencies, other interest groups and individuals moving from one system and culture to another.

There are major obstacles to mutual understanding in this field. One is national stereotypes. Too often the selection of news seems designed to reinforce them. We need to break them down through a deeper under-standing of the varied character of particular countries, their qualities and variety of peoples, their institutions, culture and problems, and in many other ways. A not inconsiderable problem lies in the understanding of foreign words and their translation. Dictionaries commonly give inadequate definitions in this field. Foreign terms often lack exact equivalents. The same word can have many and often conflicting meanings, so that its use confuses more than helps if an understanding is lacking of the national context in which it is used. Apparent similarities between words in different languages are often 'false friends' that mislead rather than help. Translations even of common terms such as 'district', 'region', 'mayor' and 'chief executive' can create utter confusion. Both the nature of local institutions and the context of their usage need some background understanding.

The book gives key facts on aspects of local and regional government in countries in Western Europe, North America, Australasia and Japan, in accordance with a standard pattern. Interrelated topics are surveyed in Part I, followed in Part II by a deeper examination of nine selected countries according to the same pattern. The aspects are the historical backgrounds of local and regional government; the status, values and concepts supporting local and regional government; the national structure of local and regional authorities; their joint organisations and the relations between them; central-local-regional relations; local and regional government competences and services; local and regional finance, including expenditure, local taxes, grants and borrowing; electoral systems and party structures of local and regional government and conditions of service for elected members; the internal organisation of authorities; the means for direct participation in local government by members of the general public; and how the problems of metropolitan governance have been approached.

I have generally held back from theorising, although the book contains descriptions of concepts and principles supported by theory in the third section of each chapter. That is not to say that, like most books on government and national characteristics, it may not carry implicit theory which readers may like to ferret out for themselves.

Its approach is essentially inter-disciplinary, as seems appropriate in an area in which economic, social, political, legal and administrative considerations intermingle. I have gone into more detail where this seems of particular value to policy-making, as for example in the field of taxation, and have in some cases moved towards conclusions on practice, as in structural innovation in the reorganisation of boundaries, principles of local taxation and the governance of metropolitan areas.

It can be disastrous in practice for politicians and administrators to fail to understand the contributions that all relevant disciplines can bring to policy decisions aimed at the well-being of communities. This justifies the use of highly varied sources. Much of the groundwork for the book came from copies of official papers that administrators passed on to me. Newspaper reports are vital for keeping in touch with new happenings. Flashes of insight can come from anywhere and quite unexpectedly. On the other hand they cannot substitute for deep knowledge of particular fields. For this one seeks the best sources practically available, both from experts within their own countries and from those who have studied situations from the outside. The work of the greatest of all writers on local government, Alexis de Toqueville, is the outstanding example of how the study of countries other than one's own can be of relevance to the wider understanding of government and society.

Part I gives a broad survey of the subjects stated above and related matters, taking in Council of Europe countries as a whole and also Australia and New Zealand. Thus, for example, §1.1 contains a short history of the origins and development of local government in these countries within a worldwide perspective. Later sections include among other things classifications of local government taxes and electoral systems and some comparative evaluation. My analysis in the first section to some extent determines the sequence of the chapters in Part II.

The book has geographical limitations. There are other democracies in the world that might well have been covered by its title. It was not practicable to include them, but I trust that its contents will be of equal interest to readers in these and in developing and industrialising countries, and that other authors will work to provide a basis for a wider view.

Alan Norton
Birmingham, 1993

Note on Style Conventions
I have made departures from some common style conventions in ways that seemed to be justified by the nature of the book. In particular, certain parts of the book are so thick with terms belonging to foreign languages, including many that have no satisfactory translations, that it seemed best to adopt the increasing practice of not italicising them — at least subsequent to their first introduction. In some cases, for example départements, régions and maires, it seemed better not to translate them in order to avoid confusion of meanings.

The references section seeks to aid literature searches as well as to fulfil the usual reference function. For this reason, entrances under main heads, such as Council of Europe, are given in alphabetical rather than date order, and the publications concerned are named in the main text. The usual lettering of references, however, is used for an author's publications which appeared in the same year.

Book references in the main text given after the last sentence in a paragraph indicate general sources of information on the subject of that paragraph as a whole.

ACKNOWLEDGEMENTS

The acknowledgements which I owe to the many administrators, politicians, writers and students at all levels who have helped me to understand their systems and benefit from their work and insights are so many that it is hardly possible to name the great majority of them. I can assure all that their contributions have been deeply appreciated, and that the failure to mention them here by name does not imply less regard for the generous help they have given me.

Chronologically my first contacts with the international world of local government were at conferences in the 1960s organised by the International Union of Local Authorities (IULA) and the Conference of European Municipalities (CEM), thanks to Henry Maddick, the Director of INLOGOV, who encouraged my attendance there, Paul Bongers, the director of the British branch of IULA and CEM and his colleagues who were largely responsible for the British contribution to their organisation, and also Jan van Putten, the former long-serving Secretary-General of IULA and his colleagues in The Hague.

Next I owe very much indeed to those who helped in the international consultancies in which I was engaged in the 1970s and early 1980s. Seeing the outcome of the adoption of foreign models in East Africa and Turkey gave me the opportunity to evaluate the results of the adoption of West European models abroad within different cultures. I am indebted here especially to members of the staff of OECD in Paris, especially Clifford Glover and Andrew Horgan, who gave valuable support to work in Istanbul and in Europe and gave me contacts in European countries at official levels in seminars and through introductions.

A third main source has been in connection with studies for English and Welsh local authority associations, and in particular the study in 1983 on the *Government and Administration of Metropolitan Areas in Western Democracies* for the English metropolitan counties and that for the three main local authority associations in 1985-86 on *Local Government in Other Western Democracies*. In these studies and afterwards I was able to draw on generous help from scholars and administrators visiting INLOGOV from abroad as well as on international visits, and also to try out my analysis of situations in their own countries on postgraduate students, particularly those from Germany and Italy. Japanese scholars seconded to and visiting INLOGOV have been a great and generous source

xvi

of help in the development of the chapter on Japan.

Among those who gave valuable help may be singled out Professor Jean-Claude Thoenig for early guidance in 1985 and some valuable recent help from Dr Christian Lefèvre in 1992; Dr Bruno Dente and Dr Emilio Samek-Lodovici of the City of Milan for frequent help on the Italian system, administration; the late Professor Frido Wagener of the Postgraduate School of Administrative Sciences in Speyer and Professor Gerhard Banner, Director of the KGSt in Cologne, for much help and advice over a long period; Professor Ernst Jonsson of the University of Stockholm; Palle Mikkelsen of the Danish Municipal Research Institute in Copenhagen; Professors T.J. Plunkett and G.M. Betts, especially for advice on Canadian sources, provincial officers in Toronto and, more recently, Dr Lionel Feldman; Professor Kano and colleagues, while seconded to the University of Birmingham, Professor Yashimoto Kawasaki of Chuo University, and, on repeated occasions, Professor Akira Kobayashi of Kanazawa University. I am also heavily indebted to many who have sent me relevant papers. For Chapter 10 I have been heavily dependent on the English publications provided by the Jichi Sogo Center in Tokyo through the courtesy of Director-General Katsuomi Obayashi, without which the Japanese chapter would hardly have been feasible. Greatly appreciated help was also given by colleagues in countries that are referred to in Part I but not included in Part II — amongst others Dr Carmel Coyle of the University College Dublin and Professors Risto Harisalo and, Paavo Hoikka and their colleagues in Finland, who produced a description of the Finnish system which parallels to some extent the chapters in Part II (details are given in the first section of the references part of this book under the name of Simo Hakamäki).

I have already mentioned the international local government associations and OECD. Other facilitators of the interchange of knowledge in this field to whom I owe a major debt include those associated with the Council for Local and Regional Authorities in Europe, the International Political Science Association, the European Council for Political Research and the Institut International d'Administration Publique of the Prime Minister's office in Paris. Also of great help have been seminars on Metropolitan Government in Oxford, sponsored by the Economic and Social Research Council and organised by L.J. Sharpe; on local government employees in Bochum organised for the European Council for Political Research by Drs Richard Balme and Vincent Hoffmann-Martinot; on a similar field at the Institut International d'Administration Publique in Paris, following which Marie-Christine Henry-Meininger of the Institut sent me valuable information; and on developments in European local government organised

Acknowledgements

by colleagues Drs Richard Batley and Gerry Stoker at INLOGOV.

I owe an outstanding debt to my colleagues in INLOGOV who have given me the opportunity to spend time on studies of local government in countries abroad and have given me much encouragement in these matters. I was most fortunate to serve as a research associate under Dr A.H. Marshall when I joined the Institute in the 1960s. He possessed a knowledge unparalleled in Britain of local government throughout the world. Recently Professor John Stewart, currently head of Birmingham University's School of Public Policy, has read and commented most helpfully on drafts of Chapter 1 in particular. But none of those named above carry any responsibility for the final text. Its faults are entirely my own.

The initial typing and word-processing of the book have also been entirely my own. I am nevertheless very indebted to the secretarial staff of INLOGOV who gave me unfailing support over the years. Also a special word of thanks to Tony Gaize of the university's Physics Department who under-took to convert the contents of discs that had evolved since the early 1980s on a now antiquated word-processing system into a language that modern laser-printers can understand — a much more time-consuming task than we initially anticipated — and Robert Wheeler who effectively undertook the conversion of my discs into the final form.

The main burden of support has fallen very much on my wife Susanne. The work has prevented me from giving her as much help as might reasonably have been expected, particularly on happy but time-consuming preoccupations with grandchildren.

INTRODUCTION

The core of local and regional government as it is understood in economically advanced liberal democracies lies in the concept of self-government and administration, as exercised by the inhabitants of territorial areas through the election of councillors, and sometimes also through the direct election of local government executives. High value is placed on individual rights and liberties and the protection of those privileges within the law. Value may also be placed on the general participation of citizens in government in a more direct way than by periodical voting. This has seemed to some the core of a democracy, enabling citizens to develop political skills and a sense of civic responsibility and so fulfil their potential as human beings. Otherwise the national systems described in the following pages differ widely in their scale, political organisation, origins and traditions. Historically the countries in which they developed include the principal nurseries of local democratic institutions throughout the world.

Writers on international comparative government commonly use countries or states as their units for comparison. Authors often identify characteristics held in common by a group of countries, seeking to make a kind of Linnaean classification into families of national systems. This procedure has the danger of setting pre-conceptions of what may be found in a particular country because it belongs, for example, to a Latin or an anglophone culture, although members of each language group always differ from each other in important respects. What is interesting within a 'family' of countries is perhaps more how its members differ from each other than what they have in common. 'Frameworks of reference', such as that tentatively sketched in the first section of Chapter 1, can therefore be misleading in the attempt to acquire an understanding of particular systems.

'Cross-classifying' nations by selected variables can nevertheless be a help towards making the field manageable and drawing out tentative hypotheses. It invariably, however, requires gross over-simplification when dealing with social phenomena and human institutions. There is a need for continuing exploration of present conditions and their relationship to the past in order to challenge received ideas and assumptions. As Heraclitus said, one cannot step into the same river twice. But we must describe and seek to understand the flows and levels of a great river if we are to cross or to bridge it. It is never the same as yesterday. Innovative measures always have a large element of the experimental. Whatever decision-makers can find by means of comparisons, analogies and the experience of others, the more they may understand what may succeed or go wrong.

I follow the route of cross-classification in the first section of this book, and my analysis to some extent determines the sequence of the following chapters. Thus Part II starts with France, followed by Italy as an example of a country deeply influenced by the Napoleonic model and sharing the corpus of Roman law. There follow countries which were deeply affected by French concepts and events but where strong indigenous traditions conditioned the evolution of their systems: Germany, Sweden and Denmark. The division is clear between these five countries and Britain, which tended to see French radicalism as a threat to its own traditions. It still does so to judge from the reaction of the British media and some historians to the bicentenary of the French Revolution. Although Britain was midwife at the birth of national self-government in many countries throughout the world, and passed on to them many of its local government and other institutional forms as well as its basic legal system, it has gone its own way in recent times, distancing itself from most of its former dependencies yet hardly coming closer to continental European culture and institutions. The principal institutions of the United States were established before the French Revolution and rapidly developed their own characteristics. In the twentieth century the USA has been a strong influence in the North Pacific. Canada and Japan have mixed characteristics.

Part I consists of a survey of a wide range of national systems. Due to problems of space and time the text can only touch briefly on developments in some countries that deserve fuller treatment, including those in the southern hemisphere. Much less can it do justice to the new multi-party democracies of Eastern Europe whose institutions and ideologies are being transformed in the early 1990s in a search for the essence of economically successful liberal democracy.

In recent years Western Europe's continental states have been particularly concerned to spell out principles of local government, and have also been active in democratising the process of regional government within the unitary state. The Council of Europe, through its Standing Conference of Local and Regional Authorities in Europe (CLRAE), has taken the lead in these matters and has achieved the high level of consensus expressed through the European Charter of Local Self-Government (see §1.2).

PART I

A General Survey

1. LOCAL AND REGIONAL GOVERNMENT IN ADVANCED COUNTRIES

1.1 HISTORY AND TRADITIONS

The origins of local government structures as we know them today lie in eleventh- and twentieth-century Europe. Some terms used for local authorities are older still, deriving from ancient Greek and Latin. *Koinotes* (community) and *demos* (people or district) are the names of Greek local authorities today. Municipality and its variants come from the ancient Roman administrative law term *municipium*. City comes from the Roman *civitas*, itself derived from *civis* (citizen). County comes from *comitates*, which is derived from *comes* (count), the office of an imperial official.

But the institutions which gave a recognised status to local government in the early Middle Ages in Europe were Teutonic or Germanic: burg, borough and the French *bourg* from the root meaning 'protect' or 'hide' which survives in the German *bergen*; town from the Old English *tun*, an enclosure; and the German *Stadt* from words for place or dwelling. The medieval *cité* or city denoted a large settlement with special privileges.

Town, borough and city all originally denoted fortified enclosures into which the local population could retreat when under external threat. Itinerant merchants found security and the possibility of developing their own way of life within or under the shelter of such enclosures, which tended to be spaced conveniently at an average of about thirty miles from each other. They served the needs of a social class — the merchants or burghers who formed what came to be called the bourgeoisie, seeking security for their activities in the boroughs or *bourgs* from which the word *bourgeoisie* was derived. They also served the needs of the kings, bishops and princes who defended and controlled wider territories. The relationship was a contractual rather than a constitutional one, based on complementary interests, although the charters which pledged the boroughs' freedoms were underpinned by doctrines of natural law derived from the legal philosophy of Roman times which underpinned rights of property and contract. The bourgeoisie was distinct from, if at first dependent on, the declining feudal

3

society within which it developed.

From the tenth century the movement for the enfranchisement of cities and towns spread northward from Italy to Picardy and Flanders and on to the North Sea and the Baltic as far as Finland and the Atlantic as far as Iceland. The Belgian historian, Henri Pirenne, gave a picture of the medieval boroughs at their peak which, although somewhat idealised, was based upon an accumulation of British, French, German and other scholarship (Pirenne, 1925 and 1939). City government was developed through associations of bourgeois families in whose success bishops and princes had an economic interest. Participation in municipal institutions spread to commercial and artisan guilds. Forms of representation developed. Most boroughs were under the government of bishops and therefore outside the jurisdiction of the princes and the counts who presided over courts, raised taxes and levied troops in the county areas outside city boundaries. It was in the financial interest of the monarch of the late Middle Ages to protect town freedoms against attacks by bishops and nobles. Many cities became virtually republican enclaves in a princely society, governing themselves under their own customary laws and charters. In a few cases freedom was achieved through insurrections by local citizens, most famously in the city of Cambrai in 1077. Typically merchant guilds took the lead in the movement towards city autonomy, gaining charters of freedom and self-government from kings and princes which gave them a right to elect their own assemblies and officials. In some cases there was a franchise of citizens which conferred individual equality of status. The cities provided the nucleus for the growth of a civic culture which transformed middle-class life nationally.

The cities controlled their own incomes subject to contributions to princes. They developed model financial systems, regulation of commerce and industry, ruthless pursuit of fraud, controls on woman and child labour, road systems, water supply, drainage and sewerage, public health systems, schools and facilities for the care of the poor and elderly. They worked to open up new and distant markets for city trade. Revenue systems included taxes on individuals according to means and taxes on consumption, sensitive to individual expenditures and circumstances in order to lighten the burden of market tolls on the poor. The German proverb *Stadtluft macht frei* (town air makes one free), originated in the later Middle Ages. Pirenne described the social legislation as 'more complete than that of any other period in history', and the economic legislation as 'assuring to the burgher the benefit of a low cost of living'.

These systems were developed by elected mayors and other repre-sentatives who also served as magistrates, applying law and regulations

4

approved by general assemblies of citizens which in their early days appear
to have expressed something that approximated to the general will of the
citizens. Pirenne described the 'extraordinary solidarity amongst the
burgesses'. 'Body and soul, they belonged to the little local *patrie*, and
with them appeared for the first time, since antiquity, in the history of
Europe, a civic sentiment' (Pirenne, 1939). The development of the
bourgeoisie resulted in the transformation of European economy, society
and culture, leading to the renovation of central government as well as
urban local government.

Later the government of the cities was largely monopolised by family
oligarchies. As municipal rights were contractual rather than constitutional
they gave little protection against strong monarchies except in mountain
and seaboard areas. In Switzerland and the Low Countries cities protected
themselves by forming leagues for self-defence which provided roots for
constitutional growth. From the fourteenth century monarchs elsewhere
succeeded in crushing the powers and rights of the new municipalities
subject to some important exceptions.

In most of Northern Europe, from Ireland to Poland and Hungary, local
government outside boroughs was carried out by country landowners, often
meeting in regular assemblies to exercise their administrative judicial
powers. England's decentralised system of rural government rested on
oligarchic commissions of the peace and parish meetings and councils
under the commissions' surveillance. English traditions shaped most of the
new local government institutions in North America. These were often
looked to as an ideal by reformers in continental Europe in the eighteenth
and nineteenth centuries.

Modern local government's inheritance from these early forms is less
than has often been assumed. The modern city authority may show some
trappings of municipal power and may even possess a medieval town hall,
but it differs greatly from the medieval model in status, powers and values.
The monopolisation of claims to power by monarchs and, in the British
case, parliament, supported by theories of sovereignty, erased most
borough freedoms. In Britain national intervention began with the reforms
of 1835 and continued with the enforcement of the *ultra vires* doctrine by
the courts. The shards of borough privilege were finally destroyed by the
Local Government Act of 1972.

Rationalism, Constitutionalism and Institutional Engineering

Modern concepts of national sovereignty developed from claims to
absolute power by royalty in the sixteenth and seventeenth centuries. The

concept of natural law, however, transmitted from the Roman Empire through the Church, sought to limit that power. Jean Bodin (1530-96) gave the classic definition of sovereignty in his *Six Books of the Republic* (1576), but the work also contained the sentence 'Monarchies become corrupted when little by little the privileges of bodies and cities are taken away, and when, instead of limiting themselves to a general supervision, which is alone worthy of a sovereign, princes want to rule everything alone without any intermediary' (quoted Wickwar, 1970). Later Montesquieu (1689-1755) wrote, 'If in a monarchy you abolish the prerogatives of the lords, the clergy, the gentry and the cities, you will have a popular state or else a despotism'. Municipalities and other local bodies 'moderate the power of the sovereign while at the same time enjoying some delegated sovereign powers' (ibid.).

But across much of Europe royal power exercised by decree cut through the structure of obligation and rights developed in the Middle Ages. Monarchs from the sixteenth to the eighteenth century sought to impose their will by decree, overriding traditional and contractual rights. They relied with varying degrees of success on local implementation by crown-appointed officers known as *intendants* in France and commissars, commissioners or governors elsewhere (Hintze, 1975; Page, 1991).

Exceptions are found in the Netherlands and Lower Germany where the power of the cities was reflected in an influential book by Althusius published in 1603 (*Politica methodica digesta*) which contributed to the ideas behind German federalisation in the latter half of the nineteenth century and foreshadowed the concept of a federal Europe. His ideal model of the state consisted of tiered levels of organisation within the political system: the family, the voluntary corporation (*collegium*), the local community, the province and the state. The lower groups in the structure set up the next higher level by agreement or contract, each level regulating only those matters necessary for its constitutional purpose.

The eighteenth century 'Age of Enlightenment' saw an international flowering of rationalist 'institutional engineering' approaches to local government. These are closely linked with developments in legal and political concepts described in §1.3 below. In Britain, David Hume (1711-76) wrote of the 'idea of the perfect commonwealth' as a country of a hundred counties, each divided into a hundred parishes, the whole ruled by a hundred senators, one from each county. Each county was to be governed by ten magistrates drawn one from each ten parishes (*Essays Moral and Political*, 1741). Turgot (1727-81), a politician of the French Enlightenment who served Louis XV as controller-general for two years, proposed a three-level hierarchy of 'municipalities'. The kingdom was to be divided into village municipalities elected by property owners. Thirty of these villages within a radius of 15 kilometres were to elect 'provincial municipalities'. Thirty of these were to form the 'great general municipality of the realm'. The system was argued to provide a practical form of civic education. Probably inspired by this plan, the first government of the United States under the influence of Jefferson (1743-1826) decided to subdivide its north-west territories geometrically with a tier-on-tier division and subdivision of governmental responsibilities 'from nation to township' (Wickwar, 1970).

Revolution and Liberalisation

The French Revolution of 1789 resulted in a short period of spontaneous decentralisation and local innovation, followed swiftly by ruthless centralisation. The main elements of the system were created within a few months (see §2.1), including the communes, with assemblies and mayors as executives for both communes and the state; local elections (soon to be abolished); *départements*; and state commissioners, predecessors of the prefects with unlimited scope in their départements. They were members of an elite corps selected for their abilities and promise without regard to social status, former occupation or political opinions. Their first instruction was to create a new France in which all divisions between Frenchmen would be abolished (Chapman, 1955).

The system developed as a compromise between local agents of central government and centrally supervised councils representing local interests. The office of prefect as both departmental executive and agent of central government lasted until the 1980s.

The earliest effect of the French Revolution on local government outside France was probably in Luxembourg where municipal autonomy was recognised in a decree of 1789 that has remained in force ever since. The prefectoral system was imposed or adopted in much of Napoleon's Empire, including puppet republics and confederations in the Lowlands, West Germany and Italy.

The most important consequences of the revolutionary years for the future history of local government were perhaps the entrenchment of the concept of national sovereignty and the seeding of ideas of local self-government of a kind proclaimed in the revolutionary movements of 1830, 1848 and the 1860s. The Napoleonic prefectoral and similar systems continued to serve as a means to enforce central authority, acceptable in monarchies as a rationalised version of the intendant system of the despotisms of the years preceding 1789. It was not foreign in principle to many traditional regimes

7

wherever crown-appointed governors or their equivalents had represented the sovereign in earlier centuries. Governors have continued to represent the notional crown in democratic, parliamentary monarchies in Northern Europe, fulfilling a role of varying importance. Examples are the royal commissioner in the Netherlands and the *fylkesmann* in Norway, who are both executives and take the chair for the provincial councils; the *lanshovding* in Sweden who has a general authority over the state institutions at provincial level; and even the British lord-lieutenant and high sheriff who play a somewhat obscure role in administrative counties.

The revolutions of 1848 had little immediate effect except in the Netherlands, Denmark and Piedmont, where King Carl Albert, associating himself with the interests of the bourgeoisie, continued to support the revolutionary constitutional law, the 'Albertine Statute' that was named after him. Piedmontese institutions formed the basis for the local government structure of the new Italian state as it developed in the 1860s. They were influenced by Belgium's exceptionally liberal constitution in 1831 and its communal law of 1836 that resulted directly from the Belgian uprising of 1830.

An Italian law of 1859 established the three-part internal structure of Italian local authorities (council, mayor or president and executive board (*giuntà*) that still continues in a revised form (see §3.4)). A form of the French prefectoral system also continued or was re-established, influenced by those in Belgium and Spain, but it never developed the strength in city areas that it possessed in France except perhaps during the fascist period.

The French prefectoral system of 1800 lasted until recent times, not least because it served the purposes of national solidarity and mobilisation: matters in which all communities in France and most other countries of Southern Europe had a compelling interest. Prefects were concerned with economic and social development from the start as well as with mobilisation of resources for Napoleon's campaigns. They continued to promote economic and social development after 1815. In other countries with prefectoral systems the prefect's role has been seen to contribute to the local good at least as much as to limit local freedom. It was seen as a political necessity that was perhaps unnecessary in a large sophisticated city authority but well appreciated in smaller ones.

The German Tradition

The German tradition also sees local interests as inseparable from central interests but has historically placed more emphasis on local autonomy and the rule of law as the conditions of freedom for individuals, families and group institutions. It may be dated from the reforms associated with the name of the Prussian Chief Minister Baron vom Stein (see §4.1). His emphasis was on the decentralistion of responsibilities as oppposed to Napoleonic centralisation, but it had the same basic purposes: national solidarity and development through local efforts. Under the Prussian Municipal Reform Act of 1808 elected town councils themselves chose their executive mayors and appointed their administrators in accordance with the principle that local autonomous administration was the most efficient way to respond to local needs and to develop national capacity. Voluntary service in local government was seen as the means to re-awaken 'the sleeping energy of passive subjects' and encourage a spirit of community, and local government 'an instrument of national education' promoting love of locality, province and country.

The Prussian approach provided a model for most German systems of local self-government in the following years. Its principles were reinforced later in the century by holding up as an ideal a flattering depiction of rural government by the English magistracy. It inspired reforms in the Russian empire and elsewhere and was a model for those undertaken in Japan in the 1880s. The emphasis on voluntary public service by local landed gentry was attractive, but Japan's strong indigenous communal tradition continued to underlie behaviour, as it did after the contribution of the Americans after the Second World War.

The Constitutionalisation of Local Government

Rights to local self-government came to be constitutionally recognised in Luxembourg (1789), Switzerland at cantonal level (1803, 1848 and 1874), Prussia (1808), France (1831), Belgium (1831), Denmark and Norway (1837), the Netherlands (1848), Sweden (1862) , Finland (1865 and 1871), the Weimar Republic (1919) and, after the Second World War, in Japan (1947), Italy (1948), the Federal Republic of Germany (1949), Portugal (1976) and Spain (1978). Local authorities thus became basic elements in national systems of government, able to appeal to the courts for their defence if state actions conflicted with their constitutional status. In Belgium and Norway local autonomy was a direct consequence of the revolutionary movements of 1830 and in the Netherlands and Denmark after the uprisings of 1848. Provisions for a national local government system were based on rights deriving from natural law traditions, unlike the crown-conferred privileges of boroughs. Universal citizen franchise came later, usually at the end of a long period during which the right to vote had been progressively detached from discriminatory qualifications. The end of discrimination on grounds of property, religion, colour or sex was achieved in Norway in 1913, Denmark in 1917-18, Sweden in 1918-21, Britain in 1928, Japan in 1947, the United States in 1965 (with the effective ending of racial discrimination by means of court decisions), and not until the 1980s in Switzerland with the general extension of the vote to women.

In continental Europe at least it was thought necessary until recently to monitor local government decisions for legality and to give guidance to local authorities through a hierarchy of prefects or provincial governors. In some cases governments appointed mayors or burgomasters. Municipalities, counties and provinces have lived in close interdependence with central or federal state governments in a relationship which still remains to a varying degree (see §1.6).

The American Tradition

Self-government was a necessity in the pioneering settlements of North America. It fitted the British tradition of non-interference by government in local goverment affairs (see §8.1). As Alexis de Toqueville wrote of his experience in the United States in the one political classic that gives local government a first place in its description of a national system of government: 'The village or township is the only association that is so perfectly natural that, wherever a number of men are collected, it seems to constitute itself' (De la *Démocratie en Amérique*, 1835; in translation *Democracy in America*, 1925). Toqueville was struck by the lack of a state administration in the French sense. There was no direction from the centre and local authorities were largely self-regulating within state law.

The constitutionalism of the United States was an important world influence, but it was based on quite different social, economic and legal systems from those of continental Europe. Although starting from British traditions it quickly became characterised by an un-British variety and has developed inventively in varying ways from state to state.

Perhaps the outstanding characteristic of the American system is the distrust of government power (Humes IV, 1991), which seems to derive above all from the popular reaction to the 'taxation without representation' exercised by the British motherland, and from the experience of state power in Europe from which so many have emigrated from the time of the Stuart kings onwards. Hence the limitation of government, systems of checks and balances, distrust of ideology and attempts to achieve popular government that can control those elected as local executives. 'Turning back the frontiers of the state', the Thatcher government's declared objective in the 1980s, reflects American historical attitudes. Linked with this is the weakness of political parties which has continued since Toqueville found in 1831 an absence of parties that contrasted sharply with contemporary France (Jardin, 1984 and 1988). One most remarkable characteristic of the population of the United States is its mobility. One in three households changes its fiscal address every year.

The British Legacy

British local institutions in earlier centuries were praised by other Europeans as a paragon of local independence, although both shire and borough governments were oligarchic in different ways and generally recognised in the early nineteenth century to be in need of radical reform. Reform acts from 1835 renovated the system and widened the franchise. Outside the reformed boroughs the option of building on the traditional parishes and small town authorities was rejected and an artificial system of district authorities established in the 1890s. This was developed mainly by abolitions and amalgamations up to 1974 into the system that existed at the beginning of the 1990s. An eminent Prussian scholar of the late nineteenth century, who wrote an influential book of some three thousand pages on the English Constitution (Rudolf von Gneist, *Das englische Verwaltungsrecht*), saw the abolition of the duty to serve in parish offices as 'a fatal step', doing away with personal obligations and responsibilities within the '*communa*' and eradicating the roots of the whole structure (see §7.1).

In eighteenth century Canada the crown administration resisted attempts to set up self-governing powers on the model of the United States and it was not until 1840 that the provinces began to establish corporate municipalities to exercise delegated powers that were withdrawable at will. No uniform pattern developed. Britain's attempts to set up elected local authorities in Australia in the mid-nineteenth century to help reduce the costs of administration were successfully resisted by the New South Wales legislative council with strong public support. 'Jealousy and competition between state and local governments is one of the main themes in Australian local government history' (Jones, 1991). The Government of Victoria Municipal Institutions Act of 1854, which allowed settlements to set up their own elected district councils with powers similar to those of the English parish councils of the time, was copied in other provinces. Local government in the large cities was for long highly fragmented between councils and ad hoc bodies. The first city-wide authority with infrastructure provision and planning powers was set up in 1926.

The development of local government in Ireland under British rule followed Britain's reforms more or less step by step until the establishment of the Republic. The Irish Republic's local authorities have been character-ised since national independence by an exceptionally weak status *vis-à-vis* central government. The Local Government Act of 1991 among other reforms released them from the *ultra vires* rule, finally distancing the system from the British tradition.

The Restoration of Local Democracy in Europe After the Dictatorships and the Creation of Regional Democracy

The inter-war Fascist and Nazi regimes destroyed local democracy in the name of national leadership. The first priority of the politicians who emerged from war-time darkness was to root public rights and freedoms in new institutions protected by entrenched constitutions. Parties in the centre and centre-left of the political spectrum placed a strong emphasis on achieving social solidarity through democratic institutions. Autonomous local government was given a new constitutional basis in Italy and Germany. This was also the case in Japan where modern local government institutions established in the 1880s had lost what freedoms they enjoyed under the militarist regime that gained ascendance in the 1930s.

The new Italian constitution provided for autonomous regional governments, as did later the new constitutions in Portugal and Spain that followed the end of the Salazar and Franco regimes. The Italian legislation to enable regions to exercise their constitutional role was delayed until the 1970s, when the process began of arranging for the transmission of implementational responsibilites to local authorities. Regionalisation has also been a principle in new constitutions in Spain and Portugal. It was adopted as the means of providing for the autonomy of regions and cultural groups in Belgium. In the 1980s France established its own form of elected regional government.

By 1992 most of continental Western Europe had experienced forty-five years of stability within a central political consensus: a fact that has provided a beneficial environment for the movement towards a decentralisation of governmental and administrative responsibilities towards regions and local communities. It was paralleled by the institution of decentralised power for Western European countries within the European Community (EC). The EC's development has had a major impact on local and regional government orientation in consequence of the benefits obtained in many areas from European policies and instruments aimed at correcting social and economic imbalance within its area.

The Main Traditions of Local Government

An analysis of the nine systems of sub-national government which this book describes in detail suggests that they belong to five groups: South European, North European, British, North American and Japanese. The Federal Republic of Germany has characteristics relating to the South and to the North European groups. Table 1.1 tentatively summarises leading characteristics of states representing these groups: British, North American, Latin or South European, North European and Japanese. An element of judgement is involved and some of the classifications may be debatable.

On nine of the thirteen characteristics in the table the North American systems match the British, but there are major differences: not least in degrees of party politicisation, pluralism, the relative weakness of central government and the form of executive. There is a concentration of central power in the United Kingdom that is now alien to most European Latin systems as well as to the American. The North and South European groups stand together in ten characteristics but differ from the British in about half of these. Japanese structures are clearly a modern synthesis from two continents working in an often awkward relationship with national traditions.

The classification resembles most others that are known in identifying a Southern European Group (Hesse and Sharpe, 1991; see also Humes IV, 1991 and Page and Goldsmith eds, 1987). The emphasis on the prefectoral role in these analyses is now out of date, although not the close organic relationship between the national, regional and local levels. A reformulation is needed which fully takes into consideration the evolution of relationships between central, regional and local governments arising from the decentralisation policies of the last twenty years and distinguishes France from other Latin nations in which *cumul des mandats* has had much less significance and in which regionalisation has been more fundamental in its effects. In many respects the latter countries are closer to Germany in their constitutions and their regional, electoral and political systems. The 'anglo' group, as Hesse and Sharpe term it, also has distinct characteristics which it shares with other English-speaking nations, but it should perhaps be split into a North American group and one relating strongly to that in Britain. The North European group has characteristics remote from those in Britain and closer to Central Europe (Austria and Germany), and so is reasonably termed German/Scandinavian. Finland and Switzerland have their own special approaches, as does Japan where European and American influences have been absorbed into a distinct pattern of structure and behaviour. It is hoped that readers will test these generalisations against the detailed material in the following chapters and their own reading and experience.

Table 1.1 Characteristics of World Systems of Local Government

	Britain	U.S.A. & Canada	France & Italy	Sweden & Denmark	Japan
Constitutional status	creature of parliament	state constitutional	national constitutional	national constitutional	national constitutional
National structure	mixed	mixed	3 tier	2 tier	2 tier
Powers	limited by statute	limited by statute	general competence & statute	general competence & statute	general competence
Control of legality by	courts	courts	regions & courts	state & courts	state & courts
Control of local policy	low	low	interlocked	interlocked	interlocked
Control of local policy historically	low	low	high	high	high
Local functions 1949-89	reduced	various	increased	increased	increased
Local authority expenditure as (UK) % of GDP, 1985*	12%	11%,9%	9%,15%	28%,30%	18%
Public expenditure as % GDP*	44%	35%	49%,50%	57%,60%	29%
Local executive authority	council	mixed	mayor or president	mixed	mayor or governor with board
Representational system	majoritarian	majoritarian	proportional representation	proportional representation	majoritarian
Party system	strong two party	weak two party	strong multi-party	strong multi-party	strong multi-party
Participation at elections	low	low	high	high	high

*Figures from Poul Erik Mouritzen and K.H. Nielsen, *Handbook of Comparative Urban Fiscal Data*, DDA, Odense, 1988

General

The current state of local government in each country has been the result of pragmatic development in response to the results of wars, invasions, revolutions, political pressures, evolving and conflicting concepts and values, economic and social demands including the development of physical and social infrastructure, the spread of affluence, increasing geographic mobility and the expansion of state efforts to promote economic growth and counteract unemployment and other contingencies. The factors of growth and more rarely of retrenchment or loss of power are interrelated and defy simple generalisation. We are describing a world in which watercourses are constantly being reshaped by unpredictable forces.

It is in the nature of local government to be closer than regional and central government to the frontiers of society and its social and environmental problems and therefore best placed to identify local needs and to assess what action is needed. Its roots lie in the self-dependence of local individual communities. As the feudal and subsequently the nation state developed, such communities became increasingly subject to central power and its policies and decisions. Local institutions of self government became more and more homogenised within national boundaries. They have become agents of national law and state executives. They are part of the tissue of the state on which central governments are dependent. In so far as they are elected by their inhabitants they have a democratic legitimacy similar to that of higher levels of government. The following sections of this book explore chief aspects of their position, relationships and competences within modern nations.

1.2 THE STATUS OF LOCAL AND REGIONAL GOVERNMENT

Constitutions and Regional and Local Government Status

By status is meant here standing in law within the governmental system as a whole and, more difficult to determine, standing in the respect of the public. There is a clear distinction between countries in which local authorities have a place in the national constitution and those where they lack this. Constitutional concepts permeate a system of government. Constitutions translate political values into entrenched law and record agreement that politicians and government officials should be required to act in accordance with constitutional provisions.

In advanced countries, excepting the United Kingdom, written constitutions control the use of power by both legislature and executive. In the United Kingdom on the other hand the 'unwritten constitution' is largely what individuals claim it to be. There is no means of legal challenge to the dogma of the 'absolute sovereignty of parliament' or, in practice, the majority in the House of Commons (Mount, 1992).

In mainland Western Europe the constitutional status of local government developed within the traditions of Roman Law and under the influence of eighteenth- and nineteenth- century principles of liberty, rights, national unity and constitutionality, sometimes linked in public debate with medieval concepts of city freedom. It is reflected in the Council of Europe's Charter of Local Government Rights which was signed by the main Western European powers in 1985, excepting the United Kingdom.

The status of local government differs in Council of Europe countries on the main European continent from that in most anglophone countries in two important ways. Written constitutions guarantee a system of local government or administration and give it a secure position within the national system. They may also guarantee not only democratic rights, freedoms and equality of opportunity as the basis for democratic pluralism, but also social democracy (not to be confused with socialist democracy or the welfare state), as in Germany and Italy. They provide as it were a philosophy within which central, legal and local governments and political parties are expected to act.

The 'social state' is by implication an interventionist one with an active role in the field of economic-social relations, taking a direct part in provision of services, prepared to intervene to correct malfunctions in the market, giving assistance to the disadvantaged and observing the rights of labour. Local authorities serve the purposes of such a state as a whole, contributing to its constitutional values (Baldassare and Mezzanotte, 1986).

Competences may be rooted in constitutions, as in the case of those of the regional level in the Italian and Spanish constitutions. Member states of federations and regional governments make provisions for local government powers and status in their own constitutions, as in North America, Germany, Italy and Spain.

The Implications of Democratic Principles for Local Government

Local government may be considered part of the body of the state, just as the individual citizen is deemed to be part of the state. It may have the status of an agency or representative of the state or of the people as a whole within the individual territories it represents. The exercise of authority at the local level, just as at the centre, may be shared between a decision-making body and an executive, instituting in miniature the separation and balance of powers between legislative and executive at national level.

The separation and balance of powers at national level constitutes a protection for the local authority as it does for the individual citizen. Abuse of power by the legislature or the executive can be checked by the judiciary, and legislature and executive can exercise mutual checks on each other's activities to local authorities' benefit.

No distinction is made here between local government and local administration in English since, as the dictionary shows, they may be synonymous or their meanings may overlap. Moreover as translations of the nearest equivalents in foreign languages they are often misleading. The term local government appears to have first gained currency in the polemics of J. Toulmin Smith in the mid-nineteenth century (*Local Self-Government and Centralisation*, 1851), who weakened his case for community-based government as against utilitarian administration through ad hoc bodies by eulogies of a romanticised past. Statements in German and French sources that their communes are not governing but administrative bodies appear to arise mainly from equating government with the exercise of sovereign powers. A Spanish source stating that 'Local government is "administrative" in that it is self-government within a legal framework determined by... the state and the region' (Alfonso, 1991), illustrates the problem of distinguishing between the two. British local government is more restricted in some ways than 'administration' as the word is often understood in countries such as France and Germany which have maintained in the past that local authorities are 'administrative' and not 'governmental' bodies, as the British refusal to allow general competence to authorities shows. It is a fact, however, that continental authorities have tended to be more bound by regulation than anglophone ones. But in some respects the situation is now reversed, as by the British legislation on compulsory contracting out of services.

In translating local government bodies as 'local authorities' an important distinction is missed between the local authority conceived as its citizens — the people who belong to its area and have the right to participate in governing themselves as a collectivity — and the body that in fact exercises power over them. Thus German *Gemeinden*, French communes, départements and regions and other local government bodies in Europe consist of their citizens, as distinct from their assemblies and the separate executives whom some elect to exercise powers in their name. The French term for the former is in fact *collectivité locale* and the Italian *collettività*.

17

Kommune and *komune* appear to be used in a similar sense in Germany and Sweden. They have in law a moral personality, possessing estate, agents and a budget, and rights and obligations. They elect organs (particularly deliberative councils and in certain cases executives) to act for them, but cannot in principle alienate themselves from their actions. In anglophone countries, on the other hand, there are no equivalent words: city or town may convey such a sense, derived from historical origins, as may the 'body of citizens' although the phrase is archaic. Moral personality is attributed, however, not to the citizens but to the council that they elect. Electoral systems in European continental countries are designed to give an effective say on who represents them to all citizens in a community as far as possible, whereas the British majority voting system frequently gives power to a party which receives a minority of votes and, taking into account abstainers, is usually voted for by a minority of all citizens (see §1.8). The low turn-outs that are usual in anglophone countries may reflect an indifference to local government policy, opting out from civic responsibility or a sense of powerlessness.

The rights of local authorities are defined in European constitutions as, for example, to look after the affairs of their communities (Denmark) or to govern and regulate their own affairs (Germany). In Spain regional and local authorities have the same constitutional status in that they possess the right of self-government and the power to manage the interests of the community. The entrenched national law on local government guarantees to municipalities and provinces the power to rule and organise themselves and to tax, finance, expropriate, research and recover their assets. Ireland conferred general competence by ordinary statute in 1991, giving a local authority the right to 'take such measures, engage in such activities or do such things in accordance with law (including incurring expenditure) as it considers necessary or desirable to promote the interests of the community'. In continental Western Europe the main case where local government has no place in the national constitution is Switzerland where internal matters are reserved for determination by individual cantons (the federal states of the Confederation). The rights of communes, however, receive general recognition there and functions such as policing, education, health and even military training are delegated to them. In the past local government was believed to have status as part of the United Kingdom's 'unwritten constitution', but it became clear under the Thatcher governments that the 'unwritten constitution' afforded them no protection. The larger British dominions have federal constitutions which again make no provision for local government.

In Australia the federal Advisory Council for Inter-Governmental Relations (ACIR) in a report of 1985 advocated that formal recognition should be given to local government within the Commonwealth's Constitution (Advisory Council for Inter-Governmental Relations, 1985). In 1988 the matter was put to national referendum, opposed by opposition parties and rejected, less than 33 per cent of the electorate having voted in favour. This would seem to have been due in no small measure to objections to federal interference in a matter that was seen as essentially one for individual states. Local authorities had, however, previously been recognised and protected against arbitrary dismissal in the constitutions of constituent states — Victoria and Western Australia in 1979, South Australia in 1979 and New South Wales in 1986. (Jones, Michael, 1981, 1989, 1991)

In the American Revolution 'the amorphous British approach' dependent on the fiction of crown sovereignty was rejected by the colonials, partly because, as they believed, it had permitted the state executive, under a tyrannical parliament, to treat them unjustly, and because it was seen 'to provide no enforceable limit to an omnicompetent legislature' (Maddox, 1989). Although there is no provision for local government in the United States or Canadian constitutions, individual states and provinces may determine in some detail structural and other conditions that must be met within the local government system. In Japan, on the other hand, the 1947 Constitution recognised local government as one of the administrative systems underpropping a new democratic system based on the rule of law.

The 1980s have seen an ideological clash in the Council of Europe between European concepts of local government's position in society and British views. The European Charter of Self-Government was developed through a long process of deliberation and accepted in 1985 by the Committee of Ministers as a covenant which member states were invited to sign (Council of Europe, 1986, Explanatory Memorandum on the European Charter of Local Self-Government). The Charter commits signatories to apply 'basic rules guaranteeing the political, administrative and financial independence of local authorities'. An explanatory report declared it to be a demonstration 'of the political will to give substance at all levels of territorial administration to the principles defended' by the Council, exercising its self-declared function of 'the keeping of Europe's democratic conscience and the defence of human rights in the widest sense'. It 'embodies the conviction that the degree of self-government enjoyed by local authorities may be regarded as a touchstone of genuine democracy'. By September 1989 the Charter had been signed by 17 member states and ratified by eight. The British government, although a somewhat embarrassed participant in the development of the Charter, failed to sign on the grounds that the approach was alien to British tradition.

The Convention encapsulates much of the West European ideal of local government status common both to the southern and the northern countries, excluding the United Kingdom. It states that the principle of local self-government should be laid down in written law and where practicable in fundamental constitutional law (Article 2). That principle is declared to denote 'the right and ability of local authorities, within the limits of the law, to regulate and manage a substantial amount of public affairs under their own responsibility and in the interests of the local population', exercised by assemblies directly elected by secret ballot with universal suffrage (Article 3). They are to have 'discretion to exercise their initiative with regard to any matter which is not excluded from their competence nor assigned to any other authority'. Their powers 'should normally be full and exclusive... not undermined or limited by another, central or regional authority except as provided for in the law'. The Charter states that public responsibilities should generally be exercised, 'in preference, by those local authorities which are closest to the citizen. Allocation of responsibilities to another authority should weigh up the extent and nature of the task and requirements of efficiency and economy' (Article 4). Changes in boundaries should be made only after consultation with the local communities concerned, possibly by referendum (Article 5). Local authorities should be able to adapt their internal administrative stuctures to local needs and to ensure effective management (Article 6). 'Any administrative supervision of the activities of the local authorities shall normally aim only at ensuring compliance with the law and constitutional principles', but may be exercised 'with regard to expediency by higher authorities in respect of tasks which are delegated to local authorities', and 'kept in proportion to the interests which it is intended to protect' (Article 8). 'Local authorities shall be entitled within national economic policy, to adequate financial resources of their own', partly at least 'derived from local taxes and charges at rates determined by them within statutory limits, which they may dispose of freely within the framework of their powers'. These should 'be commensurate with the responsibilities provided for by the constitution and the law' (Article 8). Although some discretion is given for a state to subscribe to the Convention without accepting every one of its paragraphs, the exceptions are strictly limited.

Less Formal Aspects of Local Government Status

Local government can be argued to be part of 'natural law' in that members of natural communities need to associate to look after their own affairs, and that not to do so deprives them of a natural right to care for their own welfare. Relevant evidence is given in Chapters 2 to 10 below of informal community status and popular regard in individual countries.

Popular status may also depend on the resources local authorities can command from central (and where appropriate regional) government. France is an outstanding case where achievement in this area and in what gets done locally is personalised in the work of leading local politicians who identify with their constituents and can often tap resources at a number of points in the national administrative system (see §2.2). Ultimately this must rest not so much on formal autonomy but on achievements and social and political values. But these are not necessarily stable: constitutional laws that include an autonomous system of adjudication provide a keel to steady relationships between the ship of state and the society it serves.

Regional Government

Regional governments, excepting those in France, are defined as 'political entities with wide-ranging diversified powers within constitutionally unitary states' (European Centre for Regional Development, 1989). Except in France they administer and legislate for their areas within the framework of the national law and constitution on matters within their boundaries, including local government. They cannot, however, override local authorities' constitutional rights. They are found in all non-federal countries covered by this survey with populations of above 16 million excepting Japan and the United Kingdom. They also include Belgium and two countries that in 1992 were in the process of developing regional structures: Greece and Portugal. Their constitutional status varies: one survey suggests that the main way in which the four most developed cases differ from states in West European federations is that they lack representation in the second chamber of a national parliament (ibid.). In Italy they have a right to initiate legislation in the National Assembly.

They, or an associated non-political body, may have what are sometimes called supervisory powers over local authorities, but in general these are limited to ensuring legality of action. Their local authorities can defend their autonomy within the courts and at national political level, sometimes very effectively.

French regions and the pending Portuguese mainland regions are described as 'more like decentralised authorities with specialised powers but still subject to the legal order of the State'. Provinces and counties in other countries on the other hand, including those in Denmark, Ireland, Norway, Sweden and Britain, have limited sectoral powers and 'their legal status is very similar to that of municipalities' (ibid.).

The newness of the European regional regimes means that their status in the community is still evolving. But there are indications that they are already well established in the public consciousness as the upholders of the interests of their areas within the wider state as well as within the national political systems. Some but not all have the enhanced 'legitimacy' of identifying with distinct regional cultures, especially when these are associated with distinct languages or dialects. There is a growing emphasis on the concept of the 'Europe of the Regions'. Their regional planning functions in many cases fit into European Community requirements for development purposes and many are succeeding in identifying themselves with regional progress.

1.3 CONCEPTS AND VALUES

Countries differ in the concepts and values that underlie their understanding of the role of local government and inter-governmental relations. Three important aspects may be distinguished: meanings and values embedded in terms in common use; ideal values; and relevant principles and doctrines.

Peoples in continental Western Europe tend to see territorial community-based administrative institutions as a natural part of an organic whole within the political aspects of society, and to stress the desirability of solidarity within and between communities. Those in anglophone countries on the other hand tend towards instrumental and pragmatic views of government and to view the national interest as no more than the outcome of competing private interests.

The former reflect 'non-economic, non-utilitarian attitudes' towards political relationships, described by one writer as the 'European' concept of the state (Dyson, 1980). Local government is seen to derive its legitimacy from local communities. There is concern about its integration within the national system as a whole in a pattern in which levels of government have complementary contributions to make to the general social good. This can be explained by the drive to create unity out of diversity, as in countries where power has been fragmented between territories, for example

Germany. But the aim to overcome divisions of interest between economic and social groups provides a more general explanation of the importance put on organic relationships. Concepts and values moulded by social, moral and political philosophies expressed through political channels have played a crucial role.

In anglophone countries, on the other hand, local government tends to be regarded as one local interest among others in an essentially competitive society in which self-interest between autonomous bodies is the driving force. Local authorities are seen as a special case because they exercise powers by which they can interfere in the competitive process. General-purpose local authorities are viewed by national governments as one means among others through which they may set conditions to secure the common good. The continental European view emphasises social action; the anglophone view action for individual interests.

The two models described above are polar types. In practice concepts and assumptions are mixed and some concepts cut across between the poles, for example the desirability of a balance of power. The approach in the American Constitution resembles that on the European continent since the Second World War in distributing power among government institutions in a pattern of checks and balances, both between central law-making, judicial and executive arms of government and territorially between the federation and the states. In Britain, on the other hand, real power has become concentrated in the de facto executive.

Local Government Terminology

The concepts embedded in 'language inform the beliefs and practices of political agents' (Ball et al., 1989). Ball quotes Alasdair MacIntyre: 'The limits of one's language mark the limits of one's world'. The French word 'commune', for example, means not an organisation controlled by elected representatives but a self-administering community of the inhabitants of the area. The idea of the commune is described as 'a natural grouping of inhabitants living in a prescribed area, leading a close collective life and possessing numerous interests in common' (translation from Bourjol and Bodard, 1984) — a meaning also embodied in the Italian and other uses of the same word. The commune possesses a social reality anterior to that of the state. The same is true of the German term *Gemeinde* and the Dutch *gemeente*, the root being the germanic word meaning 'common'. 'Sociologically speaking it is a community — a collective entity based on a neighbourhood within defined boundaries whose citizens view themselves as distinct from those in other communities' (Nassmacher and Norton,

1985). The German *Gemeinde*, Dutch *gemeente*, the *municipio* of Spain and the communes of Scandinavia and France and other countries all carry this meaning, together with connotations of a corporate legal entity which, if it does not exercise 'direct democracy', elects a council to take decisions on affairs of common local concern.

Variants of the word 'commune' are also used in Germany and Scandinavia in a somewhat different sense. They are in this case borrowed from another culture and lack the same significance. This is generally true also of the word 'municipality', excepting the use of *municipio*, the basic authority in Spain which is traced back to the ninth century. Such words need to be used and understood with caution since they can mean different things in different languages (as well as in the same language). Some other words that denote medieval contractual status, such as city and borough, are however an exception, reflecting special privileges although the title in the twentieth century is generally no more than honorary and symbolic. The word 'corporation', known to be in use in the fifteenth century in England, appears to have been generally limited to town or city 'governments' possessing a *corporate* responsibility for decision-making and administration for the interest of its area.

Values and Concepts and Their Impact on History

In the use of language by politicians it seems important to distinguish between mere rhetoric and real influence in decision-making. But rhetoric commonly embodies ideal principles and values that have meaning to the public: otherwise it would have no power. There is ample evidence that words such as the famous 'liberty, equality and fraternity' (or in the case of the last its close relation, 'solidarity') have had momentous influence in history. They are still much alive in discourse on the autonomy of local communities, especially in Latin countries as the evidence given elsewhere in this book shows. Chapter 2 shows how the slogan of the French revolutionaries embodied concepts that are still at the centre of French debate on the nature and future of local government. Ylvisaker, an American writer, replaces 'fraternity' with 'welfare' — an interesting substitution with quite a different meaning. In removing fraternity from the trinity he loses the sense of a social bonding force within nature: the sociability that complements liberty and prevents liberty and equality from being mutually destructive in a society within which individuals pursue their self-interests.

The principle of solidarity and its associated concepts remain very much alive in European political discourse, as speeches by continental politicians and texts from European Community offices show. For example a European Commission paper in 1991 on regional programmes (Commission of the European Communities, 1991) places a heavy stress on partnership ('participation of all parties involved at regional and national level at the different stages of the process') and on subsidiarity (the placing of responsibility 'as close as possible to the level of concrete reality, where action can best be tailored to suit the situation'). It ends with a statement that 'solidarity is indispensable'.

Underlying Ideologies

The understanding of these concepts and principles requires an appreciation of the philosophy of natural law in which they are rooted. Cicero (106-430 BC) gave a natural law definition of the purpose of the state developed from the writings of Aristotle and the Stoic philosophers. He saw it as a moral self-governing community of individuals with mutual obligations relating to the common good. St Thomas Aquinas (1225-74) wrote of society as a system of ends and purposes in which the lower level serves the higher and the higher serves and guides the lower to the end of a happy and virtuous life. Suarez (1548-1617), the Jesuit jurist, opened the way to the application of natural law principles to relations within states and between states. The basis of natural law was defined as within human nature. What was right conduct according to that law was proved by the consequences of human action. Such arguments opened the way to natural law becoming the ground of constitutional theory and international law. Natural law theory was made independent of theology and sovereign power, arising from innate human propensities and the force behind social structure. Its application was developed by the Dutch school of lawyers, the most eminent of whom was Grotius (1583-1645), along with the concept that the exercise of political power was based upon an assumption of a contract between rulers and ruled. As the concept of absolute sovereignty was undermined, so the way was opened to constitutionalism and the theory of the state enshrined in revolutionary constitutions in North America, France and other West European countries. Most important to the more modern development of relevant concepts of national development were the works of French and English writers of the eighteenth century and those who followed them in the nineteenth century. Locke (1632-1704) embraced a view of government and other political agencies as responsible to the community which they serve and of natural law as implying innate rights to 'life, liberty and estate' (*Essay concerning Human Understanding*, 1690). He gave special stress to the right of property, underpinning the interests of the land-owning classes which dominated both local and central government in the United Kingdom. The consent of each individual to be part of a body politic obligates him to obey the decisions of the majority. The representatives in the legislature control the executive.

The principles defined by Locke in his *Treatises of Government* were quickly absorbed by French intellectuals. Montesquieu (1689-1755; *L'Esprit des Lois*, 1748), probably the most influential eighteenth-century French writer on the development of political thought and on constitutionalism generally, based his concept of the separation and autonomy of the legislature, executive and judiciary on his understanding of Locke and the British system of government as one of checks and balances that secured the liberty of the citizen.

Concurrently in Britain and France a psychology of action based on the pleasure-pain system developed which cut across natural law theory, although it was itself based on 'self-evident' principles, just as was natural law. It was basic to utilitarianism, the theory developed in France as an instrument of reform by the Swiss, Helvetius (1715-71; *De l'Esprit*, 1758). Bentham (1748-1832; *Introduction to the Principles of Morals and Legislation*, 1789) adopted it enthusiastically, advocating that pain and pleasure 'alone' should 'point out what we ought to do, as well as... determine what we shall do'. This justified generations of British administrators in continuing reorganisations which had little regard to the principles of local social responsibility. It also cut Britain off from the constitutionalism of the continent.

Against the trend John Stuart Mill developed an enlightened utilitarian approach which stressed the necessity of local representative bodies with wide discretion, but based on a theory of their utility for political education and as a means of controlling local executives in the common interest (Mill, 1861). A British utilitarian challenge to this 'ideal' approach can be found in Sharpe (1970). There is a contrasting nineteenth-century British tradition (cf. Toulmin Smith, 1851) 'espousing a vision of local self-government based on a highly romanticised, if not Gothic, vision of British history' (*Against the Over-Mighty State*, 1988). The authors of the American Constitution, the French Declaration of the Rights of Man and the Citizen and subsequent constitutions in France and elsewhere were all imbued in natural law assumptions of the eighteenth century. A common aim was to secure human rights by means of the control of the executive under an assembly delivering the common will of the people expressed through law as interpreted by an independent judiciary. They provided the basis for theories of popular decentralised self-government as an aspect of the freedom of local communities. The separation of territorial powers could be seen as a check on the power of the central state: the dangers implicit in the 'tyranny of the majority' as exercised by central government against the interests of local areas whose own overwhelming majorities were opposed to its policies. They also provided the model of checks and balances in the relationship between local government councils and mayoral and other executives acting within the limits set by national law. The American stress on the division of powers between levels of government could be extended to some extent to local government as mitigating the dominance of the sovereign.

Ylvisaker uses his own trinity of 'liberty, equality and welfare' as a rationale for local government by bringing in other American values : 'Liberty (Constitutionalism, with a good mixture of laissez-faire); Equality (especially as embodied in its corollary of democracy and the axiom of wide-spread participation)'; and 'Welfare (service)' as commented on above (Ylvisaker, 1959).

There is a bifurcation between its use by rationalists in the tradition of John Locke in eighteenth-century Britain and the fathers of the American Constitution who placed a strong emphasis on the right to property and non-interference by the state on the one hand, and on the other theorists of the revolutionary movement in Europe to whom personal liberty and the role of the state in securing the conditions of liberty were pre-eminent issues.

The German tradition was distinct but influenced by an interpretation of British practice rather than utilitarianism. Baron vom Stein (1757-1831), the statesman who inspired early nineteenth-century reforms of local government in Prussia, made assertions of values in local government which have continued to be quoted there (see §§ 4.2 and 4.3).

One North European school of thought little known further west is that of the German historical law school of the early nineteenth century. It had a deep influence on Dutch scholars, particularly Johan Rudolf Thorbecke, a former Professor in History and Public Law who was prime minister at the time of the adoption of the modern Dutch Constitution in 1848 and largely responsible for the local government legislation that followed it. The Dutch stance is said to have arisen from 'reaction to both the rationalism of the French Enlightenment and the bureaucratic-centralist approach of the Napoleonic era' (Toonen, 1991, 1987). The Dutch term, used to describe the system introduced in the 1848 Constitution, may be translated as 'the decentralised unitary state'. The theory stresses that the state and its component parts (including local governments) cannot be seen as 'passive machines or will-less instruments, subject to outside steering and hierarchical control'. They are rather 'living and dynamic entities': the state and its components being 'best seen as relatively autonomous from their environments'. But 'unity among the component parts and elements is necessary to generate state unity'. 'State authority is not the source, but the outcome of unity... among the relatively autonomous parts'. 'The need of the unitary state refers to the need for arrangements for conflict resolution, consensus building, and mutual adjustment'. The 'organic municipality has a relative autonomy and independent strength of its own.... Its viability needs to be recognised and authorised by other parts of the state system... municipal autonomy is not reflected in the insulation of local government from "higher" governments'. Thorbecke stressed instead 'the municipal right to initiative in conducting its own affairs, as the embodiment of the principle of municipal autonomy'. But to prevent harm to other parts of the state, including other municipalities, autonomy must be 'bounded' by a supervisory authority exercising 'negative power' at provincial level. 'Supervision powers enable the complex configuration of parts — citizens, municipalities, and others which constitute a province, to tell any single authority what it should not do, not what it should do'. Toonen suggests that Thorbecke's concept of the unitary state would probably be better represented as 'the consensus state' rather than the 'decentralised unitary state'(Toonen, 1991). Despite stress on the 'separateness' from each other of the three main levels of government in the Dutch system, the concept of 'organic' relationships implies a high level of mutual understanding between them in matters of mutual concern. It demonstrates again the importance of the concept of community with its connotation of power-sharing.

In Sharpe's words, 'it is possible to hypothesise, without doing flagrant injustice to reality, that local government's primordial role is no different from that of other polities in that it reflects a sense of common identity among its citizens which at its most basic may be defined as the consciousness that they have more in common with each other than they have with people living beyond their communal boundary'; and that 'such consciousness can be given tangible expression (and be tested) by the establishment of a tax on all citizens for the provision of public goods and other forms of collective consumption that the same citizens do not wish to have provided voluntarily or by the market' (Sharpe, 1988).

Subsidiarity

One principle applicable to local government conceived as the local community is that of subsidiarity. It was used in the debate on the Council of Europe Charter described in §1.2. The principle has wide connotations that have become deeply rooted in political thinking over much of Western Europe since 1945.

It was in the nineteenth century that a somewhat different but related distinction developed between characteristically British utilitarian thinking that tended to assume that human institutions should be justified in terms of individual self-interest and that the role of the state should be minimalised, and the characteristically continental philosophy of man as in essence a social animal — a member of a society and of a state responsible for creating the conditions in conformity with natural law by which he was enabled to realise a virtuous life. Catholic social and legal philosophers in Germany from the second half of the nineteenth century, steeped in Cicero and Aquinas, appear to have been mainly responsible for formulating social principles consistent with this view of the relations between society and the state (Alexander, 1953). They saw the primary purpose of society as the dignity and self-fulfilment of individual human persons working together responsibly within a community directed towards the common good: an essentially social individualism as opposed to one based on individual self-interest. Their view was in even stronger opposition to the contemporary Hegelian approach which subordinated the concept of society and so of the individual to the ideal of the state, and led directly to Hitlerism on the one hand and to Marxism on the other.

The Catholic principles of subsidiarity and solidarity were formulated within the framework of natural law theory by German members of the Society of Jesus who exercised a direct influence on papal thinking (Adonis and Jones, 1991; Wilke and Wallace, 1990). That of subsidiarity comes into prominence in the papal encyclical, 'Quadragesimo anno', of Pius XI in 1931, within the context of the social pronouncements of Leo XVIII (1878-1903). It assumes that social responsibility rests primarily on the individual or that level of society nearest to the individual person. Pope Pius XII (1939-58) declared the principle of subsidiarity to be 'valid for social life in all its organisations'. John XXIII (1958-63) employed the principle in the encyclical *Mater et Magistra* of 1961 in connection with the proper role of public authorities in economic affairs as 'to encourage, stimulate, regulate, supplement and complement, not replace, individual efforts (remarkably similar to the 'enabling role' which has been extensively coined as a chief local authority function in Britain during the 1980s), and also to regional aid by central governments.

The main carriers of the concepts into the world of politics were the German Centre Party and later the Christian Democrat and Social Union Parties representing Protestant as well as Catholic views across continental Europe. These parties, normally working with non-Marxist socialist and

French centre parties who have to some extent acknowledged the same principles, have been the dominant political influence on the development of the European Community.

Jacques Delors, President of the Commission of European Communities, gave in a Colloquium at Maastricht in 1991 an authoritative interpretation of the subsidiarity principle that bridges between its use as a principle of moral guidance regarding the location of authority and responsibility in social matters on the one hand and of authority and responsibilities in inter-governmental affairs on the other (Delors, 1991). In the latter respect it retains its moral force in so far as governments accept the ethical requirement that, in Delors' words, 'the dignity and responsibility of the people who make up society is the final goal of that society' and that it is their responsibility to serve this end. Delors, reflecting the encyclical, states that subsidiarity has two 'infrangible aspects':

- the right of each to exercise his responsibilities there where he can perform them best;
- the obligations of the public authorities to give to each the means to reach his full capacity.

He adds that it 'is not simply a limit to intervention by a higher authority *vis-à-vis* a person or a community in a position to act for itself, it is also an obligation for this authority to act *vis-à-vis* this person or this group to see that it is given the means to achieve its ends'. But 'the smaller unit's right to act is operative to the extent, and only to the extent... that it alone can act better than a large unit in achieving the aims to be pursued.' He has also said that the extension of the competences of the European Union to areas which are 'federal' by nature should imply 'a recentring of the European construction towards real equilibrium between the Community level, the national level and the local level'.

Individualism and Decentralisation

The word *individualism* is used in this book in different senses. To generalise, individualism in the Anglo-American tradition tends to connote an independence of authority. It fits in with the liberal economists' basic premise of minimalisation of control, and perhaps also the minimalisation of society, as in Margaret Thatcher's reported remark that 'there is no such thing as society'. John Stuart Mill in his early years (1848) gave a classic expression to it in his *Principles of Political Economy*, the handbook of mid-Victorian liberalism: 'Laisser-faire, in short, should be the general practice: every departure from it, unless required by some great good, is a certain evil.' (Compare this with the intervention for the good of individuals implied by the 'social state' concept.) It is the rationale for 'Tiebout theory', much quoted in the United States, that postulates that local governments are like private firms competing for customers by means of the attractiveness and prices of the services they provide, or individuals competing between themselves for maximisation of goods guided by the principle of economic advantage. The best performing local authorities will attract residents and property investment, thereby promoting excellence. (Tiebout, 1959)

Take by contrast the case of Sweden's 'co-operative individualism' which emphasises above all the exercise of autonomy by the individual to follow his own bent but co-operatively rather than competitively. The French stress the right to individual autonomy while at the same time exhorting social solidarity, more perhaps than any other nation. The 'One and Indivisible Republic' is not inconsistent with nonconformity. The approach can be related both to the support a local authority should make available to the individual and the support the state should supply to the authority itself. There is an underlying concept of a moral, organic society in which all members are interdependent and seek common goods through both private and public bodies as a condition of well-being and individual freedom under the law.

Ideally in such a society all its members should be involved in ensuring the public interest. Decentralisation of power and local solidarity are principal means to counteract the threats to freedom that any gap between rulers and the ruled implies. The shreds of full citizen participation in government in industrialised countries are now small historical curiosities. Representative systems are widespread, but the extent to which they represent the diversity of interests in modern society is generally very limited.

The proportion of members of a local community involved in government has shrunk rapidly during the last three decades or so in most countries reviewed in this book. There is a danger that political elites are isolated from popular wishes. Party systems with high levels of popular involvement and sensitivity, as described in §1.10, are one means by which the vertical gap between local politician and the public can be bridged. Involvement of sectoral bodies representing business, labour and voluntary bodies is another. Both are given great importance in many of the Council of Europe countries and Japan. Both may be constitutionally recognised and supported legally and financially in the interests of solidarity and national achievement.

The concept of ***decentralisation*** is one that has been closely associated with developments described in the following section. In Europe it has permeated into political thinking increasingly since the war: the reforms of the past two decades especially have seen it acquiring real definition in practice, closely supported by arguments of solidarity and subsidiarity. Its virtues are at the heart of the case for local and regional government.

The events of the early 1990s, however, have put both principles under great strain in their West European heartlands. It seems possible that the mutual social support and decentralisation that they imply have developed in forms that are too expensive to defend and sustain against forces that have been released by the opening up of Eastern Europe and discontents arising from the economic recession. In so far as social and political collaboration lose force against those in which individual and national interests dominate, they deeply threaten the authority of decentralised elected authorities.

1.4 NATIONAL STRUCTURES OF LOCAL AND REGIONAL GOVERNMENT

The Variety of Structures

The simplest democratic structure is that of the city-state which is both state and local government. This still exists in San Marino, founded in AD 310 and today a city of 23,000 people. The world's oldest republic, it has enjoyed a form of constitutional government since the year 1600. It possesses nine zonal sub-governments called 'castles'. Within Germany the cities of Berlin, Hamburg and Bremen also combine state with municipal status (see §4.12). The largest, Berlin, has a population of some 3,380 thousand, and the smallest, Bremen, one of 667 thousand. Like San Marino each contains sub-municipalities.

The simplest structure below central government is a single tier of all-purpose municipalities. A single tier has obvious attractions. It makes it possible, in theory at least, for each local authority to work to a comprehensive and well-integrated set of aims and policies that takes into account the full range of local needs and sets overall priorities. Overall co-ordination and, where desirable, integration of services to achieve the greatest effectiveness and efficiency should be much simpler than in a multi-tier structure. All-purpose authorities should be able to represent the needs of their areas to central government with a single authoritative voice. They should make it clear to the public where responsibility for a service lies and may be expected to attract stronger candidates for political office and management posts. Yet this form of sub-national government is rare in advanced countries. It exists universally only in three of the states mentioned in this book: Iceland since the late 1980s (population 257 thousand), Luxembourg (population 338 thousand) and Finland, which has a single autonomous tier of 480 municipalities for a population of under five million. Finland, however, has a provincial level consisting of strong special-purpose joint bodies and centrally appointed bureaucracies.

Australia and Switzerland have single-tier local government structures within their member states. In Canada, the United States, Germany, Austria, Denmark, Norway, Sweden and Ireland a general-purpose level can be found combining functions that elsewhere in the same country are divided between basic and intermediate tiers of self-government. These resemble the British county boroughs that were abolished in 1974. London boroughs and metropolitan districts would be similar if it were not that important functions are carried out by joint bodies. The three Scottish island authorities are all-purpose authorities. Island authorities here and elsewhere are a special case due to their separation from the mainland.

Multi-tier systems predominate in four out of five of the countries listed in Table 1.2. The most important argument for multi-tier systems is perhaps the need to keep as many functions as possible in authorities easily accessible to local inhabitants, while separating to an intermediate level those functions where there are clear benefits available from larger-scale authorities. Such benefits include greater ability to make large-scale investments, appoint more specialised staff and afford more specialised equipment. Multi-tier systems may also arguably avoid unsatisfactory alternatives such as large-scale amalgamations of existing authorities, joint authorities, special-purpose authorities, direct provision of services by government departments or agencies and large-scale amalgamations. It has also been argued that a second tier is desirable to achieve a 'wider area of discourse', and that the optimum number of levels of power is three because 'Two is an invitation to abiding conflict and stymie, or at the other extreme to subordination and acquiescence'. The same author commented that two-level systems 'inevitably tend to progress toward the establishment of a middle level' (Ylvisaker, 1959).

The French départements and German Landkreise have developed an important role in supporting and complementing the work of smaller communes by providing services beyond the latter's resources under mutual agreements. In California counties contract extensively to provide services for small municipalities.

Table 1.2: Classes and Numbers of Sub-National Authorities

N.B.: Foreign words are given in the singular with plural forms in brackets around pluralising suffixes. Where this is not possible the full plural words are given in brackets.

	Basic Level	*Intermediate or General Purpose*	*State or Region*

Countries with mixed types of structure

England	non-metropolitan districts 296	counties 45 London boroughs and City of London 32 metropolitan districts 36	
Wales	non-metropolitan districts 37	counties 8	
Scotland	districts 53	regions 9 islands 3	
Germany	Gemeinde(n) 8846	Kreise 428 Kreisfreie Stadt (Städte) 121	Land (Länder) 16 incl. 3 city-states
Irish Republic	non-county bor-oughs 6; towns 28; urban district councils 49	counties 27 county boroughs 5	
USA[1]	municipalities 19,200; towns/ towns/town-ships 16,691	counties incl. 'city-counties' 3,043	states 50

Countries with predominantly uniform multi-tier structures

Austria		Gemeinde(n) 2,304	Land (Länder) 9
Belgium	commune(s)/ gemeente(n) 596	provincie(s) 9	region(s) 3 communities 3
Denmark	primaer kommune(r) 273	amtskommune(r) 14	

France	commune(s) 36,433	département(s) 96 incl. Ville de Paris	région(s) 22
Greece	demos (demoi) 264; koinotes (koinotetes) 6,022	nomos (nomoi) 51	
Italy	comune (comuni) 8,074[2]	provincia (provincie) 94 to be restructur- ed in early 1990s[1]	regione (regioni) 20
Japan	shi (cities) 653 cho (towns) 2006 son (villages) 594 Tokyo wards	fu, ken and to Tokyo-to	
Netherlands	gemeente(n) 714	provincie(n) 12	
Norway	kommune(r) 448	fylkeskommune(r) 18	
Portugal[3]	conselho(s)/ municipio(s) 275		regione(s) 2 for islands
Spain	municipio(s) 8,027[2]	provincia(s) 50[2]	comidad(es) autonoma(s) 17
Sweden	kommune(r) 284	Landstingkommune(r) 23	
Switzer- land	commune(s) 3,000		cantons 23

All-purpose authority structures
Finland: municipalities ('kunta' in Finnish and 'kommuner' in Swedish) 460, including 94 towns and cities and 366 of other types
Iceland: baer (towns) 23 and hrappar (rural districts) 199
Luxembourg: communes 126

Other
Australia: a wide range of types of authority but in general single-tier under the six state governments. Types include metropolitan and non-metro-politan cities; municipalities, towns and boroughs; and shires or district councils. County councils have been formed consisting of representatives of a group of local authorities to carry out special functions. In 1986 the total number of basic authorities was calculated from censuses as 836 (Jones, 1989).
Canada: the main Canadian source, the *Canada Year Book 1990*, classifies as unitary authorities many that appear to be in the bottom tier of a two-tier system (unitary: cities 200, towns 885, villages 1,062, rural municipalities

2,089; regional municipalities (upper tier): metropolitan and regional municipalities 165, counties and regional districts 150).

Notes
1. In the case of the USA the terms used for categories of local authority in the national census are given. There is a great variety of names and distinctions throughout the States. Australia and Canada are omitted from the table because their complexity defies summary within the format.
2. In both Italy and Spain responsibility for structural reorganisation within the law and constitution has passed to the regional authorities. The figures given are consistent with the position in 1987 but have been changing since then.
3. Portugal has in addition to its districts 3,848 parish authorities with an average population of about 2,500. They carry out a range of statutory functions by delegation in addition to exercising discretionary powers. They have much wider scope than the English parish and Welsh community authorities whose functions are entirely discretionary and not comparable with any of the authorities listed above.

In most cases multi-tier systems are not hierarchies in the sense that the higher level governs the lower. Whatever may have been the case in the past there remains in general no element of political control by an intermediate tier over the basic authorities in its area. In many countries it is now a principle that all levels of authority have equal autonomy (see §1.2).

In some cases structures are mixed in the sense that authorities at a particular level are found in some parts of a country but not in others. The tendency among the most economically successful major countries in Western Europe since the Second World War has been to increase rather than decrease the number of levels. In certain cases as many as five directly elected levels of administration are found, including France, Germany and Italy where there can be national, regional, provincial or county, municipal or most-purpose and also sub-municipal councils in certain cases.

Italy, France, Spain and Belgium have well-established systems of regional government. Portugal and Greece are in the course of developing them (see §1.2). Except in France they are primarily responsible for regional planning and development. The elected regional assemblies legislate for their areas on domestic matters within a framework of national law which they and their executives have participated in developing. These matters include local government structure and services, as in the case of governments of member states in federal countries such as Germany and the USA.

The establishment of the regional level in Western Europe since the 1950s has been effected mainly by the devolution of functions from central government to a level where there is less administrative congestion and a more intimate appreciation of popular needs. Regional governments are generally required to delegate onwards to local authorities the exercise of functions which do not require administration across a region as a whole. Regions are thus generally different in purpose and essence from counties and European provinces and also from the regional council authorities to be found in Canada and New Zealand. They should not be confused with regions defined by the European Community for structural fund purposes, although they have become increasingly involved in different ways in development programming to qualify for economic and social funding from the EC.

Terminological confusion can arise in other structural matters. The translation 'district' has often been used for the German and Austrian 'county' (*Landkreis*) levels and for Scandinavian counties or provinces, but in the United Kingdom and New Zealand districts are basic authorities. The character and names of authorities in the Republic of Ireland derive from English terminology.

Community, neighbourhood or parish councils (and 'town councils' in England and Wales) have in general no mandatory powers. They may be an autonomous level, as in Britain, or have been set up by municipalities to carry out minor functions in their areas and represent local interests.

Countries which give most emphasis to utilitarian values tend to favour large-scale authorities, while complex, multi-tier systems with large numbers of small basic authorities with general competence are characteristic of countries which tend to emphasise the relationship of basic authorities to communities, the principle of equality of powers between authorities, 'solidarity' and consensus formation.

Table 1.2 shows the terms used for authorities above the neighbourhood or parish level country by country, grouping them according to whether they have mixed types of basic authority, uniform types in multi-tier systems or all- or most-purpose authorities. Countries are listed together that have mixed systems at basic level (that is both all- or most-purpose and limited-purpose authorities). For simplicity's sake joint authorities and special-purpose authorities are omitted from the table.

Structural Reform After 1950

In Western Europe the Second World War initiated a period of migration between and within nations that mingled cultures and in many areas transformed the nature of local society. Demographic, economic and social change and technical progress, including the mobility brought by ownership of private cars and the provision of public transport, 'made local structures based on a vanished world seem suddenly antiquated, out of date and obsolete' (Zehetner in Council of Europe, *The Reforms of Local and Regional Authorities in the Europe: Theory, Practice and Critical Appraisal*, 1983). Administrative areas ceased to relate satisfactorily to the amenities sought by inhabitants or came to be seen by policy-makers as incompatible with the reform of services. National reports made 'it fairly clear that, primarily, the size of a local authority is a function of the services expected from it' (ibid.). Small local authorities, the legacy of previous centuries, were believed to be incompatible with professional standards and the high level of investment and efficiency required if society was to attain the economic, physical and social standards which rising wealth had brought within the public's reach.

In West Germany (see §4.4) and Scandinavia (§§5.4 and 6.4) extensive reorganisations were justified in part as a condition of decentralisation of powers from the centre. Minimum population size targets were set in the 1960s for basic authorities of 8, 10, 12 or 20 thousand inhabitants, justified by the numbers considered necessary to provide primary schools and other basic social facilities. The Japanese government also rationalised boundaries and raised the average population size to above 32 thousand, although the great majority of basic authorities remained well below that. The extreme case was Great Britain where the reorganisation in the early 1970s sought a general minimum population size of 80 thousand for shire districts and around 200 thousand for districts and boroughs in the largest conurbations, although in the event some cases survived that were below these levels. Although in most cases great efforts were made to persuade authorities to merge of their own free will, amalgamations were often enforced against local wishes.

In Southern Europe, local opposition to amalgamations, supported in some cases by court rulings, protected small authorities against amalgamation, so that other means had to be found to achieve the desired concentration of resources. Small authorities were encouraged to form joint bodies to exercise functions requiring larger areas and resources, delegate functions upwards, contract services out and adopt other means by which limitations of smallness might be overcome. But the result could be that although communal powers were maintained in principle, effective communal control of key services was lost.

At the same time a movement developed in Southern Europe towards decentralisation of power from the centre to new regional authorities. Motives included the diffusion of power to block the way to new dictatorships, the breaking up of monolithic and inefficient national bureaucracies, overcoming political congestion at the national level, instituting regional planning processes to replace national ones which had been seen to fail, and responding to pressures for autonomy from regionally-based cultural and linguistic movements.

Existing intermediate authorities — county, provincial and departmental councils — were at first seen as under threat from the expansion of basic authorities below and the new regional governments above, but the threats failed to materialise. In the end intermediate authorities not only survived but came to be seen in the Mediterranean as the most suitable level from which to provide certain services.

Basic Local Authorities

'Basic' local authorities all possess the core of responsibilities shown in Table 1.3 below but they vary greatly in their resources and ability to carry out their tasks. Their size ranges from a tiny homestead or hamlet in France up to the *Ville de Paris* with around 3 million inhabitants, and in North America up to the City of New York with a population of over 7 million.

The size of a local authority determines its qualities more than any other single factor. It affects the extent to which leading elected representatives and paid employees can be expected to have a grasp of the local authority's business as a whole, the scale and level of specialisation of the officer organisation and many other matters.

As Table 1.3 indicates, countries differ widely in the sizes of their basic authorities. The Mediterranean countries have in general shown the strongest resistance to pressures to increase scale. France is the outstanding example, having over 36 thousand communes in a country of some 54 million people, giving an average population per commune of about 1,540. The United States has an average not far below that of Italy but a much greater range in the size of its local authorities. Germany and the United States stand between Southern and Northern Europe in this analysis. Germany illustrates among its own *Länder* the tendency for the average scale of authorities to grow larger as one moves north. Great Britain 'diverges dramatically from the European norm. The average district in the shire counties is over thirteen times as large in population terms (96,000) as the average of all the German and Italian municipalities (somewhat over 7,000), five times the size of the average French commune' (Blair, 1991). The great discrepancies in scale between basic authorities raise major problems over the distribution and implementation of responsibilities, a matter central to the problems of decentralisation of power.

Table 1.3: Size and Populations of Basic Local Authorities

Country	Number Authorities	av. pop. (approx.)	% less than 100 thou. pop.
Southern Europe			
France	36,757	1,560	38
Greece	6,022	1,827	81
Switzerland	3,000	2,122	60
Luxembourg	126	2,905	41
Austria	2,304	3,000	97
Spain	8,027	4,700	58
Italy	8,074	7,019	23
Germany	8,846[1]	8,845	37
Portugal	275[2]	34,180	0
Northern Europe			
Norway	448	9,421	4
Finland	460	10,770	5
Belgium	589	16,740	0.2
Netherlands	800	17,860	3
Denmark	273	18,811	0
Sweden	284	30,249	0
European Islands			
Iceland	222	1,100	n.a.
Ireland	92	41,190	2
Northern Ireland	26	60,480	0
Wales	37	75,870	0
Scotland	56	91,620	0
England	365	127,000	0
Around the Pacific			
Canada[3]	4,238	5,594	n.a.
USA	35,800[4]	6,600	n.a.
Australia	836	19,114	n.a.
Japan	3,245	37,200	n.a.
New Zealand[5]	70	46,729	n.a.

All figures are approximated from data available in the late 1980s.

Notes
1. Includes 91 combined towns and counties.
2. Portugal has in addition to its Districts 3,848 parish authorities with an average population of about 2,500 which carry out a range of statutory functions under delegations in addition to their discretionary powers. They have much wider scope than the English parish and Welsh community authorities whose functions are entirely discretionary and not comparable with the other authorities above.
3. There were 3,913 unitary municipalities under 10,000 pop. in 1988 (*Canada Yearbook 1990*).
4. Municipalities and townships, 1986 (*Statistical Abstract of the United States, 1991*)
5. Recommended by New Zealand Local Government Commission Report, 1989, and subject to subsequent policy changes.

Table 1.4: Numbers, Populations and Areas of Intermediate Authorities

Country	Number	av. pop. (000s)	Av. Area sq. km.
Southern Europe			
Italian provinces (*provincie*)	94	611	3,202
French (*départements*)	100	556	5,490
Greek prefectures (*nomoi*)	51	216	2,538
Spanish provinces (*provincias*)	50	780	10,100
West German (*Landkreise*)	428	170	834
Northern Europe			
Belgian provinces	9	1,095	3,390
Danish *amter*	14	365	3,076
Norwegian *fylker*	18	234	18,477
Swedish *landstingskomuner*	24	358	18,741
The Islands			
English counties	39	724	3,133
Irish counties[1]	27	n.a.	n.a.
Scottish regions	91	561	8,111
Welsh counties	8	351	2,595
Around the Pacific			
US counties	3,041	n.a.	n.a.
Japanese prefectures	47	37,200	8,036
New Zealand	14	234	19,191

The figures are approximated from the latest data available to the author from the 1980s.

Note
1. A two-tier system exists only in 84 small urban areas.

In some countries larger towns constitute a special statutory class of authority, possessing county or provincial responsibilities as well as municipal ones. In the majority of Council of Europe countries however, and especially in Latin countries, the principle of uniformity or equality of status and privileges has been maintained, subject in some cases to special provisions for the capital city. This has not prevented a recognition of the de facto political power of the 'great cities'. In France they have their own association and their mayors are often powerful national politicians.

Intermediate Authorities

The development of intermediate authorities over the last two centuries has been accompanied by transfers of state responsibilities to their assemblies or executives. The following arrangements are found for county or provincial administrations:

(1) *A state-appointed governor or other high-level official responsible for state functions over a large area without an elected council of its own.* The area may include many sub-areas with autonomous local assemblies, as found in Austria, Finland and the larger West German Länder. In Luxembourg there is a state-appointed commissioner for each of the three administrative districts whose purpose is liaison with communes, the only form of local government in the country.

(2) *A state-appointed governor for each province who acts as executive for and presides over an elected provincial council,* as in Portugal pending the setting up of regional governments on the mainland. In Belgium there is a state-appointed governor for each province who heads a provincial executive board, but the provincial assemblies elect their own chairmen.

(3) *A governor or prefect who is responsible for central government functions in a county or province in parallel with an autonomous assembly which provides major services and elects its own chairman and executive.* In some cases he or she presides over boards of representatives chosen by the local assembly, so that there is close involvement of local councillors in decisions and advice given on central government actions affecting the area. This is now a widespread arrangement found in Denmark, Sweden,

Italy, Spain and Greece.

In France the classical prefectoral system was superseded in 1983 by one in which the council appoints its own executive and chairman (see §§2.1 and 2.6).

All these systems in different ways provide for a close and often inter-locking relationship between state-appointed officials and local government executives. Basic authorities in most if not all countries have often argued that intermediate authorities lack the status of true local government bodies in that they are not truly local, being used predominantly to provide state-controlled mandatory services and subject to detailed government regulation and interference by service ministries.

Intermediate authorities can be of high importance in the national organisation of political parties. Without the means for coming together at this level the small authorities typical of Latin countries would lack a strong means to represent their needs to state government and relate to the decentralised officers of central ministries. They provide a meaningful level for government and party consultation and the exercise of influence upwards and downwards. In a complex organic system they can be the main nerve-centres that link the periphery and centre. They can provide a ladder of advancement for mayors even of quite small communes if they possess the necessary political abilities.

Where cities are all- or most-purpose authorities with a special status independent of the general county system (termed in Germany 'county-free'), the intermediate level is much weaker and may be predominantly associated with rural interests, despite the fact that it may in many cases include large and wealthy town and suburban populations.

Special-Purpose Authorities

Special-purpose authorities have been set up where governments have not wished to confer responsibility on a general-purpose type of authority or where such authorities do not exist. They may be called local government bodies where they consist wholly or substantially of directly elected members or members of local authorities appointed from within their councils. They may include members appointed by government or representatives of non-governmental organisations. Most are single purpose or responsible for a closely related group of functions such as water-supply, drainage and sewage disposal.

Such authorities cannot 'govern' their areas in the sense of determining priorities or making trade-offs between a range of functions for the good of the community as a whole. They are generally dependent on a small range of professionals. Their areas are often determined on grounds of functional efficiency and not coterminous with other local authority boundaries. They usually work to a central ministry or branch of a ministry interested only in its own area of interest and may be subject to detailed regulations drafted in that ministry. In general they are not favoured in Western Europe if there is a suitable level of multi-purpose elected authority that can reasonably undertake the services concerned.

In England special-purpose authorities were set up in order to take over the responsibilities of the previous metropolitan county authorities on their abolition. They are statutory joint boards for the police, fire, civil defence and transportation purposes in the English metropolitan counties, and, in Greater London, for fire and civil defence combined (see §7.13).

By far the most highly developed networks of special-purpose authorities are found in the United States, where they outnumber any other form of local government. They administer one in ten of national school districts and have been growing in number for other purposes (see §8.4). The pattern of criss-crossing boundaries of service authorities has been described as 'organised chaos' (Owens and Norregaard, 1991).

Governments of Autonomous Regions

In nine of the countries listed in Table 1.2 local authorities are subject to legislation by member states of federations or by a regional level of government. In two others, Greece and Portugal, regional governments are being established for all areas. In France regions have acquired importance for local authorities because of their planning and other functions.

In countries which possess federal constitutions (the Federal Republic of Germany, Austria, Switzerland, Australia, the United States and Canada) local authorities are subject to the laws of their federal states. They normally participate in national decision-making through representatives in central assemblies. It may be noted that many local authorities are larger in population than some member states within federal constitutions. In Switzerland, an outstanding example, nine of the cantons have fewer than a hundred thousand inhabitants.

Table 1.5: Member States in Federal Constitutions: Populations, Areas

Country	Number	Av. Pop. (000s)	Av. Area sq. kms
Swiss cantons	26	248	1,588
German Länder	16	4,905	22,297
Austrian Länder	9	849	9,286
Australian states[1]	6	2,495	1,058
Canadian provinces[1]	10	2,533	6,059
United States[2]	50	5,008	187,452

Notes
1. Figures exclude very large non-autonomous areas ('territories') and their generally sparse populations, and also the Australian Capital Territory.
2. Excludes District of Columbia.

Regional governments constitute a legal order subject to discretionary supervision by central government (European Centre for Economic Development, 1989). In Belgium a regional system was initiated in 1980 and revised in 1988. The three regions are Flanders (population 5,676,000), Wallonia (3,206,000) and Brussels (976,000). The members of these and their partner bodies, the cultural communities, are drawn from the membership of the National Assembly and Senate.

Spain's regionalisation under the 1978 Constitution is the most radical short of federalism except perhaps that of Belgium. The regional authorities are the 17 'autonomous communities', ranging in population from La Rioja (260,000) to Andalucia (6,573,000) and averaging 3,331,000. The French and Italian regions are described in Chapters 2 and 3 below.

Table 1.6: Autonomous Regions: Populations and Areas

Country	Number	Av. pop. (000s)	Av. Area (sq. kms)
Southern Europe			
French regions	22	2,521	30,750
Greek regions	16	1,081	14,660
Spanish autonomous communities	17	2,142	28,042
Italian regions	20	2,833	15,505
Northern Europe			
Belgian regions[1]	3	3,286	10,174

The figures are approximated from the latest data available to the author since the 1980s.

Note

1. These figures are for the political and administrative regions: there are three overlapping cultural and linguistic communities in parallel which determine policy in appropriate fields: Flemish, Walloon and German.

Note on Criteria for the Reform of Local Authority Areas

It is arguable that national structures of regional and local government should be based on areas which facilitate the democratic process and enable services to be provided efficiently and economically, relating area and population to authorities' powers and responsibilities. A prior issue is the width and nature of the functions which local authorities are meant to exercise. If these are minimal there is no case for large authorities. But if a high level of decentralisation is intended and responsibilities and the control of services are to be brought as close as reasonable to members of the public in accordance with principles outlined in §1.3, then the need to reconcile purposes of effectiveness and efficiency with those of democracy becomes crucial.

Considerations relating to economic efficiency include: (1) low travel and other communication costs; (2) how far local authorities can meet their needs for financial, land and other resources from within their areas and therefore minimise economic dependence; (3) minimalisation of costs arising from the effects of activities in one area which spill over and cause costs in others; (4) facilitation of collaboration and co-ordination between services; and (5) matching of areas with those of private, voluntary and other public bodies with related interests to facilitate co-operation and co-ordination in matters of mutual interest and interdependence.

Democratic effectiveness criteria tend to overlap each other and in some cases those for economic efficiency. They are in some respects interdependent but in others conflicting. Boundaries may be drawn to secure: (1) what voters favour; (2) fair representation of significant minorities; (3) easy accessibility for inhabitants to elected members and the staff of the authority; (4) public understanding of the system and its purposes; and (5) a range of powers and responsibilities enabling a local authority to respond to the present and future needs of local inhabitants and to trade off one public good against others.

Two additional considerations have a special importance regarding both democratic and economic efficiency: (1) stability: how far the system will prove stable in coming years and avoid the heavy cost of new reorganisations; and (2) flexibility and responsiveness: how far the system has the potential to adapt to fulfil future needs by incremental change, avoiding the necessity of radical upheaval.

The principle of subsidiarity (see §1.3) implies that areas should be preferred that are as close to the individual as possible, provided that the resulting authorities possess the competence to fulfil other requisites. It can also be argued to favour the maintenance of natural and historic communities where a consciousness of communal solidarity exists.

1.5 INTER-AUTHORITY RELATIONS AND ORGANISATION

Working Together

In theory local authorities should be able to achieve the optimum size and geographical areas for any service by decentralisation within their own areas, sharing facilities and expert staff, setting up joint organisations with other authorities and delegating functions to other existing levels. They can also contract out services to firms in the private sector or set up mixed public-private bodies (see §1.8). Local practice depends on various factors including the size and competences of the authorities concerned, pressure by governments, statutory requirements, the legal forms available for joint action and the willingness of authorities to work together and share responsibility through representation on a joint organisation or to accept a contractual relationship. Most of all, perhaps, it depends on financial and other incentives to make joint working worthwhile.

The nature of inter-authority relationships appears to differ significantly in continental Europe from that in the United States, as might be predicted from the characteristics described in §1.3. Local governments are often pictured in the American literature as in an individualistic, competitive, bargaining relationship with each other, behaving very much as do private firms. There is much contracting between local authorities as well as with the private sector. The well-known case of Lakewood in California contracting out almost all its services to the county is an example (see §8.5). Joint public organisations appear not to be at all as plentiful in the United States as in most of Western Europe, although authorities may be represented on joint boards and some special purpose agencies.

Relationships between municipalities and between levels of local government seem closer in continental Europe, involving more personal contact and often much joint working. This has not always been the result of spontaneous collaboration between local authorities. Strong resistance to compromising identities and freedom of action seems as strong in Europe as elsewhere. Rather it has been the result of persuasion, incentives and sometimes legal requirements. In France, where leading politicians have traditionally served on authorities at more than one level, close working between region, *département* and commune appears to be typical, both in planning and execution, with the regions and *départements* passing responsibilities within regional programmes to a lower level and channelling financial support.

In Italy inter-authority collaboration is a basic principle laid down in the 1990 Local Government Law: 'regional law will control (*disciplina*) the cooperation of communes and provinces between themselves and with the region, with the purpose of achieving an efficient system of local authorities (*autonomie*) in the service of economic, social and civil development' (Article 3). The law repeatedly requires inter-level consultation. In Sweden the law requires sharing of responsibility between authorities for regional and local transport and some corrective institutions. Such duties are usually carried out there through jointly owned limited companies or other joint bodies. Governments in many countries have sought to persuade small local authorities to form joint bodies to overcome problems of economic scale and area. Multi- and single-purpose agencies are numerous in France, Italy and Germany, especially among their smaller communes. Legal forms have been designed to facilitate the movement of responsibilities for development and management to a joint body with suitable areas and adequate resources for effective and efficient investment and administration. Among those of particular importance for rural areas are the French *syndicat*, the Italian *communità montana* and the Spanish *comarco*. The Italian local government law of 1990 provides for several types of institution for the exercise of joint powers: forms of co-operative, consortia, unions preliminary to the amalgamation of small communes.

In general, Scandinavian countries have preferred amalgamations. In Denmark the government has discouraged local authorities from signing away their accountability to joint education boards.

The other main field in which governments have promoted inter-authority joint working is that of metropolitan areas, in which strategies for large and complex areas require collaboration between authorities that differ widely in scale and resources (see §1.13).

International Inter-Authority Associations

The need to represent local government interests at higher levels makes regional or national associations essential. In Europe international institutions have provided major new tasks for national local government associations, particularly the Council of Europe's Standing Conference of Local and Regional Authorities in Europe and the European Community with its interest in the involvement of all levels of government in the implementation of its policies for remedying imbalances in economic and social well-being between areas. A means of communication between local government in Europe as a whole and the European Commission has been established in the Consultative Committee of Local and Regional Authorities of the Member Countries of the European Community on regional and transport policies and other interests. The two main international associations in Europe are the International Union of Local Authorities (IULA, 41 Wassenaarseweg, 2596CG The Hague, Nether-lands), founded in Ghent in 1913, and the Council of European Municipalities and Regions (Conseil des Communes et Régions d'Europe (CEMR)), 41 Quai d'Orsay, 75007 Paris), founded in Geneva in 1951 as CEM with the main purpose of building up collaboration between authorities in the reconstruction of Europe after the Second World War.

Regional associations such as the Assembly of European Regions (Immeuble Europe, 20 place des Halles, F-67000 Strasbourg) have also been formed.

National Associations of Local Authorities

In the multi-tier systems, with one or two exceptions, each tier has its own association. In Austria and Switzerland, as in France, there is an organisational division among the basic authorities between towns and rural communes or, as in France, between the large towns and the others. The division of interests is built into the representational system.

The most essential task of local authority associations is to represent their members as a whole and fight for their interests. This may involve lobbying at all levels of government wherever policy-makers are accessible to them, right up to European Community level. They have been powerful in the United States in the lobbying field but relatively weak and fragmented in Canada. They normally work closely with state governments in a consultative and advisory capacity. In general they carry responsibility for determining a national stance on behalf of their members and channelling their views upwards. They may also provide national services for their members, as described in §6.5 on Denmark.

Details of national associations in the countries are given in §5 of each of the following chapters. Other national associations are:

Europe
Austria: Union of Austrian Towns (Österreichische Städtebund), Rathaus, I 1082, Vienna; Union of Austrian Rural Municipalities (Österreichische Gemeindebund), Johannesgasse 15, A 1010, Vienna

Belgium: Union des Villes et Communes Belges, 53 rue d'Arlon, 1040 Brussels

Greece: KEDKE, Union of Municipalities and Communities of Greece, Odos Acadimias 65, Athens TT142

Iceland: Association of Local Authorities, Háleitisbrunt 11, 128 Reykjavik

Ireland, Republic of: County Councils' General Council, c/o Institute of Public Administration, 57-61 Lansdowne Road, Dublin 4; Association of Municipal Authorities of Ireland, Hon. Sec., County Offices, Fermoy, County Cork

Luxembourg: Association des Villes et Communes Luxembourgeoises, 11 Bld Grande Duchesse Charlotte, 1331 Luxembourg

Netherlands: Association of Netherlands Municipalities (Vereniging van Nederlandse Gemeenten), de Willemshof, Nassaulaan 12, 2514JS The Hague

Norway: Norwegian Local Authorities Association, Kommunenes Hus, Haakon VII gatan 9, PB 1378, 0161 Oslo 1

Portugal: Associaçao Naçional de Municipios Portugueses, Av. Marnoco e Soma 52, 3000 Coimbra

Spain: Federaçion Española de Municipios y Provincias, Calle del Nuncio 28005, Madrid

Switzerland: Union of Swiss Towns (Union des Villes Suisses), Junkerngasse 56, 3011 Berne; Association of Swiss Communes (Association des Communes Suisses), Zentrumsplatz, 3322 Schönbühl

Around the Pacific

Australia: Australian Council of Local Government Associations, Churchill House, 218, Northbourne Av., Canberra, ACT 2601 (comprising two representatives of associations in each state); Australian Institute of Municipal Administration, 32 Vincent St, Oak Pk, Victoria 3046

New Zealand: New Zealand Local Government Association, PO Box 1214, Local Government Building, 9th floor, 114-118, Lambton Quay, Wellington; New Zealand Counties Association, PO Box 1012, CML Building, Custom House Quay, Wellington.

1.6 INTER-GOVERNMENTAL RELATIONS

Their Nature and Complexity

The scope and effectiveness of local government and therefore the contribution it can make to community, regional and national well-being rests largely on the nature of inter-governmental relations. There are relations concerning the exercise of power: delegation and constraints imposed by one level on another, typically by a national or federal state on local authorities by law and regulation and under executive discretion. The converse of this is the scope for free autonomous action available to a lower-level authority. Secondly there are financial relationships, in particular the transfer of finance and other resources and their conditions. Thirdly there is influence by means of advice, by the provision of information or by persuasion as opposed to the exercise of mandatory power.

There is a simple model of two-pole central-local relations which bears little resemblance to reality. Each level of government is fragmented and complex. Relations cross each other in what is a diagonal and tangled pattern rather than a vertical one. Given the great variety and complexity of the institutions at any one level of government, the range of channels and the modes of communication that can be used downwards and upwards in any one case and the extent to which many of the channels used are invisible to researchers as well as to the general public, it is clear that even if a study is sharply focused, light can only be thrown on limited aspects of interaction (see for example the description of the British case in Rhodes,

1986).

At the centre are the legislature, which in most cases consists of two chambers of distinct composition, the national executive, which always includes a complex of state institutions varying in closeness to the centre of power, and also the judiciary which interprets the law and resolves conflicts in its interpretation. The last has often been extremely important in its adjudications, some of which have put a lasting stamp on local government powers, as for example the development of doctrines of *ultra vires* in the United Kingdom and the USA and decisions blocking amalgamations of unwilling communes in Latin countries.

The executive can be dominant if it controls the legislature, shaping the law to overcome legal obstacles in its way. However it is itself fragmented between ministries, departments of state and a large number of other government agencies, both central and provincial. The extent to which even members of a ministerial cabinet act corporately varies greatly.

At regional and local government level the complexity is even greater. Among many thousands of elected local authorities there are sharp differences in type and structure, and within each authority internal divisions in political and administrative institutions, all of which may formally or informally communicate with central institutions. In a very small one-party authority with a one-person executive it is perhaps possible that communication with other levels of government may be limited to a single channel, but in an authority of any size there are many avenues to the centre, both official and political. The associations described in §1.5 and other chapters and many others representing aspects of regional and local government attempt to articulate and act for these interests but are often divided within themselves in different ways. There are communities of interest between institutions at different levels sharing party, professional and other common concerns. Not least important are those of paid central, regional and local departmental officers. Configurations of power vary widely from country to country within each main group.

Despite the limitations of meaningful comparison, studies relating to this field can be influential, as in the case of Montesquieu and others' understanding of the British system and Toqueville's of America which, if it partly reflected reality at the time, quickly became obsolete. Toqueville, however, was concerned primarily with underlying behavioural factors and also the impact they have on the qualities of national society. His work and others' have demonstrably contributed to national thinking on the value of decentralisation.

The terminology used in discussions on the subject is often tendentious, or at least felt to be so. Even the word 'sub-level' can be resented by some who feel that it offends against the principle of local or regional autonomy. Like a diagram showing one tier of government under another it is a spatial metaphor that in no way need indicate power relationships or any other form of superiority. The description of non-central government as 'peripheral' is another metaphor that has had general circulation among political scientists since the book of 1977 titled *Between Center and Periphery* (Tarrow, 1977). Non-central government is not peripheral in any sense given in the Oxford English Dictionary. 'From a service delivery perspective central government is not the peripheral institution of government' (Rose, 1985). Moreover 'decentral' government can dominate the centre and in a real sense be part of it. It has increasingly set the agenda for national politics in some countries (§§2.6 and 4.6).

States which have in the past three centuries used local government as a means for the mobilisation of resources and an agent for the implementation of change tend to have a well-integrated relationship with local authorities — one that reflects a history in which governors and prefects exercised the powers of the state at local level; or, as seen in the Dutch case described in §1.3, the state has looked to municipalities to exercise initiative subject to the provincial government acting as watchdog to guard common interests within the province. In English-speaking countries, on the contrary, the executive arm of government has lacked a significant local presence. Government neglect was the basis of the self-dependence of the early American local governments. Wickwar (1970), generalising across countries in the late 1960s, could write that the 'Characteristic twentieth-century approach to local government is to take Local Government for granted as a going concern within its limits but' try 'to improve on its efficiency'.

The distinction between anglophone and continental European countries largely coincides with that of countries in which the power of the centre was hardly challenged and those that have experienced a history of revolution and invasion in the last two hundred years. The classical European system was one in which governors, prefects or other government officials supervised local authorities to ensure that their actions were in accordance with the law and government regulations or not otherwise faulty, exercising powers to annul or refer upwards decisions which they considered failed to meet legal conditions. The administrators concerned were also usually presidents and executives of the provincial or departmental councils. In most cases some supervisory powers still remain, but they are generally limited to ensuring legality, sometimes in retrospect.

The exercise of supervision by governors or prefects has not generally been oppressive in recent years: it tends to be one of advice, liaison and maintaining the mutual interests of state and local authorities by joint agreements and the co-ordination of their services. The offices of governors and prefects have been modified to fulfil what is essentially a liaison role between the national executive and the locality and between deconcentrated state offices in each area. The result is an intermeshing between central and local administrative functions within each locality which is difficult to unravel.

The British system has been described as a 'dual polity' behind which lies the assumption that local and central governent are two separate realms, each defining its own purposes (Bulpitt, 1983). This leads easily to the idea that they are competitive, fighting for a limited sum of resources in a 'zero-sum game', as to some extent they must be regarding their claims on the financial resources of the centre. But this is unrealistic: central government is dependent upon sub-levels for implementation of policies, and most of its expenditures are for the maintenance and implementation of policies, at least where expensive services such as education, policing and social services are within the competence of local government.

In federal systems where local government has no constitutional status, as in the United States and Australia, there are frequent controversies as to how far the centre can by-pass member states to implement federal policies and the extent of the financial liability of states regarding local govenment's role in implementing national policies. In the continental Western European tradition there is a clear concept of the need for national unity, implying that solidarity is an important goal of national policy. This means that by and large levels of government are expected to work together to fulfil national as well as local purposes. The terms used to describe the general constitutional function of local and regional government reflect this, particularly the use of those implying implementation of a central purpose (e.g. *administration* and *Verwaltung*). Yet local authorities have an underlying general competence to serve the interests of their citizens and wide discretion in fulfilling a wide range of legal competences, and can fall back on the courts if that discretion is challenged. In fact in Germany and the Netherlands at least there is a strong conception of the separateness of the functions at different levels. In France, where the interpenetration of the business and administration of the 'state' has been historically strong, the events of the 1980s have led to a clearer and broader definition of expanded competences, but they have also demonstrated the interdependence of government levels.

Prefectoral powers were by no means inconsistent with local self-government or with the assumption of the responsibility and general competence of local authorities to meet the needs of their inhabitants in ways within national law. The powers of central government, as well as those of local government, were controlled under the system of administrative law and counterbalanced by the political weight of local authorities. Local government could exercise counterbalancing powers, helped by constitutional guarantees and its influence through associations and national party networks. Central government depended on it for the implementation of policies 'which ensured stability and continuity in the system' (Council of Europe, 1984, *The Relationship between the Various Levels of Local Administration under a Regional Organisation*). In practice central influence has tended to be exercised more by persuasion or political manipulation than by compulsion. Decentralisation of responsibility during recent decades was seen to be in the joint interest, but this did not necessarily mean a loss of influence at the centre. In fact power-sharing between levels was expected to heighten effectiveness at all levels.

In modern jargon, the distribution of power is not a 'zero-sum game'. In the Italian case in the 1970s for example 'there was a simultaneous centralization of the decision-making process and decentralization of financial resources' in which 'the financial centralization was supported by the local authorities, who feared the more dangerous regional centralization'. 'New administrative powers granted to central departments were jointly managed with representatives of the local authority associations, as in the case of personnel policy.... One may say that the Italian communes and provinces were able to to transform an attempt to centralize powers into an opportunity to strengthen their role and their access to power'. (Dente, 1985b)

The term Dutch scholars have used to describe the system introduced in the Netherlands Constitution of 1848 is translated as 'the decentralised unitary state', 'which — marginal adaptations left aside — still applies to the present day' (Toonen, 1991; see also §1.3). The theory stresses that the state and its component parts cannot be seen as passive machines or instruments without a will of their own, subject to outside steering and hierarchical control. It stresses 'higher authority as a means of conflict resolution, consensus building, and mutual adjustment' (ibid.).

The theory may seem to suggest a passive role for the state, turning the Latin concept of it as a mobiliser of national development upside down. After the end of the Second World War decentralisation of power in Europe became an accepted principle in reaction against autocratic regimes, and in some cases against the inefficient bureaucracy inherited from them, but at the same time Europe and Japan had the colossal task of rebuilding and modernisation through national physical and social policies. The need for local authorities to act as the chief agents in the task was obvious. There was a joint interest between levels of government in sharing resources and acting together for reconstruction. There was also a strong motivation to work together to redress the economic imbalances between regions resulting from the decline of traditional industries. The European Community was not only founded as a means to address these problems across national frontiers but also as an epitome of the new approach of international sharing of power and initiative.

The context for the development of such relationships has been a constitutional one. As described in §1.2, local government has a guaranteed legal status and prerogatives that vary from country to country. In Germany and Italy national framework laws for implementation through member states or regions are designed at the centre in close joint consultation. The member states or regions design the detailed law within the framework, devising their own legal instruments to suit the local conditions, needs and wishes of their areas and the political preferences of the parties. Procedures are characterised by a high level of consultation, much of it required by framework legislation.

The 'state based on law' as intended by the constitution makers does not in itself ensure true representation of local interests at the centre: this is more the task of the 'state based on party' (*Parteienstaat* as the Germans call it). The parties, representing the diversity of political interests within the state, are themselves organised into parallel hierarchies, each party level feeding into and participating in the articulation of policy, but at the same time exploring and articulating the views of other party levels through vertical channels from top to bottom. The aim to involve a wide and representative spread of interests in government is implicit in European electoral systems, especially proportional representation (see §1.10).

Systems in continental Europe tend to assume joint working between levels. In France the Senate, which is constituted by an electoral process that brings local leaders together in cantons and provinces, has been termed the 'house of the communes'. In Germany local political influence is exerted less directly through parties and the representation of *Länder* in the upper house. Italian regional council presidents come together in national cabinet offices to work through the implications of proposed measures among themselves and with members of the cabinet. The joint working may be at the top, in parliament or the committee rooms of ministries as the implications of proposals are analysed and worked out. Or it may be at the intermediate levels of region, county and province, or at all these levels. Inter-governmental consultative committees on finance and different aspects of services are a frequent feature. The executive arms of the state may have close relationships with local and regional associations and with local chief executives and departmental heads through its civil servants.

The elements of this approach are common to both federal and unitary states in continental Western Europe. In fact different forms of state seem less important than the philosophy of government. Both federal and unitary forms are also found in the English-speaking group, but in general members of the latter have a very different political philosophy, which sees local government as unintegrated with the centre.

Working Relationships and National and Regional Planning in Continental Western Europe

European Community norms and instruments require the participation of local and regional bodies in the procedures for the allocation and implementation of development aids to correct economic imbalances. This has been influential in bringing interests together in Britain as well as in other member states of the Community. Regional development plans have been important in providing a framework within which regional and local authorities have been involved, both in contributions to their content and in their implementation, diffusing responsibilities in a calculated way by contracting and other methods. On the other hand financial stringencies, especially since the 1970s, have led to sharp pressures on spending: a case where central economic policy clashes sharply with the implications of local government's concern with local interests.

Germany and Sweden are among countries which have inter-governmental councils for planning and expenditure control. Inter-governmental negotiations on financial planning and taxation seek to achieve consensus in these and other cases, balancing in discussion local government's estimate of needs and what central government considers the nation can afford. Financial implications of new proposals may be scrutinised jointly and the principle accepted that new burdens placed on local government by the state are conditional on new means of funding.

The transfer of new functions to local government in Scandinavia, France and elsewhere and the sharing of responsibility between levels has been accompanied by a great volume of government regulation which may be seen as oppressive and inconducive to innovations aimed at increasing efficiency and effectiveness. 'Free local government' experiments in Sweden, Denmark and Norway were initiated in the mid-1980s to test possibilities of releasing the hold of the centre on local authorities and helping to overcome initially disappointing results of the amalgamation of communes (see §§5.6 and 6.6).

Japan is a special case in that local officials are also government officials.

The system is highly integrated, and chief executives were estimated in 1982 to spend 70 to 80 per cent of their time handling matters for which they were responsible to central ministries (Shindo, 1982). The system has been described as one of 'high delegation, high direction, high dependence and resources' (Humes IV, 1991).

In general the expansion of the functions of local authorities in Western Europe appears to have resulted in a new and more positive concept of partnership between levels of government: a realisation of mutual dependence rather than increased independence.

The English-Speaking Countries

National advisory bodies have been set up in Australia and the United States to research and make recommendations on the problems of inter-governmental relations. In 1967 Australia's Advisory Council for Inter-Government Relations was asked to report to the states and the Australian Council of Local Government Associations (see §1.2). The Advisory Council of Inter-Governmental Relations of the United States (ACIR), a principal source of the information given in Chapter 8 below, monitors and advises on issues that arise due to the tangled web of relationships and the inequalities within the system. The evidence from these commissions shows much weaker relationships between levels than in West European federations, although relations between local governments and member states of the federations can be close. In the United States state governments often co-ordinate municipal planning and housing intiatives and provide transport infrastructure and health and welfare services themselves through field agencies (Humes IV, 1991). The local government lobbying function, however, is highly organised at both state and Washington levels. The 'role of local broker' played by local political leaders in winning grants and other favours through influence in state capitals and Washington may be regarded as a measure of their success.

The style of relations in the United States is influenced by the segregation of the capital market between the federal and state levels under the constitutional doctrine that different levels of government cannot tax each other. The notion of general public finance hardly exists. Nevertheless tensions between state and local government on service support were strong in the 1980s. President Reagan's policies of 'cutting back the state' were understood to achieve a degree of decentralisation whereas Mrs Thatcher's resulted in increasing centralisation (see §8.6; also Wolman, 1988).

The British 'dual polity' tradition, with centre and local government at the poles and without mediation has been described above. The Irish and New Zealand national governments are much closer to local government. In Ireland's case the centralisation of the selection of local authority chief executives is accompanied by close contacts with central departments (see §1.11). There is a similar closeness between local authorities and state and provincial governments in Australia and Canada. By 1991 a state attack on local government's freedom to choose its own means of service provision is not known by me to have occurred other than in Britain (see §7.6), although financial crises and a movement of politics to the right in some countries in the early 1990s suggest that this might not be the case in the future.

Central-Regional Relationships

Post-war regional governments in Western Europe were designed to take over responsibilities for the implementation of services within their regions within frameworks of national policy. National government cannot relinquish its responsibility for the well-being of the nation as a whole and must therefore be concerned in the development of policy in close relationship with the regional governments. For this reason organic relationships of different kinds are built into the structure. The members of regional councils may be members of national parliaments as in Belgium, or they may elect members of the upper house of parliament as in the Netherlands and Spain. The state may be represented in each regional government by a crown representative as in the Netherlands, or by a minister of state as in the Portuguese regions.

The national government may be represented at administrative levels by a high-ranking civil servant, as in the case of the government delegates and civil governors in Spain and the regional prefects in France and Italy who have responsibility for reviewing, directing and co-ordinating the administrative functions of central government in the region and for coordination between state and regional services. The Portuguese Constitution requires regional bodies set up by national government to consult and work with regionally elected bodies. In France the political responsibility for co-ordination of state and regional services lies with the president of the regional council. He or she and the regional prefect have a duty to promote the shared use of state and regional staff.

In all cases the functions of state and regional bodies are fixed in the national constitution or, in France's case, by statute law. The central state may supervise a region's legislation to ensure conformity with the law, or regions may be required to submit drafts of proposed laws to the council of state as in Belgium; but it is open to a region to challenge the constitutional legality of the central state's decisions. In each case there are high-level judicial bodies designated to hear challenges on legality: for example a constitutional or administrative court and a court of auditors on financial matters, as in Spain. (European Centre for Regional Development, 1989)

Normally more significant on a day-to-day basis are the ongoing relationships between the two levels of government. In France there is national co-operation on provisions in the National Plan, the regional presidents being members of the National Planning Commission. Contracts are made for implementation under the Plan between central and local government which are designed to ensure common objectives. There is similarly close working on national planning between the central ministries and the regions in Italy by means of sectoral joint consultative bodies. The general aim of central government and regions has been that the overall actions of central government and the regions should be consistent through a combination of co-operation, supervision and guidance in which consensus is a guiding principle.

1.7 LOCAL AND REGIONAL GOVERNMENT SERVICES

Local Government Services

Local government activities have often been grouped according to purpose, process or specialism. No such classification is attempted here since they often fulfil more than a single purpose and involve shared specialisms and joint processes. Housing services, for example, aim at both social welfare and a healthy environment, involve building, maintenance and welfare functions and require more than one profession. Again, physical planning is not to plan but to pursue a range of purposes. No limit can be put on what local authorities undertake unless by law. Local authorities exist to meet common and special needs, and such needs are unpredictable since they change with time and conditions. Their overall purpose is the good of individuals and the community as a whole. Recognising that municipalities are best placed to recognise local needs, countries such as those of continental Western Europe for this reason allow them to act in any matter which has not been specifically excluded by law.

The services detailed below are those known to be provided by local authorities in at least two or three countries. This type of listing misses some activities that may be important. Regulating public behaviour by

60

means of by-laws etc. is an example, a matter given prominence among responsibilities in Ontario but hardly mentioned today in most accounts of British local government.

The information used in this section comes from a large range of sources, most notably a survey of services in fifteen Council of Europe countries by the Steering Committee for Regional and Municipal Matters (Council of Europe, 1988, *Allocation of powers to the local and regional levels of government in the member states of the Council of Europe*).

The main difference in the services which local authorities provide lies between Europe, including Great Britain, together with Japan on the one hand, and the English-speaking countries in America and the Pacific on the other. In the former group a substantial proportion of the education and social welfare functions are provided by locally elected general-purpose authorities, but heavily subsidised voluntary agencies may play a major role, as in Germany. In the second group these services are provided predominantly by elected ad hoc special-purpose bodies or directly by states or Canadian provinces. Since their local authorities work are limited by the *ultra vires* rule, as are those in Great Britain, what they can provide for their citizens tends to lack elasticity.

On the Western European continent and to some extent in Canada there has been a general movement towards decentralisation of functions from the state to local authorities in recent decades, often linked with the local authority amalgamations described in §1.4. A Council of Europe report of 1981 generalised, 'A strong movement towards decentralised services can be discerned in 10 of the 14 countries.... In all the five countries which have completed reforms, these have been generally successful... Transfers of powers have gone quite somoothly.... Central administration has to some extent benefitted from the shedding of services.... it seems clear that the most successful changes are those where particular attention has been paid to situating the transfer of power within an overall reform designed to create local and regional authorities with sufficient financial administrative strength to operate new services effectively' (Council of Europe, 1981, *Functional Decentralisation at Local and Regional Level*, 1981). The most substantial decentralisation appears to have been carried out in France and Italy where amalgamations have been rare and other means, including those mentioned in §1.5, have served to make this possible.

The 1988 Council of Europe survey found that there was 'a certain homogeneity' between functions performed at the basic level of local government', whether or not local authorities worked under a general mandate of power or a list of specific responsibilities. The sharpest contrasts are found among intermediate authorities. These authorities tend to provide large-scale social sevices which are seen as beyond the resources and ability of most basic authorities and which otherwise would probably be undertaken by state government direct — in particular health, social security and secondary education. In Sweden, Norway and Denmark the counties are chiefly responsible for hospitals and other health services. In Finland, which has no intermediate-level authorities, authorities are statutorily required to be members of joint authorities in 'general hospital regions'. They are therefore at least involved in an institutional network which brings together all aspects of health care. Responsibility for hospitals, and in some cases the employment and payment of teachers and lecturers, determine above all else the much higher relative expenditure by local government in Scandinavia. In Italy and Spain it came to be accepted after the provinces were under threat that in most areas they could probably provide some major services better than alternative arrangements. In Germany the Landkreise relate closely to the Gemeinden, providing public utility, cultural and other services that elsewhere are provided predominantly by the basic level. They help to achieve a rational distribution of responsibilities in accordance with the subsidiarity principle. Authorities considered large enough to provide Kreis functions themselves (*Stadtkreise* or *kreisfrei* Gemeinden) combine the functions of both levels.

Table 1.7, derived from the 1988 Council of Europe survey, shows how far particular functions are undertaken by local government in the 15 countries covered. In some cases functions may be delegated to or performed under delegation from another level of government. Others may be shared between levels or divided between them. Some functions on which individual countries may place high importance were not specified in the questionnaire (e.g. non-university adult education).

British authorities no longer undertake water, gas and electricity supply, hospital and other aspects of personal health care and social assistance involving income support (although they have wide responsibilities for social care for disadvantaged groups in the population). These are competences for basic levels of service in all or nearly all the continental systems.

Table 1.7: Distribution of Local Government Functions in 15 Council of Europe Countries

N.B. The figures in brackets give the number of countries in which a particular function is legally mandatory.

The core functions in all or nearly all countries (12-15)
All 15 countries: primary schools — construction and upkeep (15), roads (15), local planning (15), building and demolition permits (15), refuse collection (15), social assistance (9), homes for the elderly (6), library services (5), tourism promotion (0), theatres (0), sport development and facilities (0)
14 countries: fire service (13), pre-primary schools — construction and upkeep (12), sewage disposal (12), water supply (11), nature and site protection/waste disposal (11), cemeteries (9), organisation and management of land transport (6), cultural and artistic heritage conservation (5), subsidised housing (4), museum services (0), nature parks, recreation and open spaces (0)
13 countries: protection of the environment (8), development or employment conservation (2 — the Netherlands and Portugal), land control (purchase, reserves etc.) (1), abattoirs (0), baths and showers (0), financial participation in public/private enterprises (0)
12 countries: disaster relief (12), planning control and building regulation (9), fairs and markets (2), financial or fiscal aid to public and private undertakings (0)

In a large majority of countries (9-11)
11 countries: pre-primary school administrative, teaching or technical staff (8)
10 countries: epidemic control (8), river or sea transport (1)
9 countries: primary school administrative, teaching and technical staff (10), hospitals (5), electricity supply (5), gas supply (4)

In a small majority of countries (8-10)
8 countries: secondary schools — construction and upkeep (4), aid for religious worship and upkeep of related premises (4), housing assistance (4), consumer protection (4)

In half or nearly half (4-7)
7 countries: involvement in regional or national planning (6)
6 countries: cinemas (0)
5 countries: secondary school administrative, teaching or technical staff (5), air transport (0)

In one country only
higher education premises — construction and upkeep (0).

Details of the Range and Distribution of Functions in 20 Countries

1. Physical Planning and Development

Physical planning in the sense of town and country planning or development planning, is a mandatory local authority function in all the 20 countries. A chief executive may have a specific legal role in this function, as in the United States where responsibilities may be delegated to planning commissions which report to the municipal chief executive. In Japan the governors of the prefectures may take over responsibility for large projects or housing developments.

2. Housing

Municipalities provide 'social', subsidised low-rent housing except in Australian states, generally through mixed building companies, public corporations, voluntary sector associations and other bodies, or through subsidies under agreements on usage. They may guarantee loans to state-aided associations as in Denmark, prepare sites or share rent allowance responsibilities with the state. Special housing authorities are often set up for this purpose by cities and counties in the United States and by provinces in Canada. Redevelopment is generally a core function of city authorities.

3. Roads

Municipalities have responsibilities for building and maintaining local roads in all countries. Counties, départements, prefectures and provinces (and in Ontario regions) are usually responsible for the wider networks that connect municipal districts within their areas. They often build or maintain sections of trunk roads for the state or region under contract or other arrangements.

4. Transport

Municipalities or bodies that act on their behalf plan and co-ordinate or provide public transport in all countries except the Netherlands. In Sweden non-profitmaking companies have been set up jointly by municipalities and counties and in Germany by the Kreise. Private companies often receive subsidies to maintain services on uneconomic routes and enjoy contracts for school transport. Some municipalities and intermediate authorities provide and run commercial and fishing ports.

5. Education

In Southern and Central Europe the state normally employs teachers and supervises the curriculum, but premises are provided and maintained by local authorities who may also have a part in deciding where new schools are built. In Canada and the United States schools are run in some cases by municipalities but in many by elected special authorities or boards. In

Britain school boards have been enabled to opt out from local authority management with government approval. In Japan municipalities and prefecturates are generally responsible for the building and management of schools.

The usual arrangement in countries where local authorities are responsible for education is for pre-primary, primary and sometimes lower secondary education to be provided by municipalities. Secondary, higher secondary and sometimes special education are provided by intermediate authorities. In Britain, however, counties and metropolitan districts are responsible for municipal schools at all levels.

6. Vocational and Adult Education

Intermediate and most-purpose authorities are generally responsible, but municipalities and states may also have a role.

7-8. Cultural Activities including Libraries and Museums

In general all main levels may involve themselves in this field in Europe. Only counties and regions, however, may provide public libraries in Britain, except in some cases in Wales.

9. Recreational Services

Responsibilities of municipalities throughout the European countries, concurrently with counties in Germany, Britain and Sweden.

10. Health and Social Assistance

Systems vary widely. With the exception of Greece and Britain preventive health services are the responsibility of local government to some extent in all countries in the survey. Hospital services are also provided by local government in most cases. Hospitals as well as preventive health are provided primarily by counties in Denmark and Sweden. Japan provides its main health services through prefectural health centres and hospitals, supplemented by some 2,600 municipal clinics.

Social assistance is provided by municipalities in all European countries in the survey and is mandatory in eight at municipal level and three at intermediate authority level. In Japan the larger authorities have a statutory responsibility to maintain comprehensive welfare provision through local offices. In Canada and the United States forms of social support are provided by local and intermediate levels.

A main problem in this field is the integration of health and social services. Denmark has perhaps the most integrated arrangements (see §6.7), unless bettered by Finland's single-tier system. In its two-tier areas Germany also has close collaboration between Kreise and municipalities in providing preventive health services. Canada has a variety of arrangements.

11. Police

In nearly all the Latin and German language countries, including

Luxembourg, local policing is a municipal duty for which the mayor has primary responsibility. It is not a local function in Portugal, Scandinavia, the Netherlands, Australia or New Zealand. It is provided by cities in the United States and more generally, and mandatorily, in Canada. Intermediate authorities maintain police forces as well as municipalities in France and Spain. Counties have administrative responsibility for policing in Britain except in Greater London, although in many cases the forces are under joint boards. Police committees in Britain are composed in part of magistrates.

12. Fire Protection

Fire services are a local government responsibility except in Italy, Australia and New Zealand. They are generally at municipal level but at intermediate level in the Netherlands, Germany and Spain. Only in Britain is the responsibility solely at intermediate level under county councils or joint boards.

13. Development of the Local Economy and Employment Promotion

These are generally local government activities in the Council of Europe countries, Australia, Canada, Japan and the United States. Japan appears to be the most interventionist of all. Intermediate authorities are involved in Belgium, France, Italy and the Netherlands.

14. Public Utilities

Municipalities provide one or more out of water, electricity and gas supply services in all countries except Britain and Australia.

15. Tourist Promotion is a general activity, often at all levels.

16. Conservation of Nature and the Environment is generally an activity at municipal level and in most cases also at intermediate level in Europe and in Japan. In the United States special districts are established for land conservation.

European Regional Authorities

Regional governments are primarily designed to decentralise state functions and plan and support local development. The functions they undertake themselves are generally in intention limited to those for which they qualify under the subsidiarity principle. In Belgium, Italy and Spain the regional assemblies legislate for their areas on all matters of domestic policy.

In France regions have above all an administrative function. They provide regional inputs into the national planning system and contract with the state for the implementation of agreed programmes. They are also active in the fields of environmental protection, preservation of heritage including the cultural heritage, financing major road development, regional plans, upper secondary, special, vocational and higher education, regional museums, major country parks, cross-country footpaths and, perhaps above all, the stimulation of economic development.

Italian regions and Spanish autonomous communities are promotional in all these fields. In Spain, for example, the autonomous communities have powers over rail and road networks and over education at every stage and level, subject to the state's ultimate powers of inspection to guarantee the provision of adequate education. In Belgium the three communities' responsibilities cover education and health as well as all matters that would normally fall under the description of 'cultural'. All other domestic matters come under the authority of the regions.

1.8 IMPLEMENTATION OF SERVICES

Options in Service Delivery

Local authorities in all the countries covered in this book have a wide range of options as to how they deliver many of their services. Broadly they can carry them out directly or delegate or transfer their implementation to other public or private bodies provided that they can meet their legal obligations. But both direct and indirect provision take many different forms.

Direct Provision

(1) The most direct form is where a service is provided by an authority's employees under the control of elected members or executive. For any but the smallest operations an organisational unit is needed, but this need not have any administrative or financial autonomy. The head of the unit, or, as it is often called, department, is responsible directly to the assembly or its executive. The organisation may have its own budget but that budget is part of the local authority's budget and not necessarily self-balancing. Details of staff or employee organisations are given in §1.11.

(2) Administrative and financial autonomy may be conferred on the organisation, when it may be responsible for controlling its own finance, balancing its budget and contracting for its own external needs. It may remain under the control of elected members or the executive; in Latin countries often through a deputy or assistant mayor. It will normally, however, be directly accountable to the authority.

(3) A service unit may have its own legal status or personality but stay close to the central administration nevertheless, under the control of a board on which the assembly or its executive is represented.

(4) An authority may set up a distinct 'public enterprise' but under local authority control, as is commonly done in Germany, Greece, Italy, the Netherlands, Portugal and Spain (Luchaire, 1991).

(5) In Canada and the United States cities usually appoint commissioners or boards to run some services, as in the cases of planning decisions and libraries. Their members may or may not be members of the council. They tend to report to the executive rather than the council or one of its committees.

(6) In Germany *Stadtwerke* are employed for running public utilities such as gas, electricity, water and passenger transport in urban areas (Sauberzweig, 1991). They may be units under the direct control of the municipality or in the form of companies controlled by representatives of the municipality who are members of their boards.

(7) In many instances local authorities adopt limited company forms in order to take advantage of their greater freedom and flexibility regarding finance, staffing, management structure etc. Political control can be retained by appointing elected members or authorities' own employees to the board of management.

(8) Joint authority bodies may be set up, sometimes as a legal requirement but often voluntarily, as described in §1.5.

Indirect or Delegated Management of Services

(9) One means of transferring the management of local government functions to agents is by *concession*. The agent can be in legal terms a moral or physical person, public or private, who becomes bound under contract to a schedule of conditions of service. This form is commonly adopted for public utilities and work projects. Concessioners are normally expected to meet investment costs, reimbursing themselves from charges to the users. The local authority fixes permitted charges and reviews the position annually. In France such concessions can be for periods of 12 to 24 years but may be ended at any time subject to compensation to the contractor. A variety is *affermage* (farming out), usually for 3 to 6 year periods, in which the works necessary for carrying out the service are made available to the *affermier* by the authority, which may also guarantee the necessary finance. The *affermier* keeps income from charges and may pay back to the authority a proportion to cover the amortisation of its investments. Or administration can be transferred to an agent who is re-

munerated according to financial results or fulfilment of objectives. Here also a contractor may undertake to manage a service for a fixed remuneration. The local authority fixes the tariffs charged and is responsible for the financial risks involved. (Luchaire, 1991; Lemas, 1991)

(10) Mixed public-private sector bodies may be set up, the best known of which are probably the French *sociétés d'économie mixtes* which have limited company status. There were over 700 of these in France in 1983, mostly in the building and development fields. Mixed-sector companies have been used extensively for city and economic development in the United States and Western Europe. A special form in which local authorities appoint a third of board members, the *HLM* ('public agencies for housing at moderate rents'), has been the mainstay of the French public housing system (see §2.8). Non-profit public interest housing companies in which the public sector holds controlling shares also have a long history in Germany. In general local authorities fill at least half the places on the board and provide at least half the capital. The use of this form appears to have increased almost everywhere within the European Community in the 1980s (Luchaire, 1991). It enables authorities to maintain some control over a service while allowing it to be run under commercial conditions and bring in private sector skills and commercial motivation as well as capital.

(11) Voluntary associations have played an important role in some countries. The contracting out of welfare services to voluntary associations has a long history in Germany, Canada and elsewhere. In Germany the principle of subsidiarity has been held to favour them. In Italy there has been a rapid growth in their number, estimated at 15,000 in the late 1980s. Most have close relationships with public bodies (France, 1987).

(12) Contracting out services to private sector businesses is universal and longstanding. It is usually justified on grounds of efficiency, although this is often disputed, especially in the case of contracts over long periods that are justified on the grounds that contractors need to recoup their initial outlays (France, 1987). The largest and most highly developed system of external services is probably to be found in France in the public utilities field.

The legal enforcement of open tendering on local authorities in selected services to maximise privatisation was a feature of the Thatcher government policies in the 1980s which has not been replicated elsewhere as far as is known. Although most services have remained under direct provision in Britain, the need for competitive tenders from within the local government organisation certainly led to the elimination of much inefficient working within local authorities, resulting in reductions in personnel. Possibly as important has been the need, associated with financial stringency, to re-examine and define practice and aims in order to set down essential requirements in invitations to tender and contracts (Wolman, 1986; Flynn and Walsh, 1988).

There is a history of the reverse tendency in the field of public transport in the history of German counties and American cities taking over subsidised companies that could not make sufficient profits to fulfil urgent public needs.

Direct provision remains general, as evidenced by the figures of local government employees in different countries. If the total of local government employees is calculated as a proportion of the population of 15 to 65 year olds (omitting teachers and general police in the American and the British cases to make them more nearly comparable), it appears that France, Great Britain, Italy and the United States all had between 3.0 and 3.7 persons in every hundred in local government employment. The United States was very close to Italy. (These figures are derived from *Statistical Abstract of the United States 1991*, 1991; Chantraine and Geuser, 1991; CIPFA, 1990 and 1991.)

1.9 LOCAL AND REGIONAL GOVERNMENT FINANCE

Unremitting Pressures

From the Gulf oil-crisis pressures onwards governments tightened their control over local resources in most countries. 'Urban fiscal strain' became an international topic for studies on the means available to local authorities to reduce their expenditures (e.g. Clark and Ferguson, 1983). Local government in the United Kingdom was especially hard hit, total municipal revenues dropping in real terms by 7.3 per cent from 1978 to 1985 whereas they tended to rise in continental Europe, most notably in France and Italy where they grew by 25.9 and 54.2 per cent respectively in the same period (Mouritzen and Nielsen, 1988, p.44). An ideological factor entered in the 1980s with the policies of the Thatcher and Reagan administrations to hold back or reverse public sector growth. Systems of national control to help check inflation have now been introduced in virtually all West European countries. The Scandinavian governments, among the most punctilious about local government's right to set its own levels of expenditure, were virtually enforcing freezes on local authority financial expansion around the end of the 1990s. The pressures show no sign of abating in the current decade.

Gross Expenditure and Revenue

Levels of per capita expenditure differ widely between countries. In seven unitary countries in Europe in 1987-88 local government accounted for from 11.5 up to 45 per cent of total government domestic expenditure, averaging 23 per cent. In Japan it was much higher: over 71 per cent in 1982. In four federal countries the national government's share of general government domestic expenditure in 1988 averaged 58 per cent, the member states' share 24.5 per cent and local government's 20.9 per cent. But there were wide variations: at national level from 48 per cent (Switzerland) to 70 per cent (Austria); at state level from 13 per cent (Austria) to 30.5 per cent (USA); and at local level from 16.5 per cent (Austria) to 28 per cent (USA) (Owens, 1991; *Statistical Abstract of the United States 1991*, 1991; *Local Public Finance in Japan*, 1984).

It is difficult to assess the real impact of enforced financial austerity on local government discretion. Expenditures on services such as education and social support may be required by law and regulation. Discretion may be shared between levels in ways difficult or impossible to disentangle. In North America the most costly local expenditures may be in the hands of ad hoc authorities, particularly the school districts which take up some 36 per cent of local government expenditure. In England and Wales 44 per cent of local outgoings went on education and 12.5 per cent on law and order services, areas of limited discretion.

Related problems arise in trying to assess local autonomy in terms of control over tax revenues. The information is available for OECD countries in terms of local and state tax revenue as percentages of total government expenditure (OECD, 1991). The average percentage of total government tax revenue taken by local and regional governments for 18 non-federal countries was 12.9 per cent, ranging from 1.4 per cent (Greece) to 30.4 per cent (Denmark). In the four federal OECD member states it averaged 10.1 per cent and ranged from 3.4 per cent (Austria) to 16.3 per cent (Switzerland).

Countries may be grouped into four classes in terms of proportions of tax revenue raised by local government. The first is of those where total government tax revenue is over 20 per cent of the total national tax income. These range from Norway's 21.1 per cent to Denmark's 30.4 per cent and include all five Scandinavian countries (including Iceland at 21.4 per cent), and also Japan (25.8 per cent). In the second class the corresponding figures run from 10.6 per cent in the United Kingdom up to Switzerland's 16.3 per cent. This group includes Spain (10.8 per cent), Austria (11 per cent), Luxembourg (11.6 per cent) and the United States (12.1 per cent).

The third group is below the average, ranging from New Zealand at 7.1 per cent to France at 8.9 per cent and includes Germany (8.7 per cent) and Canada (8.8 per cent). The bottom group ranges from Greece at 1.4 per cent to Portugal at 5.1 per cent. It also includes Italy (2.2 per cent), Ireland (2.6 per cent), Australia (3.4 per cent) and Belgium (4.7 per cent).

Japan and Finland stand with the German/Scandinavian group in their willingness to decentralise taxation. If decentralised state taxation uptake is included with local government's, Austria (21.4 per cent), Germany (30.9 per cent) and Switzerland (38.3 per cent) may be included. The Latin countries' decentralised tax uptakes were at less than half these levels, ranging from 2.2 to 8.9 per cent. The anglophone group in general stands in a midway position, although mostly well below average, ranging from 2.6 per cent (Ireland) to 12.1 per cent (USA).

In terms of the direction of change during the previous fifteen years, however, the Latins were the gainers and the anglophone group the losers. Proportions of national tax uptake by local government increased between 1975 and 1989 from 4.3 to 10.8 per cent in Spain, from 7.6 per cent to 8.9 per cent in France, from an unknown but extremely low level to over 5 per cent in Portugal and from 0.9 to 2.2 per cent in Italy. On the other hand the proportion of tax intake dropped in all six anglophone countries over the same period: in Ireland from 7.3 to 2.6 per cent, in Australia from 4.2 to 3.4 per cent, in New Zealand from 7.7 to 7.1 per cent, in Canada from 9.7 to 8.8 per cent, in the United Kingdom from 11.0 to 10.6 per cent and in the United States from 13.9 to 12.1 per cent. The German, Scandinavian and Japanese group's take-up changed little. It ranged from 8.7 to 30.4 per cent in 1989 as against 9.1 to 29.8 per cent in 1975.

How much does the proportion of local authorities' own tax revenue within overall government budgets vary between countries? In seven OECD non-federal local government systems in 1988 the percentage of local government's own tax revenue in its overall revenues ranged from 4 to 70 per cent; non-tax revenue from 5 to 20 per cent; and grant revenue from 10 to 80 per cent. In federal countries member state and local revenues combined ranged from 30 to 70 per cent; non-tax revenue from 10 to 30 per cent; and grants from 12 to 30 per cent.

The relationship between local control over revenues and local autonomy is far from clear. The reasons for the differences are obviously political, but behind these lie economic, social and other factors. Observation seems to suggest that the Latin group has been moving up in terms of investment in services while the anglophone group has been lagging behind. But what the differences mean in practice is another matter. Are Amsterdam and Milan really less autonomous than London boroughs or Aarhus? Differences would appear to relate more to the total sources available, local needs, competences, locally defined objectives, the extent to which areas of activity are controlled by regulation and no doubt other factors. The subject requires detailed analysis and case studies before definitive conclusions are possible, assuming that levels of autonomy can be measured satisfactorily at all.

Perhaps the public investment for which local authorities are responsible is more significant than levels of autonomous taxation. An inquiry directed to eight countries in the European Community found that the local government share in the gross formation of fixed public capital ranged from 39.4 per cent to 79.3 per cent of total expenditures, the lowest figure being that of the United Kingdom and the highest that of Italy. The countries raising least in terms of their own revenue scored very high in this respect: Ireland, where local government raises only 2.7 per cent of expenditure from its own revenues scored 73.4 per cent, Italy 79.3 per cent and the Netherlands 72.2 per cent (Chantraine and Geuser, 1991).

The Justification of Local Taxes

Means of taxation available at local level differ widely between countries. The main types of tax employed and their international distribution are considered below, but it may be helpful first to state some of the criteria by which they can be evaluated.

Equity A tax should be a fair one. If fairness relates to means the fairest tax is on income or property values or both, it being possible normally to convert one into the other. On the other hand the community charge ('poll tax') introduced by the Thatcher government at the end of the 1980s was justified on the principle that it was fair for individuals to pay for the costs of the benefits they received from local government and that these tended to be equal, so that the richest man in Britain should pay the same as his butler. Unfairness also arises when current relative values drift away from earlier assessment rates, a reason why many countries have introduced annual updating systems on valuations. Different taxes affect individuals unequally, and therefore there is a strong argument for a variety of taxes to even out the injustices involved.

Collectability An aspect of fairness is that a tax should be difficult to evade. Factors combine: many people believed that the community charge was flagrantly unfair and some claimed to resist payment on conscientious grounds even when it was very much against their personal financial interest to do so. Apart from such cases avoidance was widespread and caused not a few people to avert electoral registration in order to avoid being on the tax register, thereby undermining the representativeness of the vote.

Efficiency A tax should give a high yield in relation to the costs of its collection. This is obviously related to its collectability and the extent to which people believe it to be fair. It is also argued that a good tax should give a high yield so as to prevent the need for a multiplicity of taxes. But efficiency has also been given a wider and much more problematic definition involving cost-benefit analysis: that additional benefit should equal the additional benefits from the services provided. But benefits cannot be quantified without gross assumptions in their measurement and about their relative values.

Taxes should be met by beneficiaries of services, that is by residents within the area of the administering authority; but since many non-residents may benefit from expenditure within the area to which they commute for work or pleasure, or even which they visit as tourists, there is a justification for taxes on outsiders who use local facilities, such as forms of consumption tax.

A tax's behavioural effects It should not be at a level that discourages people from living in, working in or visiting a district, or businesses from moving into it.

Buoyancy or elasticity Its yield should as far as possible rise with levels of income and inflation, or at least be flexible so that it can be adjusted inexpensively at frequent intervals to cope with changes in real income and need.

Immobility of tax base, otherwise residents may opt to change residence or shopping centres to avoid it.

Perceptibility and accountability Taxes should be of a kind that can be clearly associated with expenditure so that payers are aware of a local authority's accountability to them for how its tax receipts are spent and vote on their judgement of how well they are used.

Compatibility with other taxes Are a tax's implications for the impact of taxes levied at other levels of government acceptable?

Types of Tax

Property Taxes
Taxes may be based on the potential or sale value of land and/or buildings, mobile possessions or tangible building assets. Such taxes were levied by local government in all 22 countries in the OECD in 1989 except Belgium, Greece, Italy and Sweden. Property may be assessed on a capital or annual value basis or in other ways. There are generally exemptions for types of

building such as schools, hospitals and places of worship. It is convenient to place liability for payment on property owners. Only in France and the United Kingdom have vacant residences been taxable. In France property tax is adjusted by family size. In the United States and the United Kingdom rebates have been given to owners or residents with low incomes. Residential properties have commonly been taxed at a lower rate than business premises, but there is reported to be a general trend towards equalising between the two types of property for economic reasons. (Owens, 1991)

Although local discretion over a tax base is unusual, local authorities often have complete discretion over the rate levied. In some cases, however, increases need government permission (in New South Wales only if an increase would be above the rate of inflation).

In 1988 the average proportion of local property taxes as a percentage of local authority tax revenues was nearly 50 per cent in federal countries and 30 per cent in unitary countries. It formed above 70 per cent of local tax revenue in the Netherlands (73.4 per cent), the USA (74.3 per cent), Canada (85.0 per cent), New Zealand (93.1 per cent), Australia (99.8 per cent), and 100 per cent in Ireland and the United Kingdom until it was abolished. It has been the predominant local government tax of the anglophone world, the main local criticisms centring on whether it should be based on assessments of rental or of capital value, the infrequency of revaluations (now not difficult to meet to some extent by annual revision in accordance with market values of types of property), and hard cases, typically elderly persons in large houses and single households benefiting from the income of several workers. But it scores high on several of the criteria detailed above.

Local and Regional Income and Profits Taxes

Local income and profits taxes are levied in 17 out of 24 OECD countries, including six at federal state level (see Table 1.8). They are efficient and flexible. Profits taxes overlap the business tax category described below, but are grouped together here in accordance with the OECD statistics. They come closest to providing for each to contribute according to his or her means. They are flexible and can be adjusted relatively closely to basic needs by a qualifying income threshold and allowances on income. Equity and welfare can be promoted by making deductions from the base not only for dependent children but for other reasonable expenses such as pension contributions and even (in Japan) losses through calamities. They can be progressive according to income levels and are buoyant in that they rise automatically with incomes and inflation. They can be related without great difficulty to location. They can, if a government wishes, be applied to all levels of income, although it is generally accepted that personal income tax should not be deducted below a level of basic need. (See Travers and Gibson, 1986).

Table 1.8: Revenue from Income and Profits Taxes as Percentages of Total Tax Income at Different Government Levels and of the GDP in Selected OECD Countries (arranged in order of national GNP growth 1980-89)

	GNP growth	% Share Total Tax Income			—————% GDP——-————>			
		local	states	centre	local	states	centre	total
(Highest growth rate in GNP)								
Japan	4.2	63.4	-	70.7	5.0	-	10.0	15.0
Norway	3.6	88.2	-	26.4	8.5	-	6.4	14.9
Finland	3.4	99.1	-	33.0	10.0	-	7.8	17.8
Canada	3.3	-	49.4	70.2	6.2	10.5	16.7	33.4
(Middling growth rate in GNP)								
USA	3.0	6.0	39.6	90.3	0.2	2.2	10.8	13.2
UK	2.7	-	55.0	-	-	-	14.2	14.2
Italy	2.3	44.4	-	56.4	0.4*	-	13.7	14.1
France	2.1	14.6	-	34.5	0.6	-	7.1	7.7
Sweden	2.1	99.6	-	27.1	15.6	-	8.4	24.0
FRG	2.0	82.4	62.7	43.8	2.7*	5.3	5.3*	13.3
(Lowest growth rate in GNP)								
Greece	1.5	27.6	-	27.6	-	-	6.1	6.1
Ireland	1.5	-	-	42.6	-	-	13.2	13.2
Netherlands	1.7	-	-	52.2	-	-	13.3	13.3
Belgium	1.8	75.4	-	55.8	1.6	-	15.1	16.7
Denmark	1.8	92.2	-	47.3	14.0	-	15.7	29.7

Note
*These figures are of taxes collected by another level of government of which a fixed proportion is transferred to other levels.

Source: Derived from OECD, 1991, *Revenue Statistics of OECD Member Countries 1965-1990*, Tables 122 to 128 and *Statistical Abstract of the United States, 1991*, Table 1.4.

It has been argued that they are a disincentive to maximising personal income and that local and regional additions on top of national tax would reduce personal work effort or add to inflation through higher wage demands. As Table 1.8 shows, international comparisons of growth in GNP and personal income tax do not seem to give any support to this proposition.

There are arrangements for automatic allocation of proportions of nationally administered income tax between lower levels of government in Austria, Germany, Luxembourg and Spain. In Belgium, Canada (except Quebec), Denmark and Norway, local authorities may levy an addition to central income tax (called 'piggy-backing'); or they may collect an income tax with a separate base, usually differing mainly in tax reliefs. In Quebec, Switzerland and the United States, state or sometimes local governments may fix their own tax bases (Owens, 1991). Although in most countries the tax is levied at a standard rate, in Japan, Switzerland and the United States, at least, rates progress with income levels.

As a proportion of GDP in 1989 income and profits taxes formed 1.5 per cent of tax revenue in federal countries and 3.9 per cent in non-federal countries, ranging in 1989 from 0.2 per cent (USA) up to 15.6 per cent (Sweden). As a proportion of local government tax revenue the range was from 6 per cent (USA) to 99.6 per cent (Sweden). In federal countries it is more a state tax, taking 6.2 per cent of GDP in Canada in 1989 and 5.3 per cent in Germany and Switzerland.

The countries where such taxes account for over 75 per cent of local government tax revenue are all either Germanic, partly Germanic or Scandinavian: in Belgium 75.4 per cent of local tax income, Germany 82.4 per cent, Luxembourg 85.1 per cent, Switzerland 86.1 per cent, Norway 88.2 per cent, Denmark 92.2 per cent, Finland 99.1 per cent and Sweden 99.6 per cent. All four Norse countries are high taxing, putting their main emphasis on income taxes but allocating most of their share of overall taxation to local government to enable it to meet the costs of administering the most expensive services (education, health and social services) from its own revenue.

Most countries are very similar in the percentage of the GDP that comes from income and profits taxes, which stands at between 13 and 15 per cent. Local government has no direct share in any of the anglophone countries' national income tax, and in Latin countries it receives below 2 per cent, most of the receipts being retained by central government. In three of the federal countries (Canada, Germany and Switzerland), the federal state level received 5 to 6 per cent of the GDP, but German local government is allotted half the state's allocation and in Switzerland 4.5 per cent of GDP.

Business Rates and Other Sources of Tax Revenue

Local authorities receive rates based on local business incomes, usually as defined by national government, in Austria, Finland, Germany, Italy, Japan, Luxembourg, Norway, Portugal, Spain, Switzerland and the United States. Other taxes on businesses are not solely or directly related to profits: in France and Germany, for example, they are combined with income rating and other variables in the business tax. As a proportion of GDP they range from 0.1 per cent in Italy and Spain to 0.6 per cent in Switzerland, and as percentages of total local tax revenue from 1.7 per cent in Denmark to 14 or 15 per cent in Belgium and Germany (Owens, 1991). Their effects on business location can be considerable.

Other Taxes

Consumption or sales taxes are not in general important except where the revenue from other taxes is unusually low. In the United States in 1989 they contributed more than income tax at 10.4 per cent of local revenue; in Spain 12.4 per cent; and in Portugal 17.4 per cent. They are not used in 15 of 22 OECD countries.

Payroll tax is levied at local level in Austria, forming 11.4 per cent of local revenue in 1989. Austrian local government was also exceptional in its use of taxes on usage, specific goods and services and other miscellaneous taxes which amounted altogether to 18 per cent of local tax income (0.5 per cent of GDP), an unparalleled level. Canadian local goverment comes second with 14.8 per cent (0.5 per cent of GNP).

The Distribution of Local Taxes in OECD Countries

Anglophone countries have conservatively depended chiefly on a tax on property for their local authorities, mostly on houses or real estate. The problem-fraught British community tax has been superseded in 1993 by council tax, a house tax combined with a capitation element. In the Germanic and Scandinavian countries and Japan, however, income tax, the most directly and fairly distributive approach, prevails, albeit in Austria and Germany the level and allocation is fixed centrally so that it is in practice close in nature to an income related grant-in-aid. A sole tax based on property was reasonable in Britain until the growth of education, social services and policing made it inadequate by itself and led to what has generally been considered an excessive dependence on central grants and thus to undermine local government autonomy. This was less of a problem in other anglophone countries where states took the main weight at least of these services and mostly financed them by raising income tax levels.

Latin countries as well as Germanic/Scandinavian also typically employ income tax as a major element, but at a lower level by combining it with a range of other taxes. Both property and income taxes can be strongly modified in the direction of greater equity by means of rebates, allowances and progressive scales. The business taxes in France and Germany, for example, have complex bases designed to avoid undue weight on a single factor. A major British inquiry into local government finance recommended a combination of a property tax with a local income tax, a means to combine the strengths and compensate for the weaknesses of both taxes (*Local Public Finance*, 1976). Central and state governments are, however, generally determined to monopolise income taxes where a precedent for local income tax has not been set, preferring to increase local dependence by funnelling money down to lower levels in the form of special-purpose or global grants.

The United States and Japan use a wide range of taxation devices (see §§8.9 and 10.9) and are laboratories for their study. The Japanese system in particular is highly complex, using scales, allowances and exceptions to a remarkable extent, even within the main 'local tax' which features a per capita sum together with graded income assessments. Perhaps high complexity can be combined with efficiency alongside equity, given the possibilities of modern data processing systems.

Borrowing

Surveys on this subject by the Standing Conference of Local and Regional Authorities in Europe (CLRAE) (Council of Europe, 1984c) and by an international banker focusing on EC countries (Cornut, 1991) show the great complexity of the subject. The field has expanded as private markets have opened up and new institutions, not least the European Investment Bank, have widened opportunities. Since the 1870s at least, borrowing from the private sector has been of great importance to development activities by local authorities in the United States (Aronson and Hilley, 1986). The CLRAE review summarised the borrowing methods found in Europe as: (1) borrowing from internal funds, as for instance Swiss local authorities on employee insurance funds, legacies and foundations; (2) borrowing from public and private banks; (3) temporary borrowing from the money market, especially in the United Kingdom and Switzerland; (4) bonds, debenture issues, a common feature of eleven countries on which information was studied; (5) in the United Kingdom stock issues; and (6) lease arrangements, apparently in Europe also special to the United Kingdom.

The CLRAE report made recommendations which seem of lasting interest. They accepted a degree of government control over borrowing activities but stressed that excessive control of capital spending could impede financial and economic management at local or regional level. They considered that disproportionate central budgetary control and reduced or delayed financial transfers from central government could jeopardise authorities' stability and credit-worthiness. They felt that borrowing to meet finance deficits on current account was imprudent and that the sole purpose should be financing capital development and re-scheduling debt. They also believed that debts incurred should be secured on the total revenues of an authority or guaranteed by government.

The study found that sources of borrowing for local authorities, for capital investment at least, were in principle uncontrolled in Germany, France and the United Kingdom, subject in Germany to their being for investments in a five-year planning system. Japan also has restrictions on loan purposes and a system of control within the framework of a yearly capital planning system within which the costs of loans are shared between levels of government (*Local Public Finance in Japan*, 1984). Government authorisation is required in Belgium, Spain, Italy, the Netherlands and Denmark, subject to exceptions. These countries, excepting Germany, had national credit institutions specialising in loans to local authorities. Long-standing preferential rates provided by such bodies have tended to decline in recent years along with the growth of privatisation of borrowing where this is permitted. The new European single market is expected to lead eventually to a fusing of loan controls. Cases of excessive indebtedness by local authorities have been reported in France and of default in Belgium, despite a government system to control borrowings. It has been suggested that in the event of such cases continuing there may be a case for a 'European financial tutelle' (Cornut, 1991).

Grants-in-Aid and Other Local Incomes Outside Local Authority Control

Transfers of finance from central to regional and local government are a universal feature in OECD countries. There is a logic to them in that the most expensive services provided by local government are to fulfil purposes defined by central government, not just for the local good but for national well-being; and they are to a large extent mandatory and without local participation in the related decision-making. As agents, willing or unwilling to fulfil national commitments (but often very willing), local authorities cannot be expected to raise all their own resources. Purposes embodied in legislation are generally shared with central government, or in any event accepted as legal obligations. But the implementing authorities will expect to have discretion to act within the framework of national law to match local provision to local needs and preferences within their area and set levels of quality beyond what may be required as a minimum by central government. This implies that they should have choice and flexibility in implementation: that they can add value well within minimal costs estimated at the centre. Moreover they are responsible to their electorates for ensuring as good a level of quality and efficiency as possible within the resources contributed. They act only as agents for certain high-cost elements, above all salaries set at national level of employees required for mandatory tasks. They also need wide scope for innovation in mandatory services as well as non-mandatory if there is to be local and national progress. It is therefore impossible to determine how much should justly be regarded as the responsibility of the centre and how much of the locality. Contributions to local finance have to be a shared commitment. To create instability in the proportions of support allowed creates instability in locally administered services and consequent inefficiency.

It is important, however, that there are frequent adjustments to levels of grant as national priorities change. The implications for local finance need to be threshed out between central, regional and local partners to ensure that relative contributions are as far as possible agreed to ensure a just distribution of financial responsibilities. In Denmark and Sweden, for example, there are inter-governmental meetings to achieve an agreement on the financial implications of new legislation for local authorities and to adjust grant levels accordingly, and also on annual revisions of grant contributions in the light of changing cost levels and central policies.

Strictly speaking the term 'financial transfers' includes state taxes divided between levels of government, such as German income and business taxes. In Japan there is a special national 'local allocation tax' that is distributed to prefectures and municipalities. Normally, however, the phrase is applied to grants made from central government's general income. The main distinction is between general-purpose and specific grants.

General-purpose or global grants can in principle be spent by authorities as freely as the income they raise for themselves. Sometimes there are separate global grants for current and capital expenditures. Their level may be related to objective criteria and in some cases to the level of an authority's own determined tax level, increasing as this rises.

Specific grants may be discretionary or related to particular fields of expenditure. The latter may be assessed as a percentage of costs incurred for a service, even up to 100 per cent. Or they may be based on standard costs, any additional expenditure being met by the authority from its own resources (Council of Europe, 1986b, *Policies with Regard to Grants to Local Authorities*). In 1981 general-purpose grants as a proportion of authorities' total grant income ranged among 17 Council of Europe countries from nil (Austria) to 94.6 per cent (Portugal). In Italy at that time 68.4 per cent was related to local authorities' own taxation efforts.

Specific grants for current expenditures or for current and capital based on standard costs were made in nine cases, ranging as a proportion of tax income from 1.8 per cent (France) to 51.2 per cent (Sweden). Specific grants related to actual costs were made in 11 countries, ranging from 3.3 (Spain) to 62.5 per cent (Denmark). Seven countries made unconditional specific grants, from 0.1 (Denmark) to 11.6 per cent (Greece). Specific capital grants were made in every one of the 17 countries except Switzerland and ranged from 0.3 per cent of grant revenue (Denmark) to 93.4 per cent (Cyprus). An indication of the proportion of total revenue on the spending over which local authorities have full discretion within the law may be given by calculating the proportions of general or global grants added to those of local tax revenues as a percentage of total revenue. A report by Graham Kelly for the Council of Europe (Council of Europe, 1981b, *Financial Apportionment and Equalisation*) showed that out of 16 countries in 1981 this 'free spending money' totalled from 37.2 per cent in the Netherlands to 95.5 per cent in Portugal. In only five of these countries, however, was local government expenditure more that 10 per cent of the GDP: 37.2 per cent in the Netherlands, 61.7 per cent in Denmark, 75.1 per cent in Sweden, 80.9 per cent in the United Kingdom and 82.8 per cent in Norway. These are of course countries where local government carries responsibility for education and other major services and the discretion over expenditure may be highly limited in practice by regulations.

Financial Equalisation

In recent decades governments have in general recognised a responsibility for reducing economic and welfare disparities between parts of their areas to help ensure that each can make its highest potential contribution to the economy, as well as on grounds of equity or equality of opportunity for all inhabitants.

Direct assistance with urban renewal programmes and infrastructure is necessarily of a specific nature. Across most local government services, however, specific grants have tended to give way to the general, block or global grants described above. These are generally assessed in proportion to the needs of areas and to raise the level of financial resources of the poorer areas towards a standard level. Put another way, they may seek to ensure that all authorities have the means to finance a comparable level of services for the same rate of local tax or taxes. Criteria relate to service costs and need. They include population mix and density (for example numbers of pre-school and school children, young people and elderly), children in one-parent families, length of roads, age of housing etc. and market conditions such as level of labour costs, selected partly according to cost factors within the range of mandatory functions possessed by authorities. Revenue support grants may seek to raise revenues to a minimum rate.

Although there may be extensive consultations on the formulas employed in fixing the rates and involvement of a wide range of experts in the determination and weighting of the criteria, a large element of subjective judgement is involved. Authorities will fight for their own interests — urban against rural, poor against affluent and so forth. Government ministers will be accused of bias in the weightings to benefit groups of authorities they favour. They will also be seen as undermining local judgement. It may be claimed that block grants can strangle local government freedom in a way that is hidden from view and beyond the comprehension of almost all professionals and politicians, unlike specific grant systems where transfers are given for particular tasks which local authorities are required to fulfil as part of national policy. The problems of general grants seem inescapable and their scale rises with the proportion of grant upon which local authorities rely (Council of Europe, 1988, *Financial Instruments and the Role of Finance in Regional Institutions*)

Grant setting is inseparable from the regulation of expenditures on mandatory services. It may also be developed to set limits on overall local authority expenditure for macro-economic and even ideological reasons, as in the case of the British Grant Related Expenditure Assessment system which, although primarily for determining an equitable distribution of block grants, has been used as the basis for judgements on how much local authorities should spend in each financial year, penalties being placed on authorities that are deemed to 'overspend' (§7.9).

Finance for Intermediate and Regional Authorities

There is a clear distinction between intermediate authorities that exist primarily for providing services that are considered unsuitable for basic authorities and those that have general powers over the authorities in their areas such as the regions in Belgium, Italy, Spain and Portugal. The latter have an essential role in planning for the development of their areas and enabling local authorities to carry out their role. The French regions are in a middle position, planning within their national systems and able to supplement local authorities' resources to a limited extent.

In the first group the Dutch provinces depend heavily on finance from central government, receiving annual transfers from a fund maintained by a fixed percentage of yield from national taxes divided among them according to their populations, areas and length of navigable waterways, with a remainder distributed in even shares. In addition they receive specific allocations for civil defence, pollution control and construction and maintenance of provincial roads. They also collect stamp duties and charges for the use of their properties. The British counties and regions precept for a proportion of the community charge (council tax from 1993) collected by district councils. A large part of their incomes come from central grants (see §7.9). In Ireland local property taxes have been abolished and counties depend for nearly all their revenues on central transfers. In Sweden and Denmark over half the county revenues have come from local income tax, supplemented in Denmark by a land tax rate set by statute (§§5.9 and 6.9). In Norway the proportion of tax income is at a much lower rate: together with charges only about one-third of income in the late 1980s. Prefectural revenue sources in Japan closely mirror those of the municipalities (§10.9). In the second group Belgian regions receive a percentage of the national personal income tax relating to the contributions of their inhabitants. In Italy the bulk of regional resources are transfers from the national government and a number of national agencies. Otherwise ordinary regions operate taxes on state and regional concessions, traffic taxes and taxes on open spaces. In Spain the autonomous communities' assets and sources of income are stipulated in their individual constitutions. They consist of the taxes they have power to levy, an allocation of central taxes levied in their areas, surcharges on state taxes and a miscellany of other sources. Overall in the late 1980s the spending levels of the regions were projected to rise from their current 20 per cent of national public expenditure to 25 per cent, as against 15 per cent by local authorities. (European Centre for Regional Development, 1989)

1.10 ELECTORAL REPRESENTATION

Representation of the interests of local inhabitants is the essence of modern local and regional democracy. The exceptions are cases, found most notably in Switzerland, where participation in key decisions is open to all citizens in a popular assembly, and, in a few countries by referendum (see

§1.12). Both of these have limitations even when practicable, especially in that they can result in the 'tyranny of the majority', a phrase coined by Toqueville after seeing oppression of minorities in small communities in the United States (Toqueville, 1835).

This section deals with three main factors which determine the extent to which the popular will is met: the political parties which put forward policies and candidates for popular choice; the conditions of service which determine how far people are attracted to the representative role and how much weight and attention they are likely to give to it; and the electoral systems that determine how individuals or party candidates are chosen to exercise power on the voters' behalf.

The Parties

National party systems fall into two main groups: multi-party systems, strongly associated with proportional representation, and those where two parties are dominant and tend to alternate in power, associated with 'first past the post', 'winner take all' selection systems (see below under Electoral Systems). Two-round systems may mix proportional and absolute majority methods.

Parties vary widely in nature. Some have sharply defined policy platforms reflecting an ideology, while others are pragmatic with only vague policy commitments and may expect people to vote chiefly for individuals rather than a party manifesto. Some have mass memberships and strong national and regional secretariats, as in the case of the larger parties in Germany and Italy, and others small memberships representing elites or a special viewpoint. Parties may also be distinguished by the nature of their grass-roots functions, for example whether they are bringing together mainly businessmen and professionals, or are 'clientelistic', seeking support by helping individuals and families to obtain jobs where possible and helping them to deal with local or national bureaucracy, most conspicuously perhaps in Italy and Japan. They may see their electoral strength as resting in the concrete benefits they bring to local or regional communities by obtaining favourable treatment from central government for local projects and in other ways — especially it seems in Latin countries and Japan,

Mass membership parties normally have an ideological base, and are often also 'clientelistic'. On the other hand a relatively small membership may be brought together for fighting elections and sharing office in political administrations, as in the United States. Britain has manifesto-type parties with local party organisations that are weak in comparison with many on the European mainland. Ideological commitment has played an

85

important part in the French system but the main parties are not of a mass-membership type. Individual personalities or reputations (*notables*) play a major role. Parties often group into alliances on lists and share participation in the political administration, leading inevitably to a somewhat pragmatic approach. In Japan parties are identified, as in Europe, with ideologies but also with individuals. However the Liberal Democrat Party, dominant at national level, is akin to the French parties in the extent to which it is governed by 'notables'. Here, also, local elections often fail to return a majority party, despite one-party dominance at national level, and coalitions are frequent.

Non-party candidates can play a crucial role in small authorities. At local level larger authorities are more likely to be dominated by party. In continental Europe many parties are often represented on a council, giving a representation of a wide range of social, economic and cultural interests. The ways in which parties achieve influence and decisions in such cases varies (Mellors and Pijnenburg (eds), 1989; Szajkowski (ed.), 1986).

Multi-party systems in which structures at local and regional levels mirror national systems often result in a plethora of organisations. In 1984 in Italy, for example, of the local authority plural executives (*giuntà*) in communes with over 5,000 inhabitants, under a third (770) were under one-party control. Among the other 1,540 there were at least 47 different combinations of parties in charge, including two formed from six different parties and over a hundred that included the two largest parties, the right-wing Christian Democrats and the Communists (Pridham, 1989). In most countries many local parties without national organisations are involved in coalitions, complicating the outcome.

Multi-party regimes became much more common in British local government in the 1980s, when support for the Conservative Party fell strongly and the grip of the two main parties weakened against strong attacks by minority parties. Overall majority control was lost in many instances (152 out of 513 authorities in 1987-88), but there was strong resistance to the formation of coalitions. A survey of 103 'hung' authorities in 1987 found that only eight had 'shared administrations' (Leach and Stewart, 1987). The 'politics of accommodation' is extraordinarily weak: party politicians in some cases prefer the head of staff to put forward decisions for acceptance and divide on a vote only occasionally (Norton, 1991).

A pragmatic approach aimed at uniting communities rather than dividing them is strongly represented in the Christian Democrat movement. This does not imply that relationships in party alliances are always harmonious (Mellors and Pijnenburg (eds), 1989). Coalition-making has been facilitated by the dropping of the Marxist principle of class war by left-wing parties. Communist parties have competed for office successfully on the grounds of their management ability or lack of corruption. This is especially so in direct elections of chief executives such as have been achieved by alliances of socialists and communists in Japan in important prefectures including Tokyo, Osaka and Kyoto. Direct elections of executives and officers in Japan, South Germany and the United States have their own special characteristics.

Where parties can be placed roughly along a single political left to right spectrum, viable and often semi-permanent coalitions may be expected often to cover a band within the spectrum representing the overall majority of the electorate. Some multi-party systems have accommodated parties with new and challenging ideologies, particularly the 'Greens', cutting across the traditional left to right spectrum and in some cases pioneering approaches that make an impact on national policy-making. For example the German Greens succeeded in introducing new issues and ideas into the national debate through their local influence, leading older parties to formulate green policies of their own.

Close relationships between levels within parties from sub-municipal up to national level can be a great strength to local and higher-level politicians, providing channels whereby local needs can be effectively expressed and supporting communities in ways that at their best may be termed 'enlightened clientelism'.

Party Groups

Since the end of the 1940s Germany has termed itself a 'party state' in which political pluralism is essential to liberty. Hence the subsidisation of political parties to help ensure that they can be effective agents of democracy. Local authorities give financial assistance to political groups in Denmark, Germany, the Netherlands, Norway and Sweden. Elsewhere they give assistance in the form of accommodation, information and office facilities. Out of the seventeen countries in a Council of Europe survey in 1988, thirteen reported that they provided accommodation for group meetings, especially in larger authorities. Only Ireland replied in the negative (information was lacking for France and Luxembourg). Austria appeared unique in not normally providing office facilities for elected members. Office accommodation was provided and financial assistance given to enable parties to provide facilities for the public, as in Sweden. In some cases office provision is limited to mayors, as in Norway and Germany, or to other senior council members, as in Belgium, the Nether-

87

lands and Luxembourg. (Council of Europe, 1988, *The Status and Working Conditions of Local and Regional Representatives*)

The Status of Elected Members and Their Conditions of Service

Ultimately the strength and success of local government depends largely on the qualities of those elected to serve it. Where it can be an avenue to advancement in society and the political system, as in France and Germany, it is particularly successful in attracting people with high abilities.

Rank and file members of party groups have many roles: not least competent representation of varied interests and talents. To maintain representativeness and commitment, enabling factors are important such as remuneration for the costs involved and the compatibility of being an elected member with current job and career prospects elsewhere in the public or private sector.

A Council of Europe survey (ibid.) showed the following conditions under which elected representatives served in all its member states except Switzerland. Terms of service lasted from three years (in Sweden) to six years (France, Belgium and Luxembourg). To stand for an election a candidate needed to be at least 18 years of age in eleven European cases, Canada and the USA, and 21 in six European countries. It was necessary to have status as a national except in Denmark, Ireland, the Netherlands and Sweden. In twelve cases a local or regional residential status was required, although having your principal place of work or paying the local tax or taxes in the area were alternative qualifications. Paying local taxes was also a qualification in France and Ireland. Grounds for disqualification were conviction for an offence punishable by imprisonment (seven cases), bankruptcy (Luxembourg and the United Kingdom), declared insanity (six cases), being a blood relation of the mayor or a councillor or related to either of them by marriage (Belgium and in France excepting spouses), and deprivation of legal capacity (three cases). In the United Kingdom candidates are disqualified by a surcharge by the statutory auditor or conviction for an electoral offence. In some Swiss cantons drunkenness can be a reason for disqualification.

Holding a seat on more than one council is illegal in Austria and Italy. Political parties restrict their members to sitting on one council only in Belgium and the Netherlands and with certain exceptions in Denmark. Combining an official job with service as an elected member in the same authority is permitted in Denmark and to an increasing extent in Switzerland. In nine other European countries an authority's employee may not be elected to its council. Portugal and the United Kingdom do not allow certain senior employees to serve as councillors in another authority. There are various other exclusions but it seems to be only in Austria that a leading position in the private sector is a disqualification.

The burdens and social rewards of being a councillor or an elected executive vary greatly. According to the replies to the Council of Europe inquiry, time spent by councillors on formal council and committee meetings averaged about six hours a month in Swedish municipalities and 40.5 hours in the Netherlands. The Swedish estimate for county councils amounted to over 40 hours. Time spent on all aspects of council business averaged 74 hours a month according to a 1985 survey. For German municipal councillors the average was 12 to 14 hours. Estimates of the average time taken over formal meetings by mayors in Denmark was from 80 to 120 hours a month, and, for full-time mayors in Germany, 40 to 60 hours. For members of executive committees in the Netherlands in 1979 it was about 60 hours.

There is an obvious case for rewarding what are virtually full-time jobs with full-time salaries, and a danger that, whether rich or poor, full-time executives may regard the exploitation of the job for gains of a dubious if not illegal kind as defensible if they do not receive just recompense for their time and efforts. Payments to elected members are often but not always described as general allowances rather than salaries, although they may be meant as direct compensation for work opportunities. No distinction is made here and the term 'general remuneration' is used for both. There are national rates of remuneration in some cases, graded by population or type of authority and job. According to the 1988 Council of Europe survey remuneration was paid to all councillors in Denmark and the Netherlands and to Italian regional councillors (60 to 100 per cent of that paid to MPs). None was paid in Ireland or France, or in the United Kingdom except modest attendance allowances for approved duties. Executive mayors, mayoral assistants and executive aldermen and some committee chairmen received general remuneration, at least in larger authorities. In Britain special payments might be made at a much higher level than attendance allowances to a limited number of councillors with special responsibilities. In Norway a full-time mayor normally received the same remuneration as the head of administration, and there and in Sweden payments were discretionary. Attendance allowances and travel expenses were usually additional.

Payments were made to members with full or part-time functions which were intended to provide them with a real income in Austria, Norway, Portugal, Spain and in some cases in Switzerland.

Private as well as public sector employers of elected representatives are required to give them leave of absence, to some extent at least, in all 17 European countries excepting Denmark, Ireland, Switzerland, Turkey and the United Kingdom. Their employers are required to bear the cost in Belgium and Luxembourg. Local authorities have to do so in Belgium, Germany (normally) and Portugal, and in some circumstances in Denmark, Ireland, Spain and the United Kingdom. Compensation for loss of earnings or other income is provided for in Austria, Denmark (as an alternative to fixed allowances), Norway and Sweden, and to members of local executives in Switzerland.

Elected representatives enjoy guarantees of job security and protection of career prospects in Austria, Denmark, Germany, Portugal and Spain, and job security at least in France. No formal protection is given in the Netherlands, Scandinavia, Turkey and the United Kingdom, and not in general in Switzerland. Assistance is specifically for retiring from professional life in Denmark, Norway and Portugal. Full-time service qualifies for a pension in Austria, Belgium, Denmark, France, Germany (mayors only) and Sweden. Ireland, Luxembourg and the United Kingdom are out of line in giving no retirement allowance or pension.

Electoral Systems

Universal and secret balloting by adult citizens has become an essential part of advanced liberal democracy in recent years. Qualification to vote for members of the local authority in the area in which one is normally resident follows on recognition as an adult. The qualifying age has fallen recently in many countries. According to latest information from various sources it stands generally at 18 but at 19 in Austria and 20 in Japan and Switzerland. Exceptions are commonly made in the case of people committed for crimes subject to the penalty of imprisonment and those of unsound mind or, as it is put in Denmark, 'unable to manage their own affairs'. Aliens have generally been excluded but progress is being made towards requiring residential qualifications alone. Drunkenness can disqualify in parts of Switzerland.

Legal qualifications rarely imply the right to vote without registration, and it is usual to find that five to ten per cent of qualified residents are unregistered for various reasons. This may be due to their not being in an area long enough to be entered in the annual revision of the register or to meet a residence condition, but it may result from deliberate evasion for some reason, including tax avoidance. The extent to which a vote is likely to have any influence on which candidates are elected depends largely on the electoral system in force. The factors involved include the boundaries of the area, the ratio between numbers of electors and people to be elected and how many seats on the council are up for election.

Electoral systems differ with tradition and the aims of those who determine them. There is a fairly sharp division between those that primarily seek to give all voters an influence on the composition of their council and those where the candidate who receives most votes wins. The former seek to ensure that the result is in accordance with the balance of wishes within the electorate by a system of proportional representation (PR) or transferable votes according to second and subsequent choices if the voter's first choice is unsuccessful. They aim at a broad representation of the spectrum of public opinion. The latter seek to ensure a strong majority for the purpose of strong government or decisiveness, as in Britain, Canada and the United States. The first group is found mainly in countries consciously seeking social unity and opposed to the divisiveness involved in putting an overall majority of the electorate or at least a large part of them in a position where they lack political effectiveness; the other where there is a belief that a strong and effective political controlling group is needed that can act decisively and without the need to build up a consensus to reconcile different sectors of opinion. A strong majority may be equated with efficiency and the view that the management of an authority should be decisive and accountability should lie clearly with a single group with a clear mandate to carry through its proposals by the next election so that voters can judge its performance on the results. Under such a system the constitution of the electorate may be such as to give one party what appears to be permanent control or, at the other extreme, result in a frequent alternation of power between parties and so instability and sharp discontinuities in policy.

Countries with the former systems generally have strong voting rates, ranging from 60 to over 90 per cent of those on the register; and countries with majoritarian systems rates between 20 and 50 per cent. This does not necessarily imply a cause and effect relationship and exceptions can be found. It is tempting to put the associations down to the nature of the local culture; but whose culture? Opinion polls have found in Britain, for example, that a substantial majority of those asked were in favour of proportional voting of some kind, although the two main parties have consistently opposed it.

The following survey of voting systems begins with those of lowest proportionality and ends with the most proportional. In most anglophone countries election by relative majority applies. Authority areas are often divided into wards, each returning one or more members of a council, giving representation of relative majorities by individual wards or electoral districts, as in Britain. Or, typical of traditional American arrangements, election can be 'at large', the top performers in council elections being returned to fill the number of the seats available. A completely non-proportional system is that where an absolute majority is required, obtainable by ruthlessly restricting choice to two candidates or lists. More choice can be built in in this case if there are 'primary' elections for the candidates who are to stand in the name of the parties involved. More liberally there can be two rounds, as has been used in Australia: one to choose the most supported candidates and, if nobody wins at least half the votes, a 'run-off election' between the two most successful.

What is called the single non-transferable vote system is used for local government elections in Japan (although a proportional representation method is used for elections to the national House of Councillors). Voters cast one vote for a single candidate in multi-seat constituencies. In Greece candidates have been put forward on lists and whichever wins an absolute majority first time takes two-thirds of the seats available and the list that comes second the remainder. If there is no majority there is a run-off election between the two top lists. A second round of elections is used in France, enabling parties together on competing lists to negotiate a common list if none wins a majority in the first round.

Proportional systems use ingenious methods to ensure that, subject to qualifications such as exclusion of small minority parties with anti-constitutional ends, no-one's vote is wasted. They normally require competing lists of candidates, usually selected by individual parties but sometimes shared by allied parties or independent non-party candidates. They tend to be drawn up by the parties with regard to achieving a representation of areas, sexes and other interests to attract a wide section of the electorate and thus give the best chance for minority or disadvantaged social groups to be represented. In a few cases voters have no option other than to choose one of the lists of candidates presented to them unaltered, as in Austria and Luxembourg. Elsewhere they are given means to express their preferences between individual candidates on the lists. In most countries the system seeks to combine the list system with a degree of choice between individuals. Voters may be able to strike out names of individual candidates on a list (*panachage*), change the order of priority for election, or substitute names from other lists, or even enter names not included. Some or all of these methods are found in Belgium, South Germany, Italy, the Netherlands, Norway and Sweden. In Denmark and Finland voters can vote both for individuals and for lists and the method of selection combines the results. The most popular 'PR' method appears to be the Sainte Laguë or modified d'Hondt system, in which seats are allocated in sequence by dividing the votes for each list by a series of numbers, for example by 1, 2.5, 3.6 and so on. Given the right divisor this system is claimed to be at least as proportional as the single transferable vote (STV) system, which appears to be otherwise the most perfect in terms of proportionality (Blondel, 1969 and 1989).

STV is used in the Irish Republic, Northern Ireland and Tasmania. Here, in order to be elected, candidates must gain at least more than the total number of votes cast divided by the number of seats to be filled. If no candidate succeeds at this stage, the second preferences of those who voted for the lowest-scoring candidates are added to the score of the others. When a candidate scores more than needed to elect a candidate, the 'surplus' is transferred according to second preferences. The procedure continues using subsequent preferences until all available seats are filled. A head of administration and electoral returning officer in Northern Ireland, where STV has been used because of the desirability of giving representation to church-related minority parties and the Alliance, informs me that the system works smoothly and impressively there, and in general to the satisfaction of a deeply divided community.

Different methods may be appropriate for different sizes and types of community, as is recognised in France, Luxembourg and most of Italy where majority voting is used in smaller communes. In Italy minority parties have been given the concession that each voter is allowed to vote for only four-fifths of the number of representatives to be elected in at-large elections.

1.11 THE INTERNAL ORGANISATION OF LOCAL AND REGIONAL AUTHORITIES

When people refer to a local authority or municipality they may mean: (1) the elected assembly or council accountable to its electorate for its decisions and the work done in its name; (2) its executive or the elected members responsible for controlling its decision-making process and services; (3) the staff to whom it delegates most of this work; or (4) two or all three of these. The functions of the assembly and executive are the universal means of local government, whether or not their membership overlaps. In many countries the name of the collectivity of citizens who elect the assembly, such as the commune or Gemeinde, may be used popularly in reference to any or all of these institutions.

The assembly and the executive provide both government and administration. Where government ends and administration begins depends on varying usage of words and their translations, so that precision requires that they are not used without specific definition or qualification. But the phrase 'local self-government' may be used to cover all the processes that go on in the name of elected local authorities (see §1.2).

Elected assemblies are similar basically in all advanced democracies apart from variations in their sizes and styles, but the executive takes a large variety of forms. The senior staff, paid servants or officers of the local authority, who are often somewhat misleadingly called the bureaucracy, normally have very close relations with the executive and are generally under its control. They may be termed 'the officer administration' to distinguish them from 'the political executive' which consists of elected politicians. Even so exceptions have to be made, as in the case of the German Magistrat (see §4.4).

Roles commonly overlap. In the British system there is no legal distinction between council and executive, so that decisions elsewhere taken by an executive such as a mayor or board may be taken by the council or its committees. In councils of no more than three to seven members, as are common in the United States, there would seem to be little scope for a separate executive, although they may appoint a general manager and executive commissions. The council in some cases has its own officers and the executive its own body of advisers and other staff, distinct from the departmental system.

Councillors may undertake service implementation that would in other cases be carried out by employees. At the other extreme there may be formal and even physical separation, with the assembly, an elected or appointed executive and the staff working in separate units occupying separate accommodation. In most cases, however, there is an overlapping or organic relationship between parts of local authorities.

The executive normally prepares business for the council, implements its decisions and represents it in formal and informal relationships. It is dependent on staff, both those who prepare the business of the council for debate and ratification and those who administer the authority's services and control its workforce on behalf of the executive.

The senior staff are normally expert professionals. Their power lies in their expertise, their relative permanence, the nature of the functions they perform for the council and executive and their status within the authority and sometimes in national law. Their effective power can be great since the political executive depends on them to prepare the business of the council, undertake many tasks of subordinate decision-making, maintain the authority's services and manage many external relationships that were formerly within the province of elected members. It is useful to distinguish between staff who work close to councillors and/or the executive and administer departments and the business of the authority as a whole from the often very large number of other council employees. The former may be members of a national corps or cadre, have a special designation within the law or, on the other hand, be entirely subject to the employment conditions determined by their authority. Anomalous cases are the burgomasters in the Netherlands and the city and county managers in Ireland, posts in which the crown and a national board are involved in their appointment respectively (see §1.6). Executive and paid officer functions merge in these cases, as in that of British chief executives and chief administrative officer posts in North America and Germany.

While the council and the political executive have not grown much in size during their history, the officer organisations in large authorities have doubled many times over, covering a complex of specialised functions that can raise critical problems of co-ordination and control. To cope with this scale and complexity councils have set up complex committee systems to which to delegate all but a few key choices in the decision-making process, and rely on them to predetermine most of their decisions. Executives have deputies, assistants and experts to help them who may be politically appointed or normal paid staff.

Political parties or their council groups mediate between citizen and institution, not only through their role in focusing and narrowing effective electoral choice of council and elected executives but also in the relationships between council and executive and in some cases staff appointments.

The Elected Assembly or Council

Assemblies embody the representative nature of local government. They make local laws, by-laws or ordinances (the meanings and emphases placed on these differ widely (see §9.7)). They take decisions that regulate behaviour and conditions within the authority and determine the nature and mode of the services to be provided beyond what may be statutorily required. They determine what taxes the public must pay, sometimes its borrowing, and other key decisions. They make the formal appointment of the executive or distribute executive functions unless the executive is directly elected by the citizens or appointed by another level of government. They monitor the work of their council, acting as 'watchdogs' for the public. They take decisions on residual matters, the taking of which has not been delegated by them elsewhere or specifically allocated by law to the executive and other institutions. They serve as a forum for discussion and the rejection of proposals put before them if they prove not to have the support of the majority.

The size of a council affects the extent to which it can represent the wishes of the electorate, contain a range of skills and abilities, educate politicians in the skills of managing the responsibilities of public office, and provide the means for members with political ability to show their talents and begin political careers. Its size also relates to its efficiency as a decision-taking body in control of a large and complex organisation if, as research has indicated, the most effective decision-making or problem-solving body has some five to seven members (Handy, 1976). North American councils of only three members would seem to be not only low in representativeness but also too small to be efficient decision-making bodies unless they co-opt other members. On the other hand the efficiency of councils of above seven members at least is likely to decrease with increasing size. But if the primary functions of a council are representing the public, serving as a forum for discussion, confirming or referring back decisions but not normally formulating them, much less implementing them, and supervising the services provided, then a much larger group would seem appropriate. Preparation of decisions, if this is not a function of a separate executive, may be given to relatively small committees of members. These will be much better able to probe deeply into matters, make futher consultations, commission more information if thought desirable, thresh out issues with officers and provide a basis for well informed decisions.

An IULA survey in 1983 showed that the minimum size of councils in thirteen of the countries mentioned in this chapter ranged from three members in the United States and five in Canada and Denmark to 60 among the English metropolitan authorities. The country with the lowest maximum was Canada at 15 and the highest Sweden at 149, excepting the combined département and commune of Paris which had 163. In the great majority of cases all council members were found in the same survey to be elected together at one time, but elections were staggered in South Australia, in certain cases in Britain and in 77 per cent of city councils in the United States. (*The Local Council*, 1983)

Council meetings are generally open to the public subject to exceptions regarding certain types of reserved business, but in many cases the pro-ceedings of all but small councils are likely to be formalised in ways that make their proceedings more or less incomprehensible to outsiders. Small American councils are another matter, and here intervention in discussions by non-members may be accepted or even welcomed.

Procedures often reflect those in the national parliament. Public petitions are received in many cases. British councils may have a 'question time' during which committee spokespersons reply to questions put by individual councillors. In most countries on the Western European continent matters for deliberation are laid out in a form similar to national draft statutes, so that the procedure resembles 'law-making' rather than the debate and approval of reports and resolutions typical of the British system.

Committees

Committees (or commissions as they are often called in continental Europe) may have standing, permanent or main committee status. They are normally the means by which decision-making and advisory work is distributed among members. They may have statutory or delegated powers or be purely advisory. They may be special committees, working groups or task forces of ad hoc nature, set up to deal with special tasks and normally disbanded when they have reported to the council or one of its permanent committees. Another distinction is between standing committees that deal with a particular area of service such as transportation or recreation (vertical or service committees in English terminology), and those concerned with general aspects of control that cut across the interests of committees of the former type, such as finance, estate and personnel matters. Some permanent committees may be required by law. Other types are statutory or voluntary joint committees or boards with memberships from more than one authority, either with delegated powers of decision and administration or advisory only. Any type of committee may have sub-committees, with or without delegated power. A committee with a range of sub-committees may become a kind of 'mini-council', with or without delegated power to make decisions on behalf of the council itself.

The size of a committee can range from one person to the full membership of the council (plus co-opted members in some cases). In smaller authorities at least a meeting of the full council 'in committee' may be used as a means for all members of the council to meet to focus on issues of general interest without the special formalities of a council meeting, or to provide for a stage in decision-making prior to formal consideration of inter related aspects of the implications of committee decisions after taking into consideration the whole range of the council's commitments.

Committees usually reflect the political composition of the council by distributing seats proportionally. They may provide a means for co-option of persons from outside the council to provide expertise and representation of interested groups, with or without the right to a vote in decision-making, or they may be present only in an advisory function.

They may be primarily orientated towards policy, planning and programming decisions, developing proposals from the executive or head officers into forms that will be acceptable to a majority on the council, or serving as 'watchdogs' or checks on the activities of the executive and employees. The nature and scope of committee business varies widely, but it is determined especially by the division of responsibility between the council and the executive and administrative functions. Committees of authorities which have no distinct executive may have put before them any communications from within or outside the authority's organisation within their defined field of concern. However the volume of business alone prevents them from being omnicompetent in practice. In general the larger the scale of the business, the higher the dependence on officers tends to be.

A distinction may be made between policy and administrative matters in determining what may be delegated to officers and what should not (without prejudicing the ability of officers to advise on the effects of policy proposals or to put up ideas and provide drafts for adoption by committee or council).

The more the activities of a council are governed by formal council or state regulations, the clearer but more rigid the system. Leaving broadly framed resolutions to interpretation by officers and progressively elaborating internal regulations to limit their discretion and make implementation more uniform can result in a spiralling of bureaucracy. On the other hand, for council committees to undertake responsibility for implementational detail can lead to decisions becoming personalised and unpredictable and result in inefficiency and the frustration of broader policy. Such problems can be resolved to some extent by limiting committee business to general policy and other key matters and giving officers scope to act subject to consultation with chairmen whenever there are doubts on interpretation of policy resolutions or new and unforeseen policy issues arise. Advice on general policy and its implementation may be placed in the hands of a team of officers including the heads of administrative services, under the leadership of an officer chief executive, working in a close relationship with the political leadership, as in the British pattern (see Norton, 1991).

Committees are inevitably very dependent on the executive since to a large extent it determines the business with which they are concerned and how their decisions are implemented. Their chairmen may be members of a corporate executive.

In general, in local authorities that function within a developed party political system, party groups expect to maintain control over the outputs of committees and commonly have their own sub-structures and leadership patterns which match the main committee structures. In anglophone countries at least, problems with the co-ordination and efficiency of committee activity have led investigatory bodies and management consultants to press for the delegation of all detail to officers and a concentration by committees on policy and other key decisions. In Britain the great majority of authorities have followed national recommendations in instituting a central policy and resources committee as a means to set priorities, co-ordinate policy and action and monitor and review performance from a viewpoint above special service interests (§7.11). This has been complemented by the development of a corporate approach through an officer management board or chief officer group working closely with policy and resources committee members in the initiation and development of the proposals and evaluation of alternatives.

Forms of Executive

The executive function as generally understood in continental Europe may control both the political and the administrative system. Where there is no statutory provision for an executive, as in Britain and some types of local management plan in the United States and Canada, local arrangements, traditions and the characters of the leading individuals within the system determine how the function is exercised.

Statutory executives may be single persons or take the form of a board or executive committee. They may be directly elected, chosen by the council, or even appointed at national level in agreement with the local authority concerned, as in the cases of Dutch burgamasters and Irish city and county managers.

In general the executive function consists of preparing the business of the council, including draft bills, by-laws or ordinances, budgets and multi-year plans; implementing the council's decisions; administering its resources; and representing it in formal and informal relations. The role may include appointing and dismissing officials and other employees. The executive is normally expected to take the key role in preparing draft decisions or ordinances and ensuring implementation. The management process for which it is responsible may be seen as a cycle in which feed-back from the community on needs, demands and the effects of policies is evaluated, policy change and innovations incorporated in plans and programmes, budgets formulated and commitments implemented, to be followed by evaluation of feedback on the results. The executive is expected to ensure that the council organisation is efficient and well-managed. The executive, however, is highly dependent on staff and the officer organisation, both in the policy definition process and in the implementation of decisions. Because accountability to the council and the community for these matters centres on the executive it is therefore essentially a political as well as a managerial one (even if, as in Ireland, it is outside the party system).

The political process is much more one of leadership, responding to events and reconciling differences between those concerned to overcome destructive conflicts. It depends on maintaining the confidence of the controlling party group or coalition or, in a non-party administration, maintaining the confidence of a majority. General confidence will rest on its performance, particularly with regard to its submissions to the council, its leadership and management functions and the reactions of the public to the performance of the authority in general. The word 'executive' is often used ambiguously. Its meaning shades into that of manager, director or administrator. This is not surprising since its functions overlap these roles. The key to its success is close working with officials on the one hand and with local political leaders on the other.

The evidence in the following chapters is that the relationships involved are often problematic. Politicians are not elected for their managerial abilities in many cases, although these are likely to be given high priority in selecting them to stand as candidates for executive office, as for instance in the case with American 'strong mayors', South German Bürgermeister, French maires and presidents of departmental and regional councils, and members of a German Magistrat.

A main challenge for an executive is to ensure that heads of individual services work together for maximum efficiency and flexibility. There is often a head of staff to take general responsibility to the executive and advise him or her on other service matters, relations with external bodies and other central functions. A critical issue is the extent to which politicians who head services identify their interests primarily with the services for which they are responsible rather than the authority as a whole, whether they are members of a corporate executive, assistant or deputy mayors or chairmen of service committees. The general interest can be frustrated by alliances between such politicians and heads of departments working against common purposes. The extent to which members of an executive should be involved in the management of particular services has often been controversial in so far as their intervention in departmental management can override expert judgement and demoralise professional officers, leading to a failure to see the overall tasks of an authority in perspective.

The ideal model is perhaps a political executive that includes politicians overseeing particular aspects of the authority's work and working together to common purposes, headed by a political leader (such as president, mayor or council leader); and a complementary group of officer heads of services led by a head of staff with a general responsibility for the functioning of the management of the organisation as a whole and the relationships between the officers and the political executive. Both the political head and the head of staff would see themselves working for the council as a whole and maintaining its confidence in their performance. The relationship between these 'twin pinnacles' would be the bond on which the unity of the organisation would depend.

In all cases the relationship of the executive to the deliberative council is crucial to the democratic logic of the system. The political leadership in the assembly may constitute the executive or in corporate models be in a position to determine decisions within the executive. Where there is no legally defined allocation of responsibilities, as in the British model, the location of the executive function has to be determined locally and tends to depend on the character, interests and abilities of the leading politicians and officials, and who holds the confidence of the majority in the assembly.

Among the models of executive found in the United States the strong mayor plan focuses and concentrates authority in a single person with great clarity. The South German mayoral (Bürgermeister) model is similar, although the strong party system results in a measure of interdependence with the controlling group on the council. Japanese directly elected governors of prefectures and municipal mayors possess particularly strong powers, being able to challenge decisions of the council and dissolve it and call a new election in certain cases. Like Central and Southern European mayors they have tasks for which they are directly responsible to state governments, but these are of a higher range and importance in Japan than elsewhere.

Executive mayors and presidents elected by their councils are found in Latin countries (excepting Italy where from 1993 they are now directly elected), and South-West Germany (§§2.11, 3.11 and 4.11). The need for a wider executive group including assistant or deputy chief executives, is recognised in all these cases. The fact that the council chooses these adjuncts to the chief executive and in most cases proportionately, so that their composition reflects the political interests of the controlling parties, gives a corporate character to the executive team as a whole and secures a close relationship with the council and the party groups.

The Italian local government law of 1990 has developed the 'checks and balances' system implicit in other Latin models by giving the corporate *giuntà* a clear and distinct set of competences, including residual matters not allocated to the mayor (§3.11). By contrast, in Japan vice-governors and deputy mayors are appointed with an assembly's approval for four-year terms of office but the chief executive has the power to dismiss them at will.

Once the mayor is elected he or she normally has tenure until the next election. There are exceptions: in the Rhineland-Palatinate *Bürgermeister* are appointed chiefly with regard to their individual abilities. They have a more permanent status, serving normally for a ten-year period and often for another ten years at least, while councils are re-elected every five years. Those appointed and their deputies have often been government officials with mixed administrative, technical and political backgrounds.

Plural executives are characteristic of northern continental Europe. Executive boards of aldermen appointed by their councils and headed by a mayor or burgamaster are found in Belgium and the Netherlands. In general their members reflect the political composition of the council. Although each member may specialise in a particular area of service, their decisions are made corporately. Scandinavian municipalities also appoint an executive board headed by an appointed chairman. In 1986 Oslo adopted a political cabinet whose members have a degree of responsibility for particular services, throwing into question the position of the overall city manager (Baldersheim, 1991).

Canada has directly elected executive bodies in Ontario known as boards of control, and executive committees of commissioners appointed by councils under the council-committee system (§9.11). Similar systems are found in the United States (§8.11).

Employee Executives

The formal definition of a political executive does not remove the need for a head of employees or chief servant of the council to take general control of staff matters (§§2.11, 3.11, 4.11 and 5.11). Such a post is a highly demanding and responsible role in any local government system. One case is that of the French secretary- or director-general who works in close liaison with the mayor or president of the departmental or regional council. In Belgium a municipal secretary has to be appointed who is said to carry responsibilities close to those of a typical English town clerk of before 1974. Such heads of staff are in some cases drawn from a national cadre or corps which guarantees their competence and abilities. In cases where there is no legal political executive, however, the role has a special importance, as in the cases of American county and city managers (§8.11). The Republic of Ireland has city managers and also county managers who serve as executives of towns within their areas as well as their county. They are selected by a state-appointed appointments commission and have intimate contacts with the Ministry for Domestic Affairs. Certain matters such as major policy issues, finance and by-laws are reserved for council decision, while other, legally designated 'executives' fall to the manager. In practice the managers usually initiate policy and members rely on them for advice. Councils can, however, challenge their decisions and may suspend them by a two-thirds majority vote, although they need the competent government minister's approval to remove them. 'Activities of the manager vis-à-vis his elected representatives.... centre on his autonomy.... His ability to formulate and conduct policy relies upon an unquestioned acceptance of his leadership by his council.' (Collins, 1987).

The Scandinavian systems stand between those of Europe to the south and those of Britain in this matter. Councils in Norway are required to appoint a chief administrator as head of staff responsible for administration and co-ordination, presentation of the budget and with the right to speak at council and executive committee meetings. Chief administrators in Sweden have less general responsibility than those in Norway and Denmark (§6.11). In both these countries elected members are closely involved in detailed administrative decision-making.

The main problem of overall staff leadership where there is a formal executive group is probably the strength and autonomy of politicians within it who carry responsibility for a particular service and sometimes for sub-areas of the authority's territory. In these circumstances an appointed head of services may be confronted with a formidable task of co-ordination and rationalisation of decision-making and implementation in the face of strong centrifugal political forces.

The problem of centrifugal forces can be at least equally strong in authorities without a distinct executive. Britain struggled for decades with the problem of achieving rational corporate decision-making in authorities with a wide range of disparate mandatory functions. In 1992 an effective informal executive function depends on the council leader, who normally leads business in a policy and resources committee in close partnership with an appointed chief executive officer who heads a management team of senior officers which assists in defining policies and co-ordinates implementation. (§7.11; Norton, 1991).

North American forms include two models where the decision-making power and the executive are fused, as in Britain. Both have been subjects of heavy criticism. One is the small elected commission or board model, often supplemented by elected officials including a popularly elected clerk, and systems where a chief administrative officer is appointed with responsibility for operations in parallel with a political board. Problems of rivalry between the 'operations manager' and the chairman of the commission or board are understood to be not unusual. The 'weak mayor plan' is closer to the British system. The mayor in practice often tends to exceed his defined responsibilities and act as chief executive for the council. The attempt to split administration from politics was a failure from the start (§§8.11 and 9.11). A similar situation arises in the North Rhine-Westphalia system where a post of *Stadtdirektor*, meant to resemble that of a British town clerk, was introduced in 1947. The case illustrates the difficulty of prescribing a system without taking the strength of local tradition into account (see §4.11). In Austria's case an equivalent post is provided for in a provision in the federal Constitution which rules that each town should have a general director (*Magistratsdirektor*), a head of the administration whose duties are laid down by law.

Local Government's Other Employees

The legal positions of the office-holders who serve a council and implement its decisions vary widely between countries. Their posts are usually grouped into classes, such as those of officers, employees and workers employed in the German system, each with separately negotiated conditions of service and status. The word 'officers', as used in Britain, excludes elected officials other than party officers and is roughly equivalent to the French *fonctionnaires*. Officers are usually classified nationally by grades according to levels of responsibility and in some cases the nature of the qualifications and the expertise required.

In northern countries employment is mostly on an individual contractual basis, although there are usually standard national conditions of service negotiated and agreed between employers' and employees' representatives. These are in principle voluntary, and in Britain at least there has been a recent tendency for authorities to set conditions individually in order to provide higher incentives for recruitment and efficiency.

In the Latin countries and Belgium there are constitutional, legal and regulatory provisions that provide for a special local government officer status within what, notionally at least, is a single local government service (in French *fonction publique territoriale*). This service is distinct from but to some extent analogous to the state service (*fonction publique de l'État*). Such services conform to codes or regulations paralleling those of state services. The development of local autonomy in France since the 1970s has to some extent loosened the system and given more autonomy in staffing matters. The greatest changes have occurred in Spain, where rights and obligations are now dependent on the administrations served instead of the national state.

The German local government service is national and its status is basically not dissimilar from the new French cadre status. Conditions are laid down in national joint conventions, thus avoiding conflict with local government's constitutional right to 'free administration' but giving some protection to officers. (§4.11; *Les Cahiers no.27*, 1989; *La Fonction Publique Locale*, 1988)

The uniformity and security in office of officials over most of Europe contrasts with conditions in English-speaking countries and Scandinavia where employment conditions are, except in a few cases where state interests are concerned, in accordance with the general law of employment and the master-servant relationship (§7.11).

1.12 CITIZEN PARTICIPATION IN LOCAL GOVERNMENT

Participation in the government of small communities has been a right and often a duty of adult free men, if not women, since early times. Direct participatory democracy still exists in most of Switzerland's three thousand municipalities and indeed in five cantons. Their citizens meet in assemblies and elect a collegiate executive to carry out their decisions. It exists in a highly attenuated form in English parish and Welsh community meetings. But for the great majority little remains of direct self-government but the right to vote for representatives whom most know only by name and party if at all.

The phrase 'participatory democracy' is sometimes used to mean ways in which citizens without political power other than through the vote may help to determine specific issues, either through group initiatives and referenda or by other means established by a representative assembly itself, such as taking part in its discussions or those of its committees, advisory committees, consultative procedures such as open meetings, opinion polls and other means of sounding public individual and group interests.

Local authorities in the United States have traditionally shown concern to involve citizens in the process of government, partly at least as a means of overcoming anti-government feelings of an extent not generally found in Western Europe. They have sought consultations with individuals, involved private organisations in their decision-making, allowed members of the public to participate in council as well as committee meetings and sought the respect of interest groups and the press. These are features of modern local government that are generally accepted but sometimes criticised for resulting in overmuch exposure of public business to biased interests and detrimental to purposeful government (Marshall, 1967; Pateman, 1970; Richardson, 1983).

Referenda and Citizen Initiatives

In some parts of the United States referenda are required on bond issues, increases in tax limits, amalgamations, and amendments to city charters including home-rule decisions. They may also be held on issues chosen by local authorities themselves or by groups of citizens exercising a legal right for a prescribed minimum number of citizens to submit draft ordinances for a general vote. Under the 'recall' system elected officials may be removed from office by a special election triggered by a petition (§8.12). Referenda provisions also exist in South Germany, Switzerland and to a small extent in Denmark (Council of Europe, 1978, *Conditions of Local Democracy and Citizen Participation in Europe*). There are arguments against them, such as their use by opposition and other interest groups who may frame them to make the options offered to voters narrow and unacceptable. They may prevent fulfilment of commitments made in elections and override long-term objectives that also have the support of a majority.

Decentralisation in Cities

The case for sub-municipal area councils or representative advisory committees has been accepted in most large European countries since the 1950s. Aims include enabling neighbourhoods to articulate their needs, bringing power closer to the people, and drawing a wider range of participants into the political system. Some countries have given area councils delegated powers to exercise and budgets to administer. Where small authorities have been amalgamated with a large city this has been seen as a way of giving them the means to maintain a measure of self-government. This has been preceded in many cases by setting up area councils within the central city area itself, working towards a general pattern of decentralisation of functions throughout the new area on the subsidiarity principle.

In Italy municipal decentralisation was pioneered by Bologna and some other cities. Area councils were set up to involve new immigrants and give the suburbs a voice in the physical development of their areas and service provisions (§3.12). In Germany around 1950, backed by the experience of similar initiatives under the Weimar Republic, six of the larger German Länder made provisions for municipal area advisory boards or committees. In the 1960s directly elected autonomous area councils were set up with a variety of functions in cities of over 95 thousand inhabitants. The main emphasis has been on environmental matters. (§4.12)

A law was enacted in the early 1980s to give Paris 20 *arrondisse-ment* councils consisting of about one-third city councillors and two-thirds members elected specially in each area. They have budgets for grant-aiding voluntary agencies, certain housing functions and rights of consultation. Similar provisions were made for Lyon and Marseille (§2.12).

Area bodies have also been set up in Danish (§6.1), Dutch, Norwegian, Spanish, Swedish (§5.12) and Swiss cities to advise on local needs, planning issues and in some cases to undertake minor responsibilities.

In European experience the make-or-break point for the success of such initiatives has often been the relationship between members of area bodies and municipal departments. If area councils are to become more than an adjunct to the party system, maintain a significant and influential role in municipal decision-making and succeed in having their value recognised by local inhabitants, businesses and voluntary organisations as the main point of reference for raising issues of local interest, they need to have a direct influence on the provision of city decision-making and local services. In large cities they need a proper recognition of their function and value by sub-offices of municipal service departments, a light rein on their work by leading municipal politicians and a proper decentralisation of political discussion on sub-area matters within the parties. Proposals coming before area councils need to be given precise definition but remain open for improvement or substitution. Officials need to appreciate that a decision-making process that may seem to them slow and burdensome may often result in conclusions that are wiser and carry more local commitment than would otherwise be the case.

In accordance with national traditions, initiatives in the United States and Britain have been more local, varied and piecemeal. In the 1960s, however, the United States federal government offered as part of its anti-poverty programme incentives to encourage participation in decision-making by the inhabitants of disadvantaged city neighbourhoods. Local administrative centres were established in a number of cities, notably in New York and Philadelphia, to encourage constructive initiatives by voluntary groups in the hope that this might develop into a degree of self-administration. Successes were limited (§8.12). In Britain some cities have decentralised administration to local suburban offices which have been expected to establish close consultative arrangements with local residents, but this is not known to have resulted in any significant impact on policy except in two or three cases (§7.12).

Consultation and Co-operation with Communities on Needs and Interests

The Council of Europe undertook a series of surveys between 1979 and 1981 relating to citizen participation, information and communication. (Council of Europe, 1978, *Conditions of Local Democracy and Citizen Participation in Europe*; Council of Europe, 1979, *Information and Communication about Municipal Affairs*; Council of Europe, 1979, *Methods of Consulting Citizens on Municipal Affairs*; and Council of Europe, 1986, *Decentralisation of Local Government at Local Level*). These cover local government publicity; other forms of relationship with the public and the media; conditions of civic participation in political parties and by voluntary or interest groups; local referenda and territorial sub-units of authorities, giving special attention to measures for uninvolved groups; information and communication in municipal planning; methods of consulting citizens; and decentralisation of administration. Control of municipal facilities by users themselves is another practice. It is beyond the scope of this book to describe even in outline the great variety of approaches that were identified.

Consultation is a central and in some cases the only function of neighbourhood councils. The model to be sought is a two-way exchange of information and ideas, whether or not they are combined with the possibility of delegated action at neighbourhood or suburban level. Ideally it should develop shared purposes between councils and inhabitants. Even where no powers are delegated by the main authority there may be a possibility of stimulating voluntary action on such matters as the improvement of the environment, including recycling of materials, perhaps through a network of voluntary groups.

One area of community involvement deserving special mention is that of arrangements to involve businesses and representative bodies in planning and development. The economic and social committees that advise French regional authorities and comparable institutions in Italian regions are an important example (§2.11; Nanetti, 1988). There have been many major and minor joint bodies set up in American cities to enable local authorities to work with business and voluntary bodies to set joint goals for the future of cities and to motivate action (§8.12). Britain provides other examples

(§7.12).

Participation as an Elected Member

The most intensive form of participation is service as an elected member. The more elected council members there are proportionally to the number of inhabitants, the more inhabitants are likely to know a councillor and the wider representation of local views can be. The ratio of councillors to population varies widely. A comparison of the overall ratios of representatives to inhabitants in different countries shows remarkable differences. In the information below English and Welsh community council members are included as well as those of main authorities, municipal area sub-councils and, in the case of Sweden, alternate councillors. On a rough calculation of the position in nine countries the ratio ranges from one elected politician to 110 inhabitants in France to one to 1,800 inhabitants in Britain. Sweden has one member or alternate member to 270 inhabitants. At one end of the range Japan has the second largest ratio of about 1,550. The totals from which these figures are calculated do of course comprehend extreme differences within countries, as in France between hamlets where there are hardly sufficient candidates to meet the membership demands of the assembly on the one hand and cities in which one councillor represents a population of tens of thousands or many times more in large North American cities where councillors are elected 'at large'.

1.13 THE GOVERNANCE OF METROPOLITAN AREAS

Solving the Problems set by Metropolitan Expansion

Metropolitan areas have in most cases grown outwards from large international business centres and include important secondary and tertiary centres. Business centres and sub-centres act as magnets for commercial activities and job-seekers, generating large-scale residential settlements over increasingly large areas. Essential transport and other infrastructural needs grow rapidly. Heavy public investment is needed to maintain or re-establish acceptable levels of efficiency for businesses and quality of life for inhabitants as a whole.

Where boundaries are redrawn they often quickly become obsolete again. Immigration and industrial and commercial growth, population spread, new technological, economic, social and cultural change and relocation of industry and habitations are among the factors that change the texture of city areas and demand continuous structural change.

A strategic approach demands rational targeting of investment, land-use planning, integrated transport systems, measures to promote a balanced economy and city-wide health, environmental and other services that meet the standards required for healthy living. Comprehensive structural reform may seem to offer great economic and social benefits, but it has proved difficult or impossible to achieve in many cases.

Economic efficiency and an environment conducive to human welfare depends on many inter relating factors. Physical, economic, social and cultural needs should ideally be tackled together, but the means to provide them are usually fragmented between authorities. High regard for the autonomy of small local authorities and their ability to defend their boundaries legally and politically can stand in the way of meeting these needs. The political problems of redrawing boundaries and transferring functions between authorities and sectors have commonly proved politically insuperable.

The number of local popularly elected bodies in modern metropolitan areas can be extremely large. In the Paris metropolitan area, for example, there are well over a thousand autonomous local authorities. Both the United States and Japan have metropolitan regions of quite exceptional scale and complexity (see §§8.13 and 10.13). Metropolitan Chicago, as defined by demographers, contained 1,172 separate governments in 1977. The Tokyo region with nearly 30 million inhabitants within a radius of 50 kilometres has relatively few main local authorities: 286 in all. In the United States above all the law, other historical factors and culture stand in the way of boundary rationalisation. In Japan governmental structure and a planning ethos have facilitated a more purposeful approach to problems of even greater magnitude. But in neither case has metropolitan governance been able to master the problems involved.

The following patterns of government exist:

(1) There may be joint multi-purpose bodies such as voluntary committees or associations of local authorities for consultative, advisory and co-ordinative purposes, sometimes exercising powers delegated to them by constituent authorities. Such delegations are usually inadequate to enable them to deal with major problems. Authorities may join or withdraw at will. Interests inevitably clash in some respects. The associations lack the general authority and ability to take or implement some key decisions relating to the development of their area as a whole. Proposed infrastructural measures to overcome their problems are seen as threats to

property values and the way of life in particular districts. There is no ultimate means of mediation between their members unless the state or a higher level of government has the power and interest to intervene and enforce implementation. This is not to say, however, that the definition of strategies by such associations cannot be of real value and provide a framework which will influence local planning, project definition and higher-level policies.

(2) A statutory multi-purpose joint body of authorities may be set up by the state for consultative and advisory purposes. Authorities may be legally required to participate and define metropolitan objectives, plans and policies and carry out implementation. Its recommendations may have to be submitted to a higher level of government for approval and made binding on all member authorities so that the higher level can ensure that they are in harmony with national or regional policy. The effectiveness of such a system will depend on the constitutional and legal powers of the higher level and the extent to which it can motivate action at the lower level by financial incentives and other means.

(3) Statutory joint inter-authority bodies for special or ad hoc purposes may be set up. This approach brings problems of collaboration and rationalisation between such bodies, municipalities and other authorities.

(4) A 'quasi-federal' structure may be set up with a metropolitan assembly consisting of members appointed by district municipalities but with direct statutory responsibility for selected functions. This will not remove the problems of collaboration and implementation mentioned in connection with approaches (1) to (3) however. It may even aggravate inter-authority relations and so reduce collaboration.

(5) A directly elected metropolitan authority may be instituted. This may possess an independent mandate but does not in itself help to promote inter-level collaboration. Like (4) it may result in less co-operative relationships than existed before. But legislation in both these instances can redefine functions and duties between services and legally require consultative and other procedures that attempt to minimise possible conflict and maximise efficiency.

(6) A single elected authority with general powers for a whole metropolitan area may be set up. A structure of sub-municipalities may undertake responsibility for the administration of particular services in their areas within a central policy framework with integrated two-tier budgeting, as for example in Berlin.

(7) Another means of achieving inter-level planning and implementation is to have the same staff serve two levels, as in the reportedly successful case of two joint institutions around Mannheim, the Raumordnungsverband and

Regionalverband Unterer Neckar.

Within most of these arrangements inter-governmental contracts may be negotiated, sometimes between large authorities and small ones, to achieve economies of scale and other benefits, as in the case of the County of Los Angeles providing services to smaller authorities in its area (§8.5).

The nature and extent of current problems vary with the scale and configuration of metropolitan areas and their patterns of growth, as do the possible solutions. For policy-makers it is a matter of considering how feasible and beneficial each organisational approach is likely to be in a particular case and selecting from among possible approaches those that best match economic, social, cultural and democratic criteria.

Criteria of success used in a recent Dutch survey of seven European metropolitan authorities were adequacy of geographic scale, the competence and authority of a 'supra-local' administration to implement decisions binding on the local authorities concerned, the ability to develop an integrated policy vision encompassing the relevant policy areas weighed against each other, democracy (defined in terms of the direct election members of the metropolitan authority), and the efficiency and effectiveness of the authority's decision-making procedures (Berg, Kink and Meer, 1992). It found that in general the arrangements studied fell well short of effective control of land use for economic development purposes, and concluded that these criteria alone were insufficient to explain a metropolitan authority's capacity to solve regional problems. It found that administrative organisation, culture, political circumstances and the quality and 'entrepreneurship' of key individuals were also important factors in explaining success. Above all willingness among local authorities to co-operate was found to be essential.

The Recent History of Metropolitan Authorities

The following survey is based on the author's experience on the subject during a study undertaken in 1983, together with recent information about subsequent experience in this field (Norton, 1983). It is limited to authorities set up under statutory provisions. It indicates which types of status have been most conducive to survival: the critical test in an area in which a number of initiatives have been terminated before there was time to evaluate their success over a reasonable period.

A first group is of metropolitan governments possessing a constitutional status that are units in a major level of state administrative structure. Their metropolitan character is incidental to their type. Two are at regional level.

One is the region around Paris (Région de l'Île-de-France), which acquired its present status with the direct election of its assembly in 1986 (§2.13). The other is the Autonomous Community of Madrid, established in 1983 in the same short period as the other Spanish autonomous communities. Both conform with type 5 above. Greater Stockholm differs only in limited ways from its constitutional peers, the other 20 Swedish counties (§5.13).

Greater Vancouver is one of 28 regional district authorities in British Columbia. It is a quasi-federal structure of type 4 above. It differs from the other cases in that the representatives constituting its council are not directly elected but chosen by the muncipalities within its area . All four in this group have wider functions than planning and regional infrastructure provision. They are well established and understood to be generally accepted. To establish them elsewhere may require major boundary changes. In the Netherlands, for example, the equivalent would require a redrawing of the historic boundaries of several of the provinces or setting up a new regional structure, a solution that has long been considered, especially in the cases of the Amsterdam and Rotterdam regions.

The Italian local government law of June 1990 provides for metropolitan authorities at provincial level in a strong version of type 5. It places the main responsibility for arrangements at regional government level, although this can be transferred to the national level in case of default (see §3.13). The projected reforms in the Netherlands and Italy both involve the division of large cities into new municipalities as part of reformed structures. Amsterdam has been working to achieve such a solution for over ten years.

The second group is of statutory exceptions designed to meet the needs of particular areas within a state structure. Like the Greater Vancouver case they possess quasi-federal structures, their members being chosen by municipal assemblies (type 4). These are the *communautés urbaines* (*CUs*) in France and Quebec. Of the nine French cases (see §2.13), the Communauté Urbaine de Lille was designated with four others in 1976. Four more were set up voluntarily under provisions in a law that enabled at least a 'qualified majority' of the communes in their areas to adopt the legislative provisions. The other cases are the Communautés Urbaines of Montreal and Quebec. That of Montreal has been the subject of much criticism but has provided much-needed services and had some success in equalising the provision of services between rich and relatively poor sub-urban areas (§9.13).

Thirdly there are 'one-off' ad hoc metropolitan authorities set up under state legislation: directly elected for Rijnmond in the Netherlands and Greater Copenhagen (§6.13) and indirectly elected in the case of the

Metropolitan Corporation of Barcelona, all of which have been abolished under political influences of various kinds; and the directly elected German Umlandverband Frankfurt (§4.13), a planning organisation which has survived against difficulties. The first three at least have left an appreciable legacy of achievements despite the difficulties of maintaining consensus between the municipalities in their areas. In the Barcelona case the work has continued under a voluntary association of a statutory type (*mancomunitat*, type 1). It has continued the implementation of previously initiated metropolitan services and projects, not least for the 1992 Barcelona Games.

The Municipality of Metropolitan Toronto, established by the Province of Ontario and justified by three independent and searching assessments of its value, has had a successful history over 35 years (§9.13). In this case its mixed membership has included leading political officials of the district authorities within its area as well as directly elected members (type 5 modified in the direction of type 4). The overlapping membership was reduced around the end of the 1980s and the district mayors disqualified from holding the powerful chairmanship of the authority, leading to increased inter-authority friction.

Judged by the criterion of survival therefore, all the authorities that were part of a national level of self-government lasted until 1992. Three out of 16 ad hoc cases have been abolished. Those that survive are the narrow-pupose Umlandverband Frankfurt and the communauté urbaines of France and the Province of Quebec. They may have passed the survival test due partly to the acceptance of their intermediate governmental status as part of the national and provincial structures.

Of the six directly elected authorities (type 5), three have survived: those in fact that were members of a national tier of government. Of the thirteen indirectly elected cases (type 4), twelve have survived. Metropolitan Toronto has not been included because of its mixed composition.

It would seem in general that being part of a national system and being indirectly elected by constituent authorities give the best chance of survival. It may well be from other evidence that in the latter cases the closely interwoven webs of participation between levels of government (including the national level) give the authorities a political strength and joint interests with their constituent authorities that are lacking in some of the other cases.

There have been cases of the failure or partial failure of voluntary unions of authorities (type 1) and joint consultative or advisory types (type 2), of which The Hague association was one (Norton, 1983). They have clearly not met the criteria set out in the Dutch study mentioned above, which was undertaken to identify a stronger and more robust model (Berg, Kink and Meer, 1992). Successful collaborative arrangements are claimed by some English groups of metropolitan districts which have preferred a voluntary basis to the imposed metropolitan county structures of the model 5 type which were abolished in the mid-1980s (Leach, Vielba and Flynn, 1987). The joint authorities set up on their abolition (type 3) suffer from deficiencies described above. The news from Holland in late 1992 is that the authorities around Rotterdam have committed themselves to a new union to which metropolitan functions will be transferred, apparently showing that local agreement on a strong federal structure is possible.

Conclusions

The main problem shown by these cases is the difficulty of achieving sufficient unity of purpose among the authorities involved. Any approach aimed at overall gains inevitably results in uneven distribution of the costs and benefits involved between areas and social groups. Some of the short-run costs fall heavily on those affected and are difficult for participants to balance against longer-term gains. People who see their interests badly affected exercise their right to oppose proposals through interest group and political pressures. They may try to undermine a metropolitan authority itself. The political opposition may crystallise within political channels able to exercise strong influence at state level. A metropolitan authority needs to carry the weight of local opinion with it as far as possible in decisions that affect local interests in matters basic to the quality of life and the local economy, such as efficiency of transportation, disposal of wastes and containment of pollution. Diffusion of information is not in itself sufficient to ensure that there is a sufficient shared understanding of decision implications among groups affected. If short-run benefits can be provided, however, they may tip the scale towards initial acceptance of a metropolitan authority. This may allow time for appreciation to spread of the longer-term benefits resulting from the authority's work.

Close relations between levels of government and administration are needed. Very good communication among the groups involved is likely to be crucial to co-operation among politicians and officers. This has been achieved to some extent in some of the French cases. Relations in Montreal and Quebec have often been acrimonious. In France the cost of maintaining six levels of government (seven in Lyon if the arrondissements are included) may horrify those in the Anglo-American tradition. Americans should not be horrified since their ad hoc authorities produce more severe fragmentation, although between authorities rather than between levels of

115

government. The principle of separateness of responsibilities which has been strong in some northern countries in the past has severe limitations in practice as interdependence between levels of government increases.

The experience gained since I studied the subject in 1983 and some knowledge of what has happened since leads me to put forward the following tentative conclusions. They assume that the structure is one in which the wishes of all authorities in the area are respected and overridden only when this is seen by a substantial majority as for the common good.

(1) The distribution of responsibilities between authorities should ensure that as far as reasonable decisions that do not need to be taken at the metropolitan level for the common good are taken at levels closer to the citizen. The justification of metropolitan authority functions would thus be in accordance with the principle of subsidiarity, that is they can of their nature only be performed adequately at metropolitan level or would be significantly more economic and effective if exercised for the area as a whole.

(2) The metropolitan authority should be responsible for the setting of overall objectives and a strategy to achieve them that commands wide support and embodies a shared vision of the optimal future for the area. All interested parties should have the full opportunity to contribute to such a strategy. It should be consistent with norms set bindingly at higher levels of government: regional, national and European, and compatible with the resources that can be made available. It should include an outline rolling programme of a general kind, with realistic estimates of the minimum resources required, leaving as many tasks as possible to municipalities without jeopardising overall objectives. Its aims and programmes are likely to be most acceptable if they are accompanied by incentives, for example bringing benefits to localities that are unlikely to be achieved by other means.

(3) Programmes and projects need to be defined with sensitivity to local preferences. Some issues may be intractable, for example location of refuse disposal plant and traffic arteries which disrupt communities. Recourse to outside mediation or mediation at regional or national government level is preferable to a break-up of collaborative working.

(4) There must be an effective executive at metropolitan level to ensure as far as possible that all avenues have been explored as far as can reasonably be expected; and, if and when the costs of delay are considered to exceed the costs of prolonging the formation of a consensus, to put proposals to the vote with clear recommendations.

(5) The voting process may be designed, as in Canadian examples, to safe-

guard to some extent the interests of the majority of the populations represented in the assembly as well as the majority of representatives present.

In most matters municipalities will retain autonomy, but in some cases they may, as in Canadian and French cases, prefer that implementation is carried out by a metropolitan agency. They may have the right to opt between metropolitan provision, self-provision and contracting out elsewhere in such matters subject to certain qualifications, as I understand to be the case under certain conditions with the communautés urbaines and regional districts in both France and Canada. On any matter that is not integral to the central purposes of a metropolitan authority there are strong reasons for not overriding local choice. Political robustness and continuity are essential to metropolitan authorities if they are to prove their potential. They must be given wide scope to deal with matters which no other level is well equipped to deal with. As shown, those with a special status have proved highly vulnerable to ministerial decisions. To give them a robust status, however, may require reform of administrative boundaries over a wider, regional or national area, and their integration into a provincial or county structure.

The choice between direct and indirect democracy is not as clear as often assumed. For them to be directly elected may not give them public support to the extent that is sometimes assumed. Because metropolitan authorities usually lack an intimate relationship with individual members of the public and may not have such strong political roots in the party system as the basic municipalities possess, the relationship with electors is likely to be a problematic one for a new metropolitan authority unless it is conspicuously involved in prestigious projects. Indirect election produces a sharing of responsibility and stronger possibilities (not always achieved) of easy inter-authority communication, resource sharing and general co-operation between levels. If there is direct election at metropolitan level special consideration must be given to achieving strong inter-authority relationships. This includes relationships between executives and senior officers at both levels.

This section is written on the assumption that metropolitan government can improve human and environmental well-being to an extent that well outweighs its costs. Where no overall metropolitan government is possible there may still be governance of a kind: a network of relationships between public authorities and other institutions whose investments are relevant to the future of the area if it is to secure its development in accordance with shared goals, such as to protect the environment, launch projects to

117

improve the efficiency of the physical infrastructure and undertake other initiatives to the common good of the area as a whole. This chapter stops short of evaluating such alternatives to metropolitan government in the sense described earlier in this section or simple reliance on the free market. It is to each reader to make a subjective evaluation based as far as possible on personal experience and observation of results. It may be that the sheer scale and complexity of principal American and Japanese metropolitan areas has taken them past a threshold beyond which the patterns described above are relevant: that they demand a new hierarchical pattern, more homologous to natural structures than to machines. If so, such patterns have hardly yet begun to be realised.

It is appropriate to end this chapter on the subject of the quality of human inter-relationships, something that together with the mix of values, concepts and resulting objectives largely determines how much local, regional and national government contributes to human happiness everywhere. Structure is important only as the means through which human communication can be improved and services made more efficient and effective.

PART II

Selected Countries

2. FRANCE

2.1 HISTORY AND TRADITIONS

The French system of local administration that was defined by statute between 1789 and 1801 became the model on which local government systems were to be based throughout most of Western Europe and the Latin empires. It resembled the Bourbon system that preceded it in its centralisation of power and in being based on the same town and village communities. It survived some ten changes of national constitution and became increasingly self-governing from the first half of the nineteenth century.

The collapse of monarchic authority in 1789 led to a brief flowering of local freedom full of variety and experimentation. This was quickly succeeded by a period in which deviation from purposes defined by the revolutionaries in Paris was crushed by state commissioners. In August 1789 the Constituent Assembly decided that 'all the particular privileges of the provinces, cities, corps and communities, be they financial advantages or any other kind' should be 'merged in the common law of all the French'. In December it laid down that there would henceforth be a municipality in each town, borough, parish or rural community to be termed a commune; and all from a hamlet to Paris itself should have the same status'. Each was to have its own assembly elected by universal suffrage; and also a mayor who was to be responsible to the central government as well as to the commune.

The gap between the communes and the government in Paris was to be filled, in accordance with a law of January 1790, by a structure of 83 départements with boundaries drawn to ensure that all local communities within their boundaries were easily accessible to state representatives from a central departmental town or city. A tier of artificial districts was defined to fill the gap between them and the communes. The departmental and district executive councils were initially elected, but Jacobin governments found the opposition encountered in elected authorities intolerable and appointed commissioners for each département with dictatorial powers to act as local executives in the name of 'the one and indivisible Republic'.

In 1799 Napoleon Bonaparte, as First Consul of the Republic, wiped out what remained of local freedom to deviate from the new model. Under his direction a new system was built on the new structures already in place. The law of 17 January 1800 (by the revolutionary calendar 28 pluviôse year VIII) provided for the commissioners to be replaced by prefects, a title derived from the Latin word *praefectus* ('man at the head'), the name of officials in the Roman Empire. Bonaparte himself signed the prefects' letters of appointment. In directing the administration of their départements they were to be assisted by general councils of 16 to 24 local '*notables*' who were to apportion direct taxes between areas and vote supplementary taxation for local expenditure on roads and other purposes. Prefectoral councils were set up with general responsibilities, among which public works were given the main emphasis. The districts were renamed *arrondissements* and given appointed councils to divide the burden of tax locally and take decisions under the supervision of sub-prefects. The implementation of the will of the people, as interpreted by central government, was to be applied equally and thoroughly everywhere, overriding local freedoms.

The prefects held their posts at the pleasure of the First Consul, later the Emperor. They were responsible for implementation of the law and administration and the maintenance of order in their départements. They received incomes at a level of those of wealthier inhabitants and formed a top elite of officials, selected for their competence and promise as future leaders of the Empire without regard to class, social status, former occupation or politics. Their scope was unlimited within the law and their instructions from the government extended to the development of their départements' welfare, education system, physical infrastructure and industry. Their first instruction was to create a new France in which all divisions between Frenchmen would be abolished. (Chapman, 1955)

The prefects have continued in their role as agents of central government and mediators between the centre and the locality until today. The law of 2 March 1982 'on the rights and liberties of the communes, départements and regions' gave them another title dating from the revolutionary era, 'commissioner of the republic', but that of prefect continued in use and has been formally restored. The law transferred most of their formal powers over local government and their role as executive of the departmental council (*conseil général*) to each council's president. Prefects have continued to head government staff within their départements with the duty to co-ordinate local branches of central government departments and between central and local government.

This system of centralised direction stayed basically unchanged for over 180 years through two imperial, two royal and four republican regimes, while local powers developed step by step towards local democracy.

Départements were recognised as local authorities in the 1830s; universal franchise was established at communal level in 1848; the power of local assemblies to make decisions in their own right was recognised in the late 1860s and 1870s; the départements were given full recognition as 'territorial collectivities' in 1871; full budgetary competence was conferred and a general competence for communal assemblies 'to regulate the affairs of the commune' in the communal charter of 1884; and freedom on budgetary matters was extended step by step from the beginning of the twentieth century.

The mayors, the executives of the communes, became popularly elected in 1882 instead of being nominated by a minister on the prefect's advice. Unlike British mayors they are both the chief executives and political leaders of their authorities. In the départements the prefects remained chief executives until the law of March 1983. They not only tended to dominate the proceedings of departmental councils (*conseils généraux*) but also exercised powers of supervision over decisions by the communes, their signatures being required before those decisions could be put into effect. Their power increased with deconcentration of responsibilities from Paris and the rationalisation of areas of service under ministries' local directors. In practice their supervisory power (*tutelle*) had been exercised more and more lightly through the years and with growing circumspection, since they were subject to political challenge and their decisions became unlikely to prevail unless based on solid grounds. Nevertheless the tutelle was a local irritant and a cause of delay (Grémion, 1976).

A class of local political leaders known as 'notables' developed through the nineteenth century. They 'managed' relations with representatives of the government, including prefects and sub-prefects and sometimes senior officials and members of the government in order to advance the interests of their areas and maintain political support. The more able and ambitious could acquire great prestige and authority, often through the accumulation of electoral offices which gave authority and influence (*le cumul des mandat*s): so much so that prefects and central ministries might ignore them at their peril and preferred to cultivate the notables as important allies. The more eminent became known as *grands notables*, able to control the power of the state in the interest of the locality by their own elective and informal power. The system has been described as 'tamed jacobinism', implying that the lion of jacobinism had been tamed by local interests (ibid.).

The Twentieth Century

Services developed rapidly in the early years of the century to cope with the effects of industrialisation. There followed a relatively stagnant period between the wars. The expansion of the welfare state was driven from the centre, with local government playing a subordinate role (Mabileau, 1991).

The French have named the years after the Second World War 'the Thirty Glorious Years' (*Les Trente Glorieuses*). Government policy was expansionist, aimed at developing growth in the provinces and correcting the imbalances between Paris and the rest of France and between wealthy areas and those which were suffering from industrial decline. A regional planning system was developed. State work was 'deconcentrated' from Paris to regional and departmental centres. Twenty-two 'programme regions' were set up in 1956. To spearhead the drive for economic development in the 1960s the départements were grouped into regions, each headed by the prefect of the central département of the group who was termed the 'prefect of the région'. He served as the leading government representative in the region, with responsibilities for co-ordinating the work of the regional branches of central government departments as well as heading the special regional machinery.

New state economic development commissions (CODERs) were set up with consultative bodies (ECOSOCs) to bring together representatives of local economic, social and cultural sectors (*'forces vives'*) with political leaders and state servants in consultative bodies to participate in regional planning and programming. This policy led to increasing collaboration and interlacing of interests between central and local government and local industry and commerce. Prefects found great difficulty in reconciling aspirations expressed from within the départements and the downward pressures from central ministries. Their power was not strong enough to overcome the government departments' lack of respect for locally expressed priorities.

In 1976 a powerful report by a government commission (*Vivre Ensemble*, the 'Guichard Report') argued that the central state had become grossly inflated through absorbing almost all administrative activities, bogged down in confidential administrative detail by a system of minute regulation and fragmented by the separate development of its own services and the multiplication of non-elected bodies. Thus it had the problems of centralisation without the benefits of unity. 'Local public life is no longer local affairs by right.... Local authorities are woven into a resistant net of financial and technical supervision...'.

The Socialist Party's subsequent election manifesto declared decentralisation, local responsibility, self-government and the organisation of a counter-balance to the centre as the policies which conditioned all others. 'We consider that if central power has served national unity in the past, it now harms it'.

The new government of 1980 saw as essential the transfer of powers, resources and associated staff to regional and local centres in order to meet the planning aspirations to be expressed in the form of the Ninth Plan. The commitment led to the appointment of Gaston Defferre, Mayor of Marseille, to head the ministry responsible for the necessary structural reforms.

The reforms gave the regional organisations the status of corporate public entities and the presidents of regional and departmental councils real executive power. Planning and schools, the main areas of domestic state activities, were transferred to the communes; social support and colleges to the départements; and vocational training, lycées and other matters to the regions. The tutelle was replaced by juridical control by administrative tribunals on reference by prefects or individuals and, in the case of financial matters, by independent chambers of accounts. Most areas of specific state subsidy were superseded by global grants (Dupuis, 1989).

In the early 1980s the regions acquired a major role in the allocation of assistance to industry and also a key role in the regional planning dimension of the Ninth National Plan and other functions (see §§2.4 and 2.7). In 1982 their presidents took over responsibilities as executives for the regional councils from the prefects. Staff and financial resources were transferred from the civil service. From 1986, as directly elected councils of regions with the special constitutional status of territorial collectivities (*collectivités territoriales*), they are directly responsible to the electorate for the planning and development of their areas. Both socialists and communists saw the election of regional councils as acceptable despite the fact that the councils were nearly all likely to be controlled by the right. In the first regional elections the right won power in 20 out of the 22. When the socialists lost control of the National Assembly that year the new government, headed by Jacques Chirac, accepted the new structure. It can be said that as far as can be forecast the regional governments are a permanent part of the state and political structure.

In principle there is now a highly integrated planning system under which priority action plans embodying locally and regionally chosen initiatives and priorities are fed into the substance of regional and national plans. In the current economic climate there must obviously be conflict between financial policy contingencies and the powers and expectations raised by the decentralised planning system. Nevertheless the system has settled down and acquired a European dimension. Communes, départements, regions, the state and the European Community have become partners in the *aménagement* of areas (aménagement is defined as the mobilisation of space and other resources to equip communities with the means to fulfil the needs of their members in accordance with agreed objectives).

General

It has often been argued that France is not a centralised state but a corporate one in which decisions are determined not so much by the centre as through influence on the centre by bodies of interests throughout the nation at large, including the private sector.

By 1991 it was clear that the legislation in the early 1980s had secured a strong shift towards regional and local autonomy, and that it was no longer justified to claim that local government institutions were administrative bodies rather than semi-autonomous governments. The law recognises only *administration locale* and never local government, but in comparison with some other states in which local authorities are described as local government French authorities have at least as much legal autonomy, especially since the early 1980s. France indubitably has a system of local government in Anglo/American terms.

The economic downturn of the early 1990s has bred wide uncertainties and disaffection with the state and politicians, working against the national solidarity that it had been hoped decentralisation would bring. Strong feelings have emerged which challenge the attempts of government to act positively towards meeting the civil and welfare rights of immigrant groups, fed by tight financial policies, the failure of businesses and widespread unemployment. A new vision is sought that is realistic but consistent with the concerns of the 1990s as well as with deeply rooted social principles.

In general French history appears to have resulted in a remarkably close-knit relationship between state, political and economic spheres at most levels. (Firms are obliged to belong to a system of representative bodies (chambers of commerce and trade) which directly advise and influence government locally, regionally and nationally.) This has been achieved through concepts of positive government and administration, with a political elite leading the nation in the achievement of common goals. Though some expected the reforms of the 1980s aimed at decentralisation to be the 'end of the notables', others have described them with hindsight as the 'consecration of the notables' (*le sacre des notables*). They have widened opportunities for people in many walks of life to enter the class of political leaders and given increased scope to exercise leadership to local politicians. Today the central position in the local system is occupied by the notables rather than by the prefects. Once in office their tenure tends to be long. In the municipal elections of 1989 only 54 out of 394 towns with over 20,000 inhabitants changed political control, but close to 90 per cent of those that did 'confirmed their confidence in the previous mayor' (Mabileau, 1991). In these ways the system has given increased scope for leadership while maintaining continuity.

A Summary of the Decentralisation Laws of the 1980s

The Law on the Rights and Liberties of Communes, Départements and Régions (2 March 1982) abolished state powers of control over administrative and financial decisions of communes and départements, provided for regional councils to become directly elected authorities, provided for the presidents of departmental general councils to replace prefects as their authorities' executives and abolished the supervisory functions of prefects over local and regional government. The prefectoral role was partly replaced by that of commissioner of the republic who was responsible for checking the legality of decisions of local elected bodies *a posteriori*. The grades of prefect and sub-prefect were, however, retained within the staff structure of the administrative corps, and the commissioners continued to be known as prefects, a fact recognised by the formal re-adoption of the title subsequently.

The Law on Administrative Organisation in Paris, Marseille and Lyon and Public Bodies for Intercommunal Cooperation (31 December 1982) provided for directly elected councils (arrondissements) to be set up in sub-areas of three cities and for a wider representation of communes in the urban communities (*communautés urbaines*) (see §§2.12-13).

The Law on Division of Competences between Communes, Départements, Régions and the State (7 January 1983) conferred on regions, départements and communes concurrently with the state responsibility for physical, economic, social, health, cultural and scientific administration and development in their areas; protection and improvement of the environment; particular functions for planning and housing in the three sub-national levels (although housing policy remains a national responsibility); and defined means of financial support for the newly transferred functions.

The Law on Transfer of Competences for Transport, Public Education, Social Services and Health (22 July 1983) conferred responsibilities on regions, départements and communes for inland waters, transportation,

127

planning, the building and maintenance of educational facilities, the environment and cultural action; and, mainly on the départements, social welfare, some health functions and libraries and museums. It defined state functions and means of financial support for the functions transferred.

The Law on the Local Government Service (26 January 1984), described by Defferre as the third in importance of the decentralisation laws, aimed to create a local government service with a status that would enable local authorities to recruit staff who measured up to the new powers and responsibilities of local authorities and regions. The fundamental principles of the law are the unity of the local government service, parity with the national civil service and a special status for local government officers (see §2.11). Original intentions have subsequently been modified to some extent.

2.2 THE STATUS OF LOCAL AND REGIONAL GOVERNMENT

The Constitutional Status of Local and Regional Governments

Communes, départements and regions share the juridical status of territorial collectivities (*collectivités territoriales*) which was created in the Constitution of 1946 and continued in the more centralising Constitution of 1958. Territorial collectivities share three characteristics: a population, territorial boundaries and legal organs which are empowered to make decisions in the name and interest of their populations. Their councils 'rule (*règlent*) by their decisions (*délibérations*)' the affairs of the commune, as do departmental councils (*conseils généraux*) the affairs of the département, and the regional assembly those of the region. There are no satisfactory English equivalents to these terms. A common translation of 'collectivité territoriale' is 'local authority', but it should be remembered that this does not convey the idea of administration being the responsibility of the community, not just of the local council, and that regional authorities, which it is misleading to call 'local', also enjoy the status of collectivities (see §1.2). A territorial collectivity is the body of people living and acting together within an administrative area — not just the elected representatives acting as a legal entity. The fundamental meaning is a 'society of citizens' — a traditional concept resting on the principle of free administration. That concept is expressed in the phrase in the 1958 Constitution that they 'administer themselves freely by means of elected councils and under the conditions provided by the law' (*s'administrent*

128

librement par des conseils élus et dans les conditions prévues par la loi).

The 1946 Constitution provided for the freedom of local authorities with the express purpose of creating a counterweight to the omnipotence of the central state. The reporter-general of the Commission on the Constitution affirmed that territorial collectivities constituted 'one of the elements of the body politic' (*corps politique de l'État*). 'The counterweight to the omnipotence of the state is strongly organised local power'. 'For us, political power comes from below', not from above. (Bourjol and Bodard, 1984)

For action the territorial collectivity depends on its corporation, the elected council including its executive, the mayor or president of its council. The corporation possesses the legal status of an 'artificial person' and can carry duties and rights accordingly. It was only in the nineteenth century that the tendency developed to regard the corporation as the authority rather than the community of citizens. The status of 'legal person' has important implications that arise from the principle of equality: legal persons enjoy the same protection of rights and liberties as the citizen group they bind together, although their different situation calls for different legal norms (ibid). Hence the title 'The Law on the Rights and Liberties of Communes, Départements and Régions' of 1982.

Local democratic power is recognised not only in the constitutional principle of self-administration but also in the composition of the Senate, the upper house of parliament. Senators are elected in each département by a 'college' consisting of national deputies and representatives of local collectivities or their substitutes. They thereby participate in the exercise of national sovereign legislative power. Thus although the French Constitution is far from federal, it contains federal elements in that territorial authorities participate through elections in the exercise of central power. '

A principal argument in favour of the decentralisation laws was that they were a means to national solidarity. According to a government spokesman, they were to define 'a new citizenship, or free adhesion and participation of the citizen, as the foundation of a common solidarity and cohesion of society... based on a concept of free choice and participation as the foundation of national social unity' (J.P. Worms, government reporter in the Chamber of Deputies, quoted by Bourjol and Bodard, 1984).

Free administration is held to imply the power to decide on administrative actions and the management activities necessary to implement them. In law these actions are specific to the affairs of the collectivity and general in that they may relate to all affairs of the collectivity. They are a manifestation of the will of the collectivity as publicly defined by its representatives. Thus free administration implies a general competence, the right to act in whatever way fulfils its needs. There is always the possibility of its undertaking new activities so far unspecified and unallocated within the law. One Anglo-French text on French public administration puts the local authority's position within the national framework of government as follows: 'The state has an inherent responsibility to provide or regulate the public services necessary for the welfare of the community. Local authorities, as branches of the state, share in this responsibility with regard to local services. The French approach to local government emphasizes the community to be administered, not the services to be run. To administer, in this sense, means not only to run existing services but to provide for new services as new needs arise.' (Ridley and Blondel, 1969)

The extent and exercise of collectivities' powers is limited by law and state regulations. The national legislature can regulate the allocation of competences between authorities and the conditions under which such competences are exercised, including authorities' internal arrangements. Until the Law of 2 March 1982 French authorities were notoriously subject to 'tutelle', that is to approval of their decisions for legality before they could come into force. But the legal controls could not be exercised in an arbitrary way. They were valued by mayors for the protection they afforded them against possible illegalities. Since 1982 decisions by communes have full force in law as soon as the legal requirements of publication or notification of interested parties have been fulfilled and, with certain exceptions, the texts have been transmitted to the appropriate state representative. State representatives can then do no more in law than refer any item whose legality they believe to be in question to an administrative tribunal which decides as to its legality. An exception is made in the case of decisions concerning the communal or departmental police or matters delegated to local authorities by the central state, in which cases state representatives can substitute a decision in the name of the state. Persons believing themselves to be wronged by a decision may also activate reference to a legal tribunal.

Central powers over financial decisions were extensive until 1982. They are now limited to the local authority budget, supplementary budget and alterations to the budget — in particular the date of voting the budget, its 'real' balance, the statement of accounts, deficits and obligatory expenditures. Action on these rests primarily with a regional court of accounts, the membership of which is designed to exclude party political influences. The law may be interpreted as implying that the freedoms of local authorities are fundamental public liberties (Bourjol and Bodard, 1984). This concept carries us well beyond that of decentralisation, which assumes that power to decentralise lies at the centre. If freedom of self-administration is a fundamental constitutional right, it is beyond the power of national law to remove it.

A fact of interest relating to the basis of community powers is that the new arrondissements in Paris, Marseille and Lyon have an authority resting not on a status as legal persons (which they are not), but on their role in expressing the will of their inhabitants (ibid). Thus, it is argued, the legal 'personality' of collectivities does not in itself underlie their powers but is only a means to enable them to exercise their constitutional right to 'free administration'.

The regulatory powers of the state obviously limit or even frustrate the constitutional intention that collectivities should be free to administer their own affairs. State regulation intrudes into wide areas which should arguably be within local competence, including the organisation of local services, local finance, the new arrangements for the local government service and obligations to the government administration and to joint bodies to which authorities belong.

Regarding personnel matters, functions have been transferred from the smaller authorities to local management centres within a national framework designed to promote the principles of equality and free movement between public sectors. The communes keep general competence over management of employees, appointments, gradings, definition of duties, promotion, discipline, dismissal and recruitment of senior administrators. In addition to action under their 'general competence', local collectivities exercise extensive powers transferred to them by the central state, and share such powers with the centre.

In general it may be said that although local authorities are subject to complex regulation they do in practice have wide scope for initiative. Such scope is especially evident in the large cities, where the mayors are expected by the public to tackle urban problems in a bold and enterprising way. In doing so they tend to work with the government administration, not against it, although there have been famous battles between government ministers and communes about the scope of local action. The crucial issue is one of legality. A highly developed system of courts is at hand to rule on where the boundary between central and local prerogatives lies.

The Status of Local Government in the Political World

It is impossible to separate the real power of local government in France from that of the notables described in §2.1. They are the people recognised by the government and its officials as able to deliver local co-operation and partnership in decision-making. The system is built on an acceptance of interdependence between local leaders, central politicians and senior government officials. Levels of government are bound together by *le cumul des mandats*. The central-local relationship is sometimes as close as it can be: many mayors and leading departmental and regional councillors are members of the legislature and some of the government itself. The number of local elected officials rose from two in 1958 to 80 per cent in 1978. Of members elected to the National Assembly in 1988, 45 per cent were mayors, 11 per cent assistant mayors, 48 per cent members of departmental councils (conseils généraux) and 24 per cent regional councillors. Ninety-seven per cent held at least an executive office and/or were members of a departmental or regional council (Knapp, 1991).

Three of Mitterrand's prime ministers were mayors and one an assistant mayor. The new socialist prime minister in 1981, Pierre Mauroy, went straight to the post from the mayoralty of Lille and political office at other levels in the Région du Nord-Pas-de-Calais. The minister entrusted to drive through the decentralisation programme was Gaston Defferre, the Mayor of Marseille, an outstanding champion of communal rights against previous governments. Most remarkably, after the centre-right parties took over the government in 1986 the prime minister was Jacques Chirac, Mayor of Paris (which is both a commune and a département). He was reported to have spent more time in his mayoral accommodation than in the prime minister's rooms during the period he held both offices. The former French president, Giscard d'Estaing, became the president of the regional council of the Auvergne after its first election. Such men may dominate the national political scene but they are strongly aware of the need to maintain local as well as national confidence and support in a highly competitive culture in which an outstanding record as a local or regional executive can be one of the strongest qualifications for government office.

Le cumul des mandats enables career politicians not only to rise to prestigious positions at national level while maintaining a secure electoral base. It also gives them the means to care for the interests of local authorities through their contacts and influence in Paris. On the other hand the many other functions attached to the post such as those in housing agencies, hospital management and inter-communal institutions, as well as in parliament in some cases, mean that they can give only scant attention to many if not most of their responsibilities.

A law of 1985 limited a deputy or senator to only one other elected post among those of MEP, regional councillor, departmental councillor, Paris councillor, mayor of a commune with 20,000 population or more or *adjoint* of one with 100,000 population or more. In the event members of parliament proved more attached to mayoralties than posts at other sub-national levels.

There are two broad national markets of political power for local politicians: the great cities on the one hand and the rural areas, towns and lesser cities and suburban authorities on the other. The great cities exercise power chiefly through their mayors. These are public testing grounds of managerial competence and ability to 'work the system'. The mayors have direct lines to central ministries, both to the ministers themselves and to the most senior officials. They are in a position to by-pass local prefects. Mayors of rural and smaller urban communes participate in power through elaborate networks of institutions, delivering support in the names of many thousands of village, town and suburban communities.

Mayors articulate local needs and co-ordinate local resources to meet those needs. The tradition is that the mayor is an integrative force above the particular interests of minorities. Mayors are, however, very dependent on their *adjoints* (assistant mayors), salaried national officials, including prefects, assistant prefects and local heads of state technical and financial services as well as the employees of their own communes (the latters' role has substantially increased in importance as service provision has been decentralised). Since 1982 a fair number of civil servants have become local government officers and advisers to mayors or presidents of local and regional authorities.

Power is shared between the two interdependent hierarchies — that of the politicians and that of the officials. Collaboration between the two is close within an authority, but otherwise communications tend to be vertical between levels of government and administration. Collaboration between authorities has in general to be secured by joint institutions. Nevertheless, the system can be described as organic in its working: the centre is alive to messages from the periphery, which is prepared to work with the centre provided that the centre can deliver.

An American writer in a comparative study of British and French policies and their implementation concludes that the French communes and departmental councils have a popular 'legitimacy' which British local authorities never possessed. 'French local politicians never relied as much as British politicians on inertia or territorial jurisdiction to influence national policy.' (Ashford, 1982)

Popular Status

The sheer number of elected representatives is remarkable. France has around half a million of them and 215,000 are mayors or assistant mayors.

Two-thirds of respondents to a survey commissioned for the Association des Maires de France believed that elected members, with the mayor at their head, played a more useful role than members of parliament (Mabileau, 1991). The communes in particular are regarded as second only to the state among levels of administration. Two American authors comment, 'Bonds of sympathy between local authorities and their constituents are strong, mostly because of administrative efficiency but also because municipal administration is the natural symbol for a community of local interests that feel forever threatened by the central government and frequently by a neighbouring town' (Almond and Powell (eds), 1988). A French authority on local government remarks that for those administered the commune and municipal government are considered as a privileged place for education in democracy, and for elected politicians they constitute the foundations of political representation (Mabileau, 1991).

2.3 CONCEPTS AND VALUES

Individualism and *Étatisme*

Individualism denotes both a doctrine which maintains the importance and rights of individuals as opposed to the state and faith in their independence and initiative. It emphasises individuality: the belief that no two people ought necessarily to behave in the same way or have the same needs. It is an assertion of autonomy and the refusal to sacrifice liberty in order to uphold a general rule. It therefore contradicts the essence of bureaucracy, which is to treat everyone according to a rule book. It rests on tolerance, as in the small and integrated commune that is typically tenacious of its rights, fearing that to merge itself into a larger unit can only lead to the loss of freedoms and valued idiosyncracies. It helps to explain why the so-called 'one and indivisible French Republic' has not given birth to a homogeneous and undifferentiated mass of citizens but boasts a hundred different types of family structure — a hundred models of behaviour absolutely independent of each other.

French individualism has often been described by the French and others in unflattering ways: in terms of self-seekingness, mistrust of others and factionalism within and between groups: characteristics leading to stratific-ation of interests and tenacious maintenance of privileges, 'organised anarchy' and parochial conservatism, thus causing political *immobilisme*. On the other hand individualism may be described as the kernel of liberal democracy in its defence of local freedoms and be thanked for sustaining the thick texture of national culture.

Intrusive regimes, including the Bourbon and Jacobin, have helped to ingrain the distrust of the centre which remains a defensive mechanism against the state in the late twentieth century. When President de Gaulle made his much-quoted complaint, 'How can one bring together a nation with 252 different cheeses?', he was expressing the pessimism of ruling elites who have for centuries worked to maintain national unity and identity. The promotion of liberties and national well-being is used to justify a strong lead from the centre: elitism, technocracy, bureaucracy and *dirigisme* (direction of the economy). Against this, commentators remark on a 'divorce between the political class and society' (for example Mabileau, 1991).

Étatisme is a term for positive intervention by the state to promote the economic, social and cultural life of the nation: something expected of all governments to some degree yet often resented (Ardagh, 1990). Dirigisme, the belief that economic life should be directed by the state, is its darker aspect.

An eminent French sociologist describes French bureaucracy as typically divided into upper and lower strata: on the one hand the higher officials who take decisions without the detailed knowledge of local needs and practical problems of implementation which should inform those decisions and, on the other hand, those who understand local circumstances but lack the power to fulfil their local needs (Crozier, 1970). Recent observation suggests that this model rings less true of central-local relationships today, at least with regard to the workings of government and administration. The decentralisation programme described in §2.1 has promoted mobility and mingled groups of administrators, forcing them to participate in joint problem-solving which crosses many of the old boundaries. But certainly it seems in the early 1990s that citizens' distrust of politicians in general has recently increased, affecting regard for both central and local government.

Liberty and Local Government

Toqueville wrote in *De la Démocratie en Amérique* (1835),

> It is in the commune that the force of free people rests. Communal institutions are to free people what primary schools are to knowledge; they put power within the reach of the people. Without communal institutions a nation can give itself a free government, but it will still lack the spirit of freedom... if you take away the force and independence of the commune you will find that there is nothing but administered people and never citizens....

The Guichard Report (*Vivre Ensemble*, 1976; see §2.1), a commission of senators, mayors and presidents of departmental councils set up by the President of the Republic to examine the question of the development of local responsibilities, put the concept of communal liberty at the centre of its argument.

The socialist government of the early eighties did not challenge individualism: in fact its policies have been interpreted as a reaction to centralising 'technocracy'. The new laws were defended as a means for the preservation and development of local individuality as a condition of French social survival. The note sounded in the first decentralisation statute, the *Law on the Rights and Liberties of Communes, Départements and Régions of 2 March, 1982* (§2.1), was one of which Toqueville would have approved. The concept of liberty is upheld by French individualism but has not prevented the toleration of complex bureaucratic regulation and may even have encouraged it through over-zealous attempts to protect individual rights. The main explanation why such a highly uniform and centralised system has been flexible in practice is that individualism and rationality have worked within it and adapted it to human purposes. Laws confer powers and impose obligations in a very general way. They are interpreted through a hierarchy of decrees and orders, but their application is shaped by local interests. A uniformity of approach unable to cope with variety of situation and therefore hampering local responses results in regular resort to 'system D' ('*débrouillard*', the art of getting round the rules). The presence of many mayors and departmental councillors within parliament helps to ensure that legislation is reasonable from the local point of view.

The Trend to Pluralism

It has been suggested that France entered a pluralist phase after it became obvious that uniformity repressed minority interests (Zeldin, 1983). Zeldin argues that the age of the minority has now arrived and that politicians are trying to institutionalise a society of diverse ethnic, recreational and ideological minority groups. Certainly the federal concept of 'unity in diversity' is a popular one, even if not much reflected in the legislation. One theory is that the conferment of new autonomies is a strategy to spike the disintegrative forces of provincial separatism that have emerged in Provence, Brittany, the Basque country, Corsica and elsewhere.

Pluralism, Equality and Elitism

Paradoxically, measures to provide equality of opportunity have tended to result in inheritance of privilege by elites, since it is elites who are best equipped to give their children the best chances to avail themselves of the opportunities made available. This occurs most obviously as a result of competition open to merit — Napoleon's *'la carrière ouverte aux talents'*. The sharply competitive system of schools for officials which Napoleon established has produced powerful elite corps of administrators and engineers, the members of which appear to dominate as much today as ever, moving between the high levels of public administration, private enterprise and politics. They form a network of old colleagues who give each other mutual support which bridges sectors and levels of government — a bonus over and above their high and proven natural abilities. There are over seven thousand active graduates of the administrative school, 'L'École Nationale d'Administration' (ÉNA), many of whom serve as mayors, presidents, departmental and regional councillors, senators and deputies, and some as ministers. Like the *cumul des mandats*, their communications network increases the capacity to overcome the complexity of the system and 'get things done' despite bureaucratisation.

The principle of equality justifies the uniformity of legislation for the communes, treating in most respects the city of Paris the same as hamlets. The need to provide for administrations of all sizes has contributed to the quantity of regulation. Paradoxically again, equality of status goes with great inequalities of power. In the case of the over 36,000 communes, defence of liberties has forced the state to resort to hard persuasion or, where that is unsuccessful, mandatory requirements to pool resources in joint bodies in order to achieve more capacity for development. But the prevalence of minuscule communes should not be exaggerated. Seventy per cent of the French population live in urban areas. The larger cities and the départements and regions can recruit officers who add to their national influence. Decentralisation has greatly increased the numbers of expert staff under their control. With large and skilled staffs of administrative and technical officers they are able to carry out projects as well as or better than central government field services. Their policies are often notable for their originality of emphasis, arising from dynamic leadership (sometimes under a mayor who has belonged to a *grand corps*). A state treasurer and paymaster general is reported as saying, 'a patient and determined mayor can do virtually anything he wishes' (Wright, 1983).

Mitterrand's government of the 1980s undertook to upgrade the status of the local government service to enable local authorities to recruit staff with the ability to help them fulfil their new responsibilities. A number of members of the prefectoral corps moved to high-level posts in large regional and local authorities. Mayor Chirac in Paris recruited a team of officials of the highest ability, some of whom moved with him into the prime minister's office and other key posts in the central ministries.

Fraternity, Solidarity and Decentralisation

Fraternity was the moral cement intended to overcome the disintegrative effects implicit in a system of liberty and equality of rights. During the latter half of the nineteenth century in particular, aspirations towards fraternity tended to be expressed in the doctrine of 'solidarity', adopted, developed and preached by moral philosophers, sociologists, scientists and politicians alike as both the explanation and the key to social progress. A French dictionary defines solidarity as the situation in which people answer for each other regarding the same things, feeling bound by common responsibility and interests. It defines it also as the relationship between people conscious of a community of interests, carrying the moral responsibility not to harm others and to give them assistance (*Le Petit Robert 1*, 1984).

In the cause of solidarity governments have encouraged mutual assurance societies, promoted and subsidised by the state and often run by local notables. Government intervention to promote collaboration between sectors and to support joint ventures has been a common strand in the policies of most political parties, supported by a broad consensus of political opinion. Joint bodies for housing and development are a conspicuous aspect of French administrative structure. It is paradoxical that France, a country of individualists, is also a country where sectoral interests are so closely intertwined. The need for inter-sectoral collaboration is recognised as much at community level as at the centre.

The ability of a mayor is commonly judged largely by his success in persuading people to overcome their disagreements and work together, and to contribute to 'solidarity' in his commune's relationship with higher authorities, technical agencies and other outside bodies.

The concept of solidarity in a broader sense recurs as a leading objective of government policies — not least in justification of the socialist government's decentralisation measures in the early 1980s. Advocacy of decentralisation has long been linked with advocacy of solidarity. At least 77 books were published on the subject of decentralisation in the 1860s alone (Zeldin, 1983).

The concepts have featured regularly in subsequent debates on local government reform. The polarisation between right-wing pressures for local autonomy and republican and left-wing pressures for action from the centre seem to have largely evaporated due to the adoption of decentralisation as a major plank of socialist policy. The acceptance of the socialist reforms by the new centre-right government in 1986 showed the extent to which they have transcended party divisions.

A cynical interpretation of the policies is not uncommon. The new system, it is argued, has resulted in no more than a re-grouping and even a reinforcement of the power of the notables and government elites at local level. It has been accompanied by a mass of new regulation and what are regarded as inadequate resources for fulfilling statutory tasks, proving, according to critics, that it is only a shell without substance and that the old vices remain. It appears to be a common view, however, that there has been a genuine shift in the balance of power in favour of local authorities. A main criticism has been the failure to make a significant advance towards popular participation, although 'power to the people' was a major slogan in Mitterrand's campaign speeches of 1980-81.

Catholic Corporatism and Humanism

Solidarity and subsidiarity (see §1.3) are both eminent parts of catholic corporatism — perhaps an unhappy term because it suggests the spectre of the state-dictated corporatism of fascist regimes and the economic dominance of commercial corporations. In fact it is in the Aristotelian tradition in that it sees the development of the individual as the purpose of society. It is concerned with the individual's social relationships which give him or her identity, meaning and belonging among other natural needs. Thus it attacks forms of liberalism, marxism and capitalism which leave the individual exposed without help to unmitigated economic forces and their political outcomes. The emphasis is on non-state bodies such as families, voluntary associations and local government structures inter-mediate between the central state and the individual. As such it is a political check on Jacobinism and economic liberalism (Soltau, 1931; Gourevitch, 1980).

Planning and Pragmatism

The French have assumed since the Monnet plan of 1947 that in a complex and uncertain world economic planning must be indicative rather than definitive: a means to activation and learning rather than simply design and implementation. The regional level of administration was developed in order to achieve balance between areas and to relate more closely to the local needs and resources. It was only with the Ninth Plan, however, that a serious attempt was made to incorporate regional policies that were as much determined from the ground upwards as from the top downwards.

The regional plan procedures were intended to achieve intensive consultation at local level, perhaps resulting in expectations well beyond what could be achieved. The interests of ministries and directorates clashed. State priority plans (PPEs) cut across those being developed in regional plans and were sometimes incorporated in planning contracts before differences were reconciled. The device of plan contracts (*contrats de plan*) between government and regions has, however, meant that provisions in key fields have benefited from the interchange of ideas and mutual criticism and bargaining between levels of government and different sectors.

The French terminology for development planning interestingly reflects their positive, perhaps engineer-led, approach to the field. The key terms are *aménagement* (see §2.1) and *équipement*, comprehending all that serves to equip for defined purposes and, where used in the phrase '*équipements collectifs*', all the provisions and installations necessary for the life of a community. The terms are not necessarily confined to physical provisions but include all the services which the definitions imply. Équipement is seen as a core purpose of a commune, with which both council and mayor are concerned. It is a corporate or community-based concept which cuts across the departmental thinking that has tended to characterise British local government.

An American student of French administration argues that the many-pronged attack on the problems of modernising the French local government system and the fact that local government is recognised as a constitutional matter with its interests well represented at national policy-making levels have led to a pragmatic approach which has been more satisfactory in its outcome than the British reorganisation of 1974. Hence the title of his book, *British Dogmatism and French Pragmatism* (Ashford, 1982).

2.4 NATIONAL STRUCTURE

Territorial Collectivities

The French system possesses an extreme number of elected bodies in relation to its size together with a complex distribution of functions between levels. The intermediate level of départements, highly urbanised areas apart, still reflects the socio-economic patterns in the provinces in 1800. Sixty-eight of the hundred départements have between 250 thousand and a million inhabitants. The departmental capitals are generally at the centre of their areas and well placed for communication with their communes as Napoleon intended. Some of the new regions fit regional geography and patterns of culture much less satisfactorily.

Table 2.1 gives details of the number, average areas and population sizes of the local and regional authorities. They are based on official figures for 1988 and include overseas France (*France d'Outremer*), consisting of the regions of Guadaloupe and Martinique in the Caribbean, French Guyane in South America and Réunion in the Indian Ocean. These regions exercise departmental powers and include respectively 34, 34, 21 and 24 communes.

The Commune

Of all French political institutions, the commune has by far the deepest roots. In the great majority of cases it genuinely corresponds with a real historic social community. As described in §2.2, it has an ancient status recognised in law many centuries before the existence of national constitutions. It is founded on the concept of a natural grouping of inhabitants living in a given area, leading a close collective life and possessing a clearly defined centre (*le chef-lieu*) which contains a town hall (*hôtel de ville*) or a mayor's office (*mairie*).

Each commune's mayor is central to the political life of the local community. He or she is also integrated into the world of departmental politics, and ultimately into that of national politics through participation in the selection of departmental councillors at cantonal level (see §2.10). Mayors therefore have at their disposal a channel of influence through which they can promote the interest of their communes within their regions and indirectly at least, in parliament.

A large part of France belongs to communes under the legal concept of communal goods (*biens communaux*), a concept distinct from those of public or private property. Many of these communal lands are wooded or mountainous. They cover over half the area of some départements.

Table 2.1: Classes, Populations and Areas of French Territorial Collectivities, 1988

	Number of Authorities	Av. Area (sq. kms)	Av.popu-lation	Population Range (000s)	%
Communes	36,763	15	1,613	under 1	79
				1-50	21
				over 50	0.3
					100
					%
Départements	100	5,490	580,935	under 100	1
				100-250	21
				250-500	31
				500-1,000	30
				1,000-2,531	17
					100
					No.
Régions	26	25,000	2,275,186	under 1,000	7
				1,000-2,500	11
				2.5-5,000	6
				5,016	1
				10,073	1

Source: Derived from figures in *Les Collectivités Territoriales en chiffres*, 1991, which are based on official sources, particularly the 1990 population census (INSEE and DGCL). The four overseas regions are included in departmental as well as regional figures since they have departmental as well as regional competences.

Communes have general competence to undertake any activities to meet the needs of their inhabitants not otherwise provided for or excluded by the law. Traditional communal services before those added in the 1980s were cemeteries and funerals, markets and slaughterhouses, fire protection, roads, refuse, water and cleansing, gas and electricity (see §2.7). The mayor serves the central state as a channel of communication to the community, registrar and protector of public order, in which last capacity he has powers of control over the communal police. He takes decisions on market matters and appoints the officers of the commune. For the provision of many of their services most communes have to rely, if they want them, on agencies outside their boundaries (see §2.8).

In 1982, 84 per cent of the population lived in communes with populations with under 100,000 inhabitants, and over 49.6 per cent in communes of under 10,000. The Guichard Report's chapter on communes begins:

> Each of the communes of France is irreplaceable. If our communes did not exist, it would be necessary to invent them.
>
> In the communes democracy is seen to be at its closest to people and to their problems: if the solutions to those problems almost always and everywhere exceed what they can do, it is certainly at their level that needs are known and expressed, their effects felt and judged, and there that problems must be posed and those responsible submit to the sanction of universal suffrage.
>
> There is another objective justification for the number of communes. In all rural France their map areas are based on where people live; ... they are only the reflection of the physical and local reality of people's lives. Although some villages have lost their population, so long as a village is inhabited it remains a community whose life and problems are distinct from those of others, and which therefore has the right to take responsibility for its future.
>
> In the urban agglomerations, swollen by a century of urbanisation, the communes, even if their boundaries perpetuate the frontiers of peasant communities that have disappeared, have rediscovered a function that is valid today and will be tomorrow: it is participation. They are, almost always, the place in which one can understand the human dimension of the city.
>
> In consequence, no authoritarian suppression of the commune must be envisaged. One of the objectives which we pursue is to make the participation of citizens more active and more effective. (*Vivre Ensemble*, 1976), cap. 19

The report argues that to wipe out communes with fewer than a thousand people would wipe from the map nearly 29 thousand of them, and also eliminate the same number of mayors and some 300 thousand councillors. 'The will to participate would indeed be compromised. Independently of all criteria of money, titles or education, people are chosen by their compatriots to take responsibility for the common interest. A nation is rich to have been able to give life to and sustain such a texture of responsible persons'.

The Département

There are 100 départements containing in all 337 arrondissements and

3,838 cantons. The arrondissements and cantons exist mainly for the purpose of central government administration although some facilities such as information technology at the canton (sub-prefect) level have been made available for use by départements. (The arrondissements should not to be confused with the sub-municipal arrondissements in the three largest cities.)

Départements in mainland France range in population from Lozère with 74,294 inhabitants to Nord with 2,520,526 (1982). They are not natural communities but political frameworks for the election of members of parliament, local self-government and general state administration under a prefect. The laws of 1982 and 1983 have enhanced the status and functions of the departmental council (see §2.7). Their presidents have replaced the prefects as executives and acquired responsibility for traffic policing and co-ordination of works.

The role of the départements was developed to give support to the communes and to provide services beyond communal resources or which needed to be organised over larger areas. Functions beyond the means of the communes have tended to move gradually upwards to departmental level for resource reasons — often without specific sanction but sometimes as a result of changes in the law, as in the cases of education, social assistance and roads.

The département, historically led by the prefect, has been the meeting place of local interests. As the Guichard Report put it, 'The prefect is the pivot of many "round tables", comprising partners such as the state, chambers of commerce, agriculture and trade, social security bodies, employers, trade unions etc. The département acts as a kind of club, a cross-roads of experience' (ibid.).

Départements have taken on the task of giving help to communes, especially where they have formed joint organisations. They have served as mediators: a place of arbitration between and among town and village interests, and also a kind of syndicate of joint communal bodies. In some matters they have carried out functions delegated to them by communes and joint communal authorities.

The Région

The 22 régions are the outstanding innovation in domestic governmental structure since the eighteenth century. One condition of their status is that they must not prejudice national unity nor the integrity and autonomy of the départements and communes.

The core function of a région is to provide a framework and support to enable local government to act more effectively: according to the Act of 2 March 1982 it can only act effectively if it pays 'respect to the integrity, autonomy and responsibilities of the départements and communes', which remain the levels of service delivery with the exception of regional planning and development, including housing, transport, colleges, lycées, higher education institutions and regional archives. Its role is complementary: co-ordinating, programming and organising development, and providing special wide area services, especially vocational training. It is essentially a means to devolve functions from the central state to governments elected by the provinces. A région has no general competence. It is largely a facilitating body, jointly planning and promoting developments and able to give modest financial aid to other bodies in some fields.

The central concern of the régions in the early years of the Mitterrand presidency was regional planning for the Ninth National Plan and for negotiating the related *contrats de plan* with central government in 1984-85. The then left-wing council of Provence-Alpes-Côte d'Azur for example set priorities to overcome unemployment, promote manpower training and qualifications, initiate research for innovation, improve the quality of the environment and develop the region generally. There was an emphasis on collaboration with local communities for the building of infrastructure and improvement of the environment. A *contrat de plan* signed in 1984 provided for sharing costs of implementation between the state and the region as follows (in millions of francs and order of size, with percentage of costs on each priority contributed by the state given in brackets): (1) development of infrastructure 1,972m. francs (62 per cent state financed); (2) improvement of the quality of daily life 1,633m. francs (60 per cent); (3) job creation 1,339m. francs (59 per cent); (4) manpower training 437m. francs (51 per cent); and (5) initiation of research on innovation 337m. francs (60 per cent). Later a contract for health and social developments of over 10m. francs was agreed covering investments to develop services for preventive and other health fields, elderly and handicapped persons, children, families and other specific groups.

The new right-wing coalition president, after the elections in March 1986, gave his principal aims as reducing costs of administration, seeking a better return on regional investment and a more equitable distribution of financial assistance to local authorities and to associations.

Départements have been apprehensive and defensive about the role of the regions. The future of regional plans is not yet clear to me at time of writing. The commitment of the state is under test in a period of financial stringency and political change.

2.5 INTER-AUTHORITY RELATIONS AND ORGANISATION

Inter-Authority Relations

An appraisal of inter-authority relations in France argues that levels of authority are inseparable: 'By their number and their fragmentation French Communes are condemned to co-operate to exercise their competences — especially in view of their powers' (Becet, 1989). Over 1,820 communes are below the figure of 10,000 inhabitants which has often been regarded as the minimum threshold at which a commune can effectively exercise its legal competences.

The decentralisation of 1983 made it more necessary than before for départements to assist small communes to exercise their competences and obliged them to co-operate to secure coherent action. There is no subordination of one level to another: communes, départements and regions have the same constitutional status and powers of self-administration. The problems and inefficiencies involved can be overcome to the extent that authorities support each other in a shared interest.

Small communes are able to draw to some extent on state and departmental technical services and the majority do so, but the small communes often pay a large town commune to supply them with particular services. Agreements (*conventions* between communes to assist each other) are frequent.

Both régions and départements have a special responsibility in this matter and have set collaboration and support of other authorities within their boundaries as primary aims. There are political and often financial incentives to joint working which contribute to the integration and success of the system as a whole. A text from French government sources dated 1979 needs no revision in the light of subsequent reforms:

> Except where the law has prescribed that a public authority has sole competence in a given sphere, parallel powers are exercised at the three levels of administration. In practice, these three levels co-operate both in planning and execution. Plans are drawn up.... in consultation.
>
> It may be said that if the definition of boundaries between the State's and local authorities' responsibilities gives rise to problems sometimes, this is not true between the départements and the communes... There is a general tendency on the part of the *conseils généraux* to leave responsibility to the communes when they are capable of assuming it and to give assistance by sharing the financial burden. (Council of Europe, 1979a)

Joint Organisations

Joint action is essential if local autonomy is to be preserved. The formation of joint or 'federal' bodies has therefore been strongly promoted. It is important to appreciate that in general the joint municipal bodies do not provide the services involved directly but through 'para-municipal organisations'— private corporations with which they act as partners as described in §2.8.

For over a century the state has promoted the alternative of co-operative institutions, beginning with single-purpose bodies in 1890. New legal forms for single- and multi-purpose syndicates called SIVUs and SIVOMs respectively were provided in 1959. Syndicates have a legal status as public authorities but they cannot raise their own revenues. They are supported by compulsory contributions from their members according to an agreed formula, income from charges and taxes relating to their functions and central and departmental grants. They are, however, subject to some state control, especially regarding formation, membership and dissolution. After several attempts met by local opposition and indifferent results the state has retreated from the idea of compelling communes to create syndicates. To remove one reason why some communes were unwilling to co-operate a law was passed in 1988 to make it easier for them to withdraw from syndicates if they wished. They may secede, given the agreement of the SIVOM committee, two-thirds of the communes in membership and a formal decision by the prefect. New communes may join a syndicate unless a third or more of its members are against. Syndicates have the power to change their own functions. From 1988 they have been able to select the services they want from a SIVOM *à-la-carte*.

By 1980 there were 542 syndicates which included private sector representatives. In 1989 11,984 SIVUs and 2,097 SIVOMs had been set up in urban and rural areas serving a population of over 20 million.

Syndicates are established by order of a prefect after the agreement of all the communes concerned, or if agreed by two-thirds of the communes represented and at least half of the population of communes representing two-thirds of the population. The prefect must seek a commune's full co-operation in formulating the provisions for powers, decision-making and operation, including sharing of costs. Appropriate communal competences are then transferred to the syndicate.

A survey in 1979 found that there were 3,971 single-purpose syndicates providing water services, 2,191 for school services, 1,627 for electricity and/or gas supply, 841 for flood control and water power services and smaller numbers for a wide variety of purposes including roadworks, transport undertakings, cultural activities, municipal personnel and funeral services.

A syndicate is administered by a joint committee in which each commune is represented by two delegates. It elects a board, including a secretary and a treasurer. It also elects a president who serves as executive in a role similar to that of a mayor in a commune. In general internal relationships and procedures resemble those of a medium-sized commune. A syndicate can be dissolved by a majority vote of its members with the consent of the departmental council or alternatively by the state. The detailed provisions deal ingeniously with procedures in case of disagreement between the members of a syndicate on revenue proposals and other matters. (Bourjol and Bodard, 1984)

Districts, of which there were 153 in 1989, are similar to multi-purpose syndicates but differ in that they can precept on their communes for a proportion of communal taxes and have a legal requirement to provide housing and fire services and services previously provided by syndicates for their members. Their origin is in a law of 1959, application of which was first restricted to urban areas such as the suburbs of large cities but has since been extended with success to use in rural areas. Districts draw income from fees and charges in connection with their services (including refuse collection charges), communal contributions and special purpose state grants, and also precept on their member communes for a share of their government general revenue support grant income, local government property tax and local duties on goods.

Communautés urbaines are joint, indirectly elected authorities created by law for the metropolitan areas of Lille, Strasbourg, Lyon and Bordeaux in 1966 and by special decree after a procedure requiring a weighted majority of the communes in their area in favour, as in the later cases of Dunkirk, Le Creusot-Montceau-les-Mines, Cherbourg, Le Mans and Brest. A description of their functions and of the case of the Communauté-Urbaine-de-Lille is given in §2.13 below.

Other forms of inter-authority association provided for by law are joint committees (*commissions syndicales*) for indivisible rights or properties, inter-communal agreements for works and institutions of common utility and special conferences (ibid.). There are analogous provisions at departmental and regional levels.

Legislation also provides for collaboration by local and regional authorities across national frontiers, following the Council of Europe's framework convention for trans-frontier matters (ibid.).

Relations Between Départements and Régions

Fears have been frequently expressed about rivalry between régions and départements despite the fact that competences have been enhanced at all sub-national levels by the decentralisation of state functions. A strong school of thought has maintained that one level must be a loser, at least in the long term. Départements have fought to represent the interests of small communes at both regional and national level, the great majority of which have no local leaders to represent them on regional councils against the strong representation of the large cities. The distribution of resources is a critical field of bargaining — particularly so in a time of expenditure cutbacks. Régions have the power to allocate aid to local authorities from their special funds. They also influence government allocations and their terms to local authorities.

Conclusion

The untidiness of the system contradicts commonly advocated principles of clarity of function and accountability. Nevertheless it ties interests together from top to bottom of the governmental ladder in networks of communication and influence. It has been highly responsive to demand. Whether it gives more in terms of real freedom of choice, responsiveness to need and distribution of resources is not a question easily answered since there has been no convincing assessment of its outputs in human terms against inputs: the only way to judge its costs and benefits.

National Associations

France has an exceptionally large number of associations which articulate local and regional views. They represent executives as well as councils and elected members generally. They include the Assemblée des Villes et Pouvoirs Locaux and the Assemblée des Présidents des Conseils Généraux de France, both at 15 rue de Vaugirard, 75291 Paris 06, the Association des Maires de France, 41 quai d'Orsay, 75007 Paris and the Mouvement National pour les Élus Locaux, 36 rue Laborde, 75008 Paris.

2.6 INTER-GOVERNMENTAL RELATIONS

The Concept of the State

As §§2.1 and 2.3 have shown, the state has traditionally conceived its role as one of positive direction through its agents, the prefects of the Ministry of the Interior and administrative officers of other ministries. Mayors and local councils have served as agents for the centre in implementing national policy.

Tutelle (supervision over decision-making by local councils) is an umbrella term that has covered various controls, some relating to the maintenance of legality, some to decisions or acts of a municipal council before or after they take effect, and some over persons, such as the suspension of a general councillor and police measures by a mayor. There is also a vague area of indirect tutelle relating to control of resources — most notably the use of financial transfers by the state for specific purposes.

In order to give a clearer understanding of what is implied in current practice the following model of the state as a legal entity may be helpful, drawn mainly from a French text (Bourjol and Bodard, 1984). The state is said to be part of an 'organic' interpretation of the constitution which is the antithesis of the polarised 'centre-periphery' model of Jacobinist domination. It is conceived as a sovereign organic unity expressed through law. In the French traditional constitutional philosophy of the national state the words 'nation' and 'state' define two faces of the same entity or 'juridical person'. 'Society' may be seen as another face that is often in conflict with the state. In relation to the state there are three main orders of organisation sharing boundaries that have in the past been defined by government. Under an interpretation of the 1958 Constitution local (and now also regional) directly elected authorities participate in the exercise of sovereignty under the national administration headed by the President.

Within the state there are three main institutional orders which to a large extent share the same administrative boundaries. One is that of private institutions represented by chambers of commerce and trade etc. The second is the national administration, whose powers have to some degree been deconcentrated to prefects and regional and departmental heads of national services in line with recent policies to overcome malign effects of over-centralisation. The third is local and regional authorities.

These institutions 'cohabit' in the areas of the 22 regions and 96 metropolitan départements, and to some extent in areas based on the more than 36 thousand communes. In the case of sub-departmental areas the central administration also works within 337 arrondissement and 3,838 canton areas.

The various public services lie under different government ministries and the directorates. In matters concerning sub-national authorities the Ministry of the Interior has the central responsibility. However other ministries are deeply involved — most notably perhaps that responsible for development (équipement), local government having been largely dependent on the services of its engineering corps except in large cities with their own technical services. The decentralisation of competences has greatly extended the dependence of local authorities on staffs under other ministries.

The main responsibilities of the Ministry of the Interior are exercised through general directorates for local authorities and law and order. A National Council for Departmental and Communal Services advises the Minister. It is divided into four sections: legislation, public service functions, information science implementation and personnel matters. The last section includes a joint commission for personnel affairs elected half by mayors and half by municipal personnel. The Council as a whole consists of eight members of parliament, eight government representatives, 22 representatives of local authorities and 11 from consumer associations.

While the local government bureaucracy has been under central control, that control has generally been exercised with sensitivity to local interests. Local political interests have often been expressed very effectively through well-used channels of influence by the larger communes, the départements and regions upwards and the central government downwards. The mayors of the great cities and the presidents of the departmental councils have exercised their powers at the centre as members of the Senate, the House of Assembly and of the government itself (see §2.2 on the *cumul des mandats*).

In the provinces prefects and officials from the various central ministries with localised staffs have co-operated closely with local political leaders, relying on their advice and support. Prefects have depended upon developing satisfactory relationships with council presidents and the mayors of the large cities in order to achieve government objectives and to fulfil the role of mediators between the provinces and Paris that was expected of them. The governmental and administrative frameworks have provided means of communication enabling local interests to be expressed upwards as well as central interests downwards.

There is constant pressure on the state to re-orientate its decisions towards local and regional interests. Mabileau writes (translated from the French) 'in no other Western democracy can relations between the centre and the periphery that tie together central power and local institutions be so direct and efficient in the regulation of the political system'. But, according to the same author, 'Central power has succeeded in incorporating local power, ways of functioning being prescribed by law and highly regulated, as in the system of *contrats de plan*' (Mabileau, 1991).

The Convergence of Interests at Departmental Level

The departmental level has been the centre of government power in the provinces since the late eighteenth century through the prefects and other government servants. The prefects have symbolised that power, although government servants under other ministries have also been powerful. It is here also that the growth of local democracy has been most critical for the state. Departmental councils have become key centres of interest for all bodies involved in local and regional government, from the central ministries and directorates down to the communes. This has been due to their acquisition of their own executive presidents who are often persons of political eminence nationally as well as in their départements, massive transfers to them of functions with accompanying staff and the possession of general competence. The anxieties of republicans that the unity of the state is under threat have centred as much on what is happening here as on what is happening at regional levels.

The régions are primarily planning and enabling bodies (see §§2.1 and 2.7). It is in the départements and communes that implementation takes place, and it is chiefly at the departmental level that the interests of the political system in central government and local government intersect. Their powers are exercised upwards as well as downwards, not only through the channels described above but also by the participation of their 22 presidents in the national commission responsible for the National Plan and in the negotiations with the state of the contracts through which the National Plan is largely implemented.

The Role of Prefects

Fears that decentralisation would lead to fragmentation and disorder arose especially from the abolition of the central role of the prefect as executive for the departmental council as well as for the government. Many felt, however, that the power of the prefect had already been undermined, not only by the power of the notables but also by the members of other ministries as they increased the strength of their local organisations. In 1982 the prefect's role was redefined in remarkably sweeping terms.

In the words of a senior member of the prefectoral corps, the prefect is the actor and guarantor (*l'acteur et le garant*) of the decentralisation reforms. As representative of the state he exercises the essential and irreducible competences of sovereignty — a role deriving from the Constitution. In accordance with decrees of 10 May 1982 he remains the representative of the state and of the government, being their 'delegate' in charge of national interests, respect for the law and public order. As such he is in charge of electoral arrangements; he plays a key part in *a posteriori* control of such local government decisions as may be referred to the administrative tribunal for judgement of their legality, and also of budgetary decisions in agreement with and under the conditions determined by the regional chamber of accounts. Consular rule must give way to dialogue and persuasion. The new prefect must accept pluralism and diversity and act for the state as arbitrator, animator and mediator..., promoting government policy, seeking the protection of minorities such as the young, the old, the handicapped and immigrants, working for employment creation and planning contracts, applying and explaining government policies and seeking co-ordination of effort and bringing the resources of the state to support the initiatives of the local and regional authorities. He is a channel of information between central and local governments. He must ensure that as far as possible matters are settled locally and do not have to be referred to Paris. He is expected to arbitrate between levels of sub-national government and between social sectors, and to help through mediation citizens whose interests have been hurt by a local authority decision. (Bernard, 1985).

But it is now the president of the departmental council or his director-general who receives the departmental mail from the public. Mayors with problems and requests now tend to come to the president, not the prefect, although they may have consulted assistant prefects first. But the prefect is still responsible for the detection of illegalities in regional and local decisions, although only about two per cent of the questions he takes up are referred to administrative tribunals (Hubricht and Malleray, 1989). The same is true of financial matters which he feels warrant submission to the regional council of accounts. A large proportion of the cases of adopted unbalanced budgets are settled without submission to the chamber of accounts.

The centre of local government business in a département is now truly within local government and likely to be in the hands of an eminent 'notable' with strong lines to Paris. The prefect's influence depends largely on the quality of the relationships he achieves with politicians and with local senior officials.

At regional level relationships between the regional prefect and presidents are reported to be virtually a carbon copy of those at departmental level.

Controls

Prefects vary widely in the extent to which they refer local authority decisions to administrative tribunals. They prefer to work by persuasion where legality might be challenged. Most references are reported to be about fees and charges, contracts and personnel matters, where trade unions can easily create a situation where a disputed interpretation of the law needs determination.

Control of financial decisions — or non-decisions — is now exercised by regional chambers of accounts (*chambres régionales de comptes*) on reference by the commissioner, treasurer-paymaster general, elected members, local authority treasurers or private citizens. Most references result from failure to decide the annual budget by the appointed date, most of the others being for failure to balance the budget or to make provision for obligatory expenditure. The chambers consist of irremovable magistrates and graduates of the École Nationale d'Administration (ÉNA), to whom may be added senior civil servants and local government administrators. Appeals go to the minister in Paris (Garrish, 1986).

Each local and regional authority must have an accountable officer for finance (*le comptable*). In the case of the communes he is appointed by the national Minister of the Budget after agreement with the mayor; at higher levels by the president of the council. His accountability is now to the collectivity, not the ministry.

There is also a pattern of control on technical grounds by the central ministries concerned. In general the dependence of communes on these services, excepting the large cities, is considerable but decreasing.

General

Power in inter-governmental relations is essentially shared power, mediated by those in influential roles at sub-national levels. The abilities of the mediators in the political system — the presidents of councils and other notables with influence at the centre — are crucial to local government interests.

The Ministry of Finance's interpretation of the national interest may of course cut across what are perceived locally as necessary expenditures, but the cutbacks in expenditure of the late 1980s do not appear to have produced anything like the clashes and bitterness that characterised British central-local relations in that decade.

2.7 LOCAL AND REGIONAL SERVICES

The laws of 1983 greatly extended the competences of local and regional authorities (§2.1). The possession of general competence means that many of the activities of communes and départements are not defined by law. This is especially so in the case of the communes, although it must be borne in mind that their achievements and use of powers vary enormously according to their size. Besides purely local matters in the care of local councils there are state activities for which mayors are responsible as local state representatives.

The competences and activities listed below are in many cases carried out by various forms of public corporation and joint body (§2.5). Special-purpose public and mixed bodies — établissements, sociétés d'économie and others — play a large part in the implementation of services. The following details relate mainly to the responsibilities of the directly elected authorities.

1. Town and Country Planning (*Urbanisme*) and Development ('*Aménagement and 'Équipement*)

Communes are responsible for the preparation of structure plans (*schémas directeurs et de secteur*) aiming to secure balanced development within zones determined by the state representative to achieve a 'community of economic and social interests'. Communes are expected to commit the preparation and revision of *schémas* to a joint communal body. They are also responsible for local land-use plans (*plans d'occupation des sols*) which must conform to the principles of schémas directeurs where they exist. Planning control is primarily through approval of building permits by the mayor of the commune unless the commune transfers this responsibility to the president of a joint body. Mayors or presidents of joint bodies are entitled to free assistance on planning matters from the state field services. Physical development is mainly undertaken by public or mixed bodies in which communes are represented and which they help to finance.

Départements have responsibility for rural development, particularly in liaison with groups of communes participating in agreements for development and investment (*chartes intercommunales d'aménagement et de développement*).

Régions are responsible for regional economic, social and cultural development. They may also be active in the field of environmental protection, preservation of heritage etc.

2. Housing *(Logement)*

Communes may prepare local housing programmes setting out needs and priorities — especially for social groups that are unsatisfactorily housed. They also play a key part in the setting up, capitalisation and management of a form of public corporation known as HLMs (*habitations à loyer modérés*, 'bureau which provide housing at moderate cost to tenants'). They may supplement state loans from which the HLM bureau draw their finance.

Départements define priorities, advise the state on the allocation of aids and play a general co-ordinating role. They may also participate in HLM bureau. They agree subsidies, loans, guarantees and securities for construction, improvements and requisitions through a special form of statutory committee.

Régions develop regional housing policy and define priorities jointly with the départements. They can supplement the state allocations by means of subventions, loans, loan guarantees and interest subsidies. They establish programmes for improvement of the quality of the environment, improvement of infrastructure etc. The state retains responsibility for the final allocation of housing finance.

3. Roads *(Voirie)*

Communes plan, build and maintain local municipal and rural roads.

Départements have responsibility for the maintenance of departmental roads. They co-ordinate roadworks and maintenance between authorities.

Régions play a part in financing major road development.

4. Transport

Communes make local passenger transport plans and provide passenger transport services, often jointly with other communes. They make traffic plans and may also undertake development of recreational ports and provide port police. They commonly provide school transport within the departmental plan.

Départements make departmental transport plans, provide for non-urban transport and organise school transport. They also provide for commercial and fishing ports.

Régions make regional transport plans after consultation with communes and départements. They contribute to joint main projects and promote road safety.

5. Education *(Eneignement)*

Education remains centralised under the Ministry for Education excepting pre-school and elementary education, but since 1983 communes appoint to state education planning councils at departmental level. They also appoint to the administrative boards of collèges, lycées and special schools. Mayors have a responsibility to ensure atttendance by pupils in their areas.

All main levels are involved in advising on the system as a whole in relation to local needs. They are represented on advisory councils at regional and departmental level which put forward general plans to the state.

The involvement of local authorities varies at different levels in the system. The following text is based on the law as it was in 1983.

Pre-School and Primary Education (Pré-Élementaire et Élémentaire)
Communes decide on the setting up of pre-school classes and elementary schools (for 6-11 year olds) but depend on state agreement to pay the salaries of the teachers. They are also responsible for building and equipping the schools and for most running expenses except salaries.

Comprehensive Secondary Schools (Collèges) and Lycées (including Mixed Ability Schools
Communes play a major part in the construction, maintenance and running of *collèges* and can claim the right to construct and provide maintenance for lycées.

Départements plan, finance, build, equip and maintain premises and advise on provision of lycées and higher education institutions.

Lycées, Special Schools and Vocational and Higher Education Institutions
Régions plan, finance, build, equip and maintain premises.

Complementary Educational, Sports and Cultural Activities
Communes, départements and regions may organise activities on educational premises in normal opening hours with the agreement of the responsible authority. Communes have a right to use premises out of academic opening hours.

Primary Teacher Training Colleges: *départements*
School Transport: *départements*
Grants to Students: *départements*
6. Vocational Training *(Formation Professionnelle)*
Communes and départements have powers to provide vocational training — particularly where there is a gap between needs and what is already provided by the national education system and otherwise.

Régions have general competence in this field and responsibility for ensuring suitable provision of vocational training and apprenticeship opportunities. The state plays only a subsidiary role, especially in ensuring that there is suitable provision for special categories such as immigrants and handicapped. Régions are required to prepare an annual programme for training, taking advice from regional and departmental committees on training, social matters and employment. They finance training institutions from a special regional fund.

7. Cultural Activities

This has been an area of rapid development in recent years. The government has set new policies and more than doubled its financial support. The rights of communes and départements to use educational premises for sport and educational and cultural activities complementary to other provisions are widely used.

Communes and départements have developed a wide range of activities, including opera, orchestras and festivals. Recently the emphasis has been away from 'prestige' projects and towards supporting private and voluntary efforts in the theatre and elsewhere.

Régions develop regional cultural policies covering music, theatre and other visual and verbal arts. They allocate resources both from their own budgets and from state grants.

8. Libraries, Museums and Archives

Communes: municipal libraries, museums and communal archives.

Départements have taken over state central libraries (the state retaining responsibility for scientific and technical salaries), and also conservation of departmental archives including private and relevant state archives.

Régions organise and support regional museums and conserve regional archives.

9. Recreation and Conservation of Environment

Communes provide sports centres, youth centres, clubs and open spaces and can institute measures for protection of historic buildings and conservation areas.

Départements prepare plans for departmental footpaths and can create forest domains.

Régions provide country parks, green spaces and country walkways.

10. Health and Social Welfare

The key local responsibilities for these services rest with the départements.

Communes run environmental health centres and implement departmental work in this field as agents. They are responsible for food hygiene, maternity and infant welfare centres, other child services, health and training centres for the mentally ill, homes for the aged etc. Under their general competence for social action they can give social help in urgent cases. Special social assistance bureaux are controlled by joint committees of councillors and state nominees. Their role is essentially supplementary to that of other providers. Some communes have experimented boldly with local policies, including minimum income guarantees and returning indigent people to the employment market.

Départements have general responsibility for social assistance and other social services (but responsibility for social security including family, health, old age, accommodation and rehabilitation benefit payments remains with the state). They plan social and socio-medical provisions and administer health and social aids and allowances (disbursement being the responsibility of the president of the council). These matters cover medical care and grants for children, families, elderly and handicapped. They can make supplements to state allowances. They are responsible for preventive health measures (immunisation etc.) and family, child and maternity health care. They also provide a range of social work activities.

Régions may also assist with services for the elderly (e.g. sheltered housing and home help) and collaborate with the state in the development of regional hospital provision.

11. Police

Communes The mayor is in charge of the municipal and rural police under the administrative control of the state representative in the département. The tasks of the municipal police are to ensure good order and public safety, security and 'salubrity'. This covers an extremely wide range of eventualities. The mayor must publicise laws and regulations and call on citizens to observe them (*rappelle les citoyens à leur observation*). He has power to call in the state police to maintain order and tranquillity if necessary. Responsibilities have in many cases been transferred to the state police in recent years. The mayor also has some traffic and conservation duties.

Départements Presidents of departmental councils have responsibilities relating to traffic control. Government policy has in general moved towards centralisation, the state having recently taken full responsibility for police salaries.

12. Fire Protection

Communes can request a branch of the national corps of firemen (*sapeurs-pompiers*) to be provided through the state representative. The branch is then subject to orders from the mayor. Local services are run under semi-autonomous bodies chaired by a councillor. Chief officers are appointed by the Minister of the Interior. The communes approve local regulations and participate in disciplinary matters. They are responsible for local recruitment and make an annual contribution to costs assessed by the state representative.

Départements The president of the departmental council now exercises what were previously the powers of the prefect in these matters, excepting call-outs for operations. There is a departmental body of mixed membership under the president's chairmanship which oversees fire provision in the département as a whole and arranges services for communes without services and help for those that have them.

13. Development of Local Economy and Employment

The Law of 2 March 1982 conferred specific powers on communes, départements and regions to intervene in local economic life in order to promote economic development and safeguard firms in difficulty, subject to not violating the freedom of commerce and industry, the principle of equality before the law or planning rules. The scope of action at all three levels is wide.

Régions have basic competence to give aid to private enterprises to the extent provided for in the National Plan.

Communes and départements may supplement aids to levels fixed by decree. Possibilities of so-called 'indirect' aid are, however, extensive, covering land provision, promotion of local products, training, provision of support services on industrial parks, aids to management, export, research and innovation, industrial buildings and under certain conditions loan guarantees, allowances in connection with industrial buildings and temporary local tax concessions. (A government manual lays down with clarity what local authorities can provide and gives practical advice.)

14. Public Utilities

Communes provide services for **water** and **drainage, gas** and **electricity** and **town heating.**

15. Tourism

Communes may make extensive provisions in this area.

16. National Plans

Régions have been responsible for research and key contributions and co-ordination for five-year plans. They assess proposals and liaise with state representatives.

17. General

Régions have planning, co-ordinative and financial allocation responsibilities which involve them in close relationships with all local authorities in their areas. They are deeply involved in financing voluntarily services of regional significance and providing public services under agreements with other levels of government.

2.8 IMPLEMENTATION OF SERVICES

The General Approach

Only a few communes are large enough to carry out the wide range of functions that they may be reasonably expected to exercise through their own employees. Nevertheless communes of all sizes have handled the great expansion of services that has occurred in the last hundred years with some success. The government has generally been promotional, assisting and filling deficiencies through the efforts and encouragement of prefects and field services and establishing and developing new forms of joint working between local authorities and other public and private institutions. But municipal initiatives have been as much the driving force for development as state services, and much more so in larger urban authorities. In other areas central ministries and field staffs have set the pace, raising local resources wherever they could.

As new needs and standards were defined, so the gap between aims and achievement increased and an increasing range of tasks was undertaken by government agencies. One of the main purposes of decentralisation in recent years was to enable local authorities to do what they wanted or were legally required to do without dependence on state employees. Mitterrand governments have given priority to building up the quality of departmental and communal staff to enable local authorities to fill that gap. While the large cities had a base and resources to build on, smaller communes had to rely on external help. The practice by which départements employ communes, especially large ones, as agents, and the communes, especially the small ones, arrange for departmental services to fulfil certain functions beyond their means, is described in §2.5.

The way in which the means of provision may be split is illustrated by the number of employees of bodies engaged in public work in the Nancy conurbation. The position at the end of the 1980s was that the city had some 2,000 employees, suburban communes another 2,000 providing services direct, a district authority (see §2.5) 660, and private companies to which public work had been contracted 800 engaged on public sector tasks. Other services were being carried out by other types of organisation including a welfare bureau with 400 employees (Lorrain, 1991).

Contracting out services to the private sector has long been an option considered by right- and left-wing authorities as a pragmatic alternative to direct provision, although on the whole more favoured by the right. The concept of solidarity (see §2.3) has frequently been cited in support of integration of responsibilities between public authorities and the private sector.

Lorrain comments regarding the municipality-private corporation relationship that the public authority is not external to the private sector but 'integrally linked to it'. There are not two separate participants, 'one who does and one who makes do', 'but two families of partners co-operating on the same projects' (Lorrain, 1992).

Modes of Implementation

The following modes are used by local authorities and the joint bodies described in §2.5.

(1) *En régie*, that is directly by the authority's own staff under the mayor or president, within the main budget or in some cases by divisions possessing their own balanced budgets under a management committee and director.

(2) Through an incorporated agency under the authority (*établissement public municipal* or *office municipal*) with a director working with a board of management consisting partly at least of representatives of the commune or département.

(3) Through private or semi-private joint stock companies and especially private corporations, subsidiaries of national groups under which there is great flexibility as to what can be provided.

(4) Non-profit associations in the welfare, sports, educational and cultural fields, both through national associations and those set up locally for a specific purpose or programme.

Sociétés d'Économie Mixte Locales (SÉMs)

SEMs are limited companies with mixed public-private participation governed by commercial law. They may be set up by one or more local or regional authorities. The Mitterrand governments sought to extend and encourage their use in a law of 1983 to bring their legal form closer to that of commercial companies. They may in principle be set up to provide any services within an authority's general competence as well as for fulfilling mandatory tasks. Over 700 of these bodies existed in 1983, 380 being for building, 180 for development (*aménagement*) and others for providing commercial, industrial and other services of general interest. Some are formed for specific projects while others are permanent features within local authorities' machinery of implementation. Where appropriate they can be transformed into independent bodies described as 'techno-structures'.

Government supervision is limited to control of legality and concern about viability. Government representatives may refer financial decisions to the regional chamber of accounts which has a duty to ensure that provisions are within the authority's resources and to verify the accounts.

Elected authorities must hold at least the majority of seats on the board and from 50 to 80 per cent of capital. Every participating authority must be represented on the board directly or through a grouping of authorities. Capital has been limited to 1.5m. francs for construction and 1m. for capital investment. Finance is provided by banks and by local organisations such as chambers of commerce as well as by local authorities.

Advantages claimed for SEMs are that they enable less well-equipped authorities to carry out complex rehabilitation schemes with expertise and access to private resources from beginning to end and without entanglement with the central bureaucracy and its legalistic procedures; and that they circumvent the dangers of lack of continuity resulting from changes in the political control of the authorities involved. On the other hand some have over-extended themselves and made serious financial misjudgements. Some are said not to have been monitored with the care that with hindsight might have been desirable — partly because central government approval of projects has been wrongly considered a guarantee of their solvency and competence. They have also been accused of operating without regard to social impact in order to achieve maximum financial returns.

Offices Publics d'Habitation à Loyers Modérés (HLMs)

HLMs ('public agencies for housing at moderate rents') are set up by decree on application by communes singly or in groups, a département or a communauté urbaine. Their employees numbered 27,288 in 1989. Their objects are building and administration of low-cost housing. They are directed by boards consisting of 15 members, five appointed by local authorities, five by the state to represent a range of knowledge and interests (including immigrants), three by tenants' representatives and two by local organisations such as family savings banks and friendly societies. Their initial endowment is in property assigned to them by local authorities and in gifts. There is state supervision and a limit on the dividends they are allowed to pay.

A larger form of development agency has also been possible for urban development purposes since 1973 termed *office public d'aménagement et de construction* (OPAC). OPACs have boards of 28 members, a quarter appointed by local authorities, half by the government representative directly or on nomination by other organisations, and the balance by local financial bodies, trades unions and tenants.

'Cocontracting', Particularly with Major Utility Undertakings

Since the mid-nineteenth century authorities have contracted with large firms to provide what are classified as public industrial and commercial services, including electricity, gas, town heating systems, transport, car parking, water, sanitation, public slaughterhouses, refuse collection and disposal financed by special charges, fairs, markets and ports. They have generally been distinguished from what are termed 'public administrative services' such as education and training, sport and leisure activities, culture, health, social assistance, libraries, archives, school meals, fire protection, public abattoirs and, characteristic of Mediterranean countries, funeral ceremonies, which were considered matters that should come directly under the elected representatives. The distinction between the two categories has been blurred by a decision of the Conseil d'État in 1986 that the administrative character of a service did not forbid implementation of a public service through private persons unless, by its nature or under legislation, it can only be assured by the local authority itself (Lemas, 1991).

The contracting out on a large scale of major public utilities such as water, sewage and waste treatment, energy supply, refuse collection, collective heating systems, urban transportation etc. started with the Compagnie Générale des Eaux in 1853. By 1975 when it had expanded beyond water services into the electricity and cleaning sectors it had a group turnover of 5.4bn francs. By 1987, after developing activities in building and public works, lighting, carparking, cable networks, cellular telephones, funeral, public health, catering and leisure sectors, its turnover had risen to 53bn francs. At the beginning of the 1990s these companies were providing for three-quarters of the water market. In overseas markets, in which the Société Lyonnaise-Dumez, formerly Lyonnaise d'Eau, has been a leader, 1987 turnover was 16.7bn francs. Their activities and investment have expanded to Italy, Spain, Belgium and the United Kingdom. They tend to aim at vertical integration within a sector: in water, for example, one company will undertake water distribution, treatment, maintenance and pipe manufacture.

How far can such commercial activities relate genuinely to public responsibility? How far can mayors and the deputy mayors responsible for 'co-contracted' functions, much less local councils themselves, have any power and accountability in matters which, once put in the hands of firms on a long-contract basis, tend to stay there for decades if not over a century? Lorrain writes that 'as long as the service works and the users do not complain, the operator is assumed to be doing the job well'. The control is thus 'based on global and political criteria rather than technical ones'. If there are no complaints the question of profits is 'of minor importance'. 'The solution has a major advantage. Each party is competent in its own sphere of action, responsibilities are clear, and there is no duplication of effort'. However the charges and records of service delivery of different companies can be compared and the municipality may be able to opt out. Regulation can be developed in ways in which it is an effective control. Certainly even for quite a large commune 'to go it alone' could be prohibitively expensive in many instances, and the companies do have a form of accountability to users which the communes can help to enforce if necessary. Moreover the companies have to comply with state norms, conditions attached to state subsidies and financial procedures. (Lorrain, 1992)

The Local and Regional Government Service (*la Fonction Publique Territoriale*)

Since 1945 the number of local government employees has progressively increased and entrants into the service have become more qualified, taking over functions previously undertaken by state employees as well as carrying out new and expanded activities. Communal employees increased threefold between 1950 and 1983. By 1989 the personnel in local and regional services as a whole was double that in 1969, having expanded to approaching 1,200,000. The number of established officers (*titulaires*) had increased from 466,554 to 813,136 (Ministère de l'Intérieur, 1991). Grade A officers, comprising heads and directors of services, their assistant chief officers in the larger authorities, directors of semi-autonomous public agencies set up to provide regional or local services (excluding the housing agencies (HLMs) except in Paris), and others of similar rank formed five per cent of the total.

Seventeen laws passed between 1983 and 1988 created a new national framework for local government employees. The general aim was to attract entrants of high ability into local and regional administration. The original intention was a single public service with two branches, one for national government and one for regional and local government, sharing a common status and open one to the other. But a law of 1987 diverged from this ideal in favour of two distinct services, 'neither comparable nor equal, and unequally open' (Bourdon, 1989). Territorial officers were not to belong to corps exterior to the authority but to be grouped into nationally agreed 'cadres', each authority being able to reconcile jobs with gradings. All local authorities have to accept the general conditions that have been drafted in consultation with representatives of local authorities and staff, but they retain the normal rights of employers. Officers share a common status of *fonctionnaire* but their appointment is the concern of their individual authorities. They possess a right to training under an ambitious decentralised system under the national training organisation.

Classes of posts are designated comparable with those in the civil service. Their remuneration is determined by orders of the Conseil d'État after consideration of proposals by the national joint Higher Council for Territorial Public Services. Entrance to higher grades is by *concours* (general written examinations) open to both internal and external candidates. The results are classified in order of merit, following the pattern of the national administrative college for the civil service.

Staff and arrangements vary considerably with the size of the authority concerned. Medium- and large-sized towns have substantial numbers of employees organised in divisions for services for which assistant mayors (*adjoints*) have executive responsibilities. A secretary-general heads the central staff and works closely with the mayor. The post has grown rapidly in responsibility with the new status and transfers of competence to départements and districts. It has attracted officers of high administrative ability from the prefectoral corps.

Formal recognition has been given to 'cabinets' of policy advisers to presidents of regional and departmental councils and mayors of large communes, analogous to those of government ministers. Members originally tended to be drawn from outside the authority but they increasingly include members of the public service. They have recently been described as meeting-places between politics and administration. A tendency towards public-private amalgamation has been observed between the work and interests of 'elected technicians' who have been appointed as adjoints and directors of services.

2.9 LOCAL AND REGIONAL FINANCE

General

The financial status of local authorities strengthened during the 1980s. They were given the freedom to fix and vary their taxes directly within limits. They were freed from hierarchical controls and able in principle to spend as they wished. State grants were increased annually in accordance with agreed formulas. In 1986 the free capital market was opened up to them and they were able to raise loans at will. Steady growth supported expansion of expenditures until the end of the decade. This was accompanied by a rise in total taxation from 41.7 per cent of the GDP in 1980 to 44.4 per cent in 1988. Local government's share of general taxation rose in this period by over 23 per cent.

The system is well-rooted in principles but it is unclear how far it can survive the recession of the early 1990s. One view is that a confusion of responsibilities had developed as public authorities at all levels exploited these new opportunities, often in competition with each other (Beltrame, 1990).

There is a national advisory committee for local finance which enables local knowledge and expertise to contribute to key government decisions. It consists of nine members from parliament, nine representatives from local authorities and nine appointed by the state and is chaired by one of the local authority members. It controls the division of the block grant for services and must be consulted on all regulatory proposals and draft legislation relating to local finance. Increased local autonomy and improved equity in the distribution of resources were sought and a series of reforms were carried out with a good level of agreement.

In 1988 the budgets of France's 36,875 local and regional authorities totalled 635 milliard francs, 37 per cent capital expenditure and 60 per cent current. Since 1982 expenditure had increased by over a fifth in real terms. Capital expenditure was 154 per cent of that by the state and recurrent expenditure 39 per cent. (*Les Collectivités Locales en Chiffres*, 1991)

That year the communes accounted for 50 per cent of expenditure by local public bodies, joint agencies 12 per cent, départements 24 per cent and regions five per cent. Of total personnel expenditures the communes spent 71 per cent, joint authorities 6.3 per cent, départements 10.6 per cent and regions 0.6 per cent.

Local Income

The critical period of financial development was during the main transfer of services from the state between 1982 and 1986. In 1983 local taxation increased by 18.2 per cent and by 24.6 per cent in 1984. Over four years the increase in real terms was 36 per cent against an increase in real expenditures of 7.8 per cent. Official figures show that state assistance and borrowing actually dropped in real terms at the same time. By 1989 growth of local budgets had fallen to 0.2 per cent.

Revenue provided for in local and regional budgets in 1989 totalled 570 milliard francs of which 46 per cent was to come from local taxes, 9 per cent from fees and charges, 19 per cent from state grants and subventions for services, 5 per cent from grant toward capital expenditure, 10 per cent from loans and the balance from other sources.

Wages and salaries took 29 per cent of expenditure, financial expenses 8 per cent, purchase of goods and services 15 per cent, social services 5 per cent, physical investments 23 per cent and reimbursement of loans 8 per cent, the balance being spent on other matters. (Durand, 1991)

Direct Local Taxation

There are four main taxes through which local and regional authorities spread their demands for tax among population groups. Levels are fixed by local authorities but collected by the national tax office and redistributed. Tax demands are set in the following four categories:

The Taxe professionnelle yielded 44.3 per cent of total tax income in 1989. It is levied on industrial, commercial, very small and one-person businesses and the liberal professions. It is made up of: (a) the rentable value of fixed assets (sites, structures, installations, vehicles, plant and other equipment costs when receipts are above a certain sum), and (b) the total wage bill paid (or in some cases receipts). Professionals in receipt of non-commercial income who employ fewer than five people have a tax base of one-tenth of their income.

Foncier bâti yielded 25.1 per cent of tax income. This is levied on owners of buildings and is assessed on the rentable value of land less 50 per cent to allow for management, maintenance etc.

Foncier non-bâti yielded 4.4 per cent of tax income. It is paid by owners of unbuilt-up land, being levied on undeveloped urban land, agricultural land, forests etc.

Taxe d'habitation yielded 26.2 per cent. It is levied on residents in respect of dwellings of individuals or families and based on full assessed rentable value, whether occupied or not. There are large inequities in incidence, with payers in poor Paris suburbs paying much higher rates than those in the affluent centre. Ceilings for each tax have been set annually by a formula relating to the national average uptake for the previous year.

There are other minor taxes: *domestic refuse disposal tax* and *transport levy* in municipalities with over 100,000 inhabitants and payable by enterprises employing ten or more people, calculated at a rate up to a maximum of one per cent of their total wage bills or 1.5 per cent in specially approved cases. It can be used for transport subsidies or transport investment.

Local capital equipment tax can be levied in communes of more than 10,000 inhabitants and in smaller ones if the council so decides. The rate is one to five per cent of the value of a site. Its proceeds must be used to finance infrastructure investment. A *levy on structures above the legal density ceiling* is charged according to the extra land that would have been covered if the ceiling limit had been observed.

Syndicates of communes, districts and communautés urbaines can enjoy shares of the standard taxes on their own account in place of or in addition to transfers from their member collectivities.

Régions draw on the four main direct taxes. They have also acquired income from driving and vehicle licence fees.

Other taxes are levied on bowling alleys and mineral water.

The tax uptake shows strong regional variations, being highest per capita in the wealthiest areas (the South-East and the Île de France), and lower by over 25 per cent in Brittany and the poorer eastern regions.

The growth of local taxes slowed down after a rapid increase in 1984-8 but grew strongly again in 1990, a year in which councillors were putting in place a new investment programme following the local elections. (*Les Collectivités Locales en Chiffres, 1991*).

Grants *(Dotations)*

The most fundamental change in recent years was in the merging or 'globalisation' of central grants to give local authorities the discretion to spend at will funds that were previously specific to particular purposes. The main case is the general grant for services, the *dotation generale de fonctionnement* (*DGF*). In origin it compensated for lost taxes but has lost this significance. It is meant to assist with all recurrent expenses and provided 20 per cent of commune incomes in 1988 and 8 per cent of départements'. A flexible grant, it has increased not least to compensate for a new liability for value added tax. For 1991 40 per cent was based on the number of inhabitants of an authority weighted according to characteristics of the commune, 37.5 per cent to equalise between differences in tax base and 22.5 per cent for costs relating to social housing, school children and road networks. It incorporates special provisions for the 'mini-communes', especially those below 10,000 in population (98 per cent of all of them and including 40 per cent of the national population).

Local authorities have been compensated for the cost of taking on more services by the *dotation générale de décentralisation* (*DGD*), a staff training grant and grants for investment in schools as well as new local fiscal resources. The amounts involved have been small in terms of commune expenditure but large in the case of the départements (74.1 per cent of total DGD) and regions (24.6 per cent).

Subsidies for capital investments have been globalised in the *dotation générale d'équipement* (*DGE*), a general grant for investments in development initiated in 1972 but first used significantly in 1983. Communes with above 2,000 population and joint bodies of communes receive aid pro rata according to their investments. Communes below this size and others up to 10,000 if they opt to take advantage of this provision, benefit from a formula which takes into account their special needs. Départements receive part of the grant for direct investment, weighted strongly in favour of the poorer regions, and a second part which is used mainly to aid investment by communes. The system has been criticised as intrinsically perverse, for it removes responsibility from both elected members and the public. No one knows who pays what. Smaller communes are forgotten. (Guillaume, 1990).

As described in §2.6, central government's attitude to local government has been promotional, and this is reflected strongly in matters of local finance. It has seen its task as the development of the wealth and well-being of the nation as a whole and overcoming imbalances between areas.

Direct financial transfers are only part of central support. Apart from the direct services provided to localities by central ministries there are subventions to other local public bodies (*établissements publics*), especially in the case of public-private sector corporations for building, development and other purposes.

Borrowing

There has been no set limit on borrowing. All but a small proportion has until recently been from a range of state established banks, amongst which the Caisse des Dépots et Consignations (CDC) is the central source. It co-ordinates its own lending with that of other public sources — in particular the savings banks and the Caisse d'Aide à l'Équipement des Collectivités Locales (CAECL), and also acts as a financial adviser. The CAECL is a branch of the CDC which finances local authority development expenditures by means of funds raised by floating bonds.

Statutory regional loans boards were set up in 1982 on which local and regional councillors form a majority. They lay down general lines for policies on loans, play a consultative role regarding the finance of investments of regional importance and can intercede when a body has refused a loan in the first instance. Authorities can also borrow from other lenders and, with Ministry permission, float their own bonds or borrow in foreign currencies on international markets. Loans are no longer available freely at special cheap rates: 71 per cent were assisted in 1983 but by 1987 only 20 per cent.

Indebtedness has grown in the 1980s. In 1986 debt charges took up 12.5 per cent of communal budgets, 8.1 per cent of departmental and 12.5 per cent of regional. Brokerage skills are required to manage the loan market successfully. There have been cases in the past of civic bankruptcies. There are indications in the early 1990s that with the rise in interest rates from a very low level a substantial number of local authorities are running into severe financial problems. Cities such as Saint-Étienne and Marseille were experiencing financial crises in 1991.

2.10 ELECTORAL REPRESENTATION

Elections

The qualification age for voting is 18. That for candidates for election is 18 in communes and 21 in départements. Councillors at local and regional levels are elected for six-year terms. For departmental councils (conseils généraux) half the council membership is elected every three years. Elections for different levels of government are spread over the years. Within the course of six years there can be theoretically four local or regional elections, two five-yearly elections to the National Assembly, two three-yearly indirect elections to the Senate and two five-yearly elections to the European Parliament: ten in all. When the turn-out in the departmental elections fell below 50 per cent in 1988 it was generally put down to 'voter fatigue' due to the heavy incidence of elections in that year.

France has changed her electoral system many times since 1789, almost every government having considered whether there might be a way of achieving greater fairness or governmental stability on the one hand and a result more compatible with its own political interest on the other. In the interest of strong government Charles de Gaulle re-introduced the majority list system for communes of over 30,000 inhabitants in which the list 'first past the post' won all the seats on a council, thereby removing all opposition. This worked against the Gaullists in the socialist successes in the 1977 elections. A law in 1982 applying to all communes with over 3,500 inhabitants sought to balance strong management against fair representation with an electoral system that produced both an effective administration and an effective opposition.

Recent systems tend to compromise between the fairness embodied in proportionality and the distinctively French system of two-round elections. The five different local and regional election systems employed in the second half of the 1980s were as follows.

In communes of under 3,500 inhabitants lists of candidates for the seats on a council are put forward by the parties or groups of citizens. In communes with populations of under 2,500 individuals may also be put forward for election. Voters can modify a list of their choice by means of *panachage* (striking out candidates on their chosen list of whom they disapprove and substituting others). In the first round of the election candidates are elected who succeed in winning an absolute majority (half plus one) of the votes and who have been voted for by at least a quarter of registered voters. In the second round candidates are elected in proportion to the number of votes received up to the number of vacant seats remaining after the first round.

In communes of over 3,500 inhabitants councillors are elected by list in two rounds by proportional representation and without panachage. If in the first round any list wins an absolute majority it wins half the seats (rounded upwards if necessary). These are allocated to the top half of the list of candidates. The remaining seats are distributed between all lists which received at least five per cent of the vote, including that which has already won half the seats, using the procedure of the 'rule of the highest average' or 'modified d'Hondt system' (see §1.10). Thus at least three-quarters of the members on the list with the absolute majority of votes will be chosen while allowing the candidates at the top of the minority lists places from which they can contribute to council debate. If there is no list with an absolute majority, any list winning at least five per cent of the vote may be submitted for a second round. The surviving lists may be amalgamated to strengthen their appeal to voters. In the second round half the seats are given to the list which wins most votes and the remainder are distributed between the other lists in accordance with the rule of the highest average. Candidates are taken from the top of the lists in downward sequence until all seats allocated to each list have been filled. In the event of a tie between lists, age determines who shall win the seat.

In departmental councils each canton (constituency) is represented by a single member. Election is by simple majority in two rounds. To be elected in the first round a candidate has to obtain a simple majority and the votes of at least 25 per cent of registered voters. Candidates in the second round must have received at least ten per cent of the vote in the initial round. The candidate with the most votes wins the seat.

In the 1986 regional elections members were elected by list in a system of proportional representation similar to that used for communes of over 3,500 inhabitants. The electoral areas were those of the départements, each département being given a number of seats proportional to its population. Mayors of communes and presidents of general councils and their assistants (adjoints) are elected at the first meetings of their newly elected councils. The mayors and departmental and regional presidents are normally the council members who headed the successful list.

Arguments for the two-round system are that it forces parties to bargain and compromise, accepting a 'second best' in the cause of solidarity while putting control into the hands of a spectrum of support that is likely to embrace a good majority of the voters. Proportional representation (rule of the highest average) was argued to produce 'an exact photographic reproduction of political opinion and allow the representation of all sentiments. It avoids excessive cleavage and allows the constitution of a variable majority' (Virieux, 1985).

Elected Representatives' Conditions of Service

The Municipal Code since 1855 lays down that councillors and mayors are to give their services gratuitously. Councillors are eligible for allowances in larger communes within set limits. Mayors are re-imbursed for loss of income due to absence from work and for costs incurred on official duties in accordance with a scale related to the population of the commune. An inquiry in 1984 found that mayors' expenses in communes with more than 15,000 residents ranged from 70,000 to 124,000 francs. A mayor may transfer part of his allowances to someone acting as his agent. Mayors and adjoints who have served at least 24 years in the same commune receive a state honorarium on their retirement.

In a survey in 1987 sent to some 500 mayors, 36 per cent of those in communes with under 2,000 inhabitants said that they spent at least four days a week on their mayoral duties. The percentage rose to 57 per cent in communes of two to five thousand and 83 per cent in communes of over five thousand. It is impossible to assess the significance of these figures without taking account of mayors' often numerous commitments in other offices they hold on public bodies (Villielm, 1989).

Of the mayors elected in 1983, 36.5 per cent worked in agriculture (cf. 1971, 45.3 per cent), 11.7 per cent in industry and commerce (1971, 14.7 per cent) 13.7 per cent as engineers or in other groups in the private sector (1971, 10.4 per cent), 5.4 per cent in the liberal professions (1971, 5.8 per cent), 7.6 per cent as teachers (1971, 4.6 per cent), 3.3 per cent as officials

(1971, 2.9 per cent) and 20.2 per cent were retired or unemployed (1971, 14.2 per cent).

Among members of departmental councils the largest group in 1985 was that of the liberal professions (24 per cent), followed by teachers (16.4 per cent), retired and unemployed (14.9 per cent), engineers and other groups in the private sector (13.4 per cent), those in industry and commerce (12.4 per cent) and those in agriculture (10.15 per cent). Among the new regional councillors of 1986 the largest groups were those from the liberal professions and teachers (both 19.9 per cent), engineers etc. (16.8 per cent) and retired and unemployed (13.6 per cent). Those in agriculture had declined to 6.3 per cent. (Ibid)

The proportion of women councillors in the municipal councils increased from 8.4 to 14.1 per cent from 1977 to 1983. The proportion in communes of under 3,500 inhabitants almost doubled between these dates. In larger communes it was around 21 per cent.

The average age of councillors is reported to have dropped markedly from 1977, accompanied by a rise in the level of education, due it is suggested to the growing technicalities involved in the management in local authorities, enforced unemployment, increased democratisation through decentralisation, increased politicisation of local elections and other factors that have changed the profile of the elected representative. (Ibid.)

The Political Parties and Local Leadership

French politics are characterised by elite political groups known largely by the names of their leaders. François Mitterrand took over the leadership of the Socialist Party (PSF) after bringing together a confederation of political clubs which he had built up himself. He was elected to the party's secretaryship as an outstanding politician who could build its constituent elements into a unity.

Giscard d'Estaing brought together a group of Conservative MPs with local power bases during the de Gaulle presidency, first known as Independent Republicans and then the Republican Party (PR), but commonly Giscardians. The Union for French Democracy (UDF) has been an alliance of a small central liberal and social democratic parties with the Republicans. Its membership's support for Giscard's liberal stance has been tempered by traditional conservatism. It inherits some of the Christian Democrat stance of the temporarily successful Popular Republican Movement (MRP) Union after the war.

Jacques Chirac led the Gaullists, the 'Rally for the French Republic' (RPR) from 1976: a mass-membership party based initially on the charisma and ideology of Charles de Gaulle. RPR policies have a 'Jacobin' tinge, emphasising the state's role internationally, the development of the economy and the overcoming of inequalities to foster national unity.

The parties on the far wings — the much weakened Communist Party and the National Front (NF), an anti-immigrant, anti-crime, anti-taxation party that advocates 'popular capitalism' — depend on strong leadership to overcome fragmentation. The NF had a whiff of power around the beginning of the 1990s as the possibility of allying with elements on the right-centre to defeat the socialists emerged, a possibility highlighted by critical situations after regional elections.

For a prospect of victory mayors and prospective mayors usually seek a balanced list of candidates that includes if possible well-known and respected persons. Socialists may be prepared to ally with Greens if the Greens are willing.

The leader of a right-wing alliance will have to weigh the acceptability of including National Front candidates if that is the price of forming a controlling alliance.

Proved performance and maintaining traditional support is generally more important than party. The mayors of one small town have shared a common ancestry since the French Revolution. Mayors have generally played down their partisan role (*apolitisme*), partly because they regard their representation of the local community as a whole as more important and partly because they may wish to obtain help from central government without being prejudiced by their party loyalties (Kesselman, 1967). It follows that communal councils and executives are not in general politically polarised and a doctrinaire stance is generally unhelpful. They are often in the grip of political personalities. Leaders typically will look for candidates who will be popular as members of their panel of *adjoints*.

Departmental and regional levels are inevitably more remote from the public and more dependent on party organisation than all but the larger communes. There can be strong polarisation at regional level between left and right parties, with the National Front and possibly communists as a factor of disequilibrium.

2.11 THE INTERNAL ORGANISATION OF LOCAL AND REGIONAL AUTHORITIES

The Commune

Each commune possesses a municipal body (*le corps municipal*) consisting of the municipal council (a deliberative and decision-making body) and an executive consisting of the mayor and one or more assistant mayors (*adjoints*). The council is elected every six years 'to regulate the affairs of its commune'. Its duty is to 'deliberate', that is to discuss and where appropriate take decisions on matters 'of general interest'. In size it ranges from nine members (for communes of under 100 inhabitants) to 69 (for communes of over 300,000) according to a fixed scale. It must meet once a quarter or on the summons of the mayor or at the demand of half its members or the request of the local assistant-prefect. Decisions are by absolute majority. One proxy vote may be registered by each member present. Voting by individual members may be recorded on a decision by a quarter of members present or kept secret if a third of the members demand it and in the case of an appointment or election.

Specific competences of communes and their general competence and its implications have been described in §§2.2, 2.4 and 2.7. In general terms decisions that fall to communal councils include:

- management of communal properties, classification and repairs to roads, plans of alignment for roads and buildings etc., and lettings and contracts as part of the management of communal properties (see also §2.7);
- budget, taxes and charges, and loans and guarantees to certain types of joint body;
- staffing and conditions of service for some classes of employees;
- organisation of communal services and regulation and direction of the services (see §§2.4 and 2.7);
- participation of the commune in private enterprises of general interest.

Councils also appoint to the posts of mayor and adjoint, and to committees, boards administering social aid bureau, hospitals, joint authorities and public/private sector bodies and some national bodies. They give opinions and advice on all matters of common interest and when required by law or by the state representative in the département, including conditions for the distribution of state aids, alignment and improvement of main roads in built-up areas, establishment and relocation of social assistance bureau, budgets and accounts of charitable institutions, new towns, HLMs (§2.8) and other public bodies.

Standing committees are usually appointed for works, finance, development, town-planning and other purposes. 'Extra-municipal' committees can be set up to involve members of the public.

The administration of a commune is the responsibility of its mayor, who acts both as the agent of the commune and of the state in some matters. Adjoints assist the mayor in his duties and stand in for him in his absence. The word 'adjoint' is often translated as deputy mayor but in practice it signifies an assistant mayor with a specific legal status, acting on delegations by the mayor which the mayor may change or withdraw and deputising in the mayor's absence. Up to 30 per cent of the members of the council may be elected to such posts. Special adjoints may also be appointed to carry out state responsibilities of the mayor, including those concerning police, for sub-areas where travel from the centre is difficult or at times impossible. They need not be councillors.

As executive a mayor manages the communal properties, carries out communal works, takes measures relating to roads, signs contracts, agreements and orders for purchases, sales and many other transactions. He prepares and manages the budget and carries responsibility for accounts. He represents the council at law where required, takes measures for destruction of dangerous animals and, according to the 'code des communes', 'in general carries out the decisions of the municipal council'.

The council can delegate certain powers to the mayor or to the mayor and adjoints jointly for the period of its mandate with the possibility of withdrawing the delegations at any time. Mayors take some actions on their own responsibility in expectation that the council will sanction them retrospectively. Delegations include loan contracts with lending institutions, fixing tariffs within limits agreed by the council, fixing revised alignments in road and land-use plans and setting up arrangements for accountable management. In some other matters a mayor has much wider discretion, such as appropriation of properties for public use, purchases and lettings within quite high limits, insurance contracts and professional fees.

A mayor directs the communal staff, appointing, suspending and revoking the appointments. He also controls the local state police for most purposes (§2.7).

As a state agent he is responsible for general security, electoral rolls and organisation of elections, census, some work for the army, hunting permits and establishing dossiers of social aid. He and his adjoints are officers of the judicial police and of the civil state. The legal provisions on some of these matters enable him to delegate tasks to municipal officers.

The wide differences in the scale of communal services make it impossible to give a general description of staff structures. The role of the commune's secretary-general is always central, whether as 'maid of all work' in a small commune (cf. Lacombe, 1980) or as head of the large and complex staff of a great city.

The Département

Departmental councils (*conseils généraux*) range in size from 14 members (Territoire de Belfort) to 76 (Nord), the number of members corresponding to the number of cantons. Each canton elects one member. Cantonal boundaries now bear little relationship to the distribution of population and result in a disproportionate representation of rural areas. A member of a departmental council can receive demands from all the mayors within his canton. He has the informal status of a local 'notable'. The members sit as individuals, not as members of a successful party list. Relationships between councillors and executive differ fundamentally from those in a commune. This arises in part from the fact that until the early 1980s their executive was the departmental prefect, the head of state services. The responsibility for political initiative therefore fell clearly on the members, who could propose expenditures and have their own propositions put to the vote. But the prefect prepared the budget, incorporating provisions agreed with a departmental committee — a kind of inner council set up to control the prefect and to take over certain of his former responsibilities, including the allocation of grants.

Views on the power of departmental councils vary. One writer (Dupuy, 1985), comments that council members do not form a body capable of formulating policy without the help of intermediaries, and in particular that of the prefect and the heads of state field services. Council meetings are 'ritualistic, formal and brief'. 'Consensus is the order of the day'. The president of the council, a 'grand notable' likely to be a senator or deputy with strong lines to Paris, provides a focus of power, but his negotiating position is weakened by the fact that he is himself a cantonal representative with 'irons in the fire'.

The transfer of duties of executive from the prefect to the president of council in 1982-83 undoubtedly resulted in a major shift of power (§2.6), but the scale, divisions of interest within the administration and complexity of internal and external relations are such that the president, the prefect, the heads of state field services, the director-general of the department's services and the directors of those services depend heavily on each other.

As described in §2.4, the departmental councils have general competence over 'all matters of departmental interest'. The Law of 2 March 1982 stated that they regulate by 'deliberation' (i.e. consideration and decision) the affairs of the département. They vote budget, taxes, loans and guarantees and offers of collaboration to other authorities, participate in the control of mixed companies and take decisions on personnel matters and the departmental services detailed in §2.7.

Restrictions on the councils' right to express views on economic interests and general administration have been lifted. The aids they can make available to communes in grants, subsidies, loans and guarantees give them a strong strategic influence on economic development. They advise on orders for the grouping of communes into syndicates, districts and communautés urbaines.

The Law of 2 March 1982 stated definitively that the president of the departmental council is the executive organ of the department. He prepares and carries out the business of the council, manages expenditure, proposes means for the collection of revenue and heads the services of the département. He can delegate powers of signature under his surveillance and responsibility. He manages the département's properties and ensures that its current affairs are dealt with if it is dissolved. He is responsible to the law for budgeting procedures, controls the departmental traffic police, co-ordinates road works and regulates the policing of departmental ports. He has taken over the prefect's responsibility for the departmental fire agency and chairs its board, a body which includes councillors, mayors, fire officers and other ranks.

The departmental bureau extends the capacity of the executive and links it with the council. It consists of the president, four to ten vice-presidents and one or two other members of the council, varying in size from ten to fifteen members in all. It is not a collegiate executive and does not share the president's executive power. Vice-presidents may be delegated executive responsibilities individually by the president but not budgeting decisions. The main task of the bureau is to prepare business for the council and to carry out tasks which the council delegates to it. It is a hybrid animal, acting for the council with individual members acting for the executive. Its decisions are implemented by the president.

Each member of the bureau is elected separately by the council. The members may be of the same party or an alliance of parties or include opposition members. (Gasnier, 1985).

The Departmental Administration

There are wide differences in the form of the administrations which presidents head. In most cases there is a clear division between the cabinet (the president's staff unit) and the administrative services. The cabinet varies from a simple type of secretariat to a 'veritable general staff furnished with *chargés de mission*, elaborating directives and giving substance to the president's policies (ibid.). In many cases the service staffs are headed by a director-general from the prefectoral corps or by the former head of the departmental staff, the ex-secretary-general. Services may be organised under two to four directorates or, in a few cases, seven to ten groupings. According to Gasnier, the former director-general for the département of the Gironde, there are four essential functions: (1) finance and budget, usually grouped with estates; (2) personnel and means (e.g. buildings, often termed the technical services); (3) co-ordination and programming, which includes co-ordination with state services and those of other authorities and may be divided into (a) infrastructure and development work (*équipement*) and (b) educational, cultural, social and recreational activities; and (4) economic action (ibid.).

As described by Gasnier, the management style during the transfer of competences in the mid-1980s was one of lateral rather than hierarchical co-ordination. The directors-general played a central role in co-ordination across the services and in guaranteeing the coherence of policy under the president. The director-general is the 'president's man', signing directives for him in 90 per cent of cases, putting into administrative form projects and ideas or gauging their feasibility. 'This complex interplay of different actors is often the result of long and repeated efforts to escape from unitary decision-making, the effectiveness of which is so much the greater in that matters are "agreed" precisely between parties. The complexity does not engender confusion but an approach of greater sharpness and subtlety which often makes execution so much the more rapid.' It is a system of integrated working, very different from that which stereotypes of French inter-personal attitudes would seem to imply.

The Région

The internal structures of the 22 regional authorities differ from those of the départements mainly in that they are bicameral. They have advisory economic and social committees (ECOSOCs) to represent the interests of main groups in their area in addition to their councils. Wide differences in their administrative arrangements are due partly to differing concepts of their role. That role however is essentially strategic, and their success in working with and through the départements and communes within their boundaries is fundamental to its achievement.

The Regional Council or Assembly

The size of the regional councils ranges from 31 members for Guyane with 91 thousand inhabitants to 197 for the Île-de-France which has over ten million. The council 'regulates the affairs of the région by its deliberations' (*'règle par ses délibérations les affaires de la région'*).

It has a duty to promote the région's development in the economic, social, health, cultural and scientific fields, while preserving its identity and respecting the integrity, independence and functions of the départements and municipalities. It budgets and fixes the levels of its taxes. It collaborates in the development and implementation of the National Plan (§§ 2.1 and 2.7) and the physical development of the region. It draws up the regional plan within the provision of the National Plan and approves it after consulting the local authorities in its area.

The assembly delegates power to a bureau under the same conditions as a departmental council.

The Economic and Social Committee

A decree of 11 October 1982 gave equal membership of the economic and social committees (ECOSOCs) to enterprises and non-salaried profess-ionals on the one hand and unions of employees on the other. An additional 25 per cent of places are allocated to representatives from a range of organisations 'participating in the collective life of the nation'. The number of members ranges from 40 to 110. Regional councils are required to consider the advice of their economic and social committees on matters connected with the National Plan and on the general structure of the region's draft budget. Committee reports are submitted to the government with those of the regional council. In addition to the committee's mandatory role it is involved in consultations on many types of economic, social and cultural projects.

The Regional Executive

The president of the regional council is its sole executive. His duties are framed in the same terms as those of the president of the departmental council, excluding the latter's specific competences regarding traffic police and co-ordination of works. He is also responsible for certain administrative matters relating to the economic and social committee.

Presidents may delegate competences and rights of signature to vice-presidents and rights of signature to officers. In a survey of 1983 the

181

'tandem of president and director-general' was shown to be tied together in mutual dependence at the top of the administration. One prefect wrote in 1983 that it was on the 'solidarity' of the 'tandem' and the confidence in each other that united them that the success of decentralisation depended (Schmitt, 1985).

Departmental structure varies widely. In 1985 Aquitaine had five different groupings (administrative and financial, technical, aids to local authorities and vocational training), while Provence-Alpes-Côte d'Azur had seven (urban planning and housing, economic intervention, local development, health and social services, education, research and lands).

A notable feature of most regions is their dependence on agencies, which in some cases are chaired by regional vice-presidents with delegated powers. In Aquitaine in the early 1980s there were ten vice-presidents with responsibilities for agriculture, energy, culture, research etc. The membership of these agencies generally includes strong representation from the departmental councils. They play an important role in decisions on assistance to local authorities. Provence-Alpes-Côte d'Azur had agencies concerned with agricultural and forest planning, tourism and leisure, transport and communications, the environment, energy, vocational training, culture, maritime matters, action on women's matters, informatics and new technology and Mediterranean co-operation and development.

The Regional Administration

Arrangements and relationships in regional administration are basically the same as those for the départements described above, but more heavily orientated towards the planning and research functions.

General

There is a clear separation of powers in law between the deliberative body (the council) and the executive (the mayor of president of the council) at all three sub-national levels. Politically the relationship between the two main organs of local government is extremely close, mayors and presidents normally leading the largest party or joint party list and both sharing the collective responsibility to meet local needs. The balance is weighted heavily in favour of the executive since the council has no power to remove the holder of the office. Moreover he or she is normally the political architect of the council majority's membership through the list system, mediator between the commune and outside institutions, public and private, in an interdependent relationship, and operator of the central channels of communication with government and the central bureaucracy.

2.12 CITIZEN PARTICIPATION AND DECENTRALISATION WITHIN CITIES

General

Participation of voters at municipal elections in the 1980s was about 70 per cent or above. That for departmental elections sank exceptionally low in 1989 to 47 per cent. The turn-out for 1986 elections by contrast was 78 per cent.

France is remarkable for the number of people who hold seats as elected representatives, some half a million (see §2.2). There are many other members of the public, probably hundreds of thousands, involved in consultative bodies, including a wide range of associations.

There is extensive corporate involvement through state-sponsored chambers of trade and commerce and trade unions. In the regions the participation of local associations is built into the structure by means of the economic and social committees described in the previous section. It is facilitated at more local levels by legislation for setting up consultative committees within the framework of municipalities or joint municipalities. Since 1976, laws have provided for associations concerned with environmental improvement and town and country planning matters to play a consultative role in municipal procedures. Public colloquia, surveys and questionnaires are also used. There are requirements for the appointment of representatives of family associations to the membership of social aid bureau and for tenants to be represented on administrative boards of low-rent housing bodies (HLMs).

Some local authorities arrange for associations to assist in or to be totally responsible for running sports centres, day nurseries, hostels, cultural centres etc. Objective criteria are used to determine approval of associations, e.g. that they have been registered for at least three years.

The new government in 1981 made participation of citizens one of its primary goals. Expectations have been largely disappointed. Nevertheless France is in comparative terms a high performer as regards citizen involvement.

Decentralisation Within the Cities

In 1982 the government decided to initiate a stronger pattern of decentralisation in the largest cities. A bill was fought through parliament against strong opposition, most notably that of Jacques Chirac, Mayor of Paris. Elected sub-municipal councils for *arrondissements* were set up in Paris, Lyon and Marseille. Their average population is 100,000 in Paris and Marseille (where there is some grouping of arrondissements under joint councils) and 60,000 in Lyon. The arrondissement councils and their mayors act 'in the name of' their city councils.

Arrondissement councils consist of 20 members in Paris, 16 in Marseille and 9 in Lyon. Two-thirds of their members are directly elected by proportional representation in accordance with the procedures for communes with populations of over 3,500 (see §2.10). The remaining third are city councillors elected for the area concerned. Each council elects its own mayor and adjoints. The mayor and one of the adjoints must be municipal councillors.

In the elections candidates' names appear on the same lists as those of candidates for council seats at the time of the communal elections. Selection is by a process of weighted proportional representation.

Each arrondissement possesses an 'initiatives and consultation committee' representing local associations and national associations active in the area. The law requires the arrondissement council to give the committee all the information it needs for its work. A mixed committee of representatives of the city council and of the arrondissements was set up to deal with some matters of joint concern. (Luchaire, 1989)

Arrondissement Powers and Functions

An arrondissement council may intervene on all matters of interest in its arrondissement by expressing wishes in writing to the mayor or orally to the municipal council. It is to be consulted by the municipal council on town planning matters, assistance to associations and conditions of admission to crèches, kindergarten, homes for the elderly etc. It may be given delegated services relating to the daily life of its inhabitants such as for young children, sports facilities etc., representation of inhabitants, allocation of social housing after consultation with associations concerned and bringing life to its area by means of committees for local initiatives and consultation. It may be noted that in general it has few substantial rights of action of its own and depends very much on delegation by the commune. The arrondissement budget is part of the city budget. Revenue consists of an obligatory grant determined in negotiations between the arrondissement and the city council.

The Mayor and Adjoints

The responsibilities of mayors of arrondissements include dealing with matters of civil status, elections, town planning and the commune's properties. They are, however, likely to be dependent on the commune's administration in these matters, being subject to communal regulations. They have responsibility for preparing commune business and carrying out their councils' decisions. They chair and serve as executives of the local schools' finance committee. They deal with school attendance matters and registration for national service. They have an important advisory role regarding land use, issuing planning permits and dealing with land and building transactions in the area; and control of arrondissement staff allocated to them by the mayor of the city. They can propose whoever they wish to serve as secretary-general to the arrondissement.

There is provision for other cities to be given similar institutions, paricularly in the case of amalgamations of communes of over 100,000 inhabitants.

Functional Decentralisation

Administrative decentralisation through local town halls and other means by which citizens can obtain local access to information and services are a common feature in larger communes. Laws provide for separate municipal bodies with individual legal status and control over their own budgets for purposes which include control of expenditure from funds for school meals services, pupil transport, vacation colonies etc.; social welfare bureau; certain health functions; and housing (HLMs (see §2.8)). In addition local authorities may delegate the provision of some local services to private corporations, a power most often used for setting up cultural and recreational associations. The mayor chairs their boards and councillors are often board members.

2.13 THE GOVERNANCE OF METROPOLITAN AREAS

General

In general French metropolitan areas have spread out from a central city like blots of ink, absorbing villages and small towns into one closely-knit economic entity. But they have not absorbed these small governmental units into a political unit. The communes have usually retained individual identities rooted in medieval institutions. The boundaries of the départements defined in the revolutionary era have also generally remained the same.

Greater Paris

The population of the Paris area has spread from its historic centre, the *Ville-de-Paris*, across three départements (the 'little crown') and into four outer départements (the 'great crown'). The outer boundaries of the eight départements defined the regional planning area of the Île-de-Paris which acquired an elected council with its own executive in 1986. It has a population of between ten and eleven million and a total area of over 12,000 square kilometres. Its inhabitants outside the boundaries of central commune and département of the Ville-de-Paris are gradually approaching four times the latter's number. The area is over 113 times the Ville-de-Paris area and includes large districts beyond about ten kilometres from the centre of Paris which retain much of their rural character.

Greater Paris has in all five levels of government: 20 arrondissements within the Ville-de-Paris (see §2.12), communes (123 within the inner départements and 1,156 in the outer ones), webs of joint authorities (*établissements publiques* (§2.5)), eight départements and the encompassing region of the Île-de-France.

The characteristics of these bodies have been described in other sections of this chapter. The region can be described as an 'enabling' authority that supports the work that is relevant to its strategies carried out by the much more than a thousand organisations concerned with the provision of public services in its area. It is responsible for regional plans covering land use and development; housing development for low-income families in the centre and outside; business and job development including training services, energy policies, development of waste land and business and job subsidies; transport by road and rail to improve circulation between internal areas and communication with outside; and improvement of the quality of life generally, including co-ordinated action to improve town centres, green spaces, noise pollution, water purification and river control, conservation of historic area and sports centres.

The powers of the Mayor of Paris are similar to those of other French mayors excepting the omission of those relating to the municipal police. He authorises expenditures and chairs various municipal bodies, including a council for public assistance and the *bureau d'aide social* (social aid bureau).

The Council of Paris votes three budgets: those of the Commune of Paris, the Département of Paris, and the police; the last being prepared and administered by the special 'Prefect of Police'.

The Urban Communities ((*Communautés Urbaines*) (*CUs*))

The nine urban communities whose status is described in §2.5 were set up under a law of 1966. Under a law of 1982 a CU can be dissolved by order of the Council of Ministers at the request of two-thirds of member municipal councils representing at least three-quarters of its population or, alternatively, of three-quarters of the councils representing at least two-thirds of its population. CUs have structures that rest on the participation of their constituent communes. But they possess fiscal powers and a long list of mandatory competences that have given rise to complaints that they are absorbing communal powers. They can transfer the development or management of facilities to one or more communes or groupings of communes and, complementarily, a member commune can transfer its development functions or the management of certain of its own services or institutions to the CU. The CU can also provide technical services relevant to its competences to a member commune on request. It can co-operate with external authorities to provide amenities, initiate services and undertake studies of common interest.

Its competences include structure and town planning instruments; housing programmes and land banks; urban renovation and rehabilitation; construction and management of school sites; fire, passenger transport, water, sewage and refuse services; lycées and collèges; cemeteries and crematoria; abattoirs and meat markets; markets of national interest; and roads, traffic signals and car parks. Communes can retain powers over roads, housing and cemeteries and crematoria when they are principally intended for the inhabitants of the commune. The structure enables responsibilities to be tiered in deals negotiated to secure an optimum division of tasks. Municipalities and private companies collaborate in its activities 'to stimulate and co-ordinate the economic development of the region, and step in where for lack of economic support and for other reasons, individual municipalities fail' (Berg, Kink and Meer, 1992).

The membership of councils varies from 50 to 140 according to the size and number of its member communes. Larger communes select their own members; smaller communes select their own in 'colleges' of mayors. In choosing members of the communauté's bureau or board, the local authorities secure balanced participation in the executive. A 'grand notable' as president can carry great advantages. For example, Pierre Mauroy, Mayor of Lille, Prime Minister of France in the government that effected the decentralisation reforms of the early 1980s and President of the Communauté-de-Lille since then, has been a great asset to local interests. He is also director of Euralille, the société d'économie mixte which has played the leading role in the development of the express rail junction area between Belgium, Britain and France.

Within the limits of their competences councils of urban communities administer their affairs under the same conditions as municipal councils. They appoint a president and four to twelve adjoints who make up the bureau. The president serves as executive under similar provisions to those of mayors. He plays a representative role for his urban community and can delegate functions to vice-presidents.

Unless all the member communes are represented on the council the president is required to call together all the mayors of the community for consultation before the vote on the budget, and also at the demand of a majority of the mayors, or alternatively of two-thirds of the mayors of the communes not directly represented. There is provision for setting up consultative committees of mayors of groups of constituent communes. Mayors of member communes without representation on the council are asked to attend in a consultative role when matters affecting their communes are under discussion.

Communautés set their own rates of tax on the same four main tax bases as the communes (§2.9) in parallel with other levels of sub-national government. They levy specific rates and charges related to functions transferred to them from the communes. They also receive shares of the block grants related to the competences they exercise for recurrent and capital expenditures and other forms of central grants. They make three year 'planning contracts' (*contrats de plan*) for urban development with the state.

Reasons have been identified at to why some CUs have been more successful than others. They clearly depend on strong and effective leadership, the ability to win finance from other levels and a certain degree of willingness among their members to work together and build consensus. The facilitatory role of the prefectoral corps and other central officials has been important. As so often, interests are so thickly intertwined in French territorial administration that it is impossible to weigh individual contributions. While by 1992 the CU de Lille had established a well-integrated regional development policy which is integral to regional and national planning, the Strasbourg CU had not found sufficient solidarity among its members to allow one to be drawn up and implemented. There have been hostile reactions to government plans to extend obligations to development and welfare of immigrant settlements beyond their existing boundaries.

In general they appear to have been a qualified success. Their motivation, however, appears to be chiefly connected with the power they can exercise in attracting finance from higher levels and spreading the benefits among their members. (Berg, Kink and Meer, 1992; Norton, 1983)

3. ITALY

3.1 HISTORY AND TRADITIONS

The Diversity of Italy

The tendency to stereotype nations is always misleading but rarely more so than in the case of Italy. The contrast between the relatively poor South and the prosperous and sophisticated cities of the North is well known, but the complexity of the country can be understood only in finer terms. Most of the areas of its twenty regional governments are more or less coterminous with social identities developed by ancient mixtures of settlers, contrasting geographies and regimes imposed on inhabitants in the years before the unification of the 1860s. It is claimed that the Italians speak at least twenty different languages.

People in the northern regions — Piedmont northwards from Tuscany to Umbria, Lombardy and Emilia-Romagna — rate themselves high on industrial dynamism, incomes, work opportunities and prospects, while the six southernmost regions are, with North-West Ireland, the gloomiest in the European Community about future prospects. The EC survey body, Eurostat, found at the beginning of the 1980s that per capita gross domestic product was higher in the same northern regions than in the South-East of England while in the six southern regions and Sardinia the per capita GDP was lower than in any region of the United Kingdom.

The great economic growth and resilience that Italy has shown since the late 1940s have been maintained until recently under what elsewhere might have been regarded as critical levels of inflation and deficit-finance. After a breakneck rate of industrial expansion in the 1950s and 1960s in which large areas around the great cities north of Rome were colonised by major industry and a great new workforce recruited predominantly from the South, the country has achieved a prominent status as a modern industrial power.

Historical Background

Modern Italy first acquired a degree of national unity in 1802 as a member of the Napoleonic Empire. That unity was lost when the empire collapsed, but recreated in the twelve years following the war of 1859. The Napoleonic prefectoral system influenced the regimes in most of the states into which Italy was re-divided in 1815-16. After 1859 a mixture of war, revolution and diplomacy brought about unification in the form of a liberal state based on the model of the Piedmontese constitutional monarchy of 1848, including its administrative and local government systems. Piedmont provided a highly centralised uniform Napoleonic model (Giannini, 1967; Bartole et al., 1984). The Rattazzi Law of 1859 based on a Piedmontese law of 1848 provided the structural framework for local administration throughout Italy, supervised by a strong prefectoral system. This has remained the formal system, modified by codifications in laws of 1911, 1915 and 1934 and reforms since 1945.

The basic element is the commune, defined as the local inhabitants of the administrative area electing their own council by direct election. The council elects an executive consisting of a mayor (*sindaco*) and a collegial board of assistant mayors (*giuntà* of *assessori*). The provinces and regions have similar structures (see §3.11), co-existing with the local offices of central government.

Until the First World War government was dominated by bourgeois elites. Universal suffrage in 1913 was followed by a period of political instability in which no mature political leadership emerged. After the First World War the king, under the claim of establishing national unity, order and purpose, invited the leader of the relatively small Fascist Party, Benito Mussolini, to take over the premiership. A manipulated referendum followed, the results of which reflected a widespread disillusionment with the results of liberal democracy. Local democracy soon became non-existent in a real sense although the previous local structures remained.

Against the background of the sudden and total collapse of the fascist dictatorship during the Second World War determination was shown by new political leaders to establish a truly representative political system with constitutionally protected individual and political rights. The Constitution of 1948 embodied that objective.

Subsequently the Christian Democratic Party dominated Italian government for over twenty-five years. Despite a mass membership cemented together by a clientelist approach it was short of a parliamentary majority and relied on coalitions with centre parties. After 1960 the Communist Party succeeded in building up local strength and national reputation by showing its capacity in achieving efficient and effective municipal management in cities and regions where it was able to form alliances with other political elements and thereby initiate long-term economic and social policies. These pragmatic approaches broke down in 1979 due to fears on the outer wings of both the Communist and Christian Democratic

Parties that association with each other would be self-defeating. The stability achieved during the mid-eighties under a coalition led by a Socialist Prime Minister showed that new patterns of political control were possible.

The 1970s and 1980s have been periods of rapid social and economic change with an economic growth rate continually above the average for the OECD. The period saw great improvements in social and health services and in the level of education. Italy could be seen in the late 1980s as a post-industrial society that has overcome the problem of basic needs and is mainly concerned with 'problems of individual freedom, opportunity and maximization of quality of life' (Nanetti, 1988). An entrepreneurial culture is unbounded by social class and there is 'widespread commitment to sustain the development that is found among diverse political, social and economic organizations'.

The year 1990 heralded radical changes in the internal structure of local authorities and in long-established patterns of political representation. A new law redefined the roles of council, giuntà and mayor. Electoral systems have been modified and the direct election of mayors introduced. The first direct election of mayors in June 1993 has no less changed the political map and, indeed, the political life of the nation. The prosecution of leading national and local politicians for corruption, most notably that connected with party funding, accelerated the growth of disaffection with the traditional parties and their popular support has collapsed dramatically — in parliamentary elections in 1992 and much more so in the first direct mayoral elections in June 1993. Christian Democrat and Socialist mayoral candidates were eliminated on a wide scale in the first stage of the electoral process. In the final round the candidates of the federalist Northern League were returned in most of the larger cities in the North while those of the Party of the Democratic Left, the ex-Communist PDS, maintained its leadership in the 'middle belt' from Emilia-Romagna to Tuscany and Umbria and replaced the Christian Democrats on a large scale in the South (see also §3.1).

Constitutional Background

The Constitution of 1948 was born of a deep and effective will to establish freedoms under the control of law. It defines Italy as a democratic republic 'founded upon labour', and gives guarantees of popular sovereignty, personal and domestic liberty and private property. The upper house, the Senate, is elected on a regional basis by direct popular vote.

One of the six main sections of the Constitution is devoted to the regions, provinces and communes (see §3.2). The last section provides for constitutional guarantees and a Constitutional Court of 15 members nominated one-third by the president, one-third by parliament and one-third by the magistrature. The Court adjudicates on the constitutionality of acts of the state, regions, president and ministers and on conflicts regarding powers between the state and the regions.

Parties

The parties provide channels of influence between localities and the centre on a broader and more comprehensive scale than perhaps in any other advanced democracy. The new Italian state that emerged from the Second World War was largely their joint creation. They are virtually part of the state and their campaign expenses have until recently been met in part by public funding.

Parties have had mass memberships: the Christian Democrats and Communists both over one and a half million members and others up to half a million, constituting in the 1980s over fifteen per cent of the electorate, although less than five per cent have been active within the parties. Party membership implies commitment to a particular political ideology, although within each main party there are opposing factions. Most parties have been linked with particular unions and associations of various kinds — even sports associations — and organise cultural festivals. They have been integrated deeply into popular life. Party authority has been achieved by a pyramid of democratic representation: village and town sections elect section heads, who elect provincial committees, who elect regional committees, who elect the national committee. Most party elections have been by proportional representation, which ensures that the strength of factions within the party is weighted according to numerical strength.

The party bureaucracy has tended to dominate at lower levels. National party leaders often have local bases of strength which they are expected in many areas to maintain by patronage. Patronage and ideological commitment have, however, been in decline in recent years. Information about individual parties is given in §3.10.

Clientelism and Corporativism

Relations within the political system have often been explained by the concepts of clientelism and corporativism. The model of clientelism is based predominantly on studies of the South, the *Mezzogiorno*. Clientelistic relationships depend on exchange of support and benefits originating in a society in which local 'notables' sought to maintain popular support by use of political office, 'bending the rules' to provide protection as well as legitimate services. Modern socio-economic developments made it necessary for them to 'capture' wider interest groups than the traditional ones. In the words of a Sicilian politician, clientelism 'now concerns entire (social) categories, coalitions of interests, groups of (private) employees, employees of public office or of regional enterprises.... In order to put this powerful machine to work the Christian Democrats have placed party men in positions at every level of power.... Today clientelism is a relationship between large groups and public power' (Graziano, 1973). This has led to a new openness of the patron class: anyone with some talent, a party connection and strong initiative can aspire to 'patronship'.

More significant nationally is the degree of corporatism: the heavy involvement of sectoral interest organisations in national and sub-national decision-making. A theoretical distinction needs to be made between clientelism on the one hand and the close horizontal or 'family' relationships between organised, politicised interest groups and political parties (*parentela*) on the other. In the latter relationship there are mutual interests and some sharing of policy aims between particular major interest groups and the parties with which they are associated. This is to be found strongly in the trade union movement, industry, commerce, catholicism and elsewhere. But in terms of political support it is important to bear in mind the significance of ideological factors and 'the more modernised patterns of relationship between the political system and the citizenry in operation mainly in northern urban areas' (Dente, 1985a).

General

As a consequence of the splitting of interests between sectors and parties and the great number of political centres involved in decision-making the system is one of extreme political fragmentation. It can, however, be argued that this is a justifiable response to the complexity of interests within modern society and therefore a condition of effective choice for the individual. Like Germany, Italy claims to be a 'state based on law'. Resting on its interpretation of the law, the administrative bureaucracy has been compartmentalised and rigidly legalistic. The chief justification for the decentralisation of power to the regions and elected provincial and communal councils was to bring decision-making into touch with the varied and wide-ranging nature of local problems.

This has been compatible with a conservative approach to structure. The

Local Government Law 142 of 8 June 1990 has re-codified and carried forward the approach which received its classic definition in the Ragazzi Law of 1859. It also initiated important changes in the internal and national structures of local government described below. Law 241 of 1990 which followed required authorities to define a locus of responsibility for stages in the decision-making process to make transparent where accountability lies.

The system has been called 'centripetal pluralism' (Farneti, 1985). It has maintained a state of stability through constitutionalism, despite what has often been called a condition of continuous crisis. In spite of its faults it has scored well in the fields of economic success and social welfare. The country has overcome many of its greatest problems and major reforms have taken place, not least in the field of local government.

3.2 THE STATUS OF LOCAL AND REGIONAL GOVERNMENT

Constitutional Status

The Constitutional Assembly of 1947 aimed to override the Napoleonic tradition of political and administrative centralisation which had been exploited so disastrously by the fascist regime. Article 5 of the 1948 Constitution declares that the 'one and indivisible Republic' recognises and promotes autonomous local authorities and is to effect the widest decentralisation of administration in the services which depend on the state and to conform in its principles and methods of legislation with the requirements of autonomy and decentralisation.

The Constitution conceives regional and local government as integral parts of a national political system based on law. It gives sweeping responsibilities to the regions in response to demands to restore power in domestic matters to areas with distinct historical identities. Thus Article 115 provides that 'The Regions are constituted as autonomous entities with their own powers and functions according to the principles determined in the Constitution'.

The intention was to retain at the centre the prerogative for legislation on aims and principles while building in flexibility at the regional level through the law-making and administrative powers of the newly conceived regional governments. Thus Article 117 states that 'The Region issues legal precepts (*norme*) for the following matters within the fundamental principles established by State laws, providing that such precepts do not conflict with the interest of the State and other Regions: the organisation of the communes, departments and the dependent administrative bodies of the Region, communal boundaries, local police, fairs and markets, public assistance and assistance for health and hospital services, vocational training, educational assistance, local museums and libraries, town planning, tourism and tourist accommodation, tramways, roads, road networks, aqueducts and public works of regional interest, inland ports and navigation, mineral and thermal waters, quarries and peat extraction, hunting and inland fishing, agriculture and forests, handicraft, and other matters defined in constitutional laws or delegated by the State. The laws of the Republic can endow the Region with the power to issue precepts (*norme*) for their implementation.' The administrative functions for these matters are to be determined by the region with delegation to communes and other local bodies excepting those that are exclusively attributed by the laws of the Republic to the provinces, communes or other local authorities (see §3.6).

The Constitution gives all sub-national levels equal dignity and autonomy. It treats them as separate entities not subordinate one to another. Yet the powers of provinces and communes are to be exercised within the 'ambit' of the region. Since the regions provide in their own constitutions and legislation for the local levels of government, there exists, in a sense, a subordination. Yet the system remains truly pluralistic in law. The provinces and communes are in no sense creatures of the state or of the regions: they are the creatures of the Republic through the Constitution, just as are the national institutions of government.

Law 142 of 1990 lays down that communes and provinces have statutory and financial autonomy within the ambit of the laws and the co-ordination of public finance. Each local authority is required to have its own statute, published in the region's official bulletin, embodying the requirements of the law on organisation and procedures, including forms of collaboration with other local authorities and arrangements for popular participation, decentralisation within its own boundaries in the case of larger communes and access of citizens to information to ensure that they are able to exercise their rights of participation.

Hierarchical Authority and Controls

The principal legislation regarding services is developed and promulgated in Rome. This provides frameworks within which regions and local authorities make their decisions. The local authority therefore acts both within national provisions and within those enacted by its regional government. The means by which the state has sought to ensure this are described in §3.6.

A regional government is required to legislate for the internal administrative organisation of its territory and to make provision for rights of referendum and initiative in its laws and administrative provisions.

The regions have financial autonomy and their own taxes, which according to the Constitution should relate to regional needs. In practice, however, they are overwhelmingly dependent on state provisions for their revenues, as are the communes. In the mid-1980s only about six per cent of regional revenues came from the regions' own taxes and charges. The corresponding figure for communes was near to ten per cent.

Real or Illusory Status?

The constitutional status of local authorities is in many ways a strong one: they exercise local functions defined by the state and carry out the functions for which their regions legislate. Their responsibilities have been built up within the constitutional provisions from what was in 1945 a very low point indeed. The creation of five 'special regions' apart, political fears and administrative delay held back the completion of regionalisation until the late 1970s. The regions were the necessary instruments through which state functions were extensively decentralised to local authorities.

There remains the subjective sense of status which is distinct from that in law. 'The progressive, but now old-established transformation of local authorities from administrative authorities into providers of services for their communities radically modifies the situation. If they are not predominantly concerned with regulating public behaviour but with transfer of values (not necessarily quantifiable in economic terms), then issues of liberty and authority are not the only (and in many cases not the principal) dimension by which communal activities may be assessed.' (Dente, 1985b, translated from Italian)

The practical scope for free exercise of statutory autonomy may appear small, given the mass of regulations which control their actions. However the controls over obligatory services are in general by no means suffocating. The able politician or officer can find much space for action within the system. Moreover there remains a tradition of autonomous competence undefined by law. The right to provide transport, pharmaceutical and other services had previously been recognised in a law of 1927. After the war the wealthy cities of the North and the central cities with communist leadership developed the provision of crèches and nursery schools, school meals and after-school activities, transport systems, preventive medicine, airports and motorways (§3.7). To quote an article in *The Times* relating to the slump of the early 1980s, 'Regions and Communes have been mostly left to themselves' but 'have shown great adaptability and flexibility in meeting recession' (16 June 1983). Against this picture is the fact that thousands of small and poor authorities lack the resources to make any use of the potential powers widely exercised by progressive cities in the North. Constitutionally the principle of equality of power and treatment applies, but in practice equality of treatment regardless of size and influence is a myth. The principle of equality has created severe problems regarding national distribution of powers, finance and collaboration.

The status of the great city confers benefits on its councillors. There is a political career movement from city and province to region and from region to national government, a *cursus honorum* which attracts the politically ambitious to attempt to demonstrate their capacity at city level as a basis for a national career. Achievement is easily recognised by party and public since mayors and to some extent other political leaders carry known responsibilities and are subject to the light of publicity. The secretariats of the political parties can spot talent and back its promotion from level to level. This does not imply that civic service enjoys the regard that may be desirable — especially among the younger generation. The reasons lie partly in the values discussed in the following section.

3.3 CONCEPTS AND VALUES

One word much used by writers on modern Italian politics is 'particularism' in the sense of putting particular personal or local interests before broader or national ones. This is hardly peculiar to Italy. Perhaps the distinguishing feature of Italian particularism is not so much individualism or localism, although these are strong, but rather the sensitivity of the political system to such interests. This relates closely to the force of clientelism and *parentela* (see §3.1).

It is said that in comparison with northern countries everything in Italian life is now politicised, that is linked with the interests of political parties. This raises the question of how the resulting conflicts have been so peacefully contained. A part of the answer lies in Italian constitutionalism. The 41 articles of the Constitution setting out the rights and duties of individuals are parts of the Italian consciousness as well as of the legal system. They not only set out liberal rights — inviolability of the home, secrecy of correspondence, and rights of assembly, religion, thought and expression, legal action, education and others, but also economic and welfare rights including trade union organisation, private property, enterprise and social assistance. This is in the context of a statement of the civic duties of the individual and the responsibilities of the Republic to the family, children, the sick, the unemployed and the disabled. It is an expression of the social commitment of the state to duties which were and remain fundamental to both the Christian Democrat and the parties-of-the-left view of the relationship between state and society.

The electoral system described in §3.10 carried fairness to all voters and parties to a point which is perhaps only equalled in Scandinavia. The sharing of benefits of participation in ruling coalitions is also finely tuned. Participation, at least in voting if not in some other ways, is extremely high (§3.12).

The combination of clientelism and interest group involvement in a society characterised by a high level of political activity and competitiveness results in a cancelling out of partisan political initiatives, and therefore by and large in a low level of achievement of distinct party aims. This is the price of the high stability of the system, as opposed to the instability of governments as hard-won coalitions fall apart and are laboriously replaced. Against this in the early 1990s there is a strong movement to break through the resistance to change that results and institute a form of majoritarian voting to make possible strong action to stem economic problems. Against this level of achievement of high-level values must be set the darker side. The Mafia and Camorra are related to clientelism but receive general moral condemnation in Italy, along with the cases of high corruption in the politico-business worlds of Rome, Milan and Turin — corruption which feeds widespread disillusionment amongst those involved in the political system and those outside it.

Political awareness seemed to reach a high point in the early 1980s. Well over half the respondents in a survey declared themselves strongly or somewhat interested in politics (58 per cent in 1981 as opposed to 37 per cent in 1958) and 62 per cent said that they often discussed politics with their friends compared with 32 per cent in 1958 (Nanetti, 1988). But a survey of the mid-1980s showed a heavy incidence of dissociation from the system, especially among the young. Almost a quarter of 15 to 19 year olds rejected parties completely, and of the remainder two-thirds were detached from or indifferent to trade unions and parties. The survey not only indicated disillusionment with institutions of a political nature but also showed a high regard for social values: 92.5 per cent view the institution of the family favourably, 78.7 per cent school, 77.3 per cent the Church and 69.2 per cent the parish. Community attachment is still strong among the great majority (*La Repubblica*, 14-15 April, reporting a national survey by CENSIS).

Another feature is the tendency, as in Germany, towards seeking answers in the law. This has had a centralising influence, clearest in the culture of the public sector where every action demands legal justification, tests of competence, decision and communication before enforcement (Dente, 1985b).

Two books summarise behavioural essentials without which Italy cannot be understood: Italians 'possess a much higher tolerance for uncertainty, confusion, and complexity than any other Western people... natural Jeffersonians,...' considering 'little and weak government safer than strong and effective government' (Spotts and Wieser, 1986); and 'This has not been an immobilist democracy, stagnating because of the incapacity of its political leadership or institutions. If the idea of a living constitution creates creative adapation to growing or unexpected challenges, without sacrifice of democracy itself in the process, I know of no postwar democracy with a better record....' (LaPalombara, 1987).

To quote from an Italian source which confirms what I have seen in practice, 'Italian municipalities have the common characteristic of being able to respond to the changing demands and needs of the community. Compared with higher levels of government, this high flexibility in municipal policy is clearly visible since, periodically, some themes emerge and develop on a local level in a relatively short time, spreading from one locality to another.... Types of social policy (from day care to home help) have followed this dynamic and only found outlet on a national level at a later stage' (Dente, 1991). This is true also of the 'spontaneous proliferation of neighbourhood councils, cultural policies, and, more recently, of new policies to foster economic growth'.

3.4 NATIONAL STRUCTURE

Italy has four principal levels of government (see Table 3.1), and also in the larger cities, a sub-municipal structure described in §3.12. There are also the large number of special joint bodies established for special functions described in §3.5.

Table 3.1: Local Authority Numbers, Average Areas and Populations

Class	Number	Average Area (sq. km.)	Average Population
Regions (*Regioni*)	20	15,064	2,887,308
Provinces (*Provincie*)	95	3,171	607,854
Communes (*Comuni*)	8,100	42	7,129

Source: Annuario Statistico Italiano, 1991, from Tables 2.13 and 2.14

The Regions

The development of regional government has had wide effects in all sectors (*Le Relazione Centro-Periferia*, 1984; Putnam, Leonardi and Nanetti, 1985; Leonardi, Nanetti and Putnam, 1987; Nanetti, 1988). Constitutional provisions were implemented quickly in 1948 and 1963 for the peripheral areas of Sicily, Sardinia, Trentino/Alto-Adige, Friuli-Venezia Giulia and Val d'Aosta. The German-speaking Province of Bolzano was given special autonomous status in 1969. These 'regions with special status' were followed in 1970 by the election of the other councils.

After the first regional elections the regional reform passed through three phases (Putnam, Leonardi and Nanetti, 1985; Leonardi, Nanetti and Putnam, 1987): the 'messianic' or 'constituent' phase when it was seen as the key to the democratisation of Italian political life and the first powers were conferred; mobilisation culminating in the victory of a 'regional front' leading to key legislation in 1975 and 1977; and managerial in which the regions came to assume major responsibilities for policies. The most important step was the 616 Decrees of 1977 which virtually redefined regional functions.

Table 3.2: Regions, Populations and Number of Communes

Region	Population (000)	Communes
Piedmont	4,356	1,207
Valle d'Aosta	116	74
Lombardy	8,939	1,546
Trento-Alto Adige	891	339
Bolzano-Bozen	442	116
Trento	450	223
Veneto	4,398	582
Friuli-Venezia Giulia	1,201	219
Liguria	1,719	235
Emilia-Romagna	3,928	341
Tuscany	3,563	287
Umbria	822	92
Marche	1,436	246
Lazio	5,191	376
Abruzzi	1,272	305
Molise	336	136
Campania	5,853	551
Puglia	4,082	257
Basilicata	625	131
Calabria	2,154	409
Sicily	5,197	390
Sardinia	1,664	375
Italy	57,576	8,098

Source: From *Annuario Statistico Italiano 1991,* 1991, Table 2.14

Details of regions and quasi-regional provinces are given in Table 3.2. The smallest is the special province, the Valle d'Aosta, which was given substantial autonomy for political and cultural reasons.

The Commune

Table 3.3: Number of Communes in population brackets and percentages of national population, 1990

Population	Number	Percentage of National Population
Under 5,000	5,095	15
5-10 000	1,149	14
10-20 000	588	13
20-50 000	311	16
50-100 000	86	9
100-500 000	44	13
Over 500 000	6	13
Total	8,100	

Source: Annuario Statistico Italiano 1991, 1991, Table 2.14

The extreme discrepancy in scale between the larger communes and the thousands of small rural communes has been a major obstacle to decentralisation of functions. The only exceptions to the principle of equality of provisions for communes regardless of size relate to the size of council, composition of the giuntà and a few fiscal and staffing matters. This has meant rigidities for the larger communes which are unjustifiable on grounds of resources, competences and the needs of the cities. It has also been the cause of much experimentation with inter-authority machinery (§3.5).

The level of fragmentation varies between regions. The average population size of communes in Puglia (15,881) is about eight times that in Piedmont (1,984). That in Central Italy is around twice that in the North. Hence the attempts to establish consortia of authorities in the North have been stronger than in the South.

Over half the communes with populations of below five thousand are in the mountains, often divided by ridges and other obstacles to communication, so that self-government is only meaningful in terms of the small village (Pola, 1984), although the problems are deeper than physical geography since geographical factors have been overridden in mountainous areas in Northern Europe.

The Provinces

Regions have from two to nine provinces within their boundaries. An original justification of the regions in 1859 was to provide for substantial decentralisation, but in practice the boundaries were fixed mainly for military convenience. Provincial councils were directly elected and appointed their own executives, but they lacked autonomy, finance and prestige.

The provinces are pivots of the political and administrative system in a number of ways: for inter-governmental co-ordination, for co-ordination between local services and for party organisation, bridging with the communal and the regional and national party levels. There was a movement for the abolition of the provincial level but agreement was reached in the mid-1980s that certain major functions, including development planning, should be under the responsibility of the provincial councils.

All but three provinces have populations within the span of 220 thousand to several million, the largest being those based on the great cities. The largest is that of Milan with a population of over four million, making up 45 per cent of its region. There are eleven with over a million inhabitants and 56 with under half a million.

With the redefinition of the status of the province has come an acceptance that major changes are necessary in its boundaries, chiefly to adjust them to the pattern of modern metropolitan areas. After repeated initiatives to overcome the problem, Law 142 of 1990 initiated a process under which regions affected were required to redefine areas to provide rational boundaries for a new form of province, to be called a 'metropolitan city'. This is to have additional powers to enable it to contribute to the economic, social and cultural balance of its area and region.

General

Little effort has been given to the reform of communal boundaries, despite the recognition that they present serious functional problems in terms of welfare standards. The only acceptable means to reorganise has been through the formation of 'unions' or communities of communes to carry out services, as described in the following section. Thus the debate has centred in recent years largely on the achievement of efficiency for the implementation of functions within a framework dating from the nineteenth century.

There would seem to be a strong case for eliminating the provincial level in the South where a combined provincial-regional level might more effectively deal with provincial level services, but feelings between areas within small regions can be strong. Each case will have a different configuration of communication and political forces to overcome.

3.5 INTER-AUTHORITY RELATIONS AND ORGANISATION

Joint Bodies

Joint boards are a long-established means of providing public utilities and cultural and environmental protection services including water purification and supply, land reclamation, solid waste disposal and recycling and country parks. They may take the private law form of companies owned entirely by local authorities or jointly with the private sector. In recent years attention has focused on finding a more satisfactory means for the provision of modern services under national and regional legislation which in most of the country require a wider area than the individual commune. The areas of provinces have been thought too big for the purpose and the functions concerned are essentially those of communes.

The 1977 Decrees provided for the regions to take the initiative in requiring communes to form joint multi-purpose inter-communal associations. One type was the mountain community (*communità montana*), of which there were some 350 in the early 1980s. They acquired responsibilities for health services where their boundaries were suitable, park administration, prevention of water pollution and administrative oversight of member communes. They are in some cases 'approaching the model of the fully-fledged all-purpose local government' (Nanetti, 1988). Regional legislation has provided for other forms, particularly for schools, special health districts (*unità sanitarie locali* (USL)) and municipal *consorzi* (consortia). The regional councils of Tuscany, Umbria and the Marche legislated for forms of multi-purpose community associations. There are also 'mega consortia' for special purposes, for example the Reggio Emilia Intercommunal Association for water and gas distribution has a membership of 42 communes.

School districts have very limited resources and powers, being in practice mainly consultative. Their members include civil servants, trade union and parents' representatives as well as local councillors.

The USLs were introduced as the local agencies in the sweeping health reform of 1978. They are joint communal associations except in the larger cities where they have a decentralised structure, as in Milan where there are twenty district health-care units with their own management committees and a central general assembly and co-ordinating body for integrated management of health and social services.

The scale and functions of such joint agencies have varied widely from region to region. Venezia has developed inter-communal bodies of a modest size to provide for basic communal functions, while Piedmont has set up bodies covering wide areas defined for economic and physical planning purposes. In some cases the joint agencies are single purpose and in others general purpose. They may be regional bodies which include representatives of the communes, or they may consist of commune representatives only. The attempts in Emilia-Romagna and Lombardy to set up joint bodies consisting of political representatives failed to mobilise sufficient support among the communes.

Inter-authority bodies are generally seen as problematic. The politicians who control them often concentrate on business which brings them electoral support, such as local investment and employment for their constituents, without regard to longer-term planning needs. The 1990 Local Government Act made new provisions for consorzi and for multi-purpose unions of communes. Constituent communes of the unions are to be generally of not more than five thousand inhabitants with the possible exception of one commune with five to ten thousand inhabitants. They are initially to form associations with their own budgets and within ten years are expected to amalgamate into a single commune.

Local Authority Associations

National associations of local authorities play an important and often powerful role in the representation of local interests. Two represent the main national levels of local government as a whole: the National Association of Italian Communes (Associazone Nazionale de Communi Italiani (ANCI), Via Prefetti 46, 00186 Roma), and the Union of Italian Provinces (Unione delle Province d'Italia (UPI), Piazza Borghese 3, 00186 Roma). Some are more specialised, including the National Association of Mountain Communes (Unione Nazionale dei Communi e degli Enti Locali (UNCEM)) and the Italian Confederation of Local Authority Public Services (Confederazione Italiana dei Servizi Pubblici degli Enti Locali (CISPEL)). All four have decentralised arrangements: *unioni*, sections, delegations and regional branches which have succeeded in evening out regional disparities of influence (Pregreffi, 1984).

They negotiate with departments on draft legislation, lobby deputies and senators to obtain amendments and assist departmental officials in their responsibilities, and play a central role in matters concerning local personnel, work with the central loans bank (Cassa Depositi e Prestiti) and the personnel control commission (ibid.). ANCI for example was founded in 1901 on the initiative of Roman Catholic and Socialist mayors. It is a statutory body whose primary objective has been to protect municipal autonomy against 'creeping centralisation' by influencing central government, parliament and the political parties. It has had remarkable success in bridging interests between communes of greatly differing sizes as well as between parties. It has developed a training function for local administrators and an information service. (Triglia, 1986)

3.6 INTER-GOVERNMENTAL RELATIONS

Central-Regional/Local Relations

In some matters national laws define practice in detail but others leave wide space for regions and local governments can define the law for their citizens. In the case of major changes such as the reorganisation of metropolitan government under Law 142 of 1990 a law may set a wide framework within which regions can legislate and provinces and communes prepare their own schemes, but it also sets a programme of action and reserves to the national executive the right to act in case of disagreement with regional proposals or a default on the time schedule. It distributes resources and to a limited extent exercises control over their use. A regional council may be dissolved if it promulgates acts which are contrary to the Constitution, commits grave violations of law or fails to replace an executive or president responsible for such offences. It can also be dissolved if it fails to function owing to resignations or the impossibility of forming a majority government or for reasons of national security. A decree for the dissolution of a regional council must include the appointment of a commission of three citizens eligible for appointment to such a council who must call an election within three months. The commission's other acts are subject to the ratification of the new council. In practice these procedures have rarely been invoked.

There are also provisions for the state or its agent to dissolve a local council and substitute a commissioner for reasons of public order or persistent legal violations, to suspend a council in cases of urgent necessity, and to suspend or remove a mayor. These powers are limited to prevent the possibility of political abuse and have also rarely been used in practice.

The main actors in matters of central policy that have a direct impact on regional and local authorities nationally are certain ministries and departments.

The Ministry of the Interior has controlled increases in and costs of local authority personnel through a control commission and the machinery for collective bargaining. It has also administered a special fund for the equalisation of local expenditures. It has tended to be regarded as the traditional enemy of local autonomy because of its legalistic approach to the subject. The advent of regional power, however, resulted in the cultivation of an alliance with local government interests to moderate the ambitions of the regions. It has had no inclination in this respect to contain communal expenditures: rather the opposite.

The Treasury has sought predictability of expenditures. The main means to achieve this has been to hold closely to incremental planning on the basis of historic expenditures. In this matter it had fair success in the early 1980s. It was much less successful in its efforts to contain local expenditure.

The Finance Department has resisted the introduction of new local taxes and maintained its quasi-monopoly of tax collection.

The Ministry and the Department of the Budget and Economic Planning have opposed the incremental system of financial transfers and have been regarded as allied with regional interests, like the Ministry for the Regions. But these ministries and the Department for Public Personnel have had no significant influence on local financial legislation.

The changes in the role of prefects are central to the development of the relationships between Rome and local authorities. Until recent times they exercised powers of tutelage and control and were regarded as the essential channel for communication downwards to and upwards from the local and provincial authorities (Fried, 1963). Remnants of prefectoral tutelage remain, particularly to ensure as far as necessary that regional and local decisions are in accordance with the principle of the rule of law. A government commissioner, successor to the prefect, resides in each region's capital city and has the duty of supervising the implementation of state functions and co-ordinating them with those exercised by the region. In cases defined by national statute the state can refer back regional acts for reconsideration by regional councils on the grounds of their merit. Any law approved by a regional council must be communicated to the state commissioner, who has thirty days in which to endorse it. After that period it may be promulgated after ten days and will then come into force twenty days later, or more quickly if it is agreed to be urgent. If the government considers that a regional law exceeds a region's competence it can return it to the regional council within a set period. If the council re-enacts the law the government can refer it to the Constitutional Court.

Prefects or commissioners still possess powers to collect and transmit information, to scrutinise the actions of public bodies and to adopt measures 'indispensable for the public interest in the different branches of the service'. Mayors have limited responsibilities as officials of central government and prefects can inspect their performance of these functions. Prefects are agents of the state and can issue emergency decrees and initiate substitutions for local bodies in some vital functions: public health and public safety and order and the local police, and also regarding registration and municipal building. Since 1981 they have been given additional powers for civil defence and public order matters and in the co-ordination of small local bodies through an advisory technical and legal service. (Sanantonio, 1987)

Regional-Local Authority Relationships

Article 118 of the Constitution states that 'the region normally exercises its administrative functions by delegating these to the provinces, communes and other local bodies'. This has been interpreted to mean that communes should be given powers of decision. Accordingly the regions have delegated service provision to local government, given financial support and attempted institutional reform.

Article 130 of the Constitution provides that an organ of the region will control the legality of the acts of the provinces, communes and other local public bodies, and that on request they can review local decisions on grounds of their merit and refer them back to local bodies for reconsideration. Quasi-autonomous regional committees of control, consisting of a number of 'experts' chosen by the regional council, a member appointed by the central government commissioner and a magistrate chosen by the regional administrative court, exercise powers of control as to legality, along with certain regional departments. They work through sub-divisions in each province. In the case of an authority failing to carry out obligatory functions the control committee can act in substitution for the authority.

Research in Lombardy found that the enormous increase in legislation and regulation resulted in a rapid expansion of cases referred to these bodies and thus overloaded them, resulting in the exclusion of minor matters, control by sampling according to the interests of members and selection by the official in charge of the preliminary inquiry. Cases are mostly referred back to an authority for elucidation or further information. The committee resorts to annulment only in extreme cases on grounds of violation of the law or lack of competence, and almost never for the 'excessive use of power' (Vandelli, 1984b). It paints a different picture from that of Sanantonio (1987), who concludes that local authorities are supervised in a very detailed way and 'that their powers of discretion are small'. The great volume of business in recent years has made comprehensive scrutiny of local acts impossible in most cases and the regional bodies concerned have limited their attention to samples, particular categories of acts or those brought specially to their notice (ibid.).

A major study on the recent history of the regions gives the uncertainty of the nature of their relations with local authorities as one of their leading problems (Putnam, Leonardi and Nanetti, 1985). The leading activity of the region was from the start conceived as planning, hence the attempt to develop *comprensori*, associations of communes by means of which planning intentions could be realised in local areas. This was a problematic area in such a highly political society. Planning ideas often failed to take account of the speed of development. An emphasis on a joint role with the communes seems a much more realistic approach, in which the regions provide 'leverage' of different kinds at different levels in the development and implementation of development programmes which have been evolved in a close relationship with communal interests. Emilia-Romagna provides a model of this approach (Leonardi and Nanetti, 1990).

A large proportion of regional income is transferred to local authorities to finance the implementation of national policy. A Council of Europe study comments that the Italian regions 'would seem to have a co-ordinating and supervisory function tied to planning, restricted to certain earmarked transfers from central to local government and applying solely to the apportionment of resources among providers of services and to supervision of the use of funds'. They are the intermediaries for transport, vocational training, social welfare and public works funding, according to agreed programmes and subject to supervision of expenditure. Regions in many cases approve schemes for which local authorities seek finance as being in accordance with the regional development plan. They apportion state finance for health among the local health authorities and have a duty to ensure that they are used efficiently and to good purpose. But the regions have no authority over the bulk of local authority funding, which is directly allocated from the centre (*The Relationships between the Various Levels of Local Administration under a Regional Organisation*, Council of Europe, 1984). They lack any but marginal financial resources of their own: Rome holds the purse strings (see §3.9). They are accused of distributing 'money provided by national laws, following the criteria established in the legislation in a more or less random way' (Dente, 1985b).

The communes have been successful in challenging regional measures in the courts and through friends in the Ministry of the Interior and the provincial prefectorate. 'They have allies in the most powerful central departments, while the friends of the regions within the central government machinery are comparatively weak' (ibid.). Primary legislative and budgetary power have remained at the centre. Hence a highly complex three-cornered game. Devolution 'has become a multifaceted bargaining arrangement involving the state, the regions, other local government bodies, and the new array of socio-economic political groups that have been organised at regional level' (Leonardi, Nanetti and Putnam, 1987).

Party Conveyor Belts

The system is extremely sensitive to changes in party support. What is commonly a fine balance between parties means that sensitivity to minority points of view and regular re-negotiation of alliances and support are necessary (§3.10).

Another characteristic is the attempts at control over matters at communal level by party leaders and bureaucrats from the centre, the regions and the provinces. But the constant need to watch local support produces a very sensitive political system dependent to a large degree on what is happening politically in the communes, provinces and regions. The parties act as effective vertical 'transmission belts' of opinion. Communes, provinces and regions have all had multi-party systems analogous to those at the centre, each with its own peculiarities but serving as political barometers, giving members of parliament and national government a constant need to consider the impact of their decisions on regions and localities.

3.7 LOCAL AND REGIONAL SERVICES

Communal, Provincial and Metropolitan City Competences

Communal and provincial functions specified by law are of two main classes: those determined by the general laws of the Republic in accordance with Article 128 of the Constitution and those on regional matters in accordance with the provisions of Article 118 (§3.2). From 1977 the allocation of functions was sought in terms of 'organically linked sectors', that is the determination of functions of 'exclusively local interest' within coherent blocks of functions detached from the central administration. (Sanantonio, 1987)

Activities are partly governed by regional laws on organisation, expenditure and implementation. They may be optional or obligatory, although the word 'obligatory' cannot be taken literally because it is often unbacked by the necessary resources. The first category also covers the vague area of general competence. (Bartole, 1984)

Law 142 of 1990, in providing for new metropolitan cities, confers on them both normal provincial functions and those of communes which possess a 'supra-communal' nature in the following areas: territorial planning of their areas, roads, traffic and transport, heritage, environment, soil and water protection, refuse disposal, water services, economic development and large-scale commerce, wide-area health, education and training functions and other services on a metropolitan level.

Regional Functions

Regional legislative powers are those within the fields set out in Article 117 of the Constitution (§3.2), the so-called 'complementary' functions allocated to the regions in other fields of legislation, and those administrative functions which can be delegated by the state by the normal legislative process in these and other fields (Article 118). Provisions differ for special regions.

Specific Activities

During the 1970s there were extensive transfers of power to the regions and local authorities. Especially important were the 616 Decrees of 1977 which redefined regional purposes in a way that has enabled the regional councils to develop the roles of their local authorities 'organically', fitting their duties and powers to local circumstances. Three main sectors have been developed since 1977: (1) social services (human development, health and hospital care, vocational and artisan education, the right to study, cultural resources, recreation and cultural activities, information and mass media and voluntarism); (2) economic development (commerce, tourism and hotels, artisanry and small industry, agriculture, forestry and mining, co-operation, advanced services to firms, energy and credit); and (3) territorial and environmental planning (conservation of agricultural land, national parks and reserves, land-use controls, transportation and roads, aqueducts, ports and public works, environmental protection, natural calamity and disaster relief and housing) (Nanetti, 1988).

Nanetti analyses the roles of regional and local authorities in terms of fulfilling what she calls a 'social capitalist' model of development: what the British might prefer to call a 'mixed economy' model. The regions, together with the communes and provinces, are identified as: (1) mediators among competing groups, aggregating interests towards consensus; (2) promoters of socio-economic activities through research and analysis, identification of objectives, their translation into multi-year programmes and their implementation; (3) experimenters, supporting new enterprises to diversify products and services; and (4) providers of consumer and advanced services to the private sector. Regions are also monitors of policy outputs and outcomes by annual evaluations of impact jointly with provinces and communes and other means.

Beyond these internal regional and local government roles are four extra-regional roles: the region as co-ordinator in partnership with other regions, e.g. on river basin and coastline projects; as ombudsman defending regional/local interests in dealing with multinational and other externally based interests; as contributors to state and EC initiatives related to regional interests; and as interpreter of state and EC initiatives to fit them into regional/local needs (ibid.).

The tendency has been to eliminate 'ad hoc' agencies and base powers squarely on the three main levels of government, with encouragement of joint arrangements where effectiveness requires larger-scale organisation than the smaller communes can provide. A general role was defined for both communes and provinces to promote the civil, social and economic development of their communities and to foster the liberty and equality of their citizens and their social development as persons (*le formazione sociali nelle quali si realizza la persona umana*). They are to adopt participative methods, exercise impartiality and good administrative conduct and openness of proceedings to the public. They are required to develop their functions through the adoption and execution of annual and multi-annual programmes in harmony with the objectives of national and regional programming, contributing to the development of regional programmes and co-ordinating their own actions with those of the region and of the state.

Table 3.4 shows the balance of expenditure within fields of responsibility in 1988 (provisional figures), together with, in brackets, the increase or decrease in expenditure from 1985 to 1988. (The rate of increase is not untypical of the previous ten years.)

Table 3.4: Current Expenditure of Local Bodies by Function (provisional figures, 1989; absolute in milliard lire), and Percentage Changes, 1985-88

	Regions	Provinces	Communes
Administration	6,575 (+8.4)	1,204 (–3.5)	10,285 (+5.8)
Public Security	-	-	2,497 (+5.5)
Education, training, culture, research	2,831(+10.1)	1,907 (+8.0)	9,592 (+8.5)
Housing Intervention	26(–37.9)	-	599 (+1.4)
Social Intervention	65,818(+11.8)	71 (–69.8)	716,155(+10.1)
Transport & Communications	6,209(+20.2)	1,431 (+3.2)	7,362(+31.6)
Intervention in Economic Field	4,151(+10.7)	661 (+8.7)	2,304(+18.3)
Other Tasks	993(+23.9)	401(+132.1)	2,736(+14.8)
Totals	86,605(+12.1)	6,168 (+8.9)	51,531(+11.7)

Source: Derived from *Annuario Statistico Italiano, 1991,* 1991, Table 19.22.

At communal level the strongest field of growth has been social intervention, reflecting responsibilities devolved from the central state through the regions. This field includes includes health, water, sewerage and sports centres. Expenditure on education and culture dominates provincial budgets. The same emphases are reflected in capital expenditures which in all formed 27 per cent of regional expenditures, 40 per cent of provincial and 44 per cent of communal costs.

Expenditures showed dramatic increases in the first half of the 1980s and continued to grow at a more modest rate subsequently.

The list of services below follows in general the numbering and sequence in the chapters on other countries. It inevitably over-simplies, given the thousands of legal provisions that have accumulated during the century (see Giovenco, 1983) and the fact that 'functions are carried out by all the bodies at the same time and in the same arena, competing, overlapping and interacting with each other, creating flexible networks for policy-making and implementation'. This complex pattern 'cannot be set out in a neat and ordered scheme' (Sanantonio, 1987).

The new metropolitan city responsibilities and transfers of competences from communes described above are not included.

1. Town and Country Planning, Development and Environmental Protection

Communes are responsible for town planning and building control; protection of nature and the environment against pollution; soil and hydro-geological protection; town development and the management of installations necessary for the performance of communal services and of public services relevant to housing settlement etc.; control and surveillance over changes in public and private land and building usage.

Provinces co-ordinate plans relating to communal decisions on matters within their own competences and regional law and programmes; determine the general direction of land-use change, indicating in particular directions of industrial development and urban expansion; development of major infrastructure and lines of transmission for water, mineral and forestry resources, and soil and water conservation; areas suitable for parks and nature reserves; and implementation of aspects of the regional plan delegated to provinces. They carry out works for soil protection, development of hydraulic resources, and control of water and atmospheric and noise pollution; protection of fauna and flora; parks and reserves and environmental protection.

Regions oversee town planning generally and control quarries and peat extraction control. (See head 16 below for regional planning).

2. Housing

Communes: location of public housing, acquisition of sites, conservation and restoration of public and private patrimony; construction and allocation of subsidised public housing; co-operation in cadastral surveys.

3. Roads

Communes: communal roads.

Provinces: inter-municipal roads.

Regions: road network and works of regional interest.

4. Transport

Communes: urban public transport, school transport, traffic management, control of transport, taxi hire and hoardings.

Provinces: transport of provincial interest.

Regions: inland ports and navigation; regional and local transport legislation.

5. Education

Education is generally under central control with the exception of the regional vocational training centres. Teachers are state employees and syllabuses determined centrally. Most children attend pre-primary schools (*scuole materne*) from 3 to 5. Besides state institutions there are important networks of local authority managed schools and colleges.

Communes build, maintain and equip schools, provide supplementary activities to the state curriculum and assistance to pupils and students. There are many civic initiatives. Milan, for example, has developed its own professional training activities parallel with those of the government.

Provinces have competences relating to secondary education under state legislation and undertake buildings for secondary schools specialising in science and technical subjects.

Regions provide educational assistance and some local schools.

6. Vocational Training

Provinces may promote vocational training.

Regions provide craft and vocational training.

7. Cultural Activities

Communes promote cultural activities and visual performances, cinemas, theatres and facilities for other visual productions, and license theatres and cinemas.

Provinces promote cultural and related social activities.

8. Libraries, Museums and Archives

Communes provide municipal libraries, art galleries and museums, preserve archives and 'contribute to the good use of the cultural heritage'.

Regions provide regional libraries and museums.

9. Recreation and Conservation of Environment

Communes provide recreation, sports and other leisure-time activities, set up and manage related sports and recreational centres and provide parks.

Provinces: sports facilities, control of hunting and freshwater fishing.

Regions: hunting and freshwater fishing legislation.

10. Health and Social Welfare.

The main responsibility for health services lies with the district health authorities, the USLs described in §3.5.

Communes have main responsibilities for protection from environmental pollution and hygiene. They share responsibility with the *regions* for social welfare. They are involved with the *provinces* and *regions* in the provision of social assistance.

Regions provide public assistance, health assistance ond hospitals.

11. Police

There are some five types of police in Italy. The main forces are the carabinieri, generally recruited from the armed forces; the Ministry of Interior police organised under provincial commands; specialist forces under other ministries; and some sixty thousand local police employed by *communes* under the control of mayors. Communal police are used for enforcement of communal responsibilities, some of them related to public security but also to public health matters. Rural communes have licensing functions, some subject to direction by prefects. (Vandelli, 1984a)

Regions have joint legislative powers for local policing except in Sardinia and the Val d'Aosta where they have exclusive powers.

12. Fire Protection is not a sub-national function except in certain special regions.

13. Development of Local Economy and Employment

Regions have a central position in economic development arising naturally from their regional planning role. Since their powers were widened in 1977 their practical activities have expanded. They have used constitutional and statutory powers relating to tourism and the hotel industry, commerce and marketing, craft and small industries, advanced services to firms (especially aiding innovation and restructuring), co-operation, agriculture, fisheries, mining and development of cultural resources to provide a wide range of specific inputs into sectoral and disadvantaged areas and vocational education. They have developed credit sources to small and medium firms where they have been able to provide leverage to businesses in connection with implementation of development plans and have played a major part in setting up and backing public private companies providing loan guarantees and technical and financial assistance. Promotion of local products has been an active area of concern where their responsibilities for fairs and markets have often dovetailed with communal competences.

They have developed close collaboration with local business and labour interest groups who find it easier to relate to government activities at this level than at state level. In a survey in 1983 increased fiscal and financial autonomy for the regions was supported by 66 per cent of bankers, 72 per cent of businessmen, 76 per cent of agricultural representatives and 93 per cent of trade unionists. A recent study by an American researcher remarks on the 'centrality of the region in creating a climate favourable to consolidation and development activities, particularly during the 1980s recession from which Italian industrial areas appear to have emerged as strongly or more strongly than those elsewhere in Europe' (Nanetti, 1988).

Communes have a key role in control of consumer prices for national and provincial committees, regulation of commercial and wholesale markets, licensing commercial activities etc. They support craft training and enterprises provided for in regional plans.

14. Public Utilities are promoted by communes and regions.

15. Tourism: communes and regions

16. Regional Plans

Regions were central in defining a new approach to wide-area planning in the 1970s. Early over-ambitious attempts at comprehensive planning were superseded with one governed by definition of objectives within sectors of production, control of territorial growth and urban and personal services, developing a 'pragmatic and management-conscious approach to planning' that was greatly abetted by their remit to delegate implementation to local authorities under the decrees of 1977 (Nanetti, 1988).

3.8 IMPLEMENTATION OF SERVICES

Communal and Provincial Services

Local authorities employ a wide range of means for the implementation of their services, including private law forms to escape from the rigidities of public law. Approaches include direct provision, companies set up by communes (e.g for water and energy distribution and refuse collection), public-private companies, concessions and contracting out. A reaction against indirect provision in the 1970s resulted in 'the nationalisation or municipalisation of nearly all the private or quasi-public bodies that provided an important part of the services together with a belief that services should be either free or subsidised and managed under politicians, particularly assistant mayors (assessori), with the City of Bologna leading the trend.

Municipal employees increased by at least 15 per cent between 1976 and 1981. The trend was not consistent with the finance available despite a massive increase in financial transfers from the centre. New legislation compelled authorities to cover costs such as those of refuse collection by user fees and meet the cost of 'individual demand services' including school meals, kindergartens and theatres by charging fees to cover at least 30 per cent of expenditure.

Besides problems of costs there were attacks on political involvement in management, including appointments, and charges of gross inefficiency. But the reaction was not Thatcherist. Flexibility has been sought through temporary appointments, employment of co-operatives consisting largely of previous employees, and increased contracting out of services such as school meals to profit or non-profit enterprises. There is also a new willingness to use voluntary services. (Dente, 1991)

Regions

Regions are also free to develop their own approaches. Economic development has become a special concern. The 'ordinary regions', unlike the longer-established 'special regions', lack general competence in this field but nevertheless involve themselves in it through their planning responsibilities. They have experimented widely with the use of powers within their competences. A common approach involves joint action with the private sector, justified as an extension and completion of decentralisation policy. Their capacity to contract under private law with such bodies as business consortia and regional holding companies has become a central avenue for the implementation of policy. Means employed include loans to SMEs below market rate from joint funds with banks administered by special bodies or banks alone; financial subventions; loan guarantees; advances on government credits; participation in private enterprises; and provision of industrial zones, buildings and services to smaller firms; grants to consortia where their powers allow, as with hotels and tourism enterprises; infrastructure incentives using regional land or on communal land using communes as agents; underwriting bonds or shares issued by SMEs; and tax incentives (Buglione and France, 1991; Sanantonio, 1987).

Policies have also been implemented by means of regional holding companies set up under regional law which can operate outside the restrictions of regional competences. In 1984 there were fourteen of these covering the whole of Central and Northern Italy and parts of the South. Participants included chambers of commerce, banks and insurance and other companies. They may be primarily loan companies participating in share capital of firms (but not empowered to undertake 'salvage' or welfare operations), or promotion and guarantee agencies.

Communes

The range and complexity of the means employed by the larger authorities can be illustrated by the implementational structures of the Commune of Milan in the late 1980s. This great and highly developed municipality appointed boards of directors of municipal companies for municipal transport, energy (electricity and gas production and supply), street-cleaning (including solid waste collection and disposal) and milk supply, processing and distribution companies. It ran municipal chemists' shops. In 1981 it owned the majority of shares in various limited companies, including those responsible for the Milan Underground, Airport Services, Milan Wholesale Food Market Provision and Management, and Controlled Sales Ltd (undertaking retail sale of foods for price-control purposes). It held 90 per cent of the shares in the Council House Institute, a public body for house building and management. It possessed minority holdings (10 to 20 per cent) in a major thermo-electrical company and the Genoa-Milan-

Ponte Chiasso Motorways and Spluga Tunnel companies. It had an important share in the management of the Milan Fair, the Triennial Exhibition, the Scala, the Piccolo Teatro di Milano, the Milan Centre for Sports and Recreational Activities and the City Universities. In addition it was involved in local health authorities and education bodies (USLs and school boards (see §3.5)).

3.9 LOCAL AND REGIONAL FINANCE

General

Expenditures by communes and provinces rose from 4.6 per cent of the GDP to around six per cent during the 1980s. The recent history of Italian local finance is nevertheless one of response to a succession of critical situations. Despite tensions this has not on the whole been an area of conflict between central and local governments because of a shared concern about economic development to combat the adverse social effects of the 'economic miracle' of Italy's rapid economic development in the 1950s and 1960s, accompanied by an acceptance of the need to decentralise responsibilities for relevant expenditure. Central governments, however, have been hamstrung by the need to control inflation and reduce state financial deficits.

There has been general agreement on the need for a fairer balance of resources between the wealthy urban authorities and poor rural ones, and between North Italy and the South, implying a major equalisation role for the centre. This has, however, met a strong challenge from northern regional parties in the early 1990s.

Before the 1970s about two-thirds of municipal income had traditionally come from local taxation. There were severe imbalances in that per capita expenditure by communes in the South were commonly only half those in the North. In pursuit of financial equity and to help local authorities finance their growing debt burdens and cover their deficits, a reform in 1972 consolidated nearly all direct and indirect local taxes into a simpler system by means of which, it was hoped, these problems could progressively be overcome. All but a few very minor local taxes such as those on dogs, occupation of public areas and forms of advertising were abolished. Taxes collected by central government were re-distributed to local authorities according to their recorded expenditures in the year before the tax reform, to which were added standard annual increases of ten per cent. As a result, between 1972 and 1976 the communes' proportion of income from central transfers doubled but communal tax revenues fell from 15.6 per cent to 3.6 per cent. Economic crises in the mid-70s substantially reduced the value of the transfers. Moreover popular demand for welfare services increased rapidly. This led to a situation in which over 60 per cent of Italian communes had deficits which they were forced to meet from loans. For several years the communes depended predominantly on borrowing up to the extent of over two-thirds of their total revenues. The government turned a blind eye even where interest payments were financed by further borrowing. The situation became critical and resulted in a series of decrees between 1977 and 1983 which wrote off a large part of local debts, consolidating and transferring them to the state. Basic financial principles were established for local authorities: balanced budgets, controls over staff, limitation of borrowing to capital investment purposes and a proportion of municipal income, and control over increases in local taxation and tariffs. Grant was stepped up annually by fixed percentage increases on previous expenditures, but with special additions for communes in the South and the mountains.

Expenditure on wages and salaries was covered in full by national transfers, but increases in numbers of employees above the 1976 figure were permitted only in accordance with reorganisation plans agreed by a joint central and local government commission. Pay and working conditions had to be in accordance with national joint agreements. Urban transportation subsidies were also covered by direct grant subject to centrally stipulated minimum fare charges. The cost of approved investments was also met by the centre. Local authorities were required to submit requests for loans to the state bank with evidence that the finance required was for projects consistent with the regional economic plan, but were allowed to seek a loan elsewhere if the bank refused funding.

Charging requirements were set for certain services: refuse collection (not disposal) at 100 per cent costs, and some social services, including nurseries, at a minimum of 30 per cent. In addition new local taxes were introduced, on electricity consumption and housing accommodation for example. The results were an increase in the reliability of expenditure forecasts, a moderate rise in expenditure in real terms and a moderate decrease in inequalities between classes of local authorities. (Dente, 1985b, 1990).

Indebtedness by communes and provinces rose steadily throughout the 1980s (*Annuario Statistico Italiano*, 1987 and 1991, Table 19.24). In 1988 the regions received 98.25 per cent of their incomes on the current account through transfers from the national budget and passed on 90.3 per cent of total income in transfers to local and provincial bodies. On the capital account nearly 99 per cent of their incomes came as national transfers and 73.6 per cent of their expenditure was passed on to lower levels (ibid., Tables 19.15 and 19.23).

Local tax income increased by 80 per cent from 1988 to 1990, but still formed a lowish proportion of revenue. In 1989 communes met 22 per cent of their expenditure from their own resources and 70 per cent in transfers. The provinces were able to meet only 11 per cent, the transfers they received amounting to 86 per cent. (Ibid., Tables 19.17 and 19.19) While financial transfers have enabled mayors and their councils to expand services, the lack of significant local taxes has held back further expenditures which local inhabitants might well be willing to pay (Dente, 1991).

The Law of 8 June 1990 recognises the financial autonomy of local government 'founded on certainty of their own and transferred resources, and their fiscal autonomy'. It lays down that 'transfers must be distributed according to objective criteria taking account of population, area and socio-economic conditions' as well as on the basis of 'an equalising distribution of resources which takes account of the unevenness of local tax resources'. (Dente, 1985b, 1991; Sanantonio, 1987)

The Finance of the Regions

Regions are independent for accounting purposes. Ordinary regions have narrow fiscal resources consisting of taxes on concessions of state land and assets, regional concessions, traffic and use of public areas and spaces — no more in fact than a token recognition of financial autonomy. Special regions have wider resources. Sicily collects all revenues for the state treasury within its region except the tobacco and production taxes and the national lotteries. The other special regions receive proportions of national taxes collected in their areas.

Regions play a key role in the distribution of resources under regional plans through the project-based implementation system. Instruments have been introduced linking administrative action to a planning methodology seeking rational use of resources to define required results (see §3.7). A multi-annual budget indicates the resources needed to achieve the programme objectives. The region legislates on expenditure norms, stipulating specific objectives and the means needed to achieve them. Methods are laid down for budgeting, economic and financial supervision, departmental accounting and programme and project accounting.

3.10 ELECTORAL REPRESENTATION

Electoral Arrangements

The national electoral system has resembled those in Belgium, the Netherlands and Scandinavia in tending towards strict proportionality on the modified d'Hondt model, subject to variations at different levels of government. Major changes have been introduced in the early 1990s to achieve greater accountability, including two-round systems as in the case of mayoral elections referred to in §3.1. Due to the changing situation the following text may in some respects be out of date.

In the Senate and provincial council elections electors have voted for single candidates chosen by parties. In all others except for small communes they vote for a number of councillors on competing lists, enabling them to express preferences between individual candidates. The Senate system has combined majoritarian and proportional methods. In the case of the Chamber of Deputies and regional elections the proportional system has been applied. A variation of this has been used in the provincial system, and also in elections in communes with populations of over five thousand. In early 1993 the courts cleared a proposal for a referendum which is expected to approve a change towards a first-past-the-post system in the Senate and larger communes which, it is widely hoped, will reduce the dominance of the long-established party machines.

In the smaller communes a majoritarian system is used enabling each elector to vote for four-fifths of the total number of councillors to be elected, thereby ensuring representation of minor parties with significant support. Exceptions are in Sicily and Trento-Adige where proportional representation applies in all cases except communes of under 1,000 population in the Province of Bolzano. Despite the dominance of the parties there is nothing to stop independent candidates or lists of independents contesting elections. The collapse of the main parties through splintering which was predicted as a result of the lack of a qualifying minimum for representation did not occur. The traditional parties continued to dominate, but the Lombard League and other new parties are making a powerful challenge at all levels in the early 1990s.

As a rule elections take place every five years, but national elections are usually called at shorter intervals in practice. Levels of voting are high. Voting is a constitutional duty although there is no effective method of compelling citizens to vote. For the Chamber of Deputies the voting turn-out was 90 per cent of electors in the 1980s and for the Senate 88.5 per cent. The national turn-out for the regional election in 1990 was 86 per cent: 89 per cent in the North and Central regions and 81 per cent in the South. The highest turnouts were 93 per cent in Emilia Romagna and Bolzano-Bozen; the lowest 76 per cent in Calabria. Only in the case of Molise, the very small region in the South, were more than half the votes cast for one party. The proportion of votes cast for the three most popular parties was overall 34 per cent for the Christian Democrats; 23 for the Communist Party and 15 for the Socialists. Centre parties were over-shadowed by the successes of the Greens (5 per cent) and the Lombard League which won nearly 7 per cent in the North-Centre and 19 per cent in Lombardy, the first breakthrough of a regionally based party. (*Annuario Statistico Italiano*, 1991)

As mentioned in §3.1 the results of the elections of 1992 and 1993 have given a major shock to the system, resulting in a division between the North and the cities of the middle belt and the South.

Status and Working Conditions of Councillors

Candidates for regional and local government election must be at least 18 years of age. Councillors may not hold seats on more than one local council. The Constitution rules that regional councillors may not hold seats in the national parliament or government. The following are excluded from council membership: civil servants and senior police officers, those exercising supervisory powers over regional and local administrations, employees of the local or regional authority concerned and senior staff of bodies dependent on that authority, government commissioners, prefects, vice-prefects, senior officers of the armed forces, ministers of religion and certain classes of judges and magistrates.

Mayors and members of municipal executives in large cities (assessori) and the president and members of provincial executives receive emoluments presupposing full-time employment. Regional councillors receive an official allowance of 60 per cent that of members of the national parliament or more according to function, rising to 100 per cent for the president and members of the executive. Mayors are voted official allowances up to a maximum on a legal scale according to size of authority. Executive members in municipalities of over 30,000 population receive half this rate. Similar provisions apply for provincial authorities. There are also daily attendance allowances for meetings.

Public employees elected to local councils are entitled to be absent on essential council work without loss of salary or, if they prefer, to take un-paid leave of absence. Those elected to regional councils, provincial presi-dents, mayors of towns of over 50 thousand and assessori of communes of over 100 thousand may be released from their employment for the duration of their public service and receive allowances from their councils related to their former salaries as well as normal councillors' allowances.

Employees in the private sector have no right to paid leave of absence but may be granted unpaid leave for the period of office or absences strictly necessary for their public duties without loss of remuneration (Council of Europe, 1983, *Report on the Status and Working Conditions of Local and Regional Elected Representatives*).

The Political Parties and Local Government

The politics of the great cities are at the forefront of Italian political life and have a significant impact on national party support. National political leaders have increasingly cited local government election results as verdicts on their national performance.

What is commonly a fine balance between parties with sensitivity to minority points of view makes a regular renegotiation of alliances and support necessary. Nevertheless the need of parties to work closely together can lead to 'unholy alliances' with a shared vested interest in resisting change and reform.

The long post-war hegemony of the Christian Democrats was associated with patronage and bureaucratic dominance, and this partly explains why in general electoral support began to fall in the 1960s. The second strongest party, the Communists (PCI), turned their emphases from national, doctrinaire policies aiming at proletarian government to competent administration, local development and participation, showing a readiness for pragmatic collaboration with a wide range of parties on the left and centre-right.

The cities of the 'red belt', which crosses the north of the Italian peninsula and comprises chiefly the regions of Tuscany and Emilia-Romagna, have displayed a dynamic innovativeness and managerial qualities in local government with a stress on the general interest which brought the Communist Party wide support on a scale that most Italians had previously believed to be impossible. Their 'flagship' was the much-publicised government of Bologna under its mayor, Renate Zangheri (§3.12).

Left-wing councils throughout the country set the pace for the development of social services and administrative reform which led to important legislation during the 1970s. Communist mayors such as Petroselli in Rome and Novelli in Turin emulated the approach in Bologna in projecting an image of integrity and concern for human problems that contrasted with the records of their predecessors (Gundle, 1986). This lay behind a surge of support in national elections, the Communist vote rising from 7.8 million in 1963 to a peak of 12.6 milion in 1976. Support for the Communists receded after the economic crises of the late 1970s, probably from a general sense of the party's failure to meet the needs of a new, increasingly prosperous but more fragmented society. A subsequent fall in support has led to a reorientation and renaming of the party as the Democratic Party of the Left (PDS) in October 1990, dropping the support of 'the hard left'.

The Socialists (PSI), the third-strongest party, up to 1992, under the leadership of Bettino Craxi, broke from a long-standing dependence on alliances with the Communists and showed in the 1980s an ability to hold together and lead centrally biased coalitions both at central and local levels without dependence on the PCI. In the 1988 election their support reached its highest level since the late 1940s at 18 per cent of votes. The corruption charges of the early 1990s, however, foreshadow wide loss of local support. The Green Party made its first significant impact at this level. The Christian Democrats remained the essential element in most coalitions, with overall support of over 35 per cent of voters: above 40 per cent in the South and the North-West. As in Latin countries generally the strength of the Christian right lies mainly outside the large cities and at its strongest at the provincial level of government. The December 1992 local elections brought great successes to the Northern League of regional parties in the North, the far right Italian Social Movement (MSI) in the South and more generally the Rete (Network), a radical left-wing organisation, with the far right looking for a regrouping with the far left in some cases. The mayoral elections of 1993 subsequently resulted in the general collapse of the Christian Democrats and Socialist support and extensive wins by the PDS, the successor party to the PCI.

3.11 THE INTERNAL ORGANISATION OF LOCAL AND REGIONAL AUTHORITIES

General

The three main levels of Italian sub-national government share a pattern of organisation based on a Piedmontese development from the French revolutionary model (see §3.1). The executive arm of communal, provincial and regional governments consists of a board (*giuntà*) and a mayor (*sindaco*) or president (*presidente*) who is appointed by and chairs both council and giuntà. Communes and provinces differ little in their formal procedures. The council appoints and has the power to remove the sindaco or president and the giuntà by means of a vote of 'no confidence'.

Law 142 of 1990 provides for the council to make plans in accordance with the demands of the local community and for the giuntà to operate as the organ of government, while the mayor or president becomes the titular head and director of services (Rolla, 1992). It requires every local authority to make a precise allocation of functions in decision-making and implementation to each of the political and administrative units.

The Law has tilted the balance of power towards the giuntà, giving it residual powers beyond those legally conferred on the council and sindaco or president. It is conceived as 'the political committee of the authority' on which internal political control hinges. However the new way as of 1993 may be expected to carry strong legitimacy and public expectations arising from their direct election.

A council can make decisions of a political and administrative nature; pursue the objectives of its electoral manifesto; exercise political-administrative control over the giuntà, the administration and services (exercising this power annually when the annual report is presented or in the event of a no-confidence vote in the executive); appoint to agencies and other bodies within its sphere or dependent on it; and take key policy and administrative measures, including those on some specified management and executive matters (Graziano, Girotti and Bonet, 1984). It may delegate its powers to mayors or presidents except for a few key responsibilities.

The giuntà is a collegiate body responsible for developing the activities of its authority. It prepares draft decisions for the council, including regulations and budget proposals. It virtually runs the authority beyond the functions given to the council, sindaco and officials by the law.

The Commune

Communal councils consist of 15 to 80 members, varying in accordance with a population scale which gives the smallest number of councillors (and members of the executive board) to communes with populations of under 3,000 and the largest to communes with over 500,000. They serve for a five-year term of office.

The giuntà consists of the sindaco and members (*assessori*) chosen by secret ballot of the council. The latter may include members from outside the council qualified to make a major contribution to its work if an authority decides to have an enabling provision included in its own statute. Their number is fixed according to a population scale, ranging from three for communes with up to 3,000 inhabitants and sixteen for those with over half a million. The term 'assessori' is translated variously as deputy or assistant mayors or aldermen. The assessore receiving the most votes becomes deputy mayor (*vicesindaco*), deputising in the mayor's absence subject to his replacement by another assessore chosen by the mayor.

Before the new legislation the role of the giuntà varied widely in practice between communes, particularly according to their size and political composition. In small communes it has tended to be dominated by the sindaco; in medium-sized communes the sindaco has been no more than 'first among equals'; in large communes the giuntà tends to be seen as the chief means for the co-ordination of decisions by individual assessori in their areas of delegation; while in largest, the metropolitan communes, it is likely to be a place of negotiation and bargaining among assessori who, with heads of department, dominate decisions in particular fields (Dente, Sharpe and Mayntz, 1977; Vandelli, 1984a).

The general administration of a commune is likely to be in the sindaco's overall charge. The sindaco will continue to exercise his or her special state functions and to deal with general relationships with other levels of government. The same seems likely also in the case of the president of a provincial council.

The sindaco calls meetings of council and giuntà, issues agendas, watches over the performance of the assessori in their spheres of delegation, carries responsibility for carrying out the decisions of the council and the giuntà, signs documents on behalf of the commune, represents the commune in legal actions, supervises the administrative departments of the council and can suspend communal employees subject to confirmation by the giuntà and council. He is responsible for the direction of administrative bodies and institutions set up by the commune and represents the commune in external relationships. Among his state responsibilities are registration, certification and health and public works matters, securing law and order and publishing state laws and other legal instruments. He or she is responsible for urgent action and co-ordination of public services in the event of emergencies.

The Province

Provinces possess two seats of government: that for decentralised state functions under a prefect who is responsible for co-ordination of government services, executing national law, maintaining security and certain health functions, and that for representative government consisting of the council, giuntà and president.

Provincial councils range in size from 24 members for provinces with under 300,000 inhabitants to 45 for provinces with over 1,400,000. The main legal provisions for the giuntà are the same as those for communes. Its size is no larger than a fifth of council members up to eight members.

The strong sectoralisation of business and close relationships with particular government ministries give a particularly strong position to individual assessori. The president lacks the prominence in local politics typical of the sindaco. (Vandelli, 1984b)

Officials (*Funzionari*) of Communes and Provinces

Law 142 of 1990 gives autonomous status to the posts to which senior officials are appointed. It lays down that officials (not politicians) must head offices and services and carry out administrative matters that have not been placed with the council, the giuntà, mayor or president by law. They have since been given the power to manage funds to improve the efficiency of services and determine financial incentives for productivity, overtime and working hours. They must also ensure the transparency of the decision-making process, the participation of all interests involved in the administrative process and the rationality and efficiency of the administration as well as the attainment of political objectives set by the executive committee. They are responsible for the monitoring of the conduct of business generally, reporting on administrative procedures, progress on programmes, staff organisation and the means to overcome inefficiencies and irregularities. (Rolla, 1992)

Secretaries or secretaries-general are members of a national corps. They are appointed to their first posts by the Ministry of the Interior after success in an open competitive examination and remain legally responsible to the government. The Ministry controls qualifications within the service and authorises promotions and transfers. Higher qualifications are required for appointment to one of the larger municipalities. In addition to acting on directives from the sindaco or president they are responsible for supervising the work of the directors of services, co-ordinating activities, the realisation of measures and preparatory work for decision-making by the giuntà and the council. Reports of decisions must include the secretary's opinion on their legality and that of the other responsible officials on their technical feasibility and financial aspects. They may refuse to implement council decisions they consider illegal. Heads of department are directly responsible to the secretary by law.

Organisational structure and personnel procedures of communes and provinces are regulated by the state. Practical arrangements vary greatly according to the size of an authority and for other reasons. None is typical.

Milan may serve as an example of the administrative patterns of the great cities. In the early 1980s there were some 48,000 communal employees, including over 20,000 in municipal utilities. The mayoral and general secretarial offices contained 111 employees. There were separate staff offices for law, programme planning and control, research, statistics and data processing and general technical matters. Internal services were provided by accounting, personnel and supply departments. External services were the responsibilities of twenty departments for tax revenue, sanitation, urban supervision, transport, decentralisation (zonal councils), education, social welfare, civil status, culture, sports, parks and gardens, trade, ecology, state property and estates, town planning, council housing, private-building control, public works and services, justices of the peace and labour and social problems.

The Region

Regions differ from communes and provinces in being primarily legislative and planning bodies, running few services directly. Although their internal governmental structures appear much the same on the surface they have developed some institutions which are closer to those of the national parliament than to local government. The basic internal structure for regional governments is laid down in the national Constitution (Article 121). Like local authorities, they have three organs: the regional council, the giuntà and the president. The council exercises the legislative and regulatory powers attributed to the region and other functions conferred on it by the Constitution and the laws. It can propose national laws to the chambers of parliament. The president of the giuntà represents the region, promulgates its laws and regulations and directs administrative functions delegated to it by the state in conformity with instructions from central government.

The size of regional councils ranges from 30 to 80 members according to population size. The giuntà for an ordinary region varies from six to twelve assessori and two to four substitutes according to scale. Special regions are free to determine the number themselves.

Each region has its own statute, which lays down its internal organisation, including provisions for public rights of initiative and a referendum on the laws and administrative provisions of the region. (Bartole, 1984)

The central work of the council lies in law-making and regulation, giving it a 'parliamentary' character. Within the council permanent legislative commissions are responsible for the development and drafting of regional law in particular fields, and temporary committees of inquiry are set up to research and examine particular problems.

The president of the giuntà combines 'mayoral'-type functions with a role analogous in some respects to that of a prime minister. He has general responsibility for preparing council business and promulgates laws and regulations. As head of the council executive he participates in the development and approval of legislation within the assembly, but must return a bill to the council if he believes it to be illegal or unconstitutional. He is the formal representative of the regional government, and indeed of the region as a whole, maintaining its interests in relations with the central state, with other regions and with the private sector. After consultation with the giuntà he may challenge provisions in national legislation or that of other regions which he believes violate the legal rights of his region. In some regions the council determines the responsibilities of individual assessori when it elects the president and the giuntà; in others this is done within the giuntà itself. The president also carries out certain functions assigned to him by the central state.

The political composition of a giuntà matches that of the governing coalition. The assessori play a much more 'ministerial' role than in local authorities, their work being much concerned with the development of regional legislation in close communication with national ministries. They maintain communication with their opposite numbers in other regions in conferences and informally. But the president of the giuntà, as the representative of the regional interest as a whole, is the spokesman to the prime minister and the council of ministers. Moreover, despite their practical power arising from their formal and informal functions, the assessori are clearly subordinate in different respects to the council, the giuntà as a corporate body and the regional president. The responsibilities of the giuntà are closely intertwined with those of its president and require realisation of consensus except where the president finds it necessary to maintain a regional or national interest over and above the degree of consensus that can be reached within its membership. Regional constitutions provide that it must make provision for the implementation of decisions of the council and superintend the management of the regional public services.

The departmental structure and staffing of the regions is not hemmed around with regulations and subjected to control by the centre, as in the case of local authorities. The nature of regional tasks and relationships have required the development of a unique approach, varying according to function. (Vandelli, 1984b)

The regions have evolved rapidly in the last twenty years and roles have changed. Asked in surveys in 1970, 1976 and 1981-82 who had much or enough influence in the political life of their regions the president of the giuntà scored much the highest, his score rising from 78 to 89 per cent over the years. The score of the regional assessori rose from 65 to 79 per cent, overtaking that of party directors. The scores of national figures in 1981-82 were ministers 59, national party directors 53, regional councillors 29 (they had scored 48 in 1970), members of the national parliament 22, other regional and local office holders 30, and the government commissioner and/or the prefecture 29. (Putnam, Leonardi and Nanetti, 1985)

3.12 CITIZEN PARTICIPATION AND DECENTRALISATION WITHIN CITIES

General

The 1990 legislation requires communes to provide the means for citizen participation in city and rural sub-areas (*quartiere* and *frazione*) and implement consultation including the means for individuals and associations to challenge decisions and submit petitions and proposals (which must be considered by authorities within a fixed timespan). They may conduct referenda and must give freedom of access to internal information except in cases where this would infringe individual rights.

Council meetings must be open to the public and decisions published in an authority's official gazette and displayed on notice boards. Other administrative documents such as those relating to building permits must be published. City councils issue quarterly journals which are supervised jointly by majority and minority members. Official records are in principle private but records may be shown to parties concerned subject to safeguarding of rights. Refusal may be overridden by the order of a magistrate.

There is extensive participation by outside interests before important decisions are taken. Politicians feel free in most cases to share inside information with the public. In Milan rules and regulations passed by the Council in 1977 relating to decentralisation and participation have been said to have virtually overturned the axiom 'everything that has not been declared to the public is confidential' by the rule 'everything that has not been declared to be confidential is public'. City area council and committee meetings are open to the public. The public have a right to examine and obtain copies of matters dealt with by area council offices. Application, however, is 'hindered by old-fashioned bureaucratic mentality' (Dente, Pregreffi and Ludovici, unpublished paper, no date).

Decentralisation in the Cities

No aspect of Italian local government has attracted so much international attention as urban decentralisation. Historical precedents existed, including district authorities in Naples before 1860 (Sabetti, 1977). Modern initiatives aimed at overcoming public alienation from political and bureaucratic elites have received multi-party support.

In a manifesto of 1956 the leader of the Christian Democratic Party in Bologna promised a new form of relationship — a greater integration between governors and governed. In the municipal election of 1960, policies of municipal decentralisation were given shape in the manifestos of the three main parties — Christian Democrat, Communist and Socialist. The Communists, who were returned as the dominant party, put stress on decentralisation as a means of activation and participation by involving neighbourhood councils in the formation of plans and programmes affecting their areas. Plans are discussed and ratified in neighbourhood assemblies. Proposals for building schools, new streets, bus routes, planning and building control are in principle subject to neighbourhood approval. Under a municipal ordinance of 1963 fifteen zones for decentralisation were created (later increased to 18), each with a council of 20 members chosen by the municipal council with representation of parties proportional to their strengths on the municipal council. An executive was chosen by the mayor for each zone with the status of assistant mayor. In 1974 the neighbourhood councils were equipped with powers to formulate budget guidelines, urban and economic development projects and other matters, and also to grant licences and building permits. At the same time provision was made for the president of each neighbourhood to be elected by its voters, subject to a two-thirds majority.

The Bolognese ordinance of 1963 was followed by decentralisation ordinances by the municipalities of Venice (1964), Rome (1966), Florence, Naples and Milan (1968) and other great cities. Over a hundred cities had introduced decentralisation schemes by 1972. In many cases the initiators felt frustrated by legal constraints on the form of these developments, particularly the lack of direct election by inhabitants of the sub-municipal areas. A national law was passed in 1976 which made this possible in municipalities with populations of at least 40,000. It also enabled authorities to delegate substantive powers to area councils in most fields of service. Sub-area councils may have up to two-fifths the number of members as the commune as a whole. Their presidents are chosen by the council of the commune from its members to chair and manage the business of the area councils, to represent them and to exercise functions

233

within the area delegated by the mayor.

Their councils are required to advise the city council on instruments affecting their areas such as budgets, multi-year plans and communal regulation. Communes may require virtually all aspects of policy-making and administration of services to be subject to consultation with sub-area councils.

Councils in cities of over 40,000 inhabitants with elected area councils may make them the principal administrative authorities for their areas. Decisions by area councils must be submitted to the communal council before implementation and may be referred back to them. If confirmed they become substantive decisions in law of the commune itself (Vandelli, 1984). In Milan, for example, it was decided that they should become the means of the commune for improving the effectiveness of its services rather than primarily a means for participation in decision-making (ibid.; Fedel and Goio, 1984b).

A study of their changing functions in Milan shows that in the early 1970s the area councils were predominantly occupied with articulating collective demands, expressing these to the centre (the commune) and responding to consultations by the commune. By 1982 the delivery of services had become their main focus. They became directly involved in public decision-making processes and in some matters they became the decision-makers. Consultative activities were extended from physical planning matters to personal services such as education, health, culture and recreation. Each area was given its own trained co-ordinator and surveyors. In some cases their officers shared premises with decentralised staff of main council departments to facilitate accessibility and joint working.

The extent to which area councils bring decision-making closer to the individual depends not least on the size of area council populations. Can Rome's areas, averaging over 142,000 population in 1972, truly be called 'neighbourhood' councils? Most big cities have areas averaging well below 100,000, and in general other cases are below the average of 27,500 which was the population of Bologna's areas in 1974. In Venice, with 31 quarters averaging only about 12,000 each, participation by the average citizen may be a more realistic goal.

One of the main problems in developing the effectiveness of area councils has been their relationship with the traditional departmental system and the assistant mayors (*aggiunti*) responsible for the political direction and development in particular fields of service for a city as a whole. The relationship of lines of administrative responsibility to sub-area council decision-making and control emerges as a central problem. Unless councils and their political executives have their own staff support and exercise some influence on what is being done by central departments in their areas, they remain very dependent on the central administration.

Communes have organised special courses for officers assigned to this work. Turin has placed an emphasis on providing 'premises of great prestige and dignity for decentralised government' as well as other measures to give the area administrations status and adequate facilities (Spagnuolo, 1982).

Although the results of the area councils have fallen short of the aims of those who saw them as the solution to problems of popular participation in decision-making and administrative efficiency and development, they remain a remarkable innovation which deserves re-assessment in the conditions of the 1990s.

3.13 THE GOVERNANCE OF METROPOLITAN AREAS

Italy possesses one of the greatest problems of metropolitan sprawl in Europe. Problems of overall planning and implementation, wide differences in the size and resources of the communes that metropolitan areas contain and the fact that the boundaries of provinces in general fail to match representative and functional needs have meant that to govern the metropolitan areas democratically requires major reforms (Norton, 1983).

The problem was for many years politically intractable. Major bills in 1975 and 1982 reached a high level in the many-layered process of state decision-making but failed after many redrafts to achieve the support required. Law 142 of 1990 grasped the bull by the horns. It introduced the status of 'metropolitan city' (*città metropolitana*) for implementation in the areas of Turin, Milan, Genoa, Bologna, Florence, Rome, Bari, Naples and Cagliari, and set an exacting programme for the redrawing of boundaries and the setting up of the new metropolitan authorities. Implementation is fraught with problems and it is too soon to know how far and how well the provisions will be implemented.

Metropolitan cities, with certain exceptions, are to have the legal attributes of a province but they will possess much wider powers than ordinary provinces (see §3.4). The law provides for them to take over from existing communes those services which have mainly a 'super-communal' character or are considered to need uniform solutions for reasons of economy or efficiency, including roads, traffic, transport, planning, conservation of environment and heritage, water and energy services, economic development and wider area services in health, school, vocational training and other urban services at the metropolitan level. They are to have the power to fix taxes, tariffs and charges in connection with their services. Communes retain their other functions and may receive delegated responsibilities from the cities for those parts of city services best carried out at communal level.

If existing provincial boundaries fail to meet stated criteria the regions concerned are required, after consultation with existing communes and provinces, to submit to the government proposals for new rational boundaries for the areas of the metropolitan cities. After agreement of the city boundaries the regions are required to determine new areas for the communes within the new cities, distinguishing between the area of the 'great commune' at the centre of the metropolitan city and the communes outside which are to be amalgamated and divided where necessary to meet defined criteria. In fulfilling these responsibilities the regions must take into consideration among other matters the ability of proposed new communes to exercise their functions, to achieve 'responsible participation of citizens' and to provide for 'a balanced relationship between their territorial and demographic dimensions'.

The national government is required, after consulting the competent parliamentary committees, to issue decrees to implement the new metropolitan arrangements within two years of the coming into force of the law.

A look at the map will show that each region concerned confronts a unique problem in defining its metropolitan area. Some, like Milan, have large areas of urbanisation sprawling out from the existing central commune. In others growth is limited to a particular direction or, as in Rome, development has been sharply constrained by geography. The loss of communal status by small communes will not necessarily deprive their inhabitants of political identity since they may expect to maintain local sub-municipal functions under the provisions for sub-municipal councils that are incorporated in the 1990 act. Nevertheless the provisions cut across many vested interests which may be expected to delay proposals that offend them by whatever means are available.

4. GERMANY

4.1 HISTORY AND TRADITIONS

Background and History

Germany has a population of over 78 million spread relatively evenly over an area much smaller than that of France. The urban clusters of settlement that are characteristic of most of the area are strikingly apparent from the air. Many are made up of individual communes of a wide range of sizes.

The Federal Republic of Germany (FRG) has had a record of steady economic progress and low unemployment up to the 1990s, and a high standard of social welfare. The absorption of East Germany in 1990 combined with a global economic depression and high levels of unemployment and, by West German standards, inflation, have subsequently disturbed that record. The outcome of the 'unification' has set great problems that have not begun to resolve themselves at the time of writing. This chapter must to a large extent be based on knowledge of the western *Länder* (regional states) up to 1990 together with recent information on the re-unified Germany where this is available.

The Basic Law of 1949, its amendments and the great corpus of legislation made within its provisions established a structure and set of explicit values into which the eastern Länder were suddenly absorbed within the places that had been waiting for them within the Basic Law of the federation.

Legally the westernisation of local government in the East preceded the unification, replacing the administrative system based on 'dual subordination' of local authorities to the state and the Communist Party with those of the West based on the principle of 'self-administration'.

Germany presents apparent contradictions. It has the highest level of cultural unity among the larger countries in this survey excepting Japan, yet it is not a unitary state but one in which power is purposely dispersed between three levels of government and within each level. Before 1990 it had been called a 'state without a centre', and one unusual in 'its absence of tensions' between the centre and its periphery. Cultural unity has been accompanied, however, by a frequent obsession with lack of a sense of German identity, which must be put down partly perhaps to its relative newness as a nation and the traumatic results of two world wars.

Power has been widely dispersed throughout Germany's history, excepting the Hitler regime (1933-45). From the early Middle Ages to the nineteenth century four main levels interacted with each other: imperial institutions, monarchies and principalities, the nobility and the cities. In 1806 Napoleon put an end to the remains of the Holy Roman Empire and imposed the Confederation of the Rhine on the German states other than Prussia and Austria: a federation in name if not reality. Some of its members reconstructed their administrations in ways that copied the French model, an influence that can still be traced in the institutions of western Länder, particularly Rheinland-Pfalz and Saarland, and through them has influenced the five new eastern Länder.

A few months after terminating the Holy Roman Empire Napoleon destroyed Prussia's army at the battle of Jena. The Prussian reaction, led at first by Chief Minister Baron vom Stein, was to reconstruct its army and also its system of urban government in accordance with a philosophy contrary to that of Napoleon. It taught that power must be decentralised in order to develop self-reliance at the grass roots. An act of 1808 placed responsibility firmly on the towns, which were expected to lead in a drive for national modernisation. Stein's approach was encapsulated in what is still a well-known text in Germany:

> Entrusting power and responsibility to a man develops his ability: continuous tutelage hampers his development. Participation in public affairs confers a sense of political significance, and the stronger this sense becomes, the greater also grows his interest in the common good and the fascination of taking part in public activities, both of which contribute to a nation's spirit.

He aimed 'to re-awaken "the sleeping energy of passive subjects", to encourage a spirit of community'. Local government was to be 'an instrument of national education', promoting love of locality, province and country. The city was conceived as an autonomous corporation, the citizens of which were to take responsibility 'for administering themselves their own sphere of activities'. The policy, as well as incidentally relieving the state budget by replacing salaried officials with unpaid citizen administrators, recognised the need to tie the growing property-owning and industrialising bourgeoisie into the web of state interests and to secure a class solidarity against interests that might subvert the authority of the state (Hesse, 1991; Gunlicks, 1986).

City administrations were to consist of councils elected by property owners and salaried professionals through a secret ballot, and an executive body (*Magistrat*) elected by the council. The Magistrat was a board of lay citizens elected for six years of office sitting with professionals elected for twelve years and possessing pension rights if removed before retirement age. Councils had general powers to deal with local matters but were subject to central supervision.

The Prussian model had a deep influence in eastern Germany, but some states in the West retained the French mayoral system. The bureaucratic element was strong everywhere. Prussia set up an intermediate administration consisting of provincial governors and districts (*Bezirke*) served by bodies of officials headed by a powerful administrator (*Oberpräsident*). The Bezirke are still retained in the larger Länder. In the South rulers in general did not favour the democratic element and aimed more at a continuation of 'enlightened despotism' implemented through expanding bureaucracies and the legal system.

Prussian laws of 1853 and 1856 allowed cities to choose between the Magistrat and Rhenish mayoral (*Bürgermeister*) models, the latter requiring the election of senior officials as well as the mayor (§4.11). A law in 1872 set up a new system of county and town governments, giving larger towns the right to claim both county and borough powers. Smaller towns shared functions with elected county councils (*Landkreise*), which undertook matters requiring larger resources. A new alignment of interests developed as a result of economic and social change. The body of middle-class entrepreneurs grew in size and importance, generally supported by rulers and traditional landlords, as did the highly respected professional bureaucracy whose status was based chiefly on their schooling in law and administration. Of a very different character was the strong development of an organised working-class to man Germany's new industries. (Hesse, 1991).

The Second German Empire, largely the creation of Bismarck and dominated by Prussia, was established in 1871 in the form of a confederation developed from the model of the Confederation of the Rhine. Its legal provisions guaranteed regional autonomy. The federal government was content to depend almost entirely on the constituent states for the implementation of domestic policies. The system provided the basis for the rapid growth of Germany as a highly efficient industrial nation and a world power that from the 1880s possessed social services which other European states sought to emulate. The new Germany was built on a diversity of systems among which stood out its strong and authoritative bureaucracies drawn largely from the Junker class, the aristocratic elite with a reputation for honesty and efficiency. Within the party system the Social Democratic Party (SPD) contested the power of conservative parties despite the handicap of a limited franchise. Direct provision of utility and other services ('municipal socialism') became well established. Many cities were developed and managed in a way that won the admiration of British and other foreign visitors, including Japanese.

The armistice and collapse of the monarchy in 1918 led to the Weimar Republic, a weak federation of eighteen states with universal suffrage and election by proportional representation. The 1919 Constitution guaranteed local self-government 'within the limits of the law'. The central government's position was a weak one in domestic matters. The Prussian state ruled most of the country and, like most other member states, was unsympathetic to the politics of the Weimar government and generally unco-operative, as was the large part of the bureaucracy that survived largely intact into the new regime. The period was one in which the strong moderates of the Christian Party centre and the SPD were challenged by extremists on both political flanks against a background of acute economic problems, unemployment and poverty. The functioning of local government was undermined in many areas due to the proliferation of warring political parties and polarisation between left and right. Local tax resources were reduced and dependence on the states greatly increased. Political turbulence led to some six hundred Prussian local authorities being replaced by state commissions.

Government weakness led directly to the seizure of power by the Nazi Party and the institution of the Third Reich in 1933. State and local autonomy was overridden in the name of the 'leadership principle', (*Führerprinzip*). A uniform system of administration was imposed with all civil servants under direct Reich control. A Nazi commissar was appointed to each municipality. Even councils loyal to the Nazis were reduced to no more than advisory bodies. The word *Gleichgeschaltung* was used to describe the suppression of local government in Germany, the word also used for the annexation of surrounding states. (Hesse, 1991; Jacob, 1963).

After the capitulation self-government and administration had to be rebuilt at all levels. The international Potsdam Agreement of August 1945 provided that administration of affairs in Germany should aim at decentralisation and development of local responsibility. Elected councils were to be rapidly restored. New local leaderships emerged in the West out of voluntary organisations including trade unions, chambers of commerce and the churches. They worked with the occupying powers to provide for resettlement and social relief and to rebuild the social and physical structure on democratic principles. The liberal doctrines of citizen-power and civic rights re-emerged from the German past, along with a determination to construct a new state on the principles of constitutionalism and administration that had been strongly developed in the previous century.

The local government forms described in §4.11 were largely built on what had existed before 1933, except in the British zone where the commission of occupation sought a new approach which, it was hoped, would break down the dualism between citizens and bureaucrats. Non-executive mayors and chairmen of county councils were to be served by professional non-political 'town and county clerks'. It was an unsucccessful attempt to separate politics and administration. The traditional bureaucracy, although purged, emerged little changed (as in 1871 and 1918), except that party membership became an important factor in senior appointments.

The *Rechtsstaat*

The Federal Republic was designed as a state within which freedoms were to be sanctioned by the law and upheld by right of appeal to the courts. Under the new constitution the rule of law was all-embracing. The system was designed as a complex pattern of checks and balances. Hence the thick web of regulations: the elaborate legal prescriptions by which German local freedoms are realised and expressed. In 1989 their enforcement employed 1,810 judges serving in federal and state administrative courts out of a total of 17,627 judges in all (*Statistisches Jahrbuch*, 1990). They seek to give a uniform interpretation of the law. The executive for county councils (*Landrat*) is responsible for ensuring the legality of local authorities in each county.

  The Law incorporates guarantees of rights, including protection of human dignity, free development of the personality, equality before the law, freedom of faith and creed and expression, protection of the family, its members, illegitimate children, the home, education, assembly and expression, privacy of post and telecommunication, free movement, choice of work, property and compensation for its acquisition by the state. These are part of the environment in which local authorities act and any perceived infringement may be referred to a court. The Federation (*Bund*) is ruled as a whole by two houses, a directly elected assembly (the *Bundestag*) and an upper house (the *Bundesrat*), which is constituted entirely of members of state (*Land*) governments who explicitly represent Land interests. The sixteen Länder have their own constitutions. They are united as members of the Federation but retain sovereign state powers of their own. Thus there is no vertical separation of powers but general interdependence in an organic relationship. Powers within Länder are shared with local government, a self-administering level of municipalities and counties. There is within the system a horizontal separation of legislative, executive and judicial powers among separate institutions. (Wagener, 1983b)

The Länder possess complementary sovereign powers and a limited area of shared power. Laws of a constitutional nature have to be passed by a two-thirds majority in both houses. The Bundesrat can veto legislation which affects Land interests. There are consultative and conciliatory procedures between the houses which make powers of veto generally unnecessary. Legislation can, however, be held up for long periods when party control of the Bundestag differs from that of the Bundesrat.

There are co-ordinative mechanisms between the Bund and the Länder: ministerial conferences covering the main areas of administrative activity, joint conferences of officials, meetings to agree federal contributions on certain 'joint tasks' and on finance for urban renewal. Attempts to discriminate at federal level between expenditures on different areas have been strongly opposed. The Länder have adequate means to prevent encroachment on their prerogatives.

The local authorities consist of communes or municipalities (*Gemeinden*) and counties (*Landkreise*). The powers of both are combined in those of the 119 county borough or county-free towns (*Stadtkreise* or *kreisfreie Städte*, not to be confused with *Kreisstädte* which are head towns of counties). Between these levels there exists a complex of institutions which derive their power from these principal authorities.

'The Basic Law provides a model for a layered democracy, based not on "the invisible will of the people" but on the principle that the will can be different in each Land and in each local authority, and common welfare interpreted in different ways' (translated from Püttner, 1982).

The *Parteienstaat*

The state based on parties, the *Parteienstaat*, derives from the system established under Bismarck. Article 21 of the Basic Law lays down that political parties should take part in the formation of the national will. The term 'party state' implies that the main inputs to the decision-making system are channelled through political parties which represent the diversity of its citizens. The parties bind the system together from top to bottom through party levels that are close and responsive to each other, sharing information and reactions.They also relate horizontally to business, social, labour and other local, regional and national interest groups, many of which are closely related to particular parties (§4.10). They manage the decision-making process by inter-party negotiation and bargaining, each seeking to maximise its contribution to law-making, regulation, financial allocations, appointments and other decisions that reflect the interests of their followers. Conventions between parties govern some of these procedures, as in the common practice of proportionate sharing of the right to make appointments to certain official posts at senior levels.

The negotiation of decisions is conducted between alliances and coalitions of parties and between the controlling majority and the minority to achieve agreement on any rights of the opposition that may be involved. Local politics play a key role within the parties and have increasingly influenced national voting in recent years and influenced Land and national policy agendas at higher levels of government.

Corporate Pluralism

Germany possesses a powerful system of interest group organisation, recognised in law and closely linked with the political parties. It includes statutory chambers of trade and industry and trade union and voluntary bodies associated with the churches. They are a recognised part of the institutional system in each Land and larger municipal area and receive support from public revenues. They work through a complex network of consultative procedures which underlie and integrate policy-making at all levels. The interweaving of interests and influence between sectors and levels of government and society (termed *Politikverflechtung*) is an outstanding aspect of German political life (see §4.6).

4.2 THE STATUS OF LOCAL GOVERNMENT

Constitutional Status

As described in the section above, the Constitution gives local authorities the status of the third level of the state. Article 28 of the Basic Law states that in each of the states (*Länder*), counties (*Kreise*) and communes (*Gemeinden*), the people must be represented by a body chosen in general, free, direct, equal and secret elections. It provides that in the communes an assembly of the people may take the place of an elected body, although this provision is generally unused. The communes are guaranteed the right to regulate on their own responsibility all the affairs of the community within the limits set by the law. Associations of communes (*Gemeindeverbände*) are also guaranteed the right of self-administration within the law. Sources and apportionment of tax revenue are constitutionally defined.

The status of local authorities is given additional support in the constitutions of the Länder. Thus the Bavarian Constitution of 1946 states that communes are primary territorial public law corporations and have rights of self-government and administration of their own affairs. A sub-article states that 'Self-administration in the communes serves to build democracy in Bavaria from the bottom up'. Another itemises but does not limit local functions to those within rights of self-administration. It states that communes have the right to meet their own requirements by public levies (taxes, imposts and fees) and that when state functions are delegated to them the necessary financial means must be made available.

The interpretation of these rights give local authorities a general competence to undertake all public affairs for their areas in so far as they are not already expressly assigned to or reserved by law for other authorities. They have power to issue regulations with the status of substantive law that are binding on citizens as long as no federal or Land law overrides them.

Where local authorities carry out tasks for the Land they come under its laws and supervision. Local administration is held to imply the exercise of the following rights and duties by a local authority:

- choice of its own form of organisation and the power to appoint, train and dismiss officials and other employees;
- its own sources of revenue and determination of expenditures and administration of its own financial affairs;
- control of land use and the type of building in its area in accordance with the law;
- provision of facilities for the benefit of the population;
- making of by-laws, although statutory authorisation may be necessary if they impose 'unusual burdens' on citizens;
- making decisions relating to individual citizens if they are necessary to enforce state or local government provisions.

Status in the Community

Local government appears to enjoy more respect in Germany than in most Western democracies. The concept of the commune as a true community of people living together in a neighbourhood who view themselves as distinct from those in other communities is still alive. The late Frido Wagener, probably the most influential of modern German experts in the field of national structures, said to me after seeing the scale of English metropolitan districts that it would be 'unthinkable' to most Germans that authorities should be made so large that they would not have a councillor as a neighbour to whom they could go easily to explain their problems. Nevertheless such factors as social change, internal migration and the arrival of refugees and workers from abroad have destroyed some of the solidarity that once existed.

Political Status

Local councils have lost discretion over many functions in which they were previously autonomous. Although constitutional law gives them a secure position within the state as a whole, it does not stop them from being hedged around with detailed regulations on the many matters on which they are dependent on the Länder. 'They are subject to many pressures encouraging them to see their role as that of contributing to a comprehensive national network of public service provision and administration' (Johnson, 1983). But since the 1960s they have discovered new 'political space'. As local environmental and other local issues have come to the fore in national politics, so local politicians have been increasingly listened to at regional and central levels.

But beyond their constitutional status and their legal competences there are other aspects of the system which contribute to local government's political status. There is the community leadership role assigned to their executives, the prestige and respect given to their professional administrators and the recognised place of their party groups as channels of influence on higher levels. Their initiatives show clearly that they exercise wide freedom in approaches to community government despite being so much integrated into systems of federal and Land law.

One reason for their strength is the recognition they enjoy as the local implementers of tasks under Bund and Land legislation. They possess a large if not dominant role as agents or administrators of services for other levels of government, especially in the case of duties that can be more or less regulated but require local adaptation of approach and administrative decision-making. On the whole it seems that the political status of local government has not been much weakened by recent developments.

The German local authority associations described in §4.5 are an important means through which local government status is maintained. They have influence and support in the Land parliaments. Many members of each Land parliament are also local councillors. There is a recognised political career from a sub-municipal or area council (see §4.12) to the full council, and thence to the Land parliament and even, for those who become members of Land governments, up to representation in the Bundesrat. One German administrator with a good knowledge of France and Britain placed the popular status of local government in Germany as below that in France but above that in Britain.

The Special Position of the *Landkreise* (Counties)

Although the counties are recognised in the Basic Law, it is disputed by some representatives of communes whether they possess the same level of guarantee. They have a long tradition and are considered a satisfactory structure for rural areas, but there are problems of inter-authority relations in more urbanised areas. On the other hand many influential Bürgermeister sit on county councils and may hold ambitions to rise to be county executive (Landrat). There is an ambivalence about the Landkreis level relating to its close association with the sub-offices of Land ministries and the state functions of the Landrat, including that of ensuring legality of communal decisions. This enhances its importance without undermining its autonomy or that of the Landrat when acting on its behalf.

4.3 CONCEPTS AND VALUES

Baron vom Stein's stress on the involvement of individuals in the purposes of the state through participation in local government (§2.1) contributed to the German tendency to see an organic relationship between citizen and state. The doctrine that local administration should be rooted in personal obligations was basic to the influential teachings of Rudolf von Gneist (1816-95), a scholar of the late nineteenth century who took as ideal models of local government the English magistracy and honorary service within the parish (quoted in Keith-Lucas (1970), from Gneist, *Das englische Verwaltungsrecht*). Another influential scholar, Otto von Gierke (1841-1921), promoted the concept of *Genossenschaft*, a term that combines the meanings of fellowship, association and co-operation as a condition of group freedom and the social solidarity that should underlie society.

The values described below appear to be more strongly evident in Germany than in most comparable countries and to underlie the attitudes and role of German local politicians and the public in relation to their expectations from government. (Wickwar, 1970)

The Value of Agreement by Negotiation

Since the Second World War Germany has enjoyed more harmonious internal social and economic relations than most large Western democracies. Research in Western Germany has shown that 'political conflict and competition are less valued than co-operation and harmony'

(Grunow, 1991; Böhret et al., 1988). This may be partly because its relatively high level of wealth and equality has moderated conflict between capital and labour, but its affluence must be at least partly attributed to behavioural characteristics, including the effectiveness of wage negotiation and the unity within the labour movement in its approaches to wage policy linked with the willingness of businesses to co-operate in the negotiation of joint settlements with the unions (at least until the industrial conflicts of 1992). To further this end, complex representation and consultation procedures are built into the system, both in industry and public administration. Differing political allegiances do not prevent parties of left, right and centre from working together in coalitions at federal, state and local levels of government. Much legislation results from bargaining behind the scenes between government and opposition.

Family Values

Certain trends cause anxiety, including the low birth-rate, the end of the period of rapid growth in the 1970s, the associated energy crisis, the onset of the unemployment problem and the decline of traditional assumptions about the work ethic and family life. The removal of the father's legal right to govern the family reflected a change to more individual autonomy and joint decision-making within the family unit. The family is still comparatively strong and recognised as the basis of society, although this is now the small, nuclear family. There remains an assumption that basic social responsibilities lie with the family first and with the local community second.

The Principle of Subsidiarity

Although the principle of subsidarity was given its most famous definition by Pope Pius XI in the encyclical *quadragesimeo anno*, it has been promoted chiefly by German clergy and academics as a means of defining the rightful distribution of authority within society and, in recent times, prominently within national government and the European community (see §1.3). It lays down that in the social order tasks should be undertaken at the lower level rather than the higher, moving upwards from the individual to the family, voluntary associations, community and nation, each level taking responsibility for a social matter where the level below is unable to respond to a particular need. Thus higher levels should give help and encouragement to the lower units when they are unable to fulfil their moral responsibilities unaided (Gretschmann, 1991). Thus it justifies the importance given in Germany to maintaining responsibilities at family, labour and employers' organisation levels and, where local government action is necessary for the public good, with local authorities. At the same time it emphasises the responsibility of the higher level to support or 'subsidise' the lower to enable it to exercise autonomous choice. Thus the principle points to a system of mutual responsibilities which holds society together within the moral law.

The principle assumes the search for consensus and joint working between higher and lower levels — in an American term 'co-operative federalism' — but without undermining the responsibilities of the lower order. It is sometimes associated with the concept of the 'social state' (*Sozialstaat*), relating to Article 20 of the Basic Law which defines the Federal Republic as a 'social federal state'. The phrase has been given conflicting interpretations. It seems that it was a compromise between those who advocated strong government intervention to achieve equal access to social resources and those who argued for no more than a residual role, limited to intervention in the interests of those without the means to help themselves to achieve acceptable social standards.

Other Values and Characteristics

The churches still have a significant influence on political attitudes, both diffusely through social contacts and the media and more specifically through their role in the CDU and CSU parties.

Policy is said to be infused by a sense of moderation and caution and a wish for gradualism, especially among the middle-aged (Edinger, 1968). One deep-rooted German characteristic is the respect and deference shown to highly trained experts and higher professional state civil servants. In the last century civil service status was made to depend on defined educational qualifications. School and university curricula were linked with entry into the civil service hierarchy. Law came to be regarded as the essential training for the levels of the public service. Civil servants were protected from arbitrary dismissal and enjoyed a remarkably high social status (which also embraced the state teaching profession). The constitutional law enshrines, without specification of their meaning, the 'traditional principles of the career civil service'. The service is well privileged but without the legal right of strike action. The civil servant is regarded as exercising state authority associated with the rule of law. The public service has been considered a balancing factor, securing the stability and security of other forces within state and society. It is seen as an important part of the checks and balances within the Constitution.

There is no clear distinction in Germany between the policy advice by public officials and the policy-making of ministers. One word, *Politik*, carries the meaning of both policy and politics. There has been no bar to officials engaging in politics. They have always been the largest single occupational group among members of parliaments consisting preponderantly of teachers, who have the status of civil servant. They formed 43 per cent of the Bundestag in the mid-1970s. Since 1949 party membership has become a condition for a wide range of senior public appointments. This has brought ambitious civil servants into parties, although at the same time it has not prevented politicians with different backgrounds from winning posts in competition with civil servants. It has brought about an intertwining (*Verflechtung*) of civil service, political and business world styles which has contributed strongly to the character of the bureaucratic and political worlds. The intertwining exists as densely at local government higher official and political levels as at state and federal levels. There is horizontal and vertical movement within the political and administrative elite, although it may be chiefly those who control party channels who open up opportunities for career change (Southern, 1979). Less happily, Verflechtung easily degenerates into 'felting' (*Verfilzung*) of interests where inter-sectoral relationships become not only intimate but also impenetrable to outsiders, and sometimes corrupt.

As implied above, the power of administrators is particularly strong in Germany and little affected by the attacks of the Greens and other radicals. In eastern Germany new local councils are reported to have been dominated by officials (Wollman, 1991). Often the bias towards the integration of views into consensual decisions has been so strong that formal opinions have rarely been challenged. It has been argued that this has resulted in rigidities and a lack of flexibility in the policy-making needed to meet the variety of local situations (Wollmann, 1984), or on the contrary that the freedom and well-being of communities depend upon a process of consensus formation that involves wide participation in general policy-making by all levels.

Almost any generalisation about German values can be challenged. There has been an evolution of values since 1945, beginning with considerable cynicism about the party system and the new Constitution, followed by increasing acceptance of both the role of the political parties and of federalism — particularly since the disturbances of the late 1960s. An analysis of surveys shows a remarkably strong growth in positive attitudes towards democracy at all educational levels and in the main religious groups, shown by questionnaire responses to have risen from 30 per cent in 1955 to 52 per cent in 1972 and 71 per cent in 1978. Surveys show, however, that the actual performance of the system falls below popularly held ideals — not so much in terms of liberal democracy as those of 'socio-economic' democracy and participation (Conradt, 1981). Nevertheless comparisons with other European countries in the European Commission's 'Euro-Barometer' have shown that Germans have tended to be more optimistic than members of other Community states about the stability and future of democracy, at least up to the unification of 1990. But the events of 1990-92 have certainly shaken complacency about the permanence of such values.

4.4 NATIONAL STRUCTURE

The national structure of local government is uniform throughout the federation. It consists of two levels — the communes (*Gemeinden*) and counties (*Landkreise*) — and the larger towns and cities, known as 'county-free towns' (*Kreisfreie Städte*) which exercise the responsibilities and powers of both these levels. Details of the numbers of authorities up to 1990 are shown in Table 4.1, including those brought in from the eastern Länder in the unification.

The Länder

The sovereign powers of the Länder cover most domestic matters, excluding principally railways and telecommunications. They range in size from the City-State of Bremen, with a population of 667,000 in 1989, to North-Rhine Westphalia with a population of 16,954,000. The average population without the eastern Länder was 4,917,000 in 1989. The five eastern Länder which joined the Bund in 1990 — Brandenburg, Mecklenburg-Vorpommern, Niedersachsen (Lower Saxony), Freistaat Sachsen (Freestate Saxony), Sachsen-Anhalt (Saxony-Anhalt) and Thüringen (Thuringia) — averaged about 2,165,000 inhabitants. The smallest Land, 'Freistadt (Freetown)' Bremen apart, is Saarland, with a population of 1,057,000. There are three city-states: Hamburg (pop. 1,610,000), Bremen (667,000) and Berlin (3,379,000). Hamburg and Berlin City Councils exercise local government functions directly although there is devolution to district authorities. Bremen has two county-free towns, a miniature local government system in itself. By contrast Bayern (Bavaria) was formerly a kingdom; Niedersachsen (Lower Saxony) was based on another kingdom; Hessen and Rheinland-Pfalz (Rhineland-Palatinate) were made up of many principalities; and Schlewig-Holstein of two Danish duchies.

Table 4.1: Administrative Structure of United Germany, 1990

Levels	number
1. Bund (Federation)	1
2. Länder (states including 3 city-states)	16
3. Landkreise (counties)	426
Stadtkreise or Kreisfreie Städte (county boroughs or cities)	117
4. Gemeinden (communes), including Städte (towns within county areas). (More than 6,000 in the West were members of unions of local authorities possessing full-time officials (*Verbände*))	16,127

Main source: Statistisches Jahrbuch für das vereinte Deutschland, 1991

In the six largest Länder in Western Germany administration is extensively decentralised to three to seven administrative districts headed by district officials (*Regierungspräsidenten*). Their main duty is to co-ordinate area administration. The districts contain Land field offices for schools, police, forest, finance and other services. There are also special-purpose administrative unions or associations of local authorities which may include Landkreise and county boroughs as well as Gemeinden (see §4.5).

In the city-state of Berlin and the metropolitan areas of Land Brandenburg around Berlin, most responsibilities have been devolved to the councils of 23 'town districts' (*Stadtbezirke*).

Landkreise (Counties)

In the western Länder the populations of the 237 Landkreise average about 160,000; those in the east average about 80,000. They are part of Land administration as well as local governments. Those in the western Länder were reduced in number from 425 in the 1960s to 237 by 1987, acquiring greater scale and more than 500 additional specific competences from the Land administrations in this period, mostly of a minor nature. Less than one-third of those in the west are now predominantly rural, and some have highly industrialised areas.

Their functions can in general be explained by the subsidiarity principle: that is they administer matters which require wider areas of control and larger resources than the Gemeinden possess, and also matters which do not require the wider scale of the Land administrative areas. Most of their administrative functions come through delegation by Länder, including vehicle licensing, building inspection and social welfare. They possess a number of mandatory functions, including promotion of vocational training and aspects of public health. Discretionary functions are highly developed, including assistance for institutions of further education, cultural and recreational amenities, homes for the elderly, youth centres and local transport, and other tasks delegated upwards by Gemeinden. As Land administrations they are responsible for state functions including public transport, civil defence and public security.

Stadtkreise or *Kreisfreie Städte* (County Boroughs or Cities)

The 117 Kreisfreie Städte are responsible for all local government tasks for their areas as well as any that may be delegated to them by Länder. They are in many cases the successors of chartered medieval boroughs.

Amalgamations and Joint Authorities

The number of Gemeinden was reduced by nearly two-thirds by amalgamation between 1968 and 1987, and the number of Landkreise by over 42 per cent. The need for the reforms had been argued on the grounds of economy and social justice (Wagener, 1969). Wagener's book culminated in a recommendation that the rural Gemeinden should have populations of at least 7,000, the middle-sized towns at least 40,000, the big all-purpose cities 200,000, the counties 170,000 to 380,000 and regional associations of authorities 2,800,000 to 5,300,000.

Länder set up their own commissions to work out the principles of reorganisation. Norms were set with functional needs in mind. In North Rhine-Westphalia the needs that determined the set minimum of 8,000 included a primary school with gymnasium and swimming pool for learners, an old people's home and a pharmacy. At a minimum size of 30,000 a secondary school, a school for the handicapped, an abattoir and a cultural centre were considered possible.

The minimum size to support an effective full-time staff was set by Länder variously at 1,500, 5,000, 7,500 and 8,000 inhabitants. The minimum distance that a citizen could be expected to travel into an administrative centre was put at seven, eight or ten kilometres.

In South Germany the stress was on voluntary amalgamation, use of joint bodies (*Verbände*) and consolidation of Landkreise. The result in rural areas was a pattern of 'federated' villages or farmstead communities around an administrative centre. Where large rural Gemeinden have been created by amalgamation it has been common to allow each of the constituent villages to retain its own council. Few services may be left for these councils to administer but there will still be a village Bürgermeister to attend to simple citizen needs, carry out administrative tasks, represent the interests of the village to the outside world and provide some leadership and ceremony.

Disadvantages of the enlarged 'unitary' Gemeinden in the North and West are given as less contact between citizens and councils, 'less dense representation' and 'a deranged sense of social membership in the citizenry' (Wagener, 1980). Loss of power by representatives to professionals may be added.

The reorganisations were intended to pave the way for increased functional decentralisation from the Land level in accordance with the principle of subsidiarity. The main potential was for transfer of functions to the Landkreise which, it was laid down in North Rhine-Westphalia, required a minimum size of 150,000 inhabitants or, in more thickly populated areas, 200,000. The boundaries should be 'so fixed that they constitute viable economic units able to play their part in the process of co-ordination within the Land's system of development centres and axes' (Siedentopf, 1981).

The fundamental principle for the process of reform was political consensus. Proposals were discussed with those to be affected. All the political parties in the North Rhine-Westphalian parliament — including the opposition — declared their willingness to participate in the reform. The foundations for acceptance were laid over a period of ten years (1964-74) against vociferous opposition from some quarters. 'This broad-based approval and the good-will of all the political parties facilitated the almost trouble-free implementation of the reform' (ibid.). Special grants were available as an incentive to voluntary amalgamation.

In South Germany a transfer of functions to joint authorities was preferred to amalgamation. As a result fewer than half of the 8,400 or so Gemeinden that remain possess their own administrations. Thus there are two classes of Gemeinden. Some two-thirds are *Grossgemeinden* (large communes), normally serving several former Gemeinden, and the others are parts of two-tier associations (*Gemeindeverbände*). Each of the five Länder which adopted the latter approach developed its own form of union. The names vary: *Amt* in Schleswig-Holstein, *Samtgemeinde* in Lower Saxony, *Verbandsgemeinde* or *Gemeindeverwaltungsverband* in Baden-Württemberg and *Verbandsgemeinschaft* in Bavaria. The boards which run these joint authorities consist of councillors appointed by member authorities in agreed proportions. Special-purpose joint bodies were also set up for such services as water supply, drainage, refuse disposal, fire protection and cultural facilities. In the Rhineland-Palatinate there are bodies of officials elected directly by the voters throughout the area (*Verbandsgemeinden*), forming a kind of 'quasi-county' authority but allowing more flexibility. The intention was that they would gradually be replaced by unitary authorities.

Table 4.2: Numbers and Populations of Gemeinden in Western Germany 1968 and 1987

Population	1968		1987	
	Number	%	Number	%
under 500	10,760	44	715	20
500-2,000	9,556	39	2,940	34.5
2,000-10,000	3,275	13.5	2,698	32
10,000-50,000	579	2	1,003	12
50,000-200,000	85	0.4	117	1
200,000 or more	27	0.1	31	0.4
Total	24,282	100	8,504	100

There are regional associations of local authorities performing tasks beyond the economic capacity of Landkreise. In 1980 they employed over 50,000 officials. There is also a very variable group of ten or so metropolitan authorities (*Stadtumlandverbände*) (§4.13).

Nearly 2,000 of the *Gemeinden* within counties have the status of 'towns' (*Städte*). The big majority are quite small — of between 5,000 and 20,000 inhabitants. Only about seventy have populations of over 50,000 and nine of between 100,000 and 200,000. Their status and the composition of their administrations are similar to those of the Kreisfreie Städte and they carry out many of the Landkreis functions under delegation. Table 4.2 shows the drastic reduction in their numbers since 1968.

Research reports suggest that management capability and achievement have improved substantially. A serious loss of local power has been averted and a higher level of decision-making has been opened up to local councillors (Wagener, 1983c). The improvements were, however, accompanied in most cases by sharp rises in the number of employees and in costs. The number of elected councillors dropped from 276,000 to 153,000. There has been a virtual end to the voluntary performance of village tasks and signs of a decline in willingness to participate in civic affairs. The apathy of the public that accompanied the reforms was described as 'reform-fatigue'. Smaller local authorities have come to be run on a political party system, which has discouraged those unsympathetic to party politics but opened up political careers to others. An American author comments that the West German Länder have in effect made a decision to emphasise equality, service delivery and planning at the expense of local determination (Gunlicks, 1981b).

One criticism is the failure to synchronise decentralisation of function with structural reform. The expectations of the degree of devolution of functions that would follow re-organisation have in many cases been disappointed. Against this the entry of new 'post-materialist' values into the political process has widened local government's concerns and contributions to higher-level politics (Hoffmann-Martinot, 1987).

The system works despite its complexity, but not without a great amount of effort given to consensus formation or, when this is impossible, aggrieved feelings about the imposition of decisions. But against this must be set the high degree of popular participation and contribution to decisions that remain at local levels, as well as the way in which the Constitution has enabled different Länder to develop individual approaches that reflect the diversity of local values and traditions.

4.5 INTER-AUTHORITY RELATIONS AND ORGANISATION

An outstanding feature of German local government is the extent to which tasks that cannot be carried out satisfactorily at one level of authority are delegated to another or to ad hoc bodies. Landkreise carry out activities on behalf of the Länder, and Gemeinden on behalf of both Länder and Landkreise, wherever the tasks involved are agreed to be most suitably undertaken at the lower level. Other functions are delegated upwards from Gemeinden to joint bodies or Landkreise to gain the economic advantages of greater scale or more efficient areas.

Joint authorities or unions (*Verbände*) provide a flexible way of adapting structures to meet functional criteria at all levels. Gemeinden have a long tradition of joint organisation. Before the reforms of the 1960s and 1970s they had joint organisations to provide for almost every matter that could benefit from administration on a wider scale than that of the individual community, including equipment-sharing, road and sewerage work, schools, residential homes and hospitals. They adopted a wide range of forms for sharing resources from both public and private law.

The details of types of association are given below, starting with those nearest to the local community and ending with national associations. They have mostly been formed voluntarily but membership may be required by law in some cases.

The commonest form of joint action is the *Zweckverband*. It is a public law corporation which can be given the power to exercise one or more of its member-authorities' functions. It has been used for running schools, special and adult education, fire services, cultural matters, roads, waste disposal, welfare and youth services, savings banks and recreational areas. It is less common since amalgamations of authorities have reduced its necessity.

'Public law agreements' provide for one authority to provide one or more services for others at communal, association or county level.

'Working groups' or 'collaborative associations' of authorities are voluntary forums for the discussion of common issues and for planning and co-ordinating matters of shared concern. They may make decisions on matters which are not legally binding on the participants.

Multi-purpose associations of authorities in metropolitan areas are described in §4.13.

Bavarian *Bezirke* (special districts) administer aspects of social services, health care, youth, environmental conservation, agriculture and other services deemed to be beyond the capacity of smaller counties and county-free cities. They are directly elected with their own executive and chief executive officer.

Regional associations of local authorities have been formed for functional purposes. Rhineland and Westphalia-Lippe, parts of North-Rhine Westphalia, have assemblies that have been elected by constituent authorities since Prussian times. The Pfalz (Palatinate) *Bezirksverband* is similar and was set up under Napoleon. Social services are administered by such bodies in Baden-Württemberg. Hesse has a municipal joint body for welfare services which covers its entire area (Rengeling, 1982).

Local authorities are also able to set up joint bodies provided for in private sector law, or to mix public and private law forms for one undertaking. The main private law forms are the public limited liability company or, in American terms, the stock corporation (*Aktiengesellschaft: (AG)*), and the private limited liability company (*Gesellschaft mit beschränkter Haftung (GmbH)*).

General Federal and State Associations

There are 'peak' associations (*Spitzverbände*) which represent the interests of local authorities at government and parliamentary levels and deal with Land and national press relations. They also provide for the exchange of experience on legal and service matters between their members and give expert advice to local authorities on request.

Three main associations at national level are deeply involved in national policy formation in Bonn and Berlin. They co-ordinate their work through a joint body. These are:

(1) Deutsche Städtetag (Association of German Cities and Towns), which includes the city-states as well as county boroughs, large and medium-sized towns and joint urban authorities (Lindenallee 13-17, 5000 Köln-Marienburg 51);
(2) Deutsche Landkreistag (County Councils Association), Adenauer Allee 136, 5300 Bonn; and
(3) Deutsche Städte- und Gemeindebund (German League of Towns and Local Communities), Postfach 2733, Kaiserswerterstrasse, 199/202, Düsseldorf 1.

They represent local government on many important national and international bodies. Membership is mostly indirect through similar Länder associations which exercise parallel functions in national policy-making.

Important specialised institutions under boards of local government representatives have been set up since 1949 to focus on the research and developmental needs of local authorities:

(1) the Joint Local Government Centre for Management Studies (*Kommunale Gemeinschaftsstelle für Verwaltungsvereinfachung*, (generally known as the KGSt)) promotes improvements in organisation and management;
(2) the German Urban Planning Institute (*Deutsche Institut für Urbanistik* (DIFU)) which undertakes urban research, documentation and consultancy and is governed by representatives of local government and the federal ministry for housing;

(3) WIBERA (*Wirtschaftsberatungs Aktiengesellschaft*), which provides audit, tax advice and management consultancy services to local authorities and public works agencies;

(4) *Verband Kommunaler Unternehmenen* (VKU), concerned with gas, electricity, water and distance heating services;

(5) *Verband Öffentliche Verkehrsbetriebe*, concerned with local public transport services;

(6) *Verband Kommunaler Arbeitgeberverbände*, representing local authorities as employers in negotiations on taxation matters.

 These bodies have been supported mainly by membership fees, research grants and/or project and consultancy contracts.

4.6 INTER-GOVERNMENTAL RELATIONS

Legal Separation and Political *Verflechtung*

Relationships between federal, Land and local government are controlled by the provisions of the Basic Law. Legally local authorities are part of the Länder. In a sense the three levels are part of the state and bound by purposes which are set at national level. Where responsibilities for the exercise of power are not defined in the law they fall to the Länder unless because of their nature they cannot be administered by individual states or unless the principles of legal or economic unity or of uniformity of conditions across the nation require federal legislation. Thus where there is agreement that there should be a national approach to a matter that is constitutionally the responsibility of the Länder to implement, the draft of a framework law is developed between the two federal houses. This must win the vote of at least two-thirds of the members of the upper house of representatives of the Länder in the Bundesrat as well as of members in the lower house. Thus national parliament legislates on most matters of importance to local government, including local taxation, but not matters where sovereignty lies with the Länder, as is the case regarding education, police and the structure and functions of local authorities.

 There are also areas of joint power between Bund and Länder, including public welfare, regulation of education and training grants, transfer of land, national resources and means of production, prevention of the abuse of economic power, agricultural matters, economic viability of hospitals and regulation of their fees, public protection in matters related to marketing of food and animals, traffic, waste disposal and air and noise pollution.

 Power which belongs neither to legislatures nor to the judiciary belongs to local authorities and other public bodies which possess the right of self-administration (*Selbstverwaltung*) and administer the law on behalf of the state. The latter include providers of public utilities and those responsible for the management of certain public funds. Domestic policy implementation is shared by the Länder and the local authorities, but the latter predominate in implementation to the extent of spending two-thirds of overall public investment and also due to the extensive functions delegated to them by the Länder.

Important as the separation of powers between territorial levels may be in law, in political terms there is the opposite: an intertwining of activities (*Verflechtung*) and a high degree of interdependence between the Bund, Länder and local government and between them and other sectoral interests. Political influence is exercised in practice more upwards than downwards. The higher levels have accepted the reality of their dependence on local government as implementer of most important domestic legislation. Decision-making in practice reflects contributions from a wide spectrum of opinions from local government and other local public and private bodies as well as that of the higher echelons of policy-makers.

A federal law of 1967 provided for the exercise of Keynesian counter-cyclic policies at national level and bound Länder and local authorities to conform with national expenditure targets. Although its implementation proved to be far short of perfect, it did provide a new legal basis for inter-governmental relations. It required joint planning, decision-making and financing to match Land and local government policies: a high degree of joint decision-making that did not in the event result in loss of power to the centre. 'Despite severe conflicts over distribution, however, inter-governmental bargaining systems have remained stable. The parliamentary arena is used either for exercising vetoes or for highlighting the financial problems of all local authorities.' 'Quantitative policies are no longer sufficient; they have been complemented by qualitative policies' (Hesse, 1991). Hesse reports evidence that local government's ability to maintain its positions 'virtually compels the central authorities to co-operate and bargain with them'. 'Motivations, communication, acceptance and dialogue are keywords of the current debate: a participative-cooperative model of politics aims for the increasingly scarce resources of "consensus".' 'The local level has been gaining ground and is becoming — as an authority of implementation, co-ordination and integration — an increasingly important part of decision-making and problem-solving.' (ibid).

What has happened has been described as a development from co-operative federalism to joint policy-making. 'The political process moves onwards towards solutions as the several actors learn and adapt their aspirations. These solutions may be described as genuine reforms but are characterised by the effort to keep costs of transaction as low as possible.' (Hesse, 1987)

The Impact of Federal Power on Local Authorities

Despite the doctrine of vertical separation of powers the federal parliament has developed national policies relating to fields within local government competences and has backed them with financial support. Grants have been provided from Bonn for low-cost housing, regional industry and agriculture, construction of university accommodation and local transport. They have been justified by the need to give substance to national priorities. Doubts about the constitutionality of such grants were put to rest in 1969 by additions to the constitutional law which specifically authorised those that met certain conditions. They needed agreement with the Länder as to who was responsible for financial support to local authorities. In practice this took the form of block grants to the Länder, who used their powers to allocate them among local authorities. They were increasingly determined on a per capita basis, and the original intention that they should promote equalisation of services between the Länder has not been realised to an appreciable extent. Distribution among the Länder by an enlargement of equalisation grants would have been a more progressive method, but this would have been against the interest of some Länder who blocked such proposals.

The recession of the early 1980s caused problems of economic management at federal level, since it reduced the revenue that local authorities could draw on through the business and trade tax and at the same time increased their liabilities for social assistance to the unemployed. Thus they lacked the resources to counter the fall in economic activity by means of public investments and so assist in implementation of 'counter-cyclical policies'. Past failures of federal attempts to prime local development by means of federal development grants have discouraged new initiatives of a similar kind. One study concludes that the requirements for high consensus in federal-state policy-making 'have prevented the introduction and the implementation of a more effective business cycle and employment policy' (Reissert and Schaefer, 1985). Another emphasises the slowness of decision-making on inter-governmental transfers and blames it on problems of federal-state consensus (Reissert, 1980). The evidence is not available at time of writing on the impact of the much greater economic problems in the early 1990s.

The Intertwining of Tax Receipts

The contradictions between the constitutional duties to support local autonomy and to equalise resources create dilemmas both at federal and at Land levels. Local government expenditure was forced down from 18.0 to 16.8 per cent from 1980 to 1987, as was Land spending to the lesser extent (from 25.5 to 24.6) (Owens, 1991, based on OECD figures). At the same time the Länder have attempted to shift the burden down to local government, while local authorities have had to cope with mounting economic and social problems. As urban problems have risen on the political agenda, the need for the exercise of joint responsibility between levels of government has become ever clearer, while at the same time growing antagonism is reported between the three levels on financial issues.

Much of the expenditure by local authorities is under mandates from higher levels and is more or less regulated or controlled from above by what Germans call the 'golden reins'. But because of the interweaving of interests and the high level of consensus achieved within the decision-making procedures, it is virtually impossible to say how much influence local government or higher government levels have in these matters.

The intertwining of interests is shown in the history of public taxation since 1969. In that year a constitutional amendment changed the pattern from one in which local authorities independently controlled their major source of finance — the business and trade tax (*Gewerbesteuer*) — to one in which main national taxes were shared between levels. Value added tax also came to be shared. In 1980 the local government share of income tax was fixed at 15 per cent and in 1984 the local share of the business and trade tax was raised to 85 per cent. Income from shared taxes made up 75 per cent of federal tax revenue, 88 per cent of state tax revenue and 85 per cent of local government tax revenue. But for local authorities tax revenue did not constitute more than a third of gross income: 25 per cent came from government grants and about 20 per cent from fees and user charges.

Administrative and Financial Relationships

Each Land governs its own system of local government. The branches of its administration are closely associated with local authority departments, especially at Kreis level. There are four main levels in the larger Länder. For example in Rheinland-Pfalz (population 3,624,000) there were in 1984: (1) Eight ministries in addition to the prime minister's office and state chancellery. One of these dealt with federal responsibilities. All are concerned in different ways with the work of local authorities.

(2) A second level of Land administration comprehending functional offices for water management, environmental protection, oversight of trade, road administration, youth and social work etc.; and three territorial administrative authorities responsible for the implementation of the general law within their areas. The latter authorities, headed by their chief officials (*Regierungspräsidenten*), comprise 57 specialist divisions within six different branches, including one for education, one for economic and physical planning and building administration, one for forestry, one for the economy and environment and one for remaining services.

(3) Twenty-four county (*Landkreis*) level administrations with responsibilities both to the Land government and to the county authorities; and also two or three hundred functional Land offices including, for example, 36 finance offices, 26 health offices, 106 forestry offices and nine road construction offices.

(4) Thirty-eight independent city and communal authorities and 163 unions of Gemeinden; and certain other statutory ad hoc authorities, such as nine police offices.

There are also county boroughs (*Stadtkreise*) which combine the responsibilities of levels (3) and (4).

Within the Länder there has been a 'massive centralisation of jurisdiction' by means of extensive and detailed laws, plans, programmes and dependency on specific grants in the 1980s connected with a great increase in mandatory tasks, although the reins of control are sometimes very light (as well as very 'golden') (Uppendahl, 1985). Activities completely free from Land controls remain important, including cultural and some health and youth services, road construction, fire protection, public utilities, economic development, land-use control and urban development. In land-use planning there is a hierarchical system of plans, but ultimately the local authority is autonomous in this field. Higher-level plans are imprecise and must be based primarily upon provisions at local level (Mayntz, 1977).

Within a Land powers are exercised in parallel by the Land, local authorities and other bodies with the right to self-administration. The Land has a responsibility to ensure that they are used legally and exercises this power through its local officials. Six of the larger Länder exercise their powers locally through the Regierungspräsidenten at the second of the levels described above. These have responsibility for the exercise of Land powers of educational administration, police and audit, and also for ensuring the legality of the decisions of local authorities and public undertakings. At a more local level their responsibilities are fulfilled by officials whose areas correspond with those of the counties.

This supervisory structure does not mean that there is any control of the substance of local authority decisions beyond checking on legality, and supervisory interpretations are subject to challenge in the courts. One provision in the Basic Law makes it a duty for a Land to provide sufficient financial resources to local authorities. The Länder have powers of budgetary control but they are not very effective. There is a common interest between local authorities and the Länder in not restricting expenditure on such matters as economic development and air pollution.

If a local authority budget is going awry the Land is both empowered and obliged to intervene. It can do this in various ways, such as ordering taxes and charges to be increased or specific service expenditures to be cut. It can even appoint a commissioner to take over decision-making for the council, although nowhere was this done during the period of local fiscal crises in the early 1980s. The Länder have been said to have generally acted weakly and too late, and in some cases 'had to divert substantial funds from their own budgets to offset local authority deficits' (Banner, 1987).

The scope for decision-making within the law and regulations, the political power of the city and rural leaders and the practical limits of control and communication — all these ensure that local authorities have considerable freedom over their policies and expenditures. The larger, reorganised local authorities have greater strength against the Länder than their smaller predecessors. The increased block grants have also enhanced their real autonomy, as have devolutions of power under programmes of functional decentralisation. Nevertheless the continuing mixture of delegated tasks which brings local executives and administration close to Land officials with 'autonomous' tasks must dilute their direct responsibility to local councils.

Länder Support to Local Government

Länder are required by the federal Constitution to pass laws providing for unconditional grants or re-allocations of tax revenue to local authorities for the purpose of equalising resources (*Finanzausgleichgesetze*). What individual Länder can do is largely dependent on equalisation measures between Länder at Bund level. From 1951 a complex formula provided for the transfer of revenues from those Länder whose 'tax potential', assessed according to nationwide per capita tax revenue, population density, urbanisation and other special burdens, was above 102 per cent of the national figure to those whose tax potential was below 95 per cent of that figure. One-quarter of receipts from VAT was also used for the financial support of states with tax revenue well below the national average to bring their tax income up to 92 per cent of the average. The Constitutional Court has accepted that to go further than had been achieved towards redistributing taxes on an average per capita basis would violate the principle of the financial autonomy of the Länder. (Details of the Land equalisation measures between local authorities are given in §4.9.)

General

To sum up, most spheres of activity are governed by federal legislation. A primary aim is equalisation of economic and social resources, but this is exercised against the power of Länder and local authorities to defend their constitutional rights and autonomy. The high levels of joint working between levels of government in most spheres of activity and reciprocal safeguards inhibit independent exercise of power. Distinctions between responsibilities have been blurred and the question of whether mixed financing should be abolished or stay has become a permanent topic of discussion between constituent governments.

According to one writer who was in the early 1980s head of the Federal Chancellor's Office, 'the advance of co-operative federalism has reached a limit which ought not, in the interest of Land sovereignty of decision-making, to be transcended' (Schreckenberger, 1983). On the system as a whole he concluded confidently that 'The federal system has proved its value in a sophisticated industrialised society as a model for a balance of power and for effective decision-making'. The question raised by many familiar with systems of much less complexity must be whether it is not exceedingly over-elaborate, expensive and unadaptive because of the strength of the vested interests which it sustains. A key issue is perhaps whether the maintenance of autonomy and rights within the system and the stability it has brought could not have been achieved by simpler means.

4.7 LOCAL SERVICES

General Competence and Flexibility

Under the principle of general competence (*Allzuständigkeit*) municipalities are free to act on all local matters within legal principles except where a task is specifically assigned to a government body in the law or not a matter for the public benefit. Otherwise tasks fall into three main groups: responsibilities exercised under general planning powers, provision of facilities for the benefit of the population and regulative responsibilities. Some are delegated from above and subject to Land regulations and usually instructions. Others are obligatory and others voluntary. There is much in common among Länder regarding tasks delegated to or placed by law on Landkreise, but less uniformity in those for which municipalities have responsibility. Differences arise largely because of the different sizes and unions of Gemeinden and the special nature of town government as opposed to rural.

There has been a strong tendency at Land level to add to the obligatory and delegated functions of local authorities, accompanied by instructions and detailed regulations for the purpose of achieving uniformity of practice. This has resulted largely from citizen pressure from those who felt that they should have services at least as good as those provided in other Gemeinden. This has whittled away the discretion of municipalities, both regarding what they undertake under the general competence principle and the type and manner of provision.

At Landkreis level certain functions are delegated to the chief executive (the *Landrat*) instead of the council.

The Growth of Local Government Functions

The fact that communal policy is social policy became fully recognised only from the end of the 1960s. The parties on the right (CDU/CSU) declared that policies of communes possessed the same validity as those of the Bund and the Land. The SPD stated that social relationships were at the kernel of communal policy and that the future of the Gemeinde would decide the future of the Land. (Böhret and Frey,1982)

The interweaving of roles and responsibilities makes it impossible to say that a particular area of administration is, as a whole, the responsibility of one or other level of government. In most matters there is interdependence. Responsibilities are divided but inter-connected, and decisions are often collective to avoid confusion.

In the past twenty years all Länder have sought in principle to decentralise as many powers as possible to local authorities and have justified amalgamation of small Gemeinden by the increased activities it should make possible to confer on them. What was achieved in transfers to the new Gemeinden was disappointing. In four Länder, however, a large number of functions were transferred from Land to Landkreis level, although mainly those that had been long decentralised elsewhere.

Where communes have insufficient resources to undertake particular legal responsibilities these are normally undertaken either by joint communal bodies (*Verbände* §4.5) or by Landkreise as what are termed 'complementary tasks'. Landkreise also give financial and administrative support for municipal functions in order to help equalise standards thoughout their areas, for example in local physical planning, health care and the preservation of monuments.

The following list indicates levels of responsibility generally but cannot cover all cases since arrangements vary under Land law and delegation. 'County-free' towns (*Kreisfreie Städte*) may be assumed to possess the competences of both Gemeinden and Landkreise where appropriate.

Distribution of Services

1. Town and Country Planning and Development
Gemeinden and *Landkreise* are responsible for zoning, urban development and landscape management.

2. Housing
Gemeinden have set up or invested in public-interest housing agencies — generally non-profitmaking companies providing subsidised housing for low-income groups with the benefit of tax concessions. Such companies (in which local government owns about half the share capital) and housing cooperatives provide a large proportion of the housing stock and often take local authority-nominated tenants under local agreements. The Gemeinden usually prepare sites for building by these agencies.

Dealing with homelessness is a communal multi-service responsibility under the social assistance law (Happe,1983).

3. Roads.
Roads are graded as federal long distance, Land, Landkreis and communal. *Gemeinden* are responsible for local streets and pathways. Those with over 80,000 inhabitants are in general responsible for the construction and maintenance of federal highways within their areas, and those with over 30,000 inhabitants for Land roads. *Landkreise* undertake road construction and maintenance work beyond the capacity of individual municipalities.

4. Transport
Gemeinden are responsible for local passenger transport. *Landkreise* provide local passenger transportation jointly with *Gemeinden*, generally by means of founding and subsidising companies to run buses and local tramways. They also provide small air fields. *Landkreise* take responsibility for intermunicipal transport.

5-6. Education
Although teachers are appointed and paid by the Länder, local authorities

are involved in virtually all other aspects of school management except curricular and teaching matters. The laws of almost all Länder specify that school administration is a matter of autonomous administration for all *Schulträger*. These are basically municipalities, but often Landkreise are involved in a 'complementary' capacity, especially from middle-school level upwards. The non-teaching aspects of the establishment, organisation and administrative direction of schools come under their own competence. They develop, build, equip and maintain schools and participate in the choice of school directors. They have strong influence on head teacher and other senior appointments. They were instrumental in developing the comprehensive school concept and are deeply involved in procedures relating to school closures (Dentzer, 1983; Siebenhorn, 1983). Their school-planning activities are intertwined with those of other levels of government. *Gemeinden* are responsible for nursery, primary, middle, advanced high, integrated, special schools and folk high schools, and for further and adult education institutions. *Landkreise* are responsible for middle schools (jointly with *Gemeinden*), higher schools and technical colleges.

7. Cultural Activities

Both *Gemeinden* and *Landkreise* regard cultural matters as a principal field of activity. The *Kreisfreie Städte* are most prominent in the provision of major institutions. Culture is traditionally regarded as fundamental to the maintenance of higher values and development of human potential, both in terms of the individual and the integration and development of society. Substantially it covers cultivation of science and learning generally, stage and musical arts, visual arts, literature, film, centres for the media, festivals and open-air performances, 'socio-cultural animation' with an emphasis on neighbourhood or group self-management and other innovative areas of activity. Policies are implemented through theatres, libraries, museums, music schools, folk high schools and other forms of institution provided directly or supported by local authorities (Hoffmann and Kramer, 1983).

8. Libraries, Museums and Archives

Libraries are provided by *Gemeinden* and, for regional usage, by the Länder. *Landkreise* provide mobile libraries. Museums are provided by all levels of government. Archive departments with their own directors exist in most towns and cities with over 30,000 inhabitants. One authority describes the town archive as an administrative office, a service undertaking, an information centre and a scientific cultural institution all in one (Klötzer, 1983).

9. Recreation and Conservation of Environment

Gemeinden and Landkreise provide and maintain sports centres, stadiums, swimming pools, ice rinks, youth hostels and subsidies to local clubs as well as parks and recreation areas, while Länder and joint authorities (*Verbände*) have created a thick network of forest, jogging and rambling paths as well as providing indoor swimming pools and other recreational facilities.

10. Health and Social Welfare

The Health Service The service is carried out by institutions which the *Bund*, *Länder*, *Gemeinden*, joint communal agencies and other public institutions provide. *Gemeinden* may provide domestic nursing for sick mothers and others. The basic level of authority is the *Landkreis* or *Kreisfreie Stadt* health office. Hospitals are a Land responsibility but are often provided by Landkreise and other local authorities or joint agencies of *Gemeinden*, with the Länder and the Bund providing subsidies. Costs are met chiefly by insurance organisations (Pfau, 1983). Public Health responsibilities at *Gemeinde* and *Landkreis* level include food safety, abattoirs, preventive health services and environmental health protection including water, land and air purity, noise and radiation. There are policies and services for health education, child health, youth, target groups (e.g. mothercare, maternity and abortion control) and medical inspection, supervision of midwives, pharmaceutical and drug control etc. Much of this work is delegated to Landkreis level.

Social Services The law lays down that social assistance (*Sozialhilfe*) is to enable the receiver of help to conduct a life which human dignity requires, including enabling the recipient to become as far as possible independent of such help. It deals with individual support required beyond what is provided through the extensive and complex social insurance system: the work that cannot be regulated in detail because of the individuality of the case (the 'safety net below the safety net'). The provision of social aid falls locally on the *Kreisfreie Städte* and the *Landkreise*. The implementation of social help is a matter of communal self-administration. A higher level of responsibility lies with the Länder with participation by joint communal agencies (*Landschaftsverbaände*, *Landeswohlfahrtsverbaände* and the Land regional authorities, the *Bezirke*). The Land responsibilities are commonly transferred to local authority level. Local authorities entrust much social work to voluntary associations under joint plans (Giese, 1983). There are general laws for particular social groups, with responsibilities focused at the county level. Support for children and youth (*Jugendhilfe*) lies within the 'self-administration' responsibilities of *Gemeinden* and joint communal authorities. Some *Gemeinden* without Kreisfreie Stadt status provide child and youth services. The word for youth (*Jugend*) embraces all the early years from infancy up to adult status. Services (*Jugendhilfe* including child welfare — *Jugendwohlfahrt*) are provided under consolidated legislation which stresses their unity of aim. It covers help to children and families, parent and family education, advice on upbringing, marriage and problems of children and young people, social work for children including care and adoption, preparation for working life, help for the socially disadvantaged, handicapped children, youth clubs and other matters which fall within the definition of aims (Jans, 1983). Homes for the elderly are commonly undertaken by *Landkreise* as a 'complementary' responsibility.

11. Police, Protection in Emergencies and Civil Defence; Maintenance of Public Law and Order

General powers and responsibilities for policing, protection in emergencies and civil defence lie with the *Bund* and the *Länder*. Powers are often delegated to *Gemeinden* and *Landkreise*. However the maintenance of public law and order is a main head of services for *Gemeinden* based on their fundamental regulatory powers. It includes traffic matters and parking control, markets and pricing of goods and public safety. *Gemeinden* can be charged for police services provided on request. *Gemeinden* and *Landkreise* are also given responsibilities under Land laws for public safety and rescue services — an area of competence which is interpreted widely.

12. Fire Protection

Under Land laws *Gemeinden* of over 100 thousand inhabitants are with certain exceptions required to provide fire agencies. Many smaller *Gemeinden* also have full-time forces. All *Gemeinden* have voluntary fire services. Fire services are also provided by *Landkreise*.

13. Development of Local Economy and Employment

This area of activity by *Gemeinden* and *Landkreise* has a long history and covers a wide range of promotional and other supportive activities including site provision, ancillary support and rent and tax concessions. No direct investment in private sector enterprise is permitted.

14. Public Utilities

Gemeinden and *Landkreise* provide water, sewerage, drainage, electricity, gas and district heating services — often jointly and through private law companies.

15. Waste Collection and Disposal: *Gemeinden* and *Landkreise*

16. Tourism.

Gemeinden provide tourist bureau, monitor accommodation facilities and take other measures designed to attract tourists.

17. Abattoirs and Veterinary Services: *Gemeinden* and *Landkreise*.

18. Markets: *Gemeinden* and *Landkreise*.

19. Cemeteries and Crematoria: *Gemeinden* and *Landkreise*.
20. Other services.

Services with which local authorities are associated but which are not part of their main budgets or direct legal responsibilities include (*Gemeinden*) savings banks, federal post offices, railway stations and branch employment offices; (*Landkreise*) savings and loans banks, local health insurance, federal employment and customs offices.

Delegated regulatory responsibilities include: (*Landkreise*) nature protection, veterinary services, land registry and survey; (*Gemeinden*) schools, police, supervision of commerce and working conditions, environmental protection and agricultural field control.

4.8 IMPLEMENTATION OF SERVICES

Local authorities can implement services through their own employees or use joint organisations or forms under private law. Joint stock companies are used extensively for energy and other public utility and local passenger transport undertakings.

Forms within an authority's own administrative structure include undertakings with wide delegated powers for such purposes such as vehicle parks, cleansing, drainage, slaughterhouses and stockyards, museums and theatres. They can transfer their competences for services to communal enterprises and use special purpose-designed forms such as that for hospital undertakings. (Püttner, 1983)

It has long been normal to contract work out, but from the 1960s its more extensive use has been strongly pursued by centre-right parties as a rational and economic approach under the name of privatisation (*Privatisierung*) (Dieckmann, 1983). All possibilities have been examined repeatedly and in great detail. Some economists and politicians argue that 80 per cent or more of public tasks can be transferred to the private sector. Practical experience indicates that most authorities, whatever their political character, wish to stop far short of that level. Both right and left wish to maintain direct and effective control over standards. Many tasks have proved uneconomic for the private sector in rural areas and problematic in large cities. Recent surveys have led to the conclusion that placing tasks outside the municipal organisation in most cases creates a 'neighbourhood monopoly' and does not lead to significant savings if equivalent quality is to be maintained. Only occasionally is there a true free market situation. Financial savings arise principally in the case of services to the well-to-do, where high prices can be charged (Grunow, 1991).

The principle of subsidiarity implies that tasks performed privately should not be pre-empted by local government. It has been used to justify the role of five national agencies which undertake important social services with the main costs being met by local authority subsidies. These are the two main confessional organisations, Caritas and Innere Mission, the Workers' Welfare Organisation (formed by the Social Democratic Party (SPD)), the German Red Cross and a federation of non-religious, non-political voluntary groups. They provide, for example, services to old people, transport for the disabled, centres for foreign workers and residential homes, guardianship services and legal aid for young people.

4.9 LOCAL GOVERNMENT FINANCE

The constitutional guarantee that communes have the right to regulate the affairs of the local community is held to imply 'financial sovereignty' (*Finanzhoheit*). The structure of local finance is largely the responsibility of the Länder, apart from the Bund's involvement in determining the share of income tax. Land local government laws lay down the structure for local decisions on finance, and annual finance laws and ordinances set the terms for the annual round of decisions on local expenditures, taxes and other sources of revenue.

As described in §4.6 above, local authorities in the late 1980s derived a little over one-third of their incomes from local taxes, around 21 per cent from fees and charges and 26 per cent from federal and state grants. Net borrowing accounted for some two to three per cent.

The main elements in tax income were the business tax which it shared with Länder (some 40 per cent of local tax revenue) and a share of national income tax which also amounted to 40 per cent.

Details of Local Taxes and Charges

Business Tax (Gewerbesteuer) formed 14.9 per cent of local government tax revenue in 1988, having risen from 13.8 per cent in 1980. It has been shared with the Länder for whom it constituted 9.2 per cent of their tax revenue in 1988. It is levied on every resident company with a fixed location. Assessment is on (1) operating profit, (2) working capital, and (3) total wage bill (subject to authorisation by the Land). The basis of assessment (unit value) is subject to occasional review. State tax offices determine the uniform tax base. Communes then apply a multiplier to this base and collect the tax. If a firm has branches in more than one municipality its revenue is shared proportionately. Municipalities pay 40 per cent of the yield to the Land.

The tax gives communes a strong economic incentive to attract and retain businesses. They have to balance the benefits of a higher rate with the loss of competitiveness against communes with lower levels of tax — a problem which has tended to work against the large core cities and in favour of location of industry in suburban communes.

Land Taxes (Grundsteuer) formed twelve per cent of local government tax income in 1988, having risen from 11.3 per cent in 1980. The tax base is also determined by the state tax offices and the multipliers decided by individual communes. Land tax A is levied on agricultural and forest estates. Land tax B is on property, including buildings forming part of working capital of industrial and commercial enterprises.

Other Taxes Some taxes may be levied at the discretion of communes. They vary from Land to Land and include dog tax, hunting tax, tax on beverages, entertainment and public house taxes.

An estate transfer tax fixed by the state is payable on real estate in addition to purchase tax.

Fee Revenue Fees are in principle calculated to cover cost of service provision except where the levels implied would be unsuitable for social or cultural reasons. The main 'economic charges' are for sewerage and refuse collection. Subsidised services include swimming-baths, adult education, theatre, kindergarten and museums.

State Grants

The general grants described in §4.6 are calculated by comparing an assessment of local spending needs calculated on a per capita basis with the fiscal potential of the business, land and other local taxes. Where real tax yield is less than the assessed need the Land meets the difference up to 90 per cent of the level of assessed need. However the Länder can vary the formula annually in ways which are said to be often politically inspired.

Specific grants are made relating to road work and capital investment on schools, hospitals, health and fire services.

Borrowing

Borrowing is permitted if other forms of finance are not possible or are inappropriate, or for investment or funding purposes. Local authorities are free to borrow from savings and other banks. Not all cities raise loans but others have run heavily into debt. Interest and capital repayments must be met from current revenue.

Expenditure

In the 1980s more than 30 per cent of expenditure was on personnel. Levels of pay are determined at national level. Local authorities have regarded maintaining local employment by direct provision of jobs as an important part of their role. Nevertheless annual increases in spending on staff have been reduced severely since 1980/81, when the rise in staff expenditure was 6.4 per cent.

Capital investment has been cut back sharply — by about a quarter in the first half of the 1980s — because of insufficiency of tax income to maintain existing facilities and reductions in federal and Land investment grants. It was argued at Bund level that needs had to a large extent been saturated by investments in the 1970s, but local authorities pointed to pressures to maintain and improve waste disposal and sewage treatment standards for ecological reasons, the need to meet new town redevelopment and housing needs and to help maintain employment levels. Expenditure on social services was the main area of growth, although local government argued that there had been a rapidly increasing gap between needs and provision, especially in areas most affected by the recession. Due to fiscal stress it was necessary to cut back discretionary expenditures in many cases on youth and other social services in order to fulfil mandatory tasks.

Financial Management

Each Land sets out the principles of communal financial management in its general local government law. The concept of *Wirtschaft*, the German word for economic management, has deep roots in local culture. Its root meaning is household management. In their introductory sections to the parts on communal economic and financial management (*Gemeindewirtschaft*), the local government laws of the Länder define the approach expected. The Baden-Württemberg statute declares, for example, that 'The financial management of the commune is to be conducted so that the constant fulfilment of the commune's responsibilities is ensured. The commune is to use its powers economically so that its finances are maintained in a sound condition, having regard to the economic capacity of its ratepayers.' The law of the Land defines budgeting and other financial principles and lays down requirements for statements of accounts, efficient financial planning, administration and control and borrowing. Five-year staffing and finance plans have been required in accordance with a communal investment programme in addition to a local budget ordinance and estimates. Länder use their influence to promote compliance with federal economic policies.

Local audit is carried out by audit offices of the communes themselves. It is supplemented by a communal supervisory agency mainly concerned with the proper use of government grants and the carrying out of tasks delegated from Land and federal levels.

Issues

A central issue has been the extent to which dependence on state grants for development purposes undermines local autonomy and choice. The Länder have determined over half of capital expenditure by means of their grant systems. These special grants are said to distort municipal priorities. The ad hoc nature of the allocations and varying provisions are argued to make it difficult or impossible to plan rationally.

The balance of the tax resources at the discretion of local government has been criticised. The business tax now falls only on big businesses. It hits them most when the economy has slackened and thereby works against economic recovery. There have been proposals to replace it with a sales tax, an addition to VAT and other forms related more closely to business incomes.

Regarding expenditure controls, supervisory authorities can refer budgets that have been voted back to local authorities if they are in deficit. There is little room for manoeuvre. The local authority constitutions in South Germany are argued to favour well-balanced budgets due to the clear accountability of the Bürgermeister and the fact that the political prospects of his party are influenced by his performance. Deficit budgets are most common in the North. It has been suggested that this happens because the 'British-type' system there results in a political process under which it is often difficult to resist pressures within the majority parties for ad hoc expenditure increases. (Banner, 1984)

Despite the strains that have occurred over expenditure problems bitter conflicts between Länder and cities were generally absent. Limiting local authority expenditures was much discussed but at the end of the 1980s at least were thought to have little chance of success given local government's constitutional rights and their political unacceptability.

Although it would be legally possible for a Land to take over a city's finances in a severe financial crisis, this never happened up to the late 1980s. It was reported to be politically unthinkable.

One reason is the closeness of the local Land officials to the individual local authority. In critical situations Land and municipal officials work out in detail ways to tide over difficulties, taking a realistic view of local political pressures. Another reason is the closeness between the Land and the municipal politicians. The means is usually found to work out a consensual solution within the framework of the party machine.

4.10 ELECTORAL REPRESENTATION

Voting

The Constitution directs that voting must be universal, direct, free, equal and secret. Otherwise the voting system for local government is laid down in the law of each Land (Meyer (1982) gives details).

The general rule is a modified system of proportional representation. The basis is the principle of the highest average (d'Hondt) system (§1.10). In Bavaria and Baden-Württemberg a one-person executive (Bürgermeister) is elected for communes separately from the local council members. Vote is by party list, but there are special arrangements to determine representation of sub-areas (for example making the lists representative of parts of the full electoral area); by exclusion of lists which gain low votes; and by providing the opportunity to give preferences for individual candidates.

Any party can compete in an election if it can gain a stated number of signatures. All except two Länder require a party list to win at least five per cent of the total votes cast to qualify for representation, thereby excluding the likelihood of extremist parties such as neo-Nazi groups winning representation and possibly holding the balance on a council. Voters can, under various arrangements, strike out the names of candidates on the list of their choice, or, in three Länder, write in names of candidates from other party lists. They can also give a second or third vote to a particular candidate in place of a vote for someone who has received a negative vote. They can if they wish give three votes to each of six candidates for a council of 18 seats. They receive a form made up of a series of strips containing the lists for all parties, on which each list normally contains as many names as there are seats on the council. They tear off and submit the list of their choice, modified to show their preferences. Choice is strictly proportional between block-lists, modified by names deleted or added and by extra votes for individuals. These possibilities of expressing individual preferences are much used. It is reported that in South Germany only about 20 per cent of lists are left unchanged. This vulnerability to being personally struck out from a list of party colleagues makes individual councillors exceptionally sensitive to electors' feelings in the few months before elections.

Although there are no electoral wards in the British sense and voting is generally, to use the American term, 'at large' for the whole of the commune area, some Länder have made provision for sub-lists of candidates for sub-areas in order to secure fair representation of local interests within party lists.

Voting for the sub-municipal councils that exist in most of the cities (§4.12) takes place simultaneously with main council elections, and voters' preferences in party terms often differ significantly from those for the city council.

The Status and Working Conditions of Representatives

These are determined in the legislation of each Land. Candidates must be at least 18 years old and resident in the area of the local authority concerned. Councillors may sit as representatives at more than one level of government simultaneously, but this is not a common practice. They may not hold a post in the administration of a local or regional authority.

Councillors receive modest allowances to cover costs of attending committee and council meetings. Full-time Bürgermeister receive general remuneration and also retirement pensions. Representatives have a right to leave of absence from their jobs, with costs borne by their authority. Their job security and prospects are protected.

A full-time Bürgermeister is reported to spend 40 to 60 hours a month in council or committee meetings; a councillor 12 to 14 hours. Meetings of party groups are provided for by local authorities. Councillors can make use of the secretariat of their group for secretarial facilities, but help may also be supplied by local authority staff. Induction programmes are provided. (Council of Europe, 1988, *On the Status and Working Conditions of Local and Regional Elected Representatives.*)

Party Groups

Party groups have full legal recognition in German local government. As well as accommodation and other material allowances they receive funds from their authority for the provision of services to members. In 1983/84, for example, payments to a party group in towns of between 150 and 450,000 Deutschmark in North Rhine-Westphalia and averaged 505,000 (very roughly 150,000 American dollars). In Hessen they received over three times this amount; in Lower Saxony a little more than half. They also receive income from their own members, provided out of the members' official allowances.

Party group staff may be financed out of municipal allowances or through their authority's administrative budget. There are normally party group managers, nearly all of them paid in authorities of over 30,000 population. They may be part-time or full-time. They are often members of the council concerned and may have under them a full-time business manager with one or two typists.

Groups commonly employ research workers to prepare reports for the political and committee work of the group. In authorities of under 100,000 population they are generally unpaid and part-time. (Martlew and Kempf, 1986)

4.11 THE INTERNAL ORGANISATION OF LOCAL AUTHORITIES

There are sharp differences between the committee and executive structures of local authorities adopted by individual Länder, but much uniformity in their departmental arrangements. In 1946 the Americans in occupation found in South Germany a strong similarity between their own 'strong mayor' system and the tradition of a Bürgermeister as a directly elected chief executive working with a deliberative council of separately elected politicians. In the South-West, which has been influenced by the French system since the 1790s, there is a mayoral executive who is not directly elected but chosen by the council for administrative ability and in some cases from outside its own membership. It is this type of system to which the five new Länder in East Germany have been most drawn. There is also in the South-West a stronger emphasis on popular participation and rights of decision. In the North-West British-occupied areas arrangements were established which have a superficial resemblance to the English type of council structure. Attempts to rate the various models in terms of performance have not been altogether convincing. (Grunow, 1992)

Local Authority Decision-Making

In most Länder systems there is a clear division of responsibility between (1) the deliberative body, which is a council elected by universal franchise, and (2) the executive or political administration, headed by an executive. Nevertheless policy formulation is a joint or complementary responsibility between the deliberative body (in the case of local authorities the council (*Stadtrat* or *Gemeinderat*)) and the executive.

277

German usage limits the term 'decision-making' to the formal act of voting in representative bodies: what in Britain is often called 'decision-taking'. The council is the deliberative body in the sense that it considers and decides on the provisions within which the executive is authorised to act. The core of the 'pre-decision' process lies in the joint work of the party groups, council committees, interest organisations and the executive. For this purpose informal groups exist which may include the chairmen of council committees and party groups, representatives of trade unions and trade associations, and politicians within the council with professional qualifications such as architects, as well as the chief executive and leading officials from the departments or 'offices' of the administration. The most important contributors to the 'pre-decision' process from outside the administration are opinion leaders in party groups, representatives of local party organisations, influential people within the local press and leaders of voluntary organisations. They participate in the process of inter-group consensus formation, identifying acceptable ways of regulating conflicts relating to choices between the purposes on which local resources are spent.

Constitutions of Municipalities

Authorities have councils or 'local parliaments' of from five to eighty elected representatives. There are four principal models for the constitution of the executive arm. (Normally mayors are called Bürgermeister in ordinary Gemeinden and *Oberbürgermeister* in Kreisfreie Städte.) In the **South German Mayoral Constitution** (*Bürgermeisterverfassung*) in Baden-Württemberg and Bavaria the council (*Gemeinderat*) has both decision-making and executive functions but shares the latter with the Bürgermeister. In Baden-Württemberg the Bürgermeister is directly elected for a six-year period of office and the councillors for 5 years. In Bavaria councillors are elected for six years and Bürgermeister (directly) for eight years. The criteria for selection of Bürgermeister are predominantly a legal qualification, party affiliation and previous performance in local politics (Wehling and Siewert, 1982, quoting Rolf-Richard Grauhan, *Politische Verwaltung*, Freiburg/Br, 1970).

In the **Rhenish Constitution** in the Rhineland-Palatinate and Saarland the political executives, like French mayors, are elected by their councils. They carry the duties of chairmanship of the council, formal representation of the municipality, headship of the administration, representation of the municipality in legal and business matters and formulation and implementation of policy, including decisions on all matters not requiring council sanction.

278

There are variations in periods of office between sizes and types of authority. The commonest lengths for councillors are five and six years. Bürgermeister normally serve for ten years.

In the **North German Constitution** (the *Ratsverfassung*) of North Rhine-Westphalia and Lower Saxony councils are elected for five years. There is no 'constitutional' separation between council and executive as elsewhere in Germany, but in the latter case a powerful administrative board has been introduced. The Bürgermeister, a role which in intention is similar to that of the English mayor, is chosen by the council from among its members. He or she is chairman of the council and represents the municipality ceremonially. The head of the administration is the chief administrative or executive officer (*Stadtdirektor* or *Gemeindedirektor*). He is an official on a fixed-term contract and may be appointed for six, eight or twelve years. The term is renewable. (In North Rhine-Westphalia no pension is due until the end of the second period of eight years.) The appointment may be terminated by a decision of two-thirds of the council. Councillors are elected for five-year periods of office.

The Stadt- or Gemeindedirektor acts for the town in legal and business matters. He is responsible for routine tasks and heads the officer administration. In North Rhine-Westphalia he also prepares the business of the council and ensures the implementation of its decisions.

In Lower Saxony there is also a strong executive committee consisting of the *Bürgermeister* and a number of councillors which is attended by the Chief Administrative Officer and often other senior officers in an advisory capacity. It takes executive decisions and formulates decision proposals for the council.

As mentioned above, the North German model has been the subject of serious criticism. Some reports have recommended its abolition. The public tend to look to the Bürgermeister as executive, despite his lack of formal powers. Many citizens approach him directly on matters for which they need help, and he himself is likely to want the satisfaction of settling individuals' problems personally rather referring them to the chief administrative officer. An important third focus of power is the leader of the majority party, who lacks statutory executive responsibilities despite his central influence in the decision-making process. In some cities the Bürgermeister dominates; in others the leader; in others (generally small ones) it is the chief administrative officer who is most important. One of the main differences between the German chief administrative officer and the British chief executive (and also the American chief administrative officer) is that his appointment is under political party auspices. There is usually inter-party agreement on the arrangement.

Whether the system is more democratic than the traditional strong mayor role is strongly contested (see §4.9 and Banner, 1984a and 1985b). There have been several minor adjustments to the system since 1946, but no fundamental changes due to the strength of vested interests (Grunow, 1992).

In the **Board Constitution** (*Magistratsverfassung*) of Hesse and Schleswig-Holstein the executive is a collegiate or 'board' executive called the Magistrat. It is a group of senior officials of the council (*Beigeordnete* or *Stadträte*) elected for six years in Hesse and six to twelve years in Schleswig-Holstein sitting as *ex officio* members together with a number of politicians appointed by the council. Although its chairman (*Vorsitz*) is called the Bürgermeister or Oberbürgermeister, it is the Magistrat as a whole that is chief executive, preparing council business and representing the town. Here periods of office are six years for the Bürgermeister (or in some cases twelve in Schleswig-Holstein), and four for the councillors. In Hesse a recent consultative referendum produced a large majority in favour of the direct election of Bürgermeister, and it was expected that this would be implemented, with accompanying changes in the institutional structure.

The city State Constitutions of Berlin, Hamburg and Bremen share dependence on collegiate executives and committee systems, both at the general city-state level and at the decentralised district councils (*Stadtbezirke*) level.

Committees, Commissions and Deputations (*Ausschüsse, Kommissionen* and *Deputationen*)

These terms are often used interchangeably, but strictly speaking commissions and deputations are made up of or include officers from within the administration and/or experts from outside the local authority. They are a means to make self-government more practicable, taking the load off councils and involving laymen in public administration. Their strengths can lie in planning, control, examination and appraisal functions; their weaknesses may be in difficulties over taking initiatives and lack of influence on the executive function.

In general councils have a free hand to appoint whatever committees they wish. Practice varies widely. In one or two Länder there are requirements for the appointment of a main committee, a finance committee, an audit or a personnel committee. Some committees prepare business to the point of decision-taking and others are appointed to study and make recommendations on a particular problem. The provisions for committees and conditions for delegated powers vary widely between Länder.

Deputy or Assistant Mayors/Directors of Services (*Dezernenten, Beigeordneten, Stadträte*)

In a town of any size one or more assistant Bürgermeister or directors of services are appointed to take responsibility for groups of services on behalf of the Bürgermeister. They are 'select officials' (*Wahlbeamter*), appointed by the council for the same term as the Bürgermeister, usually politically. Although appointments are not strictly proportional to party strengths some directors of services are usually appointed who belong to opposition parties. The departments or offices (*Ämte*) are grouped under them in accordance with the general budget and financial planning headings: general administration; public order and safety; schools; learning (*Wissenschaft*), research and cultural responsibilities; social security; health, sport and recreation; building, housing and traffic matters; public establishments and economic developments; economic undertakings and capital and other special investments; and general financial management.

Departments (*Ämte*)

Departments are headed by *Amtsleiter*, not to be confused with deputy or assistant Bürgermeister or directors of services. Local authorities have in general adopted the pattern worked out at the local government management institute, the *KGSt* (see §4.5). Thus, for example, under grouping four of eight standard groupings will be found the social services office, the youth office, the sports office, the public health office, the hospitals organisation and the office responsible for administering a range of insurance benefits, allowances, compensations and other social payments. The grouping thus brings together under common direction services with overlapping purposes (*Verwaltungsorganisation der Gemeinden*, 1979).

The Status of Senior Office-Holders

The post of Bürgermeister, as indicated above, has a popular status which adheres to it even where the holder lacks executive powers. Where it is an executive post it carries substantial remuneration in large authorities. Gradings of posts are fixed by the Land. Their scope, challenge and status may, however, be assumed to be more important than money in attracting people of high ability. A high proportion of Oberbürgermeister and Bürgermeister of towns of any size have legal training, but the post is by no means a monopoly of lawyers. The number of lawyers holding it is partly a reflection of the fact that they hold a high proportion of senior public posts in general. It is common to find lawyers in charge of the finance, security and public order, health and social welfare and public services groups of functions. National scales apply in common to Bund, Land and local government posts, and mobility between them is therefore easier.

Landkreis Institutions

County councils have generally 40 to 90 members. A county council (*Kreistag*) appoints a county committee (*Kreisausschuss*). It consists of 7 to 17 members and is chaired by the senior political official of the Land, the county council chairman (*Landrat* or, as he is called in the cases of North Rhine-Westphalia and Lower Saxony, *Oberkreisdirektor*). This official is the chief executive of his authority except in the Länder with Magistrat Constitutions (Hesse and Schleswig-Holstein) where the county committee serves as a collegiate executive. In other Länder the county committee is generally responsible for day-to-day decisions.

A Landrat (county chairman and executive) is head of the county administration and responsible for implementation of county council decisions and tasks delegated to the county by the Land or federal government, supervisory authority of the municipalities as to the legality of their decisions, and responsible for certain Land functions as a subordinate Land authority.

In Bavaria he is elected by popular vote. Elsewhere he is chosen by the county council except in Rhineland-Palatinate where he is appointed by the Land. Periods of office are the same as for the Bürgermeister in each Land.

The Local Government Service

There is no head of administration in the sense of a British chief executive or French secretary-general in authorities with a one-person executive, since the latter formally combines the duties of head of officer administration and political executive. But there is of course a senior officer who works especially closely with the executive on matters of general policy.

Appointment and promotion of employees is a matter within the discretion of the council, but not dismissals. Public servants within the federal, Land and local government services all have a common status distinct from the categories of 'employees' and 'workers', whose conditions are governed by private law. There is a national system of qualification involving academic studies, a professional training period of from six months to three years followed by an examination and assessment of suitability by a board and then a probationary period of one to three years according to category. Confirmation as satisfactory for admission to a national class of officers is then required before appointment by a body within the public system to a particular post. Local authorities can select candidates at their discretion, but political affiliation may be taken into consideration. Proportionality between parties is required by some Länder and generally exercised to some extent in other cases. But there is security of tenure once appointed. Senior officers sometimes move to a more congenial authority on their own initiative when there is a change of political control.

The justification of the system, which generally stops short of 'clientelism', lies in the Basic Law provision that 'political parties will take part in the formation of the national will', and the concern to prevent the experiences of the Weimar and Nazi periods when officials dominated local councils. The role of senior officials is regarded as within the political sphere of public decision-making, but certainly not as partisan. (Degen, 1988; Henry-Meininger, 1988).

4.12 CITIZEN PARTICIPATION AND DECENTRALISATION WITHIN CITIES

Representation

The social activism of the 1960s led to a new emphasis on involving the general public in the local government decision-making process, often associated with the amalgamations of authorities described in §4.4 and the wish to maintain a local government presence in the small communities that were losing Gemeinde status. In the fourteen years up to 1980 the number of elected representatives in local authorities was reduced from 276,000 to 153,000. In the mid-1980s there was on average about one councillor to every 400 inhabitants, as against one to under two hundred in the 1960s.

The structural reforms have not, however, reduced levels of voting. The turn-out in the national elections in the 1980s was near to 90 per cent: the local government turn-out was around 70 to 76 per cent.

Citizens' Assemblies

There is an old tradition of town and village meetings to discuss matters of concern. In Bavaria and Baden-Württemberg a stipulated number or proportion of the citizens of communes of up to a certain size and of districts of larger towns have the right to require the summonsing of such meetings.

Citizen Propositions, Initiatives, Referenda and Surveys

In most Länder citizens have the power to require an issue concerning their locality to be considered and decided by their local council. In most cases a proposition (*Antrag*) must be dealt with within three months. In Hesse it must be considered within six months and a decision taken within the following six. A requirement may be made that it be supported by reasons and an estimate of the costs of implementation. Referenda can be activated on an issue in Baden-Württemberg by means of a decision by two-thirds of a council or an initiative signed by 15 per cent of the local voters. It must include a statement of the issue to be decided, the background to the issue and a proposal as to how the necessary resources should be raised. An initiative can be directed against a council decision within four weeks of its publication. There are a number of matters that are excluded, including some financial matters. The council has the power to rule on admissibility. It can also forestall a referendum by adopting the proposal in the initiative. A vote of 30 per cent of the electorate is required for the result to be valid. Local authorities can and do carry out surveys of public opinion on matters of doubt or conflict.

Municipal Decentralisation

Germany has a long history of decentralising responsibilities within cities. The Prussian ordinance of 1808 laid down that each town of more than 800 inhabitants was to be divided into quarters for the purpose of self-administration. The first major urban decentralisation in the twentieth century was the setting up of the districts for Berlin in 1920. At the end of the Second World War citizens' committees sprang up spontaneously in city districts in many parts of Western Germany to deal with the enormous problems of local reconstruction and resettlement. They preceded the setting up of new city governments, just as the city governments preceded the setting up of elected Land and federal government. Around 1950 six of the Länder made regulations to provide a legal form for area bodies. These took the shape of advisory boards or committees appointed by town councils with the duty of giving advice to the city administration. Their declared aims were greater closeness to citizens, greater collaboration between the city government and citizens and closer oversight of civic administration.

A leap forward came in the later 1960s with the boundary reforms, which not only created larger cities but also reduced the number of councillors elected to county borough-type authorities from 5,441 to 4,169. From 1970 sub-municipal government became a live issue in party politics. The concept of area bodies as no more than accessories to civic government began to be replaced by that of autonomous councils with independent responsibilities. Direct election to such bodies was made a legal possibility. By 1982 60 out of the 71 towns with populations of more than 95,000 inhabitants had set up area executive bodies, and in 40 cases these covered the whole of their areas.

The Berlin and Hamburg systems allocate administrative powers that are not required by law to be exercised at city-state level to large sub-municipal districts (*Stadtbezirke*) — fourteen in Berlin with populations averaging 243,500 population and seven in Hamburg with populations averaging about 237,000. In Berlin district decision-making powers lie with assemblies, each of which has 45 directly elected members. The assembly elects a district collegiate executive (*Bezirksamt*) consisting of the district Bürgermeister and seven councillors (*Bezirksstadträte*). The assemblies are not autonomous, being subject to central guidelines and city supervisory authorities and dependent on the city parliament for voting their budgets. The Hamburg system is similar. The city states have elaborate committee systems with wide participation beyond that of the elected members. In 1985 the city claimed to have 17,500 citizens involved in administrative responsibilities through the committee system: one for every 95 members of the population. Bremen City is not dissimilar except that its locally self-administered areas are much smaller and therefore more dependent on the city, ranging from about 300 to 3,000 inhabitants.

City-states apart, three patterns were distinguished in a detailed survey of provisions throughout the Federal Republic (Schäfer, 1982). The first is of cities whose areas are only partly covered by district councils. The second is the South German type with comparatively large numbers of small districts based on traditional boundaries, for example Munich with 41 districts (average population 33,700), Stuttgart with 23 (average population 25,300) and Wiesbaden with 25 (average population 10,800). The third is the North German type with large areas, normally closely related to the pattern of administrative decentralisation (e.g. Duisburg 10 (average population 60,000), Cologne 9 (average population 108,700) and Hanover 13 (average population 41,400)).

In 1981, in towns where all districts had local councils 30 out of 40 were directly elected and 32 had certain rights of decision-making. In 14 cases where there were local bodies for only parts of a town, 13 local councils were directly elected and 15 had rights to make decisions. Altogether 8,642 representatives were elected under these arrangements (ibid.). It is reported that political careers often start in area councils, leading on to election to a town or city council.

All types of sub-municipality are designed to increase closeness to the citizen, effective control of the administration and popular participation. Specific functions are to articulate and follow through local interests, control and support municipal institutions in their areas, achieve integration of activities with the all-city government and administration and recruit new politicians (ibid.).

Studies have indicated that district councils cannot expect to direct services but can successfully develop their role in promoting policies for their areas, especially when supported by officials, local associations and press. Schäfer recommends that district councils should work towards formulating coherent policies for their areas. They should improve their relationships with their city councils so that there is more mutual understanding and a willingness to allow them to assume more of their potential areas of responsibility. He advances the case for them all to be directly elected, as was the case in the 1980s in Berlin, Hamburg, Hesse, Lower Saxony, Saarland and Kreisfreie Städte in North Rhine-Westphalia.

4.13 THE GOVERNANCE OF METROPOLITAN AREAS

Some conurbations have large dominant central cities (e.g. Berlin, Hamburg, Munich, Stuttgart and Hanover). Others have a number of centres clustered together (e.g. the Ruhrgebiet and Rhine Valley conurbations). The Frankfurt region is dominated by the city but includes other centres, notably Offenbach, which often oppose Frankfurt's policies. Greater Berlin has the well-integrated decentralised structure described in §4.12. Hamburg, sandwiched between Lower Saxony and Schlewig-Holstein, has to meet the problem of co-ordinating metropolitan policy with other Länder and their local authorities.

Dense settlement and high demands on infrastructure, communication and recreation facilities create a *prima facie* case for effective framework planning and service areas, but the political difficulties have hindered achievement. Nevertheless, using the forms of inter-authority collaboration described in §4.5, a complex pattern of joint action has been established, with collaborative bodies crossing Land boundaries in some instances.

In particular joint agencies have been promoted for sub-regional, conurbation-based planning, especially framework planning based on and implemented under the delegated or transferred powers of Gemeinden and Landkreise which help them to achieve efficient public transportation, industrial development and refuse and sewage disposal throughout their sub-regions.

Agencies for regional planning include the Rhine-Neckar Raumordnungsverband for framework planning which provides for an area of over 1,700,000 inhabitants stretching across the boundaries of three Länder. It co-ordinates the sub-regional planning of the Länder. It is a joint planning organisation and its success in laying a common basis for local plans has been attributed partly to the fact that its director was an official jointly appointed by the Länder concerned who was also the head planner for the three individual planning bodies of the Länder: a regional Verband, a regional planning agency and a Landkreis.

Other metropolitan Verbände are also regional planning agencies under joint political control, notably the regional Munich planning Verband and the Hanover area Zweckverband Grossraum Hannover, which provides for the city and the surrounding county including 20 municipalities. Until 1980 there was a directly elected metropolitan 'parliament' of 75 members for the latter area which has been replaced, against the wishes of its main members, by the Zweckverband with 28 members on a council appointed by the constituent authorities. It continued as a multi-purpose body responsible for public transport, sub-regional planning and promotion of economic development and recreation.

The joint Ruhr Authority (*Kommunalverband Ruhrgebiet*) was set up in 1979 for this polycentric area of five and a half million inhabitants. It is responsible for regional planning and the increased planning functions of its members. Its central purpose is the protection of green spaces and participation in the establishment and management of public recreational areas of supra-local importance. It provides technical planning services for its member authorities. Its costs are apportioned between members according to the work undertaken. It is controlled by an assembly of delegates proportionate to party strengths among the 11 cities and four Landkreise of the Ruhrland.

The most powerful model of a directly elected multi-purpose metropolitan joint body is the Zweckverband, Umlandverband Frankfurt (Berg, Klink and Meer, 1991; Fürst, 1991; Norton, 1983). Its area has a highly fragmented administration with a dense tangle of roads and railways that is the economic centre of Germany, some say of Europe. It includes 43 municipalities and innumerable joint bodies. The Umlandverband is a weak solution to the needs of a sub-region of such complexity which covers 3,200 square kilometres and contains a population of 3,100,000 of whom 640,000 live in Frankfurt.

The Umlandverband was set up in 1974 under a Land law. Its primary function is planning, including a zoning scheme, a general traffic scheme and a landscape plan, together with supporting water, waste-processing and leisure functions. It advises local authorities and co-ordinates their economic development and environmental protection measures. Its staff numbered 190 in 1991. It has two representative assemblies: one directly elected council of 105 members and the second a chamber of municipalities with one member from each of the 43 member authorities. Its political executive, a board of fifteen members, is led by the director of the union, a politician from Frankfurt. According to a recent study (Berg, Klink and Meer, 1991) it has come to be regarded by its directors mostly as a resource for undertaking advisory, co-ordinating and consulting tasks. It has had some success in this field and in mediating over differences between local governments where the result can give mutual benefits. But it has had little success where disadvantages accrue to individual members from projects such as waste disposal sites, pollutant factories and new road routes. Its economic development role is said to have been negligible. It lacks the 'competences, funds and especially municipal support to plan an important role in socio-economic policy'. Its frustrations have been largely due to the negative attitudes of Frankfurt and suspicion of that city's ambitions among the surrounding authorities. Despite the large scale of its area it is too small to cope with the major strategic issues that it confronts.

A study of these metropolitan bodies finds a main source of support for them lies in the proved value of the agency work that they undertake for member authorities. It emphasises the importance of the personal abilities of their officials in mediating between interests and building a consensus. Success is seen to depend much more on working through regional networks to secure generally acceptable outcomes than on the use of power. The effects of direct election were found to be ambivalent because it raises frustrating conflicts between parties at different levels. But the entry of wide environmental and ecological concerns into planning heightens the importance of democratic participation and public participation in mediation between interests and decision-making at regional levels. (Fürst, 1991)

5. SWEDEN

5.1 HISTORY AND TRADITIONS

National Background

In area Sweden is the fourth largest country in Western Europe, but its population of under eight and a half million is less than that of the London region, having an average density of under 19 people to the square kilometre. Not more than ten per cent of its land is cultivated, but the country is self-sufficient in food as well as one of the most highly industrialised in the world. Seven-eighths of the inhabitants live in its southern half, and over one in six in the area of Greater Stockholm.

In the past Sweden has been famous for its social homogeneity (Rustow, 1955). In recent years, however, there has been an influx of over a million immigrants, mainly coming from Finland, the Mediterranean countries and Chile. Over a third of all immigrants live in Stockholm County. Income distribution is the most even in Western Europe. Average per capita purchasing power in the 1980s was higher than that of other European countries excepting Norway and Luxembourg, but its rate of growth has declined to a point where its high level of social welfare has become too expensive for the economy. The GDP fell 1.3 per cent in 1991 and the country experienced an economic crisis in 1992. In 1990 public consumption formed 35 per cent. Local government's share alone was 19.4 per cent.

History

Swedish local government has deep popular roots. In the fourteenth century mutual rights bound together king, council and peasants in a system of mutual obligations. Peasants possessed personal and economic freedom and political rights and were involved in provincial assemblies (*landstinger*). They won back land ownership from the aristocracy following clashes between the crown and the aristocracy. From the 1760s each parish acquired formal responsibility for public services — first social welfare and care of the poor and subsequently education and book distribution.

Sweden's unbroken traditions of local democracy were given a new legal

289

form in the 1862 Local Government Ordinances which established 2,500 municipalities and self-governing provincial and city councils. The councils represented social classes, including the artisans in the cities. Local authorities were given the right to decide issues within their territories and to levy taxes. The structure remained largely undisturbed until the 1960s, proving itself compatible with rapid industrialisation in the twentieth century. The main changes came between 1962 and 1973 when the number of local authorities was drastically reduced (see §5.4).

Politics and Corporatism

The Social Democratic Party (SAP) became the largest party in the *Riksdag* (parliament) in 1914. It continued to govern alone or in coalitions from 1916 until 1976, returning to power in 1982 until support fell away drastically in the 1991 election. A four-party minority government took over with only 170 of the 349 seats in the Riksdag, dependent on the freshly formed New Democracy Party, a 'party of discontent', to martial a majority (§5.10).

Until very recently at least Sweden has demonsrated a remarkable ability to harmonise social interests. This was due particularly to the success of the patient, pragmatic Social Democrat leadership which reconciled the interests of the most unionised non-agrarian workforce in Europe with those of capitalists in the development of comprehensive welfare and wage policies (Ashford, 1986).

The degree of popular involvement in political parties changed little in the fifteen years before 1990, but voluntary group activity grew strongly. A high degree of individualism is complemented by a strong inclination towards membership of voluntary associations. Interest organisations such as those of white-collar workers, employers, farmers and academics are involved in the decision-making process of the state and local authorities. Local party organisations have sought to provide channels for these and other interests but have found this difficult in recent years due to the problems of reconciling divergent interests with the party system. Voluntary bodies have become more directly integrated into a joint decision-making process with state bodies. Sweden has been identified as 'partly' an archetype of corporatism, 'with big interest organisations conducting far-reaching negotiations to reconcile interests peacefully and participating in various forms of government policy-making in the framing and implementation of policies in formally defined channels' — the opposite of 'the classical image of pure type American pressure groups in a pluralist society' (Stromberg and Westerstahl, 1984). Nevertheless 'the basic form is still the expression of citizen preferences for political parties competing for seats in the Riksdag'. The system is said to have resulted in 'increasing institutional sclerosis and decision-making inertia'. (Lane and Ersson, 1987)

The Constitution

The Swedish Bill of Rights was based on the fourteenth-century Oath of Coronation which protected personal liberty and well-being, property, privacy and conscience from executive action, subject to the law. The Riksdag dates from the fifteenth century and has dominated policy-making since then, gaining effective budgetary control in the early nineteenth century. Executive and legislature work closely together. The power of the national executive is also moderated by the autonomy of national boards and local authorities exercising traditional authority and responsibility.

The constitutional law, which was confirmed in 1975 after twenty years of gestation and thirty re-draftings, consists of three documents: the new Instrument of Government (*Regeringsform*), the Act of Succession dating from 1810 and, remarkably, the Freedom of the Press Act of 1949 which provides for freedom of expression and the openness of all public documents at all levels of public authority. Agreement was reached between the four main parties on a single chamber parliament to be elected every three years at the same time as the elections to the municipal and county councils. A general local authority act followed in 1977 aimed at implementing the values in the new constitutional documents.

5.2 THE STATUS OF LOCAL GOVERNMENT

Local Autonomy

'Local self-government has long been one of the cornerstones of the Swedish constitution. The decentralized decision-making which this has made possible has meant a great deal for the country's economic, social and cultural development.' (Gustafsson, Agne, 1988)

The basic principles of local autonomy are expressed in the Instrument of Government, which lays down that municipalities and counties are entitled to levy taxation and that decision-making powers are to be exercised by elected representatives in municipal and county councils. The provision of the 1977 Local Government Act that local councils 'shall conduct their own affairs' has been given the interpretation of general authority or competence to act in the interest of local residents. Decisions must, however, concern matters of public interest in the authority's area, relate to non-profitmaking and non-speculative activities, not encroach on the rights of individuals and not be oppressive. And they must treat all citizens equally.

Any member of a municipal or county council (but no one else) can appeal against a decision up to the level of the Supreme Administrative Court on the grounds that it is beyond the authority's general powers. A judgment applies only to the municipality concerned. A member of another authority may however effectively challenge and so invalidate a decision on the grounds of a legal precedent elsewhere.

A deliberate decision was made in the early 1930s to base social and economic reforms on local rather than national authorities. A main reason for the decision was to take advantage of the scope and flexibility of local authority competences in order to avoid unnecessary state bureaucracy.

A government commission in the mid-1970s defined the following principles which, it claimed, reflected the results of general debate on relations between central, regional and local levels:

- It is a matter of national interest for all citizens to be assured of a certain minimum standard of security, safety and welfare.
- No issue should be decided at a higher level than necessary in relation to the persons affected by that decision.
- Matters requiring a considerable degree of uniformity or a national overview should be placed at central level.
- Matters requiring a considerable amount of local and specific, detailed knowledge should be transferred to local authorities.
- Closely related matters should be administered at the same decision-making level and handled by the same agency if efficiency can be improved in this way.

Finance and Autonomy

Local income tax is regarded as the foundation of local autonomy. Arguments for fixing a limit on local expenditures were rejected until the 'temporary' tax freeze of 1991-92. But strongly expressed support for local government has been said to represent a cultural attitude of deeper importance than fiscal freedom. It maintains the basis for fiscal freedom. (Greenwood, 1980)

Government powers to control local authority financial decisions were removed by a law of 1976. A local authority's freedom to set its rate of local income tax is accepted as a hallmark of its status. This is possible because there is an active concept of the common interest, both between government levels and between parties. Conflicts are controlled if not invariably resolved through constitutional and political channels.

In the 1970s local government acquired greatly increased responsibilities for the services of the welfare state, including the most expensive ones: education, health and housing. The rapid expansion of mandatory functions brought with it regulatory controls and an expanding bureaucracy. Some 70 per cent of local authority expenditure falls within the area of state-regulated activities.

Growth in local expenditures averaged six per cent a year between 1965 and 1980, well above that of the GDP. The growth in the expenditure of county councils in real terms between 1972 and 1981 was 336 per cent. Central grant covered about 28 per cent of the cost. From 1982 to the end of 1985 local government consumption rose by over eight per cent while that of national government fell by over one per cent. This greatly stretched local capacity to raise revenue (Lane and Magnusson, 1987). In June 1991 the parliament overrode fiscal freedom by imposing an unprecedented freeze on tax increases for 1991 and 1992.

The great expansion of services brought local authorities more discretion within the government system because they gained increased choice over means of implementation. This was justified by the argument that the extent and detail of government regulation had imposed heavy costs on the municipalities. If central government wished to avoid such costs, local government had to be given discretion to adopt the most effective means of reducing expenditure (ibid.).

The Results of Expansion of Local Activities

One study concludes that the improved economic, administrative and political resources brought about by increased municipal scale have strengthened the national status of local authorities (Gustafsson, Gunnel, 1981), and therefore also its power if this is measured against that of the centre.

The question of where power should lie remains a matter of debate. 'Both county council and state regional administration can be said to have been reinforced in the past few years' (Gustafsson, Agne, 1984a or b). There have been significant movements towards hybridisation or power-sharing, reflecting the tendency to reconcile contradictions in a synthesis.

To summarise, local government is well rooted in the law and Constitution and also in the local economy of the country. It has a high level of autonomy in some respects, although subject to detailed regulation over the bulk of its activities. Not only is its role accepted by the public but it appears to be the general belief that its powers should be strong. However boundary changes in amalgamations have made it much more artificial and distant from local communities. The sharp increase in functional activities and the extent to which they are regulated at national level have led to much greater dependence on officials. Local government has not been kept close to the community, as in most of France, but closer than in Britain. Possibilities of change in any direction are always open and continuously under debate.

5.3 CONCEPTS AND VALUES

In general the Swedes regard the law as indicating 'rightness': in fact the common Swedish word for 'suitable' or 'appropriate' means literally 'according to the laws'. Law has been used to realise an ancient folk ideal of the elimination of social class in the cause of social solidarity as well as of equality (Scott, 1977).

  The search for consensus is linked with the value of solidarity, expressed in the ideal of *folkhem*, the community as home of the people 'in which all members should live in harmony without antipathy between classes (ibid.). It is also linked with 'matter-of-factness' (*saklighet*), meaning a cool, objective and dispassionate approach to questions of public policy, as to be seen in the care taken in setting out the rationale behind government proposals. High levels of taxation are of course controversial, but 'distributive capacity' in social welfare and insurance has not been seriously questioned by the centre-right opposition, at least until the early 1990s. Nevertheless local government housing and social welfare policies are prominent electoral issues and divide the parties without undermining their willingness to seek accommodation after issues have been thoroughly discussed and fought out.

  Typically decisions are preceded by much preliminary research and deliberation. The process has often taken years before reaching conclusion. The consultation process is remarkably comprehensive. The case of the Commission on the Constitution in the 1950s and 1960s was typical in this respect but extreme on account of its importance and complexity. There is a willingness to compromise and decisions are designed to avoid lasting opposition (Anton, 1980). This is the view of an American. A Scandinavian perspective emphasises the split between social democratic, integrated welfare-planning values and those emphasising conservation and family interests, as in the long debate on local government reform (Kjellberg, 1983).

Citizen participation has been regarded as a crucial value, and local government's position makes it a chief means of fulfilling that value (but §5.12 below shows that this description needs qualification). In recent years interest has turned to achieving not just citizen participation but requiring public servants to consult clients systematically on the service they need, reach agreement on the service to be given with a right to appeal in case of disagreement, and determine what is provided within regulations or guidelines and is consistent with the responsible use of available resources (Gustafsson, Lennart, 1987).

Thus Sweden is a country of 'co-operative individualists', prosperous egalitarians, radical rationalists rooted in long historical traditions and participators in an increasing number of regulated activities.

An opinion survey in 1979 highlighted incompatibility of values on local-national issues. Local variations in services are sharp and often conflict with concepts of distributive justice. Almost all agreed that 'the resources of society can best be adapted to local needs through local self-government' and about half agreed with the statement that 'all communes should be forced to maintain the same level of service and have the same tax-rate'. (Stromberg and Westerstahl, 1984)

Conflicting values, principles and aspirations that are commonly held with such firmness and conviction inevitably cause much stress, but the stress does not usually produce breakdowns in relationships, at least of a public or political nature. The explanation can be sought in 'matter-of-factness', collaboration, acceptance of hard-won compromise and also very importantly the closely related legal tradition already mentioned — the belief that rightness must be expressed by a law which formulates an outcome that is just and acceptable. As one writer puts it, 'The meticulous regard for "law" has not meant rigid subservience to established codes, but, rather, continuing efforts by public officials to adapt the legal foundation of the state to the ongoing character and needs of society' (Hancock, 1972). He quotes Rustow's *The Politics of Compromise*: 'Whatever its merits or defects the politics of compromise is rooted in tradition.... The essence of that tradition is a strict and often meticulous regard for law and legal procedure, expressed in the old adage, *Land skall med lag byggas*, — "Country shall be built with law"' (Rustow, 1955). The security of individual rights is seen to lie largely in a legal framework which guarantees security and defines the powers of individuals and local institutions as much as central competences, the values on which that framework is based having been developed purposefully and held secure since the Middle Ages. Within this framework Swedish citizens do not see an inconsistency between the dominant role played by the state in provision of personal welfare services and their firm opposition to the infringement of individual liberties. They do not favour the extension of government into the private sector and are proud of an economy based on private enterprise. They look on the great co-operatives, for example, as privately owned and non-governmental in character. It must be questioned, however, how much the economic crisis beginning at the end of the 1980s has undermined fundamental assumptions.

5.4 NATIONAL STRUCTURE

General

Sweden has three basic levels of government and administration: the central state, the counties (*landsting*) and the municipalities (*kommune*). The two local government levels date from 1862. There is a landsting for every county region except the Island of Gotland and the cities of Gothenburg and Malmö, which have county as well as municipal status.

Central government functions are administered by the 23 county administrative boards described below. The governor (*landshövding*), appointed centrally for a six-year period, is head of the board but has only a casting vote on general policy issues which require the board's approval.

Local government, however, is carried out by the county and municipal councils. The municipality is termed the primary authority and the county the secondary authority since its role is to fulfil interests of the community which are beyond the capacity of the primary authorities in its area. The central legislative power lies with the Riksdag. Governmental power lies with the cabinet, headed by the prime minister, who is accountable to parliament. Ministries are small, with average staff, including clerical workers, of around one hundred. For the preparation of new legislation the cabinet defines guidelines and entrusts the drafting to commissions of enquiry which include politicians of governing parties and the opposition, officials and outside experts. The commissions normally sit for two or more years. Their reports and drafts are submitted to administrative bodies and non-governmental organisations for comment (the *Remiss* procedure), and the replies are summarised and submitted to parliament with the revised bill. Implementation of government decisions is entrusted to some seventy or eighty agencies which carry out their responsibilities in accordance with laws and regulations prepared and steered through by the appropriate ministries.

Table 5.1 Local Authority Numbers, Populations and Areas

	Number	Average Population	Population Range
Counties	24	346,580	55,346 to 1,528,200
Municipalities	284	29,300	3,156 to 653,578

Size of Local Authority Areas (sq. miles)

	Average Size	Size Range
Counties	66,220	1,127 to 38,187
Municipalities	552	not available

Source: Figures for 1983, *Årsbok för Sveriges kommuner*, 1985.

The County as a State Administrative Region

All but three counties have populations of under 500,000. Each county administrative board is headed by a county governor who is appointed by central government for a six-year term. He or she may be a former cabinet minister, civil servant or eminent local inhabitant. Each board has fourteen members elected for three years by the county council and in two cases by cities independently of the local county. Its duties include regional planning, police and administration of justice. It promotes the co-ordination of national, county and municipal administration in the county and is expected to represent the interests of its area to central government and parliament.

The main emphasis in the past has been on its comprehensive planning role, bringing together and co-ordinating regional policies and physical and sectoral planning in co-operation with local authorities. Boards' other executive and supervisory responsibilities include the adoption of site development plans, nature conservation, water conservation, environmental protection, health protection including food inspection, social care and roads and traffic. They also administer tax activities, civil registration and civil defence. They are tribunals for certain administrative appeals, for example against decisions by local authorities and state agencies, with further appeal possible to separate tribunals and central authorities.

Each county also has a number of functional boards for education, employment promotion, housing, agriculture and forestry which possess lay directorates appointed by central government, central boards and the county councils.

The County as a Self-Governing Authority (*Landstingkommune*)

A county council has independent legal personality. It is elected every three years and elects its own chairman and executive.

Although there were reforms in county organisation in 1971 no alterations were made to boundaries. County activities have increased greatly in recent decades, especially in the fields of health care and medical services, which together account for four-fifths of county council expenditure. Although the services provided by the counties are well-known and appreciated, the county councils themselves are little known among the public (Strömberg and Westerstahl, 1984).

Municipalities and the Results of Reform

Municipalities are independent corporate bodies elected every three years. They have a monopoly of decision-making rights at sub-national level in town and country planning, housing, public utilities and social welfare. About two-thirds are in the population range from ten to fifty thousand.

The number of municipalities in Sweden was progressively reduced by amalgamations. Between 1862 and 1951 there were about 2,500, of which 2,200 were rural. Rural municipalities had in general the same boundaries as church parishes (*forsamlingar*), which have the same status in law as municipalities including independent powers of taxation. In 1946 parliament resolved unanimously that boundaries should be revised to give rural municipalities the resources to run major services. The aim was a minimum population of 2,000. The reform took effect in 1952, reducing the total number to 1,006, including 133 towns and 88 boroughs whose boundaries were unaffected.

The 1962 reforms were based on the principle that each municipality should be a coherent economic and geographical unit consisting of a natural region held together by economic, social, cultural and other relations, with a central locality serving the surrounding area. The work was dominated by planners who sought to centre the new areas on 'growth centres perceived as the crucial element for a balanced economic and occupational development' and 'the Social Democrat view of local authorities as integrated parts of public administration'. Although there was a clash between this approach and the emphasis of the opposition on local autonomy, the 'planners and the Social Democrats won the day'. (Kjellberg, 1984). The government decided that the desirable minimum was to be 8,000 residents, which was regarded as sufficient to support a reform of elementary education.

The attempt to achieve voluntary amalgamations failed and a statutory plan was made backed by enforcement powers. By 1974 numbers had been reduced to 278. A few amalgamations proved unworkable and were split, five of them since 1980, increasing the total to 284. About one-quarter of the population still live in municipalities with under 20,000 residents.

Some population minima for different services may be of interest to policy-makers. Comprehensive schools were considered to need a population base of 6,500 to 7,500 inhabitants; for social welfare services 5,000 to 6,000; for health administration (excluding county inputs) 8,000 to 10,000, and for employment policies 7,000 to 8,000.

The effects of the reforms have been researched, with a particular stress on their impact on local democracy (Gustafsson, Gunnel, 1980; Strömberg and Westerstahl, 1984). The conclusions were that the new municipalities had acquired improved financial and administrative resources and that the need for grants-in-aid had been reduced. Planning was more efficient and much less help and supervision from the state was thought necessary. The services provided for residents are more fairly distributed. But the number of directly and indirectly elected political representatives dropped from about 200,000 in 1951 to about 50,000 in 1974. As a reaction to the last fact measures were introduced between 1974 and 1980 that increased the number to 70,000 (§5.12). One scholar concludes from empirical research that a population of 8,000 may be assumed to be 'the upper limit for the existence of a municipal system where contact still exists on a primarily informal level' (Gustafsson, Gunnel, 1981).

The consequent decrease in the number of representatives is said to have impaired relations between politicians and voters. The proportion of officials to 'full-time' working councillors was found to have varied sharply with size: it was four to one in small communes and sixty to one in towns with more than 30,000 inhabitants (Gustafsson, Agne, 1984a). One Swedish source states that local authorities were transformed into 'heavily bureaucratised organisations' with big budgets and a large number of employees' (Lane and Ersson, 1987); another that they became 'bureaucratic machines, rulebound and displaying considerable inertia in decision-making' (Lane and Magnusson, 1987). Another again found that the amalgamations did not lead to a relative decrease in costs, except in respect of administrative charges (Lane and Magnusson, 1982, quoted in Lane and Magnusson, 1987).

5.5 INTER-AUTHORITY RELATIONS AND ORGANISATION

In order to increase the capacity of local authorities to provide efficient services the Swedish government has generally resorted to effecting amalgamations. However joint limited companies or 'foundations' have been used in certain cases, particularly for public transport undertakings, as a means to increase flexibility by escaping from public sector legal restrictions. Sharing of responsibility between county and municipal councils has been required for regional and local transport, temperance care institutions and approved schools. These services may be provided by means of municipally owned companies, foundations or federations. In 1982 there were 19 such agencies, mostly concerned with regional planning, water supply, public transport and fire prevention.

The Swedish Association of County Councils (Svenska Landsförbundet) (Gavlegatan 16, Box 6606, 11384 Stockholm) and the Association of Swedish Local Authorities (Svenska Kommunförbundet) (Hornsgatan 15, 11647 Stockholm) provide a wide range of common services: advice and assistance in administrative, technical, legal, auditing and other financial matters; representation of national interests nationally; collective negotiations with employees; and training and education of elected members and local government employees.

Local authorities have transferred tasks to the following national organisations:

The Municipal Group Life Insurance Company (KFA), set up by the associations, issues group insurance policies for municipal and county council employees and provides other services.

The Municipal Credits Company Ltd (Kommunkredit AB) is owned by the local authority associations and savings banks. It makes loans to municipalities and county councils and to enterprises in which they participate.

The Planning and Rationalisation Institute for Health and Social Services (Spri). This is financed and operated under an agreement between the State and the Federation of County Councils. It supports, co-ordinates and participates in the planning and effective operation of health and medical services, gathers and disseminates information in this area and sets standards for hospital care.

The County Council Purchasing Centre (LIC) is a trade association whose members are the Federation of County Councils, individual county councils and a number of municipalities and other organisations. Among other things it sells goods and in some cases develops and produces them for use by its members.

The Institute for Disabled Persons (Handikappinstitutet), operated jointly by the State and the Federation of County Councils, researches, develops, tests and supplies information about technical aids for handicapped persons.

Kommun-Data AB was set up jointly by the two local authority associations to provide data-processing services for local authorities.

5.6 INTER-GOVERNMENTAL RELATIONS

The government's principle has been to limit the role of central government departments to national policy-making and allocation of resources, hence the smallness of central ministries by international standards. The corollary is that the centre must trust and depend on the provinces. But as shown in §5.4 the state is strongly represented at county level. Responsibilities are intertwined there between state agencies and locally elected bodies so that it is hardly possible to define boundaries between central and local interests in most matters. In the words of a government commission,

> The relationship between state and local authorities is no longer character-
> ised by a permanent segregation of duties and fundamentally different
> interests, but by a common endeavour to promote the best interests of citizens,
> by constant shifts in the mutual division of labour, by continuous co-operation
> in a variety of forms and by mutual dependence. (Gustafsson, Agne 1984b)

Sometimes responsibility is explicitly shared between the state and county councils, as in the case of regional development funds set up to support local commerce and industry. There are many overlaps of membership among local bodies and between them and state institutions, for example a politician may be a municipal councillor and a member of the municipal executive, managing director of a public housing company, member of the county council and a regular participant in several government housing and urban study commissions (Anton, 1974).

About 80 per cent of members of parliament have served as local councillors (Lane and Magnusson, 1987). Channels of influence, both upwards and downwards, are therefore not limited to national associations at the centre but widely diffused, through multiple role-holding, frequent contacts between councillors and local officials and civil servants within state hierarchies, and meetings between leading councillors and ministers. Local government issues are continuously present at the centre of national politics and powerfully represented. They are also the life-blood of the national parties.

Central government both promotes its own policies for service development and seeks to constrain local taxation by negotiation and persuasion through the local authority associations. Policies of fiscal restraint, however, have often been accompanied by increases in central grant to ensure that modest growth can continue (Greenwood, 1980). There is an ordinance which prohibits new regulations liable to raise local and regional bodies' expenses directly or indirectly without direct government approval. The principle has been that local authorities should be reimbursed by the state when new duties are conferred on them by legislation (Lane and Magnusson, 1987). Assumptions relating to this kind of provision have, however, led to acute problems regarding macroeconomic control (see §5.9).

The principles of the system do not preclude central government from issuing large numbers of directives to local authorities on how services under national legislation should be administered. Laws and regulations set minimum standards of service but to different extents in particular fields. Moreover the administrative boards may be described as the eyes and ears of central government, although their role in relation to local government is not a controlling but a collaborative one. The substance of local autonomy has increased through an increasing tendency for the Riksdag to make framework laws that leave decisions on means of implementation to local councils.

The growth of local authority powers that are exercised in the capacity of agent for the national state has greatly increased the identification of local government with the purposes of national government. This led to its serving as a 'whipping-boy' for sectors of the public represented by local interest groups, especially during the 1970s. The tension between democratic values and national welfare state ambitions became acute. Recent reforms, such as provisions for neighbourhood councils and other forms of decentralisation of local powers (see §5.12), have aimed to reduce gaps that had arisen between municipalities and the people.

The case has continued to be argued for reduction of control and forcing more responsibility for levels of service back on to local authorities. This is seen to require some acceptance of inequalities and variety of approach between areas as against the stress on efficiency and national standards (Lane and Magnusson, 1987). It does not imply that the government has lost concern about the quality of local administration and the promotion of norms orientated towards understanding and, as far as reasonable, meeting clients' perceptions of their needs. The government's 'programme for the renewal of the public sector' launched in 1985 lays great stress on reduced state control and increased exercise of freedom to adopt new forms of organisation at local level. Building on the experience of a pilot project involving twelve local authorities the government promoted legislation in 1988 to involve 23 authorities, aiming at removing obstacles to novel approaches to committee and departmental structures, the reduction of financial and other controls, exemption from state regulations for reasons of efficiency and improving inter-governmental co-operation generally (Gustafsson, Agne, 1991; Gustafsson, Lennart, 1987; Clarke and Stewart, 1985).

5.7 LOCAL GOVERNMENT SERVICES

Local government has lost functions since 1945, including road maintenance, employment services, labour market matters, police, prosecutions and local courts administration. But the gains in this period have far outweighed the losses: it has acquired responsibility for schools, health and medical care and some specialised training, and at county level increased scope for the development of commerce and industry, transport, cultural and social amenities and certain special education services. Transfers of services to local government in the last three decades have greatly increased the scale of local government services. The number of local employees rose from 725,000 in 1972 to 1,149,000 in 1982. After a fall in the early 1980s numbers rose again to 1,145,000 by 1989. Education and social welfare constituted about 62 per cent of total local government expenditure. About two-thirds of expenditures are on mandatory functions.

Gothenburg provides an overall picture of local government activities because, unlike nearly all other local authorities, it combines responsibility for both county and municipal functions. It is a city of about 430,000 inhabitants (Sweden's second largest). (One krone may be taken as a little more than one-tenth of a pound sterling at the time.)

Table 5.2: City of Gothenburg — Expenditures, 1987 Estimates

Service	Operating Expenditure (SKr.mn)	%	Capital Expenditure (SKr.mn)	%
Education	2,228	12.1	36	3.7
Leisure and culture	894	5.1	24	2.5
Health, Medical and Social Services	8,698	50.0	287	29.9
Housing	8	-	48	5.0
Public Utilities	2,489	14.2	300	31.2
Public Safety	161	0.9	14	1.5
Commerce	10	0.1	54	5.6
Public Transport	1,601	9.2	155	16.1
Land and Real Estate Administration	574	3.3	40	4.2
Central Administration	821	4.7	4	0.1
Totals	17,486		961	

Source: City of Gothenburg, 1987.

Legal Powers to Provide Services

Because local authorities possess general competence within the limits described in §5.2 their activities in the interest of their own areas cannot be comprehensively defined. There are over twenty general enactments with accompanying legal instruments for particular fields of activity, including education, building, fire protection, public sanitation, environmental protection, social services, health and medical care and care of the mentally retarded. Some make detailed requirements while others go no further than laying down guidelines. In addition there are many enabling acts, including those giving powers and limits for levying of charges in public places, and aid to political parties, industry and commerce, foreign students and international disaster relief. There are very few matters left where state or county administrative board approval is required: a notable exception being adoption of site improvement plans.

1. Town and Country Planning and Development

Municipalities have a monopoly of land-use and development control excluding state land. Subject to state approval of site plans they exercise building control. The counties share regional planning responsibilities with the county administrative board. There is no hierarchical control.

2. Housing

Municipalities design programmes for housing provision on the basis of comprehensive local assessments of housing needs. Housing allowances are jointly financed with the state. They have powers of compulsory purchase and first refusal on property put up for sale; submit applications for government loans and grants with comments; and promote housing production through special municipal housing bodies.

3. Roads

Municipalities undertake construction and maintenance of streets where there are site development plans. (General roadworks and maintenance are carried out by state county road boards.)

4. Transport

Municipalities and *counties* participate in special authorities that are responsible for regional and local transport excluding surface railroads (mainly county transport corporations).

5-6. Education and Vocational Training

Municipalities are responsible for comprehensive schools (ages 7-16) and upper secondary schools (attended by over 90 per cent of young people); adult education and some specialised forms of higher education; school meals; preventive school health care; educational welfare and psychological services.

County councils run about a half of adult education colleges (folk high schools) and grant-aid others; special schools; much of in-service teacher training; nursing and upper secondary agricultural, horticultural and forestry education; and sponsor a third of all higher education, especially that in auxiliary medical fields.

7-8. Cultural Activities, Libraries and Museums

Municipalities provide libraries which generally house a variety of cultural activities for all age groups. They assist theatres, museums, art galleries, musical and other voluntary organisations, including cultural and adult education associations. Counties provide cultural activities and grants to cultural and educational organisations.

9. Recreation

Municipalities provide sports facilities, public baths, ice rinks and youth recreation centres and support recreational associations. Counties provide sports and leisure centres.

10. Health and Social Welfare

The approach is national, administered by the National Board of Health and Welfare to secure the best contributions at the most appropriate levels.

Health

Municipalities implement environmental protection and public health services under a mandatory committee which plays a role in public planning and carries out a wide range of environmental activities including the promotion of domestic hygiene, enforcement of industrial and handicraft standards and air, water and noise monitoring and control.

Counties and three large cities have general responsibility for health services and medical care, including all hospitals and primary health care; school health services; psychiatric, dental and ambulance services; and district health care centres responsible for preventive health care.

Social Welfare

Municipalities administer social assistance benefits, 'safety net' help to anyone in need without other available aid, home help to families with children, alcohol and drug abuse prevention and domestic and other help for the disabled. They prepare five-year plans for child care including day nurseries and support for those in need of care.

Counties provide care and assistance for specific groups, including the mentally handicapped (education, care and employment), diabetics and other physically handicapped persons.

11. Police

Policing and local justice were transferred to the state in 1965.

12. Fire Protection is undertaken by *municipalities*, often through joint bodies.

13. Development of Local Economy and Employment

Municipalities take measures to attract commerce and industry, provide industrial estates and facilities for hire, support to new technology and consultancy help to small firms. Subsidisation of businesses is not legal but support may be given if closure or cutbacks would lead to heavy local unemployment.

14. Public Utilities

Municipalities provide water services, sewerage and sanitation, gas and electricity supply, town heating, refuse disposal (often jointly with other authorities), abattoirs, refrigeration plant.

15. Cemeteries are a parish authority responsibility

16. Tourism

Municipalities provide publicity and services.

County councils provide some finance for tourist facilities.

5.8 IMPLEMENTATION OF SERVICES

Local government employed a quarter of the Swedish workforce in 1985. Core services are mainly supplied directly by local authority departments. Utility and other services are commonly provided by fully or partly owned companies, while some housing and other functions are carried out by foundations or non-profit companies. In many cases the directors are all local authority members or officials. Around 1983 there were some 1,300 commercial-type enterprises in which municipalities and county councils had controlling interests.

Companies are legally and financially distinct from municipal administration, with separate staffs, budgets and financial arrangements, and are expected to operate on a self-financing basis. Fresh share capital may be supplied through the municipal budgets. Long-term capital is raised mostly from mortgage companies or government institutions.

The City of Stockholm in 1986 had fifteen fully owned companies in the housing and building sector and a 25 per cent interest in another; nine fully or predominantly owned harbour and industrial companies, 16 with a minority interest and two with a 50 per cent interest; and 13 other fully owned companies including city theatre and garage companies, plus a 50 per cent interest in television, information, tourist and five other companies and a minority interest in three other cases.

The work of Gothenburg's 22 companies included building, management of properties, administration of a community centre, public auctions, port services, passenger ferries, coach tours, an amusement park, operas, concerts, theatre, sports, technological research and development, public relations, sewage purification, refuse disposal, real estate management, and purchase and storage of fuel and oil. The City also owned a 50 per cent holding in the Gothenborg and region bus company.

Advantages cited for joint participation with external interests in such businesses include use of outside capital and expertise, avoidance of bureaucratic regulation and the need to obtain government approval for loans and confidentiality in land purchases and other sensitive matters, thereby avoiding the public scrutiny which the law would otherwise require.

5.9 LOCAL GOVERNMENT FINANCE

General

Local government expenditure is principally financed from local authorities' own autonomous revenues. There is one single local government tax, the local income tax. From 1975 to 1987 this provided for 40 per cent or more of municipal current expenditure and around 60 per cent of that of the county councils. By 1989, however, it covered only 47 per cent of municipalities' revenue. During the same period income from the second largest source of revenue, fees and charges, rose from 18 to 22 per cent of current costs and from 15 to 25 per cent in the case of the counties. It formed 18 per cent of municipal revenue in 1989. In 1989 the municipalities received 21 per cent of revenue from state subsidies as against 28 per cent in 1985.

The financial position can only be appreciated in the context of inter-governmental relations (see §5.6). There was no legal constraint on the level of income tax which local authorities could raise until the years 1990-91, but for reasons of macro-economic control the local authority associations had agreed with the government on voluntary tax limits in two previous years which are understood not to have been entirely observed. On occasion central grant has been raised to fend off threatened increases in local tax levels. There is said to have been fierce competition for resources between levels of government during the 1980s (Lane and Magnusson, 1987).

Of total local government expenditure, municipalities spend about two-thirds and the counties one-third. State-regulated activities account for about 70 per cent of local government expenditure. In the municipalities education consumes about a quarter of expenditure; energy, water and refuse disposal 13 per cent and recreational and cultural amenities 7 per cent. Whereas these proportions remained fairly steady over the decade, social services expenditure rose rapidly from 22 per cent in 1980 to 27 per cent. Over three-quarters of county expenditure is on health services and medical care (see Table 5.2 for Gothenburg).

The decentralisation of functions from 1967 and response to local demand have produced a pattern of rising expenditure by local government against falling expenditure by central government. Hence, due to government macro-economic policies to boost the competitive strength of the private sector and thereby real economic growth and to counter problems arising from balance of payments deficits and growing foreign debts, there has been general agreement on the need to dampen down public expenditure.

Attention has inevitably focused on local government costs. From 1986 the government used reductions in grant linked with agreements with local government to restrain local tax demands with the aim of limiting growth to some one per cent annually. The level of income tax was generally thought to be as high as could be tolerated, so that the reductions in grant have inevitably forced local authorities to sharpen priorities in a search for savings. The exemption of business income from local taxation has also been an important influence on service expenditures, especially in areas such as Stockholm which are well endowed with industry.

Sources of Revenue

While national income tax is levied on a progressive scale, local income tax is assessed as a fixed proportion of income. Its burden on citizens has been around double that of the national income tax. The tax base includes not only a fixed proportion of income but also a small percentage of property value. The property value is normally assessed every five years at an amount corresponding to three-quarters of a property's probable market value at a sale in the free market in relation to the average price two years before the assessment year. Net capital gains, with certain exceptions, are also subject to the tax. (Council of Europe, 1985, *Financial Resources for Local and Regional Authorities*)

Income tax levies are fixed by municipal, county, and parish councils. Councils deduct sources of income other than income tax from estimated revenue needs and then assess the income tax rate on the total taxable amount on which the tax is to be levied (the tax base). Before 1986 this tax base included income of bodies with agricultural or other property or carrying on business in the municipal area concerned during the tax year.

Assessment, charging and collection are handled by the national tax authority along with national taxation, but members of the local tax assessment committees are appointed by local councils. Most decisions are made by the committee's chairman, who is appointed by the county administrative board. Controversial cases are put to the committee.The formal responsibility for the assessment work lies with the tax director, who is head of the administrative board's tax department. (Ibid.)

Charges and Reimbursement for Services

Around 19 per cent of municipal and 25 per cent of county expenditure are covered by charges and client reimbursements. In principle charges for utility services such as electricity, heating, water and sewerage cover costs but should not yield a profit. Charges for social services such as nurseries, care of the elderly and patients' fees are often abated on welfare grounds. Charging in these fields is a controversial issue.

Central Grants

In 1989 state grants accounted for around 21 per cent of municipal incomes and somewhat less of county incomes, the big majority of which are in the form of specific grants for mandatory services such as child care, medical care and education under conditions set out in parliamentary regulations. The latter have been used as open-ended incentives to encourage local authorities to provide permissive services such as care for the elderly. In the 1980s there was a tendency to increase general grant modestly against reductions in specific grants.

General grants are primarily tax equalisation subsidies. In 1985 they amounted on average to four per cent of municipal current costs and six per cent of county costs. They compensated about 90 per cent of authorities with low average tax bases and/or with special needs due to the age composition of their populations and problems concerning building stock. In 1986 a 'Robin Hood' tax was imposed on the wealthiest municipalities, the proceeds being transferred to municipalities with the lowest tax base (which lie particularly in Northern Sweden).

As well as promoting equality between areas, general grant has been used as an instrument of macro-economic control. For example in 1986 the total grant was frozen with the aim of achieving reductions in local government expenditure of one or two per cent a year.

Capital Finance

Most capital finance is covered by revenue sources. In the early 1980s loans amounted to around four per cent of gross investment by municipalities and less than fourteen per cent of that by county councils. Net debt, however, rose substantially year by year.

Financial and Regional Planning

The annual budget has become a medium-term overall planning process. A rolling multi-year plan has been adopted annually. Thus Gothenburg, for example, has prepared a four-year plan aiming to maximise the effective allocation of resources. It is based on data which include population projections, service needs by population groups and housing needs, and employment, industrial development and land-use predictions. Data from long-term plans are supplied to the county administrative boards by municipalities and thence to the National Housing Board and the Central Bureau of Statistics; and also by the counties through the Federation of County Councils. County administrative boards are required to produce county development plans in co-operation with county councils and municipalities. It would be interesting to establish how far these rational planning procedures have been upset by or assisted the national response to the financial crisis of the early 1990s.

5.10 ELECTORAL REPRESENTATION

Electoral Arrangements

Since an inter-party agreement in 1967, elections have been held for all three levels of government on the same day every three years. This helps to secure a high turn-out: in 1982 91.4 per cent of the population for parliament, 89.9 per cent for the county elections and 89.6 per cent for the municipal elections. According to figures for 1979, 10 per cent of voters for parliament supported a different party in the municipal elections and 7 per cent did so in the county elections. It is probable that there will be new provisions on timing of elections in the 1990s.

The national electoral system, as in Denmark and Norway, is based on the Sainte Laguë, modified d'Hondt or 'largest remainder' method (see §1.10). In Sweden voters can cross out names on a party list but a candidate is only excluded if at least half the voters cross his or her name out.

Who represents the voters is obviously determined largely by the order of names on the party lists. The practice in the Social Democratic Party in Lund, for example, has been for the choice to be determined by meetings of about a hundred party members. Each member votes for 25 candidates after a general discussion of the principles governing the list, and especially the balance between sexes and geographical areas. The rank order in the results is then scrutinised to determine how far it is consistent with the agreed criteria. It may then be modified by agreement. In recent years a 'limited majority' rule has been generally adopted under which majority parties or coalitions hold the committee chairmanships and the majority of full-time posts (Strömberg and Westerstahl, 1984).

The Party System

The local party organisations adopt party platforms and have the main say in nominating candidates for the party lists. They are consulted on nominations to committees. Party groups are well organised and meet to discuss business before meetings of committees, councils and joint bodies.

Party groups on councils include deputy members who are elected in the local elections to replace full members on councils or committees when the latter are absent. Non-elected party members are also co-opted to committees as well as other people with relevant skills and experience.

Since 1970 municipal and county councils have possessed the power to pay subsidies to parties at a uniform rate per seat, and these have been paid by all councils since 1977. In the early 1980s local subsidies ranged from 500 kronor per seat (about 48 pounds sterling) to, in Stockholm, 110,000 (about ten and a half thousand pounds). The money covers salaries of party officials and helps finance accommodation, training of representatives, party propaganda etc. State and press subsidies add to party resources. The Local Government Act enables local authorities to organise courses related to the interests of political parties and groups and to put premises, materials, political secretaries and administrative services at their disposal. Party offices make secretarial assistance available to enable councillors to fulfil their responsibilities.

In the 1980s the balance was often fine between right- and left-wing coalitions, but the advent of new parties, especially the Greens whose vote cannot be relied upon by either side, has produced cases in which there is no controlling majority or coalition.The biggest party, at least up to the end of the 1980s, the Social Democrats (SAP), believe in the maintenance of the welfare state, increasing equality and the promotion of 'economic democracy'. Although traditionally representing trade union interest, it has championed local democratic control in recent years, which it sees threatened by right-wing policies including customer-oriented reforms. The Moderate and Liberal Parties, stronger among white-collar workers, professionals and business people, argue for depoliticisation of local government and privatisation. The Centre Party's strongest support is among farmers, but it has won votes from substantial minorities in other sectors. It has traditionally stressed decentralisation, egalitarianism, co-determination in industry and the protection of the environment. There is a strong cross-party representation of 'economisers' that wish to end public sector expansion, a trend that has gained in strength. (Montin, 1992)

The balance in the past has been very stable in most instances, as in the City of Stockholm where the Social Democrats held from 39 to 41 seats continuously between 1976 and 1988. With the arrival of new parties and a leading emphasis on tax-cutting it may be expected that the 1990s will be more turbulent although the Social Democrats have moved towards the centre and continued to seek consensus.

Working Conditions of Councillors

In most counties and larger municipalities there are full-time political commissioners and chairmen or mayors.

Councillors have job security during their periods of office. According to a survey at the end of the 1970s municipal councillors spent an average of about sixteen hours a month on council duties and county councillors about ten hours. Indications are that the extent to which they take up specific cases to help individual members of the community was surprisingly low, at least by British standards, but the helpfulness of local party offices may compensate for this.

Councillors receive attendance and mileage allowances. At county level full-time councillors receive salaries. Full-time commissioners (see §5.11) could in 1983 expect to receive around 130,000 Swedish kronor a month (about 12,000 pounds sterling). They are entitled to social security and health insurance benefits and a full pension after twelve years of service (Council of Europe, 1983; Malmsten, 1983; Calmfors, 1972).

5.11 THE INTERNAL ORGANISATION OF LOCAL AUTHORITIES

Since 1977 laws requiring local authorities to adopt standard forms of organisation have been relaxed. The 'Free Municipality Experiment' mentioned in §5.8 promises more radical reforms. (Gustafsson, Agne, 1991; Gustafsson, Lennart, 1987; Peterson, no date).

Co-ordination and policy definition have increasingly come to depend on party organisation, without an understanding of which the functioning of a particular authority's decision-making system cannot be properly understood (see §5.10).

The Council (*Fullmäktige*)

The directly elected council appoints all committees (*nämnder*), proportionally to party strengths if a minority requires. It also appoints its chairman, commissioners and representatives to state and other bodies. A

313

municipal council can appoint local bodies in geographically defined parts of its area and confer on them certain independent decion-making powers (see §5.12). It decides the budget, fixes the rate of local income tax and charges and appoints its own auditors. It determines the details of administrative structure and responds to consultations by the government and national and county administrative boards, often on important issues of government policy. The municipal council adopts site development plans and issues by-laws on fire prevention, traffic, environmental health and other matters. Councils can delegate to committees but not on matters of principle or other key issues.

A council is free within limits to decide its number of members, but the minimum membership is 31 and the number must be an odd one. Deputy members are returned at elections to stand in for full members when necessary. Chairmen of councils and of their executive committees are regarded as the foremost representatives of their authorities. Council meetings are generally monthly, or in counties less frequent.

All committees or boards (both translations are often used) exercise independent prerogatives. The elected members are involved through the committee system in the decision-making process at all levels.

The Chief Executive Committee or Board (*kommunstyrelse or landstyrelse*)

The law requires the appointment by the council of a chief executive committee as its supreme executive authority. This is not a distinct executive but it has responsibility for leading and co-ordinating council business and activities, including the administration and supervision of the activities of other committees. It is a powerful and respected body which develops its own initiatives and combines responsibilities for overall finance, policy and property. People may speak of it as 'governing' the municipal area. It may not interfere in the business of other committees that are required by law when they are carrying out duties under special legislation, but it may make recommendations and suggestions and request statements and information. Its budgetary responsibilities and other powers give it a degree of control, but ultimately a disagreement within another committee's area of legal competence can only be settled by the council. It frequently makes use of special sub-committees and delegation of tasks to individual members. The City of Stockholm has a board of nine commissioners, each heading a department and chairing the committee which controls it.

Committees or Boards

Committees or boards carry out most authority business and in most cases have a department or office at their disposal. They draft business to be decided by council, put council decisions into effect and attend to administrative business. Elected members participate directly in handling matters at all levels, from drafting to decision-making and implementation. Unlike the council they meet without the public present because this is believed to be necessary for frank and unprejudiced discussion.

In the 1980s most municipalities had between nine and fourteen committees, but the largest might have as many as 30, each with eleven or twelve members and the same number of deputies. County councils had from five to thirteen committees. Municipal special statutory committees have been required for building and town planning, environmental and health protection, social welfare, education, elections and sometimes for fire, civil defence, transport and unemployment. Other committees are likely to cover recreation, the arts, personnel, works, property, streets and parks, sanitation, harbours, consumer affairs and environmental protection.

Stockholm had about 25 committees or boards, including service, resource management, audit and election committees. It also had 18 district committees for welfare services and 18 for education. There were two joint committees for the Greater Stockholm area and a mixed Council for Cultural and Natural Values. Gothenburg, with its county responsibilities, had over 35 committees. Some had very specific and detailed areas of responsibility, such as the 'Keillers Park Committee' and the 'Immigrant Services Committee'.

County councils have statutory committees for public health, medical matters (with local hospital committees), mental and social welfare, and education (with local education committees). In addition they are likely to appoint personnel, arts, construction and appeals committees. In the health field committee structures vary widely.

Paid Political Commissioners

Larger municipalities and county councils have sought to overcome problems of over-reliance on staff, which they believe has impaired the power of elected members to exercise the degree of control appropriate to their democratic responsibilities. To this end they have appointed some councillors as full-time and part-time commissioners, normally for the life of a council and renewable subject to the results of the next elections. Stockholm appointed municipal commissioners in 1920. By 1980 there were 491 full-time and 143 part-time commissioners. The county had 95 full-time and 84 part-time county council commissioners (Malmsten, 1983). Municipalities with under 20,000 residents usually have one commissioner while those with populations of over 50,000 usually three or more. Where committee chairmanships are held by a majority party there is usually one 'commissioner for the opposition' without administrative duties (Council of Europe, 1985, *Management Structures in Local and Regional Government*).

Administrative Organisation

Local councils vary in their administrative arrangements. The commonest arrangement in small and medium-sized authorities is for each committee to control its own department through a head officer. In large municipalities the committees, including the executive committee, are often divided into sub-committees for separate departments. Sometimes the commissioners act as a drafting committee which forms a kind of inner cabinet within the executive committee. There may be an integrated secretarial committee, but public health and medical normally committees have their own secretarial offices under an administrative officer directly responsible to the medical committee. (Gustafsson, Agne, 1984b)

The chief executive or town clerk is an officer who together with the treasurer is responsible to the executive committee. As chief officer for the committee responsible for the general control of resources he or she exercises a general co-ordinative role throughout the organisation. Most chief executives are lawyers. Professional influence is strong because heads of department belong to the main professions: it is, for example, the town architect who is head of the building department. In most but not all cases a local authority is free to decide the qualifications it requires of its heads of department as well as to appoint them. One of the exceptions is the chief education officer whose salary has been partly met in the past by central government. (Council of Europe, 1985b, *Management Structures in Local and Regional Government*)

5.12 CITIZEN PARTICIPATION AND DECENTRALISATION WITHIN CITIES

Direct Participation in Local Government

Participation in local elections has been around 90 per cent. Sweden has some 70,000 elected representatives — one to about 270 inhabitants. This has been achieved by policies deliberately aimed at increasing participation that were introduced after the amalgamations described in §5.4 which reduced the number of local councillors by more than 100,000.

Research shows that the changes reduced the representativeness of councillors in terms of sex, age, social background and education among other variables. 'Those elected or appointed became even more a "social elite" after the amalgamations than was the case before'. The amalgamations also had a negative effect on representation of public opinions and local party organisations, and consequently on communication of citizens with local politicians and party groups, increasing their dependence on officers and interest organisations. (Gustafsson, Gunnel, 1980)

All documents in possession of a public authority, received or deemed compiled by that authority, are public unless within the purview of secrecy legislation. Computerised information is treated similarly and public authorities have a duty to assist members of the public to gain access to computerised data which rank as public documents.

From the mid-1970s the government sought to increase active participation in decision-making by providing more political roles open to citizens within local government. Provision for 'substitute' committee members doubled the numbers representing the public. By 1991 area committees had been set up in 23 authorities with responsibilities under main service committees, most notably in the fields of social welfare and leisure.

'Institutional committees' have been set up to take charge of sports centres, day nurseries and elderly people's homes. They are said to help in adapting activities to local needs and variation, improve conditions and provide motivation for local party members, give more opportunity for contact with residents and bring in residents in under-represented groups to play a less demanding role than that of central committee members. (Gustafsson, Gunnel, 1981, Montin, 1992)

The right of tabling business for councils is generally restricted to committees, auditors or government bodies, but there is provision for individual councillors to table motions. A letter from the public can be discussed if endorsed by a member as a motion. Councillors can lodge

317

appeals for adjudication against council decisions and administrative appeals can be made by parties indirectly affected under sectoral legislation to local and national boards and administrative courts and tribunals up to supreme judicial level and to government. Appeals may be against the content or advisability of a decision and a tribunal may not only quash a decision but may also substitute a new one. Appeals by councillors are limited to issues of legality and may be taken up to the Supreme Administrative Court, where a ruling has the status of case law.

Councils or committees may decide to put issues to popular referenda, in which a 60 to 70 per cent response is normal. They may also commission opinion polls on a policy topic. With one exception popular consultation is not a legal requirement, but it is very common to invite written opinions from local voluntary bodies and to hold open meetings, or to set up study groups, sometimes in association with adult education activities.

Decentralisation

The first consultative multi-purpose neighbourhood councils were set up in Lulea in 1969. Although some 30 other municipalities set up similar bodies, the results tended to be rather discouraging and most were disbanded. An act in 1980 enabled councils to delegate decision-making powers to multi-purpose sub-district councils as well as to raise local issues and respond to consultations. They may be enabled to take responsibility for a large part of municipal tasks within their areas. Members are appointed by municipal councils, usually in accordance with party nominations proportional to party strength. Members need not live in the district and are responsible for arranging public meetings to give information and answer questions about their activities. They have an allocation of funds to spend as they wish in their area's interest. In most cases they have their own administrative office, a chief co-ordinating officer and responsibilities for personnel. By 1987 some twenty authorities had established such councils. (Kolam, 1987)

As concern about the rising costs of government increased, they were supported as a means to greater effectiveness and efficiency through inter-service co-ordination, enlistment of voluntary services and extending officers' contributions beyond their purely professional roles. Arguments against them have included increase in bureaucracy and expense, difficulty of state supervision, stifling of grass-roots movements, weakening of small parties and tendencies to inequality between neighbourhood areas. Opposition tends to lie within parties, not between them or within the bureaucracy. Kolam's conclusions are that some of the objectives of these councils have been achieved although not as fully as had been hoped by the decision-makers. Popular knowledge of their activities has been low, and most residents have failed to use them as mediators of needs and demands or for other purposes.

Eight out of ten Swedes have in recent decades been found to be members of at least one association. Political activity often grows out of representation of interests at sub-municipality level towards wider political concern. Nevertheless interest appears not to be channelled primarily through the parties.

By the end of the 1980s political interest had turned from neighbourhood councils to 'user democracy', and in particular allowing decentralisation of decision-making to junior officers provided that they worked with the advice of consumer groups. The results have been mixed and the move has not necessarily reduced costs unless it has served as a stimulus to improvement through self-help. 'Consumer choice' has been advocated as an alternative to participation in the delivery of public services. (Montin, 1992)

5.13 THE GOVERNANCE OF METROPOLITAN AREAS

Sweden's two main conurbations, Stockholm and Gothenburg, include one-fifth of the country's population. In both cases there is extensive settlement of people outside the boundaries of the old city, but there are no spreading conglomerations to the extent found in larger industrial countries. The central city contains 48 per cent of metropolitan area inhabitants in Stockholm's case and 60 per cent in Gothenburg's. The patterns of government organisation have been quite different. Gothenburg has remained an all-purpose or 'county borough' -type authority, and the surrounding suburbs have remained under the national two-tier pattern of municipalities and counties (§5.11).

Greater Stockholm has a special form of county which, subject to a small exception, covers the areas of twenty municipalities. It has health, vocational and adult education, children's homes, special schools, public transport and cultural competences and sponsors some regional funds for economic development.

The central municipality, the City of Stockholm, spreads over several islands and opens into an archipelago of twenty-four thousand islands and islets. It has a population of about six and a half thousand and the urban areas outside its boundaries provide for around nine hundred thousand, nearly all of whom live within the area of Stockholm County.

The metropolitan region is well planned, with high living standards, mostly modern housing, a good health record and a balance of industry and commerce. The main differences between Stockholm county and other counties arise from the special needs of the metropolitan region. Land-use and other key planning powers lie with the municipalities and the county represents as it were the joint planning interest of all twenty municipalities. It ties the area's planning into the needs of state planning bodies. A national law requires a regional plan to guide land-use decisions, indicating where development should take place. The planning activities are the basis for consultation and discussion within the county. Disputes can be settled by the county administrative board which, on the national model, consists of fourteen county-appointed members and a government-appointed chairman (see §5.11).

The county council has 149 members. Its committees for regional planning and enterprise, health and dental care, transport, certification, real estate and personnel submit proposals to the executive committee and implement the council's decisions.

Other forms of metropolitan organisation include the Suburban Committee (a voluntary regional committee), the Stockholm Municipal Association for Housing Supply (based on inter-governmental contracts) and the inter-municipal Greater Stockholm Energy Corporation, which is a special-purpose ad hoc authority that develops and supplies hot water heating systems (Norton, 1983).

6. DENMARK

6.1 HISTORY AND TRADITIONS

National Characteristics

Denmark has a population of a little more than five million, some three-quarters that of Greater London. Its area of 43,000 square kilometres is also relatively small. It is a homogeneous country with a strong central state. Factors which might have led to a high degree of centralisation have been countered in recent years by the perceived need for strong autonomous local government.

The state is a monarchy with popular control based on institutions, rights and procedures defined in a written constitution. There is a provision, hardly ever used, for a third of the members of the *Folketing* (parliament) to require a referendum within three days of the final reading of a parliamentary bill, excluding financial and nationality matters. Why this has hardly been used must lie largely in the nature of the finely tuned system of proportional representation and the party system on which it depends.

Voter choice has grown volatile in recent years and related to opinions on issues rather than social allegiances. The country has a remarkably broad spectrum of parties and a corresponding range of distinct minority approaches (see §6.10) (Thomas, 1987). Since 1973 at least ten parties have been represented in parliament (see §6.10). Between 1975 and 1982 the Social Democrats were the dominant party, with some support from the Liberals. A centre-right coalition followed including conservatives, centre democrats, liberals and the Christian People's Party.

There is intense involvement of organised interests in national decision-making, both through party channels and direct relationships with government ministries. In this it stands with other Scandinavian countries in its high degree of corporatism (Lane and Ersson, 1987).

History and Constitution

The origins of modern local government are found in medieval popular assemblies for mutual assistance and in the royal granting of borough charters. During the succeeding centuries a series of royal despots, mostly with enlightened views of government, maintained a system of local administration. The structure of 20 counties, each under the control of a governor (*amtmand*), dates from 1793. Feudalism was abolished in the late eighteenth century and a class of farmers and indigent crofters developed. The spread of liberalism which followed the American and French Revolutions reinforced concepts of self-administration and local autonomy. Local committees were set up to administer the 1803 Poor Law and statutory educational functions. In 1837 popularly elected councils were introduced to advise the ruling magistracy. Four years later parish councils were given responsibility for running schools, assisting the poor and maintaining roads.

The 1848 revolution resulted in the end of absolute monarchy. The 1849 Constitution declared 'the right of local authorities to manage their own affairs under the control of the state'. A slow transfer of central responsibilities to local elected representatives followed. A reorganisation in 1869 put town administration into the hands of elected councils. The steady expansion of municipal functions was under way. Nevertheless chairmen of borough councils (*burgomaster*) continued to be appointed by the crown until 1919.

The second era of structural reform came in the 1970s, involving the merging of authorities described in §6.4, transfers of functions (§6.7) and a weakening of the role of the governors (§6.6), part of a comprehensive policy to decentralise functions which could be better carried out autonomously by county and municipal authorities through their own means. The aim was to rationalise the rules concerning formal state control of local authorities and lift control from local government finance and resources (§6.6 and 6.9). The reforms marked a sharp break with the past and are remarkable for their comprehensive approach.

6.2 THE STATUS OF LOCAL GOVERNMENT

Legal Status

The local authority (*kommune*) is a corporation consisting of the inhabitants of an administrative area. Its functions are exercised by a council elected by its inhabitants as their sole agent. It has possessed fiscal autonomy in that there has been no statutory limitation on the extent to which it may raise local taxes. (It should be noted that the use of the English term 'local authority' for kommune is general in Danish translations and that in this case it does not normally include the county or province level.)

Most powers exercised by local authorities are statutory but both counties and municipalities have general competence within the law to provide benefits in the interest of local inhabitants beyond those given in the law. A local authority may not, however, restrict the liberty of citizens by regulating their conduct or undertaking any activity dependent on a licence without a statutory basis. It may not take actions forbidden by law or 'administrative (supervisory) practice'. Conformity to centrally defined standards may be required in the case of non-obligatory as well as mandatory statutory functions (Bogason, 1987).

Under the Constitution of 1849 local authorities were incorporated to take care of the affairs of the local community under supervision of the state. It has been accepted that they are limited by their objects, even if certain objects are to be found in common law rather than in statutes. The principles governing their powers are broadly that they may only spend money to the benefit of individual persons if provided for in the law. Paying a subsidy to an individual firm to avoid its closing down would be *ultra vires*.

Local authorities may not undertake activities belonging to the private sector — in particular trading and enterprise. Utilities such as water, gas, electricity and district heating are permitted provided that they are required in priniciple to meet their expenditures from income, at least in the long term. Facilities for common use such as parks, fire services, markets and libraries are traditional objects which may be supported by subsidy provided that they are open for use by the general public. Fees may be charged.

Ninety per cent of local authority expenditure is in practice spent on services that are mandatory under the law. Municipalities determine their own rate of local income tax and assess individual liabilities in accordance with a national code.

Concepts of Autonomy

A report of the National Association of Local Authorities in Denmark published in 1981 defines the ideas on which local government has traditionally been based. The first is self-government, that is that local authorities are entitled to manage their own affairs without interference by other authorities, particularly central authorities. The second is a comprehensive and unitary administration where almost all local tasks are managed by the local council. The third is representative government, 'where the citizens state their own views leaving it to the representatives to manage the local affairs'. The crux of representatives' authority is said to be the rights of taxation and deciding what amounts may be spent on particular services.

A view is said to have been held that the power of local bodies is 'absolute'. But new power centres cut across local authority responsibilities based on new social groupings with interests stronger than the sense of community. Other factors are seen to undermine local autonomy, in particular official machinery, the limits on the capability of elected representatives to deal with the mass of business, and the county and national planning processes to which local authorities contribute but which inevitably impose constraints on their decision-making. The fear is expressed that new demands are leading to a canalisation of power through professional groupings rather than through the party system, thereby turning representative democracy into something of a myth.

Hence a call for a redefinition of local government's purpose. The Association singled out labour market intervention through measures which fit local social conditions and new forms of support for domestic life and ensuring reasonable conditions for disadvantaged groups. The line, it argued, should be drawn between investigation, treatment and preventive action and unjustified 'guardianship' — particularly by professional bureaucracies and others concerned in the implementation of services.

New tasks in which local authorities are likely to be involved are defined as 'catalysts in relations to citizens and business', including urban renewal and employment policies, and 'the normalisation of life for individuals suffering from various types of handicap within the community environment'. But the central issue is defined as the extent to which the local council can act as a mediator between concentrations of power outside local bodies, handling their manifestations 'at a local level where things are of clear and human dimensions'.

To fulfil these objectives new developments were said to be needed with deliberate efforts to increase representation of women and age groups on councils, clearer majority rule in a parliamentary sense and more direct citizen representation.

6.3 CONCEPTS AND VALUES

The Complex of Values

The Danes have many things in common with their Swedish neighbours, including pragmatism, tolerance, willingness to sort out problems by negotiation, and practical competence. The same may be said to some extent about their orientation to social welfare, although the 'welfarist consensus' came under strong attack in Denmark before this happened in Sweden. The Conservative People's Party has attacked 'welfarism' from the point of view of economic liberalism and argued that it undermines family responsibility and fosters a materialist outlook. Nevertheless political consensus has marked the structural reforms of government in recent decades, reached through political planning and lengthy negotiations with all interested parties. (Kjellberg, 1983) The laborious seeking of consensus before decisions are made is as striking here as in Sweden, if not more so. It has been said to have arisen from the nature of the close rural communities from which local society developed.

Denmark's character is epitomised in the maintenance and enhancement of the traditional in Copenhagen as against the modern architecture of Stockholm. Small-scale enterprise is typical and has often been highly successful. Design is more 'homely'. The high value on the home and the domestic is more evident than in Sweden.

Denmark's brainchild, proportional representation, reflects a tradition of scrupulous representation of a diversity of values and high competence in negotiating and ultimately reaching conclusions which are acceptable to a wide part of the political spectrum, an approach which may be called voluntary political integration of values.

Political commitment to local government autonomy is not over-whelming, even among councillors. In 1981, 31 per cent of a sample survey of councillors agreed with the statement, 'The state must control local government effectively', as against 42 per cent who disagreed and 27 per cent who were neutral or who 'didn't know'. Most citizens in a sample of 1,500 respondents considered that there was too little spending by local authorities; 19 per cent felt spending was adequate; but 37 per cent thought there was too much. (Villadsen, no date)

However the values of new groupings in society, professionalism and regional planning are not always in harmony with the values of the small authority. 'The ideology of local self-determination is being sacrificed at the expense of efficient fiscal policies and planning' (Bruun and Skovsgaard, 1980). This is despite the fact that the role of planner appears to have been more modest than in other Scandinavian reform processes (Kjellberg, 1983).

Crucial Concepts

A handbook provided by the National Association of Local Authorities in Denmark (1984, *Local Government in Denmark*) describes Danish local government as rooted in the following concepts.

(1) The concept of community: 'All local government builds on the concept of community. According to an ancient tradition, everybody shares a responsibility for those they live and work together with.
Help to people in distress and the construction of local roads have always called for joint, solidary action.
(2) Self-government: 'Central and local politics must be coherent but within a broad, general framework the local authorities should be free to decide and control local policy.'
(3) Representative democracy: 'Among the powers vested in the representatives, those related to the levying of taxes and making of grants are of decisive importance'.
(4) Unitary authorities: 'in principle local authorities may deal with all domestic issues for which the public sector is responsible, right from taxation assessments to water and air purification.'

Regional and National Planning

Planning is included here in that it reflects values and attempts a comprehensive integration of interests in a highly rational and sophisticated way. But, as described in §6.7, the planning system has in many ways cut across concepts of local self-government in the pursuit of wider interests. 'Regional policy, understood as a national policy for balancing economic development between different geographical areas, is incorporated in almost every relevant act' (Mikkelsen and Steenstrup, 1982). A comprehensive reform of the planning system from the 1970s sought to replace detailed management by rules 'from above' with more flexible management by means of general limits for activities at the regional and local levels and comprehensive planning methods'. An initiative by the National Association of Local Authorities led to the development of a planning/budgeting system, facilitated by a national system of data management, under which local authorities were given flexibility to fix their priorities and determine the base of a pyramid constituting a national budget.

Hence a uniform planning system was brought into being for almost all public activities in Denmark, containing short- and long-term plans for sectors such as education and health. Standardised categories made it possible to make fairly precise comparisons between local budgets and sum them into a total national public sector budget. (*Norton, 1977; Bogason, 1987*)

In the 'fiscal squeeze' of the 1980s, however, politicians' sectoral priorities and also their party loyalties were undermined and the overall perspective on the system became more important (Mouritzen, 1982). But there was a tendency for relative changes on each item to catch their eye rather than 'the size of the budget per se': budgetary policy makers seem to share an incrementally oriented notion of equal misery all round' (Bogason, 1987).

6.4 NATIONAL STRUCTURE

Table 6.1: Local Government Structure

	Number	Average Population	Population Range
Counties	14	321,000	46,105 to 603,046
Local Authorities	273	18,700[1]	2,508 to 259,493

Cities with County Status

	Population
Copenhagen	482,950
Frederiksberg	88,100

Source: figures mainly from *Local Government in Nordic Countries: Facts and Figures, 1991.*

Notes: 1. Average includes the cities of Copenhagen and Frederiksberg, making 275 authorities.

The local government reforms of 1970 reduced the number of basic authorities from 1,300 to 275 and standardised their form. At the same time the number of counties was reduced from 25 to 14. The aim was to minimise the need for communities to depend on help from state agencies and inter-authority collaboration.

The Primary Local Authorities (*Primaer Kommuner*)

The Reform Commission's principle was 'one community — one municipality'. It aimed at the establishment of larger units with the capacity to deal with industrial, economic and other types of problem and form an efficient basis for the primary school system. In 1966 it suggested a minimum of five to six thousand inhabitants but would accept three to four thousand in certain circumstances. A law of 1967 stated that boundaries should be drawn so that 'normally' areas integrated in terms of population and occupational structure should form one municipality and assure possibilities of expansion within their boundaries.

A reform law in 1970 amalgamated small rural authorities with central towns and reduced the number of those with under three thousand inhabitants from 821 to three. Ninety-three per cent of the new authorities had populations of between three and forty thousand. Eighty-eight per cent were amalgamations of up to ten parishes with long histories of self-government. The picture drawn by Scandinavian writers is of new authorities absorbing large numbers of previously autonomous communities into city organisations dependent on large bureaucracies. (Harder, 1973; Kjellberg, 1983; Kjellberg and Taylor, 1984; Skovsgaard, 1984)

County Authorities (*Amtskommuner*)

The law on the revision of county boundaries in 1967 was the first of a series of reform laws. Counties extended their services to urban areas. New boundaries were fixed on the basis of population, industrial and economic characteristics. Location of hospitals was important in deciding boundaries, a convenient size stated by the commission being 200 to 250 thousand inhabitants. Greater Copenhagen was excepted (see §6.13).

The Reforms Considered

Under the reforms local councils were to take over all powers which they were fitted to administer. The amalgamations of parishes met muted resistance. The treatment of all issues together has been interpreted as the *sine qua non* of the political success (Kjellberg, 1983, attributed to Bruun). A National Association of Local Authorities Report (1981) stressed that the Reform Act was an administrative reform that left the traditional political system and its principles unchanged apart from alterations in the committee structure (§6.11) and shifted administrative burdens on to the local and county authorities, leading to increases in local bureaucracy that had in practice decreased the decision-making responsibilities of elected members. It questioned the assumptions made in the 1960s that a strengthened version of traditional local government could become the cornerstone of a decentralised public administration 'which on the basis of considerations of rationalisation and efficiency would be able to manage the public tasks in the modern welfare state.' These views reflected the stresses felt by part-time councillors generated by the burden of work. The turnover rate among mayors and councillors increased while more power gravitated into the hands of professional and technical staff (Morlan, 1981).

By 1980 the debate on local government reform had shifted to the roles of councillor and professional. A leading question was how local councillors could best serve the public interest in a time when, because of the squeeze on resources which dominated the early years of the 1980s, it was no longer possible to meet many public demands. The size and efficiency arguments had been taken to the furthest point acceptable by politicians and the public and had still not solved the problems of efficiency in a complex modern society. (Skovsgaard, 1983a).

6.5 INTER-AUTHORITY RELATIONS AND ORGANISATION

Municipalities are subordinated to counties only in so far as municipal plans are required to be consistent with regional plans. Close inter-relationships exist, most notably through municipal centres which provide a single gate of entry to integrated county health and social services (see §6.7).

The use of local joint organisations is small except through joint companies which run public utilities. The Local Government Act requires authorities to obtain government approval for joint action in the performance of any local activity. This is to safeguard against local authorities signing away their accountabilities to a quasi-autonomous body.

The work of the two local authority associations is extensive. The National Association of Local Authorities (Kommunernes Landsforening (KL), Gyldenlovesgade 11, 1600 Copenhagen) is an amalgamation of the separate associations which represented urban and rural districts and towns before 1970. The County Councils Association (Amtsradsforeningen, Landesmaerket 10, 1119 Copenhagen) was founded in 1913 and amalgamated with the Association of Hospitals in 1970. The two associations voice the interests of their members in a representational and consultative capacity, advising parliament, the government and central administration on bills, regulations, circulars and other matters. They participate directly in central government working groups and committees, often drafting parliamentary bills, regulations and circulars for adoption by central government. They provide services, advice, general information and training programmes for councillors and local government employees, conduct negotiations on salaries, wages and conditions of employment, make recommendations to government on the membership of the Local Authority Pay Board (all members of which are local government politicians) and are involved in determining applications for staff re-grading in individual local authorities. The National Association provides the secretariat for a state commission with the responsibility of regulating career structures in local government (Bogason, 1987).

The National Association of Local Authorities is an umbrella organisation for county associations of municipalities which act partly as advisory bodies to the National Association on local and national issues and partly as co-operative bodies, providing training facilities for councillors and local government staff (information supplied by the Association of County Councils, 1985, Copenhagen).

Inter-municipal agencies have tended to become national in scale over the last few decades. They include self-governing institutions, partnerships and limited companies. In particular there are the Kommunekemi A/S (an organisation for handling and treatment of waste oils and chemical wastes), Local Government Mutual Insurance Company, Government Pension Insurance Company, Local Government Auditing Department, Kommunetryk (publishing and sales department for publications, forms etc.), Local Government Research Institute on Public Finance and Administration, Danish Institute for Technical Aids, Danish Gas Works Tar Company Ltd, Municipal Natural Gas Company and Local Government Credit Association.

There are also associations with which the two general national associations are closely involved for electricity and gas works, ports, social welfare and libraries (National Association of Local Authorities in Denmark, 1984).

6.6 INTER-GOVERNMENTAL RELATIONS

Danish local government has maintained a strong ethos of autonomy despite a prefectoral system. In recent years both the sense of autonomy and the prefectoral characteristics have decreased and the contemporary picture is one of a highly integrated central-local government system whose strands are difficult to separate. The literature of the national associations defines a model of central-local relationships based upon co-operation. The County Councils' Association stated in a paper in 1984 that the division of tasks between state, county councils and municipalities assumes co-operation between public bodies on a day-to-day basis, and that the local government associations form an important link in the collaboration. The National Association of Local Authorities describes in a report on economic and political trends how parliament and central administration became accustomed to fixing local government standards, rules of approval etc. in order to manage public activities in detail, and that this respected the idea of local self-government because it was primarily a legal-administrative control of whether decisions were legal and proper which did not much affect the content of decisions. As tasks were delegated under decentralisation policies procedures of approval, norms and standards and intricate reimbursement schemes were abandoned. Central resources thereby released were spent on the improvement and co-ordination of functions, and especially on planning systems.

There remains a legal responsibility for government to supervise local authorities, but this is now exercised very narrowly, applying predominantly to the legality of local government decisions, standing orders, working arrangements with other local authorities, and budgeting and accounting guidelines (National Association of Local Authorities in Denmark, 1984). Frameworks for such matters are laid down by law, but there is much scope for adaptation to local wishes and conditions within the legal framework.

General supervisory functions lie with the Ministry of the Interior in respect of county councils and for municipalities with county supervisory committees which are corporate bodies consisting of four members elected by county councils from among their members and chaired by county prefects (*Amtmand*). County prefects are senior civil servants with legal training. In the case of a local dispute the matter is referred to the Ministry of the Interior. The supervisory authority may annul decisions as illegal or fine members of councils until obligations are fulfilled. Use of these powers is extremely rare because matters of doubt are raised for consultation in advance. Final authority lies with the courts.

Local state administrative committees in each county, which include representatives of local authorities and voluntary associations in their memberships, fulfil statutory functions for public health, children's welfare, education and further education and leisure services. Municipalities can call on a government district chief of police if force is needed to carry out their duties. His responsibilities include licensing and inspection of vehicles, drivers and exhibitions and veterinary work jointly with a district veterinary officer.

Particular ministers have power to approve schemes, plans and special actions in respect of certain grants, but central intervention has been greatly reduced. There are supervisory powers over borrowing, guarantees and land dealing and adjudication in conflicts between local authorities and members of the public or other bodies. An appeals system is available to special administrative/judicial bodies of appeal and review.

There is a government-local authority liaison committee of ministers, chairmen of the municipal and county council associations and the mayors of Copenhagen and Frederiksberg, the critical area of business being levels of expenditure and directly related matters.

Details of the strains between central and local government since attempts were made to damp down local government expenditures to benefit the private sector are given in §6.9. They have led to controls on local expenditure from above. (Bogason, 1991)

The General Character of Central-Local Relations

Local authorities by no means conform to national norms, as is shown by the large variations between authorities in expenditure patterns on major services that cannot be accounted for by differences in need (Mouritzen, 1983; Skovsgaard and Sondergaard, 1983; Bogason, 1987). Attempts to fix outputs by fixing standards and norms declined during the 1980s.

Regarding the party system, local parties act for national parties and also influence individuals and groups within the party at national level. As previously mentioned, about a quarter of leading local politicians had positions in county and central party organisations in the early 1980s (Villadsen, no date). Local lobbying by Social Democrats is reported to be heavily weighted towards obtaining amendments to acts and circulars rather than obtaining increased local investments or resources.

There are 'communities' of professional and individual service interests between local government and central departments, linked with sectoral interests among members of parliament (Mouritzen, 1983). Ministries often ask local officials to draft legislation, national regulations and circulars for them. A head of administration in a major Danish municipality declared himself extremely satisfied with circulars issued in one government domain since he had written most of them himself (Mouritzen, 1983).

The picture overall shows a remarkable degree of solidarity between political and officer elites, each 'taking in each other's washing'. There has been apprehension among opposition parties and many local politicians that the system, although in principle widening local democratic choice, has taken them much too far along the road to domination by officials and squeezed out much of the meaningful local participation which they knew in the past.

6.7 LOCAL GOVERNMENT SERVICES

Between 1970 and the mid-1980s municipalities took over all secondary education and hospitals with the exception of one or two state institutions. Counties and municipalities share social welfare provision. Reforms described above have sought to allocate tasks between levels of government in a rational way. The main principle was that responsibilities should be brought as near to the citizen as possible. It was believed that in principle only one level of authority should be responsible for services within a policy area (Mikkelsen and Steenstrup, 1982).

The highest local expenditures are on social welfare (34 per cent in 1989), health (18 per cent), education and research (15 per cent), environment and housing (9 per cent) and public utilities (6 per cent). Of these it is social welfare and educational expenditures that dominate district council expenditures. Health (particularly hospital expenditures) dominate in those of counties.

1. Town and Country Planning and Development
There is an integrated three-level structure: national, regional or county and municipal.
Municipalities provide drafts for the regional plan and prepare a municipal area plan within the structure of the regional plan. No higher-level permission is required if the lower-level plan is consistent with the higher. Local plans set out details including directives for size and use of buildings.
County councils carry out regional planning under a committee of economic affairs. They prepare drafts for, consult on and adopt the regional plan which is approved by the Minister for the Environment after

consultation with other departments.

2. Housing

Municipalities act mainly under discretionary powers. Few have used direct housing construction but they have frequently contributed to establishing independent building companies by advances and loan guarantees. State assistance to social housing associations which provide about 15 per cent of Danish housing has been conditional on municipal co-guarantees or grant contributions. Cost of an income-related family rent-grant scheme is divided between state and municipality. Clearance schemes have been financed by state/municipal grants to the companies carrying out the work.

3. Roads

Municipalities construct, administer and pay for all roads used for local transportation.

County councils construct and maintain the more important roads outside the state trunk road system. Both municipalities and counties are responsible for the day-to-day administration of trunk roads and motorways with reimbursement of costs by government.

4. Transport

Municipalities support uneconomic routes at their discretion, mainly by means of non-profitmaking companies under municipal control and bus stations, and provide goods centres run as non-profitmaking co-operatives.

County councils make traffic plans for public transportation schemes and run them, often through private sub-contractors.

5. Education

Municipalities are responsible for comprehensive schools (ages 7-16) and general leisure-time education; nursery, kindergarten and pre-school classes. Pre-school classes are free and attended by 90 per cent of the age group; mandatory 'youth schools' for 14 to 18 year olds after school hours; 'interest groups' for children and young persons and some upper secondary schools. The weight given to subjects in primary school teaching is determined locally and teachers choose their own teaching methods.

County councils have taken over the 'gymnasia' (upper secondary schools) from the government and provide special and hospital education and part of adult education facilities.

6. Vocational Education is generally run by independent institutions under boards of representatives of employers, employees, central government and county councils.

7. Cultural Activities

Municipalities and *county councils* subsidise associations which provide for theatre, music and the fine arts.

8. Libraries, Museums and Art Galleries

Municipalities and *county* councils are required to provide and finance local and county library services in collaboration. Both give support to museums and art galleries.

9. Recreation

Municipalities and *county councils* run most sports grounds and centres and swimming baths and subsidise others.

10. Health and Social Welfare

Municipalities and *county councils* run the primary health and social welfare services under joint plans. There is a single centre for social welfare and health services in each area from which a citizen can obtain necessary assistance, full regard being paid to family as well as to individuals' needs.

County councils are responsible for the planning and co-ordination of the social welfare and health services throughout their areas; running the hospital service and administering the social security system; the care of handicapped people; residential centres for children and young people; free transportation to hospitals; abortion and adoption consultation services; and rehabilitation and pension boards.

Municipalities administer social services through a statutory social services committee. They have discretion to give cash benefits (generally limited to the maximum employment benefit rate) and practical help. They administer temporary relief (which can be quite long term), and by exception permanent relief according to the retirement pension scale, and also rehabilitation benefit for the disabled and special payments for essential needs of parents and children. They also provide remedial teaching, personal guidance services, home help and other forms of support for old and disabled people, community and day-care in centres and family homes, nursing-homes and residential homes, flat-rate benefits such as retirement, disablement and widows' pensions, sickness, maternity and child benefits and rent subsidies to pensioners.

Environmental Health is a concern of both local and county councils including environmental protection, food control, inspection, authorisation and control of sources of pollution and quality in shops, restaurants, institution kitchens etc. Local and county councils decide whether heavily polluting services may start or expand production, determine water quality standards for water courses and lakes etc. and must provide efficient treatment to maintain water quality.

11. Police are a central government responsibility.

12. Fire Protection
Municipalities are responsible, often employing joint bodies or contracting out to the Falck Rescue Company.

13. Development of Local Economy and Employment
Municipalities traditionally provide work in times of high unemployment. They can buy and service land for use by trade and industry, use tax and service policies to attract businesses, provide premises at an economic rate, make loans for industrial building with state support, provide cheap loans in conjunction with the State Regional Development Council, provide guarantees to new commercial undertakings and collaborate with institutes to set up technological advisory centres. In 1977 they were legally required to spend a per capita amount on combating youth unemployment.

14. Public Utilities
Except in urban areas *water supply* is mainly by co-operative societies whose capital expenditure is financed by loans backed by municipal guarantees. *Drainage* is an obligatory function. *Electricity*: in West Denmark local authorities collaborated with co-operative societies in building seven large power stations; in the East there is an integrated system in which municipalities have arrangements with three large companies, in some cases supported by municipal capital, and also with co-operative societies. Fifty of some 1,100 **district heating stations** are run by municipalities and supply 60 per cent of this form of heating. **Refuse disposal** is mandatory.

15. Cemeteries are a responsibility of municipal and church authorities.

16. Tourism Services are often supported by local authorities.

17. Conservation and Agriculture
County councils may protect cultural-historical sites and natural habitats, map geological raw materials and control usage, and evaluate soil for agricultural planning.

6.8 IMPLEMENTATION OF SERVICES

Most services are provided direct through local government departments. §6.7 shows the extent to which private company and co-operative forms are used to provide local authority services of different kinds. In many cases there is joint involvement between levels of government and/or between authorities at the same level, and between public and private (especially non-profitmaking) sectors. The pattern of employment of independent organisations as agencies but within a comprehensive jointly planned scheme controlled by local government is particularly well developed in transport provision. The development of electricity provision in recent years is a remarkable example of public-private partnership and collaborative initiative.

The Danish government has learnt from Sweden in encouraging local authorities to experiment by relaxing its controls over services and encouraging locally motivated innovations. The main emphasis has been on decentralisation of competences within local government to schools and local committees.

6.9 LOCAL FINANCE

The largest field of local expenditure is social welfare where in 1989 over 200,000 staff were employed and the costs took up over a third of the budget. Health employed some 34,500 people and took up 18 per cent. Environmental services and housing and public utilities accounted for nine and six per cent respectively.

National tax yield is equal to about half of Denmark's aggregate income. About half is from income tax. The counties account for ten per cent of net public expenditure and the municipalities for 41 per cent. In 1984 they levied together 30.5 per cent of total taxes and duties. The counties depend heavily on block grant, which in the mid-1980s provided nearly 30 per cent of their revenue. In the case of the municipalities it amounted to nearly ten per cent.

Local authorities are free to decide the standard of their services and to fix a tax level to cover the costs. Thus they are free in principle to determine the priorities and balance of their activities. The underlying philosophy is that financial responsibility depends on local taxation rights. It is believed that if equity is ensured by measures of equalisation according to needs and resources, then decentralisation will lead to higher efficiency through voter control.

Local Taxes

Local income tax was introduced over eighty years ago. It is a non-graduated tax on personal income and each council fixes its own rate. Personal allowances are deducted from the tax base and the result is described as 'slightly progressive' (Council of Europe, 1985). Tax rates (excluding Copenhagen) varied in 1985 from 13 to 22 per cent of net income. The county rate ranged from eight to ten per cent. The tax is deducted at source by employers and paid by the self-employed in monthly instalments at post offices. The same tax base and form of tax is used for local income tax as for the national tax.

Assessment is carried out by local committees, appointed by municipalities but autonomous in their decisions. The same forms are used nationally and the same officials collect both national and local income tax. The municipal tax department acts as secretariat and calculates personal allowances and liabilities. Assessment has to be strictly in accordance with national regulations. The central general commissioners of taxes exercise supreme authority for assessments, working through the Danish State Taxation Directorate. There are 65 boards of commissioners of taxes, each of five or seven members appointed by the Ministry for Internal Revenue, Customs and Excise. They hear appeals on assessment decisions by the local tax committees. Beyond this level there is a right of appeal to the national Tax Tribunal and finally to the courts. Taxes are collected centrally and then distributed to counties and municipalities according to the rates set locally and the places of residence of the tax-payers.

The *property* or *land tax* is based on land values. The rate is fixed annually by municipalities along with the income tax rate after budget demands have been assessed. The tax unit is one-thousandth of assessed value. Amounts levied have ranged from nil to 44 thousandths in recent years. The county rate is fixed statutorily every year, providing one means for regulation of the national economy. In 1985 it was ten-thousandths. Collection is by the municipalities, both for themselves and for the counties.

There is also a shared corporation or company profits tax from which municipalities received 20 per cent of proceeds in the mid-1980s, and also a shared capital gains tax. If the local share cannot be allocated to branches of national firms it is allocated proportionally according to numbers of employees in each municipal area or, in the case of capital gains tax, proportionally to local wage bills.

Financial Transfers

A substantial but declining amount of revenue has come in the form of refunds for expenditure on matters for which the state accepts financial responsibility. Pension benefits are refunded in their entirety and social security payments and expenditure on social institutions are refunded 50 per cent.

Otherwise there are three kinds of financial transfers from the centre: equalisation grants, block grants based on objective needs criteria and special funds to meet particular situations such as those of island communities with specific problems.

For the purposes of the equalisation grants municipalities are assessed according to their tax bases. Grants are payable to authorities below the national average at one-half the rate of what would be required to bring them fully up to that average. Payments are from a fund consisting of levies on authorities with tax resources above the average. In the case of the counties equalisation is not through a general fund but by direct subsidy from central revenue which in principle brings the weaker counties up to the average.

Block grants are made according to a formula which places heaviest weight on demographic factors, particularly numbers of children and over-75s. This grant has been used effectively as a macro-economic regulator on expenditures.

Recent Financial Reforms and Macro-Economic Control

The local government grants system was examined in depth by a government commission in the 1960s, concurrently with the planning of the structural reforms described in §6.4. The commission makes an interesting contrast with the Layfield Committee on Local Government Finance in Britain, which, in accordance with British conventions, included no representatives of government departments. It was made up of members of the Ministries of the Interior, Finance, Social Security, Education, Transport and Economics. Broad political agreement was reached that state functions should be transferred to local authorities as far as suitable and that an extension of local autonomy should be sought within legally regulated services. The commission favoured general grants but doubted if a reform would be equitable without a reform of local government structure which would make possible a change to general grants based on objective criteria, supplemented by moderate tax equalisation support.

Subsequently there have been a number of changes in the criteria adopted for apportioning the grant. In the mid-1970s a working group from three ministries and local authorities was set up which argued that socially determined expenditure levels should be taken into account in the grants formula as well as objective ones such as population, age groups, road length and area. It also argued that this should be accompanied by a strengthening of the local taxation base in order to equalise expenditure needs. A bill based on this proposal was presented by the Social Democrat government and passed against opposition, but in 1983 after a rightward swing of the political pendulum legislation was passed basing equalisation grant on relative taxation bases, as described above.

Financial Planning and the Wrestle over Expenditures

From 1977 all local authorities have used a four-year budgeting system based on population and local income development forecasts. At the same time planning systems for the different sectors such as health, child care, schools and roads were introduced. They include position statements and multi-year programmes. Plans are adjusted annually and thoroughly revised every fourth year (the year in which the local government elections occur). The sector plans have been submitted to the ministries and served as a communication system between the three levels of government. From 1979 the planning system was linked to the central government's budgeting and financial planning system. Budgeting and accounting data for the whole public service were computerised by mutual agreement. A main concern about the system has been the way in which the sectoral planning procedures appear to strengthen barriers between sectors while the recession and low growth rate appear to require non-traditional methods, often outside or across sectoral boundaries.

Towards the end of the 1970s government economic policy turned from Keynesian control of the business-cycle to restructuring national expenditure in attempts to restrain public expenditure in favour of private sector investment. Ministries' demands on local authority implementation were held in check by the Ministries of Finance and the Interior through the co-ordination of central department guidelines. Ceilings were imposed on local government investments, borrowing, taxes and staffing levels. Some government control has also been exercised through limitations on use of liquid assets and borrowing.

Annual increases in local government expenditure peaked in 1978-79 with an eight per cent rise in local government budgets after allowing for price and wage inflation. Negotiations between the state and the local authority associations led to a voluntary agreement on a ceiling for local economic growth. It was left to individual authorities to decide if they would keep in line. Local government expenditure was held against pressures through new inter-governmental negotiations carried on several times a year.

The new government in 1982 made an onslaught on unnecessary ministry controls and regulations in order to reduce service pressures on local authorities from above, backed by a survey of further opportunities for deregulation in co-operation with local authorities. But in 1983-86 a mandatory freeze was met by limiting liquidity and a reduction of nearly a third in block grant. Penalties were set for those failing to meet the agreements.

In 1985 it was accepted that there should be no real growth in expend-

340

itures and that, as in the preceding year, there should be no increase in income tax levy. On the other hand central government agreed not to initiate any new policies involving significant expenditures by local authorities unless an option was opened to cut back on a particular mandatory service.

From the economic point of view the policy was successful in the 1980s as the growth rate of not more than one per cent has been maintained almost throughout the decade. But tax ceilings had been introduced and traditional 'budgetary co-operation' had been heavily compromised by the beginning of the 1990s. (Bogason, 1991)

6.10 ELECTORAL REPRESENTATION

The Parties

The Social Democrats (SD) advocate democratic control of economic decisions and eventual communal ownership of the means of production and of housing land, but are strong on liberal rights, public access to the administration, equality and social welfare. The opposing political forces on the right-centre are the Conservative People's Party (KF) which has upper-class origins and aims at stabilising the public sector at its present level by making small reductions while improving public services by the decentralisation of responsibility and increasing reliance on market forces. It is strong on reduction of taxation and private property ownership but has supported worker participation in industry and decentralised wage-bargaining. Its effective power depends on support from the Liberal Party which also emphasises the desirability of reducing the public sector, along with upholding individual rights, care for the weak, co-operative housing and the market economy. It accepts the necessity of an incomes policy in certain circumstances. To the left is the Socialist People's Party, anti-Marxist and aiming at a high level of decentralisation of power; and also the Left Socialists with their novel libertarian socialism. Other significant parties include the Centre Democrats, whose breakaway from the Social Democrats precipitated a general election in 1973. They represent middle-class electors with social democratic values who nevertheless wish to hold on to the tax advantages of owner-occupation. They seek a balance between public and private sectors and employers and employees. The Christian People's Party is strong on defence of traditional morality and emphasises respect for the individual, the family and property. There are also the radical liberal Justice Party, the populist, anti-

341

income tax and anti-bureaucratic Progress Party, and the Radical Liberals who combine social and liberal orientations. This of course takes no account of the many minor parties involved in local politics.

Electoral Arrangements

All municipal and county councillors are elected for a four-year term of office throughout the country on the same day in November and take over on the first of January. Suffrage is extended to all nationalised Danes aged above 18 years, including foreigners who have been in residence for three years before an election. Any local elector can be nominated as a candidate. Unless he is exempt or no longer eligible on any grounds he is obliged to accept nomination. If a councillor dies, is disqualified or ceases to be resident, he is replaced by a substitute. The substitute is the next candidate on the party list in line for election according to the votes cast at the election.

Denmark led the world in its search for an electoral system which gave equal weight of influence over central and local government to every voter, subject only to the exclusion of small 'splinter' parties from representation. An act of 1924 provided for a system of proportional representation by lists of candidates. The system of selection is similar to that described in §1.10: the Sainte Laguë, modified d'Hondt or 'largest remainder' method.

Lists are for municipal areas as a whole, undivided by wards. Voters can vote either for a party as such or for an individual candidate. They have only one vote each, but a vote for a candidate who fails to get elected is added to the party list on which the candidate's name is included. Candidates on a qualifying list who are not elected may acquire substitute status.

Party groups on councils are assisted at a rate which in 1987 was fixed at two kroner a vote received in municipal elections (roughly 22 pence sterling or 28 US cents), and half as much again for county votes. (Council of Europe, 1988, *Elected Representatives*)

Councillors' Status and Conditions of Service

Council chairmen or burgomasters and their deputies work full-time in their local government offices, as do chairmen of certain county council committees. They receive salaries for full-time service. In municipalities committee chairmanship is considered a part-time job, but nevertheless standing committee chairmen receive appropriate salaries. In reaction to a survey which showed that large numbers of councillors were not intending to be candidates at the next election it was decided that, in order to encourage them to continue in office, all council members from 1984 would receive fixed sums in part payment for loss of earnings as an addition to flat-rate attendance allowances. The payments were fixed initially at an amount equivalent to about £125 sterling a month.

Councillors who are public sector employees have a right to absence of up to 30 days a year to fulfil their duties on the council. They have no special job protection. There is no restriction on other offices which a councillor may hold.

Mayors become entitled to a pension after eight years of office and are given severance pay for a period after their retirement.

A councillor can be disqualified from council membership if convicted for an offence which is regarded as unbefitting for a member of a council. An electoral court including representatives of the local authority associations was set up in 1965 which has to decide what should be regarded as 'unbefitting'. It has been called to adjudicate mainly on less serious offences and has disqualified members particularly in cases where the offence is an infringement of regulations administered by the council itself, for example a false income tax return.

The law restricts the grounds for exemption or withdrawal from council membership if elected. Anyone who has served as a councillor for eight years and over may refuse to accept re-election for two electoral periods, and anyone aged sixty or over can also refuse. A county councillor can refuse election to a municipal council. A council can also relieve anyone from standing on grounds of ill-health, business commitments and other factors which hinder attendance, but there is no exemption on grounds of a political reverse or dissatisfaction with a council's work.

Office facilities and secretarial services are available for chairmen of committees, and secretarial services sometimes for councillors if the council so decides. Financial assistance may be given to individual councillors for legitimate expenses at a council's discretion, but is not given to political groups. (Council of Europe, 1982, *Synopsis of the Replies to the Questionnaire on Status and Working Conditions of Local and Regional Elected Representatives*)

6.11 THE INTERNAL ORGANISATION OF LOCAL AUTHORITIES

The pattern of internal organisation is similar for all local authorities, both municipalities and county councils with the exception of four large cities,

Copenhagen, Arhus, Odense and Aalborg. In arrangements for executive responsibilities Denmark stands midway between certain German and the Swedish systems. There is a burgomaster or strong mayor (*borgmester*) who carries general administrative responsibility, but there is also to an important extent administration by committee.

The Council

Danish municipal councils are small by international standards. The Local Government Act stipulates a general minimum of five and a maximum of 25 members except in the case of Odense, Aalborg and Arhus where the minimum is 13 and the maximum 31. Councils decide their own size within these limits. Copenhagen is an exception and must have 55 members.

Municipal councils are required to programme meetings for at least once a month but may cancel scheduled meetings. County councils must hold at least eight meetings a year. They meet in public but may resolve to go into closed session for individual items.

Local authority employees may be elected to a council but may not sit on committees responsible for matters connected with their work, or on the finance committee because of its supervisory authority over all the authority's employees.

A council can decide to submit a matter to an advisory referendum, and there are certain specified matters on which a referendum is legally required before decision, although the result does not bind the council. Such referenda are usually carried out at the same time as local or general election, probably a main reason why the numbers voting tend to be quite high.

Substitutes

If a member of a council dies or leaves the district, the candidate on his or her party list for the last election who came highest in order among those not elected is called on to take the place vacated. That candidate will also be called on to substitute for an absent member at the council's general meeting when appointments are made to the burgomaster's and other offices, and may also be required to sit on the council when a member is absent for two months or more.

Committees

The law requires the appointment of standing committees which may be empowered to make decisions on behalf of the local council. Wide use is made of delegation to committee although the only compulsory delegations are those to the social services committee. Committees tend to be small and board-like. Their number is limited and there are generally no more than three to five in addition to the finance committee. The scope of each is wide in order to facilitate co-ordination of decisions. They can make immediate use of funds, the control of which is delegated to them as provided for in the budget unless the finance committee imposes restrictions. Any committee member can require that a question relating to the committee's activities is submitted to the council. In the event of a conflict between a service committee and the finance committee the council must resolve the matter, but the finance committee submits its recommendation last when the matter is put before the council.

All councils must appoint a finance committee with legally defined powers and authority over all other committees on budgeting matters. Its functions include financial matters, appointments, dismissal of staff and salaries. It has five or six members and is chaired by the burgomaster. It draws up financial estimates and long-term plans and submits its aggregate draft budget and plans to the council.

There is a statutory duty for municipalities to appoint a social services committee and, if there is a municipal port, a harbour committee. Councils also appoint a committee for education and cultural affairs (including libraries, cinemas and museums), commonly of 13 members including at least four councillors and one parent). A technical or public utilities committee is also normal. There is usually an environmental or building and planning committee responsible for local planning and development and property administration, although this work is in some cases undertaken by the finance committee.

In addition other boards or committees are set up with specified powers. School boards of five or seven members with supervisory powers are elected by parents for every school and possess the right to make recommendations to the education committee. Adult education boards with the duty of making recommendations on leisure-time education consist of one councillor and four members elected by the associations providing courses. Youth school boards and leisure-time activity boards are similarly constituted and fulfil the same type of function.

A local assessment committee consisting of five to fifteen members is responsible for provisional tax assessments. There is likely to be a municipal fire service supervisory committee which includes the local chief of police and four councillors, and a civil defence committee consisting of the burgomaster, four councillors and two members from voluntary organisations, or alternatively a civil emergency committee performing both functions. Other advisory committees are appointed to bring wider sources of knowledge and experience into the decision-making process.

Counties appoint hospital committees and single committees for technical matters. Committee size is usually five or seven, all being members of the council selected by proportional representation according to party strengths.

Committees have normally been closed to the public. They commonly meet weekly or fortnightly. The burgomaster has the right to attend any of them.

The Burgomaster

Burgomasters are chairmen of the council and the finance committee and also political leaders. They exercise general executive responsibility, convene council meetings, prepare council business, ensure that council decisions are communicated to all concerned and are responsible for action on all matters not delegated to committees and for the authority's day-to-day administration. They possess the necessary legal powers to ensure prompt action. They are, however, dependent on the finance committee, which has the duty to ensure the effective functioning of all administrative departments. They are expected to secure inter-departmental co-ordination and deal with matters under consideration before they are brought to the council, but possess no power to take unauthorised action on matters under consideration by the authority or on those that are legally or by delegation the responsibility of a committee. Committees may, however, delegate matters to them. There is also a deputy burgomaster in each municipality and two in a county to whom the council can give the responsibility of deputising as chairman, but not as head of administration.

The Administration

Councils are free to decide their own administrative organisation except that the law requires a social services and a taxation department. There are a great variety of local arrangements, but in general only one department with responsibilities relating to those of a particular standing committee.

The finance department is headed by the clerk or chief executive, who is also secretary to the council and the finance committee and head of the burgomaster's secretariat. He may also be the chief personnel officer. Usually the clerk's main qualification is practical administrative experience in local government. In larger authorities graduates in law or economics have been appointed to the post. Heads of department have commonly been of equal status, and co-ordination has been formalised by establishment of a planning committee of chief officers.

The law lays down requirements for appointments to two posts: the head of the social services department and the medical superintendent of hospitals have to be appointed by special boards. Direct involvement of politicians in administrative matters and the extent of delegation to officers vary widely between authorities.

Arrangements in the Four Largest Cities

The municipalities of Odense, Aalborg and Arhus have their own constitutions. Each possesses a corporate executive consisting of the burgomaster and four or five aldermen. It carries out functions which are elsewhere the responsibility of the finance committee. More significantly, the burgomaster and aldermen carry out functions which elsewhere are the responsibility of standing committees. The committees are not executive but investigatory and advisory. Copenhagen has similar arrangements except that in place of the aldermen there are six burgomasters and a chief burgomaster who is responsible for the day-to-day management and financial administration of the authority.

6.12 CITIZEN PARTICIPATION AND DECENTRALISATION WITHIN CITIES

Direct Participation in Local Government

Denmark has about 4,750 local councillors compared with 11,529 before reorganisation: a little below one for each thousand inhabitants. The turn-out at local elections in the 1970s was about two-thirds of the total electorate as against 90 per cent in national elections.

There is no special legislation to empower or require municipalities to set up neighbourhood or sub-municipal councils. The matter has been discussed in parliament but the house decided to accept the conclusions of a parliamentary commission set up to examine the adequacy of present means of public participation that sufficient means existed already for citizens to exercise influence in municipal matters. Each school has its own board. In the case of primary schools all members are elected by parents except one chosen by the local council. Powers relating to the curriculum are divided between the local council, the education committee, the school board and the teachers' council. A pupils' council in each primary school has the right to give opinions.

Referenda and Consultation

Referenda are no more than consultative except in the case of school closures, in which case 50 per cent of a school district can demand a referendum on a council's decision to close a school. If at least 60 per cent of the voters in the school district vote against the closure the school must remain open until the next election, when the new council may take action contrary to the outcome of the referendum.

There is wide use of public meetings, opinion polls and other means for consultation. Study circles have been set up as part of the municipal and local planning processes. Consultation exercises have also been used in connection with regional plans and appear to have been exceptionally successful in terms of the response and constructive dialogue that they achieved. The results appear to disprove the common generalisation that consultation is only effective on local matters (Illeris, 1983 and the author's own interview evidence).

Public libraries are obliged to supply information on state and local political matters and in most cases display county and local council budgets, minutes, agendas, plans and other documents.

There is an act on public access to documents which gives anyone a right to examine at request documents currently or earlier under consideration by an administrative body. As a general rule transcripts and the making of photocopies are allowed.

6.13 THE GOVERNANCE OF METROPOLITAN AREAS

Denmark has only one area which may described as metropolitan in an international sense: that which includes and surrounds the capital. For nearly three-quarters of its length its boundaries are set by the sea and a wide fjord. It contains more than one-third of the national population, with substantially more inhabitants than Greater Stockholm. Local government within the area consists of three counties (*amter*) and two cities.

A special act established a metropolitan authority for the area, the Greater Copenhagen Metropolitan Authority, which was first elected in 1974. The case for such a council had been discussed for the previous fifty years. Its composition was a compromise between parties that wanted a directly elected council with its own taxing powers and the conservatives who wanted the members to be appointed by the local authorities of the area. The members were eventually agreed to be selected by the political parties of the area according to their overall strengths in the local government elections. The arrangements are a good example of how a metropolitan authority can be grafted on to a complex double tier of government without disturbing the main well-established purposes of the existing authorities, given the will and the right political background.

The council was responsible for regional planning, public transportation and participation in traffic planning, environmental protection, water supply and comprehensive hospital planning. It carried out successful work in all these areas, undoubtedly solving problems that would have been difficult to achieve by other means.

An unexpected ministerial decision at the end of the 1980s, fuelled by demands for reductions in public expenditure, led to its dissolution around the end of the 1980s, its functions being redistributed to existing authorities. To a large extent it seems to have been a victim of its own success in establishing new structures and procedures for overcoming the problems for which it was set up. (Norton, 1983)

7. BRITAIN

7.1 HISTORY AND TRADITIONS

Great Britain has over 55 million inhabitants, very unevenly distributed over an area of some 151,000 sq. km. More than 85 per cent live in England, nine per cent in Scotland and five per cent in Wales.

England and Wales share the same system of law and their local government structure differs only in minor respects. Wales has its own government department in Cardiff dealing with Welsh domestic affairs but no political assembly of its own. Scotland has a separate legal system and an administration centred in Edinburgh, but like Wales it has no devolution of powers. Since 1707 the three countries have been ruled by the same parliament and national government in Westminster and Whitehall. They are parts of the United Kingdom of Great Britain and Northern Ireland, a unitary parliamentary democracy.

(Northern Ireland, which has been under direct rule from Westminster since 1972, is not included in this survey. Its local authorities have few competences. Other functions that are the responsibility of local government almost everywhere else in Europe are under the control of appointed boards which include representatives of local government and the government administration centred in Stormont.)

The United Kingdom is exceptionally centralised for a nation of its size, politically and administratively and in terms of its human geography. London, in the south-eastern corner of Great Britain, is geographically remote from most of the national population. The main national roadways radiate outwards from London through the comparatively rich South-East and then through regions of lesser prosperity to a thinly peopled periphery. Forty-three per cent of the population live in the well-to-do South. The Midlands, South Wales and the North contain the heartlands of the eighteenth-century Industrial Revolution, their wealth having been built on extractive and other heavy industries which have declined greatly during the decades since the Second World War.

The picture painted in this chapter is of the legacy of the 1980s. After a period of rapid inflation towards the end of the 1980s, a phase of economic recession and unemployment followed, the end of which is uncertain at the time of writing.

Compared with other countries covered in this handbook, Britain's history shows remarkable continuity. Since 1066 it has suffered no invasion or imposition of foreign institutions. It has experienced no violent revolution since the puritan revolution in the 1640s, which was but an interruption in its evolution as a parliamentary monarchy. The ancient elements of the constitution have changed by pragmatic adjustment and an accumulation of precedents and conventions.

In the early Middle Ages the government of the counties by earls under oaths of fealty to the king was replaced by government by crown officers, called sheriffs. A crucial reform in the fourteenth century placed responsibility for the maintenance of law and the 'keeping of the peace' on magistrates or justices of the peace appointed by the crown: mostly minor land-owners of the county (the 'squirearchy') and burgesses, the so-called 'commoners', whose representatives sat in the House of Commons during the occasional sessions of parliament. For more than four hundred years the counties were governed by the justices of the peace meeting at the quarterly assizes of the county and more locally in petty sessions.

During the Middle Ages many English and Welsh towns won autonomy by royal charter. Local church districts provided the basis for the parish administration system from the early Middle Ages. They managed their own affairs, to some extent under the supervision of the bench of justices. Parish governments based on communities lost their place in the national system to new district authorities in 1894. Formal responsibilities for social care had been placed on them by the Elizabethan Poor Law of 1601, sometimes claimed to be the beginning of the welfare state. Every parishioner had the right to participate in communal decision-making, and inhabitants were required to carry out the duties of parish officials. The parish raised its income through a local rate levied 'according to the visible estate of the inhabitants both real and personal'. This tax on property according to value lasted until it was abolished by the Thatcher administration in 1988 (see below and in §7.9).

The industrial revolution set problems which the existing system was totally unfitted to solve. A proliferation of private acts provided for the setting up of bodies of improvement commissioners who could take measures to abate and transform the uneconomic and insanitary conditions of the larger towns. The Municipal Corporations Act of 1835 provided a model organisation for elected councils which was subsequently applied generally throughout local government. The new municipal boroughs, responsible for policing, lighting and by-laws to ensure good behaviour and suppression of nuisances, quickly acquired a wide range of new powers. Larger boroughs won extensions of their competences by means of private acts promoted in parliament, often pioneering new forms of public activity with powers which were eventually conferred on local authorities throughout the country.

The Poor Law Amendment Act of 1834 replaced the parish Poor Law with a system of unions of parishes set up by a central agency, the Poor Law Board. From the mid-nineteenth century a wave of reforming legislation was launched. Where suitable municipalities were not available to provide the services required, ad hoc special-purpose authorities were set up. In 1848 borough councils became the chief providers of public health services. Area boards of health carried out the same function outside their boundaries. School boards were set up to provide elementary education under an act of 1870.

Engineers and medical men, with the support of public service-orientated lawyers and local politicians, used newly developing technical knowledge to transform unhealthy urban environments. The outstanding instance is Birmingham, where Joseph Chamberlain galvanised the council and its staff into legendary achievements during his three-year term of mayoral office from 1873 to 1876 (Garvin, 1932). In direct consequence the city acquired an international reputation in the 1870s as 'the best-governed city in the world' (Briggs, 1968). It was not alone in its enterprise. In many cities public services were municipalised and developed by committed politicians and officials, usually against much opposition to the taxation and borrowing which was necessary to finance the reforms.

Universal household suffrage followed. The Local Government Act of 1888 created 62 county councils which, except the London County Council, were based on historic shire counties. Government by crown-appointed justices of the peace was ended and, in theory at least, aristocracy or squirearchy were replaced by democracy. The Local Government Act of 1894 set up the county district system to take over from the parishes and develop the less-costly services. This was a critical distancing of small communities from local government of a kind such as never happened in the greater part of Western Europe. The Act also extended the right to vote in local government elections to women.

The new system remained for some eighty years, boundary adjustments being made incrementally but often acrimonously through private acts of parliament and by government initiatives after consideration of the advice of national commissions. The greatest expansion came in 1902 when the counties and county boroughs became comprehensive local education authorities.

The period from the 1890s to the 1930s has been called the golden age of local government. Local authorities were generally recognised to be the direct providers of a growing number of public services, including hospitals, public education (excepting universities which they nevertheless sponsored), youth employment, labour bureaux, low-income housing, relief of the poor, town and country planning, and other functions inherited from ad hoc agencies. Under private acts they developed and controlled public transport, water, gas and electricity supply, docks and many other services. Some of their innovations, such as the clean air controls pioneered by Birmingham, provided models for national policies.

But the recognition of local government as all-purpose local provider began to fade from the 1930s. Functions were lost one by one: assistance to the unemployed (1934); hospitals (1946); relieving destitution and assisting need; control of river pollution (1948); electricity and gas supply around the same time; water supply and conservation and sewage disposal (1974); and London passenger transport (1984). Some other municipal services, however, expanded rapidly. There was much innovation within the scope that remained. The root causes for loss of functions were perhaps local government's political weakness, the low weight given to local autonomy and control, and the belief that most of the existing local authorities did not provide an efficient means of implementing new reform programmes.

The drastic reorganisations of local government in London in the 1960s and in the rest of Britain in the 1970s are described in §§7.4 and 7.13.

Before and after the nationalisations of the immediate post-war period a large measure of consensus prevailed about the mixed economy and the role of local government within it. From 1979 that consensus was destroyed. Central legislation assumed a different character, largely dictated by a prime minister with a non-traditional ideology (see §7.6).

Britain has often before been described as a 'class-ridden' society of two nations divided by culture and the distribution of property. The explicit aim of the Conservative governments was to absorb as much of the population as possible into the property-owning class through privatisation of publicly owned goods, both housing and industry, thus forming a large capital-owning majority. In terms of contribution to the economy there was a great change in the 1980s: private investment rose from 71.3 in 1979 to an estimated 87 per cent in 1989 (Tim Congdon, *The Times*, 30 January 1990). In the same period average real household income rose 50 per cent for the top 10 per cent, hardly at all for the bottom 10 per cent and under 20 per cent for the bands in between (Family Expenditure Survey, 1991). In 1987 came a national budget which cut back income tax rates sharply, most of all for those in the higher income bands. It contributed to an expenditure boom with rapid inflation, leading to a rapid rise in indebtedness affecting especially the housing market where there was a rapid escalation in house mortgage take-up and house prices: a trend that ended by 1990 and was followed by a housing slump, a fast rise in unemployment, bankruptcies and housing repossessions by lenders.

Against this background local government had lost a large part of its housing stock, its cushioning abilities against rises in unemployment and its flexibility as a means to respond to economic depression. Control over its fiscal capacity had begun several years before 1987 when the government started a system of 'grant-related expenditure assessment' and penalties on 'high-spending authorities' (see §7.9).

In 1987 provisions were made for the community charge, generally known as the poll tax, to replace domestic rates. This rejected the principle of payment according to means, allowing rebates only for individuals already recognised by the state as in need of social assistance. Results generally attributed to the tax were an appreciable fall in numbers registering for the electoral role that was put as high as a million by some, and also the loss of many people from the decennial census, argued to arise partly from the fear of poll tax demands if there was public knowledge of their whereabouts. The loss of these and others from recognition by the system severely reduced local government incomes and the cost of collection led to the levy of a higher rate on those registered and a great excess in costs of collection over what had been estimated.

At the time of the final revision of this text in 1993, the poll tax had been replaced by a new tax combining property valuation with a capitation element. Bankruptcies, unemployment growth and housing repossessions by banks and building societies continued into 1993. Pressure on national finances has continued together with a growing balance of payments deficit. Reduction of public service expenditure and privatisation programmes are at the forefront of government policies, as in the 1980s. Despite the policy of recent governments to cut back local authority expenditure, it has continued to rise, at least until the early 1990s.

Scottish Local Government

Local government began early in Scotland with the foundation of fourteen *burghs* by King David I (c.1080-1153), including Aberdeen, Dundee, Edinburgh and Perth — fortified towns inhabited by a cosmopolitan mixture of Celts, Norsemen and some Flemings. They developed their own form of the English language and culture, which was to develop into the sophisticated literature and form of civil society which flowered in recent centuries. The pattern of local government was similar to that in England, with chartered burghs, parishes and counties set up for the more effective implementation of power from Edinburgh in the sixteenth century.

After 1833 any community of 2,000 inhabitants or more could apply for a charter. Parishes were abolished in 1929 and small burghs lost most of their functions to the counties. The general reorganisation of the mid-1970s is described in §7.4 (Keating and Midwinter, 1983; Kellas, 1984). The government introduced the community charge a year earlier in Scotland than in England and Wales, a fact much resented in Scotland.

The British Constitution

Lord Hailsham, the Lord Chancellor (head of the judicial arm of government), said Britain had a constitution 'of the utmost flexibility'. It is unwritten and therefore presumed from experience or interpretations of history. Statutes bearing on constitutional prerogatives are in no way entrenched and can be changed by simple majorities in parliament. Power normally centres on the leader of the majority party in the House of Commons, who is normally able to ensure a majority in the four- or five-year general elections. This arises from a constitutional principle generally assumed since the nineteenth century: the omnipotence of parliament. It was Lord Hailsham again who called the system 'an elective dictatorship'.

British politics has been based since the eighteenth century on confrontation between two parties. Power is won in an adversarial contest, and the style in parliament is sharply adversarial as opposed to consensual since the governing party has no need to reach agreement with other parties unless it is short of a majority, something rare in post-war years. General and local elections (except in Northern Ireland) are based on the 'first-past-the-post system' (§7.10). Not untypically, in the 1987 election the Conservatives won power with 43 per cent of the national vote and, because a large part of qualified voters failed to vote, the active support of about one-third of the registered electorate. Proportional representation or any of the systems described in Chapters 2 to 6 of this book would produce a quite different pattern of control, probably preventing one party from monopolising power for much of the time.

7.2 THE STATUS OF LOCAL GOVERNMENT

Legal Status

Britain has two historically distinct levels of self-government and administration: central and local, both originating in appointments and grants of liberties by the crown. There is no ministry of the interior with a corps of officials to supervise and link together central and local aims and action. However local authorities have no independent rights and are since 1974 (1975 in Scotland) all creations of parliamentary statutes; or, as described above, in terms of real power in the 1980s and early 1990s at least, of a government with majority support in the House of Commons led by the Leader of the Conservative Party.

Britain never felt the need for a binding statement of civil rights, nor a systems of checks and balances to prevent abuse of power. It was content with the theory of the omnipotence of parliament. British administrative law is a collection of ad hoc statutes and court rulings, and has not been sharpened, as in the United States, France and Germany for example, by the judicial interpretation of an entrenched constitution. There is no written constitutional underpropping of doctrines about local government's status and rights, nor any statement defining its role within the local community. Moreover, 'The cumulative effect of (Conservative) governments' values has been significantly to devalue the importance of the constitutional position of local government' (Loughlin, 1986). The chairman of the Association of County Chief Executives said in 1987, that if the move towards centralism continued, 'it will inevitably sound the death-knell of local government as we know it today' (Alistair Stone, quoted in *Against the Over-Mighty State*, 1988): a prophesy which little has happened to contradict in subsequent years.

In general, until the 1980s local government had been content to regard itself as part of the established order — an essential area of government working under powers conferred by parliament though subject to an excessive degree of control by central government. There was no restriction on its freedom to set its level of income by the level of its single tax, the 'rates'. It assumed that it was free to provide services direct to the public by whatever means it liked subject to a few exceptions, and that in fundamental areas of service such as inner city development it had a monopoly subject to appeals to the courts regarding its exercise of powers beyond legal provisions and matters statutorily requiring ministerial consent. As §7.1 has shown, these assumptions have been disproved. Local government has failed to win protection of its powers through the courts in some areas previously untested. Where it has succeeded the government has used its control of parliament to change the law to enforce its will.

The government has seen local authorities as little more than agencies: thus there is no assumption that local authorities have a right to act in the interests of their inhabitants unless they can quote legal justification or limit their 'free' expenditure to a low statutory level. The position rests on the doctrine of *ultra vires*, that is that a creature of statute may do only

356

what it is authorised to do by statute, as it has been developed in the courts from the end of the eighteenth century (at first primarily, it seems, out of the need to control the many ad hoc incorporated bodies that parliament was setting up for purposes such as road-building). No special legal status was recognised for elected local authorities acting for the general well-being of their areas. The powers they use to further their objectives must be either expressly conferred or derived by reasonable implication from legal provisions.

The competence of a local authority was defined in the Local Government Act of 1972 as 'power to do anything... which is calculated to facilitate, or is conducive or instrumental to, the discharge of any of its functions'. The rigour of the doctrine has been somewhat softened by the provision that a local authority may spend from the local taxes to a specified maximum, set in 1991 at from £2.50 to £5 for specified types of authority, multiplied by the population of its area for the benefit of that area or some or all of its inhabitants, provided that the activity concerned does not conflict with other legal provisions.

Historically British cities have exercised considerable autonomy and built up a range of services which were for long admired abroad. The powers exercised derived from provisions of royal charters, private laws they had promoted in parliament and general acts of parliament. Many general acts gave general application to powers previously exercised by particular authorities under their own private acts. As in all Western countries, far-reaching powers were conferred on local authorities by governments as a means of implementing national services. Powers exercised by chartered municipal corporations under the law of trusts, which had become a minor and obscure area of competences, were removed by the Local Government Act of 1972.

There had previously been an assumption that the elective nature of local authorities gave them a mandate to decide on policy: that there is a sphere of governmental freedom in which they have a democratic right to exercise power. But since they exist only at the will of parliament such arguments have been shown to have little force in practice. The unwillingness of central government to accept that local government has any reasonable rights and powers beyond those conferred on it by parliament is illustrated by the refusal to sign the Council of Europe's Charter of Local Self-Government, on the grounds that it is alien to the British tradition (see §1.2).

Local Governent Status in Society

Opinion polls show local government to be in comparatively good regard by the public. A Gallup poll in 1985 found that 79 per cent of those interviewed supported the retention of the Greater London Council contrary to the government's policy of its abolition. In another 1985 survey 80 per cent of the sample of electors considered that their county council or its equivalent ran things very or fairly well, while 75 per cent said the same of their district councils (*The Conduct of Local Authority Business, Research Vol. III*, 1986).

Where legislation permits and sufficient resources can be identified many local authorities have developed bold and innovative initiatives during the 1980s. In order to fight unemployment and loss of industry, for example, they have launched a wide range of initiatives to help restore local economies to a healthy condition and to work with industry, without specific support from the law until the legislation of 1989 codified and limited this important area of action.

Local Government's Status under Attack

Local government's traditional role has been attacked under policies described by the Conservative government as 'rolling back the frontiers of the state' and 'increasing local choice'. Legal rights have been conferred on tenants to buy municipal housing they occupy at a heavily discounted price or to opt to transfer the accommodation to other landlords. A scheme has been introduced to enable schools to move out of local authority control with ministerial approval if they can obtain a majority vote from pupils' parents, and large amounts of money have been transferred from the budget for 'council schools' to 'opted-out' schools as an incentive to do so. Local authorities have been required to put service provision out to tender in a number of fields (but their own workforces have been allowed to tender against outsiders and have in fact won contracts against private competition in a large majority of cases). Responsibilities have been transferred to state-appointed agencies for development of designated areas. Local government financial independence has been curbed and the Greater London Council and Metropolitan County Councils, have been abolished without popular support. In various ways local authority discretion has decreased and local authorities prevented from increasing the quantity and quality of their services. (A fuller list of constrictions on local authorities is given in §7.6 below.)

Many of these central government measures have had less success than anticipated. The head of the state local authority 'watchdog', the Audit Commission, estimated in 1987 that by 1992 the number of local government jobs could fall from 1.9 million to 1.2 million. This proved wide of the mark. Local government's employees actually grew from about 1,821,000 to 1,913,000 between 1980 and 1990. Some of this was accounted for by an increase in social services staff from 208,000 to 250,000, and this should grow further as community care services are expanded, although it seems that in 1993 constrictions on local resources will deny local authorities the means to implement the policy to a large extent. But what has happened in practice is far from the goal of some liberal economists to reduce local government's functions to a residuary core, executed by a small body of elected executives. In practice most local authorities have not forsaken their unique leadership role in responding to local needs in ways that are outside the capacity of either the private sector or central government.

7.3 CONCEPTS AND VALUES

Three streams of thought characterise much of British theory about local government. One is generally linked with Edmund Burke (1729-97). It emphasises tradition and preservation of loyalty. This has been much weakened by the mobility of the population, the size of new authorities and the artificiality of boundaries in many cases. The boundaries of the new authorities imposed in 1974 ran roughshod over local tradition (although purporting to retain existing boundaries as far as convenient). They resulted in authorities so remote from local communities in most instances that belief of their value as a focus for identification and loyalty lacks credibility.

Another stream of thought is concerned primarily with the justification of local government in terms of its effectiveness and efficiency for the provision of services. L.J. Sharpe gave this primary importance in a paper in 1970 (Sharpe, 1970), although he has since changed his views on the subject. It relates closely to Bentham's utilitarianism (see §1.3).

The third stream places a high value on active citizenship. John Stuart Mill (1806-73), its chief representative, developed his general theory of government from Bentham's individualism. He placed a primary importance on maximisation of liberty and creating the opportunity for self-realisation. He argued the need for division of labour between central and local authorities and popular control over executive officers through municipal and provincial bodies which should control the supplies for their operations. He saw main functions of local authorities in 'the nourishment of public spirit' and 'the public education of citizens' of which they should be the chief instrument, arguing that the 'mental discipline' involved for participants 'from the lower grades of society' was of greater weight than the quality of administration (J.S. Mill, 1861). A recent development of the argument for the values of local citizenship drawing on twentieth-century British and American sources may be found in Ranson and Stewart (1989).

Arguments on the grounds of local government's relative efficiency, effectiveness and accountability have been most to the fore in recent times. Members of Thatcher governments have, however, attacked local authorities for their failure to provide just those same qualities. In the cause of local government the arguments for pluralism or the diffusion of powers, public participation, responsiveness to local needs and perceptions, local accountability, learning through diversity, local accessibility and control over bureaucracy, the benefits and efficiencies of smaller scale and other justifications have been strongly put forward against largely unsupported claims for the alternatives (e.g. *The Conduct of Local Authority Business, Report*, 1986; Jones and Stewart, 1985).

In the late 1940s Britain came to be seen as a 'welfare state', primarily concerned with securing a basic standard of well-being for all. This differed from centre-party views on the European continent in lacking a complementary emphasis on the autonomy of the individual and the local community with which he or she is in an organic relationship. Local government was seen as an instrument of state welfare policy rather than a means of local self-administration.

The 'welfare' approach to some extent characterised both left and right governments until the 1980s. Margaret Thatcher's version of economic liberalism cut across these shared values. It was a philosophy of individual self-help, supported by theories of the so-called 'New Right' who argued for the 'minimal state' on grounds of personal choice and the maximisation of economic efficiency. In practice policies justified on these grounds did not result in the decline in state intervention which was predicated as desirable. Nor were they generally accepted. A Gallup poll, for example, showed that only 17 per cent of respondents shared the view of Margaret Thatcher that welfare benefits had gone too far, and 54 per cent believed that they had not gone far enough; 66 per cent believed that health, education and welfare services should be extended as against 11 per cent who preferred a cut in taxes. A poll in September 1988 showed that little more than a fifth of the electorate supported the main government policies (*Sunday Times*, 17 September 1988).

The Conservative Party especially has traditionally placed a high value on leadership. A study of opinion among Conservative members of parliament in 1990 showed that only 19 per cent were firm 'Thatcherites' and concluded that 'Loyalty will flow to the new Leader as leader, regardless of which particular section of the party he or she is drawn from' (Norton, Philip, 1990). (But events under the John Major leadership appear to contradict this since the Thatcherites themselves have split from cabinet policy on European matters.) The general failure to assert contrary values effectively seems to confirm the findings of an international comparative study in the 1960s that found Britain's culture tilted towards subjective deferential values leading to the acceptance of strong government (Almond and Verba, 1963).

As noted above, the traditional decision-making style in Britain has been adversarial: between proposer and opposer, prosecution and defence, government and opposition, without much value being given to the positions between these poles. Proportionality, the weighting of the opinions of all parties to a decision, is alien to this principle. Hence a basis is lacking for the distribution of benefits through the decision-making process. There has been relatively little support for the accommodative/ liberal corporative polity characteristic of West European continental states which requires an open process of search for 'information, clarification and analysis among interests to broaden their perspectives' (Dyson, 1980).

Central government has been seen as adopting an adversarial stance to local government. Roy Jenkins (Lord Jenkins of Hillhead, former Commissioner-General of the European Commission) has remarked on 'The government's steady attrition of councils resulting in the threat of civic degradation which it is almost impossible to imagine being imposed in any other country' (*Local Government Chronicle* 10 March 1989). The concept of local self-government has been opposed to that of central dominance in a way that gives scant acknowledgement to their interdependence. As a report of a Federal Trust study group states, 'the British tradition of seeking a system within which local government can be autonomous, weakens rather than strengthens the case for local government; for in an interdependent world, there can be no such sphere' *Against the Over-Mighty State*, 1988). British governments, entrenched behind their parliamentary majorities, tend to reject the seeking of consensus: more so in the 1980s than in the previous three decades. The effects are fundamental to the position of local government and to politics in many of our local authorities.

Britain, formerly the epitome of a society of traditional values supporting a stable way of life, has in the 1980s experienced a government intent on effecting sharp cultural change. Local government can only thrive if the values that support it thrive and are expressed through national institutions. The crumbling of its status has shown that it not only lacks protection in the unwritten and uncertain constitution, but that it also lacks protection within a system of values shared by the ruling elite and the electorate.

7.4 NATIONAL STRUCTURE

National Administrative Structure

Since 1974 England has had two main types of local government structure: that of the metropolitan counties including Greater London, which contain a little under two-fifths of the population, and that of the areas of the non-metropolitan counties. The metropolitan areas are, with some exceptions, defined to correspond to continuous urban settlements. They include the heartlands of English industry and commerce whose economies, apart from that of London, have suffered heavy decline since the Second World War. Greater London and the six metropolitan counties lost their elected county councils in 1986 (§7.13). Their structure is now based on general-purpose authorities which appoint members to joint statutory and voluntary authorities for the provision of certain services within provided for the county areas as a whole. These most-purpose authorities, as they are often called, are the 32 London boroughs and the Corporation of London (the City) and the 36 metropolitan districts.

The Greater London authorities, excluding the City, have populations ranging from about 133,800 (Kingston-upon-Thames) to 380,000 (Croydon). Westminster has borough status but carries the honorary title of City of Westminster. Its council is presided over by a 'lord mayor', as is the Common Council of the Corporation of London which has a night-time population of around 5,000 and a day-time one of some 340,000.

The metropolitan districts range in population from about 157,000 (South Tyneside) to nearly one million (Birmingham). Six have populations of over 450,000: in descending order of size Birmingham, Leeds, Sheffield, Liverpool, Bradford and Manchester. Seven others have over 300,000 inhabitants. Twenty-seven are in the population band 200,000 to 300,000. Six lie between 150,000 and 200,000. Statutory joint authorities are responsible for fire, civil defence and public transport, and also for police senior appointments (subject to determination of short-lists of candidates for posts to be interviewed by the Home Office), budgets and other administrative matters.

The councils of Birmingham, Bradford, Coventry, Leeds, Newcastle upon

Tyne and Sheffield have the honorary status of city and their councils are presided over by 'lord mayors'. Liverpool and Manchester are also cities but abolished the office of lord mayor in the 1980s as an obsolete and pointless honour. Other metropolitan district councils have the honorary title of borough.

Non-Metropolitan Areas

There are 39 county councils in England. Their populations range from 124,600 (the Isle of Wight) to 1,528,700 (Hampshire). Seven have populations of over one million, 17 half to one million, and six others between 300,000 and 500,000. The Isle of Wight stands alone with only about 150,000 inhabitants. Wales has eight counties with populations from the very rural Powys (112,400) to the exceptionally urban Mid Glamorgan (534,500) which includes Cardiff, the Welsh capital with a population of about 279,500. They are responsible for education, social services, highways and transportation, fire services, trading standards services, refuse disposal, structure planning and, indirectly through joint committees, police administration.

The 296 English District Councils range in population from 24,800 (Teesdale) to 391,500 (Bristol). Most were formed by amalgamations of authorities in 1974. When they were set up in the early 1970s the guideline for their size in typical areas was between 80,000 and 120,000 inhabitants. In 1986, 140 were within those limits. Ninety-four were smaller and 62 larger. Twenty-seven of these districts carry the honorary title of city and 94 that of borough. Some large cities possess this status, including Bristol, Leicester, Nottingham, Hull, Plymouth, Stoke-on-Trent, Derby, Southampton and Portsmouth. These have subsequently pressed hard to regain something like county borough status. If they became 'county-free', however, the counties that include them would fall below viability according to the standards applied in the 1970s.

All English non-metropolitan districts are responsible for the same functions, notably housing, environmental health, refuse collection and development control. Some other services are shared or concurrent with those of counties: local planning (in general undertaken by the districts), town development, recreational facilities including country parks, museums and art galleries.

The position is similar in Wales which has 37 district councils ranging in population from 21,700 (Radnor) to 279,500 (Cardiff). All except nine have fewer than 80,000 inhabitants. Twenty-three are boroughs and two (Cardiff and Swansea) are cities. Unlike the English non-metropolitan districts they have responsibility for refuse disposal as well as collection, and the secretary of state for Wales may confer on individual authorities library, some food and drugs and weights and measures functions.

Local Councils

The English parishes and Welsh communities have the status of 'local councils' as opposed to that of the 'principal' authorities described above. They have no mandatory functions but can provide or contribute towards community activities including halls, arts and crafts, cemeteries and crematoria, cleansing the environment, public conveniences, car parks, footpath creation and maintenance and a few other minor matters. They may raise a very small proportion of the local government tax for this purpose. They must be informed about planning applications and certain types of action proposed by district and county councils, but have no right of consultation except on footpath surveys. Possibly their most important function is to discuss local affairs and represent their interests to the district council and other bodies.

There are about 10,200 English parishes and 800 Welsh community councils. In principle they were regarded as rural institutions and could not normally be established for communities with populations of above 20,000 or a fifth of those of the district council area concerned. They range in population from nil to about 41,000. Few exist in urban areas larger than small towns, where their councils may have the honorary title of 'town council' and their chairmen and deputy chairmen may be called mayor and deputy-mayor. Seven town councils with cathedrals in their areas have the honorary status of city.

They are obliged to hold general meetings to raise tax and elect councils of five members or above where appopriate. Some 7,200 in England elect councils or joint councils. Boundary matters and creation of new parishes involve the District Council, the Local Government Boundary Commission and require action including orders by the Secretary of State, but not referenda. District Councils can establish new local councils that fulfil certain conditions. (Byrne, 1990)

Scotland

The Scottish reorganisation in 1974-75 involved the amalgamation of thirty-three county councils into nine so-called regional and three islands councils. Region populations range from about 100,000 (Borders) to 742,000 (Lothian) and, by far the largest local authority in Britain, Strathclyde with a population of 2,344,600. The regions contain 53 districts with populations of from 10,000 (Badenoch and Strathspey) to 718,500 (Glasgow). Four (Glasgow, Edinburgh, Aberdeen and Dundee) have the title of city.

Distribution of functions is similar to that between counties and districts in England with a few exceptions. Scottish districts have sole duties in the fields of culture and recreation, including libraries, art galleries and museums, and are responsible for refuse disposal as well as collection.

The Islands authorities — Orkney (19,300 inhabitants), Shetland (23,000) and Western Isles (31,500) — are unique in Britain as all-purpose local authorities.

Parish councils were swept away in 1929 but a new form of community council was instituted in the 1970s. Under local schemes there can be up to 1,343 community councils, but at least ten per cent of these have not been formed. They have no mandatory functions or right to draw on public funds. (Byrne, 1990)

The Reorganisation Process

The gradual adaptation of the system to new needs and conditions and the draconian reorganisation of the 1970s have been described briefly in §7.1 and in more detail in a number of sources (e.g. Keith-Lucas and Richards, 1978; Keating and Midwinter, 1983; Norton, 1986a). Around 1,300 district and borough authorities in England and Wales and 59 county councils vanished into history on 31 March 1974, to be replaced by 369 districts and 53 counties: a reduction by two-thirds. Taken in crude averages this meant that the average-size authority was increased from about 36,200 population to 107,500, almost tripling in size. In Scotland a year later 430 local authorities were replaced by 68, changing the average population size from about 11,860 to 75,000.

The reorganisations followed reports from Royal Commissions which argued that existing administrative boundaries were obsolete and related little to economic, demographic and social change, and that existing authorities were generally too small for the financial and specialised staff resources needed. The English Redcliffe-Maud Commission argued that a single-tier system of government was preferable to a tiered one on the grounds that services were interrelated and required overall control and direction, and that the city nucleus and the surrounding countryside which contained many of the people who worked in and depended on the services of the conurbation should be included within overall planning and services structures, evening out the costs involved and giving space for rational patterns of future development. Central government departments strongly supported this view. In England public reaction was generally muted; in Scotland it was generally hostile. The English Commission advocated that metropolitan areas as an exception needed county authorities with wide areas stretching beyond the built-up conurbations as well as most-purpose district authorities. The government decided to set up metropolitan county authorities but with boundaries cut back to the edges of the built-up areas where practicable (undermining the Commission's intentions for sub-regional planning and development functions), and to retain a two-tier system of county and districts in the rest of England. The remoteness of most of the new authorities from their inhabitants was not regarded as a major problem.

The main subsequent change was the abolition of the Greater London Council and metropolitan counties in 1986. A new commission under the former head of the Confederation of British Industry and Director-General of the National Local Government Audit Commission started a new review in 1992 which is expected to result in a more flexible approach and, in some instances at least, an extension of the single-tier system.

7.5 INTER-AUTHORITY RELATIONS AND ORGANISATION

All local authorities are equal in legal status and there is no supervision of the district level by the counties, or of the parishes and community councils by the principal authority levels. There are with a few exceptions no statutory provisions for joint working. In physical planning there is close interdependence between county and non-metropolitan district councils, the latter being required to prepare local plans within the framework of county structure plans approved by central government but in the preparation of which districts are closely involved. Districts may serve as agents of the counties if the latter so wish, a limitation on their role much resented by them. In refuse matters the districts collect and the counties dispose of the waste. Agency relationships are unpopular and there is little scope for them under the legislation in the major county services of education and social services. However there have been joint projects in which county social services have worked closely with housing departments on special housing schemes for the elderly and the infirm.

In Britain local joint bodies have tended to operate as independent officer-led organisations with no more than loose links with their parent authorities. According to research findings they have operated most efficiently when the parent authorities have chosen to co-operate voluntarily, have compatible interests, where the issues concerned have low political salience, where there is policy consensus or where the purpose is limited to information collection, is profitmaking or is low cost (Flynn and Leach, 1984).

Joint boards are created by statute or by the secretary of state by statutory order. Joint authorities set up for police, fire and civil defence in the Greater London and metropolitan counties in 1985 consist of large boards of representatives of the boroughs or districts in their area. They have autonomous status, as also have the ten combined police authorities. As in the case of county police committees, one-third of members of the joint police committees represent the magistrates' boards.

The most usual arrangement is for one of the member authorities of a joint body to take responsibility for its administration.

Local Authority Associations

Since the second half of the nineteenth century the main formal means of consultation between local government interests and central government has been the local authority associations. They see their main responsibilities as interchange of views between members and promoting agreed policies to the public, government, parliament, outside interest groups and, increasingly in recent years, international bodies: above all the European Community and the Council of Europe. Their work includes briefing and lobbying on bills in parliament, responses to government proposals and evidence to parliamentary committees and national commissions and committees.

The local authority associations for England and Wales represent separate groups of authorities and have often differed strongly in their representations to government. The Convention of Scottish Local Authorities (Rosebery House, 9 Haymarket Terrace, Edinburgh EH12 5XZ) on the other hand has all Scottish local authorities in its membership and so has been able to represent their views as a whole when consensus can be reached between them.

The other main British associations are the Association of County Councils (Eaton House, 66A Eaton Square, London SW1W 9BH), which represents all county councils except one or two whose councils have withdrawn over political disagreements; the Association of District Councils (26 Chapter Street, London SW1P 4ND), the Association of Metropolitan Authorities (35 Great Smith Street, London SW1P 3BJ) representing metropolitan district councils and London authorities; the

Association of London Authorities (36 Old Queen Street, London SW1H 9JF), representing the City of London and boroughs normally controlled by the Conservative Party; and the London Boroughs Association (23 Buckingham Gate, London SW1E 6LB), representing the boroughs normally controlled by the Labour Party.

The Local Government Management Board took over the work of the Local Government Training Board and the Local Government Conditions of Service Advisory Board in 1991, resulting in a body concerned not only with training and the negotiation of employee conditions of service but also with the development of human resources and management improvement in a broad sense. Other important organisations are the Local Authorities Co-ordinating Body on Trading Standards (LACOTS) and the Local Government International Bureau (which also functions as the British Section of the International Union of Local Authorities (IULA)) and the Conference of European Municipalities and Regions (CEMR)). The last, a company limited by guarantee, organises participation in international bodies such as the Council of Local and Regional Authorities in Europe (CLRAE), formulates collective views, monitors European policies, collects and diffuses information internationally, serves as a municipal twinning agency and aims to promote and assist 'the practice of effective local self-government thoughout the world'.

7.6 INTER-GOVERNMENTAL RELATIONS

Historically British local government has owed its independence to benign neglect by central government. Crown ministers and parliament relied on chartered civic corporations and justices of the peace to maintain at least the minimal conditions for public well-being. As nineteenth- and early twentieth-century governments grew increasingly concerned with the road system, public health, education and many other matters, they came to depend heavily on local government for the implementation of their policies. The nationalisation of functions after the Second World War is described in §7.1. Although local authorities lost many competences however, both Labour and Conservative Party governments continued to rely on them to carry out national policies, as in the case of housing programmes up to the 1960s for which they were pressed to deliver nationally set targets at a speed that often went against the interests of quality. Local government initiatives were taken as models for national legislation, as in clean air legislation and the comprehensivisation of secondary schools.

The tide turned in the early 1970s, as assumptions of economic and demographic growth collapsed. The reining in of expenditure after the oil crisis was in principle by mutual agreement. In 1975 the Consultative Committee on Local Government Finance was established consisting of representatives of both central and local government to concert estimates of future local expenditure with national economic planning. After 1979 this became little more than a means to inform local authorities of new restrictions on expenditure. Central government ceased to expect to learn and weigh the experience of local government but rather sought to force through a reorientation of policy. It tended to judge local authorities on the lowness of their expenditures and the extent of their privatisation of services rather than on the quality of their social provisions.

A long list can be made of ways in which the powers of local authorities were weakened under Thatcher governments: abolition of major authorities in which the Labour Party had entrenched power (the Metropolitan County Councils, GLC and Inner London Education Authority); central control over the school curriculum; capping of expenditures of certain local authorities which were 'over-spending' according to ministerial judgement; the implications of the community charge and uniform business rate; controls over capital expenditure; powers to force local authorities to dispose of land ruled as surplus to requirement; requiring local authorities to put provision of services out to competitive tender; mandatory sale of housing to sitting tenants; providing for the transfer of rented housing away from local authority ownership at the option of a majority of tenants voting in ballots; powers for schools to opt out of local government control subject to government approval; movement of polytechnics out of the local government sector and transfer of part of local authority grant to a national government-appointed agency for expenditure on aspects of further education; greatly increased regulation in some matters; prevention of subsidisation to move rents towards market level; increased powers over senior education appointments and management structures of Inner London Boroughs; the transfer of development areas to government-appointed agencies (urban development corporations and housing action trusts); the establishment of enterprise zones outside local authority control; restrictions on the power of local authorities to work in partnership with private industry in joint companies; and so forth in 50 to 60 acts of parliament which governments drove through parliament with limited discussion and modification. The story is filled in in other sections of this chapter.

The position in early 1993 appears to be that the central government is denying local authorities the means to fulfil their obligations under the law regarding the most expensive mandatory services, education and social services, by setting the growth of support at a lower level than the increase in inflation. In education this is critical for the staffing of municipal schools, much aggravated by the 'clawback' from local authority budgets of a special subsidy of 15 per cent above the standard grant allowance to schools which have opted out from municipal management. Many education authorities are expected to be forced not only to make very unsatisfactory provision for the maintenance of school premises but also to reduce the teacher workforce, making some thousands of teachers redundant who are considered as needed to meet their legal obligations. Even more desperate is the situation regarding the new legal duties on local authorities for the care of the elderly and disabled in the community. Local councils are being advised not to disclose to 'clients' assessments of their needs because this would enable the latter to sue them for failure to meet statutory obligations that are beyond the councils' financial means.

Besides the factors mentioned above, the failure of local government to achieve major changes in the government legislative proposals must be put down to lack of local government support in parliament. Of those members of parliament who were councillors at the time of election, few have retained their council seats. Local government interests have had a low priority in the policy strategies of the major national parties. (There is a large literature on the subject. A review will be found in Jones, 1991.) In some cases Conservative MPs who formerly sat on local councils strongly support such government measures as are described above. This arises in part from the reaction to the policies of assertive left-wing local authorities which see themselves as exercising legitimate powers against government policy, but it also arises from a free market philosophy under which local authorities are believed not to have a right to redistribute incomes raised from the public to reduce the disadvantages of the poorer members of society and pursue social justice in other ways. The result is that local government has been disorientated and destabilised, although this has not prevented it from continuing to play a vital role in local services and urban development.

Government Controls

Local government in Britain lacks a close 'organic' relationship with central government levels for reasons indicated in earlier parts of this chapter. Central government may use the language of partnership but after the accession of the Conservatives to power in 1979, it has in general treated local councils as agents without a valid political mandate. This it has justified in the name of individual choice and the diversity of the market.

Central government has always been able to apply for writs in the courts that order authorities to submit their proceedings for review on the issue of legality. The courts can quash decisions found to have been made illegally (*a certiorari*) or compel a decision on a legal duty that had been evaded or omitted (*mandamus*). Such writs can also be sought by private individuals. But the government now exercises control mainly by means of statutory powers, first introduced with regard to police forces but spreading to other fields as the scope of domestic legislation widened.

Local by-laws and statutory schemes and orders are subject to ministerial confirmation. Planning permissions may be revoked or modified by the Secretary of State. Loan sanctions have been necessary for borrowing. Directions may be given to local authorities on planning applications and where an education authority appears to the Secretary of State for the Environment to have acted unreasonably. Appeals to the Secretary and ministerial inquiries on planning matters are frequent.

There are no underlying general principles. Secretaries of state usually have a number of broad legal duties to pursue, but these in themselves do not imply powers of control. A court judgment relating to general ministerial responsibilities under the 1944 Education Act confirmed that local education authorities had a broad discretion to choose what in their judgement are the means best suited to their areas for providing the variety of instruction called for by provisions in the Act. But the freedom available in education and elsewhere has been much reduced by recent legislation.

Central government has duties to ensure inspection of education establishments, police forces and fire services, and control over the appointment of chief police and fire officers. Personal social services provided by local authorities are expected to conform to guidance given by the Secretary of State, who has wide powers to order local inquiries. There are rarely used ministerial powers in the event of a local authority defaulting on a legal duty and for appointing commissioners to act in place of the authority and charge the costs to it.

A large part of ministerial influence, however, is exercised by advice in circulars and other informal means. In general local authorities have tended to regard government circulars as they would instructions. In most cases these embody advice given by civil servants in consultation with local authority associations, professional and other national representative bodies and professionals in local authorities.

The Department of the Environment is the main multi-purpose body of control, being concerned with housing, environmental health and other environmental matters, town and country planning, recreation and the countryside. The largest services, however, come under the Home Office and Departments of Education and Social Security. The resolution of rival claims between departments for financial resources for local government services is a matter for inter-departmental committees, the Treasury and often in recent times the prime minister.

The position in Scotland and Wales is somewhat different. The Scottish Office under the Secretary of State for Scotland bears a general responsibility for Scottish services, which are provided through the Departments of Scottish Development, Education, Home and Health, Industry, Agriculture and Fisheries, all based in Edinburgh. Most Welsh services which concern local authorities are carried out by the Welsh Office in Cardiff under the Secretary of State for Wales. There is closer inter-governmental consultation and integration of policy in these countries and a focus of responsibility which is lacking in England. Yet the results in Britain in general have, in financial terms, been much less severe for local government in terms of total expenditure than might have been predicted, as indicated in the staffing figures given in §7.2. In early 1993, however, it appears that there will have to be heavy cutbacks in the workforce in 1993-94.

Independent Controls on Administration and Management

The 'ombudsman' function is exercised by Commissions for Local Government Administration in England and Wales set up in 1974. Each commission is matched by a 'representative body' composed of association-nominated representatives of local authorities and other local public agencies. If a commission finds that 'a written complaint made by or on behalf of a member of the public who claims to have sustained injustice in consequence of maladministration' is justified it can compel members and officers of an authority to give evidence. If the complaint is upheld the authority concerned must notify what action they are taking. There is no remedy in law against an authority's refusal to make amends or to change its arrangements as a result of a report: the sanction lies only in public opinion and the electoral process.

The independent statutory Audit Commission for Local Authorities in England and Wales was set up in 1983 to replace previous government audit arrangements. Its members are industry, the accounting professions, trade unions and local government. The Commission appoints auditors for local authorities from the private sector as well as from the public District Audit Service, and has the duty of helping local authorities to improve the efficiency of their services through management audit and 'value for money' studies. Its independence has enabled it to criticise the inefficiencies arising for local authorities from central government practices as well as those due to the management failings of local authorities.

7.7 LOCAL GOVERNMENT SERVICES

Under the principle of *ultra vires* the services that local authorities may provide are limited to those defined in statute and such matters as can be reasonably inferred from the text of statutes (see §7.2).

The budgets of county councils are dominated by education, which around the end of the 1980s took up over 58 per cent of total spending. Social services and police expenditures followed, each at around 12 per cent. Roads absorbed between 5 and 6 per cent, fire services 3 per cent and libraries 1.5 per cent. Other service expenditures were substantially lower. The pattern is similar for Scottish regions and islands.

In the most-purpose metropolitan districts and London boroughs education also dominated at 44 per cent. There followed social services (13.5 per cent), police (6.5 per cent), roads (3.5 per cent), fire services (3 per cent), refuse services (2 per cent), parks and open spaces (2 per cent), museums and art galleries (around 1.5 per cent) and environmental health (1.5 per cent).

In English and Welsh district budgets environmental health (often closely linked with housing) and refuse services stood out at 18.5 to 19 per cent in each case. Parks and open spaces followed at 14.5 per cent, sports facilities etc. at 12.5 per cent and physical planning and rate collection, each at 11 per cent. The picture is broadly similar for Scottish districts, subject to small differences in functions.

The following details of services cover nearly all authorities. The Corporation of the City of London has in general the same functions as London boroughs.

1. Town and Country Planning and Development and Environmental Protection

County and Scottish regional councils prepare and revise structure plans of a broad strategic character based on surveys and projections of need, which define planning policies for their areas for ten-year periods.

Non-metropolitan district councils excepting three small Scottish Regional councils where responsibilities are at regional level, prepare and revise local plans for their areas, defining the detailed planning structure, boundaries for land use etc. subject to regard for the county structure plan; grant planning permission for developments and enforce compliance with regulations (subject to government 'call-in' of applications or appeals); establish country parks and nature reserves; designate conservation areas of special architectural or historic interest to preserve or enhance their character, and protect trees and woodlands by preservation orders; exercise control over maintenance of and changes to government-listed buildings of special architectural or historical interest or importance, and may under certain circumstances purchase them compulsorily.

London borough, metropolitan district and Scottish islands councils possess both the county and district competences described above, being responsible for 'unitary development plans' which combine structure and local plan provisions. Planning for London and other metropolitan counties as a whole is left to voluntary joint bodies formed by the boroughs and districts.

2. Housing

District and Scottish islands councils are the principal housing authorities. They must periodically review housing conditions and needs, including those of the chronically sick and disabled; help meet these needs and submit housing investment plans to government as a basis for agreement of investment needs; and may clear slums and rehabilitate areas. Central government has severely reduced local government capacity to provide new housing, transferring public low-cost housing provisions to voluntary associations, although provision for low-income tenants, personal government housing benefit is administered by local authorities as it's agents. Housing authorities also undertake housing conservation, improvement and renovation, and have a statutory duty to provide accommodation for the homeless.

3. Roads

Non-metropolitan county, London borough, metropolitan district councils and, in Scotland, Regional and Islands authorities are responsible for the building and maintenance of all roads and bridges (except motorways and trunk roads) and traffic management.

Non-metropolitan district councils are often employed by highways authorities as agents for local road and ancillary work.

4. Transport

Non-metropolitan county, London borough, metropolitan district and Scottish regional and islands councils co-ordinate and rationalise passenger transport provision in their areas under five-year plans, but their scope for action was reduced in 1985. *London boroughs and metropolitan districts* carry out this task through joint agencies.

All local authorities may subsidise passenger transport services. *Joint metropolitan county passenger transport authorities and some fifty larger districts* have provided their own passenger transport services, but the scope is now limited by open-tendering requirements.

5. Education

Non-metropolitan counties, London borough, metropolitan district and Scottish regional and islands councils are designated local education authorities (LEAs) for their areas. They are responsible for providing free primary and secondary education (compulsory for ages 5 to 16), post-school education and training in colleges of a wide range of types, both vocational and non-vocational; maintenance and tuition grants to students for university and post-school education; and career advisory services for pupils. New legislation from 1988 has severely reduced their discretion, including the transfer of management powers to school boards, a national school curriculum and a tier of independent state-financed schools that have been allowed to opt out from local authority management.

6. Vocational Training

County, Scottish region, metropolitan district and London borough councils, as local education authorities, working with advice from local industry and commerce, have been a mainstay of training in vocational skills. However the new National Training Agency and locally appointed training and enterprise councils (TECs), mostly consisting of local business representatives and staffed by government civil servants, have made LEA provision subsidiary to policies formed elsewhere.

7. Cultural Activities

All types of local authority provide entertainments, facilities for dancing, theatres, concert halls and other places for entertainment, bands and orchestras, and foster arts and crafts.

8. Libraries, Museums and Archives *County, metropolitan district, London borough and certain Welsh district councils* provide comprehensive public library services with free book loans and may provide and charge for loans of gramophone records, cassettes, films and pictures. *Scottish districts* and three small *regions* exercise similar functions. *Counties, metropolitan districts and London Boroughs* are archives authorities. *All types of local authority including parish and community councils* may provide and finance museums and art galleries.

9. Recreation and Conservation of Environment

All types of authority may provide urban and country parks, recreation grounds, open spaces and other amenities for recreation.

County, regional and English and Welsh district councils may provide countryside parks with ancillary sport facilities and for other recreational activities.

District, London borough, parish and community councils must provide allotments for gardening activities except in Inner London.

10. Health and Social Welfare

Local authorities are required to work together with Health Service bodies to advance popular health and welfare, for which purpose statutory joint committees are established.

County, metropolitan district and Scottish regional councils are required to set up social services (in Scotland termed social work) committees, and fulfil requirements for residential institutions for old, infirm and mentally disordered persons and others in need of care and attention, either directly or through other public or voluntary bodies; and provide facilities to help the permanently handicapped and mentally disordered, home helps and meals. They provide for children in need of care, including residential accommodation, adoption and fostering arrangements where desirable. From 1993 they have the primary responsibility for the care of the elderly and mentally handicapped in the community, aided by special grants, thereby overcoming the problems of split duties between the health service and local authorities.

District councils are required to provide environmental health services and have duties related to health and safety at work.

11. Police

One general police service exists in Britain, resourced and administered through the Home Office and Scottish Office jointly with local authorities, except in Greater London where the Home Office is the sole authority.

County and regional councils or joint county and regional committees are responsible for accommodating, staffing and equipping the police, and for appointing heads of police (chief constables), subject to approval of a short list of candidates by central government, and also appointing their assistants. The head of each force is responsible for police policy and operations within policy guidelines and advice and directions from the Home Office. Administration is subject to regulations and other controls, with government inspection and powers of intervention.

12. Fire Prevention

County and Scottish regional councils are the fire authorities except in the metropolitan counties, London and two areas in Scotland where there are joint or combined authorities.

13. Development of Local Economy and Employment

Until 1989 local authorities had no specific powers to undertake intervention, although the general power to spend in the interest of their areas up to a fixed level enabled them to provide grants, loans, equity capital and enterprise boards and to finance co-operatives, business advice, innovation centres and a wide variety of training and community development projects and activities. They also possessed powers regarding land and property which they could employ for this purpose. Since 1989 categories of local authorities have specific powers to act for economic development. They have been principal agents of central government urban development programmes.

14. Public Services
Little remains of power and water service powers apart from *district and London borough council* competences to provide and maintain markets and *county council* powers to provide agricultural smallholdings.

Refuse collection, largely free to the public, is undertaken by *all district and London borough councils* and *refuse disposal* by *county, metropolitan, Welsh and Scottish district and London borough councils.*

15. Consumer Protection and Trading Standards
County, regional, islands, metropolitan district and London borough councils enforce consumer protection and trading standards legislation and can provide consumer advice to the public. They have become deeply involved in enforcement of European Community legislation in these matters.

16. Other Powers and Duties
Burials and cremations: districts, London borough, parish and community councils.

Administration of magistrates' courts: county, metropolitan district, outer London borough and Scottish district and islands councils.

Control of animal diseases county, metropolitan district, London borough and Scottish regional and islands councils.

Licensing and registration of births, marriages and deaths: county, London borough and Scottish regional and islands councils.

Licensing theatres, cinemas, and camping sites: all types of district, London borough and islands coucils.

Residential homes, nurseries and child-minders: county, regional, metropolitan district and London borough councils.

7.8 IMPLEMENTATION OF SERVICES

British local authorities have traditionally preferred to provide their services direct to the public under their own management rather than through agencies or contracts with the private sector. Conservative governments from 1979 attacked 'municipal empires' and sought to cut back local government employment by persuasion and increasing intervention. Their aims included weakening the national bargaining power of the public sector trades unions, holding down wage costs and increasing efficiency. The enforcement of open tendering for service activities did not significantly decrease direct provision in the 1980s except in the fields of transport, education, environmental health and refuse collection (due here mostly to contracting out). There were increases in England and Wales of over 20 per cent in social services staff and surprisingly over 30 per cent in housing (CIPFA, 1990). But sharp cutbacks are expected in 1993 as a result of fiscal controls and reduced grant income.

Pressure on local authorities to contract work out has been increased year by year from the early 1980s. In the mid-1980s local authorities running bus services and airports were required to set up companies to manage them. Statutory provisions in 1988 gave the Secretary of State powers to intervene in cases where local authorities appeared to be restricting competition for services. Areas of 'compulsory competitive tendering' were extended to refuse collection, street cleaning, ground maintenance, building cleaning, vehicle repair and maintenance and catering including school meals. Councils with five or more employees in their direct labour organisations (DLOs) were forced to put work out to private tender. Local authority employees have generally had to compete with standards in the private sector, and in most cases seem to have done so successfully. All but about a fifth of services opened to tender were won by the same authorities' direct service organisations. In some cases existing staff formed co-operatives or private companies which bought out services from their local authority and sometimes won contracts with other authorities.

Service provision through grant-aiding voluntary bodies catering for particular needs has a long history. Services provided in this way include cultural activities, meals on wheels, recreational, youth and other services. Well before the 1980s many housing needs were met by grant-aided housing associations. The 1980s have seen a great increase but also strong centralisation of central control in this field through the state-appointed agency, the Housing Corporation.

Local authorities have shown great flexibility in modes of service provision in recent years, experimenting with partnerships for running facilities with local communities and using 'arms-length' companies, co-operatives and other means not previously normal in Britain. By 1989 over forty local authorities were known to have set up or been involved in 'arms-length' organisations, most commonly in the fields of economic and urban development, including boards, agencies of different kinds and trusts. However the government acquired powers in 1989 to restrict the ability of local authorities to establish or participate in private law companies.

There was a drive, encouraged by the Local Government Training Board (now absorbed into the Local Government Management Board), to make services more sensitive to public choice by systematic identification of the wishes of individuals, training of staff in regular direct contact with members of the public, monitoring the quality of services provided and making services more accessible and generally in touch with local communities by decentralisation of offices, decision-making and accountability.

In general there was much new thinking about the quality of service provision around the end of the 1980s, leading to a wide range of innovations in service delivery in response to the obstacles to provision raised by financial stringency and regulations which narrowed traditional options.

7.9 LOCAL GOVERNMENT FINANCE

Expenditure

In the 1970s local government was responsible for over a quarter of public expenditure. The Conservative governments of the 1980s attempted to force this down in various ways. They appear, however, to have been much less successful than their Labour Party predecessors in 1974-79 who reduced local expenditure in real terms by ten per cent. Spending rose again by nearly eight per cent in real terms between 1979 and 1989: faster than prices but less than earnings. The net capital element, however, fell in the same period by nearly 60 per cent (Travers, 1989).

Income

At the end of the 1980s about a quarter of local authority revenue (excepting that from fees and charges) came from the domestic rate, another quarter from the business rate and half from central grants. Under the new system introduced for the 1990s local government will be able to set the level of only one-quarter of its total tax and grant income. It has no discretion over the business rate which is allocated according to government formulas, and the rate support grant (RSG).

Local authorities have long possessed only one tax of their own. This was until 1989 'the rates', a local property tax levied on domestic and non-domestic fixed properties (real estate) excepting crown and agricultural buildings. It was levied on an assessed value based on the notional market rent which buildings could earn during one year. Low-income tenants qualified for rebates on their rate liabilities up to a hundred per cent. The rates system was replaced in 1989 by a very different and narrower source, the 'community charge' on individual adults (see §7.1).

There were great differences between regions in the level of rate levied. In 1983-85 London's domestic rate bills were 53 per cent above the average for England and Wales, but the difference fell to 16 per cent in 1988-89, due mainly to changes in central grant distribution and rate limitation measures (CIPFA, 1988).

The Community charge or 'poll tax' (see also §7.6) was a flat rate tax levied on all individual persons aged 18 or over (excepting those under 19 still at school), monks and nuns in enclosed orders, long-stay hospital patients, prisoners unless imprisoned for non-payment of fines or the community charge, and people in certain hostels and night shelters or without any normal sleeping accommodation. District and borough councils were required to prepare a special community charges register of all liable for payment, separate from the electoral register although in practice this should have included much the same people.

Those eligible for social security income support and some others on low incomes qualified for rebates on a scale to a minimum of 80 per cent. Income support was calculated to cover up to the whole of this. Students were required to pay 20 per cent. Failure to pay could result in direct deduction of the charge from income and ultimately imprisonment. Failure to return the registration form could lead to a penalty of £50 rising to £200, repeatable in the event of continued failure.

Estimates of the rate payable per head, given current rates of expenditure, show wide differences between areas, from, for example, under £200 in rural towns to £600 in the London Borough of Camden in 1989-90. The government claimed that if the tax had been in force in 1988-89 councils could have charged about £250 per person that year. The government grant was claimed to be specially calculated to cover particular needs in each area, and hence 'each council could provide the same standard of services for the same level of charge everywhere' (*The Community Charge*, Department of the Environment, 1989). The level of the tax should therefore relate to the level of efficiency in each authority. The claim that central government was able to determine 'the particular needs of each area' overrides the proposition that only local people can determine the needs of their area: a basic justification of local government. The community charge carried costs of collection that have been estimated at two or more times higher than for the rates. It was shown by opinion polls to be against the wishes of considerably more than half the population and, it is reported, against the judgement of half the British Cabinet. Arrears in payment, it is expected by some local authority treasurers, will continue well into the 1990s if not to the year 2000.

The *council tax* that replaced it in 1993 has a 'property part' and a 'personal part'. The former is based on a value assigned to a dwelling within each of eight bands relating to a valuation according to the estimated price the property would have fetched if sold on the open market on 1 April 1991. The personal part is 50 per cent of the tax rate if two or more over-18s are living in a dwelling. A single resident and certain other categories qualify for a 25 per cent tax reduction and other rebates are available up to 100 per cent for a 'liable person' where there is a low household income. Discounts are also given for full-time students, apprentices, government trainees. Exemptions are as for the community charge plus some additions. A 50 per cent reduction is made for a second home. One person in each dwelling (the 'liable person') is responsible for payment. The person should be, in order of preference, an owner-occupier, a resident leaseholder, a council or private tenant, a resident licensee of a public house or another type of resident.

The Uniform Business Rate (UBR)

The uniform business rate was introduced simultaneously with the community charge as a means to transfer to local government sums to compensate for their loss of the previous rate charges on business properties. The poundage on the rate is determined by central government, but the revenue is collected by local government. Each district council retains a sum up to the entitlement determined by central government. The balance is remitted to a national pool redistributed by the Secretary of State for the Environment to equalise the resources of local authorities in accordance with their needs as assessed by the Secretary of State's formula.

Central-Local Grants

Government financial transfers to local government as a whole are chiefly in the form of the 'block grant'. This is calculated to compensate authorities for differences in their rateable resources and their spending needs. The block grant has also been used in recent years to damp down local authority expenditure for macro-economic reasons under a formula which reduces a local authority's grant entitlement as its expenditure increases.

Other elements in the rate support grant are the domestic relief grant, calculated to maintain rate charges to householders at a level below that charged to non-domestic ratepayers; and specific grants to help in the finance of services where the government wishes to keep control on how the money is spent, for example police forces.

In 1990-91 government revenue support and other government transfers in England and Wales amounted to 46 per cent, which with the redistributed business rate put 69 per cent of income outside local control. Community charge income constituted 30 per cent (CIPFA, 1992).

Capital expenditure is met predominantly by borrowing, supplemented in recent years by large sales of land and property that have been strongly encouraged by government under its privatisation policies, and also by leasing. Contributions may be made from the revenue account. Loan interest has taken up about 15 per cent of recurrent expenditure.

The government has used a system of capital control to limit capital expenditure. Each authority is given an annual allocation for capital spending divided into blocks for groups of services. Allocations may be transferred by local authorities from one block to another and from one year to the next. Borrowing has declined in recent years more than other sources of finance.

A system of expenditure targets was introduced in the early 1980s as part of government attempts to achieve what it regarded as 'reasonable' expenditure levels. Grant penalties were also set for 'overspending'. The devices were much less successful than expected. From 1985 authorities which spent appreciably higher than the government claimed they needed to spend had a ceiling put upon their rate call. This 'rate-capping', as it was called, reached a peak in 1987/88 with 40 authorities being rate-capped, fourteen of them in London. Many authorities used all their ingenuity, often with the help of private sector sources of finance, to 'beat the system' by maintaining their spending without incurring the penalties that otherwise would have been inflicted on them.

It is strange that a government which through its strength in parliament exercises virtually absolute power in the country has had such mediocre success in its battle with authorities committed to high levels of staffing and services. There does not appear to be any sound reason why it should not have simply limited permissible rate-calls instead of playing a 'cat and mouse game'. The history of financial struggle has illustrated vividly the polarisation between the values of the 1980s Conservative governments and those of most opposition local councillors. It has also shown the weakness of the local authority associations which have battled against central control in this field, even when they have been controlled by Conservative majorities.

7.10 ELECTORAL REPRESENTATION

Britain has about 25,400 councillors on main councils, some 70,000 on parish councils and those on the Welsh and Scottish community councils. In 1985 81 per cent of those on main councils were male. Their average age had dropped in the previous eight years except in the English shire districts and Welsh counties. The averages differ widely according to the type of local authority they serve. In London boroughs the under-45s formed 50 per cent of councils and the over-60s 19 per cent. County councillors were much older, under-45s forming 22 per cent and over-60s 37 per cent. Two-thirds were or had been in non-manual occupations. Thirty-two per cent were employers or managers (42 per cent of Conservatives); 21 per cent manual workers (35 per cent of Labour Party members). (*The Conduct of Local Authority Business: Research Vol.I*, 1986)

Candidates for election must be British or Irish citizens and aged at least 21. They must also be electors, owners or tenants of property or workers or residents in the area for twelve months before the nomination day. Disqualifications from serving as a councillor are employment by the authority or by a joint body on which it is represented, bankruptcy and a prison sentence of not less than three months in the previous five years for a crime, corruption and certain other offences connected with council business. In 1989 these disqualifications were extended, controversially, to local authority employees paid £13,500 or more a year and involved in political activities defined in government regulations. This provision has been estimated to have taken away the right of serving as a councillor or participating in defined local political activities from over 70,000 council employees. One of its aims was to prevent local authorities from giving jobs to councillors on party political grounds.

The Status and Working Conditions of Representatives

Legally a member of a council has no executive powers in his individual capacity and can exercise no lawful authority on behalf of the council. But there are conventions or accepted practices which enable members, particularly committee chairmen, to give undertakings on behalf of the council subject to legal ratification. Taxable allowances are payable to members in respect of attendance at meetings subject to a daily maximum set by the Secretary of State (£18.25 a day in 1988-89), or alternatively an untaxed loss of income allowance (maximum £29.70 in the same year). In 1991 councillors with special responsibilities, such as chairmen, may be paid special allowances up to maxima varying from £525 to £5,215 according to the type of authority and its population.

The Electoral System

Principal local authorities' areas are divided into electoral areas or wards, as they are called in district authorities. Party candidates for council seats are selected by area or ward parties, subject to supervision by the parliamentary constituency or borough party.

Most British councils are elected every four years. Metropolitan district councils and 118 of the non-metropolitan district councils are elected in thirds in three successive years, followed by a year with no elections — for example 1994, 1995, 1996, 1998, 1999 and so on.

Local government elections for seats on main authorities are mostly contests between party candidates. In counties one candidate is returned for each electoral area for a four-year term. Thus if 2,500 votes are cast for a Conservative candidate, 2,700 for a Labour one, 2,300 for a Liberal Democrat and 2,000 for an Independent, the Labour candidate wins the seat although he or she is supported by no more than 28 per cent of those voting. The position is similar in metropolitan districts, although because of the system of election in thirds there are three councillors for each ward who, because elected in different years, may not all represent the same party. London boroughs and non-metropolitan districts may have multi-member wards.

Party candidates usually fight elections on policies decided by their constituency or borough committees which have been incorporated into their parties' electoral manifestos.

Political support can be very volatile. In 1977, for example, Labour lost 55 per cent of the 1,100 seats it had held on the 39 English county councils, losing control of all but one. In 1981 the Conservatives lost control of 18 counties and in 1993 all but one or two. Turnover of councillors can be very heavy in some cases, due mainly to political swings and loss in voter motivation (Gyford, Leach and Game, 1989). In 1985 65 per cent of councillors had less than ten years experience in the role.

The Councillor's Role

The ward or constituency system can and often does lead to a close relationship between councillor and ward. Most councillors see themselves as mediators between citizens and the council and its bureaucracy. The service they give to their constituents is considered a chief measure by which their performance should be judged at the next election.

It is generally recognised that a councillor's role involves a group of tasks: as representative, citizens' referee, policy-maker, politician and overseer of the officer administration to see that it is efficient and effective and fair in its actions; and that the time and effort given to particular types of task will vary widely between members. It was found in 1985 that on average councillors spent 74 hours a month on council matters — somewhat less than the 79 hours found by a survey in 1976. Office-holders averaged about 80 hours and other councillors 64 (*The Conduct of Local Authority Business: Research Vol.II*, 1986).

Nearly 90 per cent of councillors are elected as representatives of a political party. They nearly all belong to party groups with their own standing orders which follow rules set by their national parties. Local Labour parties are expected to abide by model standing orders in the party's rulebook. Local Labour parties in many cases send representatives to council group meetings, as do Conservative Party branches in about half of all cases. The Widdecombe Committee research found that non-councillors attended group meetings in 72 per cent of cases and had voting rights in 14 per cent (ibid.). The groups usually meet before council meetings and in some cases before committee meetings. Decisions taken by them before council meetings are normally expected to be binding on members. Not voting as decided by the group may lead to penalties.

Political Change

Party politics of a kind was present in many boroughs throughout the nineteenth century, but it was only with the rise of the Labour Party in the early twentieth century that it assumed the typical two-party pattern which became characteristic of English county boroughs and other urban authorities. With the amalgamation of authorities in the reorganisation of the 1970s many of the remaining non-party traditions vanished.

However local parties are highly autonomous. There is no machinery to make local parties accountable to the centre or the centre accountable to local party members.

The 1980s saw the rise of a strong challenge from the Liberal and Social

Democrat Parties. In many cases the third party upset the conventions on which councils had conducted their business. With three parties achieving substantial representation, the first-past-the-post system gives an insensitive relationship between votes and seats on a council as a whole.

The Conservative position in local government has been much weaker in local government during the 1980s than in the House of Commons. Its support in many traditional Conservative strongholds became volatile. The successes of the centre parties in 1985 for example deprived Conservatives of control in all but eleven of the 47 county councils in England and Wales and in 1993 they lost all but one. They also failed to win control in any Scottish region. In the metropolitan districts they held a majority in only one out of 36 councils and in another by the casting vote of the mayor.

Between 1985 and 1989 one in four of all councils in England and Wales were 'hung', the term used for the situation where no party has an overall majority. Two-thirds of these were shire districts, but over half the county councils were also 'hung' (Gyford, Leach and Game, 1989; Leach et al., 1989). True coalition control is uncommon. Only nine per cent of hung authorities were found to be characterised by 'high' partisanship in September 1987. Two-thirds operated through a minority administration on which one party was allowed to take chairmanships and vice-chairmanships and lead in policy initiatives and budget proposals. Politics have also become diversified by divisions within party groups, with polarisation between 'soft' and 'hard' or 'new' left in the Labour Party and 'new right', and in the case of the Conservatives between the 'wets' and the 'drys'. (Gyford and James, 1983)

7.11 THE INTERNAL ORGANISATION OF LOCAL AUTHORITIES

All local government decisions, whether executive or deliberative, are the responsibility of a council as a whole. Councils of English and Welsh main authorities range in size from 28 to 117 members and in Scotland from 10 to 103. There is no distinct legally defined executive body. The distribution of duties within councils is partly laid down in each authority's standing orders and by ad hoc decisions by councils and by committees within their delegated powers. The council leader (normally the leader of the largest party) and committee chairmen, supported by officers who often take a dominant role, steer the process of decision-making. Roughly speaking the de facto executive consists of the leader (or more than one leader where there is no overall party control), working closely with the chief executive and committee chairmen (see Norton, 1991).

The Committee System

Most formal decisions are determined in committees; hence the expression used by one writer on British administrative systems, 'government by committee' (Wheare, 1955). Committee decisions may be made under powers delegated by the council, or submitted to the council for ratification. Informally power lies with the ruling party group consisting of councillors belonging to the party with an absolute majority, where one exists. The disruption of the British two-party system in recent years that has been described in §7.10 has greatly complicated the power structure in many authorities.

Senior party politicians fill committee chairmanships and the party posts of secretary, treasurer and the 'whips' whose job is to secure effective presentation of the group's case in council and disciplined voting. Members who chair committees, briefed by senior council officers, defend their committees' recommendations. There is often tension between a leading politician who chairs a committee working for his or her committee's interests and a group leadership which seeks to enforce priorities between services. Where there is no controlling majority, who-ever is in the chair lacks the same strength and there are varied arrangements for filling the position, including choosing a chairman only at the beginning of each committee meeting.

In accordance with the recommendations of the Bains Report (*The New Local Authorities, 1972*) the great majority of authorities now have a policy and resources committee. This usually includes chairmen of other main committees. Since 1989 its membership, like that of other committees, has been legally required to be representative of the party composition of the council. The council leader often steers the work of this committee, helped by the chief executive. Its functions are commonly to advise the council on setting plans, objectives and priorities; exercise control over the major resources of the authority; and co-ordinate and control the implementation of the council's programmes. Its sub-committees, according to the report, are to 'exercise day to day control over staff, finance and land and review areas of performance'.

Also in line with the report's recommendations, committees responsible for functional areas are far fewer than was often the case before 1974. They number from about four in some small districts to sixteen or so in a complex metropolitan authority. The report envisaged these as 'programme committees', covering closely interrelated areas of service, so that priorities

387

could be considered together in the policy-making and planning process.

County and Scottish regional councils will typically appoint committees for education, social services, highways and transportation, planning and public protection, and one concerned with recreation, library, archive and museum services. County councils also have a police committee if there is no joint committee with other counties. Metropolitan districts and London boroughs will have in addition committees for housing and environmental services.

Shire and Scottish districts are likely to have leisure, housing and environmental services committees. One committee may represent the direct works interests that bid for services specified by other committees in the open competitive tendering process. In metropolitan districts covering all these functions, excepting those that lie statutorily with joint committees, there may be a strong grouping of functions, as in Bolton which has management and finance, education and arts, social services, housing, environmental services, planning and industrial development committees; or there may be a much wider structure as in Birmingham where there were sixteen committees in 1988 including those for economic development, urban development, the National Exhibition and International Convention Centres, personnel and equal opportunities, appeals and trading services. Committee sizes vary widely, ranging in 1975 from 20 to 29 members in counties, 15 to 29 members in metropolitan districts and 10 to 24 members in county districts (Greenwood, Lomer, Hinings and Ranson, 1975).

A tendency to move towards the 'cabinet' concept by appointing one-party committees, as were found in 24 authorities, and one-party sub-committees, found in 38, was nipped in the bud by legislation in 1989 (*The Conduct of Local Authority Business: Research Vol.1: The Political Organisation of Local Authorities*, 1986).

In addition to committees and sub-committees some local authorities have more informal bodies bodies such as working groups, leadership groups and member-officer groups.

A recommendation of the Bains Report that groups of service departments should be integrated into directorates to match the span of 'programme committees' has been followed to some extent in many authorities, although others have created directorates without matching committee structures. The directorates create an additional horizontal layer of organisation, subordinating some expert professional or quasi-professional heads to a director who may not have direct experience of some of the fields concerned.

Bains recommended a collective approach at officer level such as had already been adopted in some authorities, with a group of chief officers designated as members of a management team, led by a chief executive, that would exercise collective responsibility for general advice and the co-ordination of service implementation. The approach was often unpopular because it weakened the relationship between committee chairmen or chairwomen and departmental officers, and seemed to some members to result in giving undue power to senior officers. Nevertheless the new pattern has come to be accepted as normal in recent years.

Council Chairmen and Mayors

The highest formal status in a council is that of its chairman or chairwoman. In English and Welsh borough councils the chairman or chairwoman carries the title of mayor, and in the largest eight cities excepting Liverpool and Manchester that of Lord Mayor. In some Scottish districts the same role carries the traditional name of convener. The cities of Aberdeen, Dundee, Edinburgh and Glasgow have lord provosts and some other districts provosts. These heads of the council normally have deputies (vice-chairmen, deputy mayors or vice- or deputy provosts). Besides presiding over council meetings they represent their authorities on formal occasions but have no real executive functions other than by locally determined convention. In counties and districts the chairman or woman may also be council leader.

The law does not allow delegation to individual elected members, whatever their status, so that all decisions other than those delegated to officers are collective in principle, although in practice they are commonly determined by the committee 'chairperson'.

The mayoral office is normally rotated among senior members annually. The mayor, male or female, chooses a 'mayoress' to accompany him or her and possibly to deputise on some formal occasions.

The Officer Administration

Top-level officers usually have a high status and are highly influential, due largely to their professional standards, training and experience as well as their position in the organisation.

Staffing is largely at the discretion of the council. Councils have almost all replaced the traditional clerk as head of the service with a chief executive who carries general responsibility for overall management, efficiency, relationships within the authority and between it and the central ministries and other outside bodies (Norton, 1991). The designated statutory 'head of the paid service', who is normally the council's chief executive, is required to report to the council on how discharge of functions is co-ordinated, the number and grades of staff required and their organisation, appointment and proper management. The chief executive or another officer must be designated 'monitoring officer' with the duty to report to council on 'ombudsman' findings and contraventions of proportional representation of parties or other requirements in the statutory code of practice. There is also a statutory requirement for a chief finance officer, normally the council's director of finance, who carries the duty of ensuring financial propriety. Other administrative arrangements are, with one or two exceptions, entirely at the authority's discretion.

Unionisation and joint employer/employee negotiation have led to agreed salary structures and other conditions for groups of officers and other employees, and a well-developed system for regular review of gradings and appeals. Local conditions tend to be determined by the strength of staff associations and the willingness of local councils to conform to national agreements. The majority of authorities accept the conditions negotiated under the arrangements by the Local Government Management Board (see §7.5), but an increasing number of authorities broke away from joint conditions after 1979 and adopted other scales and conditions, most notably for the post of chief executive. (Bras, 1988; Norton, 1988 and 1991)

7.12 CITIZEN PARTICIPATION AND DECENTRALISATION WITHIN CITIES

About 90 per cent of over-18s are on the electoral role, but only 80 per cent or so in Inner London. Average turn-out appears to have varied little since the 1960s. Between 1973 and 1978 average turn-out in local elections was lowest in metropolitan districts (36 per cent) and highest in Welsh shire counties (53 per cent). Otherwise the averages are close to 40 per cent in English authorities and 50 per cent in Welsh and Scottish authorities (*The Conduct of Local Authority Business*, 1986). In the late 1980s the government showed its lack of interest in the level of local voting by ceasing to collect and publish turn-out figures. Council, committee and sub-committee meetings are open to the public. Local authorities are required to make minutes, abstracts of accounts, information about expenditures and information about planning proposals open to the public and to give members of the public access to papers, including agendas of meetings, reports, and related memoranda and other background documents. They have a duty since 1985 to publish certain financial information and an annual general report.

Decentralisation in Local Authorities

A few large cities have set up suburban offices as points of contact and co-ordination of services, including Birmingham. There has nowhere been direct election of sub-municipal councils, other than statutory parish councils which are independent and not part of the civic organisation (see §7.4). A few authorities have, however, developed locally decentralised political and administrative institutions that have had significant impacts on policy and administration, among them Middlesbrough District Council, the London Borough of Tower Hamlets and Glasgow.

7.13 THE GOVERNANCE OF METROPOLITAN AREAS

The United Kingdom has lacked elected governments concerned with larger metropolitan areas as a whole since the abolition of the Greater London Council and the metropolitan county councils. Aspects of the London boroughs and metropolitan districts are described in §§7.4 and 7.7. The remaining joint institutions are detailed in §7.5.

A study of inter-authority relations in metropolitan areas during the 1980s found that extensive voluntary interaction between tiers was unusual and what existed tended generally to be at operational rather than policy-making levels and dominated by officials. Politicians were seldom involved. Informal relations have proved more fruitful than formal ones. (Leach, Vielba and Flynn, 1987; Leach, Davis, Game and Skelcher, 1991).

8. THE UNITED STATES OF AMERICA

8.1 HISTORY AND TRADITIONS

Despite its great area the United States is a highly urbanised country. It has 41 continuous built-up areas of over a million inhabitants. Their populations average well over two million and they account for 62 per cent of the national population. None has a single administrative centre and only six have core city governments serving more than a million inhabitants (*US Bureau of the Census*, 1991, Tables 33 and 36). In general their governance depends on an historical accumulation of ad hoc institutions, diverse in type and function and without political coherence.

The importance of the great areas lying outside the agglomerations should not be overlooked. Research and evaluation of local government structures, however, mostly focus on the metropolitan areas, and inevitably a sketch of American local government as a whole must depend on the main sources available.

Although the national language is English and the origins of its local political institutions were chiefly British, probably less than one in nine of present-day citizens have clear British ancestry. The United States is a country of great geographical, industrial and cultural variety. Its member states vary widely in history, character and way of life. The character of local authorities varies regionally in accordance with these influences. Nevertheless national identity is strong and reflects remarkable historical continuity and stability. Local government institutions and behaviour, although extraordinarily varied, have much in common that can be clearly appreciated when contrasted with their West European equivalents.

Governments at all levels are part of a competitive milieu, mediating between social, environmental, property, business, labour and other interests. They may strive to improve the social and physical environment on the one hand but to meet the often conflicting needs of private enterprises on the other. A main key to the success of organised interests lies in lobbying to make needs and demands known and to strike political bargains. At state level as well as at national level there are parliamentary assemblies with loosely grouped political parties made up of politicians eager to maintain support in their home constituencies. Their executive institutions are often highly complex and in larger cases often consist of a plethora of sub-administrations which inevitably tend in most cases to have conflicting interests. There is a layered judiciary and the ultimate possibility of taking key issues up to the Supreme Court where cases can be argued on interpretations of the law and constitution.

American administrative systems appear to be distinct from European in a number of ways. They emerge strongly from the contrasting histories of local government reform. In Europe there is a strong urge to consolidate systems from the top and establish a uniform order, while in the United States competitive conflict and variety are regarded as normal. In general:

- in Europe structural changes have tended to be imposed from above, uniformly and nationally; while in the United States they have often moved in different directions and required voter approval or referenda;
- in Europe reforms have tended towards consolidation and integration of structures and services while in the United States they have tended towards special-purpose authorities and have relied on voluntary negotiated co-operation;
- in Europe reduction of local inequities has been sought by party and parliamentary action while in the United States the courts are more often the active agents (cf. Gunlicks, 1980);
- in Western Europe political parties provide an institutional framework for defining optional political agendas, bargaining between representatives of competing interests and allocating leadership functions; while in the United States the parties have only a superficial resemblance to European models. They are a microcosm of the United States — full of individualists, entrepreneurs, 'wheelers and dealers', vigilantes of civil rights and other typical public figures.

In the 1960s and 1970s the power of local political parties tended to decline sharply with a loss of control over nominations, undermining by referenda, increased regulation of party finances and a marked drop in the number of citizens willing to identify themselves with party policies. Yet local authorities still carry massive responsibilities and are alive with initiatives reflecting contrasting orientations (see for example Clark and Ferguson, 1983).

Historical Outline of Local City Government

An event-by-event history of American local government is hardly possible, given its fragmentation within and between regions, and state structures with sharply different characteristics. Its origins were predominantly rural. At the end of the eighteenth century all but one in twenty inhabitants lived in rural areas, 95 per cent of inhabitants lived outside areas classified as urban. Small settlements spread across the continent, leading to administrative structures that remain virtually unchanged in most areas despite their mismatch with modern patterns of settlement (Richards, 1967). Self-reliance was the essence of the early settlements.

Diversity of culture and contrasting economies led to wide variations in the structure and style of government. The town governments of New England derive from European borough government. Local government in the plantation areas to the South was a development from British shire county institutions. The Middle Atlantic States have a mixture of these town and county institutions. (Gunlicks, 1991)

Settlers often brought a distrust of higher government with them. The American Revolution was fought to defend autonomy, industry and trade against a centralised executive. At first councillors tended to be as involved in detailed administration as were those in British boroughs and counties. They or the state governor appointed their officials. Growth in scale led to increasing dependence on officials and from about 1820 there was widespread adoption of popular direct election of financial controllers, attorneys-general, superintendents of education, department heads, judges, sheriffs and others. In the cities party machines were created, exercising patronage through the control of public employment and the award of contracts. Many authorities became notorious for political manipulation and corruption.

A reaction in the 1870s led to state restrictions and a policy of appointing new employees on grounds of competence rather than party (Kaufman, 1963). Attempts were made to isolate administration from politics by setting up boards and commissions with wide powers rather than single administrators, especially where regulatory functions were involved. These developments led to an extreme fragmentation of responsibilities and accountability with no overall direction. Citizens were bewildered by the maze of local agencies and the long list of offices for which they were required to choose among candidates. Overall control was sought by the creation of strong executives: a mayor or chief executive at the apex of an administrative pyramid, with a manageable span of integrated departments below. Chief executives acquired staff assistants and units to help them plan, control and manage relationships. Four-year terms were instituted. By the 1960s integrated planning and budgeting processes had been developed in some authorities. In larger authorities the assembly or council might be expected to focus its attention on legislation, regulation and key decisions, including budget approval, leaving management and execution to the executive. These developments may have characterised large city governments to some extent, but small authorities with strong participation by council members still existed in very large numbers.

From the 1960s at least the literature on city government reflects a general sense of political crisis over reconciling financial need with dwindling resources. This was above all the case for the great cities. They lost resources on a drastic scale through emigration of internal resources to industry and more affluent inhabitants to outside their borders. Their ability to service poorer inhabitants and fend off serious breakdowns of order and protect property declined sharply. They became rapidly more dependent on state and federal grants. Their credit slumped and they desperately needed strong and enterprising leadership to hold together fragmented interests and draw in new sources of aid. In the 1980s a state of financial crisis spread from the Northwestern 'frostbelt' cities to the 'sunbelt' cities which had previously been fairly immune. Imminent collapse of the 'ungovernable city' has been forecast over three decades, and is still being so into the 1990s.

It is against such a model, incorporating an ethos of good, ambitious management to be judged by success at the ballot box and working against strong pressures towards fragmentation, abuse of power and breakdown of financial viability that the work of American city governance has to be understood. But it must be emphasised that this is an extremely simplified model of history, and that very different models may be appropriate to rural and indeed many urban areas.

8.2 THE STATUS OF LOCAL GOVERNMENT

Legal Status

Local governments are the creatures of their states and depend on their states' laws and constitutions for their status, rights and privileges. Thus there are fifty different state systems of local government, each quite separate from the other forty-nine. In theory a state can abolish and supersede a local authority, but in practice the law and politics place limits on the possibility.

The electorate, through their right to determine the state constitution by referendum, can and do limit the powers of its legislature over local authorities. The federal constitution can also be instrumental in checking a legislature's intentions. Legislation must apply to a class of local authorities, not a particular case. Thus moving a county seat of government and abolishing direct election of officials have in some cases been judged to be *ultra vires*.

The functions of local authorities are in general specifically defined, and local authorities if challenged must be able to demonstrate in the courts that they have legal authority for their activities. This strict application of the *ultra vires* doctrine received its classical formulation in Judge Dillon's rule of the 1870s which laid down categorically that a municipal corporation can exercise only 'powers granted in express words', 'necessarily or fairly implied in or incident to the powers expressly granted', or 'those essential to the accomplishment of the declared objectives and purposes of the corporation — not simply convenient but indispensable. Any fair, reasonable, substantial doubt concerning the existence of power is resolved by the courts against the corporation, and the power is denied'. The impact of the 'Dillon rule' has been softened to some extent by subsequent judgments and by provisions in the state constitutions; and, perhaps more importantly, by means of enabling legislation that widens local authority discretion. Moreover special charters granted to individual authorities, general charters applicable to all municipalities in a state and 'constitutional' home-rule charters have equal or superior authority over state legislation in municipal affairs. Home rule gives a municipality freedom to frame its own charter within state guidelines and recognises broad discretionary authority. In general it confers the right to determine how things are done within the law.

Both multi-purpose local authorities (municipal corporations) and special-purpose bodies, of which there are a great number, are regarded as both public corporations and local governments. They have legal personality separate from their citizens.

The principles of organisation for towns, townships and counties are laid down by their states. Some states have 'county home-rule' plans which enable counties to choose from a number of schemes of organisation. Some have gone further, as in Ohio, which allows the people of a county to 'frame and adopt or amend a charter' in order to provide a form of government which 'may provide for the concurrent or exclusive exercise by the county... of all or of any designated powers invested by the constitution or laws of Ohio in municipalities; it may provide for the organization of the county as a municipal corporation'. Powers and services of special districts (see §8.4) are sharply defined.

Taxation laws define fiscal powers and impose restrictions such as maxima on property taxation for specific purposes and limits to indebtedness up to a percentage of the property tax base (see §8.9).

Forms of government for municipalities may be established by special act of a state legislature, by a general act laying down a common form, by prescribed forms applying to defined classes of municipalities, by optional forms defined by law or by 'home rule'. Most states provide for 'home rule' to some extent, usually in the constitution but in some cases by statutes under which municipalities may enjoy control of 'municipal officers', or authority to manage their 'local affairs and government', or generally 'powers of local self-government'. They may give special authority to pass regulatory ordinances in matters such as town planning, building regulations, nuisances, public order and protection of property, control of brothels and disorderly behaviour. Under home rule local governments are usually able to exercise any power that the legislature is capable of devolving subject to prescription or suppression by general law. Home rule does not, however, give general competence. Grants of authority to set taxes are restricted, and the subjects on which taxation can be levied are in general defined by the state. It has been argued that home rule's effects on attitudes have been more important than the specific freedoms it confers.

Provisions for referenda and initiatives may also be argued to affect the status of local governments (see §8.12).

Political Status

A federal report describes the local governments of the United States as federalism's thousand workhorses of government, and the 50 states, with their frequent adjustments to the frameworks of local provision, as the laboratories of federalism (ACIR, 1982). It is perhaps impossible to generalise on their political status as distinct from their legal or utilitarian status. It depends on the power that individual politicans or elite groups can exercise or the strength they can hold in bargaining for resources. Local government leaders know that members of Congress or the state legislature must listen to them if they are to maintain popular support. That some are gainers and others are losers is the essence of the political culture. If one channel of influence is blocked, there is always another in the executive, legislature or indeed in the judiciary, and at the extreme in the people through a referendum or initiative.

The political system may be a ladder to high office at state or Congress level, but multiple holding of electoral offices is unusual. Nevertheless local government has its own strong constituency in both state and national legislatures, which it uses to fight encroachments on local freedoms in the traditional manner. And it is no step down in public esteem to move from Congress to a major mayoralty such as that of New York City. National and international reputations can be more effectively made as the executive of a great city than as a member of Congress. National characteristics such as the nature of American individualism (see §8.3), the traditional 'anti-government' stance, cases of major corruption and limitations on resources militate against popular status, but in most areas local authorities are understood to benefit from their closeness to the citizen and the influence they can bring to bear on politicians at other levels of government.

8.3 CONCEPTS AND VALUES

Thomas Jefferson (1743-1826), a lawyer who drafted the Declaration of Independence (1774), assisted Virginia in drawing up its state constitution and became elected its governor (1779-81), secured the adoption of the decimal system of coinage (1783), was the first head of the Republican Party, and was chosen as the third president of the United States in 1801 and saw through the prohibition of the slave trade, has been described as 'the first, and also the foremost, advocate of local self-government' (Syed, 1966). He put forward a plan to divide counties into wards of five to six square miles which citizens would govern under a system of direct democracy and would, expressing their preferences through 'wardens', determine major state-wide matters of government. The wards would be responsible for care of the poor, roads, police, administration of petty justice and elementary exercise for the militia. They would govern 'all matters which, being under their eye, they would better manage than the large republics of the county or state' (letter to John Adams, 28 October 1813). But he rejected the concept of historic, corporate communities (ibid.).

The Declaration of Independence gives the classic statement of the rights of individuals to pursue their own ends. Government is accepted subject to 'the Right of the People to alter or abolish it'. It contains the text for the conservatism that counters the radicalism of a country built on a revolution: 'Prudence, indeed, will dictate that Governments long established should not be changed for light or transient Causes': but the popular right to over-throw the executive if it fails to respond or acts against the popular will is proclaimed in peremptory terms.

In 1871 Judge Cooley gave a famous judgment in which he concluded that 'The state may mould local institutions according to its views of policy or expediency: but local government is a matter of absolute right, and the state cannot take it away'. This obviously clashes with the Dillon Rule quoted in §8.2 above. The federal Supreme Court has followed Dillon. (ibid.)

The rights endowed by constitutional amendments have been kept alive by the courts, and periodically extended by referenda and court inter- pretations. The definition of the 'one-man, one-vote' principle, along with the fundamental provisions for civil equality and against discrimination, have protected minorities and given them the means to establish themselves as parts of the political system, often in the face of entrenched prejudice.

Constitutional provisions have enabled the popular interest in a competitive, wealth-seeking, free enterprise economy and political system to prevail. The pursuit of wealth and property has been accepted as a leading dynamic force within society. It relates to the belief in growth — and 'growth is progress, bigness is goodness, expand or decline' (Adrian, 1972).

The other side of the coin has been the bias against collective action, but not necessarily against municipalities when they fight for their existence or for popular values. 'Boosterism', the enhancement of property and pursuit of growth, was often the leading strand in campaigns for executive office.

There is little concept of the state as more than the sum of its parts. 'The general idea has been that no-one should govern, or failing that, that everyone should govern together' (Banfield, 1985). There is a lack of deference to political authority, derived from respect for the self-made rather than the traditional. Strong leadership is admired as long as it is accountable and often tolerated in any event if it is successful. Against this there is the national 'super-ego': the clean government and efficiency movement which has in the end wiped out most political gangsterism and established what are by and large upright standards of management.

Phrases such as the 'social service state' have been used to describe the pluralistic welfare initiatives that have been generated in a pragmatic, ad hoc fashion, particularly in the Roosevelt era. Up to the Reagan presidencies the federal government spawned minority, urban aid and redevelopment schemes in the interest of city minorities with common needs, displaying a city orientation in its attempts to reverse the decay of city centres in the face of the movement of wealth to the suburbs and the new economies of the West Coast.

Social policy has been generally designed to play a derivative and residual role (Wolman, 1975), providing only for those without means to look after themselves, out of harmony with the French concept of *solidarité* or the German *Sozialstaat* which theoretically involve the whole population in a rational system of mutual security. But interests concerned with maintaining standards of social welfare have in practice been strong enough to resist the more draconian threats of Reagan policies in the 1980s. Moral imperatives have been evident in states' efforts to compensate for withdrawal of federal welfare support for local communities. Drives for economy, efficiency and effectiveness, the search for new resources and profitable investment, competitive lobbying and attempts to exert influence through all available channels have become more patently necessary as the financial position of local government has deteriorated.

A report of the federal Advisory Commission on Intergovernmental Relations summarises some main characteristics which condition the environment within which American local government lives:

> Liberty and equality, individualism and collectivism, majority rule and minority rights, national unity and diversity... these pairs of potentially, if not actually, antithetical values in our 200 years old system clearly reveal a perennial American propensity simultaneously to seek out and sustain opposites. Moreover, the apparent intellectual inconsistencies implicit in this behaviour have never bothered us much. The prime reason for this, of course, is that with one notable and bloody exception in the 1860s — the system with all its ambivalences worked. But signs of dysfunction-ality now are everywhere, as the foregoing probe of paradoxes illustrates. (ACIR, 1979)

Another principle is that of competition. In a report of 1987 (ACIR, 1987) the ACIR sees the fragmentation of local government as a means to individual choice and also as a means to foster 'key values of democratic government': efficiency, equity, responsiveness, accountability and self-governance (see §§8.5 and 8.13). This suggests another antithetical pairing: competition and co-operation.

8.4 NATIONAL STRUCTURE

The Structural 'Jungle'

Washington's Advisory Commission on Inter-Governmental Relations has described the national local government system as a jungle (ACIR, 1976a). Its complexity has continued to increase. In 1987 there were over 83,237 local governments, an increase of over 3,300 in ten years. State by state totals of local authorities range from 18 in Hawaii to 6,627 in Illinois. There are ten states with more than three thousand local governments each. The basic units are as follows:

Table 8.1: Types and Numbers of Decentralised Governments

	1977	1987
State governments	50	50
Counties	3,042	3,041
Municipalities	18,862	19,200
Towns and townships	16,822	16,691
School districts	15,174	14,721
Special districts	25,962	29,532
Totals	79,912	83,23

Source: U.S.Bureau of the Census, 1991, Table 464.

In 1986 the total populations of the 19,200 municipal governments was close to 150 million. Much the largest group by size of population was the 9,369 with under 1,000 inhabitants. These, however, provided for only 2.6 per cent of people under municipal governments. The 61 with over a quarter of a million inhabitants provided for nearly 30 per cent of the total. Townships, which in total provide for over 52 million people, average 3,120 inhabitants. More than half (9,143) have under one thousand inhabitants, but four have over 250,000. Half the total population belong to those with between five and fifty thousand inhabitants (ibid., Table 488).

The most rapid growth between 1977 and 1987 was in special districts (excluding school districts). They rose in number from 25,962 to 29,532. Nearly all of these are for single or dual purposes (most commonly water and sewerage). In most cases they are not coterminous with other administrative areas. Most lack full-time employees.

Counties

County governments cover nearly all the area of the United States. In 1986 their total population was over 227 million. One hundred and sixty-seven had populations of over a quarter of a million, 52 per cent of the total for all counties. At the other extreme 698 had populations of under ten thousand, under 2 per cent of the total population. Nearly six hundred counties have 100,000 inhabitants or above. In 1987, 167 of these had populations of over 250,000 and 2,644 of under 50,000.

Counties are found in every state except Connecticut, Rhode Island and Alaska. Lousiana's parishes and Alaska's districts are similar. In 'unincorporated' areas counties are the only form of government between the individual and the state. They were originally state sub-divisions established for judicial, military and fiscal purposes, but moved increasingly into the role of local service providers. They are more creatures of the state than are the municipalities, lacking a base in a particular community and liable to be abolished or have their powers changed by the state legislature. Their activities and importance grew as they acquired new tasks, often transferred from municipalities seeking the advantages of larger-scale organisation. Typical new functions are planning, recreational services and libraries.

Two-thirds of 'standard metropolitan areas' are located within single counties, although their areas do not in most cases provide a good basis for integrated metropolitan government since they also cover wide rural tracts and the main built-up areas are rarely located at the centre of their territories. In other cases the metropolitan area stretches across several counties. Hybrid forms of government have been developed to meet particular administrative problems, in particular city-counties and areas with county offices and 'governments organised on a regional basis', some of which are classified as 'county type areas'. (Florestano and Marando, 1981).

Towns and Townships

Towns and townships are sub-divisions of counties whose boundaries were originally marked out on the map by county surveyors for road building and maintenance. They now often provide library, sewage treatment and disposal, landfill and water-supply services. In New England they are municipal corporations; in the Midwest special districts. Originating mainly in the East they have assumed major responsibilities, developing 'city-type' services to meet inhabitants' demands which in some cases include fire and police, recreation and social services. (Ibid., 1981).

Municipalities

Municipalities are mostly communities incorporated by charter at the request of their members. Areas with sufficient population and density may be allowed municipal status in accordance with a procedure which usually involves voter choice. If small they may be called villages or towns. In some western states they may possess the title of 'borough'. The larger ones are usually termed cities. National attention and much of relevant academic work on local government matters centres on the cities.

Special Districts

Special-purpose districts are set up to provide one or two services — sometimes by state law, sometimes by other local governments, and sometimes as a result of private petitions and meetings leading to approval by an authorised body (frequently a court). In addition to those for schools there are districts for fire protection, conservation of natural resources, parks and recreation, water, sewerage, drainage, irrigation, libraries, school buildings, mosquito abatement, housing, community development, ports and other purposes.

In most cases the members of boards are elected officials chosen by authorities involved in setting them up from among their councillors, or are appointed as representatives of interest groups. They may be directly elected, especially in the West and Midwest, and likely to possess powers to set and levy taxes. They have been established to protect or foster an activity, to deal with problems that cross the boundaries of multi-functional authorities and to hive off activities that are considered to be able to support themselves from fees and charges. California and Illinois each have over 2,700 of them. It has been said that their popularity lies in their ability to raise money for services while at the same time 'maintaining low political and financial visibility'. They can be used to escape state restrictions on counties and municipalities through their own tax and borrowing powers. Normally counties undertake to collect their taxes for them. Highways, school building and national resources management are leading functions. They have also been used increasingly for health service delivery in recent years (see also §8.13). (Harrigan, 1985).

School districts administer nearly one in ten of the 17,000 school systems in the United States. They are a world of their own with an enormous total expenditure.

Two criticisms of special districts are that they have been an unsatis-factory substitute for the consolidation of small authorities into effective general-purpose municipalities, and that they are not in most cases accountable to an electorate (Harrigan, 1985; Florestano and Marando, 1981).

Comparisons of Structure and Performance

There is a large literature which attempts to relate forms of structure to levels of efficiency by comparing groups of local authorities within the United States. Degrees of 'horizontal integration' are compared, chiefly differences in population size or 'fragmentation' of service providers against integration of services at the same level of authority; and also 'vertical integration', especially single-tier against multi-tier systems. In general no convincing measures have been identified for gauging comparative quality of output against costs, or able to cope with the complexity of cultural, geographical and other factors. One survey of the literature concludes that 'empirical evidence from the USA suggests that local government systems which are fragmented and deconcentrated are generally associated with lower spending and greater efficiency' (Boyne, 1992). This inevitably omits consideration of wider factors of service impact, differences among types of service and 'before reform and after' analysis for which Europe is a much richer source.

8.5 INTER-AUTHORITY RELATIONS AND ORGANISATION

Collaboration and Joint Bodies

An American term for joint voluntary arrangements between local authorities is 'volunteerism'. One form, the COG, is described in §8.13. Inter-authority collaboration has been hedged around with state conditions but in general these have been liberalised during the last two decades.

A survey in 1983 showed that transfers of services between authorities required referendum approval in eleven states, a provision which damped down initiatives of this kind (ACIR, 1985). The same survey showed that among 2,039 cities and counties that replied out of 3,419 the most frequent services being contracted out by one authority to another were 'jails and detention homes' (227), sewage disposal (267), animal control (218), tax assessment (210), waste disposal (209), water supply (201), police and fire communications (186), fire services (159), processing of draft laws (157) and sanitary inspection (150). The commonest services delivered to cities under inter-governmental contracts out of a total of 3,419 contracts were public works and utilities (955), public safety and correction (805), health and welfare (785), general government and finance (492), transportation (170), education and culture (119) and parks and recreation (93). Among 909 contracts by the counties public safety and health and welfare services were the commonest subjects. Contracting tends to be lacking in fields of social welfare such as housing and action against poverty and unemployment.

Relationships are contracted on a pragmatic basis and success is evaluated by subsequent costs and benefits. Formal and informal joint arrangements often aim at improving or economising on the cost of services. They may be made between municipalities, between counties and municipalities, between central cities and suburban authorities and in some cases between states, local authorities and special districts. A survey in the 1970s showed that 61 per cent out of 2,248 municipalities had entered into such agreements, usually to achieve economies of scale. They are employed especially for sewage and refuse collection and disposal, police radio facilities and standby assistance in the case of special police and fire problems. Core cities sell water to suburban municipalities or direct to suburban residents. There are informal agreements regarding traffic flow arrangements (Adrian and Press, 1977). True joint organisations are few except for water, sewage and mass transit services.

The county is the most frequent provider of services to other levels. One well-publicised approach to combining small-scale local government with the benefits of large-scale provision is named after the municipality of Lakewood in Los Angeles County. Los Angeles County has provided contract services to municipalities since 1907 (Zimmerman, 1979). The Lakewood Plan provides for municipalities to purchase packages of services from the County. More than sixteen hundred agreements have been signed with 77 municipalities for more than 58 kinds of service to be supplied by the County. The Plan guarantees the autonomy of suburban authorities and gives them the freedom to choose between buying in a service, carrying it out themselves, entering into a joint scheme with another municipality or purchasing the service from the private sector.

The availability of the Plan has been an inducement to incorporation of new local authorities because it gives them the benefits of autonomy, tax advantages, improved information and collaboration with county departments, together with the established quality of county services (Harrigan, 1985). One advantage claimed for the approach is uniformity of provision, but non-contracting authorities argue that they prefer better services than those supplied as 'standard', and the facility to adapt services to special local circumstances.

Other types of competitive activity have been examined by the ACIR without leading to any adverse judgements (ACIR, 1987). Competition between states and local authorities can result in '"bidding wars" for job-producing facilities' and competition for business through negotiated tax packages, services and regulation. It was found that these did not necessarily depress service levels and could reduce reliance on 'ability-to-pay' taxes. (Reeves, 1992)

Local Authority Associations

The associations which together represent state and local government interests in Washington exercise formidable lobbying power. The local government associations are principally the National League of Cities (1301 Pennsylvania Avenue, NW, Washington, DC20004), the National Association of Counties (1753 New York Avenue, NW, Washington, DC20006), the National Association of Towns and Townships (1527 18th Street, NW, Washington, DC20036), the National Association of Regional Councils (1700 K Street, NW, Washington, DC20006, the Conference of Mayors (1620 Eye Street, NW, Washington, DC20006, the International City Management Association (1120 G Street, NW, Washington, DC20005). They work with the National Legislative Conference, the Council of State Governments and the National Governors' Conference in the development and representation of nation-wide policies.

8.6 INTER-GOVERNMENTAL RELATIONS

Inter-governmental relations in the United States are more a tangled web than a layered structure. They can be understood only in terms of untidy fragmentation of authority, competitive relationships and bargaining processes between interests. According to a member of the ACIR, the relationship between 'the federal government and the states moved from cooperation to coercion' during the 1980s (Reeves, 1992).

State legislation defines boundaries, forms of government and administrative structure, local election arrangements, ethical standards, provision of services to people beyond an authority's own jurisdiction (due, for example, to overspill effects in education provision and environmental matters), land use, modes of taxation, tax assessment, indebtedness, personnel regulations such as salaries and wages, pensions, housing, personnel standards and working conditions. There are wide variations between states in the discretion they permit in these matters. States may inspect local authority activities, require approval for projects, appoint local officials and substitute administrators. Some powers are hardly ever used, such as those for the removal of officials, approval and review of programmes, withdrawal of grants and substituting administration by the National Guard in the case of civil order crises.

State constitutions often require the full valuation of property, grant property tax exemptions, set tax, deficit and debt limits and restrict gifts and loans of money or property by municipalities to individuals or corporations, associations or undertakings.

It is the 'lids on taxes' which were imposed by 35 states in 1977, together with limits on spending, that have caused most concern (ACIR, 1978). State mandates along with court decisions protecting local conditions of service for employees have been central to local budgetary problems. The ACIR asserted its belief that 'permanent lids' were justified only if a state was willing to compensate by conferring new taxing ability or by a substantial revenue-sharing programme. They stressed the value of fiscal impact statements on bills: 'What is required is Marquis of Queensberry Rules' to govern state-local fiscal relations, 'thereby ensuring that neither side hits the other below the belt' (ACIR, 1978).

Since the success of the California Proposition 13 limiting property taxation in 1978, citizen initiatives have also set limits on levels of property taxes (the principal source of locally-raised revenue) and on general expenditure, forcing states to assume greater responsibility for the finance of local services. Successful initiatives in some states which limited state or both state and local spending have moreover restricted the ability of state governments to compensate for loss of federal finance.

A review of state limitations on local fiscal autonomy in 1985 concluded that the states continued to 'play a crucial role in the well-being of their local governments', bear 'a significant proportion of the cost of local operations' and assist in management, co-ordination and supervision of local administration of programmes, to a major degree ensuring good government (Florestano, 1985). It quotes another source: 'The states, after all, are the chief architects, by conscious or unconscious action or inaction, of the welter of servicing, financial and institutional arrangements that form the sub-state governance of this nation' (Walker and Walker, 1975).

The federal level has limited powers to interfere at state or local levels on grounds of national economic interest. State and local capital expenditure and borrowing are seen as separate from federal expenditure. 'The structure of the American market... helps American sub-national governments to retain substantial policy discretion... and makes it relatively difficult for the Treasury to take such control out of local hands' (Sbragia, 1985, quoted in Lee, 1985). One consequence is that American local authorities are able to issue tax-exempt bonds to finance low-interest loans in order to attract new firms, and thereby to create local jobs in a recession.

Nevertheless the old model of 'dual federalism' has been replaced by increasingly mixed responsibilities — the 'marble cake' pattern as it has been called. Federal grants for specific services have a major impact on local government and are alleged to 'distort' local budgets by 'stick-and-carrot' subsidy and regulation. They began in the 1930s with programmes which propelled local authorities into the areas of welfare housing, and were subsequently used as instruments for the implementation of urban renewal, health, education and economic development policies. By the 1980s hardly any service sector remained the exclusive province of a single level. Grants became the focus of bargaining processes over the provision and conditions of finance.

Reagan's 'new federalism' aimed to transfer responsibility for a large number of grant programmes from Washington to the states. The states blocked it because of its financial implications. Less restrictive forms of grant-aid were introduced. Three main types under the 'new federal policy' were entitlement programmes, such as welfare and food stamps administered by states and local authorities; 'operating programmes' comprising grants to states and local government for education, public health and other social services, largely replacing block grants; and capital programmes of aid for highways and other public facilities.

The new policies increased state power, gave more discretion on spending, added a new job-training role at state level, reduced regulations and federal oversight and cut out specific funding for local projects. But they also involved increased mandates on states without commensurate funding. Washington had the power to trap local politicians more deeply by requiring higher standards and then cutting finance. Labour laws and state restrictions mean that however much they can find through improving efficiency they are likely to be left with the inability to meet essential standards while maintaining what may be regarded as a minimum degree of equity. Unfunded mandates passed by states to local authorities caused 'widespread insolvency and distress' in authorities of all sizes (a Pennsylvania report quoted in Cahill and James, 1992). Reports of the federal General Accounting Office give evidence that traditional services were 'declining in quality or disappearing altogether, and that there was 'deferral or abandonment of critical capital investments' including 'street resurfacing, water and sewer lines, bridges and municipally-funded buildings including jails and senior citizens centres'. High tax demands were found to be accompanied by decaying standards up to a level where they were causing a significant exodus of residents and businesses from municipalities.

Many states have fiscal stress laws which seek to provide the means to avert financial crises. Commonly these provide for the appointment of a commissioner or special board to help steer a municipality out of insolvency. They cannot, however, take over an authority's powers.

The ideas and practice of 'the new federalism' contained contradictions between the aim of enhancing local autonomy and assisting local governments with local initiatives. In the view of many politicians, policies directed towards national equity demand both local autonomy and federal and state aids. Others argue that attempting to combine aids with local autonomy removes any prospect of making the system 'more functional, more accountable and more comprehensible' (Walker, 1983).

8.7 LOCAL SERVICES

Local authorities are responsible for all public fire services, three-quarters of expenditure on policing and two-thirds of that on education. They also spend heavily on sanitation, parks and recreation, airports, parking control and libraries. States spend more than local authorities on highways, hospitals and health. The local government workforce for housing and urban renewal work at the end of the 1980s was four times larger than that of the states. Arrangements vary a great deal at state level, and in more than ten cases there is no dominant provider of highways, health and hospital, police, sewerage, parks and library services.

In 1988-89 local government employed in all well over twice the number of employees as the states: some 10.2 million as against the states' 4.2 million. By comparison the number of civilian employees in federal government was 3.1 million (US Bureau of the Census, 1991, Table 497).

By far the biggest employers in local government are the school districts, with 8.3 million employees. They are followed by municipalities with 5 million, the counties with 3.6 million, non-education special districts with one million and the townships with 5.6 million.

The counties have increased their role since the 1960s, particularly in preventive medicine, fire protection, social services and vocational training. In 1988 health and hospitals was the most expensive liability in the counties, taking up 16 per cent of spending as against 8.4 per cent in the cities. This was followed by education and public welfare at 14.5 and 14.3 per cent in the counties, as against 4.6 per cent in the cities. Highways was also proportionately a more expensive commitment for the counties at 8 per cent against the cities' 6.2 per cent.

The balance is tilted against the cities on these heads partly because of the role of special districts in metropolitan areas. Electricity supply and policing lead the list of city services at 9.2 and 9.0 per cent of expenditure, county spending here being nil and 5.3 per cent of budgets respectively. Sewerage and sanitation also stand high in the cities at 8.5 per cent. There follow gas supply (5.7 per cent), fire protection (4.7 per cent), housing and community development (3.8 per cent), parks and recreation (3.7 per cent against the counties' 1.9) and transit systems (2.4 per cent). The only other individual city service large enough to appear in the national statistics is airports (1.4 per cent). The heavy county expenditures on works and police are mainly explained by responsibilities in suburbs which have not been incorporated into city government. (US Bureau of the Census, 1991, Table 472)

1. Town and Country Planning and Development
Municipalities undertake planning through commissions, commonly of five to seven part-time members who may include designated public officials, unpaid citizens or both. Major work may be contracted out to firms, often using standard pattern plans, or to local consultants. Large cities, however, have substantial planning departments (Adrian and Press, 1977).

2. Housing and Urban Renewal
Most municipalities have not traditionally seen housing as a routine function of local government, 'certainly not in social service terms' (Wolman, 1975). In the 1970s federal incentives were used to encourage them to meet social housing needs. Special housing authorities are commonly set up by city or county councils who issue bonds backed by a federal guarantee to finance construction.

3. Highways and Other Roads
All levels of government are involved, including special districts. Work may be contracted out to the private sector, often under agreements for 20 or 30-year periods to cover long development programmes. Groups of many local councils, boards and commissions may be involved in expressway projects together with state and federal engineers.

4. Transport
Larger cities operate transport undertakings directly or through public mass transit authorities. All subways and remaining tramways and trolley lines are under public ownership for legal reasons. Fewer than 3 per cent of

municipalities operate other forms of transport. Subsidies to private bus services are normally essential, but cities have often taken over when operators have abandoned tramlines as uneconomic — sometimes assisted by the negotiation of a federal grant for vehicle purchase. The prevalence of flat rate fares makes subsidies essential.

5-6. Education and Training

Each state has an education department responsible for enforcing state statutes. They delegate responsibilities to local *school districts*. Most districts operate autonomously under elected school boards. A state board provides outlines of courses and lists of textbooks, which are used by local boards to work out their curricula. State and local inspection has been replaced by advisory services. School boards may have the power to precept on the city or county government for their revenue. Most school districts are small. In some cases intermediate units exist between state and district levels. New York and seven other large cities are exceptional in running their own education services under appointed boards.

Local governments administer community colleges which provide further education, including vocational courses. *Counties* have moved into the provision of vocational training.

Higher Education is provided predominantly by state governments. Private colleges provide for a fifth of students, commonly assisted by state grants. Local government employs a little under one-fifth of staff and other employees in this sector. Universities and higher education colleges are normally run by boards of governors.

7. Cultural Activities are provided by local governments ad hoc and sporadically. Individual music and arts activities are supported. Art Commissions are appointed in the big cities.

8. Libraries and Museums are commonly financed by local authorities and administered by appointed trustees. There are also *special districts* for library services. *Cities* run a large proportion of American museums.

9. Recreation

Parks are administered by *cities* and *counties*. Most large cities have recreation departments which administer swimming pools, golf courses and other sports amenities. There are also *special district authorities* for parks and recreation.

10. Health and Social Welfare

In most areas *counties* play a larger role than *municipalities* in health and welfare activities, including public assistance. Health services are also provided through *special district authorities*. *City health departments* are concerned mostly with preventive health e.g. inspection of restaurants and vector control. Most municipalities appoint boards of health but often only in an advisory capacity, services being controlled by a medically qualified head reporting to the chief executive.

Major public welfare functions are now mainly financed by states and counties, but some cities play a supplementary role.

11. Police

Most policing is under the jurisdiction of the *cities* or the *counties*. Police forces are commonly under a city chief police officer or a lay head reporting to the chief executive, the custom previously having been control by semi-autonomous boards.

12. Fire Protection

Most *city* fire departments now come under city chief executives although traditionally appointment has been by a council or fire board. *Counties* or *special districts* supply the service in rural and suburban areas.

13. Development of Local Economy and Employment

Local economies have often been promoted vigorously by *cities* through tax abatement, seed money, land acquisition, development and leaseback arrangements.

14. Public Utilities

Local governments, including special districts, possess important regulatory powers relating to 'natural monopoly' utilities. Around 15 per cent of municipal revenues may be derived from them. The fields are chiefly water supply, gas, electricity, sewage disposal, drainage and airports. These services may be provided directly by a municipal government, by a special district, or, most commonly, by a private company operating under state regulation (an 'investor-owned utility'). Provision of utilities may be made under municipal licence with a flat charge or percentage of profit returned to the municipality. In some cases cities have separate utility bodies for administration with some autonomy and fiscal independence, e.g. water commissioners and airport authorities.

15. Markets are sometimes placed under a commissioner.

16. Cemeteries and Crematoria are often a municipal function. They may be run by a semi-autonomous cemetery commission.

17. Other Services

Correctional Services are in general a county responsibility, although there are city jails, often within police departments.

Pollution Control is effected by various means. New York City has a board and a commissioner of air pollution control with powers of regulation and ability to compel witnesses.

Conservation and Control of Natural Resources is commonly undertaken by *special districts*, of which there are some six and a half thousand, two-thirds of them for soil conservation.

8.8 IMPLEMENTATION OF SERVICES

The search for and experimentation with new modes of policy implementation consonant with local values has been described and analysed elsewhere (see, for example, Clark and Ferguson, 1983). Clark and Ferguson's classification of innovations in response to financial stress contains nothing unfamiliar to Western European local government, including adjusting user charges, privatisation, contracting out, use of volunteers, adjustments between employment of labour and of capital, and promotion of income-earning services. Joint agreements between authorities are described in §8.5, particularly the Lakewood Plan. Contracting out and joint agreements are by far the commonest alternatives to direct provision.

Service provision by authorities' own employees is most usual where resources allow. The extent of direct supervision by elected members varies widely according to personalities and management plans, as indicated in §8.11. The position of professional heads of department is often strong, although it can be insecure where contracts of employment are short term or dismissals are a common part of the local culture.

The normal fields of contracting-out are refuse collection and disposal, street lighting and electricity supply, engineering, legal and ambulance services, animal control, computer services and equipment maintenance. Some contracting out initiatives have been more controversial, such as fire protection and running hospitals and jails. The administration of 15 of California's 39 county hospitals was contracted out between 1973 and 1980, but a study found no significant overall cost savings or quality changes, although there were gains in revenues through better accounting and billing systems and better handling of state and federal reimbursements. In many cases contracts have been for delivery to sub-areas, sometimes pitting direct provision against contractors, and the results have by no means been all one way. (Hatry, 1983; Morgan, 1985)

The use of commissions or commissioners for particular services is common practice (see §8.7), as are joint public/private arrangements under which urban governments undertake land assembly, road works and other infrastructure provision, issue of permits and possibly financing, while private firms handle marketing risks and contribute to the construction of infrastructure and environmental amenities. The trend has been encouraged by federal funding programmes and special bond schemes supported indirectly through the tax system (OECD, 1984).

8.9 LOCAL GOVERNMENT FINANCE

As indicated in §§8.1, 8.6 and elsewhere in this chapter, financial pressures are a central preoccupation — most of all in the great cities. Greater expectations, inflationary pressure, external influences out of local control and the draining away of internal and external resources. This section is chiefly concerned with the elements of the local government system rather than the wide state or national position.

Table 8.2: Sources of Local Government Revenue, 1988

	%
Revenue from own sources	67.1
Charges, fees and misc. revenue	20.1
Property taxes	25.7
Utility revenues	9.3
Other	12.0
Inter-governmental transfers	32.9
	100.0

Source: US Bureau of the Census, 1991, Table 466

Local Taxes

Property tax is the most important local tax. It originated as a state tax and has been gradually transferred to local authorities. There have been pressures to make it entirely a local government tax on the grounds that it is best administered at local level. In 1988 it formed 74.1 per cent of all local tax income as against 9.3 per cent of that of the states (US Bureau of the Census, 1991, Table 466).

It was introduced as a state tax around 1830 when the tax base consisted in principle of the value of all citizen's property taxed as a percentage of its market value. It varies from state to state but usually takes two forms: real property tax levied on the assessed value of taxable land and improvements thereon, and personal property tax levied on the assessed value of (1) taxable personal property such as furniture, business inventories, equipment, vehicles and animals, and (2) personal property such as money, stocks and shares and other non-tangible properties. In city areas about half the yield goes to education authorities and in rural areas as much as 80 per cent.

Assessment is usually carried out at local government level as most simple and effective, but there can be overlaps between assessments by different local authorities. In 1989 the effective rate ranged in 51 large cities from 0.53 per hundred dollars of the asessment (Charleston) to 4.4 per cent (Detroit) (ibid., Table 495).

Personal property tax has been much criticised as difficult for assessors to identify and assess equitably. Evasion is extensive. In practice little is taxed other than land, buildings and vehicles. Its contribution to total property tax yields fell from 13.4 per cent in 1973 to 10.2 per cent in 1981 (Aronson and Hilley, 1986).

The use of automatic indexing of property values is the main reason for the high elasticity of this tax in the United States. Thereby assessments go up annually instead of the tariffs. Exceptions have been made to reduce the impact on elderly home owners and also to allow for the special case of the wholesaling and distributive trades. In defence of the tax at least four American textbooks quote the adage 'an old tax is a good tax'; one refers to Danegeld and the Doomsday Book! It is defended as a reasonably progressive tax compared with alternatives (Maxwell and Aronson, 1977). Its yield, however, fell from 43 per cent of state and local taxes in 1967 to 34 per cent in 1978, and again to 30 per cent in 1988 (see also Lindholm and Wignjowijoto, 1979).

A *local sales tax* is the second most important local tax. It is generally levied on retail sales, but in Hawaii, Louisiana and Mississippi also on wholesale transactions. It is available to local governments in ten states, sometimes only for cities. In California it has been set at 0.5 to 1 per cent and in New York at 1 to 3 per cent. Food and other necessities are usually exempt, giving it a fairly neutral impact. Public utility sales are also often exempt but subject to other forms of taxation. (Ibid; Aronson and Hilley, 1986).

Local income tax can be levied by local authorities in some thirteen states. Levels of federal and state income taxes have discouraged its use as an additional deduction on payrolls because of the growth of other charges and the effects of inflation. There is no deduction of personal allowances. It is in general simply a percentage of earnings, although in some cases investment income is included.

Local business taxes are of three types: (1) taxes on franchises of public utilities, justified by the monopoly privileges which such franchises confer and costs to the community as a whole resulting from business operations; (2) fees and other payments to meet the costs of regulatory activities and to enforce 'the polluter pays' principle; and (3) taxes applied selectively to commercial activities where the return is significant in relation to administrative costs.

Criteria laid down by the courts are that differentiation between businesses must be reasonable and not confiscatory. Businesses may be taxed either according to place of production or place of consumption of the products. Wages, properties and sales may be taken into account in the tax base. (Lindholm and Wignjowijoto, 1979)

The most rapid increase in sources of revenue in the last two decades has been in uptake from *fees and charges*. They rose by an average of 11.4 per cent a year between 1977 and 1983. This has 'substituted for rather than augmented local taxes'. Unlike local taxes these are not deductible from federal tax liabilities. Moreover they are claimed to be not only more regressive in terms of equity but to result in less favour being given to tax funding of services to meet the needs of the poor. (Aronson and Hilley, 1986)

There has been a trend among states towards setting specific limits on the revenue that may be raised on a tax base by each public authority. However in many cases some expenditure categories have been excluded and referenda results have allowed local government expenditures above state limitations (see also §8.6 on 'tax-lids').

Grants-in-Aid

The history of federal and state grants-in-aid, including their relative ups and downs as a proportion of local revenues, is touched on in §8.6. Total aid as a proportion of state and local government revenue fell from 18.4 to 13.3 per cent from 1980 to 1988. In the same period federal aid to counties fell from 9.1 per cent to 2.5 per cent of revenue. That to cities fell from 13 per cent to 5.9 per cent. Transfers from states to counties fell relatively slightly from 34.8 per cent to 32.5 per cent of revenues in the same period and from states to cities from 16.6 to 15.9 per cent. The main cuts were in the early 1980s, the states compensating for these to some extent in later years. Local finance has become very much a 'game' between the three levels of government.

There have been many *specific categorical and project grants* from the federal level. Conditions are imposed such as matching funds, use of technically qualified staff, output standards and strict specification on use. But some state grants are simply for the general support of local administration. States use conditions to influence spending in directions they consider desirable.

Borrowing

Interest paid by counties on general debt rose from 2.8 per cent of expenditure in 1980 to 6.8 per cent in 1988. The rise in interest payments by city governments rose from 4.5 to 7.03 per cent (US Bureau of the Census, 1991, Tables 489 and 490). Borrowing is often heavy, not infrequently because a local authority wishes to spend beyond the maximum taxing levels allowed by the state in addition to financing specific capital projects. A variety of bond types are issued, particularly general obligation bonds against future tax revenue, mortgage bonds against utilities which serve as securities, and revenue bonds secured by a pledge of revenue from a self-liquidating project such as a toll bridge or new electric power system.

8.10 ELECTORAL REPRESENTATION

The Supreme Court has defined voting as a fundamental right and left little ground for disqualification other than for criminal conviction or mental deficiency. The Twenty-Sixth Amendment fixed the voting age at eighteen.

The United States differs sharply from Europe or Japan in the weakness and in many areas the virtual non-existence of party politics in local government. In fact in nearly three-quarters of cities with more than 2,500 inhabitants political parties are not allowed to run candidates. Only in the Middle Atlantic region (New York, New Jersey and Pennsylvania), where ethnic groups have party traditions, does a majority of cities hold elections structured on the party system. This situation resulted from attacks on corrupt party machines after 1900. It may in part at least account for the low turn-outs in elections in view of a study in the 1970s which found that turn-out was higher in partisan elections (34 per cent) than in non-partisan (25 per cent) (Karnig, 1977 quoted in Gunlicks, 1991).

Failing party organisation, the recruitment of candidates depends mostly on the individual ambitions, personal resources and often persuasion to stand by friends, neighbours and sectoral interests. A would-be elective official announces his intention to run by means of a press advertisement or a circular letter. He or she must have his or her qualifications guaranteed by a number of voters and pay a filing fee.

Primary elections may be partisan or non-partisan. Partisan primaries are restricted to candidates and voters registered as favouring one party or another. Candidates gaining majorities in a non-partisan primary are usually declared winners without need for further election. Normally the two candidates with the highest votes in the primary go forward for the general election. Primary election systems vary in their provisions, for example some require a run-off election if no candidate wins an absolute majority of the votes.

Elections may be in wards or districts (13 per cent of cities), city-wide or 'at large' (60 per cent) or a mixture (27 per cent). Wards are often dominated by one party. They enable specific local interests to be represented. It is argued that if boundaries are fair, single-member districts should help minority groups to win a place for at least one representative on a city council. They may also provide at least one member who may be expected to represent citizens on small matters of detail such as are of special importance to small neighbourhoods. In counties they provide for the representation of the remoter rural areas. In urban areas where party organisation is strong they encourage the formation of small-party grass-roots clubs. They allow for short ballot papers and avoid the situation in an eastern state where ballot papers overwhelm the voter with choices among candidates for seventy or more different posts every four years.

At-large elections were used in the early part of this century to break the party machines that controlled cities by means of patronage. They eliminate the opportunities for gerrymandering boundaries which single wards provide. They encourage councillors to take into consideration the interests of the whole city and make decisions with longer-term views in mind. They favour candidates well known through the media or who have the resources to run expensive campaigns. On the other hand the result can give power to a narrow, privileged and unrepresentative elite which lacks understanding of problems of local minorities. In counties at-large elections often foster political machines — the opposite from their usual effect in the cities. The at-large system has been disqualified as discriminatory by the Supreme Court in recent years in cases brought by black citizens in the South. This has led to the introduction of a ward system (Lee, 1985). This, together with court decisions against gerrymandering boundaries, such as in Chicago in 1986 where wards had been defined to minimise the chances for black candidates within the Democratic Party, has resulted in fairer representation.

Councillors may be nominated by districts and elected at large, ensuring local representation and wide support. Candidates may contest a specific numbered seat unattached to a sub-area against others who choose to run for the same seat (the 'place system'). Under another modification ('cumulative voting') each voter may be given a number of votes to cast equal to the number of representatives to be elected, which he or she can cast for one candidate or divide among candidates. In counties, votes in council by councillors representing county districts may be given weightings according to the number of inhabitants of their districts. Voters may be given fewer votes than the number of seats on the list: say two-thirds of the number of council seats, thereby ensuring control by the majority party but enabling minorities to win seats. A council may be made up of both ward representatives and at-large representatives.

Proportional representation is known to have been in use in recent decades only in Cambridge, Massachusetts and for New York City's community school board elections. (Boyd, 1976; Zimmerman, 1983b).

Periods of office may be staggered so that they overlap and prevent a change of all office-holders at one time. Voting is almost everywhere by the 'first-past-the-post' rule but sometimes a second, 'run-off' election is stipulated wherever no candidate wins more than half the votes.

The Chicago decision of 1968 referred to above has led to strict application of the 'one man, one vote' principle with regard to warding: that is, wards in a full electoral area have to be equal in terms of numbers of electors. This does not of course prevent gerrymandering under which boundary drawing can be used to ensure representation of a minority or to cut through neighbourhoods to ruin a minority's chances of a seat.

Where candidates are elected by wards, city mayors are voted for at-large. Thus as mayoral executives they can claim against the councillors that they represent the whole, whereas councillors represent only parts of the city.

Turn-outs are small and ballot papers long. Candidates often win at the end of the course with only a small number of votes.

Many cities are dominated by one party, so that party affiliation tends to be essential for success. On the other hand parties are very fragmented and differences within and between them are not generally stated in partisan terms. Democrats tend to be strong in central cities, so that President Carter's inner-city programmes can be said to have favoured citadels of Democratic Party strength while President Reagan's favouring of the state level can be seen as opening up options to Republican strongholds. Nevertheless, within a given area the political party factor tends not to be a major influence in city-suburban relationships. With the 'one man, one vote' principle in operation the big cities have a fair representation at state levels.

One virtue of the decentralised politics of the United States is that it provides great opportunities for the reflection of local interests and needs rather than merely serving as a barometer of local feelings about national party performance (Lee, 1985).

8.11 THE INTERNAL ORGANISATION OF LOCAL AUTHORITIES

Changes in values and increases in the scale and variety of services have led to waves of innovation in administrative structures. A system characterised by 'the involvement of everybody' in the election of officials was changed due to the felt need for a strong unitary executive, typically in the shape of the 'strong mayor'. This was followed from the 1870s by a drive for morality in government as well as for the business values of efficiency, effectiveness and economy. The quality of non-partisan 'neutral competence' was sought in the professionalisation of management and a new decentralisation among specialised units resulting in a proliferation of special-purpose boards. These tendencies continue to reappear and inspire changes in administrative structure in the name of different and often opposed values.

County Government

Nearly 80 per cent among the over three thousand counties and similar bodies which form the basic administrative divisions of states follow the traditional *board* or *commission* pattern, which in eight states in the late 1970s was the only type allowed. This provides for elected boards which have ranged in size from two to over a hundred members. They have legislative power and take responsibility for the budget, administrative and supervisory powers over some departments and powers of appointment for some administrative staff. They may share responsibility with independently elected officers such as the county clerk, auditor and recorder, assessor, treasurer, prosecuting attorney, sheriff and coroner. The form is claimed to combine the values of representativeness and neutral competence. (Duncombe, 1977)

Many different political patterns have been identified within commissions: the strong chairman whose decisions the commission rubberstamps, co-equal commissioners who reach decisions by consensus or voting, commissions made up of supervisors of the towns and townships within a county, a council whose routine business is carried out by a strong supporting official (typically a county clerk who may be directly elected or appointed by the commissioners), and commissions chaired by an elected judge who undertakes administrative responsibilities for the commission (Garnett, 1985).

County agencies for welfare, hospitals, public health, highways etc. have developed large bureaucracies and become powerful representatives of professional interests. Smaller agencies for tax assessment, licensing etc. have often become instruments of patronage.

In recent years forms with elected or appointed chief executives have increasingly been adopted, particularly in the larger counties. Their number rose from eight in 1950 to around 150 in the late 1970s.

Under the *county-manager plan*, a form dating from 1927, a board appoints a manager with 'neutral competence' to serve at its pleasure. The manager prepares the budget, appoints heads of department, is responsible for presenting programmes and policy proposals and generally runs the administration, referring only the budget and other key decisions to commissioners (Kaufman, 1963). This form has served counties of up to 1.7 million inhabitants, the largest in the mid-1980s being Dade County, Florida. *County-administrator plans* are much more common. These are similar except that the administrator lacks competence to appoint and supervise heads of department.

In the *council-elected executive model* a county executive is elected in addition to the council. He or she presides over the executive branch in a scaled-down model of a state government. County executives are usually given the power to veto council bills subject to veto powers by a council majority of two-thirds. The form is favoured by some large counties in the East.

Forms without a single executive predominate in counties with under 100,000 population. Over that figure the single executive form is most usual, rising in popularity in proportion to size of county. In the late 1970s about a quarter of the counties with over one million population had no single administrator.

Municipal Government

The universal pattern of elected council (or board as it is often termed) and chairman or mayor takes a number of forms which differ according to nature and strength of the executive and its implications for the role of the council. City councils are small, with an average membership of around six. Numbers rise with populations, but the average is no more than nine for cities of 200 to 500 thousand inhabitants. For cities over that size the average is fifteen.

Five main types of executive may be distinguished. Three are described as *mayor-council plans*: 'strong mayor', 'strong mayor with chief administrative or chief executive officer' and 'weak mayor' forms. Local variations blur their distinctness to some extent. They are used by over 41 per cent of municipalities with over 2,500 inhabitants and nearly 60 per cent of those with over 250,000 (Municipal Year Book, 1988).

The *strong mayor-council plan* concentrates the executive role in the office of directly elected mayor, strongly reflecting the separation of powers principle that was basic to the national constitution. The mayor appoints and dismisses department heads, proposes budget and policy measures and implements decisions. The council is confined to legislative policy-making. Terms of office are usually four years in order to give members time to prove their effectiveness. The council is a watchdog, empowered to make investigations into departments and other aspects of administration. There are many variations on this plan. Its case rests on the belief that in a complex organisation, the parts of which are frequently at cross-purposes and subject to deviations, there is a need to give responsibility to a strong directly accountable politician. Strong mayors are generally paid a 'decent' salary but not a high one by business standards.

The *strong mayor-council with chief administrative or chief executive officer plan* is the second type. Here the mayor is supported by a powerful chief officer, often termed the controller, who may have wide supervisory powers over heads of department, budget preparation and personnel direction. He or she may be called Chief Administrative Officer (CAO) or Deputy Mayor of Operations. This was first instituted in San Francisco in 1931 and evolved into a distinct system with powers divided between the city council or board, the mayor as chief executive officer and a CAO responsible for some departments and not others (Reed, 1985). The CAO may be appointed and serve at the pleasure of either the mayor or the council. A main criticism is the likelihood of conflict between CAO and mayor.

The *weak-mayor* form, in which several principal city officer posts are normally filled by direct election, predominates in cities with under 25,000 inhabitants. At elections voters may choose members of a number of boards and possibly their clerk, treasurer, assessor, controller and attorney. The mayor lacks administrative power and has little control over staff. The plan was originally introduced to overcome corruption and inefficiency. Councillors tend to take a more active role in administration and management and in policy-making than in other types of mayor plan (Svara, 1990). Paradoxically it led to machine politics and autocratic control in some cases, such as in Chicago as exercised by Mayor Daley of Chicago for 22 years up to 1976. The system has survived mainly in some large southern cities and in smaller cities and villages.

One analysis of council-mayor forms in cities with populations ranging from 163 to 616 thousand inhabitants, half of them below 200,000, finds that an executive mayor can be expected to be the driving force in city government and has at least some formal power resources to support such a position. A 'facilitative mayor is potentially a guiding force who... helps to deliver a high level of performance'. Types of mayor have been classified, such as 'initiator' of new policies; 'broker', strong on implementation; and 'innovator', strong on both aspects of the policy process. The plan generally tends to produce a more open and conflictual pattern of decision-making than others in so far as officials have conflicting interests. This makes the system more permeable to pressures from external interests. (Ibid.)

Some models have no separation of powers. Under the *commission plan*, dating from 1900, power is given to a small directly elected board of three to seven members, one of whom chairs the council as mayor. He may be elected for office on the ballot paper or chosen by the board from among its members. Commissioners serve as the legislature and individually administer departments or functions. Use of the plan has declined since 1930. In the 1980s it was used only by some three per cent of municipalities with over 2,500 inhabitants. In some large cities a chief administrative officer is employed to help co-ordinate services (Press and Verburg, 1979).

The *council-manager plan*, a form dating from 1908, is the main alternative. An elected council of five to nine members appoints a chief administrator or manager. The manager holds his job 'at the pleasure of the council' and carries out duties as delegated by the council. Most large cities under this plan now elect their mayors directly.

The archetypal *city manager* possesses full authority over the administrative resources of a city, appoints and removes heads of departments and other key officers, makes recommendations on who should be appointed to the many bodies to which administrative responsibilities are decentralised, prepares and presents reports to the council pre-eminently including the budget, may advise on any matter, and is responsible for enforcing a city's laws and ordinances. Managers are expected to be non-partisan and to have the skills and values of a professional.

The councils they serve tend to interpret their own role as an executive one, making it desirable that there is informal agreement on respective roles and a good personal relationship between the manager and the mayor and council. In principle the councillors decide policy and the city manager generally accepts an obligation to provide policy leadership (Svara, 1990) and so needs to be in harmony with the values of the council. Managers are very weak compared with elected mayors as they have neither the legitimacy of popular election to justify their actions nor much public visibility or symbolic assets. Citizens are said to like the plan because of its clarity and emphasis on integrated management and efficiency. The form has appealed to business interests because of its business-like nature. It is found in about half of cities with over 2,500 inhabitants, mostly in the South and West. Large cases are Dallas, San Diego and San Jose, California and Rochester, New York State (Garnett, 1985). On the other hand it tends to be relatively insulated from the community. It was found in some cases that managers discourage council members from placing a dominant role on constituency service as against supporting the council's 'governance and supervisory activities' (Svara, 1990).

The pure form has not been adopted or maintained in big cities on the whole, a fact attributed to the unwillingness of some city managers to open up processes of decision-making to the public and the opinion that the theory of managerial neutrality is consonant with consensual government but not necessarily with the dialectic between interests which is the essence of the political process. Moreover the scale and complexity of great city staffs and interests are likely to be beyond the potential grasp of a single, non-political executive. In 1983 the form was used by 35 per cent of cities as against 56 per cent who used mayor-council forms, but its popularity diminishes with the size of the authority, being adopted by only sixteen per cent of cities with populations of over half a million (Reed, 1985).

Svara concludes from his survey of matched cases that city councils appear to play similar roles regardless of the systems of government, and that differences of impact between the two general types of arrangement appear to be negligible (Svara, 1990). Nevertheless, in the great cities at least the trend has been towards high-profile strong mayors, due to the declining role of political parties which favours personalities over issue and team politics, the media, and the felt need for centralised leadership to overcome conflict (Savitch and Thomas eds, 1991).

Town and Township Governments

Town and township meetings still replace councils in parts of the six New England states and in a few other regions, especially in areas with below ten thousand population, although rising in some cases to well above 25 thousand. A meeting is convened once or twice a year which elects a board of three to nine 'select men' or 'councilmen' and other officials. The board sits in public. Non-elected citizens may join in the voting at board meetings in some instances. Special town meetings can be called during the year to determine matters of policy. There is a modification of the form in which voters choose a representative meeting, often of a hundred or more citizens,

424

to debate and determine policy. In some cases *township council administrators* or *managers* are appointed to take care of business on behalf of boards between meetings. This practice has increased in recent years.

Special Districts

Special districts normally have a business type of organisation. A board of directors or commissioners is responsible for deciding on policies. Their members are normally appointed by the councils or executives of general-purpose local authorities for whose areas the board or commission provides services. They are often a mixture of private citizens and elected councillors or other officials. Or they may be directly elected, especially in the West and Midwest, when they are likely to possess tax-setting powers. They serve part-time and often their periods of office are staggered and overlap those of the officials who appoint them. They normally seek to take decisions by consensus. They appoint a general manager or executive director with responsibilities resembling in principle those of a city manager.

General

Most Americans are reported to prefer an elected mayor to the alternatives because the office gives strong executive leadership and ability to 'get things done', has a symbolic value for a city and carries clear accountability to the electorate. Against this strong mayors are not usually professional administrators, may be too concerned with politics rather than administration, abuse the centralised power they enjoy and be involved in corrupt machine politics. One important consideration is the potential ability of an elected mayor to secure benefits for an authority by use of influence at other levels of government.

There has been a general tendency to centralise powers of administration under a chief executive, but also a reaction against moving responsibilities away from council control in some cases. There has also been a loosening of detailed control at most levels, with delegation of powers to enable centres of responsibility themselves to work out the best organisation for their purposes. (Garnett, 1985; ACIR, 1982)

8.12 CITIZEN PARTICIPATION AND DECENTRALISATION WITHIN CITIES

Participation Including Voting

Participation is warmly accepted as a principle and actively propagated in the United States, but widespread cynicism is reported about the chances of influencing government (the 'you can't beat city hall' attitude). This has been used to explain the low turn-out in elections, usually about one-third and in general varying between 20 and 40 per cent or so. The business emphasis and power of the professionals, which can be related to the high valuation of 'neutral competence' in municipal administration, may be argued to run against the principle of political choice and therefore against accountability to the electorate on choice of policy. Other reasons may be a high rate of residential migration, the staggering of elections, the length and confusing nature of ballot papers and the lack of party organisation (see §8.10).

Forms of Direct Democracy

The Initiative
(1) An action group may organise a *petition*. The petition may be required to include a draft ordinance signed by a minimum number or percentage of electors as defined in a state law or the city charter. The proposed law or charter amendment has to be printed on a ballot-paper and becomes law if a majority votes for it. Thus it can by-pass the council on an issue where a majority of councillors is not in line with the majority of the citizens who are motivated to vote for it. Thirty-five per cent of municipalities and counties reported initiatives providing for changes in local tax limits in the period 1975 to 1977 (ACIR, 1979). (2) A government may be petitioned to take a defined action and the details left to be defined by the council.

The Referendum
This may take the forms of (1) a compulsory or mandatory referendum required by the state constitution, law or city charter with respect to a particular kind of decision, for example borrowings, tax increases, annexations or liquor consumption regulations; (2) an advisory or optional referendum initiated by a council to determine the balance of public opinion, for example requiring animals to be kept on reins; or (3) a petition referendum requiring a measure passed by a council to be submitted to popular vote within a specified period.

The Recall

This is a means by which an elected official can be removed from office by a special election triggered by a petition supported by a required percentage of those voting for the official's appointment in the last local election.

Governmental Efforts to Promote Participation

Federal aid programmes in all sectors have required participatory initiatives. A report by the Advisory Council on Inter-Governmental Relations (ACIR, 1979), lists and classifies the following forms of governmental initiatives to achieve participation.

(1) Citizen, special interest and specific clientele groups and official citizen committees.
(2) Individual forms: working in public projects, lobbying, appeals, court actions and demonstrations.
(3) (Information dissemination: open government, meetings, conferences, publications, use of mass media, displays, advertisements, 'hot-lines', drop-in centres, correspondence, and word of mouth.
(4) Information collection: hearings, workshops, meetings and conferences, consultation, government records, participant observers and surveys.

Openness of business is a value much stressed in the courts and as a principle of public administration in general. The press is seen as a natural ally in this regard. There is a special emphasis on openness of budget-making processes to the public. Whatever rights exist, actual participation in these matters has been found to be generally very low.

Citizen advisory committees are a frequent feature. The average municipality has been found to have one to five committees with 25 to 49 citizens on each, and counties also have prolific arrangements for large-scale citizen consultancy committees.

Interest Groups

The thick texture of social and political interest groups that covers much of the United States is in itself a net of participation within which influential action can be mobilised wherever there is a will. Chambers of commerce and many other private-sector associations have become deeply associated with reform programmes, often in collaboration with business-orientated city governments. 'Social conscience' and social and environmental impact analysis have been promoted as movements by and within business corporations.

Neighbourhood Government and Mini-City Halls

Neighbourhood government exists in practice in the United States in many of the thousands of administrative areas with very low populations. From 1961 the federal government sought to stimulate community self-help in large cities, using its programmes to finance self-help and encourage participation in decision-making by the inhabitants of disadvantaged neighbourhoods, especially ethnic groups and the poor. Anti-poverty programmes encouraged the 'maximum feasible participation' of the poor. 'Little city halls' and 'neighbourhood service centres' were opened in the hope of building elected 'community corporations' out of voluntary action groups which would advise local government officials and initiate self-help (Magnusson, 1979). Much has been written on attempts to promote sub-municipal government in large cities, much of it relating to New York where a bold decentralisation of administration to one-purpose agencies and community boards was initiated. They were given responsibilities for service monitoring and preparing improvement plans for their areas, submission of priorities for capital and revenue budgets, participation in project planning and review, reviewing planning applications, assisting in the preparation of service statements by city agencies, dissemination of information about city services and programmes, processing complaints and dealing with residents' inquiries. Service boundaries were rationalised as far as practicable so that they did not cut across board districts, excepting those of school districts (Zimmerman, 1983a).

The results have generally disappointed expectations. The disillusionment of authorities with such attempts to encourage independence from city hall and innovation springing from neighbourhood organisations led to priority being transferred to achieving administrative co-ordination between fragmented and traditionally autonomous services (Mudd, 1985).

8.13 THE GOVERNANCE OF METROPOLITAN AREAS

The United States is unique among Western democracies in the scale and complexity of its metropolitan areas. They are agglomerations of local authorities which usually centre on core cities. They are largely the result of the spontaneous growth of innumerable complementary economic activities and the residential patterns which have sprung up to service them.

Defining metropolitan areas in relation to a centre is a means the United States Bureau of the Census has used to help map metropolitan statistical areas, setting a minimum population of 50,000 for each central city and at least 100,000 inclusive of its urban surrounds (a low level of scale by international standards). More comparable with international definitions is that of a consolidated statistical metropolitan area (CSMA). In 1989 there were 35 of these with populations of one million or more, of which 12 had populations of over 2,500,000 (US Bureau of the Census, 1991, Table 33).

A city such as Houston, which was able to establish some unity over its metropolitan area by annexing surrounding land and settlements, stands out as an exception. The many forms of elected authority and board providing services rarely have matching boundaries. Their areas in any event cannot stay economically efficient for the complex and evolving patterns of settlement, communication and needs.

Between the mid-1970s and 1990 city-county consolidations had been achieved in fewer than ten cases. Earlier, out of 68 attempts to amalgamate city areas with counties between 1945 and 1977, fifty-one were defeated in referenda — in most cases by a big majority (Florestano and Marando, 1981). ACIR, which fought for consolidation in earlier years, changed its stance in 1987, accepting the Tiebout public choice argument that 'differentiation' (a term now preferred to fragmentation) benefits citizens through the competition it engenders, and that problems can generally be solved by distinguishing between providers who contract for services and producers who tender for them. Hence a 'crazy-quilt' is put forward as a logical pattern for optimisation of the public good. The argument is questionable on grounds both of efficiency and, more important perhaps, equal rights (see Gunlicks, 1991, for a summary of the controversy).

States have at times limited but also facilitated attempts to reorganise metropolitan government. In some cases they have initiated them. They have encouraged co-operation and thereby abated the case for the restructuring of boundaries. Partly due to lack of metropolitan regional authorities they have taken over a number of functions — most frequently public health, public welfare, courts, pollution abatement, property tax assessment standards, building codes and land-use regulations (ACIR, 1976a). They have also created area-wide state-controlled public authorities for transportation, parks, water, liquid and solid waste disposal and other services. These have added significantly to the problems of fragmentation of government described in §8.4. Recent important decisions at state level have tightened standards and criteria for the incorporation of new municipalities, facilitated annexations to municipal areas and created boundary review boards.

There are cases of state-created regional councils: the 'twin-cities', Minneapolis-St Paul in 1967, and the Atlanta Regional Commission in 1971. These are policy-making bodies which leave the provision of services to the basic authorities subject to approval of plans and veto powers. The Metropolitan Council of Minneapolis-St Paul has broad review powers over other districts in its region, appoints commissions to administer transit, sewage disposal and regional parks systems and to exercise control over authorities regarding airport and sports facility authorities. It is also active in other areas, not least culture.

Special districts, found in Boston, Chicago, New York, San Francisco and Washington, DC, are a means by which particular services can be rationalised across boundaries, transcending the maze of municipal administrations and drawing upon the wealth of a great area economy in whatever way the law allows. They may take on mass transportation, water and air pollution control responsibilities in response to generally felt need. Their boards may consist of members appointed by constituent authorities or state governors. They may or may not have taxation powers. In the latter case they are usually called authorities rather than districts and are able to raise revenues through charges and bonds.

Councils of Government (COGs) are voluntary associations of counties and municipalities for the purpose of co-ordinating members' activities on regional problems. They have been set up in Detroit, Washington, DC, San Francisco, Seattle, Los Angeles, Atlanta, Philadelphia, New York and elsewhere. They have undertaken metropolitan planning functions and until the early 1980s were designated as review agencies for federal grants, acting as a clearing-house for applications. Between 1977 and the mid-1980s their number dropped from 650 to about 450. Gunlicks has suggested that fundamental disagreements between experts had resulted in 'a kind of paralysis' on the subject in recent years (Gunlicks, 1991).

9. CANADA

9.1 HISTORY AND TRADITIONS

Canada has a population of 25 million people, very small in relation to its vast territories which stretch some three and a half thousand miles from East to West and two and a half thousand from South to North. Politically it consists of ten provinces joined together as member states of a federation. Six provinces have over a million inhabitants and stretch from the border with the United States to the latitude which touches the southern point of Greenland, north of which, between Greenland and Alaska, lie the great and almost uninhabited Northwest Territories and the Yukon.

The great majority of Canadians live within two or three hundred miles of the United States border. Over 55 per cent live in cities of over a hundred thousand. More than two-thirds are found along the St Lawrence River and the Great Lakes in Canada's South-East. The residents of the metropolitan areas of Toronto and Montreal together constitute about a quarter of the national population. Six other metropolitan areas have populations of over half a million.

Each province has its own culture, or rather its own mixture of cultures. The major division is between the 60 per cent of English-speaking Canadians and the nearly 25 per cent whose native language is French and who live predominantly in Quebec, the second-largest province. The balance is a mixture of indigenous Indians and large numbers of mostly recent immigrants from Europe, Asia and elsewhere.

The most striking social development of the last few decades has been suburbanisation, bringing a new emphasis on the importance of education, health, housing, culture and recreational services and leading to increasing problems of traffic congestion, high land costs and the need for urban rehabilitation, all matters for which responsibility rests primarily with the provinces and the local government systems which they control.

Historical Background

Canada developed out of British and French settlements administered as a colony after the British victory over the French Army in 1760. Early attempts by the colonists to set up autonomous local governments were

431

quickly wiped out. Popular uprisings in Ontario and Quebec in the 1830s against domination by a small property-owning class led, after a crown inquiry, to the District Councils Act of 1841 and the Municipal Corporations (Baldwin) Act of 1849. These provided for a British-type structure of municipal councils with an indirectly elected county tier.

The main milestone in the political history of Canada is the British North America Act of 1867 (renamed the Constitution Act 1867 in the Constitution Act 1982). It set up a confederation of Ontario, Quebec, New Brunswick and Nova Scotia, afterwards joined by British Columbia and Prince Edward Island and the new province of Manitoba in the 1870s, Alberta and Saskatchewan in 1905, and finally Newfoundland in 1949.

Significant modifications to their local government systems waited until the 1950s. In Ontario at least, which in some respects led the way, the main motivation appears to have been anxiety to move the cost of local services on to local communities rather than a response to popular demand.

Constitution and Politics

Under the Constitution Act each province has an equal say in decisions on constitutional amendments. The Act gives provinces exclusive control over natural resources, forests and production of electrical energy. The bicameral constitution resembles that in Westminster in that the 'Crown', represented by the governor-general, since 1959 alternately francophone and anglophone, appoints a prime minister who forms a government that acts as the political executive. Parliament consists of the House of Commons and the Senate. Senators are appointed by the governor-general on the recommendation of the prime minister in accordance with quotas fixed for each province.

The Yukon and Northwest Territories have been given elected bodies of different kinds as adjuncts to federally appointed commissioners who act as chief executives.

Provinces are empowered to levy taxes other than the largest, a personal income tax which is set at federal level and partly redistributed to the provinces.

Local government is entirely the affair of the provinces. The subject is not specifically covered in the Constitution. Co-ordination of services between governments falls chiefly to 'shared jurisdictions' set up by the federal government and the provinces. Standing federal-provincial conferences plan, co-ordinate and carry out overlapping programmes.

Canada's single-member constituency, first-past-the post electoral system (§1.10), tends to give clear one-party majorities consisting of either

Liberals or Progressive Conservatives. These have been the only parties to hold power in Ontario. A third party, the New Democratic Party, is relatively weak but has held the balance of power in some provinces. A fourth, Social Credit, has been strong only in the West. Parties are generally weak and not much involved in local elections (see §9.10).

Provincial systems show wide variations. To focus on Ontario, the province has the typical organs of a British-type national state although there is only one house of parliament, the legislative assembly. The lieutenant-general carries out crown functions.

Table 9.1: Area, Population and Representation of the Provinces and the Territories of the North

	Area sq. m.	Population 1988 (provisional)	Representatives House of Commons 1988
Ontario	344,090	9,431,000	99
Quebec	523,860	6,639,000	75
British Columbia	359,970	2,984,000	32
The Maritime Provences			
Newfoundland	143,510	568,000	7
Nova Scotia	20,400	884,000	11
New Brunswick	27,840	714,000	10
Prince Edward Island	2,180	129,000	4
The Prairie Provinces			
Manitoba	211,720	1,085,000	14
Saskatchewan	220,350	1,011,000	14
Alberta	248,800	2,401,000	26
North-west Territories	1,273,440	52,000	2
Yukon Territories	184,930	25,000	1
Totals	3,558,090	25,903,000	295

Source: Canada Year Book, 1990, Tables 1.1, 2.1, 19.3.

9.2 THE STATUS OF LOCAL GOVERNMENT

Canadian local authorities inherited the constraints of the *ultra vires* doctrine from British law (§§1.2 and 7.2). They are creations of federated provinces, subject to their province's jurisdiction and dependent on it for their form and powers and the legal conditions under which they work. All exercise of power by local authorities is subject to direct or indirect approval or query. Areas of competence tend to be narrowly defined. Powers are not only fragmented between levels but also between overlapping local jurisdictions. Notably school boards deny local authorities the intimate involvement in educational matters which local authorities possess in Northern Europe. It has been suggested that this deficit in their social responsibilities is one reason why local politics in big cities are predominantly orientated towards the enhancement of property values — 'boosterism' as it is termed in North America (Magnusson and Sancton (eds), 1983). Nevertheless §9.7 shows that municipalities have a much wider sphere of action. Social concerns exist and are expressed in a wide range of community services undertaken in response to non-economic interests. Financially, however, local government is weak and dependent (see §§9.6 and 9.9).

The little evidence there is on the degree of importance attached to local government by the public shows it to be at a much lower level than for federal and provincial government. The public appears to rate local government elections as appreciably less important than those at higher levels (Higgins, 1991). The proportion of members of the federal House of Commons engaged in local government fell from 50 per cent in 1940 to 26 per cent in 1975. At provincial level the proportion of councillors in the Ontario House in 1975 stood at 46 per cent, but in some other provincial Houses it was much lower. In Quebec it was only 13 per cent (Higgins, 1986).

Some provincial governments have concerned themselves with promoting public interest and involvement in local government, recognising that the status of local government in the community is not as strong as it should be. One recent work generalises that local government has never been strong in Quebec and Newfoundland, but has a long and honourable tradition in Ontario and the West (Masson, 1985).

It can only be concluded, however, that local government has a particularly low status compared with that in other countries in this survey, a major qualification being that in individual provinces or cities and elsewhere it may well be higher than is here indicated.

434

9.3 CONCEPTS AND VALUES

Canada inherited British liberal and conservative attitudes, and in Quebec a radical French admixture. Influences from the United States became strong in the nineteenth century, not surprisingly due to proximity and the fact that Canadians faced similar problems of pioneering, creating wealth out of a raw economy and absorbing a great and heterogeneous inflow of immigrants. The most remarkable fact is that the core, traditional cultures of the earlier immigrants from Britain and France survived so strongly and that values expressed in Canadian culture, art and institutions remain significantly different from those of the USA even in the English-speaking provinces.

There is no doubting the belief and trust in liberal democracy, individual rights and the rule of law. The Constitution epitomises the fact by embodying both references to the British unwritten constitution and a code of rights. But otherwise emphases vary strongly. In one direction they are orientated towards conservation of traditional society with only cautious change, and in the other towards radicalism and the pursuit of equal opportunities. Equalisation demands expensive development investments to overcome the disadvantages of poorer communities that are often difficult to reconcile with policies for stable overall growth. More profound perhaps is the conflict between cultural unity and cultural diversity, at its sharpest in the antagonism between the traditions of the French speaking Québécois and those of the other provinces. It is also substantial regarding the strong differences between individual English-speaking provinces such as Ontario and Alberta and reinforced by regional variations in economic character. Further tensions have arisen from recent social and legal emphases on the rights of the native Indian and Inuit Eskimo peoples.

One Canadian writer argues that the nation has effectively avoided a 'tyranny of the majority' by creating a situation in which the ten provinces and the thousands of local authorities have enabled the many minorities at national level to become majorities at provincial and local levels, thus crediting local government with the virtue of 'maintaining a viable system of democracy' (Masson, 1985).

In the big cities there was for decades a much needed emphasis on fostering development. This promoted an entrepreneurial style and a stress on facilitating the creation of wealth. Social interests were relatively peripheral — particularly until the advent of large-scale chronic long-term unemployment in the late 1970s and the 1980s.

A philosophy of civic enhancement under the influence of the United States 'city beautiful' movement arose around 1900, aiming to convert inner city squalor into an environment which people could take pride in. A second philosophy of civic enhancement, 'the city healthy', stressed the imperative need for urban infrastructure to remove the persistent threat of epidemics. A third was 'the city efficient' — rational, scientific planning to enhance the values sought by the cities' controlling elites (Tindal and Tindal, 1984). There was also a drive against civic corruption (see §9.11). Apolitical 'rational management' built up the power of professionals within local government, centralising authority in expert groups who had a strong self-interest in the success of the reform movement. In Vancouver, for example, 'not only have professionals come from the civic elite but the activity of civic politics has itself become a profession' (Tennant, 1980).

As in the United States the business ethos is strong. A writer from Alberta comments, 'Today, in many Alberta communities, the functions of government are equated with those of the private firm; a refrain frequently heard in council chambers is, 'We should keep this matter out of politics and proceed in a business-like manner"(Masson, 1985).

An anti-party bias developed, partly because of association of parties with corruption but also argued on grounds of avoiding conflict with provincial governments and the irrelevance of ideological differences to municipal tasks. A counter argument has been that excessive individualism has made for 'headline hunters who lack the saving graces of relevance and coherence' (O'Brien, 1980). Masson links this with the justification of 'at-large' elections through the argument that they attract people with community-wide interests rather than ideological ones. There are exceptions to the picture: in Quebec and Vancouver the fact that party allegiances are not visible is reported to disguise the fact that federal and provincial politicians and party organisers are often deeply involved in election campaigns. But there is little to challenge Higgins' generalisation that 'In the Canadian culture, political parties are generally thought to be inappropriate, if not antithetical, to local government', local authorities being seen mainly as a means to solve public grievances, or a sort of corporation providing only services that can be justified economically, or a kind of administrative adjunct to higher-level governments (Higgins, 1991).

Alongside this must be put the respect and acceptance of basic rights and democratic principles and the conscientious search for participation and efficiency which characterise much of official literature.

9.4 NATIONAL STRUCTURE

Local authorities may be grouped into the following classes:

(1) local municipalities, including cities, towns or boroughs and villages, townships, parishes, communities or authorities with other names;
(2) counties and regional municipalities;
(3) school boards;
(4) special agencies, joint boards and commissions which provide specific services to groups of municipalities.

Cities, towns or boroughs and villages are generally based on urban communities. Townships, districts and parishes are essentially rural authorities.

County or regional authorities have been set up in five provinces to make possible a pooling of the resources of municipal areas to provide functions over wide areas, particularly roads and planning. The counties do not generally include larger urban authorities in their areas, but the regional municipalities in Ontario and British Columbia include all types of basic authority. In most instances they conform to the pattern of federations of municipalities under councils consisting of representatives from constituent units.

Sparsely populated areas have various types of appointed and elected boards and other agencies for the provision of services. Boards with specialised functions have been set up in more thickly populated areas, side by side with established municipalities.

The general picture is of a basic traditional structure overlaid with special-purpose and new-type authorities. Where reforms have occurred they have been much bolder than in the United States and only undertaken after substantial inquiries — usually due to 'a servicing crisis' (Feldman and Graham, 1979). Other objectives defined by Feldman and Graham are overcoming harmful fragmentation in service delivery and parochialism, the quest for efficiency, planning crises when 'the rate of growth has exceeded the ability to respond', the wish to overcome 'fractionalisation' to special agencies in the search of greater effectiveness, and responses to fiscal crises. In a survey of reforms they remark that the most prominent characteristics overall are reliance on a structural or institutional approach and municipal resistance where an initiative is seen as a unilateral one by the provincial government.

No case is typical. Details of Ontario are given below if only because it has the largest population and possibly the most diverse structure.

Ontario's existing structure evolved from provisions in a law of 1849. It resembled the pre-1974 English shire county structure. The basic level authorities had various designations. Cities, like county boroughs, stood outside the county system. Since the establishment of Metropolitan Toronto in the 1950s, 'modernised' two-tier systems have been developed for thirteen regions which comprehend cities and so-called 'separated towns' that previously had a full range of powers. Both the counties and the post-war 'regional' top-tier councils are conceived as federal authorities, their members being the senior political leaders or executives from the lower-tier units. Ontario has some 830 lower-tier municipalities, 659 of them being under a two-tier system originating in 1849. Forty-nine of all the municipalities include two-thirds of the province's population.

The 478 townships were designed for rural areas and can be incorporated when the population reaches one thousand. Some have been absorbed into city suburbs. Other authorities qualify for incorporation on grounds of population size. Villages, of which there are 119, have between 500 and 2,000 inhabitants. The 145 towns have between 2,000 and 6,000 inhabitants. Cities, of which there were 50 in the late 1980s, qualify for incorporation if there is a population of 15,000, or 25,000 if their area already has a township. They were originally all-purpose authorities but those in regionalised areas have lost the more expensive services to regional authorities.

The 27 counties and similar authorities form an upper tier in the long-established two-tier system of Southern Ontario. In law they are incorporated municipalities with jurisdiction over townships, villages and towns in their areas for specified purposes. Since 1949 the principle of the county has been to provide services which are beyond the ability of individual municipalities to provide effectively, or where there is a common interest between a group of municipalities such as a road network. Responsibilities have spread over time to welfare provision, including old people's homes, building inspection and regional or strategic planning.

County councils consist of elected officials from basic authorities, including mayors, reeves and deputy reeves (see §§9.10 and 9.11). They and the regions raise income through a levy on lower-tier municipalities.

From the 1960s regional municipalities, of which there are ten, were designed to replace particular counties. They differ in having jurisdiction over cities and separated towns in their areas. They take responsibility for water supply and sewage disposal, police, parks, public transportation systems, capital borrowing and regional or strategic planning services, and they may also have some delegated planning approval powers. This is also true of the County of Oxford except that it was formed by local initiative instead of provincial.

In addition to municipalities, some two thousand or so special-purpose bodies have been set up, generally termed boards or commissions. They may serve one or more municipal areas. They operate outside the main municipal structure — generally for a single function or a limited range of functions. Health units and school boards in most cases cover all municipalities in one or two counties. A city and its surrounding area may have a joint planning board. School boards and utility commissions are directly elected. Others are elected or, more commonly, appointed by municipal councils, the provincial government or other special-purpose bodies. They may be advisory or operational, or regulatory with significant powers.

Health and conservation authorities have the power to levy revenues on municipalities. These have mixed memberships and draw most of their finance from the province. Boards of education also precept on municipalities and can levy their own property tax. Others are funded by municipalities, the province or in some cases user charges. Some are mandatory, such as school boards and health units. Others such as library boards are mandatory if electors vote for such powers.

Conservation boards for the management of rivers and their tributaries including flood lands must be set up if a majority of voters in a watershed area vote for one. They may provide extensive parks to fulfil regional needs. A board of commissioners of police is optional for municipal areas with populations of between five and fifteen thousand. Other types of service provided by boards are transportation, museums and art galleries, housing and hospitals. Some are quasi-judicial, as for planning control and assessment review.

Improvement districts, of which there were eight in 1990, were first set up in 1943 to meet the needs of developing areas without settled communities on which to establish municipal institutions, being dependent on private or public mining or pulp and paper corporations. Each district is under a provincially appointed board of three or five trustees, and was expected to attain the status of a township, village or town in due course.

The North of the province consists largely of unorganised territory without municipal institutions. Local road area boards and local service boards may be set up as small elected bodies with taxation powers in remote areas to provide roads and other specified services.

Other provinces with regional structures are Quebec and British Columbia. Quebec has concentrated on rationalisation. After attempts to amalgamate authorities failed, the provincial government sought to restructure the county councils to give them major responsibilities in regional planning. The new model was called the MRC (*municipalité régionale de comté*). In 1988 there were 258 cities and towns, 1,242 municipalities, 38 Indian reserves and 118 unorganised territories. Since 1970 three *communautés urbaines* have been set up (see §9.13). The host of municipalities derives from the conversion of church parishes into civil authorities to emulate the British system as it existed around 1840.

British Columbia adopted 'a strategy of gentle imposition' of 28 regional districts of sizes from 800 to 80,000 square miles in 1965. Greater Vancouver Regional District has a population of well over one million people. Mandatory functions are regional planning and community planning, building inspection, contract services and grants-in-aid. In 1990 the province had 37 cities, 12 towns, 48 villages and 47 districts, some of which near the cities are urban in character. There are also some 28 regional districts (see §9.13).

Of the Maritime Provinces, Newfoundland, Nova Scotia and Prince Edward Island have carried out no major reforms. Newfoundland has three cities, 167 towns, 142 'communities', a metropolitan area with an appointed board and over a hundred elected special service authorities. Nova Scotia has three cities, 39 towns independent of counties and six counties, each divided into two districts. Prince Edward Island has one city, eight towns, 77 communities previously styled villages or improvement committees. There are five separate education regions. New Brunswick implemented a thorough reorganisation in 1963. The system is single tier and has been described as the result of 'the most comprehensive and dramatic form of structural and redistributive reform in Canada' (ibid.). The province has six cities, 25 towns, 83 villages and 282 unincorporated special districts.

Of the Prairie Provinces, Alberta has 30 counties responsible for all local government functions including education, 15 cities, 108 towns, 172 villages, 20 municipal districts, 19 improvement districts and three areas under special boards. The cities of Edmonton and Calgary have progressively annexed their surrounding areas. Manitoba has generally remained single tier, proceeding by annexations. It has five cities, 35 towns, 39 villages, 105 rural municipalities and 17 local districts under provincial control with elected advisory boards. Saskatchewan has also remained single tier with 12 cities, 144 towns, 2 'northern towns', 14 'northern hamlets' and 299 rural municipalities.

9.5 INTER-AUTHORITY RELATIONS AND ORGANISATION

Joint organisations set up by local authorities appear to be relatively few. The status of a joint authority is not mentioned in the sources consulted, but the federal-type constitutions of counties and regions and the fact that, as mentioned in §9.4, members of special-purpose authorities are often nominated by municipalities in their areas, implies a network of elected members who link up inter-authority interests. In Toronto many earlier special joint agencies were subsumed into metropolitan bodies. The Ontario Planning Act 1983 provided for joint planning boards, but they have been slow to develop.

There are nevertheless close networks of inter-authority relationships that have been formed pragmatically and formalised to some extent, both in the Toronto area and elsewhere. The 1975 Royal Commission reported that 'inter-municipal cooperation is effective and extensive. The maintenance of a comprehensive list of all bodies involved in such cooperation could be a monumental and continuous task.' (Sancton, 1975).

Provincial local authority associations have been set up to serve as consultative bodies with the provincial governments, to promote and protect local government interests and to perform a range of other activities. Most provinces have one or two associations whose representatives meet fairly frequently with provincial cabinets, ministers of municipal affairs and departmental officials (Higgins, 1977). Ontario had seven such associations in the 1970s. The need for co-ordination led to the setting up of an inter-association liaison committee and subsequently the Provincial-Municipal Liaison Committee which became heavily involved in important discussions on revenue sharing. However the largest of the associations withdrew in 1979 and ended the practice of regular monthly meetings. A new umbrella organisation of the five main groupings of local authorities, the Association of the Municipalities of Ontario (AMO), was founded in 1981 with the object of finding common purposes among the diverse types of local authority. Regular meetings with the Provincial Government were not resumed (Tindal and Tindal, 1984).

One study concludes that municipalities have been ineffective in their relationships with their provinces. They have tended to focus on providing information and services. They have not succeeded in defining positions and achieving much needed change. There is no rational, planned policy-making process at the association level (Feldman and Graham, 1979).

The national local authority association is the Federation of Canadian Municipalities (Suite 1318, Tower B, Place de Ville, 112 Kent Street,

Ottawa, Ontario K1P 5PT). It aims to raise efficiency and standards in municipal administration throughout the Dominion, represent the interests of Canadian local authorities 'before the Federal Government' and serve as a research organisation for local government.

9.6 INTER-GOVERNMENTAL RELATIONS

General municipal acts specify discretionary and mandatory functions, the basic internal institutional structure for decision-making, term of office, qualifications for voters and candidates, and revenue-raising powers. Functions previously considered to be basic have been taken from local authorities, including justice and policing, and other traditional local services have become shared responsibilities. Almost all municipal actions are presumed to be approved and there is no provincial intervention. A rare exception was regarded as sensational: Ontario's veto on a Toronto expressway in 1971.

Provinces tend to control matters of general concern such as justice, health, welfare and education policy but not educational administration although it relies heavily on financial support from provincial level. In other local matters municipalities exercise full control (see §9.7).

Provinces have ministries of local affairs to deal with local government matters. They supervise local authorities on a continuous day-to-day basis and usually in considerable detail, even as far as on the colour of policemen's socks (Higgins, 1977 and 1991). They may arrange training for officers, provide property assessment services and help with local plans.

There are provincial municipal boards: autonomous administrative tribunals that hear appeals on municipal zoning by-laws and assessments and decide applications for boundary changes, amalgamations and annexations of municipalities. They may be given powers relating to municipal debt and borrowing. Members are appointed by provincial governments.

Local government has sometimes been happy to accept loss of services to reduce demands on local property tax (Higgins, 1986). In Quebec education has been taken over by the province, freeing property tax revenue for other uses. Tax sharing by percentages of income and other taxes has been introduced in Manitoba, British Columbia and Saskatchewan. The inflexibility of the single tax base is the villain in the situation. The optimal solution is to widen the base, but no progress had been made on this, at least by 1991 (Higgins, 1991; Tindal and Tindal,

1984).

Municipalities are affected by a wide range of federal policies which can raise acute policy problems at municipal level, including wage and price control, rail-line closures, redevelopment of federal lands and regional economic expansion programmes. Modest conditional grants have been made for transportation and communications, recreation and culture, environment and housing, but nothing approaching the extent of transfers in the United States.

The Canada Mortgage and Housing Corporation (CMHC) has financed a third to a half of all housing built in Canada in some years. It has also shared the cost of slum clearance with the provinces, who have generally passed on the finance to the municipalities. It has made loans to municipalities for construction, sewage treatment, rehabilitation, senior citizen and student accommodation programmes, has financed land assembly and neighbourhood improvement, and has assisted home ownership programmes.

Local government's means to influence central policy have in general been no more than informal (Feldman and Graham, 1979). Lobbying appears to have had much lower success than in the United States and continental Western Europe.

9.7 LOCAL SERVICES

Local government competences have grown piecemeal as provincial governments have accepted the case for meeting social needs. Local authorities have frequently resisted the imposition of new responsibilities, generally because of the unpopularity of raising the level of the property tax. Provinces have made support for the poor, provision and maintenance of roads and educational administration mandatory — not least to compel communities to meet essential needs from their own tax resources.

Ontario law requires that the powers of a council shall be exercised by by-law except where otherwise provided. There have been numerous court decisions invalidating council actions which were authorised only by resolution, and, according to a guidebook prepared by the Ontario Ministry of Local Affairs, it is likely that a resolution would not be enforceable beyond the term of the council enforcing it.

In 1984 41 per cent of the total outgoings of local government went on education services, mostly by special school authorities. Percentages spent on other functions were, in descending order, transportation and communications 10, fiscal services 10, protection of persons and property 8, environment 7.4, recreation and culture 6, health 6, general government 5.6, social welfare 3.5, regional planning and development 0.9, resource conservation and industrial development 1, housing assistance 0.7 and other services 0.4 (*Canada Year Book 1990,* Table 22.22).

The following list of services in the 1980s is derived from a number of sources. It is not exhaustive.

1. Town and Country Planning and Development is a basic responsibility of municipalities of all types. *Counties* prepare official plans dealing with county-wide concerns. *Regional councils* carry out regional planning and are sometimes delegated provincial planning powers.
Building Control: *municipalities of all types.*

2. Housing is carried out by *municipalities of all types. Cities* undertake especially assisted 'rent-geared-to-income' housing and housing for the elderly. (In Metropolitan Toronto social housing is built by the Metropolitan Toronto Housing Company, the City of Toronto Housing Department, co-operatives and private non-profit suppliers.)

3. Roads
Municipalities are responsible for urban streets and street lighting in all provinces and for rural roads in six. *Regional councils* are usually responsible for major arterial roads in their areas.

4. Transport: *municipalities* in all provinces except one in which a crown corporation is the transport authority.

5. Education
Municipalities and school boards in seven provinces. Administration is usually through school boards with varied constitutions and powers. In Ontario directly elected school boards are responsible except in designated city areas.

6. Vocational Training is in general undertaken by the provinces.

7. Cultural Activities are generally supported by *municipalities* with assistance from agencies such as the Canada Council and provincial arts councils.

8. Libraries and Museums: *cities, counties and museum and library boards.*

9. Recreation Services: *municipalities, park boards, regional municipalities and conservation authorities.*

10. Health
There is a mixture of providers. **Public Health** may be a provincial responsibility with or without minor municipal involvement; shared with the province; or *municipal* with provincial grants. **Hospitals** may be *provincial or municipal*, with or without provincial finance. **Ambulance**

Services are *provincial, municipal or private* with provincial grants, or voluntary. In Ontario health services are mostly administered by *district health authorities* responsible to the provincial Ministry of Health.

Social Welfare is wholly provincial in four provinces; shared with *municipalities* in four; and *municipal* with provincial grants in two. *Assistance for short-term unemployed* tends to be run by *municipalities* and *assistance for long-term unemployed* by the *provinces*.

11. Policing: a *municipal* responsibility in all provinces except Ontario and Quebec. Some *municipalities* contract out to provincial forces or to the federal Royal Canadian Mounted Police. In Ontario there is a crown force, the Ontario Provincial Police — the third largest police force in North America. Toronto has a Board of Commisioners of Police.

12. Fire Protection is a *municipal* responsibility that is sometimes provided by voluntary brigades which raise their own income. Co-operative inter-municipal contracts are not uncommon.

13. Development of Local Economy and Employment: *municipalities* with provincial support.

14. Public Utilities

Water Supply and Sewage Disposal: *municipalities of all types* with provincial supervision and some funding for capital projects.

Drainage may be a responsibility of *municipalities* with provincial assistance, as in Ontario.

Gas: in Ontario *municipalities* and private suppliers.

Electricity is distributed by *cities and some inter-municipal agencies*.

District Heating: *some cities* provide partial distribution.

Refuse Collection and Disposal: *municipalities of all types*. In Ontario regions undertake disposal and municipalities collection.

15. Other Services

Tourism Services are provided by all levels of government.

Conservation is defined as management of resources rather than protection of amenity and is a concern of all three main levels of government. *Metropolitan Toronto and Region Conservation Authority* is a joint provincial-municipal agency.

Conservation of Heritage: In Ontario *municipalities* are empowered to establish advisory committees to assist in designating buildings and areas of historical and architectural significance.

Licensing of all types is carried out at *municipal* level for about a hundred activities from amusement arcades to wheeled vehicles and dogs.

Telephone Services: *a few cities* run services feeding into the provincial system.

9.8 IMPLEMENTATION OF SERVICES

There has been a varied and non-doctrinal approach to the way in which services are implemented. Quasi-autonomous boards and commissions and municipal corporations take the form of limited companies. Voluntary bodies are also extensively supported as a means of providing communal services. Although such arrangements have been criticised as 'ad-hoccery' and for fragmentation, obscurity and distancing functions from account-ability to voters, they are defended for spreading community involvement, co-opting expertise and ability, pinpointing responsibility for well-defined tasks and in some cases distancing a service from politics, notably in the case of quasi-judicial functions. Direct provision, however, remains the normal mode of implementation for main services.

Public utility authorities in Toronto include: (1) the Toronto Transit Commission, responsible for all public transportation excluding railways and taxis, which is controlled by a five-member board appointed by the Metropolitan Council and reporting through its Transportation Committee on matters of policy. It receives substantial subsidies from provincial and municipal revenue for socially orientated policies and general operations; (2) Toronto Harbour Commissioners, appointed by the City (3 members) and the province (2 members); (3) hydro-electric and other utility commissions to which municipalities delegate operations, either directly elected or appointed; (4) parking and housing commissions; and (5) housing corporations.

Service authorities include: (1) local boards of health including 'taxpayer' members as well as councillors (Palmer, 1979); (2) conservation authorities, including joint provincial and municipal conservation and heritage bodies; (3) public library boards; and (4) roads commissions, largely replaced by county highway departments; and (5) children's aid societies.

Regulatory bodies include: (1) regulatory boards, mentioned in §9.6, including the Ontario Municipal, Energy and Environmental Assessment Boards; and (2) police commissions (Palmer, 1979).

Management authorities include boards to manage parks and/or community centres, commonly of three to seven residents, one of whom is in some cases the head of the council. Employees are appointed and paid by boards but work is carried out by municipal departments.

Promotional authorities include: (1) industrial development boards; (2) tourist bureaux; and (3) chambers of commerce and boards of trade.

9.9 LOCAL GOVERNMENT FINANCE

In 1986 property and related taxes met 37.3 per cent of local government's gross general revenue as against grant income which amounted to 46.9 per cent. Income from utilities, goods and services was 10.3 per cent and, excepting 'investment returns etc.' which yielded 2.55 per cent, there was no other specific item above one per cent. (Higgins, 1991, derived from national public sources)

The property tax on which Canadian local authorities are so dependent for their autonomous resources has been widely criticised as inherently regressive, inelastic and inadequate. Its yield in the 1980s had fallen to around a third of local revenues from two-thirds in 1960. It provided 79.7 per cent of local tax revenue in 1988, having dropped from 82.5 per cent in 1980. Provinces on the other hand had increased their take-up of the tax to 1.8 per cent of their revenues from 0.4 per cent in 1980 (Owens, 1991).

The rate of the tax is fixed in mills, that is in one-tenths of one per cent. Its base is the assessed value of taxable real property. Assessment in Ontario is by Ministry of Revenue staff and is meant to reflect the price that would be paid for the property, given willing buyers and sellers and a free market. Tax exemptions include property owned by churches, cemeteries, charitable and non-profit institutions and private schools, and government property for which compensation is paid by higher governments in lieu of tax. Elsewhere, as in Alberta, municipalities are responsible for assessment and can make their own exemptions in addition to those mandatory under provincial law.

Levels of grant income differ widely from province to province, ranging in the early 1980s from about 28 per cent in British Columbia to 80 per cent in Prince Edward Island. In 1986 some 88 per cent of grants was in specific or conditional grants. (Higgins, 1991)

In Ontario financial assistance to municipalities, boards and commissions is provided by sixteen different provincial ministries. In all there are 111 categories of grant, excluding six types of grants-in-aid in lieu of taxes. In the 1970s Ontario introduced unconditional grants for general support, resource equalisation grant and a special grant for very sparsely populated areas.

An attempt to relate provincial assistance to the growth rate of Ontario's total resources had collapsed in the late 1970s. Subsequently aids were fixed ad hoc, and municipalities have had to wait for the annual decision on allocations before knowing what their financial position would be. This has made something of a farce of long-term planning such as is associated with the six-year plan data that were required by provincial planning departments during the 1980s at least. (Ibid.)

The gap between local authority spending and revenues steadily increased, at least from the 1960s to the 1980s. Borrowing was sharply restricted by provincial governments (ibid.). There seemed no way of escaping from increasing dependence on provincial transfers. Nevertheless fiscal crises were not evident in Canada in the 1980s as compared with the United States, and experts forecast in 1983 that they were not likely to occur with the same force (Bird and Slack, 1983). But in the economic recession of the early 1990s the economic growth factor is missing that helped to improve incomes in earlier years. An escape from the financial dilemma would appear to require drastic reductions in expenditure and/or radical changes in provincial financial policies.

9.10 ELECTORAL REPRESENTATION

The non-partisan character of Canadian local government is described in §9.3. Local elections have rarely been fought on party issues. Attempts by the major national and provincial parties to run campaigning elections locally have in general been a failure, being 'inconsistent with the usual expectations of the civic electorate' (Higgins, 1977). In larger cities 'civic parties' can be prominent. In Montreal the local Civic Party has won almost all places on the council.

In Ontario the right to vote has been attached to the possession of property in a ward, so that in some cases one land-owner has had the right to vote in every ward in the city. In Montreal companies that own property have been entitled to vote through the firm's representative. (Ibid.)

Provincial ballots tend to produce between 66 and 80 per cent turnout; civic from 23 to 66 per cent with an average of 41.9 per cent (Higgins, 1986).

Traditionally manifesto policies have included promises to keep down the tax rate, but this has been less effective now that the electorate is no longer dominated by property owners. As in the United States, the most important aim of a candidate in an election is to get his name known. Ability to rally volunteer support adds to or substitutes for financial power. 'The property industry has long been the largest contributor to city election campaigns' (Higgins, 1977). Expenditures are unregulated.

Qualifications for candidature include Canadian or British nationality, age of 18 or over and residence in the municipality, or being married to a property owner or tenant. Disqualifications include employment by the municipality on one of its boards (excepting school boards); being a commissioner, superintendent or overseer of certain municipal works, a judge or a member of the provincial or Canadian parliament, certain high levels of government employee, undischarged bankrupts, an inmate of a penal or correctional institution and in some cases a patient in psychiatric care.

Councillors' terms of office are commonly three years (four years in Newfoundland and Quebec). One-year terms were blamed for preventing effective planning and the accountability they were meant to achieve. Short terms were adopted in some places in the United States as a result of Canadian influence, and then abandoned as unworkable. (Tindal and Tindal, 1984)

It has been argued that the professionalisation of leading municipal roles, with mayors being paid salaries of $24,300 to $57,500 a year in the early 1980s in municipalities of over 100,000 people, domination by the business ethos and lack of choice between distinct political platforms have resulted in a reduction in the representative character of local government and its responsiveness. It seems likely that the strong influence of local business interests through local chambers of commerce and boards of trade and associated pressures for construction and stimulation of commercial activity have not been counter-balanced by other less organised points of view. 'Municipal views are given little coverage in the press', and 'what coverage there is tends to be almost totally lacking in analysis'. Editorial backing is for pro-development candidates. (Andrew, 1983)

The system generally in use is the simple majority, plurality or 'first-past-the-post' system. The single transferable vote system has been used in Calgary and Edmonton for municipal and ward elections, but is reported to have been opposed because of lack of understanding of the procedures among electors and the delay in declaring results (Masson, 1985).

In a big majority of cases the head of a council, mayor, reeve, warden or chairman, is elected by the general vote of the entire municipality. Exceptions are county elections in Quebec and Ontario where the counties elect their own chairmen.

Other members of the council may be elected either in the municipality at large or in wards. The choice between methods may be set down in statute, left to the council itself or to the council subject to the approval of the electorate. In the large cities the problems of knowledge of candidates and campaign costs mean that a ward system seems necessary, although Vancouver still elects its councillors at large. Smaller communities usually have at-large elections because the population is considered homogeneous. Boundary gerrymandering has been an issue in Toronto, Winnipeg, Edmonton and elsewhere. (Magnusson and Sancton (eds), 1983; Tindal and

Tindal, 1984; Lightbody, 1983)

In Ontario candidates who are directly elected to the posts of reeve (mayor or chairman) automatically become members of the upper-tier county, regional or metropolitan council, creating an 'organic relationship' between levels. A similar system operates in Quebec and British Columbia. The ballot paper can specify both local and regional office, so that the voter is fully aware of the implications of his or her choice.

9.11 THE INTERNAL ORGANISATION OF LOCAL AUTHORITIES

The British council-committee system is generally employed except in some of the larger cities. It has been criticised for the extent to which committees tend to get immersed in administrative detail and the lack of overall control: 'Attempting to pinpoint responsibility in the council-committee system is a fruitless task' (Masson, 1985).

Councils are small in size, most having eight to twelve members including the mayor. Montreal once had a council of 100 that has been reduced to 57 and the mayor. Winnipeg Unicity reduced its council from 51 members to 27. There is a conflict between those who argue for a small business-style board and those favouring wider representation of citizens and the chance for minorities to participate.

Municipalities generally have a mayor, warden, reeve or chairman; councillors or aldermen; standing committees, usually of three to eight members; special committees appointed by the council; and appointed staff.

A mayor may have a chairman and civic representation role like that of an English mayor or, if supported by a civic party, he may serve as leader of a group within the council. Election at large gives mayors a strong local political status. They may dominate business despite their weak statutory role, taking the lead in negotiations with government and other authorities and initiating legislation. Personality is obviously a main factor. In larger cities the post is a full-time one and paid as such. There are no 'strong-mayor' systems in Canada although there are cases where mayors are designated 'chief executive officer'. In some provinces they have power to veto the council's legislative decisions. In Alberta they are often charged with implementation of laws and supervising and inspecting the conduct of officials of the council in the performance of their duties (ibid.). They may have power to suspend officials.

Council managers, typical of Quebec and medium-sized and smaller municipalities in Alberta, are professionals to whom the council delegates responsibility for carrying out its programmes. They present budgets, are responsible for expenditures, supervise and co-ordinate the departments, make policy recommendations and submit reports to council regarding operations. Unlike some cases in the United States there is no separation in principle between policy and administration. Councillors as well as the manager have a direct relationship with heads of department and appoint staff.

Chief Administrative Officers (CAOs) are found in Ontario and elsewhere. In this case powers are delegated to the officer, not assigned. Legislation in Alberta enables a council to combine the responsibilities of municipal secretary and treasurer in a CAO-type arrangement. (Ibid.)

In the council-commissioner system found in Western Canada, particularly Winnipeg, Alberta and Saskatchewan, the council appoints one, three or four senior administrators as commissioners to whom it delegates administrative responsibilities. In plural executives each commissioner is responsible for a span of services. Masson criticises the system for poorly defined lines of accountability and its secrecy (Masson, 1985).

The most distinctive Canadian form of municipal management is the board of control, although it has fallen out of favour in recent years. It has two levels of elected member: ordinary councillor and member of the board. A board consists of the head of council and two or four members elected at large who are also members of the council. The board acts as the executive of the authority. Such boards have lacked collective purpose and been generally ineffective in co-ordinating complex administrative structures. Of the twenty-five cities required or authorised to adopt the system, all or nearly all have dropped it.

Executive committees are appointed by the council but their collective responsibility to it seems to some commentators to be a vain hope in the absence of a party system (Higgins, 1977; Tindal and Tindal, 1984).

Departmental structures vary but are generally similar to the traditional English model. Where there is no manager or commissioners, the clerk and treasurer may become pivots between the political and administrative levels on issues of policy-making, responsibility for implementation and co-ordination. The difficulty of achieving integrated action in authorities that may have over 20 departments has been a reason for adopting the executive committee system to establish common policies for the authority as a whole.

9.12 CITIZEN PARTICIPATION AND DECENTRALISATION WITHIN CITIES

Given an estimate of over 4,000 municipalities in Canada one may perhaps assume, subject to the availability of more exact figures, that there are somewhere between thirty and fifty thousand elected councillors in the country. To these may be added members of directly elected special-purpose bodies. One estimate puts the number of citizen participants in official city bodies at 25,000 to 50,000 (unpublished paper by P.H. Wichern Jr quoted in Higgins, 1977). This suggests a very rough estimate of between sixty and a hundred and ten formal participants in the processes of local decision-making, or say one Canadian local representative to every 220 to 400 inhabitants, comparable with the French figure but even more tilted in favour of the rural situation.

Attendance by the public at council meetings is low and it is common for there to be no spectators at small town council meetings (Tindal and Tindal, 1984). Committees do not have to be open to the public.

Alberta's provision for plebiscites was repealed in 1958 because it was thought to short-circuit representative democracy, make councillors reticent about controversial decisions, cause loss of respect for elected bodies and discourage people from standing for election (Masson, 1985).

A large number of strong and active interest groups sprang up in the 1960s concerned with environmental and other matters. Neighbourhood groups have fought expressway proposals, urban renewal projects, high-rise and low-cost housing plans, often with success. (Andrew, 1983)

Winnipeg is perhaps unique in having experimented with a scheme to provide machinery for the participation of sub-municipal communities in city decision-making. Twelve community committees of three to five representatives each were set up together with residents' advisory groups for areas that included those of municipalities that were superseded when the Greater Winnipeg municipality was set up in the early 1970s. They have possessed the power to allocate a small block grant (25 cents per capita) to local cultural and recreational groups. According to the *Municipal Manual* (1982) their local officials, the community clerks, have a primary responsibility to 'develop communication between the City and the residents of the Community' (Masson, 1985).

Citizen participation has been accepted as an essential good and given much space in the literature of Canadian local government. It is statutorily required in planning procedures. The Ontario Ministry of Municipal Affairs has put much effort into promoting it, grant-aiding municipal efforts to inform the public about municipal organisation and channels for contact with councils. It has provided local authorities with promotional material and supplied relevant copy to the local press. A manual for councillors details means of involving the public, including recruiting them to serve as volunteers.

A general conclusion is that the opening up of the local political debate by interest groups has been beneficial but that, by the early 1980s, its intensity had fallen off. The balance between 'efficiency' and participation has continued to be in favour of 'efficiency' (Andrew, 1983).

9.13 THE GOVERNANCE OF METROPOLITAN AREAS

Manitoba and Alberta have unitary metropolitan authorities and Ontario, Quebec and British Columbia two-tier structures. The Alberta cases, Calgary (636,000 inhabitants in 1986) and Edmonton (574,000) have grown by annexation. Regional planning commissions have been set up to deal with wider area development issues. Winnipeg (594,500) for twelve years possessed a directly elected metropolitan authority with extensive functions. Hostility to the authority from both the city and the suburbs led to its replacement in 1972 by a unitary authority, Winnipeg Unicity, which has received much criticism due to its remoteness from the public despite the system of local citizen committees described in §9.12. One complaint is that the direct election of the mayor removes him from the central leadership and the accountability essential to the parliamentary model (Axworthy, 1980; Tindal and Tindal, 1984; Kiernan and Walker, 1983).

In Quebec a variation of a French concept was adopted, the *communauté urbaine*, introduced by the French government in 1966, three years before Quebec (§2.13; Norton, 1983). The Montreal *communauté urbaine* is an imposed federal authority with a council of 84 members including the mayor and councillors of Montreal and the mayor or a delegate from each of the 29 other municipalities in its area. Each councillor has a quota of votes proportional to the size of his or her authority. It has a powerful executive committee of 12. Decisions are subject to approval or amendment by the council (Richmond, 1982). Quebec City and Hull *communautés urbaines* are other examples (Magnusson and Sancton (eds), 1983).

The Greater Vancouver Regional District has membership open to local authorities within the designated area on a voluntary basis. Hospital services are a mandatory function and participation in other matters is voluntary. It is administered by a board of directors chosen by its 18 member authorities, membership and voting power being weighted according to their populations.

Ontario has three special metropolitan authorities that are similar in structure: Hamilton, Ottawa and Metropolitan Toronto. The last-named was founded in 1953 and is by reputation the most successful metropolitan authority in North America. In 1984 it was taken as the model for metropolitan authorities in Turkey, including the Municipality of Greater Istanbul, an authority of over five million people. 'Metro' has a population of some 2,200,000 within a metropolitan area projected to have around 3,200,000 inhabitants by the year 2000. It had a federal structure in which mayors and other leading politicians from its constituent cities were dominant. In 1988 it was changed to a directly elected authority of 28 councillors elected from two specially drawn electoral wards together with the six city mayors *ex officio*. The mayors were ineligible for election as chairman of the council: a provision that led to much acrimony between the province and the authorities of the metropolitan area.

Functions at Metro level are debenture borrowing, public transit, expressways, bridges, traffic control, policing, ambulance services, welfare assistance, housing including homes for the elderly, hostels, business and taxi-licensing, regional libraries, refuse disposal, regional parks, golf courses, the zoo, water purification and trunk distribution. Other functions are shared with the cities, namely official plans and subdivision approval, arterial roads, snow removal, economic development, grants for cultural activities and social services, hospital grants, trunk sewerage and treatment plants, drainage and collection of fines (Barlow, 1991; Feldman, 1991; Norton, 1983).

10. JAPAN

10.1 HISTORY AND TRADITIONS

Japan, with around 118 million inhabitants, has the tenth largest population in the world and, since the 1960s, the second largest per capita gross domestic product. Its area is one and a half times that of the United Kingdom and its population over twice as large, giving it an overall population density comparable to that of the Netherlands. It is a country of mountainous islands. Two-thirds of its people live on the largest, Honshu. Nearly half are concentrated in three metropolitan areas on that island. Nationally around 80 per cent now live in urban settlements. It follows that pressures on development are extreme in the cities and their environs. Land costs are high and traffic heavily congested.

Like Britain, Japan has been isolated by the sea from mainland influences. Like most of North-Western Europe it has institutionalised national sovereignty in a monarch who is a potent symbol of unity although possessing few vestiges of royal authority.

Order was traditionally maintained and self-help exercised within the family, or more exactly the 'household', which included closely related families and retainers. Associated groups or family hierarchies co-operated to undertake tasks beyond the ability of the single family. These were the roots of the neighbourhood associations (*burakukai* in rural areas and *chounaiki* in urban areas) which played a fundamental role in rural and urban Japanese society until modern times. These associations normally consist of groupings of families or 'households', interrelated and embracing more than one generation. The pattern of family and inter-family solidarity has continued and is connected with the modern exercise of political patronage or clientelism. When citizens have problems or needs which they believe can be solved by government they tend to approach eminent figures in the community for intercession with the authorities, as the French may approach their *notables*.

Decisions in the family have been traditionally reached by open discussion in which the aim was to determine a decision shared by all through a conclusion expressed by the family head (see §10.3). The relationships between the Ministry of Home Affairs and the governors of the prefectures, and also those between those governors and local councils, may still be understood by conservatives in a similar way.

The village-based institutions of local government on which the Meiji ministers of the 1860s and the military government in 1940 attempted to build have in general lost their importance. Yet it is reported that 'even if one lives in the center of a major city, a "village-like" feeling nurtured on the basis of the natural village order continues to survive' (Abe, 1975). Neighbourhood associations or their analogies have continued to be cultivated within modern Japanese society, both rural and urban. Their heads are generally elected from within by secret ballot. They run many self-help co-operative services in both rural and urban society.

Innovations from the West such as emphasis on individual rights and Marxist concepts of class conflict with cultural assumptions and are difficult to reconcile with Japanese traditional behaviour. But Western concepts of liberal rights have been accepted in general without undermining important traditional values. The Japanese are now among the most equal peoples in the world. According to surveys some 80 or 90 per cent consider themselves middle class. They enjoy one of the highest levels of civic rights in the world, and surveys show that they are the most literate of the world's peoples and the most well-educated in modern sciences.

From 1867 the reforming 'Meiji Restoration' introduced a revolutionary commitment to industrialisation as a means of achieving parity of power with Western nations. Feudal institutions were abolished by decree and feudal domains amalgamated into units of local government ('prefectures') under governors appointed by central government. A pupil of the Prussian scholar, Rudolf von Gneist (see §1.1), had a direct influence on the new system. In 1871 districts were established within prefectures for conscription purposes, overriding the traditional headships which had provided for a form of communal participation in local decision-making. National administrative responsibility was given to a Ministry of Home Affairs on the French model. Ministers saw the mobilisation of action through local authorities as a means of creating a defence against radicalism in national government. Districts were replaced by counties (*gun*) comprising towns (*cho*) and villages (*son*), each under its own authority. Heads of towns and villages were elected subject to the approval of centrally appointed governors. Chiefly for fiscal and budgeting purposes each of these new units was provided with its own council but was given little independent authority except in welfare matters. Acts in 1888, 1889 and 1890 defined three tiers: 47 prefectures controlling counties (which were abolished in 1923) and below them municipalities (cities, towns and villages). Rapid mergers reduced the number of municipalities to a fifth of the previous number. The minimum size for a village authority was set at three to four hundred households. But traditional small village functions still persisted, particularly in rural areas.

Central government delegated limited functions to the new authorities, including public works and the maintenance and management of primary schools. Mayors and chief executives acted as agents of central government to some extent. A movement towards radical reform developed between the wars which was frustrated when the government adopted strongly militarist policies.

Universal suffrage for men and women was introduced after the Second World War. The 1947 Constitution committed Japan to the promotion of social welfare. The Local Autonomy Law came into force on the same day as the Constitution. It defined the basis for the current system of local government. There was a sweeping decentralisation of the administration of police and education services which was subsequently suspended in 1956. Between 1953 and 1956 a reorganisation of municipalities was effected with the aim of eliminating as far as practicable authorities with fewer than 8,000 inhabitants, the minimum size considered necessary to run a junior high school. By 1979 the number of municipalities had been brought down to 3,255, less than a third of the number existing in 1953.

The Japanese people moved faster than most others into the unparalleled problems of a world dominated by the effects of advanced technology. New social problems have arisen as a result. The recent history of the financial relationships underlying these problems is described in §10.6. The failure of local government institutions to respond to new demands has resulted in popular protest and action by voluntary action groups, especially on environmental matters. The country faces a great challenge to develop local government into a means of responding quickly and sensitively to the new challenges. Against this local authorities have developed an extremely high level of debt. Government policies have sometimes been paradoxical, seeking to rein back spending severely in principle but also to win electoral support through new expenditures. An extreme example of the latter was a brainchild of a former prime minitser: the offer of yen equivalent to nearly 400 thousand sterling to every city, town and village to spend 'imaginatively'.

A Note on the Constitution and Politics

Japan's parliament or diet consists of two houses. The lower one, the House of Representatives, consists of 512 members elected at four-year intervals. The upper house, the House of Councillors, consists of 100 members elected by proportional representation by the electorate as a whole and a further 152, half of whom are elected at three-year intervals in multi-member constituencies. Executive power lies with a cabinet of about twenty members which is drawn predominantly from the lower house, selected and led by a prime minister who is normally also from the same house. The prime minister's usual style has been one of 'quietly seeking and building agreements on policy' in the diet 'with the minimum of open controversy and confrontation'. (Weinstein, 1987)

Party systems date from the late nineteenth century except for a long break from the 1920s to 1946. The Liberal Democratic Party (LDP) and the Liberal and Democrat Parties from which it was formed in 1955 held power continuously from 1947 to 1993. It is a centre conservative party with local offices throughout the country and a large secretariat. Its main objective has been said to be 'to keep the socialists out of power' and to maintain a climate favourable to business. By Western political standards it may be described as left of centre, since it is welfare orientated and has espoused radical policies for environmental protection. However attempts to control local expenditures in the face of national economic problems have brought it into conflict with local authorities. The Socialist Democratic Party (formerly the Japanese Socialist Party (JSP)) came second in size up to 1993. Much of voters' loyalty has in the past gone to individual political notables and tends to be retained by them even when they change their parties.(Weinstein, 1987; Boyd, 1986)

In June 1993 the LDP split, dissident leaders forming a new party, the Shinsei ('newly born') Party, and in July both the LDP and JSP lost heavily in the Tokyo metropolitan and the national elections, seemingly breaking the mould of the long-established system.

10.2 THE STATUS OF LOCAL GOVERNMENT

In Japan aspects of local government status appear to be more sharply defined than in other countries in these studies. One writer describes its local authorities as 'sovereign entities.... Today, the national government is not regarded as essentially different from the local public entities' (Kisa, 1991). But the realities do not match such a status. They reflect a history of superimposed administrative culture and values. The traditional approach to decision-making has not proved capable of resolving the contradictions involved, but it has helped to facilitate the co-existence of clashing concepts.

In 1947 a revolutionary change in central-local government relations was sought as a main plank of democratisation (Steiner, 1965). The Constitution attempted to install a democratic and autonomous system of local government and to effect the transformation of Japan into a welfare state. It recognised local government as one of the administrative systems under-propping a new democratic system based on the rule of law. It defined the basic principles of the system of local government (Isakoda, 1980), laying down that the 'organization and operation of local public entities shall be fixed by law in accordance with the principle of local autonomy' (Article 92). 'Local public entities shall establish assemblies as their deliberative organs, in accordance with the law. The chief executive officers of all public entities, the members of their assemblies, and such other local officials as may be determined by law shall be elected by direct popular vote within their respective communities' (Article 93). 'Local public entities shall have the right to manage their property, affairs and administration and to enact their own legislation within the law' (Article 94). A special law, applicable to only one public entity, cannot be enacted by the diet without the consent of the majority of the voters of the local public entity concerned (Article 95).

But obscurities remain. An issue raised by Article 92 is the meaning of 'the principle of local autonomy' (Shibata, 1986). It is argued variously that the Constitution recognises that local authorities have inherent rights by their very nature, but also that these derive from the Constitution. If the implication is that operations of local authorities cannot be subordinated to central government, then this has been overridden extensively in practice. It is clear, however, that national government cannot intervene in autonomous matters except through writs of mandamus. Article 94 has not received detailed legal interpretation of the kind given to a similar provision in the German Basic Law. The meaning of 'affairs and administration' is extremely elastic.

Local authorities have the right to enact ordinances or by-laws and to carry out administrative activities. Ordinances are enacted by the local assembly; regulations are made by the chief executive or other executive bodies of the local authority in matters within their jurisdiction. Any restriction on the rights and liberties of people must be defined in an ordinance. Affairs delegated by central government to a chief executive or other organ of a local public body ('agency delegated functions') must be stipulated by regulation: they cannot be the subjects of local ordinances (Isakoda, 1980).

Two types of local ordinance that have been promulgated demonstrate the validity of local powers. One is that of public safety ordinances dealing with mass gatherings and demonstrations, and the other lays down local standards for pollution by factories of a more exacting kind than that pro-

459

vided for in national legislation. Violation of a local ordinance can result in 'up to two years imprisonment with or without hard labour, a fine of up to 100,000 yen or detention or confiscation.' (Kisa, 1991).

10.3 CONCEPTS AND VALUES

Of traditional values the most basic is group solidarity, cultivated through harmonious relationships, consensual decision-making and the discouragement of disruptive behaviour. The second is acceptance of seniority or headship. The basic model is that of the family group or household comprising extended family and retainers, as described in §10.1. Deference is expected to the head, who carries a responsibility to seek an appreciation of the interests of the household members and to listen to members and guide the group to a consensus. All members have an equal right to be heard and express their opinions on an issue, but expression of self-interested dissent without paying regard to the good of the whole is frowned upon and in extreme cases may lead to ostracism by the group. Weight is given to attributes of seniority within the group. Collaboration is expected in the carrying out of joint decisions. The head is responsible for representing the interests of the household in the external world and making the collaborative arrangements by which it plays its part within the wider community. This is the traditional ideal model, never far away from mind within social, economic and governmental institutions.

  The statement of rights in the Constitution goes as far or further in its conferment of freedoms and protection of individuals than any in the West. There was a basis for this in the traditional rights within the family group described above. However Western interpretations of human rights in terms of unbridled individualism run counter to the traditional Japanese approach. In particular the confrontational behaviour of party members in Western-style elections and parliaments runs against the grain of the culture. Values put obstacles in the way of the confrontational system exemplified, for example, by the United States with its open airing of policy issues, public testing of the character and qualities of candidates for election and public examination of political executives. On the other hand characteristics of the anglophone approach, such as the tendency to condemn compromise and seeking of consensus, the assumption that winning a majority vote, however narrowly, justifies the overriding of minority opinions and the high level of dependence on the judgement and decision-taking of the individual political leader such as a Margaret Thatcher or a George Bush, seem contrary to the seeking of solidarity that is basic to Japanese values and that has worked to great national advantage.

Respect and deference to government authority have in the past been deeply rooted values in Japan, but at present, according to comments by Japanese colleagues on a draft of this text, there is a lack of respect for political authority: a cynical or ironical reaction to the behaviour of politicians. This has been reinforced by corruption cases among leading politicians in 1992. There is said to be a failing in support for parties generally.

A paper in Japan's Local Government Review (Abe, 1975) suggests semantic difficulties that have to be overcome if Western-style politics are to develop. Abe argues that the special cultural characteristics of Japanese local government are rooted in the denial of local politics in the Meiji local government system, and that 'local autonomy' never possessed the meaning of 'self-rule' in Japan but rather that it is understood as 'natural rule'. Concepts such as 'local politics' and 'local government' have Japanese translations but have not come into general use, the Meiji term for local self-government having been retained. There is a close analogy with the German term *Selbstverwaltung*, 'self-administration', which suggests to some people a restricted apolitical role which is not borne out by evidence of practice. Whereas German local authorities have been quick to flesh out its meaning by reference to the courts when their powers have been challenged, Japanese authorities have been slow to do so. It has been suggested that this is due to the deference of local government bodies to the government and also to the fact that the status of the central senior official is higher in the public mind than that of the judges: a survival from historical conditioning and a reflection of the dislike of public conflict. Steiner suggests that the mutually related concepts of hierarchy and harmony are antagonistic to the status of law (Steiner, 1965).

Abe quotes a Tokyo assemblyman's statement that the term 'government' suggests a consciousness of resistance against central government, 'leaving the impression that there is a duplication of authority', 'a denial of the state structure as it is presently constituted'. This is perhaps an extreme case. Pragmatically chief executives and local assemblies may reconcile themselves to the fact that confrontational policies are self-defeating: that the winning of benefits from central government requires quite different tactics from those that are normal in the West.

The Japanese reputation for deference in the face of authority is by no means borne out by their history. There were turbulence and fears of violence both from right and left during the later nineteenth century, and they had a strong impact on policy-making. In post-war times there has been strong opposition to centralisation expressed through disorders in the

461

diet, a decline in the prestige of parliamentary government, waves of public agitation and the alienation of some population groups. The last three decades have seen the emergence of citizens' movements in many urban areas, presenting a challenge to the traditions of bureaucratic administration. The question is now whether these energies can be directed into participation and a new community consciousness infused through the party system.

10.4 NATIONAL STRUCTURE

Japan has three tiers of government: central, prefectural and municipal. Prefectures and municipalities are classified as 'ordinary local public entities' and in principle have equality of status, a point emphasised in 1947 to stress that the prefectures had been given the same local democratic base as the municipalities in contrast to their former position as arms of the government bureaucracy, and that the municipalities were not to be subordinated to the higher level.

Table 10.1: Local Authorities Average Areas and Populations

Class	Number	Average Population (approx.)
Prefectures (*to, do, fu* & *ken*)	47	2,603,900
Municipalities (*shi, cho* & *son*)	3,241	37,700
Cities over 1 million inhabitants	11	
Cities of 100-199,999 inhabitants	197	
Cities of 30-99,999 inhabitants	447	
Towns (*cho*) and villages (*son*)	2,586	

Source: Data supplied by Akira Kobayashi from official sources, September 1992

Beside 'ordinary public entities' there is a class of 'special public entities' comprising: (1) Tokyo's special wards (similar in organisation to the largest class of municipality, the city); (2) property wards set up to dispose of properties after local authority mergers; (3) joint bodies or unions which run particular services considered to require larger resources or areas than those of constituent municipalities; and (4) joint local development corporations for carrying out projects involving more than one local public entity. Their special charters enable them to employ more flexible forms of management than other public institutions.

The number of prefectures has remained constant for more than a hundred years, but that of municipalities has been substantially reduced. Between 1883 and 1898 it was almost halved and between 1953 and 1966 it was reduced from 9,582 to 2,814.

The Prefectures

Despite the four different names by which prefectural level authorities are called (*to, do, fu* and *ken*), they have virtually the same legal status and are similar in structure and function. The main difference is the case of Tokyo-to with its system of ward governments. *To* is translated as metropolis, *do* used in the case of Hokkaido, the most northern and least developed of the prefectures, *fu* as urban prefecture (Kyoto and Osaka), and *Ken* for the 42 rural prefectures.

Seven prefectures have under one million inhabitants, the smallest of which (Tottori) has 620,000. Twenty-two have from one to two million, eight from two to three million, two from three to five million, seven from five to ten million and Tokyo-to over eleven and a half million. Central-local relationships hinge on the prefectures. Until 1947 they were administered by governors appointed by the Emperor on the nomination of the Minister of Home Affairs. The governors could override decisions of the prefectural assemblies. They drafted and controlled the prefectural budgets and other aspects of municipal administration. Subsequently they have been elected but retain executive responsibilities for central government in addition to their role as chief political executives for their local authorities.

The Municipalities

Municipalities, the basic level of local government, had populations in 1980 ranging from two hundred (the village of Aogashima in Tokyo) to 2,773,822 (Yokohama). They are classified into villages (*mura* or *son*), towns (*machi* or *cho*) and cities (*shi*). The conditions a municipality has to meet to qualify as a city are a population of at least 50,000; having at least 60 per cent of its housing within its urban centre; at least 60 per cent of its population engaged in or dependent on commercial, industrial or other urban activities; and the provision of certain urban facilities and other amenities specified in prefectural by-laws. If a city has a population of over

500,000 it may be designated by order of the cabinet to take over prefectural functions, including social welfare and urban planning. The designated cities in 1985 were Osaka, Nagoya, Kyoto, Yokahama, Kobe, Kitayushu, Sapporo, Kawasaki, Fukuoka and Hiroshima.

To be upgraded to a town, a village must meet certain requirements stipulated in a by-law of its prefecture. In general towns have better urban facilities than the villages. The latter consist predominantly of agricultural, forestry and fishing settlements.

Special Local Public Entities

Tokyo-to's 23 special wards (*ku*) have a range of functions similar to that of cities but modified by the need for a division of responsibilities that is better suited to the nature of the metropolitan system. They lack competences for water, sewerage and fire control services and certain planning powers.

Joint special public entities, unions and development corporations are described in §10.5. In 1980 there were 2,992 joint entities for specific functions and 16 local development corporations. Another class of special local public entity is the property ward, of which some 4,500 function within municipalities. Governors have the power to implement changes in the status of authorities, make boundary revisions and merge or divide local public entities on application by the municipalities concerned.

Structural Reorganisation

Changes in the scale of municipalities have occurred piecemeal within a legal framework which allows each case to be dealt with on its own merits. Cities multiplied rapidly from the 1940s to the 1980s due to the rapid immigration from rural areas. A survey as early as 1952 showed that only 20 per cent of the inhabitants of the Tokyo wards and 43 per cent of those in Osaka were born within those cities. Between 1950 and 1960 the area occupied by cities nearly tripled, reaching 18 per cent of the total national land area.

Communities have achieved the qualifying size for city status chiefly through amalgamations. Overall city density has increased less than might have been expected, but this is not true of density in city centres, which has been calculated at 8,700 people per square kilometre, nearly five times the nearest equivalent for the United States (Mills and Ohta, 1976).

Villages and Towns

The reduction in the number of villages and towns was effected mainly through persuasion by prefectural governors. 'Amalgamation acceleration committees' were set up consisting of mayors and elected members recommended by prefectural associations, nominees of boards of education, prefectural government staff and 'persons of learning and experience'. Groups of municipalities were allowed to define their own plans provided that they obtained the opinion of the governor in advance. 'Autonomy conflict mediation committees' were established to overcome inter-authority disagreements and make reasonable concessions to local feelings. Methods of persuasion included extolling 'such traditional virtues as harmony, sincerity and cooperation'. (Steiner, 1965; Isakoda, 1980)

By European standards the reorganisations have not resulted in large basic authorities. The results have, however, in most cases distanced local government from its traditional roots.

10.5 INTER-AUTHORITY RELATIONS AND ORGANISATION

Joint Associations

The Local Autonomy Law provided for unions or associations of local authorities with the status of judicial persons distinct from those of their constituent local authorities. They have generally been set up under agreed articles of association. They require the permission of the governor or, in the case of unions of prefectures, that of the prime minister. They may exercise powers delegated by central government and the powers of the local authorities they represent.

Unions for a limited number of functions may also be effected by the prefectural governor if considered necessary in the public interest. General-purpose unions have been rare and have foreshadowed amalgamations. In practice they amount to amalgamations since all functions are removed from their constituent authorities.

Although the administrative structure of unions is similar to that of municipalities, their chief executives are not always elected. Some have a mixed membership of municipalities and prefectures. In 1980 the main functions for which they were used were, in order of numbers, sanitation and refuse disposal (796), fire and flood protection (443), hospitals for infectious diseases (251), general affairs (238), education (201), agriculture, forestry and fisheries (182), social welfare (165) and some other miscellaneous purposes (84) (*Statistical Abstract of Japanese Local Government*, 1982).

There have been few voluntary joint unions for reasons familiar in Western countries: traditional jealousies and fear that they would seem to show that separate constituent authorities were unnecessary. Another reason is reported to be lack of initiative and guidance from above. Governors have tended to prefer amalgamations (Steiner, 1965).

Ad hoc local development corporations are few. They can be set up by charter and are responsible for project execution in such fields as housing, roads, parks, water and sewerage provision within regional integrated development plans. Their charters allow for more flexible forms of organisation and accounting.

An amendment to the Local Autonomy Law in 1952 provided for joint councils for liaison and joint management of functions. They can be set up in a much less cumbersome way than unions. They are not judicial persons and can act only in the name of and through their constituent members. Joint organs and commissioning of services by one local authority from another are also permitted, mainly for purposes of economy.

Relationships Between Prefectures and Municipalities

In principle the relationship between levels of local government is one of equality and voluntary collaboration. Prefectures are credited with general responsibility for co-ordination of affairs with and between municipalities in their areas and for providing them with advice (*Local Public Administration in Japan*, 1986). Relationships are coloured, however, by the fact that governors possess extensive delegated powers from central government which involve supervision of municipal functions. Although there is no subordination of mayors to governors in principle, a governor may supervise and direct a mayor in his exercise of centrally delegated responsibilities (Isakoda, 1980). Prefectural influence is generally through administrative guidance and financial aid. On the other hand prefectures often delegate authority to mayors by means of administrative orders.

10.6 INTER-GOVERNMENTAL RELATIONS

Distribution and Control of Functions

National government has the power to issue reports on the affairs and administration of local authorities; give technical advice and recommendations on organisation and management; request corrective action if authorities fail to observe the law or carry out responsibilities adequately; demand reports and investigation of local authorities' financial affairs; and refuse permission for the issue of local bonds or the levy of taxes of types not provided for in the law.

Some 80 per cent of functions at prefectural level and 50 per cent at local level have been acquired by delegation from central government (Kisa, 1991). Ministers direct and supervise governors, who are similarly responsible for directing and supervising the mayors to whom they delegate tasks within their responsibility. Thus there is a three-tier hierarchy of executives under central control parallel with the three-tier government system. Local authorities cannot intervene in delegated affairs: all they can do is to demand explanations from the executives and express their opinions.

Control of delegated matters is secured by a so-called 'mandamus' system: if a governor acts contrary to the provisions of the law the competent minister may order him to take appropriate action, and if he fails to act accordingly he may, after confirmation by a high court, be removed from office by the prime minister. Governors are empowered to take similar action in case of failure to observe the law by mayors.

Although popularly elected, some half of the forty-seven governors are ex-civil servants. The senior local administrators who work with them are in many cases seconded from government departments and normally return to the government civil service as a further step in their careers. They often show considerable independence while seconded, however, fighting against their own departments' directives (Kitamura, 1983).

The form of prefectural administration is laid down by law. By 1982 there were eighty-five laws administered by fourteen ministries and agencies which required local authorities to set up a wide range of special local administrative agencies. In 1955 there were 122 types of these.

Local government receives some 60 per cent of its income by transfers from national government, including in principle full reimbursement for expenditures under agency arrangements. Government pays 'obligatory shares' and grants of aid in the range of services where there is shared responsibility (see §10.9).

467

The problem of reconciling central responsibility with local autonomy, particularly in fields of shared responsibility, is reflected by Article 2 of the Local Finance Law which states that central government shall refrain from any action prejudicial to the financial autonomy of local governments or from shifting its responsibilities on to local government. The ensuing problems are reflected in an article by a prefectural governor who writes, 'The enforcement of too many obligatory tasks takes priority over the autonomous selection of work. The minimum budget for this work is paid for under strict conditions'. The grants are generally considered inadequate, and the additional costs of obligatory activities severely narrow authorities' ability to undertake autonomous functions. Moreover autonomous functions are subject to restrictive supervision. The general picture is of local executives overburdened with ever-increasing requirements by central ministries. In theory local authorities could refuse to co-operate, but there is hardly a case where they have done so. (Nagano, 1987)

There are few provisions in law for local authorities to be consulted by national government. Relationships are not of the open and structured kind found for example in the French system.

A Brief History of Relationships

In the late 1940s the governors and mayors acquired a mandate from and accountablity to the local electorate in addition to those they carried as agents for national government. Their closely related functions as adviser and as manager for their local councils inevitably meant that they were an integral part of the national system of government administration. The problems of implementing welfare systems and of economic control increased central government's dependence on them. Although local government was an essential means for rebuilding the structure of a modern state, it found itself crushed by the contradictions of national policies. Powers of local choice were strong in theory but weak in practice.

From 1955 the aim of economic growth came to dominate national policies. Local government was enjoined to collaborate with business to achieve 'total mobilisation of society' and was given delegated functions to this end (Kitamura, 1983). Following the 'economic miracle' of the 1960s new welfare policies were developed in which local authorities were deeply involved. The extensive delegations and subsidies this involved led to the new policies being labelled 'the new centralism'.

The early 1970s have been defined as the 'Age of Localism'. The oil crisis and the related rapid deceleration of growth while welfare expenditures expanded led to a critical period for local finance. Government sought to restrain local expenditure by issuing special deficit bonds and the setting of zero-growth and even 'minus-growth' ceilings on budgets. Specific grants were reduced.

From the mid-1970s local politics lost much of their earlier party political character. Mayors and governors came to receive cross-party support, resulting in a 'de-politicisation' or 'administrationalisation' (*sic*) of local government. (Kisa, 1991)

A 'new, new centralism' developed in the 1980s, linked with a report of the Second Extraordinary Administrative Research Council (SEARC), 1981-83. The council's members and its research workers came from the financial world and the state bureaucracy and are said to have considered local government as just one part of overall government and administration. It is alleged that most of the important matters were decided by the chairman in consultation with the prime minister. Rationalisation of structure and personnel matters including salaries were, it is reported, 'handled from the national perspective, with the purpose of weakening the democratic function and the reduction of local expenditures'. Critics said that the 'new, new centralism' featured 'the non-recognition of local politics', 'the unification of local autonomy', 'interference with the rights of local government' and a 'shift of financial obligations to the localities'.

From 1985 the tactic of postponing reimbursements was succeeded by fixed-rate reductions in financial transfers. The policy was difficult to agree against the opposition of ministries committed to maintaining special subsidies. Local government expenditure as a proportion of the GDP fell by about seven per cent between 1981 and 1985 against a fall in the national ratio of only five per cent (Mouritzen and Nielsen, 1988). In some respects local authorities have been more fortunate than the centre financially. Their tax incomes have been more stable and their services given priority. Minor taxes have been revised to their benefit. Some delegated functions have been transferred from local executives to the care of local assemblies, although not with a clear increase in local choice (Hoshino, 1987).

By the last years of the 1980s central-local relationships were not seen from the centre as having achieved the level of collaboration and harmony that was considered basic to future progress. There was no clear way ahead. A large burden of finance fell on local authorities who were hard pressed by demands to restrict expenditure on the one hand and to maintain the quality of services on the other. In social welfare the dilemma of fixing charges at levels which prevented delivery to the needy or overburdening tax resources is one only too familiar in the West.

10.7 LOCAL SERVICES

Japanese local authorities provide a range of services probably as wide if not wider than those in any other Western-type democracy. Responsibilities are divided between assemblies and chief executives. Complexities are increased by the many delegations from central government to local assemblies and local executives, sub-delegations from governors to mayors, and a lack of clarity in the relevant provisions of the Constitution and the Local Autonomy Law. A number of functions are allocated concurrently to prefectures and municipalities, and often to central government also.

The Constitution is interpreted to give a general competence to local authorities to take action for the good of communities, similar to that in countries of western continental Europe (see also §10.2). It is taken to imply 'that a function be attributed to the state only where there is a reasonable need for doing so, considering the prevailing objective circumstances at a given time' (Steiner, 1965), but such implications have received little testing in law.

Functions with which local authorities are empowered to deal 'in general' are included in the Local Autonomy Law of 1948, but the implications of 'in general' are unclear. Many laws cut across the list and provide for arrangements independently. In most functional areas the interdependence of prefectures and municipalities is recognised and the need for collaboration is frequently stressed. Public utilities are generally provided under specific provisions of national laws. Local authorities direct and administer these through 'local public enterprises' (see §10.8).

The information on individual services given below is taken mainly from the publications of the Jichi Sogo General Center for Local Autonomy (*Local Public Administration in Japan*, 1990; *Local Public Finance in Japan*, 1984; and Isakoda, 1980. Other sources are specified below.)

1. Planning and Development
There is an integrated national planning system in which local government plays the most important part. 'Comprehensive National Development Plans' by the National Land Agency have been approved by the cabinet every few years, as stipulated in the Comprehensive National Land Development Act of 1950. They lay down tasks to be carried out to meet their analysis of regional needs concerning land management and the 'basic life necessities of the people, including educational, cultural and medical matters, and defining those in metropolitan areas and those in urban and rural areas separately. Many local government activities are undertaken

within the context of general framework plans defined by *prefectures*. These may examine trends, postulate the needs of twenty-first century society, define goals for action and put forward a basic plan with guidelines and a five-year implementation plan including particulars of major projects within sub-regions, all within the provision of national development plans and associated legislation. (*The 2nd New Kanagawa Plan*, 1987; Saito, 1978; *Regional Development in Japan*, 1991)

Governors of prefectures designate city planning areas and give permission for developments and implementation of certain city planning projects too difficult for municipalities.

Municipalities undertake city planning other than that determined by governors, and the execution of city planning projects.

2. Housing

Governors of prefectures approve housing sites. Municipalities construct and administer public low-rent housing for people in lower-income brackets. Local government in the late 1980s was constructing some seven per cent of houses built with public funds. Most of housing was provided by municipalities. Nearly all units were government subsidised.

3. Roads

are graded as national, prefectural and municipal, and built and maintained accordingly. In percentage of kilometres, excluding national highways, the Ministry of Construction builds and maintains about four per cent of roads, prefectures twelve per cent and the municipalities 85 per cent.

4. Transport

Municipalities provide services through public enterprises under national laws for tramways, local railway and bus systems.

5-6. Education

Municipalities construct and administer all but one per cent of Japanese primary schools, provide 96 per cent of junior high schools and about a quarter of all kindergarten. *Prefectures* are the main providers and managers of senior high schools. They also provide special schools and pay subsidies to private schools to preserve and improve educational standards and reduce the financial burden on parents. (See under 13A below for vocational training.)

7-8. Social Education, Cultural Activities, Libraries and Museums

Local authorities provide social education, a category which takes more than six per cent of the education budget. This term includes libraries and museums as well as courses and is closely linked to promotion of cultural activities. 'Citizens' public halls', of which there were more than 12,300 in the early 1980s, were provided by municipalities, being regarded as 'a key facility for social educational activities for neighbourhood life'. In the early

1980s there were 79 prefectural and 1,316 municipal libraries, and 77 prefectural and 257 municipal museums. One hundred prefectural and 1,628 municipal auditoriums provided facilities for exhibitions, concert halls, theatres and art collections.

9. Health and Social Welfare

In 1987 there were 1,076 local authority hospitals as against 402 administered from national level. Most were operated as public enterprises. *Municipalities* provided a large number of clinics. *Prefectures, designated cities and the 23 special wards of Tokyo-to* provide health offices under a national scheme in accordance with a national standard of one per 100,000 inhabitants. They are also responsible for a full range of preventive measures. *Local authorities* are generally responsible for welfare centres providing services stipulated in six welfare codes, including facilities and allowance schemes for the elderly, children and mothers, the physically handicapped and relief of the needy. The role of national government is generally limited to planning, guidance, subsidies etc. *Governors and mayors of cities and towns with welfare offices* have run a scheme to guarantee a minimum standard of living, costs being shared between central and local government. *Municipalities* operate the National Health Insurance scheme locally.

10. Police

Police services are provided under *prefectural governments* and planned and coordinated by the National Police Agency. There is a Public Safety Commission in each prefecture adminstered by the governor.

11. Fire and Other Disaster Protection and Aid are the responsibility of *municipalities* and joint fire-fighting organisations set up by *adjacent municipalities*.

12. Development of the Local Economy through promotion of industries is a leading responsibility of *municipalities* in fulfilment of development plans prepared at national level. They have the central role in promotion of local industries, particularly small and medium-size enterprises and those in the high-technology fields. They may be given exemption from taxation for a period as an incentive. *Prefectures* promote and give guidance to organisations concerned with help to small and medium-size enterprises, including free or low-cost loans and loan guarantees for modernisation purposes, introduction of special products etc.

Municipalities seek to promote and enhance local industry and commerce by guidance to small and medium-size enterprises, development of new industrial areas, exhibitions of local products etc. in co-ordination with prefectures and national government.

Prefectures undertake research, agricultural extension work and soil

472

improvement etc.

Municipalities set up commissions to adjust and co-ordinate use of farm land, control production of crops and livestock etc. in close co-operation with other public and voluntary agencies.

Labour Services are provided to improve the welfare of workers. *Prefectures* set up vocational training schools for jobless school leavers and other unemployed people and provide loans to workers for education, health and social expenses and sport and recreation facilities. Aspects of labour administration, including trade union matters and industrial disputes, are dealt with by local authorities, governors or mayors as well as national government.

13-16. Public Utilities.

All types of local public enterprise are provided by *prefectural, designated city and other municipal levels,* and in many cases by *associations of local authorities* as well. In 1983 they included the following enterprises: water supply (3,639), industrial water supply (91), sewerage (1,096), transportation (137), electricity (33), gas (73), harbour improvement (187), markets (184), tourist facilities (774), housing site preparation (469), toll roads (29), parking lots (24), hospitals (724), slaughterhouses (287) and others (46).

17. Tourist Promotion is provided generally by local public enterprises set up at both *prefecture* and *municipality* level.

18. Waste Collection and Disposal is undertaken by *municipalities.*

19. Abattoirs and Veterinary Services are provided through local public enterprises by *prefectures, municipalities and associations.*

20. Markets are provided through local public enterprises by *prefectures, municipalities and associations.*

21. Other Services include environmental protection for which local authorities make plans and take measures against pollution; and river control for which governors are responsible for supervising 6,733 rivers and mayors for 12,077 smaller rivers. Local authorities construct dams for flood control, development of water resources and irrigation.

10.8 IMPLEMENTATION OF SERVICES

Services to the public have been carried out predominantly by local authority employees. Numbers of local employees grew steadily through the post-war years until 1982 when they started to decline. In 1986 they formed 2.65 per cent of the population. The education service accounted for well over one-third of these. After excluding education, police, fire services and employees of public enterprises, the remainder amounted to a little under one per cent. The fall in numbers is accounted for partly by attempts to reduce expenditure, including privatisation measures which were recommended by national reports in 1983 and 1985 (Shibata, 1990).

Of 111 authorities replying to a questionnaire on austerity strategies in 1986, the proportions classifying various strategies as 'very' or 'somewhat important' were: 73 per cent contracting out; 54 per cent reduction of workforce by attrition; 39 per cent reduction of services funded from their own revenues; 32 per cent reduction of services funded from inter-government revenue; and 62 per cent elimination of programmes. There was a fairly strong movement to transfer work and responsibilities to the private sector. The real level of current expenditure had, however, risen yearly by 25.6 per cent between 1978 and 1985, while capital expenditure was brought down by 14 per cent from 1981 to 1985 (Mouritzen and Nielsen, 1988; *Local Public Service Personnel System in Japan*, 1988).

Local public enterprises are the main means for providing public utilities and to a lesser extent some other services. They are distinct from general public services in that they satisfy the needs of individuals rather than of society as a whole. Unlike normal departments of local authorities they work in competition with private enterprise. Although required to pursue economic efficiency and earn income by charging for services, their primary object is to promote public welfare. They are preferred to private enterprise in that they guarantee a stable response to residents' needs. They also often need resources on a scale beyond the capacity of competitive private enterprise. Their types and numbers are given in §10.7, heads 14-17.

The accounting systems used are similar to those of private companies, including profit and loss accounts. Their general managers are appointed by prefectural governors and mayors. Managers appoint their workforce under the same legislation as private enterprises. In principle an enterprise is self-financing but it may receive transfers from the general administrative account of a local authority to meet unprofitable business undertaken to meet public needs. Profits are transferred to the general account for the benefit of the community as a whole.

Local development corporations are established by local authorities for project execution. They are supported by investment, loans, guarantees, grants etc. In 1982 there were 2,149 set up by municipalities, 163 by designated cities and 1,048 by prefectures. Special laws provide for land development corporations, local housing provision corporations and local road corporations. Twenty-five per cent or more of their capital fund must be supplied by one local authority.

An article in the *Local Government Review in Japan* discusses and recommends cautious privatisation of some local public enterprise activities (Shibata 1990).

10.9 LOCAL GOVERNMENT FINANCE

Note. This section relies mainly on the following sources for which details are given in the References listed after this chapter: Ishihara, 1980; *Local Public Finance in Japan*, 1984; *Local Tax System in Japan*, 1990; Maruyama, 1986; Ministry of Home Affairs, 1982; *An Outline of Japanese Taxes*, 1989; Tohru, 1983; Tsuda, 1987; Yano, 1987. I owe a special debt to Professor Akira Kobayashi for his advice and the unpublished papers he copied to me in 1992.

From 1980 local government was responsible for between 18 and 19 per cent of national expenditure. A drop of nearly one per cent in 1984 was followed by a further decline, after which the level rose to 17.7 per cent in 1990. As a proportion of public expenditure alone local government's share fell from 66 per cent in 1984 to 62 per cent in 1990. Expenditures are shared fairly equally between municipalities and prefectures.

After the Gulf oil crisis revenues fell but needs increased. Central government facilitated borrowing by paying the interest on loans raised to meet the deficits in whole or in part. The subsequent aims in the 1980s were to curb the level of local taxes and reduce specific grants. A policy of 'financial rehabilitation without tax rises' increased financial pressures by delaying reimbursement of local government interest support grants. In 1985 a fixed rate reduction started, bringing central transfers down from 23 to 13 per cent.

Local tax revenues have been more stable than national government revenues and debt expenditures have been reduced. Some reform measures favoured local government, including the transfer of delegated powers from governors and mayors to local councils and a relaxation of government requirements regarding permits and approvals and mandatory regulations. But little was done to reduce local dependence on national transfers or to increase local government's autonomous resources.

Local Revenues

Japanese local authorities have three main sources of finance. In 1990 some 42 per cent of revenue came from local taxes, imposed and collected under local ordinances. A further 22 per cent came from national local allocation and transfer taxes. The third was national disbursements or transfers to local authorities for specific purposes. These accounted for some 13 per cent of income in 1990. Other sources included borrowing through local bonds (8 per cent) and fees and charges (2.4 per cent). Dependence on local taxes rose from 34 per cent in 1980 to 42 per cent in 1990 and allocation and transfer taxes from 18 to 20 per cent, while national disbursements had fallen in the same period from 23 to 13 per cent.

Local taxes are either defined by national statutes or have been designed locally and implemented with the approval of the Ministry for Local Government. A local freedom to adjust nationally defined taxes has been little used.

There are 15 prefectoral taxes and 17 municipal taxes. This multiplicity provides a reasonable and fairly stable economic base and evens out inequities, or 'spreads the pain', across the community. On the other hand important national and local taxes share the same bases of property and income and obscure where responsibility lies among the levels of government.

The tax system was based on the Shoup Report, written by an American expert in 1949. Its principles were minimisation of the number of taxes, 'sufficient' tax revenues with priorities going to the municipalities, strict separation of national, prefectural and municipal taxes from each other, clarity of tax base and local freedom to control tax rates. It was later modified, particularly to promote capital investment.

The Local Tax Law and regulations provide a framework within which local authorities promulgate ordinances on tax objects, tax bases, tax rates and related matters.

There is close collaboration between levels on arrangements. Municipalities collect the prefectural local inhabitants tax along with their own and transfer it to the prefecture. The same tax base is used for the prefectural property acquisition tax and the municipal fixed assets tax. (*Local Tax System in Japan*, 1990)

The *local residents or inhabitants tax* accounted in 1990 for 32.5 per cent of prefectural and 54.3 per cent of municipal revenues. It is levied on residents and also on businesses and unincorporated associations and foundations with offices and premises in a local authority's area. That on individuals also has a dual basis: (1) per capita charges on a scale relating to the size of municipality — citizens of cities with over 500,000 inhabitants have to pay two-thirds more a head than those in local authorities with under 50,000 inhabitants; and (2) on income according to a graduated scale. The levy on businesses etc. also has two bases: (1) employees per capita and capital, and (2) corporation rate related to the level of the national corporation tax payable. The rate on individual incomes is similar to national income tax but has a less progressive structure. It is levied according to income on all inhabitants except those aided under the Social Aid Law.

Enterprise Tax (prefectural) is levied on both small unincorporated businesses and corporations. The former is income-based but small in total (one per cent of total tax). The latter constituted 40 per cent of the total tax income of prefectures in 1990. The Law allows prefectures to substitute other tax bases. A prefectural assembly can increase its tax rate up to 110 per cent of the national standard rates.

The *municipal fixed assets tax* provided 34 per cent of municipal tax income in 1990. It is based on land and building assets (assessed every three years) and tangible business assets (assessed annually). It provides a fairly stable revenue and the base is spread fairly evenly over the country. It is payable by any owner of taxable assets, assessments being made by the tax officers of a municipality in accordance with a national standard method. Exemption is given for assets below a certain level. The standard rate has been 1.4 per cent in the 1980s, with a top rate of 2.1 per cent.

Special land-owning tax was designed to discourage land speculation. Land acquired in compliance with land-use policies is exempt, as is land below a stipulated area. Its yield has been below one per cent.

Automobile tax is imposed on possession of vehicles according to type and cylinder capacity. It raised 8 per cent of prefectural tax revenue in 1987. An *automobile acquisiton tax* raised 4 per cent of tax revenue. A *light oil delivery tax* yields 5 per cent and a *golf course tax* 0.3 per cent.

The *tobacco consumption tax* raises 2 per cent of tax income for prefectures and 4 per cent for municipalities and the *meals and hotel tax* 5 per cent of prefectural tax revenues. An *amusement tax* yields one per cent. The *city planning tax* of up to 0.3 per cent of the tax base of the fixed assets tax raises 5 per cent of municipal revenue, specifically to finance city planning expenditure. A *business office tax* is levied in larger cities on the construction of offices with above 2,000 sq. metres floor space and business activities in offices of over 1,000 sq. metres floor area and over 100 employees.

A *municipal health insurance tax* paid by a householder insured under a municipal government health programme provided 65 per cent of expenditure on health care. It is accounted for outside other general municipal revenues. It consists of a per capita sum per taxpayer and ratings on income and the value of assets.

Discretionary taxes devised by the municipalities themselves include advertisement and nuclear fuel taxes and account for about 0.1 per cent of local tax income.

National and Prefectural Transfers

Apart from the local allocation taxes mentioned above, financial transfers are made in lieu of local taxes and inter-governmental contracts. There are also financial transfers to local authorities in the form of 'obligatory shares' of the cost of mandatory services, grants-in-aid and contributions to mandatory services.

Prefectural transfers to municipalities are similar in nature. Finance for welfare, medical care, public works and disaster restoration works is distributed from national level to prefectures and then in part onwards with matching contributions from prefectures to municipalities. By far the largest transfers are to the prefectures in respect of public works and compulsory education.

Treasury obligatory shares are of three kinds:

(1) *ordinary shares* to maintain fixed levels of provision by local councils or their executives nation-wide and contribute to costs (e.g. of compulsory education and livelihood protection), and for public works to enable authorities to carry out works in accordance with national plans, including road construction, river conservation, harbour construction, land improvement and unemployment relief works; (2) *grants-in-aid*, in principle to encourage provision of new services ('encouragement subsidies') or to meet special needs such as relief on interest payments ('financial assistance subsidies'); (3) *payments for agency tasks*. Agency tasks range from registration of foreigners, running national elections and the national census to functions relating to the national pension scheme and other social security services.

Local transfer taxes include those on fuels, in particular benzine and naphtha, petroleum gas, aviation fuel and on special ship tonnage and motor vehicle tonnage. All are collected nationally and distributed to local authorities on objective criteria.

Local Authority Borrowing

Borrowing is nationally controlled. An authority with tax rates lower than the national standards may not raise loans for construction purposes, and those with budget deficits of a certain percentage are not allowed to borrow unless they reconstruct their finances in accordance with financial plans authorised by the Ministry of Home Affairs. There are other restrictions, including conformity to a national loan plan under conditions that vary year by year.

A Public Enterprise Finance Corporation provides loans at stable low interest rates and there are no restrictions in the law on sources that local authorities may use for local loans. Larger cities and prefectures are allowed to raise their own bonds on the open market.

The Local Public Finance Programme

Annual estimates of the expenditures and revenues from local authorities are consolidated into the Local Public Finance Programme which provides a guarantee to local governments of sufficient revenues to enable them to supply services to a stipulated standard. The Programme facilitates collaboration between national and local expenditures to enable national macro-economic policies to be implemented. Capital expenditures are not included in the Plan, nor are the affairs of public enterprises. It is meant to provide an 'ideal' or standard level of revenue and expenditure. Many authorities spend higher than what is assumed in the Plan.

10.10 ELECTORAL REPRESENTATION

The origins of Japan's national electoral system lie in provisions adopted in 1878 for representative prefectural assemblies, ten years before elections to a national parliament were instituted. Town and village mayors were first elected by local assemblies in 1888. Direct, single and secret ballots were introduced in 1899. Universal franchise for males came in 1926 and for women in 1946. Direct election of governors and mayors was introduced at the same time. The Public Offices Election Law lays down that 'One person shall have only a single vote at each election'.

Candidates at municipal elections must be at least 25 years of age, have been resident for three months in the prefectural area and be qualified to vote in the local assembly. Mayors and governors have to be at least 30 years of age. They need have no local residential qualification but may not be members of the National Diet or of other local assemblies, or regularly employed staff of any local authority. They are prohibited from under-taking commercial work for their authority. Their emoluments, expenses of office and 'term-end allowances' are set by their authorities' by-laws. The payments have now 'reached relatively high levels, partly to ensure living wages' (*Local Public Administration in Japan*, 1990).

Local elections are held over a short period every four years for all levels of government. Voting is generally at large across the whole area of a municipality, but in designated cities voting for assemblymen is by administrative wards. Other cities may establish multiple electoral districts by ordinance. As a general rule electoral districts in prefectures are defined by the boundaries of cities and former county authorities. All governors and mayors are elected at large. There is one permanent voters' list for elections of all types, prepared by scrutiny of records. Supplementary lists are added before each election. Citizens have rights that enable them to ensure that they are entered on the list.

No door-to-door canvassing is allowed, or publication of opinion polls. A national Election Management Commission of four members has general responsibility for diet and prefecture elections and supervises the prefectural municipal election management commissions. These local commissions, also of four members, are responsible for the conduct of municipal elections. They have in many cases financed 'competitive speech meetings' at which each candidate has an opportunity to make his or her views known. Candidates receive a free supply of postcards, posters and bus or rail tickets. There are strict regulations on expenditures and the number of newspaper advertisements, posters, election cards, radio and television speeches, vehicles used and other matters. At the polling booth each voter presents an entry ticket and is given a ballot paper on which to write the name of the candidate chosen. There is provision for braille writing and also the employment of a deputy by someone who is unable to write.

The candidates who receive the most votes are elected. (Proportional representation is used only in the elections for the national House of Councillors.) The at-large basis gives the opportunity for minority parties within an electoral area to be represented if they have sufficient local strength. Electoral systems were, however, under review in 1993.

Independents predominate in city and even more so in town and village assemblies where they held nearly 90 per cent of the votes in the 1980s. But they held only four per cent in Tokyo's special wards. Liberal Democrat Party members hold the largest number of seats in other assemblies without overall majorities. In towns and villages the communists had the largest number of party seats in 1979, although their numbers have since fallen against advances by socialists and other groups nearer to the political centre.

Chief executives are frequently re-elected: in the case of heads of towns and villages for up to ten terms (40 years). In 1980 70 per cent of mayors of cities and special wards had served previous terms of office, and in 17 per cent of cases more than three terms.

Independents predominate in elections of governors. Many are far from conservative. Thirteen governorships were held by Liberal Democrat Party (LDP) members in 1980. Since the 1970s there has been a tendency for all the five centre parties including the socialists (termed 'the five political parties riding together') to back mayors and governors, leaving opposition to the communists. Few mayors or heads stand as party representatives in smaller types of authority.

Personal and traditional factors have a major effect on the distribution of votes. Independents may win who hold highly radical opinions. Candidates' administrative ability and the extent to which they are thought to be able to win help for the area from central ministries are traditionally important.

10.11 THE INTERNAL ORGANISATION OF LOCAL AUTHORITIES

The basic pattern of internal organisation is the same both at prefectural and municipal levels: that is, an assembly and a one-person executive. Within this pattern power is highly dispersed among a variety of sub-institutions and there is little subordination of one body of elected members to another. Both executive and assembly have mandates by direct election. Commissions for specific areas of administration are also autonomous. They were instituted partly with the aim of limiting the executive scope of governors and mayors who otherwise, it was thought, might possess excessive personal power. They therefore have a different status from British local government committees.

A set of checks and balances, sometimes called mutual controls, has been established between chief executives and assemblies in order to contain each others' power. The executive submits bills but the council may reject them. The assembly can inspect and investigate the executive's administration. It can enforce the attendance of the executive at one of its meetings to present explanations. On the other hand the executive can require the reconsideration of an assembly resolution. If it is re-voted (in some cases a two-thirds majority is required), governors and mayors must in general accept the decision. But if they believe a decision to be illegal they may appeal to higher authority or file a suit in a law court for the decision's annulment. An assembly can pass a resolution of no-confidence in the executive subject to a three-quarters majority of its members and a two-thirds quorum. But a governor or mayor has the right to dissolve the assembly, thereby forcing an election. Failure to do so within ten days leads to automatic loss of office. If the new assembly adopts a resolution of no-confidence in the executive at its first meeting he or she also loses office.

Local Assemblies

The sizes of local assemblies are in accordance with a national scale relating to populations. They range from 12 members for a town or village with under 2,000 inhabitants to 120 for the largest prefecture. City councils range from 30 for cities of under 30,000 inhabitants to 100 in the largest cases. They are described as legislative and decision-making bodies, their central activity being the enactment of ordinances.

Their major powers and responsibilities are: (1) to enact, amend and abolish ordinances; (2) to amend and pass the budget; (3) to authorise the annual accounts; (4) to decide matters concerning the levy and collection of local taxes, fees and charges etc.; (5) to approve contracts and acquisition and disposal of certain assets; (6) to order audits; (7) to investigate administrative affairs; (8) to consider petitions from residents; and (9) to submit opinions on matters concerning the interests of local authorities.

Assemblies hold four statutory meetings a year and extraordinary meetings if requested by at least a quarter of their members. They appoint chairmen and vice-chairmen for their four-year terms of office, standing committees specified in the Local Autonomy Law and ad hoc committees for specific matters.

Voting is by simple majority with a chairman's casting vote, except in the case of certain decisions which require the votes of three-quarters of members present who must form two-thirds of the total assembly membership. These exceptions include the expulsion of members, a vote of no-confidence in the executive and dismissal of his deputy and other major officials consequent on a demand for recall (see §10.11). Other decisions require the support of two-thirds of members with at least half of all members present. These include changes in offices, secret meetings, decisions on members' qualifications, abolition of important public facilities and the granting of the exclusive right to use such facilities. In principle sessions are open to the public. (Isakoda, 1980; *Local Public Administration in Japan*, 1986)

Executives of Local Authorities

Governors and mayors supervise and administer the affairs of their authorities. They have the power and duty to submit bills to their assemblies; prepare and execute budgets; levy and collect taxes, fees and charges etc.; supervise accounts; acquire, administer and dispose of assets; establish, manage or abolish public facilities; and appoint and dismiss officials and other employees.

They serve as agents of national government for carrying out state responsibilities delegated to them, including registration, surveys and national road supervision (see §10.6) (Isakoda, 1980).

Vice-governors and deputy mayors are appointed with an assembly's approval for four-year terms of office concurrently with the chief executive, who is able to dismiss them if he wishes. Chief accountants are appointed in prefectures and treasurers in municipalities for four-year terms, subject to the consent of the assemblies. They have independent powers and cannot be dismissed by governors or mayors although they are subject to the latter's supervision.

Local Authority Commissions

Commissions are small but powerful bodies, mostly of three to five members, which administer specific functional areas. Education, public safety (police), inspection, personnel, expropriation and realty valuation re-examination commissions are appointed by executives with the approval of their assemblies. The much larger agricultural and fisheries commissions are partly elected and partly appointed by the executive. Assemblies appoint members of the election administration commission. For local labour commissions five to eleven members are appointed by the executive to represent labour, employers' and general public interests.

An education commission manages schools, with responsibilities for organisation of school structure, management of educational institutions and employment and dismissal of teachers, social education and scientific and cultural matters. It appoints, supervises and controls its own superintendent of education. A prefectural public safety commission is appointed for a three-year term of office to manage the administration and operation of the police. Law enforcement is the responsibility of the police headquarters. Inspection commissions inspect the performance of financial matters within their authorities and the management of their public enterprises. Personnel Commissions are responsible for investigation, research, evaluation, planning and programming for staff matters and measures relating to working conditions.

The commissions are reported to have vague responsibilities and to be inefficient. Although intended to limit the power of governors and mayors it is said that they tend to be dominated by them, particularly through the executive's function of preparing and executing the commissions' budgets. (Isakoda, 1980).

The Local Public Service

The Local Public Service Law of 1950 established the current status of local government officers. They cannot be retired against their will, subjected to pay reductions or demoted except under certain conditions. Each local authority is required to establish a personnel or equity commission to arbitrate beween the authority and its employees, which is in principle a neutral, third-party body (Miyao, 1980). These protective clauses were justified as compensations for lack of the right to strike.

A large proportion of local government employees receive better salaries and other emoluments than they would enjoy for equivalent jobs in the central civil service. The Ministry of Home Affairs during the 1980s placed heavy pressures on local government to reduce salaries to a standard level, including persuasion of the highest paying authorities to implement three-year salary 'correction plans' (Katayama, 1985; Ikenouchi, 1985).

Local administrations, apart from the staffs of commissions, are organised on a departmental pattern which resembles that usual in the West. A typical prefecture will have departments for planning, welfare and labour, health, environmental protection, commerce and industry, agriculture and forestry, engineering and general affairs (including finance, personnel and property matters). Each department is divided into a number of divisions. Cities have a similar structure. The arrangements are not rigid: in the 1980s many authorities set up special committees to rationalise their departmental structures. (Isakoda, 1980)

10.12 CITIZEN PARTICIPATION AND DECENTRALISATION WITHIN CITIES

Direct Participation in Local Government

At the end of 1983 Japan had 70,711 elected representatives in local authority assemblies and 3,325 directly elected local government executives (mayors and governors). Thus on average there was one elected local public official to every 1,594 inhabitants.

Voters must be aged 20 or over and have lived in the electoral district for over three months. Turn-out in local government elections is relatively high, although it has fallen somewhat over the years. It is highest for heads of town and village assemblies (92 per cent in 1979), followed by that for city assemblies (76 per cent), mayors (75 per cent), prefectural assemblies (69 per cent), mayors of designated cities (69 per cent), governors (64 per cent), designated city assemblies (58 per cent), special ward assemblies (56 per cent) and heads of special wards (55 per cent). Thus voting levels decrease with size of authority, excepting the Tokyo special wards which are doubtless affected by the special character of Tokyo. In 1991 overall turn-out was 61 per cent, that of women being remarkably higher than that of men. (*Election System in Japan*, 1986).

Direct Democracy

Voters have the right to present demands which, if signed by specified numbers of residents, have to be considered and acted upon. Direct demands were introduced on an American proposal after the Second World War. An opinion in 1965 was that 'the institution has served its purpose reasonably well, although it is sometimes used in ways that were probably not anticipated by its proponents' (Steiner, 1965). A popular demand in 1982 forced a mayor to adopt the opinion of the majority of voters on the construction of a nuclear power station.

One form of initiative of this kind which requires the signatures of one-fiftieth of the electorate can call for the enactment, amendment and abrogation of a local ordinance. In early years demands to reduce taxes and charges caused problems and were quickly excluded from the scope of this provision. Demands can be rejected or accepted in a modified form by assemblies who will have before them advice on the matter from their executive.

Another type of citizen demand, also requiring one-fifth of voters' signatures, is for the inspection of the management of a local public enterprise by the commissioners. A third type is a 'recall' demand for the dismissal of the governor or mayor, their deputies, members of commissions and officials such as the chief accountant or treasurer. This needs the signatures of one-third of voters. In the case of a demand for the unseating of elected members or executives the municipal election administration committee, after satisfying itself of the legitimacy of the demand, submits it to a popular referendum, which determines the matter by a simple majority. In the case of non-elected officials the success of the demand requires a three-quarters majority vote in the assembly with two-thirds of its members present.

Another type is for the dismissal of the assembly, requiring one-third of electors' signatures at least one year after the election of the assembly or the last demand of this type. Such demands have to be supported in a referendum. The dissolution follows in the event of a positive vote by a simple majority. Between 1947 and 1960 ballots on the dismissal of an assembly occurred 110 times and succeeded in 74 of those cases. In 51 cases no ballot was held because the assembly resigned *en bloc*. In others individual councillors resigned (28 cases) or the mayor himself (82 cases). There were hardly any demands for the dismissal of non-elected officials. (Steiner, 1965)

Citizen Movements

At periods there has been a ferment of local movements challenging municipal policies. According to one authority, 'residents, especially new residents, are organising a group whenever a new problem arises and conducting negotiations directly with the mayor or the administrative personnel, bypassing the assembly'. The leaders of the groups are often professors, teachers, lawyers, doctors and trade union officials 'and therefore more formidable to the executive than members of the assembly'. (Kato, 1980).

Concerned about the absence of community feelings in the cities in the 1970s the Ministry of Home Affairs launched community-building measures. 'Model communities' were adopted across the country to experiment with community-building. Prefectures and municipalities followed the lead, feeding groups with information, holding training meetings and organising opportunities for exchanges of opinion with the administration. This community activation has worked in both directions: to promote community influence on the bureaucracy and to encourage citizens to contribute to the improvement of local life through neighbourly assistance, improvement of leisure facilities etc. (Ibid.)

As elsewhere in the world initial optimism for this kind of initiative appears to have led to critical evaluation if not admission of failure. In the late 1980s it seemed that popular movements regarding cleanliness of the environment had nevertheless been a main motive force in putting these issues at the centre of policy-making and programmes.

Many authorities have community relations departments. That for Kanagawa Prefecture, for example, one of twelve main departments, has responsibility for the promotion of civic movements, freedom of information, public relations and public hearings, complaints and advisory services along with private schools and religions, traffic safety and cultural, women's, youth and consumer affairs (*The 2nd New Kanagawa Plan*, 1987).

10.13 THE GOVERNANCE OF METROPOLITAN AREAS

The Three Great Metropolitan Regions

Half of Japan's inhabitants live in three metropolitan areas which occupy some fourteen per cent of its area. About a quarter live in Tokyo Metropolitan Region. The other metropolitan planning regions are those of Osaka and Chukyo. They comprise four and five prefectures respectively. Osaka Region includes the 'designated cities' of Osaka (population 2.65m. in 1980) and Kyoto (1.47m.). Chukyu Region centres on the city of Nagoya (2.09m.). Like the Tokyo area these regions have no elected governments for their areas as a whole. As in the rest of the country, local government is two tier, made up of prefectures and the large numbers of municipalities of city, ward, town and village status that their areas contain.

The designated city status possessed by Osaka, Kyoto and Nagoya can be conferred by the government on cities with over a million inhabitants. It carries with it administrative powers, planning and other functions that elsewhere lie with prefectures. They are divided into wards which form the basis of a system of administrative decentralisation but which have no elected assemblies or mayors.

Tokyo and its Region

The heart of Tokyo lies in the highly developed area, which consists administratively of 23 special wards that possess a unique legal status similar to that of cities. At its centre lies the Toshin area of three wards, surrounded by the 'up-town' Yamanote area of five wards. This in its turn is surrounded by the fifteen outer wards which form a crescent, the horns of which end at points on Tokyo Bay. The wards lie within the Metropolis of Tokyo (Tokyo-to), a special prefecture which includes within its boundaries the 'Tama' area of 26 cities and other municipalities to the west of the wards, including nine small islands and a rural area containing seven town and four village authorities.

The Metropolis of Tokyo is part of an administrative planning area, the

Tokyo Metropolitan Region (28.7 million inhabitants in 1980), whose boundaries stretch landwards about fifty kilometres outwards from the Tokyo Wards. This includes three other prefectures which surround Tokyo-to on its landward side. The urbanised area of the Metropolitan Region extends from Tokyo-to into other large areas of high density in surrounding prefectures, especially the prefecture of Kanagawa which includes Yokahama and that of Chiba. The whole of the Tokyo Metropolitan Region in its turn lies within a wider planning area, the National Capital Region, which includes three more prefectures.

The Governmental and Administrative Structure of Tokyo-to

The political and administrative system of Tokyo resulted from a series of major reorganisations. Edo, as Tokyo was called before 1868, reached a population of 1,100,000 in 1705. In 1878 its administration was organised into fifteen wards and eight counties containing towns and villages. The wards were within a city authority with its own council which acquired independent status in 1889. The City elected its own mayor to replace the prefectural governor in 1898. In 1932 the counties surrounding the city were reorganised into wards and amalgamated with the city. In 1943 the city and prefecture were finally amalgamated as Tokyo-to (Tokyo Metropolitan Government).

Tokyo-to has had a fairly stable population of over 11,600,000 in recent years, but it has nevertheless been subject to enormous pressures through the effects of increased economic prosperity and personal affluence. The area of the wards contains 8.65 million people, about 74 per cent of Tokyo's population, at a density of 14,900 inhabitants per square kilometre. The ward populations average some 376 thousand.

The executive arms comprise the governor and various executive commissions. In 1947 elections were held for the office of governor for the first time. The ward boundaries were redefined, providing the basis for the 23 present wards, each of which has its own mayor. From 1975 the chief executives of the special wards also became directly elected and acquired the right to administer municipal affairs free of the governor's control. Their powers were increased so that in general they matched those of cities. Tokyo-to retained the responsibility for affairs relating to wider areas than those of the wards: those that require integrated handling, matters of 'liaison and adjustment' and affairs in other ways regarded as unsuitable for municipality-type authorities. Thus the Metropolitan Government administers the fire service, water supply, sewage treatment and refuse disposal, functioning both as a prefectural and a kind of special-purpose city. The generality of services described in §10.7 remained with the wards.

As executive for the national metropolis the governor carries special responsibilities in addition to those in a normal prefecture, including the guarding of the Imperial Household, the National Diet, government offices, foreign diplomats, international receptions and 'the maintenance of Tokyo's cityscape befitting the national metropolis' (*Plain Talk about Tokyo*, 1980 and 1987). In addition to these and the normal responsibilities of a prefectural governor described in §10.4 above, he has the right to direct and supervise the heads of state services in matters relating to the Metropolis.

The executive commissions are the Board of Education and the Electoral Management, Civil Service, Public Security, Local Labour Relations, Land Expropriation, Sea Area Fisheries Adjustment, Fresh Water Fishing Ground Management, Audit and Fixed Property Assessment Commissions. In most cases their members are appointed by the governor with the approval of the assembly, but they have independent legal status (Nomura, 1982).

The Tokyo-to Assembly has 127 members. The Liberal Democrat Party won an overall majority by one seat in the late 1980s. But in the 1993 elections it was left with only 44 seats, although it remained the largest party in the assembly. In descending order the other parties were Komeito (Clean Government Party) with 25 seats, the Japan New Party with 20 seats, the Japan Communist Party with 15 and the Japan Socialist Party with 13. In the 1980s a standing committee related to each of nine departments. The President of the Assembly is elected from within by its members. He represents the assembly outside and controls its secretariat. (See also §10.11.)

The governor administers Tokyo's prefectural services by means of a span of bureaux, numbering 15 in 1987. They are for policy planning, information, general affairs (including the university secretariat), finance, taxation, citizen and cultural affairs, city planning, environmental protection, social welfare, public health, labour and economic affairs, housing, construction, port and harbour and public cleansing. The governor exercises his responsibilities through two or more vice-governors and a chief accountant.

Since Tokyo-to carries out functions for the wards that would elsewhere be municipal functions, it receives certain municipal taxes in addition to prefectural taxes: in particular the business establishment and city planning taxes and part of the corporate resident, fixed property and special land holding taxes. Because of its wealth the authority does not qualify for a share of the national local allocation tax and receives only about half of the national average of financial transfers from the national treasury. It does, however, operate its own system of resource equalisation transfers to wards, equalising their resources against assessments of need according to a formula similar to that used by the national government for the local allocation tax. Wards whose resource assessments exceed their needs contribute to a fund distributed to wards which have financial deficiencies.

REFERENCES

Note

The following lists are not meant to be comprehensive and do not in general include official non-published and publicity sources except where it seems desirable to indicate the context of the material used. The bias is towards works in English since it is assumed that they will be the most easily available to the great majority of potential readers and the most universally understood. They include some references not indicated in the main text which have influenced my own appreciation of the subjects of the book and they may be useful to readers seeking a deeper appreciation of the topics dealt with. One or two were published too late to have been an influence on the text.

More detailed lists of recent publications which are especially good on sources other than in English will be found in the country-by-country references appended to the chapters in Joachim Jens Hesse (ed.), *Local Government and Urban Affairs in International Perspective* (in English except one chapter in French), published in 1991 by Nomos Verlagsgesellschaft, Baden-Baden.

It should be noted that multiple references under the name of one author are in alphabetical order by title, not in date order as is customary. This is to facilitate reference where a large number of entries fall under one name, as in the case of those under the Council of Europe, where the titles are given also in the main text for the reader's convenience.

1. AN INTERNATIONAL SURVEY

Adonis, A. and A. Tyrie (1990) *Subsidiarity as History and Policy*, Institute of Economic Affairs, London

Adonis, Andrew and Stuart Jones (1991), *Subsidiarity and the Community' Constitutional Future*, Discussion Paper No. 2, *Centre for European Studies*, Nuffield College, Oxford

Advisory Council for Inter-Governmental Relations (1985) *Report 8: Implications of Constitutional Recognition for Australian Local Government*, Tasmanian Government Printer, Hobart

Against the Over-Mighty State: a future for local government in Britain (1988), Federal Trust for Education and Research, London

Alexander, Edgar (1953) 'Church and Society in Germany' *Church and Society*, Arts Inc., New York

Alfonso, Luciano Parejo (1991) 'Local Government in Spain: Implementing the Basic Law', Hesse (ed.), op. cit.

References

Aronson, J. Richard and John L. Hilley (1986) *Financing State and Local Governments* 4th edition, The Brookings Institution, Washington, DC

Baldassare, A. and C. Mezzanotte (1986) *Introduzione alla Costituzione*, Editore Laterza, Roma/Bari

Baldersheim, Harald (1991) 'Aldermen into Ministers: Oslo's Experiment with a City Cabinet', *Local Government Studies* vol.18 no.1

Ball, Terence, J. Farr and R.L. Hanson (1989) *Political Innovation and Conceptual Change*, Cambridge University Press, Cambridge

Balme, Richard and Vincent Hoffmann-Martinot (eds) (1991) *Local and Regional Bureaucracies in Western Europe*, Centre d'Études et de Recherches sur la Vie Locale, Talence, France

Batley, Richard and Gerry Stoker (eds) (1991), *Local Government in Europe: Trends and Developments*, Macmillan, Basingstoke

Berg, L. van den, H.A. van Kink and J. van der Meer (1991) *Governing Metropolitan Regions*, Euricur, Erasmus University, Rotterdam

Blair, Philip (1991) 'Trends in Local Autonomy and Democracy: Reflections from a European Perspective', Batley and Stoker (eds), op. cit.

Blondel, Jean (1969) *An Introduction to Comparative Government*, Weidenfeld & Nicholson, London

Blondel, Jean (1989) *Comparative Government: an Introduction*, Philip Alan, Hemel Hempstead

Bourjol, Maurice and Serge Bodard (1984) *Droits et libertés des collectivités territoriales*, Masson, Paris

Bulpitt, J. (1983) *Territory and Power in the United Kingdom*, Manchester University Press, Manchester

Les Cahiers no.27 (1989) 'La Formation et le Recrutement des Agents territoriaux dans l'Europe des Douze Perspectives 1992', Centre National de la Fonction Publique Territoriale, Paris

Canada Year Book 1990 (1991), Ministry of Supply and Services, Ottawa

Chantraine, Alain and F. de Geuser (1991) 'Le partage entre administrations centrale et locale: une mesure statistique délicate', *Revue Française d'Administration Publique no.60* (IIAP, Paris)

Chapman, Brian (1955) *The Prefects and Provincial France*, Allen & Unwin, London

CIPFA (1990, 1991), *Local Government Trends*, Chartered Institute of Local Government Finance and Accountancy

Clark, T.N. and L.C. Ferguson (1983) *City Money*, Columbia University Press, New York

Collins, Neil (1987) *Local Government Managers at Work*, Institute of

References

Public Administration, Dublin

Commission of the European Communities (1991) *Working with the Regions*, Office for Official Publications of the European Community, Luxembourg

Cornut, Charles (1991) 'Les collectivités locales et le secteur bancaire' *Revue Française d'Administration Publique* 60

Council of Europe (1988a) *Allocation of Powers to the Local and Regional Levels of Governments in the Member States of the Council of Europe*, Council of Local and Regional Authorities of Europe, Strasbourg

Council of Europe (1979a) *The Apportionment of Public Resources between the State and the Local and Regional Authorities and its Evaluation*, Council of Europe, Strasbourg

Council of Europe (1989) *Conference on 'Free Local Government: Deregulation, Efficiency, Democracy': Working Documents and Conclusions*, Council of Europe, Strasbourg

Council of Europe (1984a) *Comparative Analysis of Experiences with Regionalisation in respect of relationships between the Regions and the Local Authorities*, Council of Europe, Strasbourg

Council of Europe (1978) *Conditions of Local Democracy and Citizen Participation in Europe*, Council of Europe, Strasbourg

Council of Europe (1982) *Constitutional and Legal Provisions Concerning the Organisation of Local Governments, Document No.6, The New Regional Structures in France*, Strasbourg

Council of Europe (1986a) *Decentralisation of Local Government at Neighbourhood Level*, Council of Europe, Strasbourg

Council of Europe (1986a) *Explanatory Memorandum on the European Charter of Local Government*, Council of Europe, Strasbourg

Council of Europe (1981b) *Financial Apportionment and Equalisation*, Council of Europe, Strasbourg

Council of Europe (1988b) *Financial Instruments and the Role of Finance in Regional Institutions*, Council of Europe, Strasbourg

Council of Europe (1981c) *Functional Decentralisation at Local and Regional Level*, Council of Europe, Strasbourg

Council of Europe (1979b) *Information and Communication about Municipal Affairs*, Council of Europe, Strasbourg

Council of Europe (1979c) *Methods of Consulting Citizens on Municipal Affairs*, Council of Europe, Strasbourg

Council of Europe (1986b) *Policies with Regard to Grants to Local Authorities*, Council of Europe, Strasbourg

Council of Europe (1980a) *Reallocation of Duties and Resources between the various levels of Government*, Council of Europe, Strasbourg

493

Council of Europe (1983a) *The Reforms of Local and Regional Authorities in Europe: Theory, Practice and Critical Appraisal*, Council of Europe, Strasbourg

Council of Europe (1984b) *The Relationships between the Various Levels of Local Administration under a Regional Organisation*, Conference of European Ministers responsible for Local Government, Rome, 1984, Council of Europe, Strasbourg

Council of Europe (1983b) *Report on the Status and Working Conditions of Local and Regional Elected Representatives*, Standing Conference of Local and Regional Authorities in Europe, XVIIIth Session, Council of Europe, Strasbourg

Council of Europe (1984c) *Report on Borrowing by Local Authorities in Europe, Appendices I and II*, Council of Europe, Strasbourg

Council of Europe (1988c) *The Status and Working Conditions of Local and Regional Elected Representatives*, Council of Europe, Strasbourg

Council of Europe (1980b) *The Strengthening of Local Structures, with Special Reference to Amalgamation and Co-operation in Council of Europe Member States*, Council of Europe, Strasbourg

Delors, Jacques (1991) 'The Principle of Subsidiarity: Contribution to the Debate', *Subsidiarity: The Challenge of Change*, op. cit.

Dente, Bruno and F. Kjellberg (eds) (1988) *The Dynamics of Institutional Change*, Sage, London

Dente, Bruno (1985a) 'Centre-Local Relations in Italy: the Impact of the Legal and Political Structures' Mény and Wright (eds), op. cit.

Dente, Bruno (1985b) *Governare la Frammentazione*, Il Mulino, Bologna

Dente, Bruno (1985c) 'Intergovernmental relations as central control policies: the case of Italian local finance', *Environment and Planning C: Government and Policy* vol.3

Dupuy, François, '*The Politico-Administrative System of the Département in France*' Mény and Wright (eds), op. cit.

Dyson, Kenneth H.F. (1980) *The State Tradition in Western Europe*, Martin Robertson, Oxford

European Centre for Regional Development (CEDRE) (1989) *Comparative Study of the Status and Powers of the Regions in Europe*, CEDRE, Strasbourg

Flynn, Norman and K. Walsh (1988) *Competitive Tendering*, Institute of Local Government Studies, University of Birmingham, Birmingham

La Fonction Publique Locale: Allemagne Fédérale, Espagne, Grande

References

Bretagne (1988) Informations & Documents no.2, Institut International d'Administration Publique, Paris

France, George (1987) 'Innovation in Local Public Services', *Local Public Services and Crisis of the Welfare State*, Maggioli Editore, Rimini

Fried, Robert C. (1974) 'Politics, Economics and Federalism: Aspects of Urban Government in Austria, Germany and Switzerland', *Comparative Community Politics*, Sage, New York

Gunlicks, A.B. (ed.) (1981) *Local Government Reform and Reorganization*, Kennikat Press, Port Washington, NY/London

Gurr, Ted R. and D.S. King (1987) *The State and the City*, Macmillan Educational, London

Gustafsson, Agne (1984) *Decentralisation in Sweden*, Swedish Institute, Stockholm

Gustafsson, Agne (1988) *Local Government in Sweden*, The Swedish Institute, Stockholm

Hakamäki, Simo, Risto Harisalo and Paavo Hoikka (1988) *An Introduction to Local Government Activities, Administration and Finance in Finland*, Tampereen Yliopisto, Tampere, Finland

Handy, Charles B. (1976) *Understanding Organisations*, Penguin Books, Harmondsworth

Harloff, Eileen Martin (undated, about 1987) *The Structure of Local Government in Europe*, International Union of Local Authorities, The Hague, Netherlands

Harris, G. Montagu (1948) *Comparative Local Government*, Hutchinson, London

Hesse, Joachim Jens (ed.) (1991) *Local Government and Urban Affairs in International Perspective*, Nomos Verlagsgesellschaft, Baden-Baden

Hesse, Joachim Jens and L.J. Sharpe (1991) 'Local Government in International Perspective: Some Comparative Observations' Hesse (ed.), op. cit.

Hintze, O. (ed.) (1962) *Staat und Verfassung* Oestreich,Vandenhoeck und Ruprecht, Göttingen

Hintze, O. (1975) 'The Commissary and his Significance in General Administrative History' *The Historical Essays of Otto Hintze*, New York, Oxford University Press, Oxford

Humes IV, Samuel (1991) *Local Government and National Power*, Harvester/Wheatsheaf, New York

Humes, Samuel and Eileen Martin (eds.) (1969) *The Structure of Local Government*, IULA, The Hague.

References

Jardin, André (1984) *Alexis de Toqueville, 1805-59*, Hachette, Paris; in English translation, *Toqueville* (1988), Peter Halban, London
Jones, Michael (1981) *Local Government and the People*, Haygreen Publishing, Melbourne
Jones, Michael (1989) *Managing Local Government*, Haygreen Publishing, Melbourne
Jones, Michael (1991) 'Australian Local Government: Waiting for a Challenge' Hesse (ed.), op. cit.

Leach, Steve and John Stewart (1987) *The Changing Patterns of Hung Authorities*, Local Government Training Board, Luton
Leach, Steve, C. Vielba and N. Flynn (1987) *Two Tier Relationships in British Local Government*, INLOGOV, University of Birmingham, Birmingham
Lemas, Pierre-René (1991) 'France', *Revue Française d'Administration Publique* 60, Institut Internationale d'Administration Publique, Paris
The Local Council (1983), International Union of Local Authorities, The Hague
Local Public Finance ('The Layfield Report') (1976), HMSO, London
Local Public Finance in Japan (1984), Jichi Sogo Center, Tokyo
Luchaire, Yves (1991) 'Les modes de gestion des grands services publiques locaux', *Revue Française d'Administration Publique* 60

Maddox, Graham (1989) 'Constitution' *Political Innovation and Conceptual Change*, Cambridge University Press, Cambridge
Marshall, A.H. (1967) *Local Government Administration Abroad, Management of Local Government* vol.4, HMSO, London
Martlew, Clive and Thomas Kempf (1986) *The Councillor's Working Environment in Scotland and West Germany*, The Planning Exchange, Glasgow
Mellors, Collin and Bert Pijnenburg (eds) (1989) *Political Parties and Coalitions in European Local Government*, Routledge, London
Mény, Yves and V.Wright (eds) (1985) *Centre-Periphery Relations in Western Europe*, Allen & Unwin, London
Mill, John Stuart (1861) *Considerations on Representative Government*, Everyman's Edition of *Utilitarianism, Liberty and Representative Government* (1910), Dent, London
Mount, Ferdinand (1992) *British Constitution: Recovery or Decline?*, Heinemann, London
Mouritzen, Poul Erik and K.H. Nielsen (1988), Handbook of Comparative Urban Fiscal Data, Danish Data Archive, Odense

References

Nanetti, Raffaella Y. (1988) *Growth and Territorial Policies: The Italian Model of Social Capitalism*, Pinter Publishers, London/New York

Nassmacher, Karl-Heinz and Alan Norton (1985) 'Background to Local Government in Western Germany ', Norton (ed.), op. cit.

Netherlands Scientific Council for Governmetnal Policy (1990) *Institutions and Cities: The Dutch Experience*, Netherlands Scientific Council for Governmental Policy, The Hague

Norton, Alan (1987) 'Decentralisation in West European Cities' *Local Government Policy-Making* vol.14 no.2

Norton, Alan (1983) *Government and Administration in Metropolitan Areas in Advanced Western Democracies*, INLOGOV, University of Birmingham, Birmingham.

Norton, Alan (1985a) 'German and British Local Government and Administration: Some Comparisons A. Norton (ed.), op. cit.

Norton, Alan (ed.) (1985b) *The Present and Future Role of Local Government in Great Britain and the Federal Republic of Germany*, Anglo-German Foundation, London/INLOGOV, University of Birmingham, Birmingham

Norton, Alan (1991) *The Role of Chief Executive in British Local Government*, INLOGOV, University of Birmingham, Birmingham

Norton, Alan (ed.) (1992) *The Principle of Subsidiarity and its Implications for Local Government*, The Local Government Management Board, Luton, England

OECD (1991) *Revenue Statistics of OECD Member Countries, 1965-1990*, OECD, Paris

Owens, Jeffrey (1991) *Local Government Taxation*, Institute of Revenues, Rating and Taxation, London

Owens, Jeffrey and John Norregaard (1991) 'The Role of Lower Levels of Government: The Experience of Selected OECD Countries' Owens and Panella (eds.), op. cit.

Owens, Jeffrey and G.Panella (eds) (1991) *Local Government: an International Perspective*, Elsevier, Amsterdam

Page, Edward C. (1991) *Localism and Centralism in Europe: the Political and Legal Bases of Local Self-Government*, Oxford University Press, Oxford

Page, E.C. and M.J. Goldsmith (eds) (1987) *Central and Local Relations: a Comparative Analysis of West European Unitary States*, Sage, London

Pateman, Carole (1970) *Participation and Democratic Theory*, Cambridge University Press, Cambridge

References

Pirenne, Henri (1939) *History of Europe*, George Allen & Unwin, London
Pirenne, Henri (1925) *Medieval Cities: their origins and the revival of trade*, Princeton University Press, Princeton, NJ
Pridham, Geoffrey (1989) 'Local and Regional Coalitions in Italy: Party Strategies and Centre-Periphery Links' Mellors and Pijnenberg (eds), op. cit.

Report of the Local Government Commission for 1989 (1989), Government Printer, Wellington, New Zealand
Revenue Statistics of OECD Countries 1965-1990 (1991), OECD, Paris
Rhodes, R.A.W. (1986) *The National World of Local Government*, Allen & Unwin, London
Rhodes, R.A.W. (1987) 'Territorial Politics in the United Kingdom: The Politics of Change, Conflict and Contradiction' Rhodes and Wright (eds), op. cit.
Rhodes, R.A.W. and V. Wright (eds) (1987) *Tensions in the Territorial Politics of Western Europe*, Frank Cass, London
Richardson, Ann (1983) *Participation*, Routledge, London
Ridley, F.F. (ed.) (1979) *Government and Administration in Western Europe*, Martin Robertson, Oxford
Robson, W.A.and D.E. Regan (eds) (1972) *Great Cities of the World, vols I & II*, Allen & Unwin, London.
Rose, Richard (1985) 'From Government at the Centre to Nationwide Government' Mény and Wright, (eds) op. cit.
Rowat, Donald C. (ed.)(1980) *International Handbook on Local Government Organization: Contemporary Developments*, Greenwood Press, Westport, Connecticut

Sauberzweig, Dieter (1991) 'Allemagne' *Revue Française d'Administration Publique* 60
Sergent, Lucien H. (1991) 'Les finances locales' *Revue Française d'Administration Publique* 60
Sharpe, L.J. (ed.) (1979) *Decentralist Trends in Western Democracies*, Sage, London/Beverly Hills
Sharpe, L.J. (1989) 'Fragmentation and Territoriality in the European State System' *International Political Science Review* vol 10 no.3
Sharpe, L.J. (1988) 'Local government reorganisation: general theory and U.K. practice' Dente and Kjellberg (eds), op. cit.
Sharpe, L.J. (1970) 'Theories and Values of Local Government' *Political Studies* vol.18 no.2
Sharpe, L.J. (1987) 'The West European State: the Territorial Dimension'

Rhodes and Wright (eds), op. cit.

Shindo (1982), 'Relations between National and Local Government' *International Review of Administrative Sciences* no.2

Smith, J. Toulmin (1851) *Local Government and Decentralization*, J. Chapman, publisher London *Statistical Abstract of the United States 1991* (1991), US Bureau of the Census, Washington, DC

Subsidiarity: The Challenge of Change (1991), European Institute of Public Administration, Maastricht

Szajkowski, Bogdan (ed.) (1986) *Marxist Local Governments in Western Europe and Japan*, Frances Pinter, London; Lynne Rienner, Boulder, Colorado

Tarrow, Sidney (1977) *Between Center and Periphery — Grassroots Politicians in Italy and France*, Yale University Press, New Haven and London

Tiebout, Charles (1959) 'A pure theory of local expenditure', *Journal of Political Economy* vol.64

Toonen, T.A.J. (1991) 'Change in Continuity: Local Government and Urban Affairs in The Netherlands' Hesse (ed.), op. cit.

Toonen, T.A.J. (1987) 'The Netherlands: a decentralised unitary state in a welfare society' Rhodes and Wright (eds), op. cit.

Toonen, T.A.J. (1990) 'The Unitary State as a System of Co-Governance' *Public Administration* vol.68

Toqueville, Baron Alexis de (1835) *De la Démocratie en Amérique*, Gosselin, Paris; (1945) *Democracy in America* (trans. H. Reeve), Saunders & Otley, London; reprint Vintage Books, New York

Travers, Tony and J. Gibson (1986) 'The Financing of Local Government' *The Future Role and Organisation of Local Government*, INLOGOV, University of Birmingham, Birmingham

Wagener, Frido (1985) 'The Administration of Metropolitan Areas' *Proceedings: XIXth International Congress of Administrative Sciences, Berlin 1983*, IIAS/Kluwer, Deventer

Wickwar, W.H. (1970) *The Political Theory of Local Government*, University of South California Press, Columbia, SC

Wilke, Marc and Helen Wallace (1990) *Subsidiarity: Approaches to Power-Sharing in the European Community*, RIIA Discussion Paper 27, The Royal Institute of International Affairs, London

Wolman, Harold (1986) 'Innovation in Local Government and Fiscal Austerity' *Journal of Public Policy* no.2

Wolman, Harold (1988) 'Understanding recent trends in central-local relations: centralisation in Great Britain and decentralisation in the United States' *European Journal of Political Research* 16

Ylvisaker, Paul (1959), 'Criteria for a "proper" areal division of powers', *Area and Power* A. Maass (ed.), The Free Press, Glencoe Ill.

Zehetner, F. (1983), 'General Report' The Council of Europe, *The Reforms of Local and Regional Authorities in Europe: Theory, Practice and Critical Appraisal*, op. cit.

2. France

Note
Most official publications are easily available in Paris at La Documentation Française, 29-31 quai Voltaire, 75340 Paris Cedex 07. The series of decentralisation laws from 'Droits et libertés des communes, des départements et des régions' of 2 March 1982 onwards is available from 26, rue Desaix, 75727 Paris Cedex 15, in booklets with the related decrees enclosed. The 'Cahiers' of the CNFPT (Centre National de la Fonction Publique Territoriale) are published from its office at 3, villa Thoréton, 75738 Paris Cédex 15 (a series which covers systematically most main aspects of local government change).

L'Administration Territoriale I — Le Système Général (1983), Documents d'Études Droit Administratif no.2.02, La Documentation Française, Paris
L'Administration Territoriale II — Les Collectivités Locales (1984), Documents d'Études Droit Administratif nos 2.02 and 2.03, La Documentation Française, Paris
Les Aides des Collectivités Locales aux Entreprises: Manuel Pratique (1984), Ministère de l'Intérieur et de la Décentralisation, La Documentation Française, Paris
Almond, Gabriel and Bingham Powell Jr. (eds)(1988) *Comparative Politics Today: a World View* 4th edn, Scott-Foreman, London/Glenview
Ardagh, John (1982) *France in the 1980s*, Penguin, Harmondsworth
Ardagh, John (1990) *France Today*, Penguin, Harmondsworth
Ashford, Douglas E. (ed.) (1980) *Financing Urban Government in the Welfare State*, Croom-Helm, London
Ashford, Douglas E. (1982) *British Dogmatism and French Pragmatism*, Allen & Unwin, London

Becet, Jean-Marie (1989) *Les collectivités territoriales: commune, département, région*, op. cit.

Beltrame, Pierre (1990) 'La Dérégulation du Système Financier Local ou la Gestion de la Complexité' *Les Cahiers* no.31, CNFPT, Paris

Berg, L. van den, H.A. van Kink, and J. van der Meer (1991) *Governing Metropolitan Regions*, Euricur, Erasmus University, Rotterdam

Bernard, Paul (1983) *L'État et la décentralisation*, Notes et Études Documentaires nos 4711-4712, La Documentation Française, Paris

Bernard, Paul (1985) 'La mission du commissaire de la Republique', *La Décentralisation en Marche*, Cahiers Français no.220, La Documentation Française, Paris

Birnbaum, Pierre (1979) 'Office Holders in the Local Politics of the French Fifth Republic' Lagroye and Wright (eds), op. cit.

Birnbaum, Pierre (1985) 'The Socialist Elite, 'les Gros', and the State' Cerny and Schain (eds), op. cit.

Booth, Philip (1985) *Decision Making and Decentralisation: Development Control in France*, Department of Town and Regional Planning, University of Sheffield, Sheffield, England

Bourdon, Jacques (1989) 'Le Point sur la Fonction Publique Territoriale' *Les Cahiers* no.28, CNFPT, Paris

Bourjol, Maurice and Serge Bodard (1984) *Droits et libertés des collectivités territoriales*, Masson, Paris

Brand, Elisabeth (1982) *Les Institutions des Grandes Villes en Angleterre, France et République Fédérale d'Allemagne,* thèse pour le Doctorat d'État, Université des Sciences Juridiques, Strasbourg

Cathelineau, J. (1979) 'Local Government Finance in France' Lagroye and Wright (eds), op. cit.

Cerny, Philip G. and Schain, M.A. (eds) (1980) *French Politics and Public Policy*, Methuen, London

Cerny, Philip G. and Schain, Martin A. (eds.) (1985) *Socialism, the State and Public Policy in France*, Frances Pinter, London

Chapman, Brian (1955) *The Prefects and Provincial France*, Allen & Unwin, London

Code des Communes et Textes Annexes (regularly updated), Berger-Levrault, Paris

Les collectivités locales en Chiffres (1991), La Documentation Française, Paris

Les collectivités territoriales: commune, département, région (1989) Les Cahiers no.239, La Documentation Française, Paris

Conseil Régional Provence-Alpes-Côte d'Azur (no date) *Sur la scène inter-*

nationale, brochure, Conseil Régional Provence-Alpes-Côte d'Azur, Marseille

Constitution Française du 4 Octobre 1958 (1976) Documents d'Études Droit Constitutionnel et Institutions Politiques no.1.04, Documentation Française, Paris

Council of Europe (1978) *Conditions of Local Democracy and Citizen Participation in Europe,* Council of Europe, Strasbourg

Council of Europe (1982) *Constitutional and Legal Provisions Concerning the Organisation of Local Governments: the New Regional Structures in France,* Council of Europe, Strasbourg

Council of Europe (1979) *Data Sheets on Regional and Local Government Structures: France,* Secretariat-General, Council of Europe, Strasbourg

Council of Europe (1981) *Functional and Regional Decentralisation at Local and Regional Level,* Council of Europe, Strasbourg

Council of Europe (1979) *Methods of Consulting Citizens on Municipal Affairs,* Council of Europe, Strasbourg

Council of Europe (1984) *Report on Borrowing by Local and Regional Authorities in Europe: Explanatory Memorandum and Appendices I and II,* Nineteenth Session Standing Conference of Local and Regional Authorities in Europe, Council of Europe, Strasbourg

Crozier, Michel (1970) *La Société Bloquée,* Éditions du Seuil, Paris

Crozier, Michel and E.Friedberg (1977) *L'acteur et le système,* Éditions Seuil, Paris; trans. (1980) *Actors and Systems,* University of Chicago Press, Chicago

Crozier, Michel and J. Thoenig (1976) 'The Regulation of Organized Complex Systems' *American Sociological Quarterly* vol.21, December

D'Arcy, François (1983) *The Administration of Metropolitan Areas in France,* Institut Français de Science Administrative, Conseil d'État, Paris (paper prepared for XIXth International Congress of Administrative Science, 1983, mimeo)

La Décentralisation (1982) Cahiers Français no.204, La Documentation Française, Paris

La Décentralisation en Marche (1985) Cahiers Français no.220, La Documentation Française, Paris

Decentralisation of Local Government at Neighbourhood Level, Answer to Questionnaire by French Delegation (1977) Steering Committee for Regional and Municipal Affairs, Council of Europe, Strasbourg

Dupuis, Georges (1989) 'Centralisation: inverser la tendance?' *Les collectivités territoriales: commune, département, région,* op. cit.

Dupuy, François (1985) 'The Political-Administrative System of the Département in France' Mény and Wright (eds), op. cit.

Durand, Patrice (1991) 'France: Local Authorities in Transition' (text in French) Joachim Jens Hesse (ed.) (1991) *Local Government and Urban Affairs in International Perspective*, Nomos Verlagsgesellschaft, Baden-Baden

Fonction Publique Territoriale (1985) Les Cahiers du C.F.P.C. no. hors série, Juin 1985, Centre de Formation des Personnels Communaux, Paris

Garrish, Stephen (1986) *Centralisation and Decentralisation in England and France*, School for Advanced Urban Studies, Bristol

Gasnier, Jacques (1985) 'Les nouvelles administrations départementales' *La Décentralisation en Marche*, op. cit.

Gourevitch, Peter Alexis (1980) *Paris and the Provinces*, Allen & Unwin, London

Grémion, Pierre (1976) *Le pouvoir périphérique: bureaucrates et notables dans le système politique français*, Éditions du Seuil, Paris

Guillaume, Gilbert (1990) 'Les Dotations Budgétaires: de la Logique de la Compensation aux Maintien des Droits Acquis' *Les Cahiers* no.31, CNFPT, Paris

Hainsworth, P. (1986) *Decentralisation and Change in Contemporary France*, Gower, Aldershot/London

Hall, Peter A. (1985) 'Socialism in One Country: Socialism and the Struggle to define a New Economic Policy for France' Cerny and Schain (eds), op. cit.

Hubricht and Malleray (1989) *Les collectivités territoriales: commune, département, région*, op. cit.

Jardin, André (1984) *Alexis de Toqueville, 1805-59*, Hachette, Paris; in English translation, *Toqueville* (1988), Peter Halban, London

Jegouzo, Yves (1989) *Les collectivités territoriales: commune, département région*, op. cit.

Kesselman, Mark (1967) *The Ambiguous Consensus*, Knopf, New York

Kesselman, Mark (1985) 'The Tranquil Revolution at Clochemerle: Socialist Revolution in France' Cerny and Schain (eds), op. cit.

Knapp, Andres F. (1986) 'A Receding Tide? France's Communist Municipalities' B. Szajkowski (ed.) *Marxist Local Governments in Western Europe and Japan*, Frances Pinter, London; Lynne Rienner, Boulder, Colorado

References

Knapp, Andrew (1991) 'The *cumul des mandats*, local power and political parties' *West European Politics* vol.14 no.1

Lagroye, J. and Wright, V. (1979a) 'Introduction: Local Government in Britain and France — the Problems of Comparisons and Contrasts' Lagroye and Wright (eds), op. cit.

Lagroye, J. and Wright, V. (eds) (1979b) *Local Government in Britain and France*, Allen & Unwin, London

Lemas, Pierre-René (1991) 'France', *Revue Française d'Administration Publique* 60

La Lettre du Conseil Provence-Alpes-Côte d'Azur nos 36-37 (1986), Le Conseil Provence-Alpes-Côte d'Azur, Marseille

Lorrain, Dominique (1991) 'Public Goods and Private Operators in France' R. Batley and G. Stoker (eds), *Local Government in Europe: Trends and Developments*, Macmillan, Basingstoke

Lorrain, Dominique (1992) 'The French Model of Public Services' *West European Politics* vol.15 no.2

Loughlin, John (1985) 'Regionalism and Ethnic Nationalism in France' Mény and Wright (eds), op. cit.

Luchaire, Yves (1989) 'La commune' *Les collectivités territoriales: commune, département, région*, Les Cahiers no. 239, La Documentation Française, Paris

Mabileau, Albert (1991) *La système local en France*, Monchrestien, Paris

Machin, Howard (1979) 'Traditional Patterns of French Local Government' Lagroye and Wright (eds), op. cit.

Machin, Howard, (1980) 'Centre and Periphery in the Policy Process' Cerny and Schain (eds), op. cit.

Marceau, Jane (1980) 'Power and Its Possessors' Cerny and Schain (eds), op. cit.

Médard, Jean-François (1981) 'Political Clientelism in France: The Centre-Periphery Nexus Reexamined' S.N. Eisenstadt and R. Lemarchand (eds) *Political Clientelism, Patronage and Development*, Sage, Beverly Hills/London

Mény, Yves (1980) 'Financial Transfer and Local Government in France' Ashford (ed.), op. cit.

Mény, Yves (1984) 'Decentralisation in Socialist France' *West European Politics* vol.7 no.1

Mény, Yves and Vincent Wright (eds) (1985) *Centre-Periphery Relations in Western Europe*, Allen & Unwin, London

Methods of Consulting Citizens on Municipal Affairs (1979), Council of

Europe, Strasbourg

Ministère de l'Intérieur, Direction Générales des Collectivités Locales (1991) *Les Collectivités Locales en Chiffres,* La Documentation Française, Paris

Ministère de l'Intérieur et de la Décentralisation (1984) *Guide Budgétaire Communal et Départemental,* La Documentation Française, Paris

Norton, Alan (1983) *The Government and Administration of Metropolitan Areas in Western Democracies,* Institute of Local Government Studies, University of Birmingham, Birmingham

Le Petit Robert 1: Dictionnaire de la Langue Français (1984), Le Robert, Paris

Pezant, Jean-Louis (1976) *Le Nouveau Statut de Paris: Loi du 31 décembre 1975* Notes et Études Documentaires No 4332-4333, La Documentation Française, Paris

Région d'Île de France (1983) *Le Conseil Régional,* Agence d'Information de la Région d'Île de France, Paris

Rémond, Bruno (1989) 'Vous avez dit "collectivités locales?"' *Les collectivités territoriales: commune, département, région* (1989), op. cit.

Reydellet, Michel (1979) 'Le Cumul des Mandats' *Revue de Droit Public*

Reydellet, Michel (1984) 'Le cumul des mandats et fonctions publiques' *Les Cahiers du C.F.P.C. No.14: Le Statut de L'Élu,* Centre de Formation des Personnels Communaux, Paris

Ridley, F.F. and J. Blondel, (1969) *Public Administration in France,* Routledge & Kegan Paul, London

Schain, Martin (1980) 'Communist Control of Municipal Councils and Urban Political Change' Cerny and Schain (eds), op. cit.

Schmitt, Dominique (1985) 'Les nouvelles administrations régionales' *La Décentralisation en Marche,* op. cit

Slater, Malcolm (1985) *Contemporary French Politics,* Macmillan, London

Soltau, Roger H. (1931) *French Political Thought in the Nineteenth Century,* E. Benn, London

Sorbets, Claude (1983) *La Communauté Urbaine: L'Institution et son Double,* XIXth International Congress of the Administrative Sciences, West Berlin, 19-23 September 1983, mimeo

Stevens, Anne (1985) '"L'Alternance" and the Higher Civil Service' Cerny and Schain (eds), op. cit.

References

Thoenig, J.C. (1979) 'Local Government Institutions and the Contemporary Evolution of French Society' Lagroye and Wright (eds), op. cit.

Thoenig, J.C. (1980) 'Local Subsidies in the Third Republic'Ashford (ed.), op. cit.

Toqueville, Alexis de (1835) *De la Démocratie en Amérique*, Charles Gosselin, Paris

Villielm, Jean-Louis (1989) 'Les élus locales' *Les collectivités territoriales: commune, département, région*, Les Cahiers no.239, op. cit.

Virieux, Jean-Marc (1985) 'Les modes de scrutin' *La Décentralisation en Marche*, op. cit.

Vivre Ensemble (Guichard Report) (1976), La Documentation Française, Paris

Wilson, Irene B. (1985) 'Decentralizing or Recentralizing the State? Urban Planning and Centre-Periphery Relations' Cerny and Schain (eds), op. cit.

Wright, Vincent (1983) *Government and Politics of France* 2nd edition, Hutchinson Educational, London

Zeldin, Theodore (1973) *France 1848-1945 Vol.I, Ambition, Love and Politics*, Oxford University Press, Oxford

Zeldin, Theodore (1983) *The French*, Collins, London

3. ITALY

Baldassare, A. and C. Mezzanotte (1986) *Introduzione alla Costituzione*, Editore Laterza, Roma/Bari

Bartole, Sergio (1984) 'Le Regioni' Bartole, Mastragostino and Vandelli, op. cit.

Bartole, Sergio, Franco Mastragostino and Luciano Vandelli (1984) *Le autonomie territoriale*, Il Mulino, Bologna

Buglione, Enrico and George France (1991) 'Italie' *Revue Française d'Administration Publique* 60

Cassese, Sabino (1983) *Il Sistema Amministrativo Italiano*, Il Mulino, Bologna

Council of Europe (1984) *Comparative Analysis of Experiences with Regionalisation in Respect of Relations between the Regions and the Local Authorities*, Council of Europe, Strasbourg

References

Council of Europe (1984c) *Report on Borrowing by Local Authorities in Europe, Appendices I and II*, Council of Europe, Strasbourg

Dente, Bruno (1985a) 'Centre-Local Relations in Italy: The Impact of the Legal and Political Structures' Y. Mény and V. Wright (eds), *Centre-Periphery Relations in Western Europe*, Allen & Unwin, London

Dente, Bruno (1985b) *Governare la Frammentazione*, il Mulino, Bologna

Dente, Bruno (1985c) 'Intergovernmental Relations as Central Control Policies: the Case of Italian Local Finance' *Environment and Planning C* vol.3

Dente, Bruno (1991) 'Italian Public Services: the Difficult Road towards Privatisation' R. Batley and G. Stoker (eds) *Local Government in Europe: Trends and Developments*, Macmillan, Basingstoke

Dente, Bruno, M.I. Pregreffi and E.S. Ludovici (no date) *Survey on popular participation in Metropolitan Areas in a Comparative Study: problems regarding methods and attempt at applying them in Milan*, mimeo, Milan

Dente, Bruno, L.J. Sharpe and Renate Mayntz (1977) *Il Governo Locale in Europa*, Edizione della Communità, Milan

Farneti, Paolo (1985) *The Italian Party System (1948-1980)*, Pinter, London

Fedel, Giorgio and Franco Goio (1984) '11. Gli effetti della legge circoscizioni: l'attività dei Consigli di Zona a Milano' *Le Relazione Centro-Periferia*, op. cit.

Fried, Robert C. (1963) *The Italian Prefects, a Study in Administrative Politics*, Yale University Press, Yale/New York

Giannini, Massimo Severo (1967) 'I Comuni' *L'Ordinamento Comunale e Provinciale*, Neri Pozza Editore, Milan

Graziano, Luigi (1973) 'Patron-Client Relationships in Southern Italy' *European Journal of Political Research* vol 1 no.1

Graziano, Luigi, F. Girotti and L. Bonet (1984) '9. I partiti come strutture di controllo: i processi di formazione delle giunte' *Le Relazione Centro-Periferia*, op. cit.

Gundle, Stephen (1986) 'Urban Dreams and Metropolitan Nightmares' B. Szajkowski (ed.) *Marxist Local Governments in Western Europe and Japan*, Frances Pinter London; Lynne Rienner, Boulder, Colorado

LaPalombara, Joseph (1987) *Democracy Italian Style*, Yale University Press, New Haven and London

References

Leonardi, Robert, Raffaella Y. Nanetti and Robert Putnam (1987) 'Territorial Politics in Post-War Years: the Case of Regional Reform' R.A.W. Rhodes, and V. Wright (eds) *Tensions in the Territorial Politics of Western Europe*, Frank Cass, London

Nanetti, Raffaella Y. (1988) *Growth and Territorial Policies: The Italian Model of Capitalism*, Pinter, London and New York

Norton, Alan (1983) *Government and Administration of Metropolitan Areas*, Institute of Local Government Studies, University of Birmingham, Birmingham

Pola, Giancarlo (1984) '23. La sottodotazione dei servizi nei piccoll communii: i costi e le risorse' *Le Relazione Centro-Periferia*, op. cit.

Pregreffi, Monica I. (1984) '10. Le Associazione nazionale dei enti locali' *Le Relazione Centro-Periferia*, op. cit.

Pridham, Geoffrey (1989) 'Local and Regional Coalitions in Italy: Party Strategies and Centre-Periphery Links' C. Mellors and B. Pijnenburg (eds), *Political Parties and Coalitions in European Local Government*, Routledge, London

Putnam, Robert D., Robert Leonardi and Raffaella Y. Nanetti (1985) *La Pianta e le Radici*, Il Mulino, Bologna

Le Relazione Centro-Periferia (1984) Istituto per la Scienza dell' Administrazione Publica/Editore Giuffrè, Milan

Rolla, Giancarlo (1992) 'The Relationship between the Political and the Executive Structure in Italy' *Local Government Studies* vol.18 no.1

Sabetti, Philip (1977) 'The Structure and Performance of Urban Systems in Italy' Vincent Ostrom and F.P. Bish (eds), *Comparing Urban Service Delivery Systems*, Sage, Beverly Hills/London

Sanantonio, Enzo (1987) 'Italy' E.C. Page and M.J. Goldsmith (eds), *Central and Local Relations: a Comparative Analysis of West European Unitary States*, Sage, London

Sassoon, Donald (1986) *Contemporary Italy*, Longman, London/New York

Spagnuolo, Carla (1982) 'Transforming the Structure of Urban Government in Turin' *Making the City work: Enterprise and Democracy in Urban Europe*, Glasgow District Council, Glasgow

Spotts, Frederic and Theodor Wieser (1986) *Italy: a Difficult Democracy*, Cambridge University Press, Cambridge

Triglia, Riccardo (1986) 'The Local Government Association — the Role of Anci in Italy' *Planning and Administration* vol.13 no.2

Vandelli, Luciano (1984a) 'I Communi e le Province' Bartole, Mastragostino and L. Vandelli, op. cit.

Vandelli, Luciano (1984b) '12. Il controllo sugli enti locali dopo le Regioni: la Lombardia' *Le Relazione Centro-Periferia*, op. cit.

4. THE FEDERAL REPUBLIC OF GERMANY

Advisory Commission on Intergovernmental Relations (ACIR) (1981), *Studies in Comparative Federalism: West Germany*, ACIR, Washington, DC

Ardagh, John (1987), *Germany and the Germans*, Hamish Hamilton, London

Banner, Gerhard (1985) 'Budgetary Imbalance and the Politics of Cutback Management in German Local Government' *Local Government Studies* vol.11 no.4

Banner, Gerhard (1984) 'Kommunale Steuerung zwischen Gemeindeordnung und Parteipolitik' *Die öffentliche Verwaltung*, May 1984

Banner, Gerhard (1987), *Political, Structural and Technological Aspects of Financial Management in German Local Government*, Council of Europe paper CDRM.Sem/Fin(87)6, Council of Europe, Strasbourg

Basic Law of the Federal Republic of Germany (periodically updated), Press and Information Office, Government of the Federal Republic of Germany, Bonn

Beer, Rüdiger R. and Eberhard Laux (1977), *Die Gemeinde*, Gunter Ölzog Verlag, Munich/Vienna

Berg, L. van den, H.A. van Kink and J. van der Meer (1991) *Governing Metropolitan Regions*, Euricur, Erasmus University, Rotterdam

Böhret, Carl (1988) *Innenpolitik und politische Theorie*, Westdeutscher V, Opladen

Böhret, Carl and Rainer Frey (1982), 'Staatspolitik' and 'Kommunalpolitik' Püttner (ed). *Bd 2*, op. cit.

Brearey, Patricia (1989) 'City Coalitions in West Germany: a Case-study of Nordrhein-Westfalen' C. Mellors and B. Pijnenburg eds *Political Parties and Coalitions in European Local Government*, Routledge, London

Clements, R.V. (1978) 'A Local Chief Executive Elected by the Citizens:

References

The Oberbürgermeister of Wurzburg' *Public Administration* 56
Conradt, David P. (1981) 'Political Culture, Legitimacy and Participation'
William E. Paterson and Gordon Smith (eds), *The West German Model*,
Frank Cass, London
Conradt, David P. (1987) *The German Polity*, 3rd edition, Longman, New
York/London

Council of Europe (1979) *The Apportionment of Public Resources between
the State and the Local and Regional Authorities and its Evaluation*,
Council of Europe, Strasbourg
Council of Europe (1978) *Conditions of Local Democracy and Citizen
Participation in Europe*, Council of Europe, Strasbourg
Council of Europe (1981), *Constitution of the Free State of Bavaria*,
Council of Europe, Strasbourg
Council of Europe (1981) *Decentralisation of Local Government at Neigh-
bourhood Level*, Council of Europe, Strasbourg
Council of Europe (1986) *Explanatory Report on the European Charter of
Local Self-Government*, Council of Europe, Strasbourg
Council of Europe (1981) *Financial Apportionment and Equalisation*,
Council of Europe, Strasbourg
Council of Europe (1981) *Functional Decentralisation at Local and
Regional Level*, Council of Europe, Strasbourg
Council of Europe (1979) *Methods of Consulting Citizens on Municipal
Affairs*, Council of Europe, Strasbourg
Council of Europe (1980) *Reallocation of Duties and Resources between
the various levels of Government*, Council of Europe, Strasbourg
Council of Europe (1983) *The Reforms of Local and Regional Authorities
in Europe: Theory, Practice and Critical Appraisal*, Council of Europe,
Strasbourg
Council of Europe (1988) *The Status and Working Conditions of Local and
Regional Elected Representatives*, Council of Europe, Strasbourg
Council of Europe (1980) *The Strengthening of Local Structures, with
Special Reference to Amalgamation and Co-operation in Council of
Europe Member States*, Council of Europe, Strasbourg

Degen, Manfred (1988) 'Réflexions sur le Statut du Personnel Local en
Allemagne Fédérale, *Informations & Documents*. November 1988, No. 2
Institut Internatioal d'Administration Publique, Paris
Dentzer, Heinrich (1983) 'Schultrügerschaft — Schulentwicklung' Püttner
(ed.) *Bd 4*, op. cit.
Deutsche Städtetag (1979) *Association of German Cities and Towns*,

References

Deutsche Städtetag, Cologne
Die Gemeindeordnungen in der Bundes Republik Deutschland (periodically updated), Kohlhammer, Stuttgart
Dieckmann, Rudolf (1983) 'Aufgabenkritik und Privatisierungsproblem' Püttner (ed.) *Bd 3*, op. cit.
Dyson, Kenneth H.F. (1980) *The State Tradition in Western Europe*, Martin Robertson, Oxford

Edinger, Lewis J. (1968) *Politics in Germany: Attitudes and Processes*, Little Brown, Boston

Fürst, Dietrich (1991) *Ausgewählte Stadt-Umland-Verbänder Bundesrepublik Deutschland im Vergleich*, paper supplied by author, Institut für Landesplanung und Raumforschung der Universität, Hannover

Giese, Dieter (1983) 'Sozialhilfe' Püttner (ed.) *Bd 4* op. cit.
Gretschmann, Klaus (1991) 'The Subsidiarity Principle: Who is to Do What in an Integrated Europe?' *Subsidiarity: The Challenge of Change,* European Institute of Public Administration, Maastricht
Grunow, Dieter (1988) *Burgnähe Verwaltung*, Campus, Frankfurt-am-Main
Grunow, Dieter (1991) 'Customer-Orientated Service Delivery in German Local Administration' R. Batley and G. Stoker (eds) (1991), *Local Government in Europe: Trends and Developments*, Macmillan, Basingstoke
Grunow, Dieter (1992) 'Constitutional Reform in Germany: the Case of North Rhine-Westphalia' *Local Government Studies* vol.18 no.1
Gunlicks, A.B. (ed.) (1981a) *Local Government Reform and Reorganization,* Kennikat Press, Port Washington, New York, London
Gunlicks, Arthur B. (1981b) 'The Reorganization of Local Governments in the Federal Republic of Germany' Gunlicks, (ed.), op. cit.
Gunlicks, Arthur B. (1986) *Local Government in the German Federal State*, Duke University Press, Durham, NC

Hamburg State Public Relations Office (1985) *Stadt & Staat*, Hamburg Staat, Hamburg
Happe, Bernhard (1983) 'Obdachlosen' Püttner (ed.) *Bd 4*, op. cit.
Henry-Meininger (1988), 'Allemagne Fédérale: Repport générale' Institut International d'Administration Publique, Paris
Hesse, Joachim Jens (1987) 'The Federal Republic of Germany: From Co-operative Federalism to Joint Policy-making' R.A.W. Rhodes and V.Wright (eds) *Tensions in the Territorial Politics of Western Europe*,

References

Frank Cass, London

Hesse, Joachim Jens (1991) 'Local Government in a Federal State' *Local Government and Urban Affairs in International Perspective*, Nomos Verlagsgesellschaft, Baden-Baden

Hoffman, Hilmar and D. Kramer (1983) 'Kulturpolitik und Kunstpflege' Püttner (ed.) *Bd 4*, op. cit.

Hoffman-Martinot, Vincent (1987) *Finances et Pouvoir Local l'Expérience Allemande*, GRAL, Paris

Jacob, Herbert (1963) *German Administration since Bismarck*, Yale University Press, New Haven/London

Jans, Karl Wilhelm (1983) 'Jugendhilfe' Püttner (ed.) *Bd 4*, op. cit.

Johnson, Nevil (1979) 'Some Effects of Decentralization in the Federal Republic of Germany' L.J. Sharpe (ed.), *Decentralist Trends in Western Democracies*, Sage, London/Beverly Hills

Johnson, Nevil (1983) *State and Government in the Federal Republic of Germany*, 2nd edn., Pergamon, Oxford

Keith-Lucas, Bryan (1970) 'Introduction' J. Redlich and F.W. Hirst *History of Local Government in England*, Macmillan, London/Basingstoke

Keith-Lucas, Bryan and P.G. Richards (1978) A History of Local Government in the Twentieth Century, Allen & Unwin, London

Klötzer (1983) 'Stadtarchive, Stadtgeschichtsschreibung' Püttner (ed.) *Bd 4*, op. cit.

Kommunale Gemeinschaftsstelle für Verwaltungsvereinfachung (KGSt) (1979) *Verwaltungsorganisation der Gemeinden*, KGSt, Cologne

Kommunale Gemeinschaftsstelle für Verwaltungsvereinfachung (KGSt) (1982) *Verwaltungsorganisation der Kreise*, KGSt, Cologne

Kommunale Gemeinschaftsstelle für Verwaltungsvereinfachung (KGSt) (1984) *Bürger und Verwaltung III: Bürgerengagement, Selbsthilfe, Helfergruppen, Bürgermitverantwortung*, KGSt, Cologne

König, Klaus, H.J. van Oertzen and F. Wagener (eds) (1983) *Public Administration in the Federal Republic of Germany*, Kluwer-Deventer, Antwerp/London/Boston/Frankfurt am Main

Kupper, Utz-Ingo (1982) 'Decentralising the City: the Experience of Cologne' B. Allan (ed.) *Making the City Work*, City of Glasgow, Glasgow

Laux, Eberhard (1980) 'Kommunal Organisation' *Öffentliche Verwaltung in der Bundesrepublik*, Wibera-Sonderdruck 129, Kluwer-Deventer, Frankfurt am Main

References

Laux, Eberhard (1983) 'Administration of Rural Areas' Klaus König, van Oertzen and Wagener (eds), op. cit.

Lehmann-Grube, Hinrich (1982) *The Administration of Metropolitan Areas*, paper for Round Table Conference, Tokyo 13-19 September 1982, German Section of the International Institute of Administrative Sciences

Lehmann-Grube, Hinrich (1983a) *Die Verwaltung von Stadtregionen*, XIX Internationaler Kongress für Verwaltungswissenschaften, Berlin, mimeo

Lehmann-Grube, Hinrich (1983b) 'The Administration of Large Towns' König, van Oertzen and Wagener (eds), op. cit.

McDermott, Raymond C.O. (1981) 'The Functions of Local Levels of Government in West Germany and their Internal Organisation' Gunlicks (ed.), op. cit.

Martlew, Clive and Thomas Kempf (1986) *The Councillor's Working Environment in Scotland and West Germany*, The Planning Exchange, Glasgow

Mayntz, Renate (1977) 'Decentramento politicale e governo locale nella Repubblica Federale Tedesca' *Il governo locale in Europa*, Edizione di Comunità, Milan

Meyer, Hans (1982) 'Kommunalwahlrecht' Püttner (ed.) *Bd 2*, op. cit.

Nassmacher, Karl-Heinz (1985) 'The Changing Functions of German Local Government' Norton (ed.), op. cit.

Nassmacher, Karl-Heinz and A. Norton (1985) 'Background to Local Government in Western Germany' Norton (ed.), op. cit.

Norton, Alan (1985a) 'German and British Local Government and Administration: Some Comparisons' Norton (ed.), op. cit.

Norton, Alan (1983) *The Government and Administration of Metropolitan Areas in Western Democracies*, INLOGOV, University of Birmingham

Norton, Alan (1987) 'Decentralisation in West European Cities' *Local Government Policy-Making* June 1987

Norton, Alan (ed.) (1985b) *The Present and Future Role of Local Government in Great Britain and the Federal Republic of Germany*, Anglo-German Foundation, London/INLOGOV, University of Birmingham, Birmingham

Owens, Jeffrey (1991) *Local Government Taxation*, Institute of Revenues, Rating and Taxation, London

References

Pappermann, Ernst (1983) 'Förderung der Wissenschaft, Bildung und Kunst' Püttner (ed.) *Bd 4*, op. cit.

Pfau, Eberhard (1983) 'Gesundheitsverwaltung' Püttner (ed.) *Bd 4*, op. cit.

Politik und kommunale Selbstverwaltung (1984) Deutsche Gemeindeverlag/Verlag W. Kohlhammer, Cologne

Püttner, Günter (ed.) *Bd 1: Gundlagen* (1981); *Bd 2: Kommunalverfassung* (1982); *Bd 3: Kommunale Aufgabe und Instrumente der Aufgabenerfullung* (1983); *Bd 4: Die Fachaufgaben* (1983); *Bd 5: Kommunale Wirtschaft* (1984), *Handbuch der Kommunalen Wissenschaft und Praxis*, Springer-Verlag, Heidelberg

Püttner, Günter (1982) 'Zum Verhältnis von Demokratie und Selbstverwaltung' Püttner (ed.) *Bd 2*, op. cit.

Püttner, Günter (1983) 'Mittel der Aufgabenerfüllung: A.Überblick' Püttner (ed.) *Bd 3*, op. cit.

Reissert, Berndt (1980) 'Federal and State Transfers to the Federal Republic of Germany' D. Ashford (ed.), Financing Urban Government in the Welfare State, Croom Helm, London

Reissert, Berndt and G.F. Schaefer (1985) 'Centre-Periphery Relations in the Federal Republic of Germany' Y. Mény and V. Wright (eds) *Centre-Periphery Relations in Western Europe*, Allen & Unwin, London

Rengeling (1982) Püttner (ed.) *Bd 2*, op. cit.

Rentdorf, von Trutz (1962) 'Kritische Erwägungen zum Subsidiaritätsprinzip' *Der Staat 4*, Duncker & Humblot, Berlin

Schäfer, Günther (1981) 'Trends in Local Government Finance in the Federal Republic of Germany since 1950' L.J. Sharpe (ed.) *The Local Fiscal Crisis in Western Europe* Sage, London/Beverly Hills

Schäfer, Rudolf (1982) *Stadtteilvertretungen in Grossstädten, Teilungen 1 and 2*, DIFU, Berlin

Schreckenberger, Waldemar (1983) 'Intergovernmental Relations' König, van Oertzen and Wagener (eds), op. cit.

Siebenhorn, Dieter (1983) 'Schulaufsicht und kommunale Selbstverwaltung' Püttner (ed.) *Bd 4*, op. cit.

Siedentopf, H. (1981) 'Federal Republic of Germany' Council of Europe *Colloquy on the Reforms of Local and Regional Authorities in Europe: Theory, Practice and Critical Appraisal: Federal States*, Council of Europe, Strasbourg

Southern, David (1979) 'Germany' *Government and Administration in Western Europe* F.F. Ridley (ed.), Martin Robertson, Oxford

Statistisches Jahrbuch für das vereinte Deutschland (1990, 1991), Metzler

References

Poeschel, Stuttgart

Thieme, Werner (1983) 'The Tasks of Public Administration' König, van Oertzen and Wagener (eds), op. cit.

Uppendahl, Herbert (1985) 'Intergovernmental Relations in the Federal Republic of Germany: an Overview' Norton (ed.) op. cit.

Verwaltungsorganisation der Gemeinden (1979) KGSt, Cologne
Voigt, Rüdiger (ed.)(1984) *Handwörterbuch zur Kommunalpolitik*, Westdeutscher Verlag, Opladen
Voigt, Rüdiger (1986) 'Politische Entscheidungstrukturen am Beilspiel einer Ländlichen Grossgemeinde in Südwestfalen' K.M. Schmals and R. Voigt (eds) *Krise weltlicher Lebenswelten*, Campus Verlag, Frankfurt/ New York

Wagener, Frido (1969) *Neubau der Verwaltung*, Duncker & Humblot, Berlin
Wagener, Frido (1980) 'West Germany: a Survey' D.C. Rowat (ed.) *International Handbook on Local Government Organization: Contemporary Developments*, Greenwood Press, Westport, Connecticut
Wagener, Frido (1983a) 'The External Structure of Administration in the Federal Republic of Germany' König, van Oertzen and Wagener (eds), op. cit.
Wagener, Frido (1983b) 'The Functions and Services of German Public Administration' *International Review of Administrative Sciences* 2
Wagener, Frido (1983c) 'Gebietsreform und kommunale Selbstverwaltung' *Die öffentliche Verwaltung* 18
Wehling, Hans-Georg and H.J. Siewert (1982) *Der Bürgermeister in Baden-Württemberg*, Kohlhammer, Stuttgart/Berlin/Cologne/Mainz
Wickwar, W.H. (1970) *The Political Theory of Local Government*, University of South Calorina Press, Columbia, SC
Wollmann, Helmut (1984) *Local Government Reform via New Implementation and Reforms?*, ECPR Workshop Salzburg 1984, Zentralinstitut für sozialwissenschaftliche Forschung, Free University, Berlin, mimeo
Wollmann, Helmut (1991) 'The Reconstruction of Municipal Administration in the Former GDR in a Period of Regime Rupture, Socio-Economic Turbulence and Paradigm Change' *Local and Regional Bureaucracies in Western Europe*, Centre d'Étude et de Recherche sur la Vie Locale, University of Bordeaux, Bordeaux

5. SWEDEN

Andren, N. (1953) *Local Government in Sweden*, University of Stockholm Texts in Political Science, Stockholm

Anton, Thomas J. (1974) *The Pursuit of Efficiency: Values and Structure in the Changing Politics of Swedish Municipalities'* Terry N. Clark (ed). *Comparative Community Politics*, Wiley, New York

Anton, Thomas J. (1980) *Administered Politics: Elite Political Culture in Sweden*, Nijhoff, Boston/The Hague/London

Årsbok för Sveriges Kommuner, 1985, Statistika Central byrån, Stockholm

Ashford, Douglas E. (1986) *The Emergence of the Welfare States*, Blackwell, Oxford

Calmfors, Hans (1972) 'Remuneration of Local Government Representatives in Sweden' *Local Government Studies* 3

City of Gothenburg (1987) *Gothenburg*, City of Gothenburg, Gothenburg. Annual report in English.

Clarke, Michael and John Stewart (1985) *The Service Programme: Report on a visit to Sweden*, Local Government Training Board, Luton, England

Council of Europe (1978) *Conditions of Local Democracy and Citizen Participation in Europe*, Council of Europe, Strasbourg

Council of Europe (1981a) *Decentralisation of Local Government at Neighbourhood Level*, Council of Europe, Strasbourg

Council of Europe (1981b) *Financial Apportionment and Equalisation*, Council of Europe, Strasbourg

Council of Europe (1985) *Financial Resources for Local and Regional Authorities*, Council of Europe, Strasbourg

Council of Europe (1985) *Management Structures in Local and Regional Government*, Council of Europe, Strasbourg

Council of Europe (1979) *Methods of Consulting Citizens on Municipal Affairs*, Council of Europe, Strasbourg

Council of Europe (1983) *Report on the Status and Working Conditions of Local and Regional Elected Representatives, Standing Conference of Local and Regional Authorities in Europe, XVIIIth Session* (1983), Council of Europe, Strasbourg

Council of Europe (1988) *The Status and Working Conditions of Local and Regional Elected Representatives*, Council of Europe, Strasbourg

Council of Europe Committee on Local Structures and Finance (1982) *Synopsis of replies to the questionnaire on Status and Working Conditions of Local and Regional Elected Representatives*, Council of Europe, Strasbourg

References

Elder, Neil C.M. (1987) *The Kingdom of Sweden World Encyclopedia of Political Systems and Parties Vol II* 2nd edition, Facts on File, New York/Oxford

Greenwood, Royston (1980) 'Relations between Central and Local Government in Sweden: The Control of Local Government' *New Approaches to the Study of Central-Local Relationships* George Jones (ed.), SSRC/Gower, Aldershot, England

Gustafsson, Agne (1984a) *Decentralisation in Sweden*, Swedish Institute, Stockholm

Gustafsson, Agne (1984b, 1988) *Local Government in Sweden*, Swedish Institute, Stockholm

Gustafsson, Agne (1991) 'The Changing Local Government and Politics of Sweden' R. Batley and G. Stoker (eds) *Local Government in Europe: Trends and Developments*, Macmillan, Basingstoke

Gustafsson, Gunnel (1980) *Local Government Reform in Sweden*, C.W.K. Gleerup, Umeå

Gustafsson, Gunnel (1981) 'Local Government Reform in Sweden' A.B. Gunlicks (ed.) *Local Government Reform and Reorganization*, Kennikat Press, Port Washington

Gustafsson, Lennart (1987) 'Renewal of the Public Sector in Sweden' *Public Administration* vol.65 no.2

Hancock, M.Donald (1972) *Sweden: The Politics of Post-Industrial Change*, The Dryden Press, Hinsdale, Illinois

Kjellberg, Francesco (1983) 'The Scandinavian Countries' Council of Europe *The Reforms of Local and Regional Authorities in Europe: Theory, Practice and Critical Appraisal*, Council of Europe, Strasbourg

Kjellberg, Francesco (1984) *Local Government Reorganization and the Development of the Welfare State*, paper to the workshop on 'Towards a Theory of Local Government Reform', ECPR-joint sessions, Salzburg 13- 18 April 1984, mimeo

Kolam, Kerstin (1987) *Lokala Organ i Norden 1968-1986: fran Ide till Verklighet*, Umeå, Universitets Tryckeri, Umeå

Lane, Jan-Erik and Svante O. Ersson (1987) *Politics and Society in Western Europe*, Sage, London

Lane, Jan-Erik and Tage Magnusson (1982) 'Kommunsammanläggning och Kommunala Kostnader', *Tvärsnitt 4*

Lane, Jan-Erik and Tage Magnusson (1987) 'Sweden' E.C. Page and M.J.

Goldsmith (eds), *Central and Local Relations: a Comparative Analysis of West European Unitary States*, Sage, London

Malmsten, Bo (1983) 'Sweden's Salaried Local Politicians', *Local Government Studies* vol.9 no.3

Montin, Stig (1992) 'Recent Trends in the Relationship between Politics and Administration in Local Government: The Case of Sweden' *Local Government Studies* vol.18 no.1

Norton, Alan (1983) *The Government and Administration of Metropolitan Areas in Western Democracies*, INLOGOV, University of Birmingham, Birmingham

OECD Technical Co-operation Service (1983) *The Relationship between the Citizen and the Administration: National Contribution to Inventory of Improvement Measures, Sweden* (CT/PUMA/201/18), Paris, mimeo

Page, Edward (1991) *Localism and Centralism in Europe*, Oxford University Press, Oxford

Peterson, Carl-Gunnar (no date) *The Free Commune Experiment Takes Shape*, mimeo supplied by author

Rustow, D.A. (1955) *The Politics of Compromise: A Study of Parties and Cabinet Governments in Sweden*, Princeton University Press, Princeton

Scott, Franklin D. (1977) *Sweden, The Nation's History*, University of Minnesota, Minneapolis

Stromberg, Lars and Jorgen Westerstahl (1984) *The New Swedish Communes*, Department of Political Science, University of Gothenburg, Liber, Stockholm

6. DENMARK

Association of County Councils (1978) *The Regional Level: Counties in Denmark*, Copenhagen

Bogason, Peter (1987) 'Denmark' E.C. Page and M.J. Goldsmith (eds) *Central and Local Relations: a Comparative Analysis of West European Unitary States*, Sage, London

Bogason, Peter (1991) *Danish Local Government: Towards an Effective and Efficient Welfare State* J.J. Hesse (ed.) *Local Government and Urban Affairs in International Perspective*, Nomos Verlagsgesellschaft, Baden-Baden

Bruun, Finn and Carl-Johan Skovsgaard (1980) 'Local Self-Determination and Central Control in Denmark' *International Political Science Review* vol.1 no.2

Council of Europe (1978) *Conditions of Local Democracy and Citizen Participation in Europe*, Council of Europe, Strasbourg

Council of Europe (1985) *Financial Resources for Local and Regional Authorities*, Council of Europe, Strasbourg

Council of Europe (1985) *Management Structures in Local and Regional Government*, Council of Europe, Strasbourg

Council of Europe (1979) *Methods of Consulting Citizens on Municipal Affairs*, Council of Europe, Strasbourg

Council of Europe (1983) *The Reforms of Local and Regional Authorities in Europe: Theory, Practice and Critical Appraisal*, Council of Europe, Strasbourg

Council of Europe (1988) *The Status and Working Conditions of Local and Regional Elected Representatives*, Council of Europe, Strasbourg

Council of Europe (Committee on Local Structures and Finance)(1982) *Synopsis of replies to the questionnaire on status and working conditions of local and regional elected representatives*, Council of Europe, Strasbourg

Council of Europe (Steering Committee for Regional and Municipal Matters) (1977) *Participation by Voluntary Associations and Groups*, Council of Europe, Strasbourg

Harder, Erik (1973) *Local Government in Denmark*, The Danish Institute, Copenhagen

Illeris, Sven (1983) *Public Participation in Denmark: Experience with the County Regional Plans'*, *Town Planning* vol.1 no.4

Kjellberg, Francesco (1983) 'The Scandinavian Countries' Council of Europe *The Reforms of Local and Regional Authorities in Europe: Theory, Practice and Critical Appraisal*, Council of Europe, Stasbourg

Kjellberg, Francesco and John G. Taylor (1984) 'Les Pays Scandinaves' *La réforme des collectivités locales en Europe*, Notes et Études Documentaires 1984-5, La Documentation Française, Paris

Kolam, Kerstin (1991) 'Neighbourhood Councils in the Nordic Countries'

References

Local Government Studies vol.17 no.3

Lane, Jan-Erik and Svante O. Ersson (1987) *Politics and Society in Western Europe*, Sage, London

Mikkelsen, Palle and Jens Erik Steenstrup (1982) *Public Sector Reforms in Denmark: The Danish Health Care Sector, Recent Trends and Efforts*, Amtskommunernes og Kommunernes Forskningsinstitut, Copenhagen

Morlan, Robert L. (1981) 'Territorial Reorganization and Administrative Reform in Denmark' A.B. Gunlicks (ed.) *Local Government Reform and Reorganization*, Kennikat Press, Port Washington

Mouritzen, Paul Erik (1982) *Local Resource Allocation: Partisan Politics or Sector Politics?*, Institute of Finance and Policy, University of Odense, Odense

Mouritzen, Paul Erik (1983) *Consequences of Fiscal Strain*, Institute of Finance and Policy, University of Odense, Odense

National Association of Local Authorities in Denmark (1981) *Economic and Political Trends in Denmark and Danish Local Government Reform*, Copenhagen

National Association of Local Authorities in Denmark (1980) *Information of the National Association of Local Authorities on Denmark and the Danish Local Government Reform*, National Association of Local Authorities in Denmark, Copenhagen

National Association of Local Authorities in Denmark (regular editions) *Local Government in Denmark*, Copenhagen, Denmark.

National Association of Local Authorities in Denmark (1975) *Rationalization in Local Government*, National Association of Local Authorities in Denmark, Copenhagen

Nissen, Ove (1991) *Key issues in the Local Government Debate in Denmark* R. Batley and G. Stoker (eds) *Local Government in Europe: Trends and Developments*, Macmillan, Basingstoke

Norton, Alan (1977) 'The Rationalization of Local Administration' *Local Government Studies* vol.3 no.1

Norton, Alan (1983) *The Government and Administration of Metropolitan Areas in Western Democracies*, Institute of Local Government Studies, Birmingham

Skovsgaard, Carl-Johan (1983a) *Budget-Making and Fiscal Austerity*, Institute of Political Science, University of Aarhus

Skovsgaard, Carl-Johan (1983b) *Reforms and Central-Local Relations*,

References

Institute of Political Science, University of Aarhus

Skovsgaard, Carl-Johan (1984) *Strategies for Centralization*, Institute of Political Science, University of Aarhus

Skovsgaard, Carl-Johan and J.Sondergaard (1983) *Danish Local Government: Recent Trends in Economy and Administration*, Institute of Political Science, University of Aarhus

Thomas, Alistair H. (1987) 'Denmark' *World Encyclopedia of Political Systems and Parties*, Facts on File, New York/Oxford

Villadsen, Soren (no date, assumed to be 1983 or 1984) *Urban Politics, Central Control versus Local Demands*, Institute of Political Studies, University of Copenhagen, Copenhagen

7. BRITAIN

Note. This section is limited to references in the text. Those interested in following up the extensive English language literature on the subject could well start with the 'Further Reading' section and 'Notes and References' in the most recent edition of Tony Byrne's (1990) *Local Government in Britain*, Penguin Books, Harmondsworth.

Against the Over-Mighty State: a Future for Local Government in Britain. Report of a Federal Trust study group (1988), Federal Trust for Education and Research, London

Almond, Gabriel and Sidney Verba (1963) *The Civic Culture*, Princeton University Press, Princeton NJ

Bras, Jean-Philippe (1988) 'Grande-Bretagne' *La Fonction Publique Locale*, Information et Documents no.2, Institut Internationale d'Administration Publique, Paris

Briggs, Asa (1968) *Victorian Cities*, Penguin, Harmondsworth

Byrne, Tony (1990) *Local Government in Britain* 5th edition, Penguin Books, Harmondsworth

CIPFA (1988, 1990) *Local Government Trends*, Chartered Institute of Public Finance and Accountancy, London

CIPFA (1992) *Local Government Transfers including Community Charge*, Chartered Institute of Public Finance and Accountancy, London

The Community Charge, Department of the Environment, London

Committee of Inquiry into Local Government in Scotland, *Report (Stodart)* (1981) Cmnd 8115, HMSO, Edinburgh

The Conduct of Local Authority Business: Report (Widdicombe) (1986) Cmnd 9797, HMSO, London

The Conduct of Local Authority Business: Research Volumes I: The Political Organisation of Local Authorities; II: The Local Government Councillor; III: The Local Government Elector; IV: Aspects of Local Democracy (1986) Cmnd 9798-801, HMSO, London

Dyson, Kenneth H.F. (1980) *The State Tradition in Western Europe*, Martin Robertson, Oxford

Flynn, Norman and Steve Leach (1984) *Joint Boards and Joint Committees*, INLOGOV, University of Birmingham, Birmingham

Flynn, Norman and Kieron Walsh (1988) *Competitive Tendering*, INLOGOV, University of Birmingham, Birmingham

La Fonction Publique Locale: Allemagne Fédérale, Espagne, Grande Bretagne (1988) Informations & Documents no. 2, Institut International d'Administration Publique, Paris

Garvin, J.L. (1932) *The Life of Joseph Chamberlain vol. 1*, Macmillan, London

Greenwood, Royston, M.A. Lomer, C.R. Hinings and S. Ranson (1975) *The Organisation of Local Government in England and Wales*, INLOGOV, University of Birmingham, Birmingham

Gyford, John (1984) *Local Politics in Britain* 2nd edition, Croom Helm, London/Sydney

Gyford, John and M. James (1983) *National Parties and Local Politics*, Allen & Unwin, London

Gyford, John, S. Leach and C. Game (1989) *The Changing Politics of Local Government*, Unwin Hyman, London

Jones, George (1991) 'Local government in Great Britain, 1988/89' J.J. Hesse (ed.) *Local Government and Urban Affairs in International Perspective*, Nomos Verlagsgesellschaft, Baden-Baden

Jones, George and John Stewart (1985) *The Case for Local Government* 2nd edition, Allen & Unwin, London

Keating, Michael and Arthur Midwinter (1983) *The Government of Scotland*, Mainstream Publishing, Edinburgh

Keith-Lucas, Bryan and Peter G. Richards (1978) *A History of Local*

References

Government in the Twentieth Century, Allen & Unwin, London

Kellas, James G. (1984) *The Scottish Political System* 3rd edition, Cambridge University Press, Cambridge

Leach, S.N., H. Davis, C. Game and C.K. Skelcher (1991) *After the Abolition: the Operation of the Post-1986 Metropolitan Government System in England*, INLOGOV, University of Birmingham, Birmingham

Leach, Steve and Chris Game (1989) *Conflict and Co-operation: Politics in the Hung Counties*, Common Voice, London

Leach, Steve and John Stewart (1987) *The Changing Patterns of Hung Authorities*, Local Government Training Board, Luton

Leach, Steve, C.Vielba and N.Flynn (1987) *Two Tier Relationships in British Local Government*, INLOGOV, University of Birmingham, Birmingham

Local Government Finance ('Layfield Report')(1975) Cmnd 6543, HMSO, London

Loughlin, Martin (1986) *Local Government in the Modern State*, Sweet and Maxwell, London

Mill, John Stuart (1861) *Considerations on Representative Government*, in Everyman's Edition of *Utilitarianism, Liberty and Representative Government* (1910), Dent, London

The New Local Authorities: Organisation and Structure ('Bains Report') (1972), HMSO, London

The New Scottish Local Authorities: Organisation and Management Structures ('Paterson Report') (1973), HMSO, Edinburgh

Norton, Alan (1986a) 'The Future Structure and Functions of Local Government' *The Future Role and Organisation of Local Government*, INLOGOV, University of Birmingham, Birmingham

Norton, Alan (1986b) 'A Century of Change in Local Government Structure' *Appendices to Report No.2, The Future Role and Organisation of Local Government*, op. cit.

Norton, Alan (1988) 'L'administration d'un district métropolitain en Grande-Bretagne' *La Fonction Publique Locale: Allemagne Fédérale, Espagne, Grande Bretagne*, op. cit.

Norton, Alan (1991) *The Role of Chief Executive in British Local Government*, INLOGOV, University of Birmingham, Birmingham

Norton, Philip (1990) 'The Lady's not for turning but what about the rest? — Margaret Thatcher and the Conservative Party 1979-89' *Parliamen-*

tary Affairs vol.43 no.1

Ranson, Stewart and John Stewart (1989) 'Citizenship and Government: The Challenge for Management in the Public Domain' *Political Studies* vol.37 no.1

Redlich, Josef and Francis W.Hirst (1903) *The History of Local Government in England* 2nd edition with 'Introduction' and 'Epilogue' by Bryan Keith-Lucas (1970) Macmillan, London

Rhodes, R.A.W. (1986) *The National World of Local Government*, Allen & Unwin, London

Royal Commission on Local Government in Scotland 1966-69 (1969) *Scotland: Local Government Reform* Cmnd 4150-I, HMSO, Edinburgh

Sharpe, L.J. (1970) 'Theories and Values of Local Government' *Political Studies* vol.18 no.2

Stewart, John (1987) 'Developments in Central-Local Relations in England and Wales' *International Review of Administrative Sciences* vol.53

Travers, Tony (1989) 'The Changing Finance World' *Local Government Chronicle*, 10 February

Webb, S. and B. (1906) *English Local Government: The Parish and the County* (2nd edition, 1963), Frank Cass, London

Wheare, K.C. (1955) *Government by Committee*, Clarendon Press, Oxford

8. THE UNITED STATES OF AMERICA

ACIR (1979) *Citizen Participation in the American Federal System*, ACIR, Washington, DC

ACIR (1976a) *Improving Urban America: a Challenge to Federalism*, ACIR, Washington, DC

ACIR (1985) *Intergovernmental Service Arrangements for Delivering Local Public Services: Update 1983*, ACIR, Washington, DC

ACIR (1987) *The Organization of Local Public Economies*, ACIR, Washington, DC

ACIR (1976b) *Pragmatic Federalism: the Reassignment of Functional Responsibilities*, ACIR, Washington, DC

ACIR (1981) *Recent Trends in Federal and State Aids to Local Government*, ACIR, Washington, DC

ACIR (1982) *State and Local Roles in the Federal System*, ACIR,

References

Washington, DC

ACIR (1978) State Mandating of Local Expenditures: a Commission Report, Washington, DC

Adrian, Charles R. (1972) *Governing Our Fifty States and Their Communities*, McGraw-Hill, New York

Adrian, Charles R. and Charles Press (1977) *Governing Urban America*, McGraw-Hill, New York

Aronson, J. Richard and John L. Hilley (1986) *Financing State and Local Governments* 4th edition, The Brookings Institution, Washington, DC

Banfield, Edward C. (1985) *How the People Rule*, Plenum Publicity, New York

Boyd, William J.D. (1976) 'Local Electoral Systems: Is There a Best Way?', *National Civic Review* vol.64 March

Boyne, George A. (1992) 'Local government structure and performance: lessons from America?' *Public Administration* vol.70 no.3

Cahill, Anthony G. and J.A. James (1992) 'Responding to Municipal Fiscal Distress: An Emerging Issue for State Governments in the '90s', *Public Administration Review* vol.52 no.1

Clark, T.N. and L.C. Ferguson (1983) *City Money*, Columbia University Press, New York

Committee for Economic Development (1966) *Modernizing Local Government*, New York

Duncombe, Herbert Spencer (1977) *Modern County Government*, National Association of Counties, Washington, DC

Flinn, Thomas A. (1970) *Local Government and Politics*, Scott Foreman, Glenview, Ill.

Florestano, Patricia S. (1985) 'State Limitations on Local Fiscal Authority' *State and Local Government Administration*, Marcel Dekker, New York

Florestano, Patricia S. (1981) 'A Survey of City and County Use of Private Contracting' *Urban Interest* 3

Florestano, Patricia S. and Vincent L. Marando (1981) *The States and the Metropolis*, Marcel Dekker, New York

Fosler, R. Scott (1984) *The Public-Private Connection: Changing Roles and Relationships among Government and Non-Government Institutions (CT/LGM/-TUR/3)*, OECD, Paris

Gargan, John J. (1985) 'Fiscal Dependency and Governmental Capacity in

References

American Cities' Rabin and Dodd (eds), op. cit.

Garnett, James L. (1985) 'Organizing and Reorganizing State and Local Government' Rabin and Dodd (eds), op. cit.

Gunlicks, Arthur B. (1991) 'Local Government in the United States of America' J.J. Hesse (ed.) *Local Government and Urban Affairs in International Perspective*, Nomos Verlagsgesellschaft, Baden-Baden

Gunlicks, Arthur B. (1981) 'Problems, Politics and Prospects of Local Government Reorganization in the United States' A.B. Gunlicks (ed.) *Local Government Reform and Reorganization*, Kennikat Press, New York

Hallman, H. (1977) *Small and Large Together — Governing the Metropolis*, Sage, London/Beverly Hills

Harrigan, John J. (1985) *Political Change in the Metropolis*, Little, Brown & Co., New York

Hatry, P. Harry (1983) *A Review of Private Approaches for the Delivery of Public Services*, Urban Institute Press, Washington, DC

Karnig, A.K. (1977) *National Civic Review* vol.66 no.4

Kaufman, H. (1963) *Politics and Policies in State and Local Governments*, Prentice-Hall, Englewood Cliffs, New Jersey

Lee, Eugene C. (1985) 'Reflections on Local Government and Politics in England and the United States', *Local Government Studies* vol.11 no.5

Lindholm, Richard W. and Hartojo Wignjowijoto (1979) *Financing and Managing State and Local Government*, Lexington Books, Lexington/Toronto

McKay, David H. (1983) 'Local Government in the U.S.A.' *Local Democracies*, Longman, Cheshire

Magnusson, Warren, (1979) 'The New Neighbourhood Democracy' L.J. Sharpe (ed.) *Decentralist Trends in Western Democracies*, Sage, London/Beverly Hills

Martin, David L. (1982) *Running City Hall*, University of Alabama Press, Alabama

Maxwell, James A. and J. Richard Aronson (3rd edition, 1977; 4th edition, 1986) *Financing State and Local Governments*, Brookings Institution, Washington, DC

Morgan, David R. (1985) 'Municipal Service Delivery Alternatives' Rabin and Dodd (eds), op. cit.

Mudd, John (1985) *Neighbourhood Services: Making Big Cities Work*,

References

Yale University Press, Yale

Municipal Year Book (1988), International City Management Association, Washington, DC

OECD (1984) *Recent Trends in the Provision of Urban Services* (*UP/S(84) 8*), OECD, Paris

Press, C. and K. Verburg, (1979) *State and Community Governments in the Federal System*, Wiley, New York

Rabin, J. and D. Dodd (eds) (1985) *State and Local Government Administration*, Marcel Dekker, New York

Reed, Alan (1985) 'Chief Executives and Administrative Officers' Rabin and Dodd (eds), op. cit.

Reeves, Andrée E. (1992) 'Enhancing Local Self-Government and State Capabilities: The U.S. Advisory Commission on Intergovernmental Relations Programme' *Public Administration Review* vol.52 no.4

Savitch, N.C. and J. Clayton Thomas (eds)(1991) *Big City Politics in Transition*, Sage, Newbury Park, Cal/London

Sbragia, Alberta (1985) *The Politics of Public Investment: An Anglo-American Comparison*, University of Strathclyde Studies in Public Policy No.139, Glasgow

Shulman, L.A. (1985) 'Alternative Approaches to Delivering Local Services' Rabin and Dodd (eds), op. cit.

Stone, N., R.K. Whelan and W.J. Munn (1986) *Urban Policy and Politics in a Bureaucratic Age* 2nd edition, Prentice-Hall, Englewood Cliffs, New Jersey

Svara, James H. (1990) *Official Leadership in the City: Patterns of Conflict and Cooperation*, Oxford University Press, New York/Oxford

Syed, Anwar Hussain (1966) *The Political Theory of American Local Government* Random House, New York

US Bureau of the Census (1991) *Statistical Abstract of the United States: 1991* 111th edition (and preceding series), US Government Printing Office, Washington, DC

Walker, David B. (1983) 'Intergovernmental Relations and Dysfunctional Federalism' Zimmerman and Zimmerman (eds), op. cit.

Walker, David and Jeanne (1975) 'Rationalizing local government powers, functions and structure' *States' Responsibilities to Local Government:*

527

An Action Agenda, Center for Policy Research of the National Governors' Association, Washington, DC

Wolman, H. (1986) *Housing and Housing Policy in the US and the UK*, D.C. Heath, Lexington, Mass.

Wolman, H. (1986) 'Innovation in Local Government and Fiscal Austerity' *Journal of Public Policy* no.2

Wolman, Harold (1988) 'Understanding recent trends in central-local relations: centralisation in Great Britain and decentralisation in the United States' *European Journal of Political Research* no.16

Zimmerman, Deirdre A. and J.F. Zimmerman (eds) (1983) *The Politics of Sub-National Governance*, University Press of America, Lanham/New York/London

Zimmerman, J.F. (1983a) 'Evolving Decentralization in New York City' Zimmerman and Zimmerman (eds), op. cit.

Zimmerman, J.F. (1983b) 'A Fair Voting System for Local Governments' Zimmerman and Zimmerman (eds), op. cit.

Zimmerman, J.F. (1979) 'The Metropolitan Governance Maze in the United States' *Urban Law and Policy* no.2

Zimmerman, J.F. (1983d) *State-Local Relations: A Partnership Approach*, Praeger, New York

Zimmerman, J.F. (1980) 'United States' Rowat, D.C. ed. *International Handbook on Local Government Reorganization: Contemporary Developments*, Greenwood Press, Westport, Connecticut

9. CANADA

Andrew, Caroline (1983) 'Local Government in Canada' Margaret Bowman and William Hampton (eds) *Local Democracies: a Study in Comparative Local Government*, Longman Cheshire, Melbourne

Antoft, Kell (ed.) (no date) *A Guide to Local Government in Nova Scotia* 2nd edition, Institute of Public Affairs, Dalhousie University, Halifax, Canada

Axworthy, Lloyd (1980) 'Canada: Winnipeg' Rowat (ed.) op. cit.

Barlow, I.M. (1991) *Metropolitan Government* Routledge, London/New York

Betts, George M. (1982), *The Structure of Local Government*, mimeo

Bird, Richard M. and N. Enid Slack (1983) *Urban Public Finance in*

References

Canada, Butterworths, Toronto

Bureau of Municipal Research (1968) *The 101 Governments of Metro Toronto*, Bureau of Municipal Research, Toronto

Canada Year Book 1990 (1989), Ministry of Supply and Services, Ottawa

Dickerson, M.O., S. Drabek and J.T. Woods (eds) (1980) *Problems of Change in Urban Government*, Wilfred Laurier University Press, Waterloo, Canada

Federation of Canadian Municipalities (1980) *Municipal Government in a New Canadian Federal System, Report of the Task Force on Constitutional Reform*, Federation of Canadian Municipalities, Ottawa

Feldman, L.D. (ed.) (1981) *Politics and Government of Urban Canada* 4th edition, Methuen, Toronto

Feldman, L.D. and K.A. Graham (1979), *Bargaining for Cities*, Institute for Research on Public Policy, Toronto

Feldman, L.D. and Michael D. Goldrick (eds) (1976) *Politics and Government of Urban Canada* 3rd edition, Methuen, Toronto

Higgins, Donald (1977) *Urban Canada: Its Government and Politics*, Macmillan/Gage, Toronto

Higgins, Donald (1980) 'Canada: New Brunswick and Nova Scotia' Rowat (ed.), op. cit.

Higgins, Donald (1986) *Local and Urban Politics in Canada*, Gage, Toronto

Higgins, Donald (1991) 'Local Government and Urban Affairs in International Perspective: The Case of Canada' J.J. Hesse (ed.) *Local Government and International Affairs in International Perspective*, Nomos Verlagsgesellschaft, Baden-Baden

Kiernan, M.J. and D.C. Walker (1983) 'Winnipeg' Magnusson and Sancton (eds), op. cit.

Lightbody, James (1983) 'Edmonton' Magnusson and Sancton (eds) (1983), op. cit.

Magnusson, Warren (1983) 'Toronto', Magnusson Sancton, (eds.) op. cit.

Magnusson, Warren and A. Sancton (1983) *City Politics in Canada*, University of Toronto Press, Toronto

Masson, Jack (1985) *Alberta's Local Governments and their Politics*, Pica

529

Pica Press, Edmonton, Alberta

Metropolitan Government (1970) *Proposals for Urban Reorganisation in the Greater Winnipeg Area*, Winnipeg

Norton, Alan (1983) *The Government and Administration of Metropolitan Areas in Western Democracies*, Institute of Local Government Studies, Birmingham University, Birmingham

O'Brien, T.D. (1980) 'Father Knows Best: A Look at Provincial-Municipal Relations in Ontario' *Problems of Political Change in Urban Government* M.O. Dickerson, Drabek and Woods (eds), op. cit.

Palmer, W.H. (1970) *The Progress of the Regional Government Reform Program in Ontario*, Department of Municipal Affairs, Toronto, mimeo
Palmer, W.H. (1979) *Report of the Waterloo Region Reform Commission*, Waterloo Region Commission, Toronto
Plunkett, T. J. (1980) 'Canada: Ontario' Rowat (ed.), op. cit.

Quesnel-Ouellet, Louise (1980), 'Canada: Quebec' Rowat (ed.), op. cit.

Richmond, Dale E. (1982) *The Administration of Metropolitan Areas: Canada*, paper presented at XIXth International Congress of Administrative Sciences, Berlin, mimeo
Rowat, Donald. C. (ed.) (1980a) *International Handbook on Local Government Organization: Contemporary Developments*, Greenwood Press, Westport, Connecticut
Rowat, Donald C. (1980b) 'Introduction' and 'Concluding Remarks' Rowat (ed.), op. cit.

Sancton, Andrew (1975) *The Organisation of Local Government in Metropolitan Toronto*, Royal Commission on Metropolitan Toronto, Toronto
Sancton, Andrew (1983) 'Montreal' Magnusson and Sancton (eds), op. cit.
Siegel (1980), 'Provincial-municipal relations in Canada: an overview' *Canadian Public Administration* vol.23 no.2

Tennant, Paul (1980) 'Canada: British Columbia' Rowat (ed.), op. cit.
Tindal, C.R. (1982), *You and Your Local Government*, Ontario Municipal Management Development Board, Ontario
Tindal, C.R. and S.Bobes Tindal (1984) *Local Government in Canada*, McGraw Hill Ryerson, Toronto

10. JAPAN

Abe, Hiroshi (1975) 'The Local Political Culture of Japan' *Local Government Review in Japan* no.3

Boyd, Richard (1986) 'The Japanese Communist Party in Local Government' B.Szajkovski (ed.) *Marxist Local Governments in Western Europe and Japan*, Frances Pinter, London; Lynne Rienner, Boulder, Colorado
Election System in Japan (1986), Jichi Sogo Center, Tokyo
'États et Collectivités Locales au Japon' (1983) *Problèmes Politiques et Sociaux*, La Documentation Française, Paris

Fire Defense in Japan (1987), Jichi Sogo Center, Tokyo

Glickman, Norman J. (1979) *The Growth and Management of the Japanese Urban System*, Academic Press, New York/London

Hoshino, Shinya (1987) 'The Costs of Social Welfare — Current Situation and Basic Issues' *Local Government Review in Japan* no.15

Ikenouchi, Yuki (1985) 'Present Situation and Rationalization of Salaries in the Local Public Service' *Local Government Review in Japan* no.13
Isakoda, Takashi (1980) 'Present Local Government System and its Problems' *Local Government Review in Japan* no.8
Ishihara, Nobuo (1980) 'Present Local Tax System and its Problems' *Local Government Review in Japan* no.8

Katayama, Toranosuke (1985) 'The Present Situation and Theme of Administrative Reform of Local Public Entities' *Local Government Review in Japan* no.13
Kato, Tomiko (1980) 'History of the Local Government System in Japan' *Local Government Review in Japan* no.8
Kawasaki, Yoshimoto (1977) 'Some Difficulties to Realize Participatory Democracy in Contemporary Japan'. Paper for second conference on participation and self-management, Paris, mimeo
Kisa, Sigeo (1991) 'Local Government in Japan: Seeking Independenceand Self-Reliance' J.J. Hesse (ed.) *Local Government and Urban Affairs in International Perspective*, Nomos Verlagsgesellschaft, Baden-Baden
Kitamura, Kimihiko (1983) 'Local Government in Japan' M. Bowman and W. Hampton (eds) *Local Democracies: a Study in Comparative Local Government*, Longman Cheshire, Melbourne

Local Public Administration in Japan (1986, 1990), Jichi Sogo Center, Tokyo

Local Public Enterprise System in Japan (1989), Jichi Sogo Center, Tokyo

Local Public Finance in Japan (1984), Jichi Sogo Center, Tokyo

Local Public Service Personnel System in Japan (1988), Jichi Sogo Center, Tokyo

Local Tax System in Japan (1990), Jichi Sogo Center, Tokyo

Maruyama, Takamitsu (1986) 'The Shoup Recommendations and the Local Tax System' *Local Government Review in Japan* no.14

Mills E.S. and K. Ohta (1976) 'Urbanization and Urban Problems' *Asia's New Giant: How the Japanese Economy Works*, Brookings Institution, Washington, DC, quoted in Glickman, op. cit.

Ministry of Home Affairs (1982) 'Local Administration and Finance' *International Review of Administrative Sciences* no.2

Miyao, Takasha (1980) 'Present Local Government Personnel System in Japan and its Problems' *Local Government Review in Japan* no.8

Mouritzen Poul Erik and K.H.Nielsen (1988), *Handbook of Comparative Urban Fiscal Data*, Danish Data Archive, Odense

Nagano, Shiro (1987) 'Consideration of a New Local Autonomy Theory', *Local Government Review in Japan* no.15

Nomura, Shinichi (1982) 'Problems of Local Administration: The Case of the Tokyo Metropolitan Government' *International Review of Administrative Sciences* no.2

An Outline of Japanese Taxes (1989), Printing Bureau, Ministry of Finance, Tokyo

Plain Talk about Tokyo (1980 and 1987), Tokyo Metropolitan Government, Tokyo

Regional Development in Japan (1991), Jichi Sogo Center, Tokyo

Saito, Tsunetaka (1978) 'Problems of making comprehensive Plans' *Local Government Review* no.6

Saka, Koji (1983) 'Brief History of the Local Public Service Law' *Local Government Review in Japan* no.11

The Second New Kanagawa Plan (1987) Kanagawa Prefectural Government, Yokohama

Shibata, Hirotsugu (1986) 'Implementation of the "Principle of Local

References

Autonomy'" *Local Government Review in Japan* no.14
Shibata, Keiji (1990) 'Small Government Theory and Local Public Enterprises' *Local Government Review in Japan* no.18
Shindo (1982) 'Relations between National and Local Government' *International Review of Administrative Sciences* no.2
Statistical Abstract of Japanese Local Government (1982) Jichi Sogo Center, Tokyo
Statistical Handbook of Japan (1981), Statistics Bureau, Prime Minister's Office, Tokyo
Steiner, Kurt (1965) *Local Government in Japan*, Stanford University Press, Stanford, California

Tohru, Hashimoto (1983) 'On the Local Tax System — Choice and Burden of Local People' *Local Government Review in Japan* no.11
Tokyo Metropolitan Government *Plain Talk about Tokyo* (1980, 1987), Tokyo Metropolitan Government, Tokyo
Tsuda, Tadashi (1987) 'Tax Reform and Local Tax', *Local Government Review in Japan* no.15

Ward, Robert E. (1978) *Japan's Political System* 2nd edition, Prentice-Hall, Englewood Cliffs, NJ
Weinstein, Martin E. (1987) 'Japan (*Nihon*)' *World Encyclopedia of Political Systems and Parties*, Facts on File, New York/Oxford

Yano, Koichiro (1987) 'Stability in Domestic Affairs and Local Finance' *Local Government Review in Japan* no.15

INDEX

The following index lists personal and place names and other topics alphabetically, subject to the following exceptions. Authors named in the main text are included excepting those in the bracketed references, which are given in the references section above. In order to facilitate comparision, institutions particular to a country are listed under the country's name. For the same reason types of executive and services are grouped together under those heads. References to taxes and characteristics and criteria for taxes are given under taxation, l.g. ('l.g.' is an abbreviation for local government).

The page numbers for general sections on a topic are given in bold print. Semicolons divide the page references for each chapter so that readers can easily identify those for particular countries.

Index